A PRACTICAL GUIDE
TO UNIX™ SYSTEM V

The Benjamin/Cummings Series in Computer Science

G. Booch
Object-Oriented Design with Applications (1989)

G. Brookshear
Computer Science: An Overview, Third Edition (1991)

F. Carrano
Assembler Language Progamming for the IBM 370 (1988)

D. M. Etter
Structured FORTRAN 77 for Engineers and Scientists, Third Edition (1990)

P. Helman and R. Veroff and F. Carrano
Intermediate Problem Solving and Data Structures: Walls and Mirrors (Pascal Edition), Second Edition (1991)

P. Helman and R. Veroff
Walls and Mirrors: Intermediate Problem Solving and Data Structures—Modula II (1988)

N. Miller and C. G. Petersen
File Structures with Ada (1990)

A. Kelley and I. Pohl
A Book on C, Programming in C, Second Edition (1990)

A. Kelley and I. Pohl
C by Dissection: The Essentials of C Programming (1988)

I. Pohl
C++ for C Programmers (1990)

I. Pohl
C++ for Pascal Programmers (1990)

I. Pohl
Turbo C++ (1991)

W. J. Savitch
Pascal: An Introduction to the Art and Science of Programming, Third Edition (1990)

W. J. Savitch
TURBO Pascal 4.0/5.0 with 5.5/6.0 Supplement (1990)

R. Sebesta
VAX: Assembly Language Programming, Second Edition (1991)

M. G. Sobell
A Practical Guide to the UNIX System, Second Edition (1989)

M. G. Sobell
A Practical Guide to UNIX System V Release 4, Second Edition (1991)

F. Zlotnick
The POSIX.1 Standard: A Programmer's Guide (1991)

A PRACTICAL GUIDE TO UNIX™ SYSTEM V

SECOND EDITION

Mark G. Sobell

The Benjamin/Cummings Publishing Company, Inc.
Redwood City, California • Menlo Park, California
Reading, Massachusetts • New York • Don Mills, Ontario • Wokingham, U.K.
Amsterdam • Bonn • Sydney • Singapore • Tokyo • Madrid • San Juan

Sponsoring Editor: John Thompson
Outside Production Coordinator: Larry Olsen
Cover Designer: Juan Vargas
Typesetting: Sobell Associates Inc.

This book was typeset by Sobell Associates Inc. using troff running on an Intel 80386-based computer running UNIX. The troff output was passed through a filter (devps) to create a PostScript file. Proof copies of the book were printed on a QMS PS-810 laser printer and final typeset output was produced on a LaserMaster 1000 printer.

DECnet is a trademark of DEC
Ethernet is a registered trademark of Xerox
Informix is a trademark of Informix Software, Inc.
OPEN LOOK, TUXEDO, XWIN, Documentor's Workbench, Instructional Workbench, and Programmer's Workbench are trademarks of UNIX System Laboratories, Inc., a subsidiary of AT&T, in the U.S. and other countries.
PostScript is a trademark of Adobe Software, Inc.
SunOS and NFS are trademarks of Sun Microsystems, Inc.
UNIX is a registered trademark of UNIX System Laboratories, Inc., a subsidiary of AT&T, in the U.S. and other countries.
XENIX and MS-DOS are trademarks of Microsoft, Inc.

Library of Congress Cataloging-in-Publication Data

Sobell, Mark G.
        A practical guide to UNIX System V / Mark G. Sobell. — 2nd ed.
            p.   cm.
        Includes index.
        ISBN 0-8053-7560-0
        1. UNIX System V (Computer operating system)   I. Title.
QA76.76.063S6   1991
005.4'3—dc20   90-29049
                                                                         CIP

        3 4 5 6 7 8 9 10 –DO– 95 94 93

The Benjamin/Cummings Publishing Company, Inc.
390 Bridge Parkway
Redwood City, California 94065

for Laura

PREFACE

This is a practical guide to UNIX System V, Release 4. This book is *practical* because it uses tutorial examples that show you what you will see on your terminal screen each step of the way. It is a *guide* because it takes you from logging in on your system (Chapter 2) through writing complex shell programs (Chapters 8 and 9), using sophisticated software development tools (Chapter 10), and administering a system (Chapter 11). Part II is a *reference guide* to 72 UNIX utilities. *A Practical Guide to UNIX System V* is intended for people with some computer experience but little or no experience with the UNIX system. More experienced UNIX system users will find the later chapters and Part II to be useful sources of information on such subjects as shell programming, C programming, and system administration.

This book is about UNIX System V Release 4. It identifies features that are changed or new to Release 4. Where practical, it also describes the way changed features worked in earlier versions of the operating system. The following list highlights some of the features the book covers.

Networking.   When you are on a network, you can exchange information with and send electronic mail to other people on the network.

The vi Editor.   This screen-oriented editor, which was originally a part of Berkeley UNIX, is now the most widely used text editor on System V.

Job Control.   The job control utilities and shell layers allow users to work on several jobs at once, switching back and forth between them as desired.

New C Shell Features.   Recent versions of the C Shell have added filename completion, which enables users to abbreviate long filenames, and directory stack manipulation, which provides shortcuts for moving around the hierarchical file system.

The Korn Shell.   The newest of the three shells, the Korn Shell, is becoming more and more popular.

Shell Functions.   A feature of the Bourne and Korn Shells, shell functions, enables users to write their own commands that are similar to the aliases provided by the C Shell.

SCCS.   The Source Code Control System (SCCS) is a convenient set of tools that enable programmers to track versions of files.

A Practical Guide to UNIX System V shows you how to use your UNIX system from your terminal. Part I comprises the first eleven chapters, which contain step-by-step tutorials covering the most important aspects of the UNIX operating system. (If you have used a UNIX system before, you may want to skim over Chapters 2 and 3.) The more advanced material in each chapter is presented in sections marked "Optional," which the reader is encouraged to return to *after* mastering the more basic material presented in the chapter. Features that are new to Release 4 are also presented in separate sections. Review exercises are included at the end of each chapter for readers who want to hone their skills. Some of the exercises test the reader's understanding of material covered in the chapter, and others challenge the reader to go beyond the material presented to develop a more thorough understanding.

Part II offers a comprehensive, detailed reference to the major UNIX utilities, with numerous examples. As in Part I of the book, features that are new to Release 4 are clearly marked. If you are already familiar with the UNIX system, this part of the book will be a valuable, easy-to-use reference. If you are not an experienced user, you will find Part II a useful supplement while you are mastering the tutorials in Part I.

Organizing Information.
In Chapters 2, 3, and 4 you will learn how to create, delete, copy, move, and search for information using your system. You will also learn how to use the UNIX system file structure to organize the information you store on your computer.

Electronic Mail and Telecommunications.
Chapter 3 and Part II include information on how to use UNIX system utilities (mailx and write) to communicate with users on your system and other systems. Appendix C, Networking, has more information about communicating with users on other systems.

Using the Shell.
In Chapter 5 you will learn how to send output from a program to the printer, to your terminal, or to a file—just by changing a command. You will also see how you can combine UNIX utilities to solve problems right from the command line.

Word Processing.
Chapters 6 and 7 show you how to use the word-processing tools that are a part of your UNIX system. Chapter 6 explains the vi editor, and Chapter 7 demonstrates the use of nroff with the **mm** macros. It also introduces you to the **ms** macro package. These chapters show you how to produce professional-looking documents, including manuscripts, letters, and reports.

Shell Programming.
Once you have mastered the basics of the UNIX system, you can use your knowledge to build more complex and specialized programs (*shell scripts*—like DOS batch files) using a shell programming language. Chapter 8 shows you how to use the Bourne Shell to write your own scripts composed of UNIX system commands. Chapter 9 covers the C Shell. Appendix A

covers the Korn Shell, which combines many of the popular features of the C Shell (such as history mechanisms and aliases) with a programming language similar to that of the Bourne Shell. The examples in Part II also demonstrate many features of the UNIX utilities that you can use in shell scripts.

Using Programming Tools.   Chapter 10 introduces you to the C compiler and the UNIX system's exceptional programming environment. This chapter describes how to use two of the most useful software development tools—make and the Source Code Control System. The make utility automates much of the drudgery involved in ensuring that a program you compile contains the latest versions of all program modules. SCCS helps you to track the versions of files involved in a project.

System Administration.   Chapter 11 explains the inner workings of the UNIX system. It details the responsibilities of the Superuser and explains how to bring up and shut down a UNIX system, add users to the system, back up files, set up new devices, check the integrity of a file system, and more. This chapter goes into detail about the structure of a file system and explains what administrative information is kept in the various files.

Using UNIX Utilities.   The UNIX system includes hundreds of utilities. Part II contains extensive examples of how to use many of these utilities to solve problems without resorting to programming in C (or another language). The example sections of awk (over 20 pages starting on page 414) and sort (page 588) give real-life examples to demonstrate how to use these utilities alone and with other utilities to generate reports, summarize data, and extract information.

Regular Expressions.   Many UNIX utilities allow you to use regular expressions to make your job easier. Appendix B explains how to use regular expressions so that you can take advantage of some of the hidden power of your UNIX system.

Networking.   Networks of computers are becoming more common. If the system you use is on a network, you can probably use other computers on your network to store and process data. You can also quickly communicate with users on other systems on the network. Appendix C presents an overview of networking and describes the networking utilities. More detail on these utilities is in Part II.

Acknowledgments

I continue to be grateful to the many people who helped with the first edition. This book would not have been possible without the help and support of everyone at Informix Software, Inc. Special thanks to Roger Sippl, Laura King, and Roy

Harrington for introducing me to the UNIX system. My mother, Dr. Helen Sobell, provided invaluable comments on the manuscript at several junctures. Isaac Rabinovitch provided a very thorough review of the system administration chapter. Prof. Raphael Finkel and Prof. Randolph Bentson each reviewed the manuscript several times, making many significant improvements. Bob Greenberg, Prof. Udo Pooch, Judy Ross, and Dr. Robert Veroff also reviewed the manuscript and made useful suggestions. In addition, the following people provided critical reviews and were generally helpful during the long haul: Dr. Mike Denny, Joe DiMartino, Dr. John Mashey, Diane Schulz, Robert Jung, and Charles Whitaker.

I am also deeply indebted to many people whose help with different parts of the revision process greatly improved the second edition. Darlene Hawkins and Diane Blass handled countless administrative details. Numerous people helped by providing technical information about both versions of the UNIX system: Don Cragun, Brian Dougherty, Dr. Robert Fish, Guy Harris, Ping Liao, Gary Lindgren, Dr. Jarrett Rosenberg, Dr. Peter Smith, and Bill Weber. Scooter Morris critiqued the chapter on system administration. Brian Reid provided the USENET map of site locations and news exchange paths shown on page 9. Clarke Echols, Oliver Grillmeyer, and Dr. Stephen Wampler reviewed a draft of the manuscript.

Dr. David Korn and Dr. Scott Weikart's reviews of the Bourne Shell chapter and the Korn Shell appendix caused me to step back and rethink my approach to shell programming, and finally to make significant revisions, particularly to Chapter 8. The quality of the final text, which presents an approach to shell programming that even experienced shell programmers will be able to learn from, was motivated by their careful technical analyses of the manuscript. Dr. Brian Kernighan and Rob Pike graciously allowed me to reprint the **bundle** script from their book, *The UNIX Programming Environment,* and Dr. Richard Curtis provided several other shell scripts used in Chapter 8.

Pat Parseghian and Mike Bianchi's reviews of all parts of the manuscript led to major improvements. The time and energy these two put into the reviews, coupled with their substantial expertise, made their reviews truly of a quality that is seldom seen. Pat Parseghian also provided many of the more difficult review exercises. She also did extensive research on exactly how features were implemented in Release 4, making sure that the book remained faithful to the new release.

Dr. Kathleen Hemenway researched, wrote, analyzed reviews and generally coordinated all the efforts that went into the second edition of this book. From her work on the UNIX system at Bell Labs and her teaching experience, she has brought a breadth to the book that greatly increases its value as a learning tool. At Bell Labs, Dr. Hemenway worked on standardizing the UNIX user interface: She studied *how* users interact with UNIX, which makes her an ideal person to *teach users* how to interact with UNIX, as she does in the introductory chapters of this book. In addition, in the process of preparing and teaching a course on shell programming, she has gained a deep understanding of this key aspect of UNIX— her knowledge is evident in chapters 8 and 9 and Appendix A. In sum, this edition of the book would not be as thorough as it is if it were not for Dr. Hemenway's work on it. Thanks, Kathy.

Finally, I must also thank the black cat without a tail who harassed me during the preparation of the manuscript and who is now sitting upstairs somewhere laughing at us mortals who work all day in front of CRTs instead of stretching out in the sun. This book is for you too, Odie.

Mark G. Sobell

BRIEF CONTENTS

CONTENTS

Chapter 2

Getting Started   23

Chapter 3

An Introduction to the Utilities   45

Chapter 4

The File Structure   67

Chapter 5

The Shell   93

Chapter 7

The nroff Text Formatter   163

Chapter 8

The Bourne Shell   221

Chapter 9

The C Shell   295

Chapter 10

Programming Tools   341

Chapter 11

System Administration   367

PART II   THE UNIX UTILITY PROGRAMS   401

Appendix A

Introduction to the Korn Shell   631

Appendix B

Regular Expressions   653

Appendix C

Networking   665

Glossary   673

Index   685

UNIX
SYSTEM V

CHAPTER

1

THE UNIX OPERATING SYSTEM

UNIX is the name of a computer operating system and its family of related utility programs. Over the past few years, the UNIX operating system has matured and gained unprecedented popularity. This chapter starts with a definition of an operating system and a brief history and overview of the UNIX system that explains why it is so popular. It continues with a discussion of some of the features that are new in the latest versions of the system.

WHAT IS AN OPERATING SYSTEM?

An operating system is a control program for a computer. It allocates computer resources and schedules tasks. Computer resources include all the hardware: the central processing unit, system memory, disk and tape storage, printers, terminals, modems, and anything else that is connected to or inside the computer. An operating system also provides an interface to the user—it gives the user a way to access the computer resources.

An operating system performs many varied functions almost simultaneously. It keeps track of filenames and where each file is located on the disk, and it monitors every keystroke on each of the terminals. Memory typically must be allocated so that only one task uses a given area of memory at a time. Other operating system functions include fulfilling requests made by users, running accounting programs that keep track of resource use, and executing backup and other maintenance utilities. An operating system schedules tasks so that the central processor is working on only one task at a given moment, although the computer may appear to be running many programs at the same time.

THE HISTORY OF THE UNIX OPERATING SYSTEM

The UNIX operating system was developed at AT&T Bell Laboratories in Murray Hill, New Jersey—one of the largest research facilities in the world. Since the original design and implementation of the UNIX system by Ken Thompson in 1969, it has gone through a maturing process. When the UNIX operating system was developed, many computers still ran single jobs in a *batch* mode. Programmers fed these computers input in the form of punch cards (these were also called IBM cards) and did not see the program again until the printer produced the output. Because these systems served only one user at a time, they did not take full advantage of the power and speed of the computers. Further, this work environment isolated programmers from each other. It made it difficult to share data and programs, and it did not promote cooperation among people working on the same project.

The UNIX time-sharing system provided three major improvements over single-user, batch systems. It allowed more than one person to use the computer at a time (the UNIX operating system is a *multiuser* operating system), it allowed a person to communicate directly with the computer via a terminal (it is *interactive*), and it made it easy for people to share data and programs.

The UNIX system was not the first interactive, multiuser operating system. An operating system named Multics was in use briefly at Bell Labs before the UNIX operating system was created. The Cambridge Multiple Access System

The AT&T 6386E/33 WorkGroup System Model S computer is based on an Intel 80386
microprocessor chip running at 33 MHz. It incorporates IBM PC AT architecture and runs
UNIX System V. (Photograph courtesy of AT&T Computer Systems)

had been developed in Europe, and the Compatible Time Sharing System (CTSS) had also been used for several years. The designers of the UNIX operating system took advantage of the work that had gone into these and other operating systems by combining the most desirable aspects of each of them.

The UNIX system was developed by researchers who needed a set of modern computing tools to help them with their projects. The system allowed a group of people working together on a project to share selected data and programs while keeping other information private.

Universities and colleges have played a major role in furthering the popularity of the UNIX operating system through the "four year effect." When the UNIX operating system became widely available in 1975, Bell Labs offered it to educational institutions at minimal cost. The schools, in turn, used it in their computer science programs, ensuring that computer science students became familiar with it. Because the UNIX system is such an advanced development system, the students became acclimated to a sophisticated programming environment. As these students graduated and went into industry, they expected to work in a similarly advanced environment. As more of these students worked their way up in the commercial world, the UNIX operating system found its way into industry.

Close-up of the bottom of an Intel 80386 microprocessor. Pins for electrical connections surround the chip itself. The inside of the chip is exposed for this photo—you cannot normally see it. This chip is the basis of many UNIX systems. (Photograph courtesy of Intel Corp.)

In addition to introducing its students to the UNIX operating system, the Computer Systems Research Group at the University of California at Berkeley made significant additions and changes to it. They made so many popular changes that one of the two most prominent versions of the system in use today is called the Berkeley Software Distribution (BSD) of the UNIX system. The other major version is AT&T's UNIX System V. This book covers the features of the latest releases of System V.

It is this heritage—development in a research environment and enhancement in a university setting—that has made the UNIX operating system such a powerful software development tool.

WHY IS THE UNIX SYSTEM POPULAR WITH MANUFACTURERS?

Two trends in the computer industry have set the stage for the recent popularity of the UNIX system. First, advances in hardware technology have created the need for an operating system that can take advantage of available hardware power. In the mid-1970s, minicomputers began challenging the large mainframe computers because in many applications minicomputers could perform the same functions less expensively. Today, microcomputers are challenging the minis in much the same way, far surpassing even newer minicomputers in cost and performance. Powerful 32-bit processor chips, plentiful, inexpensive memory, and lower-priced

This is a multi-port, intelligent Input/Output board that is designed to be used in 80386- and
80486-based UNIX systems. It will allow from 4 to 32 users to access the computer.
(Photograph courtesy of Stallion Technologies, Inc.)

hard-disk storage have allowed manufacturers to install multiuser operating systems on microcomputers.

Second, with the cost of hardware continually dropping, hardware manufacturers can no longer afford to develop and support proprietary operating systems. They need a generic system that they can easily adapt to their machines. In turn, software manufacturers need to keep the prices of their product down—they cannot afford to convert their products to run under many different proprietary operating systems. Like hardware manufacturers, software manufacturers need a generic operating system.

The UNIX system satisfies both needs: It is a generic operating system and it takes advantage of available hardware power. Because the UNIX system was written almost entirely in a machine-independent language, it can easily be adapted to different machines, and it can easily be adapted to meet special requirements. Because the UNIX system was initially designed for minicomputers, the file structure takes full advantage of large, fast hard disks. Equally important, it was originally designed as a multiuser operating system—it was not modified to serve several users as an afterthought. Sharing the computer's power among many users and giving users the ability to share data and programs are central features of the system. Because the UNIX system is easily adapted and because it can take advantage of the available hardware, it now runs on a wide range of machines—from microcomputers to supercomputers.

The UNIX system offers an additional advantage to software companies: Having been originally designed by highly skilled programmers to support their own projects, it provides an ideal software development environment.

The advent of a standard operating system aided the development of the software industry. Now software manufacturers can afford to make one version of one product available on many different machines. No longer does one speak of "the company that makes the MRP package for the IBM machine" but rather "the company that makes the MRP package for the UNIX operating system." The hardware manufacturer who offers a UNIX-based system can count on third-party software being available to run on the new machine.

THE UNIX SYSTEM IS WIDELY ACCEPTED

The UNIX operating system has gained widespread commercial acceptance. UNIX system user groups have been started in many cities throughout the world; national and international organizations have been established; several conferences and trade shows are held each year; UNIX system magazines can be found in bookstores; and articles on the UNIX operating system are abundant. The UNIX operating system is available on many machines, including microcomputers, mini-computers, mainframes, and supercomputers. Even non-UNIX operating systems, such as MS-DOS, have adopted some of the traits of the UNIX system.

The UNIX system has become so important in the computer industry that in recent years there has been widespread concern that the UNIX system itself be standardized. While hardware manufacturers were adapting the UNIX system to their hardware, many of them made changes to it. Ironically, these changes make it difficult for software developers to develop applications that will run on all versions of the system. In the process of making the generic operating system a standard for a variety of machine architectures, changes were made to it that made it less standard. To standardize the UNIX system, and in turn improve the market for applications, AT&T has melded their version of the system, System V, with features of other prominent versions: XENIX, Berkeley Software Distribution (BSD), and SunOS. The result is System V Release 4. AT&T has also established a written standard, the System V Interface Definition (SVID). Meanwhile, individuals from companies throughout the industry have joined together to develop a standard called POSIX (Portable Operating System Interface for Computer Environments), which is largely based on the System V Interface Definition and other earlier standardization efforts. These efforts have been spurred by the federal government, which needs a standard computing environment in order to minimize training and procurement costs. As these standards gain widespread acceptance, software developers will be able to develop applications that run on all conforming versions of the UNIX system.

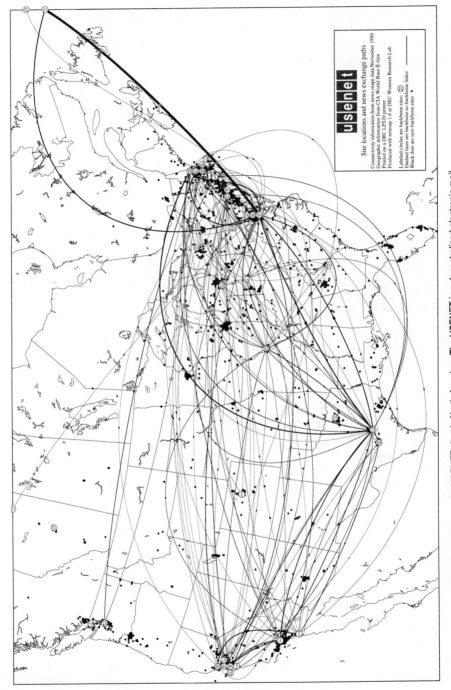

usenet

Site locations and news exchange paths

Connectivity information from news.maps data November 1990
Geographic information from CIA World Base II data
Printed on a DEC LPS20 printer
Produced with netmap 1.6 at DEC Western Research Lab

Labeled circles are backbone sites: ⊕
Dashed lines are backbone-to-backbone links: ———
Black dots are non-backbone sites •

Site locations and news exchange paths for major USENET sites in North America. The USENET is a decentralized electronic mail and news network that links more than 200,000 UNIX users worldwide. (Map courtesy of Brian Reid.)

HOW CAN IT RUN ON SO MANY MACHINES?

An operating system that can run on many different machines is said to be portable. About 95 percent of the UNIX operating system is written in the C programming language, and C is portable because it is written in a higher-level, machine-independent language. (Even the C compiler is written in C.)

The C Programming Language

Ken Thompson originally wrote the UNIX operating system in PDP-7 assembly language. Assembly language is a machine-dependent language—programs written in assembly language work on only one machine or, at best, one family of machines. Therefore, the original UNIX operating system could not easily be transported to run on other machines.

In order to make the UNIX system portable, Thompson developed the B programming language, a machine-independent language. Dennis Ritchie developed the C programming language by modifying B and, with Thompson, rewrote the UNIX system in C. After this rewrite, the operating system could be transported more easily to run on other machines.

That was the start of C. You can see in its roots some of the reasons why it is such a powerful tool. C can be used to write machine-independent programs. A programmer who designs a program to be portable can easily move it to any computer that has a C compiler. As C and the UNIX operating system become more popular, more machines have C compilers.

C is a modern systems language. You can write a compiler or an operating system in C. It is highly structured, but it is not necessarily a high-level language. C allows a programmer to manipulate bits and bytes, as is necessary when writing an operating system. But it also has high-level constructs that allow efficient, modular programming.

C is becoming popular for the same reasons the UNIX operating system is successful. It is portable, standard, and powerful. It has high-level features for flexibility and can still be used for systems programming. These features make it both useful and usable.

OVERVIEW OF THE UNIX SYSTEM

The UNIX operating system has many unique features. Like other operating systems, the UNIX system is a control program for computers. But it is also a well-thought-out family of utility programs (see Figure 1-1) and a set of tools that allows users to connect and use these utilities to build systems and applications.

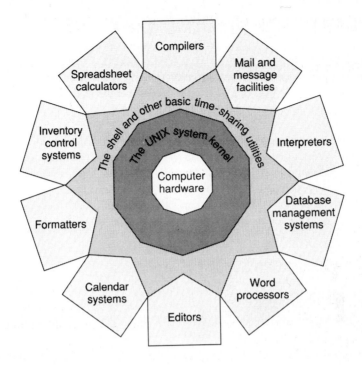

FIGURE 1-1   The UNIX System

This section discusses both the common and unique features of the UNIX operating system.

Utilities

The UNIX system includes a family of several hundred utility programs, often referred to as commands. These utilities perform functions that are universally required by users. An example is sort. The sort utility puts lists (or groups of lists) in order. It can put lists in alphabetical or numerical order and thus can be used to sort by part number, author, last name, city, ZIP code, telephone number, age, size, cost, and so forth. The sort utility is an important programming tool and is part of the standard UNIX system. Other utilities allow users to create, display, print, copy, search, and delete files. There are also text editing, formatting, and typesetting utilities. The man (for manual) utility provides on-line documentation of the UNIX system itself.

The UNIX System Can Support Many Users

Depending on the machine being used, a UNIX system can support from one to over one hundred users, each concurrently running a different set of programs. The cost of a computer that can be used by many people at the same time is less per user than that of a computer that can be used by only a single person at a time. The cost is less because one person cannot generally use all of the resources a computer has to offer. No one can keep the printer going constantly, keep all the system memory in use, keep the disk busy reading and writing, keep the tape drives spinning, and keep the terminals busy. A multiuser operating system allows many people to use the system resources almost simultaneously. Thus, utilization of costly resources can be maximized, and the cost per user minimized. These are the primary objectives of a multiuser operating system.

The UNIX System Can Support Many Tasks

The UNIX operating system allows each user to run more than one job at a time. You can run several jobs in the background while giving all your attention to the job being displayed on your terminal, and you can even switch back and forth between jobs. This *multitasking* capability enables users to be more productive.

The Shell

The shell is a command interpreter that acts as an interface between users and the operating system. When you enter a command at a terminal, the shell interprets the command and calls the program you want. There are three popular shells in use today: the Bourne Shell, the C Shell, and the Korn Shell. Other shells are available, however, including menu shells such as FACE (Framed Access Command Environment) that provide easy-to-use interfaces for computer-naive users. Because different users can use different shells at the same time on one system, a system can appear different to different users. The choice of shells demonstrates one of the powers of the UNIX operating system: the ability to provide a customized user interface.

Besides its regular function of interpreting commands from a terminal keyboard and sending them to the operating system, the shell can be used as a high-level programming language. Shell commands can be arranged in a file for later execution as a high-level program. This flexibility allows users to perform complex operations with relative ease, often with rather short commands, or to build elaborate programs that perform highly complex operations, with surprisingly little effort.

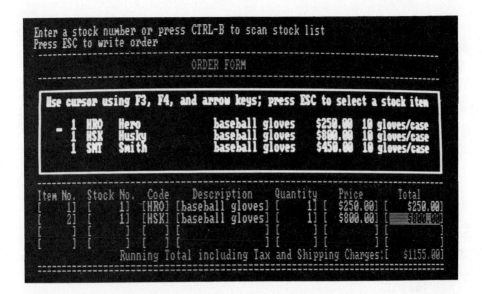

This terminal screen was generated by Informix-4GL, a fourth-generation language. Fourth-generation languages speed development time through the use of high-level, intuitive programming constructs. This fourth-generation language accesses a relational database management system (RDBMS), a necessary component of a wide range of application programs. Informix-4GL is written in C, enabling it to run on many different machines. (Photograph courtesy of Informix Software, Inc.)

File Structure

A *file* is a collection of information, such as text for a memo or report, an accumulation of sales figures, or object code created by a compiler. Each file is stored under a unique name, usually on a disk storage device. The UNIX file system provides a structure where files are arranged under directories, and directories in turn are arranged under other directories, and so forth, in a treelike organization. This structure assists users in keeping track of large numbers of files by enabling them to group related files into directories. Each user has one primary directory and as many subdirectories as required.

Another mechanism, *links*, allows a given file to be accessed by means of two or more different names. The alternative names can be located in the same directory as the original file or in another directory. Links can be used to make the same file appear in several users' directories, enabling them to share the file easily.

Security—Private and Shared Files

Like most multiuser operating systems, the UNIX system allows users to protect their data from access by other users. The UNIX system also allows users to share selected data and programs with certain other users by means of a simple but effective protection scheme.

Filename Generation

When you are typing commands to be processed by the shell, you can construct patterns using special characters that have special meanings to the shell. These patterns are a kind of shorthand: Rather than typing in complete filenames, users can type in patterns and the shell will fill them in, generating matching filenames. A pattern can save you the effort of typing in a long filename or a long series of similar filenames. Patterns can also be useful when you know only part of a filename and when you cannot remember the exact spelling.

Device-Independent Input and Output

Devices (such as a printer or terminal) and disk files all appear as files to UNIX programs. When you give the UNIX operating system a command, you can instruct it to send the output to any one of several devices or files. This diversion is called output *redirection.*

In a similar manner, a program's input that normally comes from a terminal can be redirected so that it comes from a disk file instead. Under the UNIX operating system, input and output are *device-independent;* they can be redirected to or from any appropriate device.

As an example, the cat utility normally displays the contents of a file on the terminal screen. When you enter a cat command, you can cause its output to go to a disk file instead of to the terminal.

Interprocess Communication

The UNIX system allows users to establish both pipes and filters on the command line. A *pipe* sends the output of one program to another program as input. A *filter* is a program designed to process a stream of input data and yield a stream of output data. Filters are often used between two pipes. A filter processes another program's output, altering it in some manner. The filter's output then becomes input to another program.

Pipes and filters frequently join utilities to perform a specific task. For example, you can use a pipe to send the output of the cat utility to sort, a filter, and then use another pipe to send the output of sort to a third utility, lp, that will send the file to a printer. Thus, in one command line you can use three utilities together to sort a file and print it.

NEW FEATURES OF THE UNIX SYSTEM

Over the years, many people have contributed to the maturation of the UNIX system. The two most prominent versions of the system in use today, Berkeley UNIX and UNIX System V, share a common ancestor—a version of the UNIX system developed by researchers at AT&T Bell Laboratories in the late 1970s called Version 7. Berkeley UNIX originated as a result of additions and modifications made to Version 7 by the Computer Systems Research Group at the University of California at Berkeley. Early versions of Berkeley UNIX added a full-screen text editor (vi), a new user interface (the C Shell), and virtual memory management, which enabled the UNIX system to support large applications. Later additions included a new file system for higher performance, and a networking subsystem for the support of a wide range of networking protocols. With the networking subsystem, users can log in on one machine and easily copy files to remote machines, run commands on remote machines, and log in on remote machines.

While the Computer Systems Research Group at Berkeley was making its changes to UNIX, AT&T was enhancing it in ways that ultimately resulted in System V. AT&T incorporated work done on the Programmer's Workbench UNIX system (originally developed for use within the Bell System) as well as features produced for other versions in use within AT&T. The result was System III, the predecessor of System V. Notable additions to System V were virtual memory management and new interprocess communication mechanisms. Recent releases of System V include a new file system that can span machines and a new networking subsystem.

Because of their common ancestry and because of the trend in recent years toward a single UNIX standard, System V and Berkeley UNIX are very similar in many ways. Following is a discussion of the most important new features of System V. Because of the trend toward consolidation, many of the features were adopted from Berkeley UNIX for inclusion in System V.

This discussion only touches the surface of what is new in UNIX System V. Many features—such as the new file system implementations, Sockets networking subsystem, remote file systems (RFS and NFS), and Streams networking subsystem—are beyond the scope of this book. Many others are significant only if you are familiar with previous versions of the UNIX system—these features are discussed at the appropriate places throughout the book. If UNIX is new to you, you may just want to scan this list of features and come back to it after reading the first few chapters.

Job Control

Job control allows users to work on several jobs at once, switching back and forth between them as desired. Frequently, when you start a job, it is in the foreground, so it is connected to your terminal. Using job control, you can move the job you are working with into the background so that you can work on or observe another job while the first is running. If a background job needs your attention, you can move it into the foreground so that it is once again attached to your terminal.

The concept of job control originated with Berkeley UNIX and has been added to System V in two forms. Prior to System V Release 4, job control was coordinated by the shell layer manager (shl). The name is derived from the concept of shell *layers*, each layer running a different job. Refer to shl in Part II for more information on the shell layer manager. System V Release 4 includes both the shell layer manager and Berkeley-style job control (see page 305).

Advanced Electronic Mail

System V incorporates many of the features of the Berkeley UNIX mail utility in the System V mailx utility. The mailx utility

- allows users to reply to a message, automatically addressing the reply to the person who sent the message
- allows users to use an editor (such as vi or emacs) to edit a piece of electronic mail while they are composing it
- presents users with a summary of all messages waiting for them when they call it up to read their mail
- can automatically keep a copy of all electronic mail users send
- allows users to create aliases that make it easier to send mail to groups of people
- allows users to customize features to suit their needs

See page 49 for a tutorial, and see mailx in Part II for a detailed summary of this utility.

Screen-Oriented Editor

Although the vi (visual) editor from Berkeley has been widely available for several years, it became an official part of AT&T UNIX only with the introduction of System V.

The vi editor is an advance over its predecessor, ed, because it displays a context for editing: Where ed displayed a line at a time, vi displays a screenful of text.

This book explains how to use vi in stages, from the introduction in Chapter 2 (page 33) through "Advanced Editing Techniques" (page 148). Most of the vi coverage is in Chapter 6, which is dedicated to the use of this editor.

Delayed Execution of Jobs

The at utility lets users schedule a job to run *at* a certain time. You can tell at you want to run the job in a few hours, next week, or even on a specific date in the future. This utility allows you to schedule jobs that slow down the machine or tie up resources, such as the printer, so that jobs can be run when your machine is not normally used (e.g., at night or on weekends).

Scrolling Through a File

System V provides a utility called pg (page) that allows users to display files on their terminals one screenful at a time. System V Release 4 has an additional, similar utility called more, adopted from Berkeley UNIX. When you finish reading what is on the screen, you ask for another screenful by pressing a single key. These utilities also have the ability to scroll backward through a file. See pg and more in Part II for more information.

Shell Functions

One of the most important features of the shell (the UNIX command interpreter) is that users can use it as a programming language. Because the shell is an interpreter, it does not compile programs written for it but interprets them each time they are loaded in from the disk. Interpreting and loading programs can be time-consuming.

Two of the most popular shells, the Bourne Shell and the Korn Shell, allow you to write shell functions that the shell will hold in memory, so it does not have to read them from the disk each time you want to execute them. The shell also keeps functions in an internal format, so it does not have to spend as much time interpreting them. Refer to page 287 for more information on shell functions.

Although the third major shell, the C Shell, does not have shell functions, it has a similar feature: aliases. Aliases allow you to define new commands and to make standard utilities perform in nonstandard ways. The C Shell provides aliases but not shell functions; the Korn Shell provides both.

SYSTEM V RELEASE 4

A major goal attained in UNIX System V Release 4 is the merging of popular features from XENIX, Berkeley UNIX, and Sun Microsystems' SunOS with System V. System V Release 4 also complies with recent standards set forth by POSIX, the ANSI C language committee, and in the X/OPEN Guide (a standard for window systems). This unification enhances the functionality of System V Release 4 and helps to simplify the UNIX product marketplace.

If you are familiar with older versions of UNIX, one of the most noticeable changes you will find in System V Release 4 is the reorganization of the file system hierarchy. Many familiar directories have been renamed, and many utilities and system files have been relocated to make it easier for systems to share data remotely over a network.

Many of the features that are new to System V Release 4 have been made available as extensions to older versions of System V by individual manufacturers and may already be familiar to you. Unfortunately, each manufacturer added features in slightly different ways, making it difficult for users to adapt to new systems or to share programs. System V Release 4 addresses these problems by incorporating the most common extensions, thus reducing the need for individual manufacturers to create new UNIX variants.

Networking Utilities

Networking utilities are a valuable addition to System V Release 4, enabling users to access remote systems over a variety of networks. System V Release 4 supports the Network File System (NFS) developed by Sun Microsystems, a remote file system that is commonly supplied on UNIX systems available from many different manufacturers.

System Administration

System administration has been made easier through extensions to the sysadm utility to help provide more guidance for the novice system administrator. There is better support for installing software, backing up and restoring files, and managing system facilities such as printers and terminal ports.

Graphical User Interface

The X window system, developed in part by researchers at the Massachusetts Institute of Technology, provides the foundation for the graphical user interface available with System V Release 4. Given a terminal or workstation screen that supports X windows, a user might interact with the computer through multiple windows on the screen, display graphical information, or use special-purpose applications to draw pictures or preview typesetter output.

WHAT ARE THE LIMITATIONS OF THE UNIX SYSTEM?

The most commonly heard complaints about the UNIX operating system are that it has an unfriendly, terse, treacherous, unforgiving, inconsistent, and nonmnemonic user interface. These complaints are well founded, but the shortcomings of the user interface were largely a by-product of the original design goals of the system. The designers of the UNIX system intended it to be used by highly skilled programmers for whom ease of use is much less important than power and flexibility.

As the UNIX system became popular with a wider variety of users, many of the worst problems were rectified by newer versions of the operating system and by some application programs. Also, new features of the shells have made them easier to use. In particular, aliases and shell functions enable you to rename and redefine commands so that they are more user-friendly and forgiving, and so you can avoid some of the peculiarities of command line syntax. Although these features make the shells easier to use, they have not changed the basic nature of the user interface. The shells have stayed basically the same for a good reason— many of the features that make them difficult to learn are the same ones that make them so useful for experienced users.

The UNIX system is called unfriendly and terse because it seems to follow the philosophy that "no news is good news." The ed editor does not prompt you for input or commands, the cp (copy) utility does not confirm that it has copied a file successfully, and the who utility does not display column headings before its list of users. It just presents information with no titles or explanation.

This terseness is useful because it facilitates the use of the *pipe* facility, which allows the output from one program to be fed into another program as input. Thus, you can find out how many people are using the system by sending the output of who into wc, a utility that counts the number of lines in a file. If who displayed a heading before it displayed the list of users, you could not make this connection. (Newer versions of who have an option that displays a heading and another that tells users how many people are using the system.)

In a similar manner, although it would be nice if ed prompted you when you were using it as an interactive editor, it would not be as useful when you wanted to feed it input from another program and have it automatically edit a group of files.

The UNIX system was originally designed for slow hard-copy terminals. The less copy a program printed out, the sooner it was done. With high-speed terminals, this is no longer a problem. Editors that display more information (e.g., vi) now run on the UNIX system with these newer high-speed terminals.

The shell user interface can still be treacherous, however. A typing mistake on a command line can easily destroy important files, and it is possible to log off the system inadvertently. You must use caution when working with a powerful operating system. If you want a foolproof system, you can use the tools the UNIX system provides to customize the shell. Some manufacturers are producing menu-driven user interfaces that make it very difficult to make mistakes that have such far-reaching consequences. The C Shell and Korn Shell have optional built-in safeguards against many of these problems.

Due to its simplicity, the UNIX operating system has had, and still has, some limitations. In versions prior to System V, mechanisms to synchronize separate jobs were poorly implemented, as were mechanisms for locking files—important features in a multiuser operating system. System V has rectified these problems. The objection that is perhaps the most serious and difficult to overcome is that the UNIX operating system does not have a guaranteed hardware-interrupt response time. This prevents a standard UNIX system from being used in some real-time applications. System V Release 4 supports a new scheduling policy and timers with a higher resolution, two features that will make the system more useful for real-time applications. Other new features that are available from certain manufacturers include concurrency, fault tolerance, and parallel processing. As the system continues to evolve, future versions will undoubtedly provide these and other new features, meeting a wider variety of users' needs.

SUMMARY

Although the UNIX operating system has some shortcomings, most of them can be rectified using the tools that the UNIX system itself provides. The unique approach that the UNIX operating system takes to the problems of standardization and portability, its strong foothold in the professional community, its power as a development tool, and its chameleonlike user interface are helping it to emerge as the standard first choice of users, hardware manufacturers, and software manufacturers.

REVIEW EXERCISES

1. What is a time-sharing system? Why are they successful?
2. Why is the UNIX system popular with manufacturers? Why is it popular in academia?

3. What language is the UNIX system written in? What does the language have to do with the success of the UNIX system?

4. What is a utility program?

5. What is the shell? Why was it designed to be terse?

6. How can you use utility programs and the shell to create your own applications?

7. Why is the UNIX file system referred to as a hierarchical (or treelike) file system?

8. Although the UNIX system is a generic operating system, there are different versions of it. Explain this apparent contradiction.

9. Why is it important to software developers that the different versions of the UNIX system converge? What is being done in the industry to promote convergence?

CHAPTER
2

GETTING STARTED

This chapter explains how to log in on, and use, the UNIX system. It discusses several important names and keyboard keys that are specific to you, your terminal, and your installation. Following a description of the conventions used in this book, this chapter leads you through a brief session with your UNIX system. After showing you how to log in and out, it explains how to correct typing mistakes and abort program execution. Finally, it guides you through a short session with the vi editor and introduces other important utilities that manipulate files. With these utilities you can obtain lists of filenames, display the contents of files, and delete files.

BEFORE YOU START

The best way to learn is by doing. You can read and use Chapters 2 through 10 while you are sitting in front of a terminal. Learn about the UNIX system by running the examples in this book and by making up your own. Feel free to experiment with different utilities. The worst thing that you can do is erase one of the files that you have created. Because these are only practice files, you can easily create another.

Before you log in on a UNIX system for the first time, take a few minutes to find out the answers to the following questions. Ask the system administrator or someone else who is familiar with your installation.

What Is My Login Name?   This is the name that you use to identify yourself to the UNIX system. It is also the name that other users use to send you electronic mail.

What Is My Password?   On systems with several users, passwords can prevent others from accessing your files. To start with, the system administrator assigns you a password. You can change your password at any time.

Which Key Ends a Line?   Different terminals use different keys to move the cursor to the beginning of the next line. This book always refers to the key that ends a line as the RETURN key. Your terminal may have a RET, NEWLINE, ENTER, or other key. Some terminals use a key with a bent arrow on it. (The key with the bent arrow is not an ARROW key. ARROW keys have arrows on straight shafts—you will use them when you use the vi editor.) Figure 2-1 shows a standard terminal keyboard. The key that ends a line on this keyboard is the RETURN key. Each time this book asks you to "press the RETURN key" or "press RETURN," press the equivalent key on your terminal.

Which Is the Erase Key?   Usually CONTROL-H (press **H** while holding the CONTROL, CNTRL, or CTRL key down) will back up over and erase the characters you just entered, one at a time. You can probably also use the BACKSPACE key. If neither CONTROL-H nor the BACKSPACE key erases characters, you may be able to use the # key or the DEL key. On most terminals the DEL key is labeled DELETE, DEL, or RUBOUT. You may have to hold the SHIFT key down while you press this key to make it work. Ask your system administrator or refer to page 603 for examples of how to determine which key is your *erase* key and how to change it to one that is more convenient.

Which Is the Line Kill Key?   Usually, the key that deletes the entire line you are entering is CONTROL-U; however, @ is used occasionally. This key is called the *line kill* or simply *kill* key. Refer to page 603 for examples of how to determine which key is your line kill key and how to change it.

Which Key Interrupts Execution?   There is one key that interrupts almost any

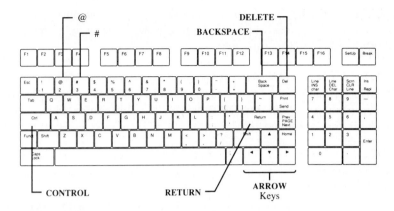

FIGURE 2-1   A Standard Terminal Keyboard (Courtesy of Wyse Technology)

program you are running. This is often the DEL key; however, if the DEL key is the erase key on your system, then another key is the interrupt key. Often CONTROL-C is used as the interrupt key. Refer to page 602 for a description of the interrupt key.

What Is the Terminfo Name for My Terminal?   On System V, a Terminfo name describes the functional characteristics of your terminal to any program that requires this information. You will need to know this name if you use vi (the visual editor). Some application programs also need this information.

Some versions that preceded System V use Termcap names in place of Terminfo names. Although the two methods for specifying a terminal are different, the way you use the names is the same. If your system uses Termcap names, use the Termcap name for your terminal when this book calls for a Terminfo name.

Which Shell Will I Be Using?   The shell interprets the commands you enter from the keyboard. You will probably be using the Bourne Shell, the C Shell, or the Korn Shell. They are similar in many respects. The examples in this book show the Bourne Shell but are generally applicable to all three shells. Chapters 5, 8, and 9 and Appendix A describe the shells and the differences between them.

Which Version of UNIX Will I Be Using?   This book tells you what to expect when you are using System V UNIX. If you are using another version of UNIX, you may notice subtle differences between what is described here and the behavior of your system.

How Can I Send Files to a Printer?   Most UNIX systems have at least one printer for producing hard copy. Typically, you will be able to use a utility called lp to send output to a printer. However, if your system has more than one printer, you will use different commands, or different variations of one command, to send output to the various printers. Ask the system administrator how the printers are set up on your system. Refer to Chapter 3 for more information about printing.

Where Can I Find the UNIX Manuals?   Most versions of the UNIX system come with reference manuals. You may want to refer to them to get more information about specific topics while reading this book or to determine what features are available on your version of UNIX.

Conventions

This book uses conventions to make its explanations shorter and clearer. The following paragraphs describe these conventions.

Keys and Characters.   This book uses SMALL CAPS to show three different kinds of items:

* Important terminal keys, such as the SPACE bar and the RETURN, ESCAPE, and TAB keys.
* The characters that keys generate, such as the SPACES generated by the SPACE bar.
* Terminal keys that you press with the CONTROL key, such as CONTROL-D. (Even though **D** is shown as an uppercase letter, you do not have to press the SHIFT key; enter CONTROL-D by holding the CONTROL key down and pressing **d**.)

Utility Names.   Within the text, names of utilities are printed in this typeface. Thus, you will see references to the sort utility and the vi editor.

Filenames.   Within the text, all filenames appear in lowercase letters in a **bold** typeface. Examples of files that appear in the text are: **memo5, letter.1283**, and **reports**. Filenames can include uppercase letters, but this book uses only lowercase filenames.

Items You Enter.   Within the text, all commands that you can enter at the terminal are printed in a **bold** typeface. This book refers to the ls utility, or just ls, but instructs you to enter **ls −a** on the terminal. Thus, a distinction is made in the text between utilities, which are programs, and the instructions you give the computer to invoke the utilities.

      In the screens and examples shown throughout this book, the items that you would enter are printed in boldface type, as they are in the text. However, unlike in the text, where items you enter are in **this boldface** type, in screens and examples the items you enter are in `this boldface` type. In the first line of Figure 2-2, for example, the word login: is printed in a regular typeface because the UNIX system displayed it. The word `jenny` is in boldface to show that the user entered it. The word **jenny** appears in the text.

Prompts and RETURNS.   All examples include the shell prompt—the signal that the UNIX system is waiting for a command—as a dollar sign ($). Your prompt may differ—another common prompt is a percent sign (%). The prompt is printed in a regular typeface because you do not enter it. Do not enter the prompt on the terminal when you are experimenting with examples from this book. If you do, the examples will not work.

Examples *omit* the RETURN keystroke that you must use to execute them. An example of a command line follows:

```
$ vi memo.1204
```

To use this example as a model for calling the vi editor, enter **vi memo.1204** and then press the RETURN key. This method of giving examples makes the example in the book and what appears on your terminal screen the same. See the next section for a complete example.

Information About New Features.   Information about features that have been introduced in System V Release 4 is presented surrounded by double lines, with the identifier NEW TO UNIX SYSTEM V Release 4. The new information is marked in this way to help you identify the descriptions of the new features easily and to enable you to skip information that may not apply to the UNIX version you are using. An example follows:

NEW TO UNIX SYSTEM V Release 4

This information applies to UNIX System V Release 4.

Optional Information.   Triple lines and the word OPTIONAL surround the information that you can skip the first time you read a chapter. Passages that are inside the triple lines are not central to the concepts presented in the chapter, and they are often difficult. A good strategy is to read a chapter, skipping the optional sections, and return to them later after you are comfortable with the main ideas presented in the chapter. An example follows:

OPTIONAL

You can skip this information the first time you read the chapter.

USING THE UNIX SYSTEM

Now that you are acquainted with some of the special characters on the keyboard and the conventions this book uses, it will be easier to start using the UNIX system. This section leads you through a brief session, explaining how to log in, change your password, and log out.

Logging In

Since many people can use the UNIX operating system at the same time, it must be able to differentiate between you and other users. You must identify yourself before the UNIX system will process your requests.

Figure 2-2 shows how a typical login procedure appears on a terminal screen. Your login procedure may look different. If your terminal does not have the word login: on it, check to see that the terminal is turned on, then press the RETURN key a few times. If login: still does not appear, try pressing CONTROL-Q. You can also try pressing the BREAK key and the RETURN key alternately. If these procedures do not work, check with the system administrator. (If LOGIN: appears in uppercase letters, proceed. This situation is covered shortly.)

```
login: jenny
Password:

Welcome to UNIX!

$
```

FIGURE 2-2   Logging In

You must end every message or command to the UNIX system by pressing the RETURN key. Pressing RETURN signals that you have completed giving an instruction and that you are ready for the operating system to execute the command or respond to the message.

The first line of Figure 2-2 shows the UNIX system login: prompt followed by the user's response. The user entered **jenny**, her login name, followed by a RETURN. Try logging in, making sure that you enter your login name exactly as it was given to you. The routine that verifies the login name and password is *case-sensitive*—it differentiates between uppercase and lowercase letters.

The second line of Figure 2-2 shows the **Password:** prompt. If your account does not require a password, you will not see this prompt. In the example, the user *did* respond to the prompt with a password followed by a RETURN. For security, the UNIX operating system never displays a password. Enter your password in response to the **Password:** prompt, then press RETURN. The characters you enter will not appear on the terminal screen.

You will see a message and a prompt when you successfully log in. The message, called the *message of the day*, is generally something like **Welcome to UNIX!** and, if you are using the Bourne Shell or the Korn Shell, the prompt is usually a dollar sign ($). The C Shell generally prompts you with a percent sign (%) or a number followed by a percent sign. Either of these prompts indicates that the system is waiting for you to give it a command.

The Uppercase LOGIN Prompt.   If the login prompt appears in all uppercase letters (LOGIN:), everything you enter will also appear in uppercase letters. The UNIX system thinks you have a terminal that can display only uppercase characters. It sends uppercase characters to the terminal and translates everything you enter to lowercase for its internal use. If you are having this problem and your terminal is capable of displaying both uppercase and lowercase characters, make sure the key on your keyboard that causes it to send uppercase characters has *not* been set. (This key is typically labeled SHIFT LOCK or CAPS LOCK.) If it is set, unset it. Once you have logged in, give the following command. Press RETURN after you enter the command.

```
$ STTY -LCASE
```

Incorrect Login.   If you enter your name or password incorrectly, the login utility displays the following message, after you finish entering both your login name *and* password:

```
Login incorrect
```

This message tells you that you have entered either the login name *or* password incorrectly or that they are not valid. The message does not differentiate between an unacceptable login name and an unacceptable password. This discourages unauthorized people from guessing names and passwords to gain access to the system.

After You Log In.   Once you log in, you are communicating with the command interpreter known as the shell. The shell plays an important part in all your communication with the UNIX operating system. When you enter a command at the terminal (in response to the shell prompt), the shell interprets the command and initiates the appropriate action. This action may be executing your program, calling a standard program such as a compiler or a UNIX utility program, or giving you an error message telling you that you have entered a command incorrectly.

Changing Your Password

When you first log in on a UNIX system, either you will not have a password or you will have a password that the system administrator assigned. In either case, it is a good idea to give yourself a new password. A good password is seven or eight characters long and contains a combination of numbers, uppercase letters, lowercase letters, and punctuation characters. Avoid using control characters (e.g., CONTROL-H) because they may collide with system operation, making it impossible for you to log in. Do not use names or other familiar words that someone can guess easily.

Figure 2-3 shows the process of changing a password using the **passwd** utility. Depending on the version of UNIX you are using, the messages the **passwd** utility presents and the sequence of the interaction may differ slightly from the examples shown on the following pages, but the gist of the interaction is the same. For security reasons, none of the passwords that you enter is ever displayed by this or any other utility.

```
$ passwd
Changing password for jenny
Old password:
New password:
Re-enter new password:
```

FIGURE 2-3   The passwd Utility

Give the command **passwd** (followed by a RETURN) in response to the shell prompt. This command causes the shell to execute the **passwd** utility. The first item **passwd** asks you for is your *old* password (it skips this question if you do not have a password yet). The **passwd** utility verifies this password to ensure that an unauthorized user is not trying to alter your password. Next, **passwd** requests the new password.

Your password must meet the following criteria:

• It must be at least six characters long.

• It must contain at least two letters and one number.

• It cannot be your login name, the reverse of your login name, or your login name shifted by one or more characters.

• If you are changing your password, the new password must differ from the old one by at least three characters. Changing the case of a character does not make it count as a different character.

After you enter your new password, passwd asks you to retype it to make sure you did not make a mistake when you entered it. If the new password is the same both times you enter it, your password is changed. If the passwords differ, it means that you made an error in one of them; passwd displays the following message:

```
They don't match; try again.
New password:
```

After you enter the new password, passwd will—as it did before—ask you to reenter it.

If your password does not meet the criteria listed above, passwd displays the following message:

```
Password is too short – must be at least 6 digits.
New password:
```

Enter a password that meets the criteria in response to the New password: prompt.

When you successfully change your password, you change the way you will log in. You must always enter your password *exactly* the way you created it. If you forget your password, the system administrator can help straighten things out. Although no one can determine what your password is, the administrator can change it and tell you your new password.

Logging Out

Once you have changed your password, log out and try logging back in using your new password. Press CONTROL-D in response to the shell prompt to log out. If CONTROL-D does not work, try giving the command **exit** or **logout**. The **logout** command is typically used with the C Shell, whereas the Bourne Shell and Korn Shell use CONTROL-D or **exit.**

CORRECTING MISTAKES

This section explains how to correct typing and other errors you may make while you are logged in. Log in on your system and try making and correcting mistakes as you read this section.

Because the shell and most other utilities do not interpret the command line (or other text) until after you press the RETURN key, you can correct typing mistakes before you press RETURN. There are two ways to correct typing mistakes. You can erase one character at a time, or you can back up to the beginning of the command line in one step. After you press the RETURN key, it is too late to correct a mistake; you can either wait for the command to run to completion or abort execution of the program. Refer to the section "Aborting Program Execution" on page 33.

Erasing Characters

While entering characters from the keyboard, you can backspace over a mistake by pressing the erase key (CONTROL-H) one time for each character you want to delete. (In place of CONTROL-H, use the erase key you identified at the start of this chapter.) As the cursor moves to the left, the characters it moves over are discounted, even if they still appear on the screen. The erase key backs up over as many characters as you wish. It does not, however, back up past the beginning of the line.

Deleting an Entire Line

You can delete the entire line you are entering, any time before you press RETURN, by pressing the line kill key (CONTROL-U). (In place of CONTROL-U, use the line kill key you identified at the start of this chapter.)

When you press CONTROL-U, the cursor moves down to the next line and all the way to the left. The shell does not give you another prompt, but it is as though the cursor is sitting just following a shell prompt. The operating system does not remove the line with the mistake on it but ignores it. Enter the command (or other text) again, from the start.

NEW TO UNIX SYSTEM V Release 4

Deleting a Word

You can delete the word you are entering by pressing CONTROL-W. When you press CONTROL-W, the cursor moves to the left to the beginning of the current word, removing the word. A *word* is any sequence of nonblank characters (that is, a sequence of characters that does not contain a SPACE or TAB). If you type CONTROL-W while in the process of typing in a word, the cursor moves to the beginning of the current word. If you type CONTROL-W after ending a word with a SPACE or TAB character, the cursor moves to the beginning of the previous word.

Redrawing a Line

If you use the erase key to change characters on the command line and the erase key on your system does not remove the characters, it may become difficult to read the command line. You can press CONTROL-R, and the cursor will move down to the next line and the system will redraw the command line. You can then continue entering characters to complete the command.

Aborting Program Execution

Sometimes you may want to terminate a running program. A UNIX program may be performing a task that takes a long time, such as displaying the contents of a file that is several hundred pages or copying a file that is not the file you meant to copy.

To terminate program execution, press the interrupt key (DEL). (In place of DEL, use the interrupt key you identified at the start of this chapter.) When you press this key, the UNIX operating system sends a terminal interrupt signal to all your programs, including the shell. Exactly what effect this signal will have depends on the program. Some programs stop execution immediately, whereas others ignore the signal. Some programs take other, appropriate actions. When the shell receives a terminal interrupt signal, it displays a prompt and waits for another command.

CREATING AND EDITING A FILE USING vi

A *file* is a collection of information that you can refer to by a *filename*. It is stored on a disk. *Text* files typically contain memos, reports, messages, program source code, lists, or manuscripts. An *editor* is a utility program that allows you to create a new text file or change a text file that already exists. Many editors are in use on UNIX systems. This section shows you how to create a file using vi (visual), a powerful (although sometimes cryptic), interactive, visually oriented text editor. This section also covers elementary vi editing commands. Chapter 6 explains how to use more advanced vi commands.

The vi editor is not a text formatting program. It does not justify margins, center titles, or provide the output formatting features of a word processing system. You can use nroff (Chapter 7) to format the text that you edit with vi.

Specifying a Terminal

Because vi takes advantage of features that are specific to various kinds of terminals, you must tell it what type of terminal you are using. The Terminfo or Termcap name for your terminal that you identified at the beginning of this chapter communicates this information to vi.

If you are using the Bourne Shell or Korn Shell, you type in commands similar to those below to identify the type of terminal you are using. You can also place these commands in your **.profile** file so the UNIX system will automatically execute them each time you log in (see Chapter 4). Replace **name** with the Terminfo or Termcap name for your terminal.

> **TERM=name**
> **export TERM**

Following are the actual commands you would enter if you were using a Digital Equipment Corporation (DEC) VT-100 terminal:

```
$ TERM=vt100
$ export TERM
```

The C Shell requires the following command format:

> **setenv TERM name**

You can place a command such as this one in your **.login** file for automatic execution (see Chapter 4). Again, replace **name** with the Terminfo name for your terminal.

An Editing Session

This section describes how to start vi, enter text, move the cursor, correct text, and exit from vi. Most vi commands take effect immediately. Except as noted, you do not need to press RETURN to end a vi command.

When giving vi a command, it is important that you distinguish between uppercase and lowercase letters. The vi editor interprets the same letter as two different commands, depending on whether you enter an uppercase or lowercase character. Beware of the key that causes your keyboard to send uppercase characters. It is typically labeled SHIFT LOCK or CAPS LOCK. If you set this key to enter uppercase text while you are in Input Mode and then you exit to Command Mode, vi will interpret your commands as uppercase letters. When this happens, it can be very confusing.

Starting vi.   Start vi with the following command line to create a file named **practice**. Terminate the command line with RETURN.

    $ vi practice

The command line will disappear, and the terminal screen will look similar to the one shown in Figure 2-4. The tildes (~) indicate that the file is empty. They will go away as you add lines to the file. If your screen looks like a distorted version of the one shown, your terminal type is probably not set correctly. If your screen looks similar to the one shown in Figure 2-5, your terminal type is probably not set at all.

```
~
~
~
~
~
~
~
"practice" [New file]
```

FIGURE 2-4   Starting vi

```
$ vi practice
[Using open mode]
"practice" [New file]
```

FIGURE 2-5   Starting vi Without Your Terminal Type Set

To set your terminal type correctly, press ESCAPE and then give the following command to exit from vi and get the shell prompt back:

:q!

When you enter the colon, vi will move the cursor to the bottom line of the screen. The characters **q!** tell vi to quit without saving your work. (You will not ordinarily exit from vi in this way because you will typically want to save your work.) You must press RETURN after you give this command. Once you get the shell prompt back, refer to the preceding section, "Specifying a Terminal," and then start vi again.

The **practice** file is new; there is no text in it yet. The vi editor displays the following message on the status (bottom) line of the terminal to show that you are creating and editing a new file. Your system may display a different message.

```
"practice" [New file]
```

When you edit an existing file, vi displays the first few lines of the file and gives status information about the file on the status line.

Command and Input Modes.
The vi editor has two modes of operation: *Command Mode* and *Input Mode*. While vi is in Command Mode, you can give vi commands. For example, in Command Mode you can delete text or exit from vi. You can also command vi to enter the Input Mode. While in the Input Mode, vi accepts anything you enter as text and displays it on the terminal screen. You can press ESCAPE to return vi to Command Mode.

The vi editor does not normally keep you informed about which mode it is in. If you are using a recent release of System V and you give the :set showmode command, vi will display INPUT MODE at the lower right of the screen while it is in Input Mode.

:set showmode

When you enter the colon, vi moves the cursor to the status line. Enter the command and press RETURN. Refer to page 146 for more information about **showmode**.

Entering Text.
After you start a new session with vi, you must put it in Input Mode before you can enter text. To put vi in Input Mode, press the **i** key. If you have not set **showmode**, vi will not respond to let you know that it is in Input Mode.

If you are not sure whether vi is in Input Mode, press the ESCAPE key; vi will return to Command Mode if it was in Input Mode or beep (some terminals flash) if it is already in Command Mode. You can put vi back in Input Mode by pressing the **i** key again.

While vi is in Input Mode, you can enter text by typing on the terminal. If the text does not appear on the screen as you type it, you are not in Input Mode.

Enter the sample paragraph shown in Figure 2-6, pressing the RETURN key to end each line. As you enter text, you should prevent lines of text from wrapping around from the right side of the screen to the left by pressing the RETURN key before the cursor reaches the far right side of the screen. Also, make sure that you do not end a line with a SPACE. Some vi commands (such as the w command) will not behave properly when they encounter a line that ends with a SPACE.

While you are using vi, you can always correct any typing mistakes you make. If you notice a mistake on the line you are entering, you can correct it before you continue. Refer to the next paragraph. You can correct other mistakes later. When you finish entering the paragraph, press the ESCAPE key to return vi to Command Mode.

Correcting Text as You Insert It.   The keys that allow you to back up and correct a shell command line serve the same functions when vi is in Input Mode. These keys include the erase and line kill keys you inquired about earlier (usually CONTROL-H and CONTROL-U) as well as the word kill key (CONTROL-W). Although vi

```
vi (visual) is a powerful,
interactive, visually oriented
text editor.
This section shows you how to create a
file using vi.
It also covers beginning editing commands.
Chapter 6 goes into detail about using
more advanced vi commands.
~
~
~
~
~
~
~
~
~
~
~
~
~                                     INPUT  MODE
"practice" New file
```

FIGURE 2-6   Entering Text with vi

may not remove deleted text from the screen as you back up over it, vi will remove it when you type over it or press ESCAPE.

OPTIONAL

There are two restrictions on the use of these correction keys. They allow you only to back up over text on the line you are entering (you cannot back up to a previous line), and they back up only over text that you just entered. As an example, assume that vi is in Input Mode—you are entering text and press the ESCAPE key to return vi to Command Mode. Then you give the **i** command to put vi back in Input Mode. Now you cannot back up over text you entered the first time you were in the Input Mode, even if the text is part of the line you are working on.

Moving the Cursor.   When you are using vi, you will need to move the cursor on the screen so that you can delete text, insert new text, and correct text. While vi is in Command Mode, you can use the RETURN key, the SPACE bar, and the ARROW keys to move the cursor. If your terminal does not have ARROW keys, you can use the **h, j, k,** and **l** keys to move the cursor left, down, up, and right, respectively.

Deleting Text.   You can delete a single character by moving the cursor until it is over the character you want to delete and then giving the command **x**. You can delete a word by positioning the cursor on the first letter of the word and giving the command **dw** (delete word). You can delete a line of text by moving the cursor until it is anywhere on the line you want to delete and then giving the command **dd**.

The Undo Command.   If you delete a character, line, or word by mistake, give the command **u** (undo) immediately after you give the Delete command, and vi will restore the deleted text. If you give the command **u** again immediately, vi will undo the undo command, and the deleted text will be gone.

Inserting Additional Text.   When you want to insert new text within text that you have already entered, move the cursor so that it is on the character that will follow the new text you plan to enter. Then give the **i** (insert) command to put vi in Input Mode, enter the new text, and press ESCAPE to return vi to Command Mode.

To enter one or more lines, position the cursor on the line above where you want the new text to go. Give the command **o** (open). The vi editor will open a blank line, put the cursor on it, and go into Input Mode. Enter the new text, ending each line with a RETURN. When you are finished entering text, press ESCAPE to return vi to Command Mode.

Correcting Text.   To correct text, use **dd, dw,** or **x** to remove the incorrect text. Then use **i** or **o** to insert the correct text.

For example, one way to change the word *beginning* to *elementary* in Figure 2-6 is to use the ARROW keys to move the cursor until it is on top of the *b* in *beginning.* Then give the command **dw** to delete the word *beginning.* Put vi in Input Mode by giving an **i** command, enter the word *elementary* followed by a SPACE, and press ESCAPE. The word is changed and vi is in Command Mode, waiting for another command.

Ending the Editing Session.   While you are editing, vi keeps the edited text in an area called the *Work Buffer.* When you finish editing, you must write out the contents of the Work Buffer to a disk file so that the edited text will be saved and available when you next want it.

Make sure vi is in Command Mode and use the **ZZ** command (you must use uppercase **Z**'s) to write your newly entered text to the disk and end the editing session. After you give the **ZZ** command, vi displays the name of the file you are editing and the number of characters in the file; then it returns control to the shell. See Figure 2-7.

```
vi (visual) is a powerful,
interactive, visually oriented
text editor.
This section shows you how to create a
file using vi.
It also covers elementary editing commands.
Chapter 6 goes into detail about using
more advanced vi commands.
~
~
~
~
~
~
~
~
~
"practice" [New file] 8 lines, 235 characters
$
```

FIGURE 2-7   Exiting from vi

LISTING THE CONTENTS OF A DIRECTORY

If you followed the preceding example, you used vi to create a file named **practice** in your directory. After exiting from vi, you can use the ls (list) utility to display a list of the names of the files in your directory. The first command in Figure 2-8 shows ls listing the name of the **practice** file. Subsequent commands in Figure 2-8 display the contents of the file and remove the file. These commands are described below.

```
$ ls
practice
$ cat practice
vi (visual) is a powerful,
interactive, visually oriented
text editor.
This section shows you how to create a
file using vi.
It also covers elementary editing commands.
Chapter 6 goes into detail about using
more advanced vi commands.
$ rm practice
$ ls
$ cat practice
cat: cannot open practice
$
```

FIGURE 2-8   Using ls, cat, and rm

DISPLAYING THE CONTENTS OF A TEXT FILE

The cat utility displays the contents of a text file. The name of the command is derived from *catenate*, which means to join together one after another. As Chapter 5 explains, one of cat's functions is to join files together in this manner. To use cat, enter cat followed by a SPACE and the name of the file that you want to display.

Figure 2-8 shows cat displaying the contents of **practice**. This figure shows the difference between the ls and cat utilities. The ls utility displays the *names* of the files in a directory, whereas cat displays the *contents* of a file.

If you want to view a file that is longer than one screenful, you can use the pg (page) utility or the more utility in place of cat. Both pg and more pause after displaying a screenful. Although they are very similar, there are subtle differences. For example, the pg utility waits for you to press RETURN before displaying another screenful, whereas more waits for you to press the SPACE bar. At the end of the file, pg displays an EOF (End Of File) message and waits for you to press RETURN before returning you to the shell, whereas more returns you directly to the shell. Give the command **pg practice** or **more practice** in place of the **cat** command in Figure 2-8 to see how it works. Part II describes both pg and more in greater detail.

DELETING A FILE

The rm (remove) utility deletes a file. Figure 2-8 shows rm deleting the **practice** file. After rm deletes the file, ls and cat show that **practice** is no longer in the directory. The ls utility does not list its filename, and cat says it cannot open the file. Consequently, you should be very careful when using rm to delete files.

SPECIAL CHARACTERS

Special characters—those that have a special meaning to the shell—are discussed in Chapter 5. These characters are mentioned here so that you can avoid accidentally using them as regular characters until you understand how the shell interprets them. For example, you should not use any of these characters in a filename. A list of the standard special characters includes:

    & ; | * ? ´ " ` [ ] ( ) $ < > { } ^ # / \

In addition, %, !, and ~ are special characters to the C Shell and the Korn Shell.

Although not considered special characters, RETURN, SPACE, and TAB also have special meanings to the shell. RETURN usually ends a command line and initiates execution of a command. The SPACE and TAB characters separate elements on the command line and are collectively known as *white space* or *blanks*.

OPTIONAL

Quoting Characters

If you need to use as a regular character one of the characters that has a special meaning to the shell, you can *quote* it. When you quote a special character, you

OPTIONAL (Continued)

keep the shell from giving it special meaning. The shell treats a quoted special character as a regular character.

To quote a character, precede it with a backslash (\). One backslash must precede each character that you are quoting. If you are using two or more special characters, you must precede each with a backslash (e.g., ** must be entered as **). You can quote a backslash just as you would quote any other special character—by preceding it with a backslash (\\).

Another way of quoting special characters is to enclose them between single quotation marks (e.g., '**'). You can quote many special and regular characters between a pair of single quotation marks (e.g., 'This is a special character: >'). The regular characters remain regular, and the shell also interprets the special characters as regular characters.

You can quote the erase character (CONTROL-H) and the line kill character (CONTROL-U) (and the exclamation point in the C Shell) by preceding any one with a backslash. Single quotation marks will not work.

SUMMARY

After reading this chapter and experimenting on your system, you should be able to log in and use the utilities and special keys listed below. Chapter 6 explains more about vi, and Part II has more information on ls, rm, and cat.

- passwd changes your password.
- CONTROL-D, logout, or exit logs you off the system.
- The CONTROL-H (or another) key is the erase key. It erases a character on the command line.
- The CONTROL-R (or another) key is the redraw line key. It redraws the current command line.
- The CONTROL-U (or another) key is the line kill key. It deletes the entire command line.
- The CONTROL-W (or another) key is the word erase key. It erases a word on the command line.
- The DEL (or another) key interrupts execution of the program you are running.
- vi creates and edits a text file.
- ls lists the names of files.
- cat catenates the contents of files and displays them.
- more or pg displays a file a screenful at a time.
- rm removes a file.

REVIEW EXERCISES

1. Is "fido" an acceptable password? Why or why not?

2. If you start vi and your screen looks strange, what is wrong? How can you fix it?

3. When you first start vi, what mode are you in?

4. When you are in vi, what are the three ways you can tell whether you are in Input Mode?

5. How can you change from Command Mode to Input Mode in vi? How can you change back again?

6. What vi command(s) would you use to:

   a. delete a line

   b. undo your last command

   c. leave the vi editor

OPTIONAL

7. What are the differences between the cat and ls utilities? What are the differences between pg (or more) and cat?

8. What is special about the *special characters*? How can you cause the shell to treat them as regular characters?

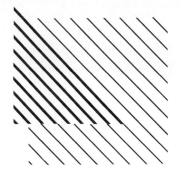

CHAPTER
3

AN
INTRODUCTION
TO THE UTILITIES

UNIX utility programs allow you to work with the UNIX system and manipulate the files you create. Chapter 2 introduced the shell, the most important UNIX utility program, and passwd, the utility that allows you to change your password. It also introduced some of the utilities that you can use to create and manipulate files: vi, ls, cat, pg, more, and rm. This chapter describes several other file manipulation utilities, as well as utilities that allow you to find out who is logged in, to communicate with other users, to display system documentation, to print files, to and perform other useful functions.

Some of the utilities included in this chapter were chosen because you can learn to use them easily and they allow you to communicate with other people using the system. Others were chosen because they were designed to help users learn UNIX. Still others were chosen because they form the bases for examples in later chapters. Part II of this book covers many of these utilities as well as other utilities more concisely and completely.

USING who TO FIND OUT
WHO IS USING THE SYSTEM

The who utility displays a list of the users currently logged in. In Figure 3-1, the first column who displays shows that hls, scott, jenny, and alex are logged in. The second column shows the designation of the terminal that each person is using. The third column shows the date and time that the person logged in. To find out which terminal you are using, or to see what time you logged in, give the command **who am i**.

```
$ who
hls              console        May  22  12:48
scott            tty2           May  21  09:07
jenny            tty3           May  22  12:53
alex             tty6           May  22  10:31
$ who  am  i
alex             tty6           May  22  10:31
```

FIGURE 3-1   The who Utility

The information that who displays is useful if you want to communicate with someone at your installation. If the person is logged in, you can use the write utility (below) to establish communication immediately. If who does not show that the person is logged in or if you do not need to communicate immediately, you can send that person UNIX system mail (page 49).

USING write TO SEND A MESSAGE

You can use the write utility to send a message to another user who is logged in. When the other user also uses write to send you a message, you establish two-way communication.

When you give a **write** command, it displays a banner on the other user's terminal saying that you are about to send a message. The format of a write command line is as follows:

write destination-user [terminal]

```
$ write alex
Hi Alex, are you there? o
```

FIGURE 3-2   The write Utility

The **destination-user** is the login name of the user you want to communicate with. You can find out the login names of the users who are logged in by using the who utility (above).

If the person you want to write to is logged in on more than one terminal, you can direct write to send your message to a specific terminal by including the **terminal** designation. Replace **terminal** on your command line with the terminal designation that who displays. Do not enter the square brackets ([])—they just indicate that the **terminal** part of the command is optional.

To establish two-way communication with another user, you and the other user must each execute write, specifying the other's login name as the **destination-user**. The write utility then copies text, line by line, from one terminal to the other. When you want to stop communicating with the other user, press CONTROL-D at the beginning of a line. CONTROL-D tells write to quit, displays EOT (End Of Transmission) on the other user's terminal, and returns you to the shell. The other user must do the same.

It is helpful to establish a protocol for carrying on communication using write. Try ending each message with **o** (for *over*) and ending the transmission with **oo** (for *over and out*). This protocol gives each user time to think and to enter a complete message, without the other user wondering if the first user is finished. Because write copies one line at a time, if you write several short lines of text rather than one long line, the other user will be reassured that you are still there.

The following example shows how one side of a two-way communication using write appears to Jenny. Figure 3-2 shows Jenny initiating communication by calling the write utility and specifying **alex** as the **destination-user**. She enters a message terminated by **o** and then waits for a reply.

As soon as Alex has a chance to respond and execute write, write sends a banner to Jenny's terminal. Then, Alex sends a message indicating that he is ready to receive Jenny's message (Figure 3-3). Following the protocol that he and Jenny have established, Alex terminates his message with **o**.

At this point, Jenny and Alex can communicate back and forth. Each time one of them types a line and presses RETURN, the line appears on the other's terminal. When they are done, Jenny enters a final message terminated by **oo** and presses CONTROL-D (as the first and only thing on a line) to sign off (see Figure 3-4).

The shell prompt appears. Then Alex signs off, and Jenny sees the EOT that results from Alex pressing CONTROL-D. Alex's final message appears after Jenny's shell prompt. Because Jenny did not give any commands, she can display another shell prompt by simply pressing the RETURN key.

```
$ write alex
Hi Alex, are you there? o
Message from alex (tty11) [Mon May 23 15:08]...
Yes Jenny, I'm here. o
```

FIGURE 3-3   The write Utility

```
$ write alex
Hi Alex, are you there? o
Message from alex (tty11) [Mon May 23 15:08]...
Yes Jenny, I'm here. o
        .

        .
Thank you, Alex - bye oo
CONTROL-D
$ Bye, Jenny oo
<EOT>
RETURN
$
```

FIGURE 3-4   The write Utility

Throughout this communication, Alex and Jenny followed the convention of using o after each message. This is just a convention and is not recognized by write. You can use any convention you please or none at all.

USING mesg TO DENY OR ACCEPT MESSAGES

If you do not want to receive messages, you can give the following command:

```
$ mesg n
```

After giving this command, another user cannot send you messages using write.

If Alex had given the preceding command before Jenny tried to send him a message, she would have seen the following:

```
$ write alex
Permission denied.
```

You can allow messages again by entering **mesg y**.

If you want to know if someone can write to you, give the command **mesg** by itself. The mesg utility will respond with a y (for yes, messages are allowed) or n (for no, messages are *not* allowed).

USING mailx TO SEND AND RECEIVE ELECTRONIC MAIL

You can use the mail utility programs to send and receive electronic mail. Electronic mail (or *e-mail* as it is sometimes called) is similar to post office mail except it is quicker and does not involve any paper or stamps. You can use it to send and receive letters, memos, reminders, invitations, and even junk mail.

You can use electronic mail to communicate with users on your system and, if your installation is part of a network, with other users on the network. Many UNIX systems are part of the uucp communications network, which is based on the uucp utility.

The mail utilities differ from the write utility, described on page 46. Although the mail utilities allow you to send a message to a user whether or not that user is logged in on the system, write allows you to send messages only if the user is logged in and willing to receive messages.

UNIX System V, Release 2, introduced a new electronic mail utility, mailx. The mailx utility is patterned after the Berkeley UNIX mail utility. The original System V mail utility, called mail, is simpler than mailx and Berkeley UNIX mail. This section describes System V mailx.

The UNIX operating system mail utilities have two distinct functions: sending electronic mail and receiving it. The following example demonstrates these two functions. Try it on your system, replacing **alex** with your login name. First, Alex uses mailx to send himself a message:

```
$ mailx alex
Subject: Test Message
This is a test message that I am sending myself.
CONTROL-D
$
```

After he starts mailx (**mailx alex**), Alex is prompted to enter the subject of the message. On your system, mailx may or may not prompt you for a subject, depending on how it is set up (refer to mailx in Part II for more information). After he types in the subject (**Test Message**) and presses RETURN, Alex types his message. He ends each line with a RETURN, and, when he is finished, he enters a CONTROL-D on a line by itself. The mailx utility sends the mail and returns Alex to the shell.

Sometimes mailx is set up to prompt you for a copy-to list after you press CONTROL-D. At that time you can enter the login names of users who should receive copies of the message. After you finish the list and press RETURN, the mailx utility will send the mail and return you to the shell.

To read his mail, Alex can run mailx without a user name (just **mailx**, not **mailx alex**). The mailx utility displays two lines of information about mailx that include the version number of the mailx program he is using, instructions for getting help, the mailbox that is being read, and the number of messages. The string **/var/mail/alex** identifies the location of Alex's mailbox in the hierarchical file system. (See Chapter 4 for an explanation of this terminology.) Following the header information is a list of any messages that are waiting for him. The list includes a header for each message, composed of the status of the message (**N** means new), the name of the person who sent it, the date it was sent and its length (number of lines/number of characters), and the subject of the message.

```
$ mailx
mailx version 4.0   Type ? for help.
"/var/mail/alex": 2 messages 2 new
>N  1 alex      Wed Aug  8 10:49   6/120    Test Message
 N  2 jenny     Wed Aug  8 10:50   6/115    lunch?
?
```

Alex has two messages, the one he just sent and one from Jenny. The *greater than* sign (>) to the left of the first header indicates that the message from Alex is the current message. After the list of headers, mailx displays a prompt (usually a question mark or ampersand) indicating that it is waiting for Alex to give it a command. Alex can simply press RETURN to look at the current message. Alex could have used the **t** (for *type*) command with a message number argument, such as **t 1,** to print a specific message. The **t** command used without an argument always prints the current message, as does RETURN by itself.

```
? RETURN
Message  1:
>From alex Wed Aug  8 10:49 PDT 1990
To: alex
Subject: Test Message
Status: R

This is a test message that I am sending myself.

? d
```

The first four lines of the message are header lines. They list: who the message is from, who it is to, the subject, and the status. Depending on how your system is set up, and depending on whether the message was sent to you from your machine or from another machine, the header may be as simple as the one above or much more complicated. In any case, the **To, From,** and **Subject** lines are the ones you will typically be interested in.

After reading his message, Alex uses a **d** command (followed by a RETURN) to delete the message. If Alex did not delete the message, mailx would have saved the message in a file called **mbox**.

As the first line of the mailx display indicates (Type ? for help.), mailx has a built-in help feature. Alex can enter **?** in response to the mailx prompt (?) to get a list of other commands he can use. Also see Part II of this book for more information on mailx commands.

After Alex presses **d** and RETURN, mailx displays the mailx prompt. Alex presses **2** RETURN to see message 2:

```
?  2 RETURN
Message   2:
>From jenny Wed Aug   8 10:50 PDT 1990
To: alex
Subject: lunch?
Status: R

Alex, can you meet me for lunch today at noon?

?  RETURN
At EOF
?  q
Saved 1 message in /var/alex/mbox
$
```

In response to this message, Alex presses RETURN. Because he has no more messages, the mailx utility displays At EOF, indicating that Alex is at the End Of his mailbox File. Alex then types q to quit reading his mail, and mailx tells him that one message (the second message) was saved in his **mbox** file. (Pathnames such as **/var/alex/mbox** are described in Chapter 4). If there were any messages left in his mailbox that Alex had not looked at, they would be there for him to read the next time he read his mail.

If Alex checks his mail after having already looked at all his messages, he will see the following:

```
$ mailx
No mail for alex
```

However, you do not have to type mailx in order to find out whether you have mail. At specified intervals (usually every ten minutes) while you are logged in, the shell checks to see whether mail has arrived since the last time you read your mail. If mail has arrived, the shell presents the following message before the next prompt:

```
You have new mail.
$
```

You can send mail to more than one person at a time. Below, Jenny sends a reminder to alex, barbara, and hls (Helen's login name). The characters :-) in the message represent a "smiley face" (look at it sideways). Because it can be difficult to tell when the writer of an electronic message is saying something in jest or in a humorously sarcastic way, electronic mail users often use :-) to indicate humor.

```
$ mailx alex barbara hls
Subject: Meeting Reminder
Please remember to bring your notes from our
last meeting to the meeting on Friday at 9:00 am
in my office.

And don't forget the doughnuts :-) ...

Jenny
CONTROL-D
$
```

When alex, barbara, and hls each log in, the system will tell them they have mail.

If your system is part of a network, you can send mail to and receive mail from users on other systems. If you are on a uucp network, you can send mail to a user on a system that is linked to yours by preceding the user's name with the name of a remote system and an exclamation point (which is commonly referred to as a *bang*). If your system is connected to a local area or other network—such as the Internet, BITNET, or CSNET—you may need to use a different format for addressing mail to users on other systems. Ask the system administrator how to address mail to other systems.

The following examples show you how to send mail to remote systems on a uucp network. The following command line sends mail to bill on the system named *bravo:*

```
$ mailx bravo!bill
```

If you are using the C Shell, you must quote the exclamation point by preceding it with a backslash:

```
% mailx bravo\!bill
```

You can also send mail to a user on a system that is not directly networked to your computer as long as your system has a uucp link to a system that, in turn, has a direct or indirect link to the destination system. Providing that you know of a path through networked computer systems from your machine to the other user's machine, you can send that user mail by listing all the systems in order on the command line. For example, if you have a login on a system that is networked to the system at the University of California at Berkeley called *ucbvax,* you can send the author mail with the following command:

```
$ mailx ucbvax!hplabs!cdp!sobell!mark
```

You can also mix the names of users on your system and on other systems on one command line:

```
$ mailx alex bravo!bill hls
```

You can obtain a list of machine names and users that are part of your network from the system administrator.

USING help OR learn
TO LEARN ABOUT UNIX

UNIX provides programs designed to introduce novice users to the system—the learn utility and the Help Facility. Although learn was developed by AT&T, today it is more commonly found on Berkeley UNIX systems than on computers running System V. The learn utility is a computer-aided instruction program that guides you through a series of lessons in several different courses. Although the courses vary somewhat from one manufacturer's system to another, the following topics are typically included:

• manipulating files
• using text editors
• formatting documents
• formatting equations
• programming in C

(To replace learn, AT&T developed a set of computer-aided learning programs called the Instructional WorkBench. Check with the system administrator to find out if the Instructional WorkBench utilities are available on your system.)

Although both learn and the Help Facility are easy and are intended to be used by novices without assistance from an experienced user or instructor, many novices prefer to use the Help Facility. The Help Facility is not organized into courses and lessons, as learn is. Rather, the Help Facility presents you with a series of menus to choose from, so that you can look at the information in any sequence you like. It includes general information to assist you in getting started as well as descriptions of specific utilities and explanations of UNIX-related terms. However, it does not give you the hands-on experience with UNIX utilities that learn does.

To use the Help Facility, type **help** on the command line. The help utility

```
help:   UNIX System On-Line Help

   choices     description

       s        starter:  general information

       l        locate:  find a command with keywords

       u        usage:  information about commands

       g        glossary:  definitions of terms

       r        Redirect to a file or a command

       q        Quit

 Enter  choice >
```

FIGURE 3-5   The Help Facility

```
$ learn


These are the available courses —
   files
   editor
   vi
   morefiles
   macros
   eqn
   C


If you want more information about the courses,
or if you have never used 'learn' before,
press RETURN; otherwise type the name of
the course you want, followed by RETURN.
```

FIGURE 3-6   The learn Utility

presents the menu shown in Figure 3-5. If you type **s, l, u,** or **g** on the command line, help will present another menu, and so on, until you reach the desired information. You can also access information in each of these selections without going through the initial menu by typing **starter, locate, usage,** or **glossary** instead of **help** on the command line.

To use the learn utility, type **learn** on the command line. It will present the information shown in Figure 3-6.

If you press RETURN without typing in a course name, learn will present descriptions of the courses and ask you to choose one. Then if you select the first course in the series, learn will present instructions about how to answer the questions it asks you, how to exit from the learn program, and so on.

USING man TO DISPLAY
THE SYSTEM MANUAL

The man (manual) utility displays pages from the system documentation on the terminal. This documentation is useful if you know what utility you want to use but have forgotten exactly how to use it. Because the descriptions in the system documentation are often quite terse, they are most helpful if you already understand basically what a utility does. If a utility is new to you, the descriptions provided by the Help Facility and by this book are typically easier to understand.

To find out more about a utility, give the command **man** followed by the name of the utility. The following command displays information about the who utility. If the information man displays runs off the top of the screen, give the second form of the command, which uses a pipe (the | symbol—pipes are explained in Chapter 5) and pg to cause the output to pause after each screenful.

```
$ man who
```

or

```
$ man who | pg
```

You can use the command **man man** (or **man man | pg**) to find out more about the man utility.

When you use the preceding format for man, the utility displays a prompt at the bottom of the screen after each screenful of text and waits for you to request another screenful. When you press RETURN, pg displays a new screenful of information from the man utility. Pressing DEL stops man and gives you a shell prompt.

As you read this book and learn new utilities, you may want to use the man command or refer to the system documentation to find out more about the utilities. Since the information displayed by the man command is an electronic version of the system documentation, the same information should be available in hard copy in the manuals that came with your system. If you would rather use paper documents than read about utilities on the screen, refer to your system manuals.

USING echo TO DISPLAY
TEXT ON THE TERMINAL

The echo utility copies to the terminal anything you put on the command line after echo. Some examples are shown in Figure 3-7.

The echo utility is a good tool for learning about the shell and other UNIX programs. In Chapter 5, echo is used to learn about special characters. In Chapter 8, it is used to learn about shell variables and about how to send messages from a shell program to the terminal.

```
$ echo Hi
Hi
$ echo This is a sentence.
This is a sentence.
$ echo Good morning.
Good morning.
```

FIGURE 3-7   The echo Utility

USING date TO DISPLAY
THE TIME AND DATE

The date utility displays the current date and time. An example of date follows:

```
$ date
Wed Aug   8 11:23:30 PDT 1990
```

USING cp TO COPY A FILE

The cp (copy) utility makes a copy of a file. It can copy any file, including text and executable program files. Among other uses, you can use cp to make a backup copy of a file or a copy to experiment with.

A cp command line specifies source and destination files. The format is as follows:

cp source-file destination-file

The **source-file** is the name of the file that cp is going to copy. The **destination-file** is the name that cp assigns to the resulting copy of the file.

If the **destination-file** exists *before* you give a cp command, cp overwrites it. Because cp overwrites (and destroys the contents of) an existing **destination-file** without warning you, you must take care not to cause cp to overwrite a file that you need.

The following command line makes a *copy of the file* named **output**. The copy is named **outputb**. The initial ls command below shows that **output** is the only file in the directory. After the cp command, the second ls shows both files, **output** and **outputb**, in the directory.

```
$ ls
output
$ cp output outputb
$ ls
output outputb
```

Sometimes it is useful to incorporate the date in the name of a copy of a file. In the following example, the period is part of the filename—just another character:

```
$ cp memo memo.0130
```

Although the date has no significance to the UNIX operating system, it can help you to find a version of a file that you saved on a certain date. It can also help you avoid overwriting existing files by providing a unique filename each day.

Chapter 4 discusses rules for naming files.

USING mv TO CHANGE
THE NAME OF A FILE

If you want to rename a file without making a duplicate copy of it, you can use the mv (move) utility.

An mv command line specifies an existing file and a new filename. The format is as follows:

mv existing-file new-file

The following command line *changes the name* of the file **memo** to **memo.0130**. The initial ls command below shows that **memo** is the only file in the current directory. Following the mv command, **memo.0130** is the only file in the current directory. Compare this with the cp example above.

```
$ ls
memo
$ mv memo memo.0130
$ ls
memo.0130
```

The mv utility can be used for much more than changing the name of a file. Refer to Chapter 4 and mv in Part II.

USING lp TO PRINT A FILE

So that several people or jobs can use a single printer, the UNIX system provides a means for *queuing* printer output so that only one job gets printed at a time. The lp (line printer) utility places a file in the printer queue for printing. (Berkeley UNIX and versions of the UNIX system that preceded System V use the lpr utility.) You should substitute the command you identified at the start of Chapter 2 for lp in the following examples.

The following command line prints the file named **report**:

```
$ lp report
request id is printer_1-450 (1 file)
```

The lp utility may display a line of information that contains a request number each time you ask it to print a file (the lines that begin with the word request in the examples). You can use these request numbers to check on the progress of or cancel a printing job.

You can send more than one file to the printer with a single command line. The following command line prints three files:

```
$ lp memo letter text
request id is printer_1-451 (3 files)
```

Refer to lp in Part II for more information.

USING grep TO FIND A STRING

The grep (global regular expression print) utility searches through a file to see if it contains a specified string of characters. This utility does not change the file it searches through but displays each line that contains the string.

The grep command in Figure 3-8 searches through the file **memo** for lines that contain the string credit, and displays a single line.

If **memo** contained words like *discredit, creditor,* and *accreditation,* grep would have displayed those lines as well because they contain the string it was searching for.

You do not need to enclose in single quotation marks the string you are searching for, but doing so allows you to put SPACES and special characters in the Search String.

The grep utility can do much more than search for a simple string. Refer to grep in Part II and to Appendix B, "Regular Expressions," for more information.

```
$ cat memo

Helen:

In our meeting on June 6th we
discussed the issue of credit.
Have you had any further thoughts
about it?

                          Alex
$ grep 'credit' memo
discussed the issue of credit.
```

FIGURE 3-8   The grep Utility

USING head TO LOOK AT THE TOP OF A FILE

NEW TO UNIX SYSTEM V Release 4

The head utility displays the first ten lines of a file. It is useful for reminding yourself about what a particular file contains. If you have a file called **months** that contains the twelve months of the year in order, head will display January through October (see Figure 3-9).

The head utility can display any number of lines, so you can use it to look at only the first line of a file or at a screenful or more. To specify the number of lines head will display, include a hyphen followed by the number of lines in the

head command. For example, the following command prints only the first line of
months:

```
$ head -1 months
Jan
```

```
$ cat months
Jan
Feb
Mar
Apr
May
Jun
Jul
Aug
Sep
Oct
Nov
Dec
$ head months
Jan
Feb
Mar
Apr
May
Jun
Jul
Aug
Sep
Oct
```

FIGURE 3-9   The head Utility

The head utility is not available on earlier releases of System V. Instead of
head, you can always use the sed command to look at the top of a file. The following command displays the first ten lines of the file **months**.

```
$ sed 10q months
```

The first argument to sed tells sed to display ten lines and quit. You can specify
any number of lines for sed to display. The next command displays only the first
line of **months**.

```
$ sed 1q months
```

Refer to Part II for more information about sed and head.

USING tail TO LOOK AT THE END OF A FILE

The tail utility displays the last ten lines of a file. It displays Mar through Dec from the **months** file (see Figure 3-10).

```
$ cat months
Jan
Feb
Mar
Apr
May
Jun
Jul
Aug
Sep
Oct
Nov
Dec
$ tail months
Mar
Apr
May
Jun
Jul
Aug
Sep
Oct
Nov
Dec
```

FIGURE 3-10   The tail Utility

Depending on how you invoke it, the tail utility can display fewer or more than ten lines, and it can also display parts of a file based on a count of blocks or characters rather than lines. Refer to tail in Part II for more information.

USING sort TO DISPLAY A FILE IN ORDER

The sort utility displays the contents of a file in order by lines. If you have a file named **days** that contains the names of each of the days of the week on a separate line, sort displays the file in alphabetical order, as shown in Figure 3-11.

```
$ cat days
Monday
Tuesday
Wednesday
Thursday
Friday
Saturday
Sunday
$ sort days
Friday
Monday
Saturday
Sunday
Thursday
Tuesday
Wednesday
```

FIGURE 3-11   The sort Utility

The sort utility is useful for putting lists in order. Within certain limits, sort can be used to order a list of numbers. Part II describes the features and limitations of sort.

USING uniq TO REMOVE
DUPLICATE LINES IN A FILE

The uniq (unique) utility displays a file, skipping adjacent duplicate lines. If the file named **phone_list** has two successive entries for the same person, uniq skips the extra lines (see Figure 3-12).

If the file has been sorted before uniq is used, uniq ensures that no two lines in the file are the same. Chapter 5 describes how to use a combination of commands, such as sort and uniq, to make changes to a file. See Part II for a description of other features of uniq.

```
$ cat phone_list
Alex      856-3462
Jenny     451-7339
Jenny     451-7339
Barbara   328-3078
Helen     249-0348
Jenny     451-7339
$ uniq phone_list
Alex      856-3462
Jenny     451-7339
Barbara   328-3078
Helen     249-0348
Jenny     451-7339
```

FIGURE 3-12   The uniq Utility

USING diff TO COMPARE TWO FILES

The diff (difference) utility compares two files and displays a list of the differences between them. This utility does not change either file; it just displays a list of the actions you would need to take to convert one file into the other. This is useful if you want to compare two versions of a letter or report, or two versions of the source code for a program.

The diff utility produces a series of lines containing instructions to add (**a**), delete (**d**), or change (**c**) followed by the lines that you need to add, delete, or change. If you have two files called **colors.1** and **colors.2** that contain names of colors, diff compares the two files and displays a list of their differences (see Figure 3-13).

The diff utility assumes that you want to convert the first file (**colors.1**) into the second file (**colors.2**). The first line that diff displays (**4d3**) indicates that you need to delete the fourth line. (You can ignore the number following the **d** since it is only important if you want to convert the second file into the first.) The next line of the display shows the line to be deleted; the *less than* symbol indicates that the line is from the first file (a *greater than* symbol is used to identify lines that are from the second file). See diff in Part II for a more complete description of its features.

```
$ cat colors.1
red
blue
green
yellow
$ cat colors.2
red
blue
green
$ diff colors.1 colors.2
4d3
< yellow
```

FIGURE 3-13   The diff Utility

SUMMARY

Below is a list of the utilities that have been introduced up to this point. Because you will be using these utilities frequently, and because they are integral to the following chapters, it is important that you become comfortable using them. The particular editor that you use is not important. If your installation has an editor other than vi that you prefer, learn to use that editor.

- **cat** displays the contents of a file on the terminal.
- **cp** makes a copy of a file.
- **date** displays the time, day of the week, and date.
- **diff** displays a list of the differences between two files.
- **echo** displays a line of text on the terminal.
- **grep** searches for a specific string in a file.
- **head** displays the beginning of a file.
- **help** displays general information about UNIX.
- **learn** provides lessons on how to use the system.
- **lp** prints text files.
- **ls** displays a list of files.
- **mailx** and **mail** send and receive mail.

- man displays information on utilities.
- mesg permits or denies messages sent by write.
- mv changes the name of a file.
- passwd changes your password.
- pg or more displays the contents of a file one screenful at a time.
- rm deletes a file.
- sed can display the beginning of a file.
- sort puts a file in order by lines.
- tail displays the end of a file.
- uniq displays the contents of a file, skipping successive duplicate lines.
- vi creates or edits a text file.
- who displays a list of who is logged in.
- write sends a message to another user who is logged in.

REVIEW EXERCISES

1. What command can you use to determine who is logged in on a specific terminal?

2. Why would you use write rather than mailx to communicate with another user? In what cases would you use mailx rather than write?

3. How can you send a single mail message to agnes on the system named cougar and to jim on the system named ucsf? Assume your computer has network links to cougar and ucsf.

4. Describe a method for synchronizing communication with another user when you are using write.

5. How can you keep other users from using write to communicate with you? Why would you want to?

6. What happens if you give the following commands when the file called **done** already exists?

```
$ cp to_do done
$ mv to_do done
```

7. What command will send the files **chapter1, chapter2,** and **chapter3** to the printer?

8. How can you find the phone number for Ace Electronics in a file called **phone** that contains a list of names and phone numbers? What command can

you use to display the entire file in alphabetical order? How can you remove adjacent duplicate lines from the file?

9. Try giving these two commands:

```
$ echo cat
$ cat echo
```

Explain the differences between them.

10. What command line displays the system documentation for the **grep** utility on your terminal one screenful at a time?

11. How can you tell whether the file **memo** is the same as the file **memo.bak**? (The **.bak** extension is often used to identify a backup copy of a file.)

12. How can you use the tail utility to display the last line of a file? (*Hint:* Refer to tail in Part II.)

13. What command can you use to look at the first few lines of a file called **status.report**? What command can you use to look at the end of the file?

CHAPTER

4

THE FILE STRUCTURE

This chapter discusses the organization and terminology of the file structure of the UNIX system. It defines ordinary and directory files and explains the rules for naming them. It shows how to create and delete directories, move through the file structure, and use pathnames to access files in different directories. This chapter also covers file access permissions that allow you to share selected files with other users. The final section describes links, which can make a single file appear in more than one directory.

THE HIERARCHICAL FILE STRUCTURE

A *hierarchical* structure frequently takes the shape of a pyramid. One example of this type of structure is found by tracing a family's lineage: A couple has a child; that child may have several children; and each of those children may have more children. This hierarchical structure, shown in Figure 4-1, is called a family tree.

Like the family tree it resembles, the UNIX system file structure is also called a *tree*. It is composed of a set of connected files. This structure allows users to organize files so they can easily find any particular one. In a standard UNIX system, each user starts with one directory. From this single directory, users can make as many subdirectories as they like, dividing subdirectories into additional subdirectories. In this manner, they can continue expanding the structure to any level according to their needs.

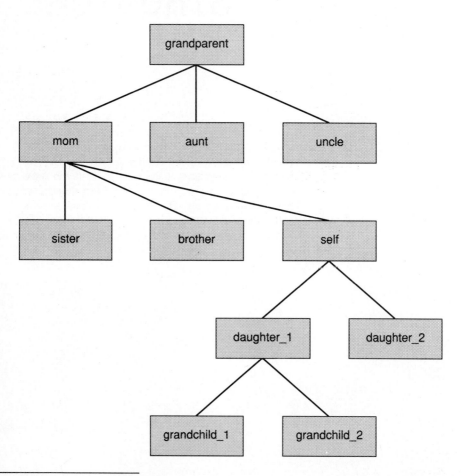

FIGURE 4-1   A Family Tree

Using the Hierarchical File Structure

Typically, each subdirectory is dedicated to a single subject. The subject dictates whether a subdirectory should be subdivided further. For instance, Figure 4-2 shows a secretary's subdirectory named **correspondence**. This directory contains three subdirectories: **business, memos,** and **personal**. The **business** directory contains files that store each letter the secretary types. If there are many letters going to one client (as is the case with **milk_co**), a subdirectory can be dedicated to that client.

One of the strengths of the UNIX system file structure is its ability to adapt to different users' needs. You can take advantage of this strength by strategically organizing your files so they are most convenient and useful for you.

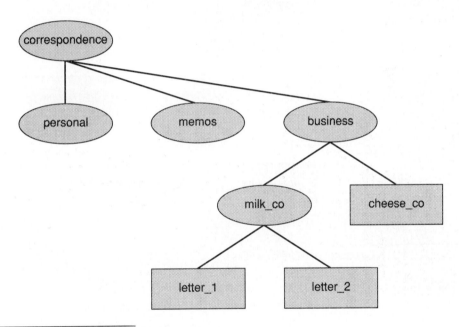

FIGURE 4-2   The Directories of a Secretary

DIRECTORY AND ORDINARY FILES

The tree representing the file structure is usually pictured upside down, with its "root" at the top. Figure 4-3 shows that the tree "grows" downward from the "root," with paths connecting the root to each of the other files. At the end of each path is an ordinary file or a directory file. *Ordinary files*, frequently just called *files*, are at the ends of paths that cannot support other paths. *Directory files*, usually referred to as *directories*, are the points that other paths *can* branch off from. (Figure 4-3 shows some empty directories.) When you refer to the tree,

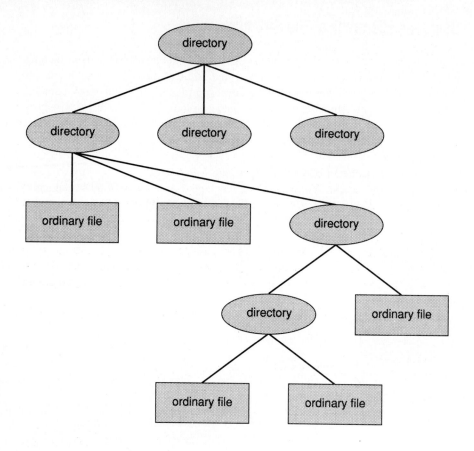

FIGURE 4-3   Directories and Ordinary Files

up is toward the root, and *down* is away from the root. Directories directly connected by a path are called parents (closer to the root) and children (farther from
the root).

Filenames

Every file has a *filename*. Older releases of System V allowed you to use up to
14 characters to name a file, although some manufacturers extended the maximum
length to 255 characters (the limit on Berkeley UNIX). System V Release 4
includes support for different types of file systems; the maximum length of a
filename will vary accordingly. On a particular file system, you will find that you
can create files with names up to 255 characters long or that you are restricted to
14-character names. Although you can use almost any character in a filename,
you will avoid confusion if you choose characters from the following list:

- uppercase letters [A-Z]
- lowercase letters [a-z]
- numbers [0-9]
- underscore [_]
- period [.]
- comma [,]

The only exception is the root directory, which is always named / and referred to by this single character. No other file can use this name.

Like children of one parent, no two files in the same directory can have the same name. (Whereas parents give their children different names because it makes good sense, UNIX requires it.) Files in different directories, like children of different parents, can have the same name.

The filenames you choose should mean something. Too often, a directory is filled with important files with names such as **foobar, wombat,** and **junk**. Names like these are poor choices because they will not help you recall what you stored in a file.

The following filenames conform to the required syntax *and* convey information about the contents of the file:

- correspondence
- january
- davis
- reports
- 1988
- acct_payable

UNIX systems that support longer filenames are becoming more common. If you share your files with users on other UNIX systems, you should probably make sure that long filenames differ within the first 14 characters. If you keep the filenames short, they will be easy to type, and later you can add extensions to them without exceeding the 14-character limit imposed by some versions of UNIX (see the following section). Of course, the disadvantage of short filenames is that they are typically less descriptive than long filenames.

NEW TO UNIX SYSTEM V Release 4

The length limit on filenames was increased to enable users to select descriptive names. A feature was added to the C Shell, filename completion, that helps users select among files in the working directory without typing in entire filenames. Refer to "Filename Completion" in Chapter 9.

Although they are not used in examples in this book, you can use uppercase letters within filenames. The UNIX operating system is case-sensitive, however, and files named **JANUARY, January,** and **january** are three distinct files.

Filename Extensions.   In the following filenames, filename extensions help describe the contents of the file. A *filename extension* is the part of the filename following an embedded period. Some programs, such as the C programming language compiler, depend on specific filename extensions. In most cases, however, filename extensions are optional.

compute.c	a C programming language source file
compute.o	the object code for the program
compute	the same program as an executable file
memo.0410	a text file

Use extensions freely to make filenames easy to understand. If you like, you can use several periods within the same filename (for example, **notes.4.10.88**).

Invisible Filenames.   A filename beginning with a period is called an *invisible filename* because **ls** does not normally display it. The command **ls –a** displays *all* filenames, even invisible ones. Startup files are usually invisible so they do not clutter a directory (see page 74). Two special invisible entries, a single and double period (**.** and **..**), appear in every directory. These entries are discussed on page 75.

Absolute Pathnames

As shown in Figure 4-4, every file has a *pathname*. Figure 4-4 shows the pathnames of directories and ordinary files in part of a file system hierarchy. You can build the pathname of a file by tracing a path from the root directory, through all the intermediate directories, to the file. String all the filenames in the path together, separating them with slashes (*/*) and preceding them with the name of the root directory (*/*).

This path of filenames is called an *absolute pathname* because it locates a file absolutely, tracing a path from the root directory to the file. The part of a pathname following the final slash is called a *simple filename*, or just a filename.

DIRECTORIES

This section covers creating, deleting, and using directories. It explains the concepts of the *working* and *home directories* and their importance in *relative pathnames*.

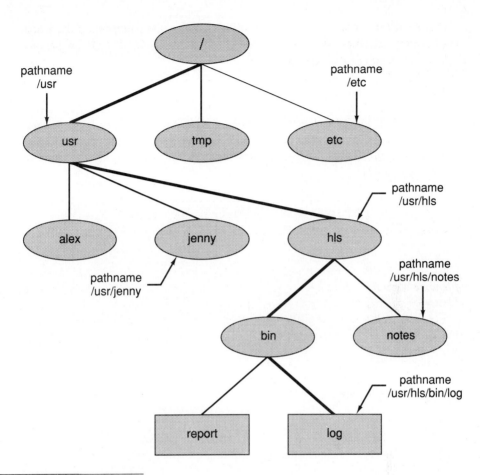

FIGURE 4-4   Pathnames

The Working Directory

While you are logged in on a UNIX system, you will always be associated with one directory or another. The directory you are associated with, or are working in, is called the *working directory*, or the *current directory*. Sometimes this association is referred to in a physical sense: "You are *in* (or *working in*) the **jenny** directory."

To access any file in the working directory, you do not need a pathname—just a simple filename. To access a file in another directory, however, you *must* use a pathname.

The pwd (print working directory) utility displays the pathname of the working directory (Figure 4-5).

Your Home Directory

When you first log in on a UNIX system, the working directory is your *home* directory. To display the absolute pathname of your home directory, use pwd just after you log in. Figure 4-5 shows Alex logging in and displaying the name of his home directory.

```
login: alex
Password:

Welcome to UNIX!

$ pwd
/home/alex
```

FIGURE 4-5   Logging In

The ls utility displays a list of the files in the working directory. Because your home directory has been the only working directory you have used so far, ls has always displayed a list of files in your home directory. (All the files you have created up to now are in your home directory.)

OPTIONAL

Startup Files.   An important file that appears in your home directory is a *startup file*. It gives the operating system specific information about you as a user. Frequently, it tells the system what kind of terminal you are using and executes the stty (set terminal) utility to establish your line kill and erase keys. Refer to Part II for more information about stty.

Either you or the system administrator can put a startup file, containing shell commands, in your home directory. The shell executes the commands in this file each time you log in. With the Bourne Shell and the Korn Shell, the filename must be **.profile**. Use **.login** with the C Shell. Because the startup files have invisible filenames, you must use the ls –a command if you want to see if either of these files is in your home directory.

For more information on startup files and other files the shell automatically executes, refer to Chapters 8 and 9 and Appendix A.

Creating a Directory

The mkdir utility creates a directory. It does *not* change your association with the working directory. The *argument* (the word following the name of the command) you use with mkdir becomes the pathname of the new directory.

Figure 4-6 shows the directory structure that is developed in the following examples. The dashed lines represent directories that are added.

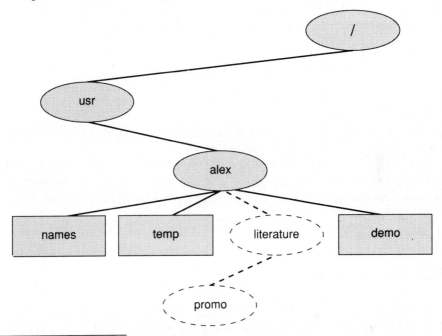

FIGURE 4-6   The File Structure Developed in the Examples

In Figure 4-7, mkdir creates a directory named **literature** as a child of the **/home/alex** directory. When you use mkdir, enter the absolute pathname of *your* home directory in place of **/home/alex**.

The ls utility verifies the presence of the new directory and shows the files Alex has been working with: **names, temp,** and **demo**.

By itself, ls does not distinguish between a directory and an ordinary file. With the **–F** option, ls displays a slash after the name of each directory (and an asterisk after each executable file). When you call ls with an argument that is the name of a directory, ls lists the contents of the directory. If there are no files in the directory, ls does not list anything.

The . and .. Directory Entries.   The mkdir utility automatically puts two entries in every directory you create. They are a single and double period, representing

```
$ mkdir /home/alex/literature
$ ls
demo              literature    names        temp
$ ls -F
demo              literature/   names        temp
$ ls literature
$
```

FIGURE 4-7   The mkdir Utility

the directory itself and the parent directory, respectively. These entries are invisible because their filenames begin with periods.

Because mkdir automatically places these entries in every directory, you can rely on their presence. The . is synonymous with the pathname of the working directory and can be used in its place; .. is synonymous with the pathname of the parent of the working directory.

Figure 4-8 lists the contents of the **/home** directory from **/home/alex** by using .. to represent the parent directory.

```
$ pwd
/home/alex
$ ls ..
alex        barbara   hls        jenny
.
.
```

FIGURE 4-8   Using .. with ls

Changing to Another Working Directory

The cd (change directory) utility makes another directory the working directory—it does *not* change the contents of the working directory. In this context, you can think of the working directory as a place marker. The first **cd** command in Figure 4-9 makes the **/home/alex/literature** directory the working directory, as verified by pwd.

Without an argument, cd makes your home directory the working directory, as it was when you first logged in. The second cd in Figure 4-9 does not have an argument and makes Alex's home directory the working directory.

```
$ cd /home/alex/literature
$ pwd
/home/alex/literature
$ cd
$ pwd
/home/alex
```

FIGURE 4-9   The cd Utility

Deleting a Directory

The rmdir (remove directory) utility deletes a directory. You cannot delete the working directory or a directory that contains files. If you need to delete a directory with files in it, first delete the files (using rm) and then delete the directory. You do not have to delete the . and .. entries; rmdir removes them automatically. The following command deletes the directory that was created in Figure 4-7.

```
$ rmdir /home/alex/literature
```

Relative Pathnames

A *relative pathname* traces a path from the working directory to a file. The pathname is *relative* to the working directory. Any pathname that does not begin with the root directory (/) is a relative pathname. Like absolute pathnames, relative pathnames can describe a path through many directories.

Alex could have created the **literature** directory (Figure 4-7) more easily using a relative pathname, as shown here:

```
$ pwd
/home/alex
$ mkdir literature
```

The pwd command shows that Alex's home directory (/home/alex) is still the working directory. The mkdir utility will display an error message if a directory or file called **literature** already exists—you cannot have two files or directories with the same name in one directory.

The pathname used in this example is a simple filename. A simple filename is a kind of relative pathname that specifies a file in the working directory.

The following commands show two ways to create the same directory, **promo,** a child of the **literature** directory that was just created. The first assumes that **/home/alex** is the working directory and uses a relative pathname; the second uses an absolute pathname.

Because the location of the file that you are accessing with a relative pathname is dependent on (relative to) the working directory, always make sure you know which is the working directory before using a relative pathname. When you use an absolute pathname, it does not matter which is the working directory.

```
$ pwd
/home/alex
$ mkdir literature/promo
```

or

```
$ mkdir /home/alex/literature/promo
```

Virtually anywhere that a UNIX utility program requires a filename or pathname, you can use an absolute or relative pathname or a simple filename. You can use any of these types of names with cd, ls, vi, mkdir, rm, rmdir, and other UNIX utilities.

Significance of the Working Directory.   Typing long pathnames is tedious and increases the chances of making mistakes. You can choose a working directory for any particular task to reduce the need for long pathnames. Your choice of a working directory does not allow you to do anything you could not do otherwise—it just makes some operations easier.

Files that are children of the working directory can be referenced by simple filenames. Grandchildren of the working directory can be referenced by relative pathnames, composed of two filenames separated by a slash. When you manipulate files in a large directory structure, short relative pathnames can save time and aggravation. If you choose a working directory that contains the files used most for a particular task, you will need to use fewer long, cumbersome pathnames.

Using Pathnames

The following example assumes that **/home/alex** is the working directory. It uses a relative pathname to copy the file **letter** to the **/home/alex/literature/promo** directory. The copy of the file has the simple filename **letter.0610**. Use vi to create a file named **letter** if you want to experiment with the examples that follow.

```
$ cp letter literature/promo/letter.0610
```

Assuming that Alex has not changed to another working directory, the following command allows him to edit the copy of the file he just made:

```
$ vi literature/promo/letter.0610
.
.
```

If Alex does not want to use a long pathname to specify the file, he can, before using vi, use cd to make the **promo** directory the working directory.

```
$ cd literature/promo
$ pwd
/home/alex/literature/promo
$ vi letter.0610
.
.
```

If Alex wants to make the parent of the working directory (**/home/alex/literature**) the new working directory, he can give the following command, which takes advantage of the **..** directory entry:

```
$ cd ..
$ pwd
/home/alex/literature
```

Moving Files from One Directory to Another

The mv (move) utility can be used to move files from one directory to another. Chapter 3 discussed the use of mv to rename files. However, the mv utility is actually much more general than that—it can be used to change the pathname of a file as well as changing the simple filename.

When it is used to move a file to a new directory, the format of the mv utility is:

mv existing-file-list directory

If the working directory is **/home/alex**, Alex can use the following command to move the files **names** and **temp** from the working directory to the directory **literature**:

$ mv names temp literature

This command changes the absolute pathname of **names** and **temp** from **/home/alex/names** and **/home/alex/temp** to **/home/alex/literature/names** and **/home/alex/literature/temp**. Like most other UNIX commands, mv accepts either absolute or relative pathnames.

As you work with the UNIX system, you will create more and more files, and you will need to create directories to keep them organized. The mv utility is a useful tool for moving files from one directory to another as you develop your directory hierarchy.

Important Standard Directories and Files

The UNIX system file structure is usually set up according to a convention. Aspects of this convention may vary from installation to installation. Figure 4-10 shows the usual locations of some important directories and files.

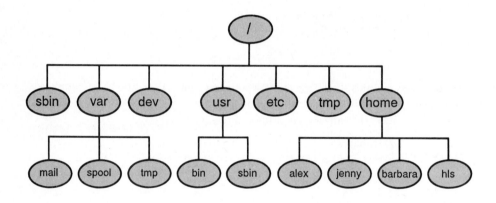

FIGURE 4-10   The Standard UNIX System File Structure

/ (root)   The root directory is present in all UNIX system file structures. It is the ancestor of all files in the file system.

NEW TO UNIX SYSTEM V Release 4

/home   Each user's home directory is typically one of many subdirectories of the **/home** directory. On some systems, the users' directories may not be under the **/home** directory (e.g., they might all be under **/inhouse,** or some might be under **/inhouse** and others under **/clients**). As an example, assuming that users' directories are under **/home,** the absolute pathname of Jenny's home directory is **/home/jenny**.

/usr This directory traditionally includes subdirectories that contain information used by the system. Files in subdirectories of **/usr** do not change often and may be shared by multiple systems.

/usr/bin This directory contains the standard UNIX utility programs. Prior to System V Release 4, some of these utilities were kept in **/bin**.

NEW TO UNIX SYSTEM V Release 4

/sbin, /usr/sbin Utilities used for system administration are stored in **/sbin** and **/usr/sbin**. The **/sbin** directory typically includes utilities needed during the booting process, and **/usr/sbin** holds those utilities that are most useful after the system is up and running. In older versions of System V, many system administration utilities were scattered through several directories that often included other system files (**/etc, /usr/bin, /usr/adm, /usr/include**).

/var Files with contents that vary as the system runs are found in subdirectories under **/var**. The most common examples are system log files, spooled files, and user mailbox files. Older versions of System V scattered such files through several subdirectories of **/usr** (**/usr/adm, /usr/mail, /usr/spool**).

/usr/ucb This directory includes utilities that are provided for compatibility with Berkeley UNIX.

/dev All files that represent peripheral devices, such as terminals and printers, are kept in this directory.

/etc Administrative, configuration, and other system files are kept here. One of the most useful is the **passwd** file, containing a list of all users who have permission to use the system. See Chapter 11 for more information.

/tmp Many programs use this directory to hold temporary files.

ACCESS PERMISSIONS

Three types of users can access a file: the owner of the file (*owner*), a member of a group to which the owner belongs (*group*—see Chapter 11 for more information on groups), and everyone else (*other*). A user can attempt to access an ordinary file in three ways—by trying to *read from, write to,* or *execute* it. Three types of users, each able to access a file in three ways, equals a total of nine possible ways to access an ordinary file:

The owner of a file can try to:
> read from the file
> write to the file
> execute the file

A member of the owner's group can try to:
            read from the file
            write to the file
            execute the file

Anyone else can try to:
            read from the file
            write to the file
            execute the file

The ls Utility and the –l Option

When you call ls with the –l (long) option and the name of a file, ls displays a line of information about the file. The following example displays information for two files. The file **letter.0610** contains the text of a letter, and **check_spell** contains a shell script (a program written in the high-level shell programming language).

```
$ ls –l letter.0610 check_spell
–rw–r––r––  1 alex    pubs    3355   May   1 10:52  letter.0610
–rwxr–xr–x  2 alex    pubs     852   May   5 14:03  check_spell
```

From left to right, the lines contain the following information.

- the type of file (first character)
- the file's access permissions (the next nine characters)
- the number of links to the file (the next section covers links)
- the name of the owner of the file (usually the person who created it)
- the name of the group that has group access to the file
- the size of the file in characters (bytes)
- the date and time the file was created or last modified
- the name of the file

    If the first character is a **d**, the file is a directory; if the character is a –, it is an ordinary file. Both of the files in the above example are ordinary files. The next three characters represent the access permission for the owner of the file: **r** indicates that the owner *has* read permission, – indicates that the owner *does not have* read permission; **w** indicates that the owner *has* write permission, – indicates that the owner *does not have* write permission; **x** indicates execute permission for the owner, and – indicates no execute permission.
    In a similar manner, the next three characters represent permissions for the group, and the final three characters represent permissions for everyone else. In the preceding example, the owner of the file **letter.0610** can read from the file or

write to it, whereas others can only read from it and no one is allowed to execute it. Although execute permissions can be allowed for any file, it does not make sense to assign execute permissions to a file that contains an ordinary document such as a letter. However, the file **check_spell** is an executable shell script, and execute permissions are appropriate. (The owner, group, and others have execute access permission.)

Changing Access Permissions

The owner of a file controls which users have permission to access the file and how they can access it. If you own a file, you can use the chmod (change mode) utility to change access permissions for that file. Below, chmod adds (+) read and write permission (**rw**) for all (**a**) users.

```
$ chmod a+rw letter.0610
$ ls -l letter.0610
-rw-rw-rw- 1 alex   pubs    3355  May  1 10:52 letter.0610
```

In the next example, chmod removes (–) read and execute (**rx**) permissions for users other than Alex and members of the pubs group (**o**).

```
$ chmod o-rx check_spell
$ ls -l check_spell
-rwxr-x--- 2 alex   pubs     852  May  5 14:03 check_spell
```

In addition to **a** (for *all*) and **o** (for *other*), you can use **g** (for *group*) and **u** (for *user*, although user actually refers to the owner of the file, who may or may not be the user of the file at any given time) in the argument to chmod. For more information on changing access permissions, refer to the discussion of chmod in Part II.

The UNIX system access permission scheme lets you give other users access to the files you want to share and keep your private files confidential. You can allow other users to read from *and* write to a file (you may be one of several people working on a joint project); only to read from a file (perhaps a project specification you are proposing); or only to write to a file (similar to an in-basket or mailbox, where you want others to be able to send you mail but you do not want them to read your mail). Similarly, you can protect entire directories from being scanned.

OPTIONAL

There is an exception to the access permissions described above. The system administrator or another user who knows the special password can log in as the *Superuser* and have full access to *all* files, regardless of owner or access permissions. Refer to Chapter 11 for more information.

Directory Access Permissions

Access permissions have slightly different meanings when used with directories. Although a directory can be accessed by the three types of users and can be read from or written to, it can never be executed. Execute access permission is redefined for a directory. It means you can search through and list the contents of the directory. It has nothing to do with executing a file.

Alex can give the following command to ensure that Jenny, or anyone else, can look through, read files from, and write files to his directory called **info**:

```
$ chmod a+rwx /home/alex/info
```

You can view the access permissions associated with a directory by using both the **–d** (directory) and **–l** options, as shown in the following example. The **d** at the left end of the line indicates that **/home/alex/info** is a directory.

```
$ ls -ld /home/alex/info
drwxrwxrwx 3 alex    pubs 112   Apr 15 11:05 /home/alex/info
```

LINKS

A *link* is a pointer to a file. Every time you create a file using vi, cp, or any other means, you are putting a pointer in a directory. This pointer associates a filename with a place on the disk. When you specify a filename in a command, you are pointing to the place on the disk where the information that you want is (to be) located.

Creating Additional Links

Sharing files can be useful if two or more people are working on a project and need to share some information. You can make it easy for other users to access one of your files by creating additional links to the file.

To share a file with another user, you first give the user permission to read and write to the file. (In addition, you may have to use the chmod utility to change the access permissions of the parent directory of the file to give the user read, write, and execute permissions.) Once the permissions are appropriately set, you allow the user to create a link to the file so that each of you can access the file from your separate directory hierarchies.

OPTIONAL

A link can also be useful to a single user with a large directory hierarchy. You can create links in order to cross-classify files in your directory hierarchy,

OPTIONAL (Continued)

using different classifications for different tasks. For example, if your directory hierarchy is the one depicted in Figure 4-2, you might have a file called **to_do** in each of the subdirectories of the **correspondence** directory—that is, in **personal**, **memos**, and **business**. Then if you find it hard to keep track of all the things you need to do, you can create a separate directory called **to_do** in the **correspondence** directory and link each to-do list into that directory. For example, you might link the file called **to_do** in the **memos** directory to a file called **memos** in the **to_do** directory. This set of links is shown in Figure 4-11.

Although this may sound complicated, in this way you can keep all of your to-do lists conveniently in one place. The appropriate list is also easily accessible in the task-related directory when you are busy composing letters, writing memos, or handling personal business.

Using ln to Create a Link

The **ln** (link) utility creates an additional link to an existing file. The link appears as another file in the file structure. If the file appears in the same directory as the one the file is linked with, the links must have different filenames. This restriction does not apply if the file is in another directory.

The following command makes the link shown in Figure 4-12. It assumes that **/home/jenny** is the working directory and that Jenny is creating a link to the

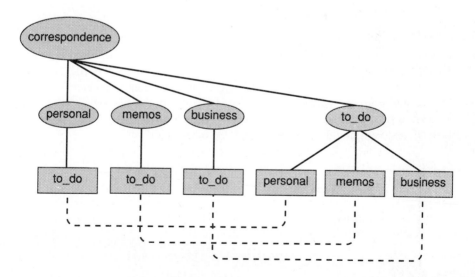

FIGURE 4-11   Cross-Classification of Files Using Links

file named **draft**. The new link appears in the **/home/alex** directory with the
filename **letter**. In practice, it may be necessary for Alex to use chmod, as
shown in the previous section, to give Jenny write access permission to the
/home/alex directory.

```
$ ln draft /home/alex/letter
```

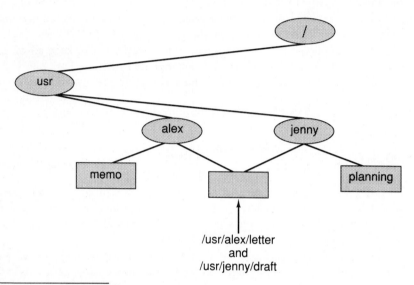

/usr/alex/letter
and
/usr/jenny/draft

FIGURE 4-12 **/home/alex/letter** and **/home/jenny/draft** Are Two Links to the
Same File

The ln utility creates an additional pointer to an existing file. It does *not*
make another copy of the file. Because there is only one file, the file status information (such as access permissions, owner, and the time the file was last
modified) is the same for all links. Only the filenames differ. You can verify that
ln does not make an additional copy of a file by creating a file, using ln to make
an additional link to the file, changing the contents of the file through one link
(use vi), and verifying the change through the other link.

```
$ cat file_a
This is file A.
$ ln file_a file_b
$ cat file_b
This is file A.
$ vi file_b
    .
    .
    .
$ cat file_b
This is file B after the change.
$ cat file_a
This is file B after the change.
```

If you try the same experiment using cp instead of ln (and make a change to a *copy* of the file), the difference between the two utilities will become clearer. Once you change a *copy* of a file, the two files are different.

```
$ cat file_c
This is file C.
$ cp file_c file_d
$ cat file_d
This is file C.
$ vi file_d
.

.
$ cat file_d
This is file D after the change.
$ cat file_c
This is file C.
```

You can also use ls with the –l option, followed by the names of the files you want to compare, to see that the status information is the same for two links to a file and is different for files that are not linked. In the following example, the 2 in the links field (just to the left of alex) shows there are two links to **file_a** and **file_b**:

```
$ ls -l file_a file_b file_c file_d
-rw-r--r-- 2 alex  pubs      33  May 24 10:52 file_a
-rw-r--r-- 2 alex  pubs      33  May 24 10:52 file_b
-rw-r--r-- 1 alex  pubs      16  May 24 10:55 file_c
-rw-r--r-- 1 alex  pubs      33  May 24 10:57 file_d
```

OPTIONAL

Although it is easy to guess which files are linked to one another in the example above, ls does not explicitly tell you. If you use ls with the –i option, you can determine without a doubt which files are linked to each other. The –i option lists the *inode number* for each file. An inode is the control structure for a file. If the two filenames have the same inode number, then they share the control structure and they are links to the same file. Conversely, if two filenames have different inode numbers, they are different files. The following example shows that **file_a** and **file_b** have the same inode number and that **file_c** and **file_d** have different inode numbers:

```
$ ls -i file_a file_b file_c file_d
3534 file_a    3534 file_b    5800 file_c    7328 file_d
```

All links to a file are of equal value—the operating system cannot distinguish the order in which two links were made. If a file has two links, you can remove either one and still access the file through the remaining link. You can even remove the link used to create the file and, as long as there is a remaining link, still access the file through that link.

Removing Links

When you first create a file, there is one link to it. You can delete the file or, using UNIX system terminology, remove the link, with the rm utility. When you remove the last link to a file, you can no longer access the information stored in the file, and the operating system releases the space the file occupied on the disk for use by other files. If there is more than one link to a file, you can remove a link and still access the file from any remaining link.

NEW TO UNIX SYSTEM V Release 4

Symbolic Links

The links that are described above are *hard links*. In addition to hard links, System V Release 4 has added support for *symbolic links*. A hard link is a pointer to a file, and a symbolic link is an *indirect pointer* to a file. It is a directory entry that contains the pathname of the pointed-to file.

Symbolic links were developed because of the limitations of hard links. Only the Superuser can create a hard link to a directory, but anyone can create a symbolic link to a directory. Also, a symbolic link can link to any file, regardless of where it is located in the file structure, but all hard links to a file must be in the same file system. Typically, the UNIX file hierarchy is composed of several file systems. Because each file system keeps separate control information (that is, separate inodes) for the files it contains, it is not possible to create hard links between files in different file systems. If you are creating links only among files in your own directories, you probably will not notice this limitation.

Although symbolic links are more general than hard links, they have some disadvantages. Whereas all hard links to a file have equal status, symbolic links do not have the same status as hard links. When a file has multiple hard links, it is like a person having multiple, full legal names (as most married women do). In contrast, symbolic links are like pseudonyms. Anybody can have one or more pseudonyms, but pseudonyms have a lesser status than legal names. Some of the peculiarities of symbolic links are described in the following sections.

Creating a Symbolic Link.   To make a symbolic link, use ln with the –s option. The example below creates a symbolic link, **/tmp/s3**, to the file **sum**. When you use the **ls –l** command to look at the symbolic link, ls displays the name of the link as well as the name of the file it is an indirect pointer to. Also, the first character of the listing shows l for link. Note that the sizes and times of last modification of the two files are different. Unlike a hard link, a symbolic link to a file does not have the same status information as the file itself.

```
$ ln -s sum /tmp/s3
$ ls -l sum /tmp/s3
-rw-r--r-- 1 alex   pubs 981 May 24 10:55 sum
lrwxrwxrwx 1 alex   pubs   4 May 24 10:57 /tmp/s3 -> sum
```

You can also use a command such as the one above to create a symbolic link to a directory. When you use the **–s** option, ln does not care whether the file you are creating a link to is a regular file or a directory.

Using Symbolic Links to Change Directories.
When you use a symbolic link as an argument to cd to change directories, the results can be confusing, particularly if you did not realize you were using a symbolic link. The pwd command lists the name of the linked-to directory rather than the name of the symbolic link.

```
$  ln  –s  /home/alex/grades  /tmp/grades.old
$  cd  /tmp/grades.old
$  pwd
/home/alex/grades
```

Because pwd does not identify the symbolic link, the C Shell provides a variable, **cwd** (current working directory), that contains the name of the symbolic link (assuming you used a symbolic link to access the working directory). If you did not use a symbolic link to access the working directory, **cwd** contains the name of the hard link to the working directory. Because it is a variable, **cwd** is preceded by a dollar sign in the following example. When you use the echo command followed by a dollar sign and a variable name, echo displays the value of the variable. Shell variables and the use of the dollar sign are explained in Chapters 8 and 9.

```
$  pwd
/home/alex/grades
$  echo  $cwd
/tmp/grades.old
```

Changing directories to the parent directory of a directory that you accessed through a symbolic link can also be confusing. When you use the **cd ..** command, the parent of the linked-to directory becomes the working directory (rather than the parent directory of the symbolic link itself). In the following example, the **cd ..** command makes the working directory the parent of the linked-to directory, **/home/alex**, rather than the parent of the symbolic link, **/tmp**:

```
$  echo  $cwd
/tmp/grades.old
$  cd  ..
$  echo  $cwd
/home/alex
```

NEW TO UNIX SYSTEM V Release 4 (Continued)

Removing Hard and Symbolic Links.   A file exists only as long as a hard link to it exists, regardless of any symbolic links. Consequently, if you remove all the hard links to a file, you will not be able to access it through a symbolic link. In the following example, cat reports that the file **total** does not exist because it is a symbolic link to a file that has been removed:

```
$ ls -l sum
-rw-r--r-- 1 alex    pubs    981   May 24 11:05 scores
$ ln -s sum total
$ rm sum
$ cat total
total: No such file or directory
$ ls -l total
lrwxrwxrwx 1 alex    pubs      6   May 24 11:09 total -> sum
```

When you remove a file, be sure to remove all symbolic links to it. You can remove a symbolic link in the same way you remove other files:

```
$ rm total
```

SUMMARY

The UNIX system has a *hierarchical*, or treelike, file structure that makes it possible to organize files so you can find them quickly and easily. The file structure contains *directory* files and *ordinary* files. Directories contain other files, including other directories, whereas ordinary files generally contain text or programs. The ancestor of all files is the *root* directory, named /.

Older releases of System V allowed you to use up to 14 characters to name a file; UNIX systems that support 255-character filenames are becoming more common. Nonetheless, it is a good idea to keep filenames simple and meaningful. *Filename extensions* help make filenames more meaningful.

An *absolute pathname* starts with the root directory and contains all the filenames that trace a path to a given file. Such a pathname starts with a slash representing the root directory and contains additional slashes between the other filenames in the path.

A *relative pathname* is similar to an absolute pathname, but the path it traces starts from the working directory. A *simple filename* is the last element of a pathname and is a form of a relative pathname.

When you are logged in, you are always associated with a *working directory*. Your *home directory* is your working directory from the time you first log in until you use cd to change directories.

A *link* is a pointer to a file. You can have several links to a single file so that you can share the file with other users or have the file appear in more than one directory. Because there is only one copy of a file with multiple links, changing the file through any one link causes the changes to appear in all the links. Hard links cannot connect directories and cannot span file systems, but symbolic links can.

This chapter introduced the following utilities:

- pwd displays the pathname of the working directory.
- mkdir creates a directory.
- cd associates you with another working directory.
- rmdir deletes a directory.
- chmod changes the access permissions on a file.
- ln makes a link to an existing file.

REVIEW EXERCISES

1. How are directories different from ordinary files?
2. Determine whether each of the following is an absolute pathname, a relative pathname, or a simple filename:
   a. **milk_co**
   b. **correspondence/business/milk_co**
   c. **/home/alex**
   d. **/home/alex/literature/promo**
   e. **..**
   f. **letter.0610**
3. Should you ordinarily start your filenames with period (.)? Why or why not?
4. List the commands you can use to:
   a. make your home directory the working directory
   b. identify the working directory

5. If your working directory is **/home/alex/literature**, what two different commands can you use to create a subdirectory called **classics**?

6. What sequence of commands can you use to remove a directory called **/home/jenny/temp** and all its contents?

7. Is the **to_do** file below a directory or an ordinary file? Do members of the pubs group have permission to read the file?

```
$ ls -l to_do
-rw-r--r-- 1 alex   pubs    1338 May 24 17:01 to_do
```

What command can Alex use to give everyone permission to write to the file? What will the **ls -l** command display after he does so?

8. What does it mean to have execute permission for a directory?

9. Can simple filenames include the character slash (/)? Why or why not?

OPTIONAL

10. Create a file called **-x** in an empty directory. Explain what happens when you try to rename it. How can you rename it?

11. If **/home/jenny/draft** is linked to **/home/alex/letter**, and Alex changes **letter**, will Jenny see the changes when she looks at **draft**? What should Jenny do if she does not want Alex's changes to **letter** to affect **draft**?

12. If **/home/jenny/draft** and **/home/alex/letter** are links to the same file and the following sequence of events occurs, what will the date be in the opening of the letter?

a. Alex gives the command **vi letter**.

b. Jenny gives the command **vi draft**.

c. Jenny changes the date in the opening of the letter to January 31, 1991, and exits from vi with the **ZZ** command.

d. Alex changes the date to February 1, 1991, and exits from vi with the **ZZ** command.

13. What problems do you run into with multiple writable links to a file?

CHAPTER
5

THE SHELL

This chapter takes a close look at the shell and explains how to use some of its features. It discusses command line syntax, how the shell processes a command line, and how it initiates execution of a command. The chapter shows how to redirect input to and output from a command, construct pipes and filters on the command line, and run a command as a background task. The final section covers filename generation and explains how you can use this feature in your everyday work. Everything in this chapter applies to the Bourne Shell, the C Shell, and the Korn Shell. Refer to Chapters 8 and 9 and Appendix A for information on using the shell programming language to write shell scripts.

THE COMMAND LINE

The shell executes a program when you give it a command in response to its prompt. For example, when you give the ls command, the shell executes the utility program called ls. You can cause the shell to execute other types of programs—such as shell scripts, application programs, and programs you have written—in the same way. The line that contains the command, including any arguments, is called the *command line*. In this book, the term *command* is used to refer to the characters you type on the command line as well as the program that action invokes.

Command Line Syntax

Command line syntax dictates the ordering and separation of the elements on a command line. When you press the RETURN key after entering a command, the shell scans the command line for proper syntax. The format for a command line is:

command [arg1] [arg2] ... [argn] RETURN

The square brackets in the example enclose optional elements. One or more SPACES or TABS must appear between elements on the command line. The **command** is the command name, **arg1** through **argn** are arguments, and RETURN is the keystroke that terminates all command lines. The arguments are enclosed in square brackets because not all commands have arguments; some commands do not allow arguments, other commands allow a variable number of arguments, and others require a specific number of arguments.

Command Name.   Some useful UNIX commands consist only of the name of the command. For example, ls without any arguments lists the contents of the current directory. However, most UNIX commands accept one or more arguments. Commands that require arguments frequently give a short error message when you use them without arguments.

Arguments.   An *argument* is a filename, string of text, number, or some other object that a command acts on. For example, the argument to a **vi** command is the name of the file you want to edit.

The following command line shows cp copying the file named **temp** to **tempcopy**:

```
$ cp temp tempcopy
```

The **cp** utility requires two arguments on the command line. The first is the name of an existing file, and the second is the name of the file that it is creating. Here, the arguments are not optional; both arguments must be present for the command to work. If you do not supply the right number or kind of arguments, **cp** displays an error message. Try it—just type **cp** and RETURN.

Options.   An option is an argument that modifies the effects of a command. Frequently, you can specify more than one option, modifying the command in several different ways. Options are specific to and interpreted by the program that the command calls.

By convention, options are separate arguments that follow the name of the command. Most UNIX utilities require you to prefix options with a hyphen. However, this requirement is specific to the utility and not the shell.

Figure 5-1 shows that the **–r** (reverse order) option causes the **ls** utility to display the list of files in reverse alphabetical order. The **–x** option causes **ls** to display the list of files in horizontally sorted columns. (The **ls** utility in UNIX System V Release 4 normally displays files in vertically sorted columns.) It allows you to view a list of many filenames sorted across the screen. (If your version of **ls** displays a list of filenames in one long column that scrolls off the screen and does not have the **–x** option, use the **–C** option or see page 110.)

```
$ ls -r
test    temp    names
$ ls -x
names   temp    test
```

FIGURE 5-1   Using Options

If you need to use several options, you can usually (but not always) group them into one argument that starts with a single hyphen; do not put SPACES between the options. Specific rules for combining options depend on the utility. Figure 5-2 shows both the **–r** and **–x** options with the **ls** utility. Together, these options generate a list of filenames in horizontally sorted columns, in reverse alphabetical order. Most utilities allow you to list options in any order; **ls –xr** produces the same results as **ls –rx**. The command **ls –x –r** will also generate the same list.

```
$ ls -rx
test    temp    names
```

FIGURE 5-2   Using Two Options at Once

OPTIONAL

Processing the Command Line

As you enter a command line, the UNIX operating system examines each character to see if it must take any action (Figure 5-3). When you enter a CONTROL-H (to
erase a character) or a CONTROL-U (to kill a line), the operating system immediately
adjusts the command line as required—the shell never sees the character you
erased or the line you killed. UNIX System V Release 4 also adjusts the line
when you enter CONTROL-W (to erase a word) or CONTROL-R (to redraw the command line). If the character does not require immediate action, the operating system stores the character in a buffer and waits for additional characters. When you
press RETURN, the operating system passes the command line to the shell for processing.

When the shell processes a command line, it looks at the line as a whole and
breaks it down into its component parts (Figure 5-4). Next, the shell looks for the
name of the command. It assumes that the name of the command is the first thing
on the command line after the prompt (that is, argument zero), so it takes the first
characters on the command line, up to the first blank (TAB or SPACE), and sees if it
can find a command with that name. On the command line, each sequence of
nonblank characters is referred to as a *word*. The command name (the first word)
can be specified on the command line either as a simple filename or as a pathname. For example, you can call the ls command in either of the following ways:

```
$ ls
$ /usr/bin/ls
```

If you give an absolute pathname on the command line or a relative pathname that
is not just a simple filename (that is, any pathname that includes at least one
slash), the shell looks in the specified directory (**/usr/bin** in this case) for a file
that has the name **ls** and that you have permission to execute. If you do not give
a pathname on the command line, the shell searches through a list of directories

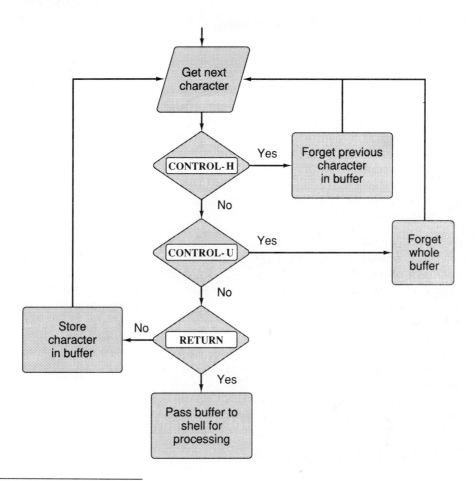

FIGURE 5-3   Entering a Command Line

for a filename that matches the name you specified and that you have execute permission for. The shell does not look through all directories—it looks only through the directories determined by a *shell variable* called the **PATH** variable. This variable is described in Chapters 8 and 9.

If the Bourne Shell cannot find the command, it displays the message xx: not found, where **xx** is the name of the command you called. If the Bourne Shell finds the program but cannot execute it (if you do not have execute access to the file that contains the program), you will see the following message: xx: execute permission denied. The messages presented by the C Shell and the Korn Shell are worded differently, but their gist is the same.

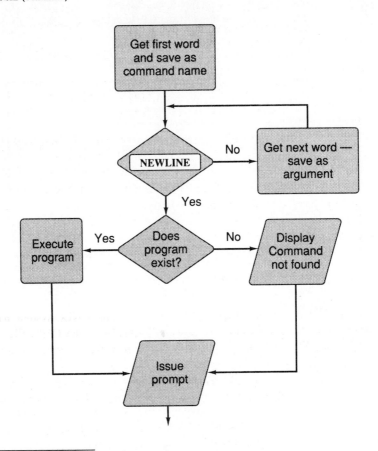

FIGURE 5-4   Processing the Command Line

The shell has no way of knowing whether a particular option or other argument is valid for a given command. Any error messages about options or arguments come from the command itself. Many UNIX utilities ignore bad options.

Executing the Command Line

If the shell finds an executable file with the same name as the command, it starts a new process. A *process* is the UNIX system execution of a program. The shell makes each command line argument, including options and the name of the command, available to the command. While the command is executing, the shell waits, inactive, for the process to finish. The shell is in a state called *sleep*. When the command finishes executing, the shell returns to an active state (wakes up), issues a prompt, and waits for another command.

STANDARD INPUT AND STANDARD OUTPUT

A command's *standard output* is a place to which it can send information, frequently text. The command never "knows" where the information it sends to its standard output is going. The information can go to a printer, an ordinary file, or a terminal. This section shows that the shell directs the standard output from a command to the terminal and describes how you can cause the shell to redirect this output to another file. It also explains how to redirect the *standard input* to a command so that it comes from an ordinary file instead of the terminal.

The Terminal as a File

Chapter 4 introduced ordinary files and directories. The UNIX system has an additional type of file, a *device file*. A device file resides in the UNIX file structure, usually in the **/dev** directory, and represents a peripheral device such as a terminal, printer, or disk drive.

The device name that the who utility displays after your login name is the filename of your terminal. If who displays the device name **tty6**, the pathname of your terminal is probably **/dev/tty6**. Although you would not normally have occasion to, you could read from and write to this file as though it were a text file. Writing to it would display what you wrote on the terminal screen, and reading from it would read what you entered on the keyboard.

The Terminal as the Standard Input and Output

When you first log in, the shell directs your commands' standard output to the device file that represents your terminal (Figure 5-5). Directing output in this manner causes it to appear on your terminal screen.

The shell also directs the standard input to come from the same file, so that your commands receive as input anything you type on your terminal keyboard.

The cat utility provides a good example of the way the terminal functions as the standard input and output. When you use cat, it copies a file to its standard output. Because the shell directs the standard output to the terminal, cat displays the file on the terminal.

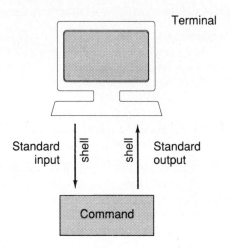

FIGURE 5-5   Standard Input and Output

Up to this point, cat has taken its input from the filename (argument) you specified on the command line. If you do not give cat an argument (that is, if you give the command cat immediately followed by a RETURN), cat takes input from its standard input.

The cat utility can now be defined as a utility that, when called without an argument, copies its standard input file to its standard output file. On most systems, it copies one line at a time.

To see how cat works, type **cat** RETURN in response to the shell prompt. Nothing happens. Enter a line of text and a RETURN. The same line appears just under the one you entered. The cat utility is working. (Some versions do not display anything until you signal the end of the file by pressing CONTROL-D; see below.) What happened is that you typed a line of text on the terminal, which the shell associated with cat's standard input, and cat copied your line of text to its standard output file, which the shell also associated with the terminal. This exchange is shown in Figure 5-6.

The cat utility keeps copying until you enter CONTROL-D on a line by itself. Pressing CONTROL-D sends an *end-of-file* signal to cat that indicates it has reached the end of the standard input file and that there is no more text for it to copy. When you enter CONTROL-D, cat finishes execution and returns control to the shell, which gives you a prompt.

```
$ cat
This is a line of text.
This is a line of text.
Cat keeps copying lines of text
Cat keeps copying lines of text
until you press CONTROL-D at the beginning
until you press CONTROL-D at the beginning
of a line.
of a line.
CONTROL-D
$
```

FIGURE 5-6   cat Copies Its Standard Input to Its Standard Output

REDIRECTION

The term *redirection* encompasses the various ways you can cause the shell to alter where a command gets its standard input from or where it sends its standard output to. As the previous section demonstrated, the shell, by default, associates a command's standard input and standard output with the terminal. Users can cause the shell to redirect the standard input and/or the standard output of any command by associating the input or output with a command or file other than the device file representing the terminal. This section demonstrates how to redirect output from and input to ordinary text files and UNIX utilities.

Redirecting the Standard Output

The *redirect output* symbol (>) instructs the shell to redirect a command's output to the specified file instead of to the terminal (Figure 5-7). The format of a command line that redirects output follows:

   command [arguments] > filename

The **command** is any executable program (e.g., an application program or a UNIX utility), **arguments** are optional arguments, and **filename** is the name of the ordinary file the shell redirects the output to.

Use caution when you redirect output. If the file already exists, the shell may overwrite it and destroy its contents.

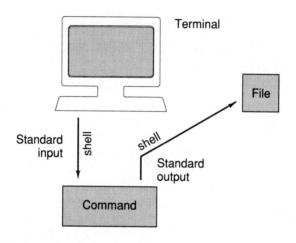

FIGURE 5-7   Redirecting the Standard Output

```
$ cat > sample.txt
This text is being entered at the keyboard.
Cat is copying it to a file.
Press CONTROL-D to indicate the
end of file.
CONTROL-D
$
```

FIGURE 5-8   cat with Its Output Redirected

In Figure 5-8, cat demonstrates output redirection. This figure contrasts with Figure 5-6, where both the standard input *and* standard output were associated with the terminal. In Figure 5-8, only the input comes from the terminal. The redirect output symbol on the command line causes the shell to associate cat's standard output with the file specified on the command line, **sample.txt**.

Now **sample.txt** contains the text you entered. You can use cat with an argument of **sample.txt** to display the file. The next section shows another way to use cat to display the file.

Figure 5-8 shows that redirecting the output from cat is a handy way to make files without using an editor. Its drawback is that, once you enter a line and press RETURN, you cannot edit the text. While you are entering a line, the erase and kill keys work to delete text. This procedure is useful for making short, simple files.

```
$ cat stationery
2000 sheets letterhead    ordered: 10/1/90
$ cat tape
1 box masking tape        ordered: 10/15/90
5 boxes filament tape     ordered: 10/29/90
$ cat pens
12 doz. black pens        ordered: 10/4/90
$ cat stationery tape pens > supply_orders
$ cat supply_orders
2000 sheets letterhead    ordered: 10/1/90
1 box masking tape        ordered: 10/15/90
5 boxes filament tape     ordered: 10/29/90
12 doz. black pens        ordered: 10/4/90
```

FIGURE 5-9   Using cat to Catenate Files

Figure 5-9 shows how to use cat and the redirect output symbol to *catenate* (join one after the other) several files into one larger file.

The first three commands display the contents of three files: **stationery**, **tape**, and **pens**. The next command shows cat with three filenames as arguments. When you call cat with more than one filename, it copies the files, one at a time, to its standard output. Here, the standard output is redirected to the file **supply_orders**. The final cat command shows that **supply_orders** contains the contents of all three files.

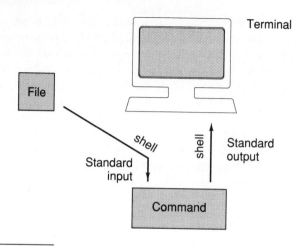

FIGURE 5-10   Redirecting the Standard Input

Redirecting the Standard Input

Just as you can redirect **cat**'s standard output, you can redirect its standard input. The *redirect input* symbol (<) instructs the shell to redirect a command's input from the specified file instead of the terminal (Figure 5-10). The format of a command line that redirects input follows:

> **command [arguments] < filename**

The **command** is any executable program (e.g., an application program or a UNIX utility), **arguments** are optional arguments, and **filename** is the name of the ordinary file the shell redirects the input from.

Figure 5-11 shows **cat** with its input redirected from the **supply_orders** file that was created in Figure 5-9 and its standard output going to the terminal. This setup causes **cat** to display the sample file on the terminal.

```
$ cat < supply_orders
2000 sheets letterhead    ordered:  10/1/90
1 box masking tape        ordered:  10/15/90
5 boxes filament tape     ordered:  10/29/90
12 doz. black pens        ordered:  10/4/90
```

FIGURE 5-11   cat with Its Input Redirected

The system automatically supplies an end-of-file signal at the end of an ordinary file, so no CONTROL-D is necessary.

Using cat with input redirected from a file yields the same result as giving a cat command with the filename as an argument. The cat utility is a member of a class of UNIX utilities that function in this manner. Other members of this class of utilities are lp, sort, and grep. These utilities first examine the command line you use to call them. If you include a filename on the command line, the utility takes its input from the file you specify. If there is no filename, the utility takes its input from its standard input. It is the program, not the shell or the operating system, that functions in this manner.

Following is an example of how to use redirected input with mailx. Frequently, it is convenient to compose your thoughts in a file before you send someone electronic mail. You can use lp to print the file, check that it is correct, and send it at your leisure. The following command sends the contents of the file **memo.alex** to Alex using mailx. The redirect input symbol redirects mailx's standard input to come from **memo.alex** instead of the terminal.

```
$ mailx alex < memo.alex
```

Cautions Regarding Redirecting Standard Output

Depending on what shell you are using and how your environment has been set up, the shell may display an error message and overwrite the **orange** file when you give the following command:

```
$ cat orange pear > orange
cat: input orange is output
```

Although cat displays an error message, it goes ahead and destroys the contents of the existing **orange** file. If you give the command above, the new **orange** file will have the same contents as **pear,** because the first action of the command is to remove the contents of the original **orange** file. If you want to catenate two files into one, use cat to put the two files into a third, temporary file, and then use mv to rename the third file as you desire.

```
$ cat orange pear > temp
$ mv temp orange
```

What happens with the typo in the next example can be even worse. The person giving the command meant to redirect the output from the nroff command (Chapter 7 covers the nroff text formatter) to the file **a.output.** Instead, the person entered the filename as **a output,** omitting the period and leaving a SPACE in its place. The shell obediently removed the contents of **a** and then called nroff. The error message takes a while to appear, giving you a sense that the command is running correctly. Even after you see the error message, though, you may not know that you destroyed the contents of **a**.

```
$ nroff -mm a b c > a output
nroff: can't open output
```

The C Shell and Korn Shell provide a feature called **noclobber** that stops you from inadvertently overwriting an existing file using redirection. If this variable is set and you attempt to redirect output to an existing file, the shell presents an error message and the command is not executed. If the examples above result in a message such as xx: file exists., then the **noclobber** variable is in effect. This feature is described on page 321.

Appending the Standard Output to a File

The *append output* symbol (>>) causes the shell to add the new information to the end of a file, leaving intact any information that was already there.

The example in Figure 5-12 shows how to create a file that contains the date and time (the output from the date utility) followed by a list of who is logged in (the output from who). The first line in Figure 5-12 redirects the output from date to the file named **whoson**. Then cat displays the file. Next, the example appends the output from who to the **whoson** file. Finally, cat displays the file containing the output of both utilities.

```
$ date > whoson
$ cat whoson
Thu Aug  9 09:24:19 PDT 1990
$ who >> whoson
$ cat whoson
Thu Aug  9 09:24:31 PDT 1990
hls           console      Aug  9 08:47
jenny         tty2         Aug  9 07:21
alex          tty6         Aug  8 11:01
```

FIGURE 5-12   Redirecting and Appending Output

The append output symbol provides a convenient way of catenating two files into one. You can use the following command to accomplish the catenation described above:

```
cat pear >> orange
```

This is simpler to use than the two-step procedure described in the previous section, but you must be careful to include both *greater than* signs. If you accidentally use only one and the **noclobber** variable is not set (or you are using the Bourne Shell), the **orange** file will be overwritten. Generally, even if you have the **noclobber** variable set, it is a good idea to keep backup copies of files you are manipulating in these ways in case you make a mistake. Although **noclobber** protects you from making an erroneous redirection, it cannot stop you from overwriting an existing file using the cp or mv utility.

NEW TO UNIX SYSTEM V Release 4

UNIX System V Release 4 provides interactive versions of cp and mv that protect users from those mistakes. Refer to cp and mv in Part II.

PIPES

The shell uses a *pipe* to connect the standard output of one command directly to the standard input of another command. A pipe has the same effect as redirecting the standard output of one command to a file and then using that file as the standard input to another command. It does away with separate commands and the intermediate file. The symbol for a pipe is a vertical bar (|). The format of a command line using a pipe follows:

command_a [arguments] | command_b [arguments]

This command line uses a pipe to generate the same result as the following command lines:

command_a [arguments] > temp
command_b [arguments] < temp
rm temp

The preceding sequence of commands first redirects the standard output from **command_a** to an intermediate file named **temp**. Then it redirects the standard input for **command_b** to come from **temp**. The final command line deletes **temp**.

You can use a pipe with a member of the class of UNIX utilities that accepts input either from a file specified on the command line or from the standard input. Other commands accept input only from the standard input, and you can also use pipes with these commands. For example, the **tr** (translate) utility takes its input only from the standard input. In its simplest usage, **tr** has the following format:

tr string1 string2

The **tr** utility translates each character in **string1** in its standard input to the corresponding character in **string2**. (The first character in **string1** is translated into the first character in **string2**, and so forth.) In the example below, **tr** displays the content of the **abstract** file with the letters a, b, and c translated into A, B, and C, respectively. Like other UNIX filters, **tr** does not change the content of the original file (see page 110 for more information about filters).

```
$ cat abstract | tr abc ABC
```

or

```
$ tr abc ABC < abstract
```

Refer to Part II for more information about **tr**.

The **lp** (line printer) utility is among the commands that accept input from either a file or the standard input. When you follow **lp** with the name of a file, it places that file in the printer queue. If you do not specify a filename on the command line, **lp** takes input from its standard input. This feature allows you to use a pipe to redirect input to **lp**. The line of information **lp** displays tells you whether it is getting its input from a file or its standard input.

The first set of commands in Figure 5-13 shows how you can use **ls** and **lp**, with an intermediate file, to send to the printer a list of the files in the working directory. The second set of commands sends the same list to the printer using a pipe.

The commands in Figure 5-14 redirect the output from the **who** utility to **temp** and then display this file in sorted order. The **sort** utility takes its input from the file specified on the command line or, if a file is not specified, from its standard input. It sends its output to its standard output. The **sort** command in Figure 5-14 specifies **temp** as the input file. The output that **sort** sends to the terminal lists the users in sorted (alphabetical) order.

Figure 5-15 achieves the same result with a pipe. Using a pipe, the shell directs the output from **who** to the input of **sort**. The **sort** utility takes input from its standard input because no filename follows it on the command line.

```
$ ls > temp
$ lp temp
request id is printer_1-452 (1 file)
$ rm temp

or

$ ls | lp
request id is printer_1-453 (standard input)
```

FIGURE 5-13   A Pipe

```
$ who > temp
$ sort temp
barbara        tty3              May 26 12:53
chas           tty6              May 26 10:31
hls            console           May 26 12:48
scott          tty2              May 25 09:07
```

FIGURE 5-14   Simulating a Pipe with who and sort

```
$ who | sort
barbara        tty3              May 26 12:53
chas           tty6              May 26 10:31
hls            console           May 26 12:48
scott          tty2              May 25 09:07
```

FIGURE 5-15   A Pipe

If a lot of people are using the system and you want information about only one of them, you can send the output from who to grep using a pipe. The grep utility will display the line containing the string you specify—chas in the following example.

```
$ who | grep 'chas'
chas           tty6              May 22 10:31
```

In early versions of System V, ls did not include the −C option for displaying a list in multiple columns. If you have a lot of files, a single column list can easily run off the top of the screen. The following command uses a pipe to list the filenames in five columns, allowing you to see all the names on the screen at once. See pr in Part II for more information on how pr works.

```
$ ls | pr −5 −t
.
.
```

Another way of handling output that is too long to fit on the screen is to use a pipe to send it through the pg or more utility:

```
$ ls | pg
```

```
$ ls | more
```

The pg and more utilities allow you to view text on your terminal a screenful at a time. If you are using pg, press RETURN to view another screenful. If you are using more, press SPACE.

Filters

A *filter* is a command that processes an input stream of data to produce an output stream of data. A command line that includes a filter uses a pipe to connect the filter's input to the standard output of one command. Another pipe connects the filter's output to the standard input of another command. Some utilities that are interactive, such as vi and mailx, cannot be used as filters.

Below, sort is a filter, taking its standard input from the standard output of who and using a pipe to redirect its standard output to the standard input of lp. The command line sends the sorted output of who to the printer.

```
$ who | sort | lp
request id is printer_1-454 (standard input)
```

This example demonstrates the power of the shell combined with the versatility of UNIX utilities. The three utilities, who, sort, and lp, were not specifically designed to work with each other, but they all use the standard input and standard output in the conventional way. By using the shell to handle input and output, you can piece standard utilities together on the command line to achieve the results you want.

The tee Utility

You can use the **tee** utility in a pipe to send the output of a command to a file while also sending it to its standard output. The utility is aptly named—it takes a single input and sends the output in two directions. In the following example, the output of who is sent via a pipe to the standard input of tee. The tee utility saves a copy of the standard input in a file called **who.out** while it also sends a copy to the standard output. The standard output of tee goes, via a pipe, to the standard input of grep, which displays lines containing the string alex.

```
$ who | tee who.out | grep alex
```

RUNNING A PROGRAM IN THE BACKGROUND

In all the examples you have seen so far in this book, commands were run in the *foreground*. When you run a command in the foreground, the shell waits for it to finish before the shell gives you another prompt and allows you to continue. When you run a command in the *background*, you do not have to wait for the command to finish before you start running another command. Running a command in the background can be useful if the command will be running a long time and does not need supervision. The terminal will be free so you can use it for other work.

To run a command in the background, type an ampersand (**&**) just before the RETURN that ends the command line. The shell will display a Process Identification (PID) number that identifies the command running in the background and give you another prompt.

The following example runs an **ls –l** command in the background. The command sends its output through a pipe to the lp utility, which sends it to the printer.

```
$ ls -l | lp &
31725
request id is printer_1-455 (standard input)
```

If a background task sends output to the standard output and you do not redirect it, the output appears on your terminal, even if you are running another job. If a background task requests input from the standard input and you have not redirected the standard input, the shell supplies a null string.

You will probably want to redirect the output of a job you run in the background or send it through a pipe to keep it from interfering with whatever you are doing at the terminal. Chapter 8 goes into more detail about background tasks in the section ''Command Separation and Grouping.''

The interrupt key (usually DEL or CONTROL-C) cannot abort a process you are running in the background; you must use the kill command for this purpose. If you want to kill *all* processes that you are running *in the background*, you can use the following command.

```
$ kill 0
```

Alternatively, when you use kill to kill selected processes, you must give it the PID number of the process you want to abort.

If you forget the PID number, you can use the ps (process status) utility to display it. The following example runs an nroff job in the background, uses ps to display the PID number of the process, and aborts the job with kill. Refer to Part II for more information on kill and ps; see Chapter 7 for nroff information.

```
$ nroff -mm textfile > textfile.out &
1466
$ ps
   PID   TTY      TIME  COMMAND
   1456  tty03    0:05  sh
   1466  tty03    0:39  nroff
   1514  tty03    0:03  ps
$ kill 1466
```

FILENAME GENERATION

When you give the shell abbreviated filenames that contain *special characters* (or *metacharacters*—characters that have a special meaning to the shell), the shell can generate filenames that match the names of existing files. When one of these special characters appears in an argument on the command line, the shell expands that argument into a list of filenames and passes the list to the program that the command line is calling. Filenames that contain these special characters are called *ambiguous file references* because they do not refer to any one specific file.

The special characters are referred to as *metacharacters* or *wild cards* because they act as the jokers do in a deck of cards. The process of expanding an ambiguous file reference used to be called *globbing*. Ambiguous file references allow you to quickly reference a group of files with similar names, saving you the effort of typing the names individually. They also allow you to reference a file whose name you do not remember in its entirety.

The ? Special Character

The question mark is a special character that causes the shell to generate filenames. It matches any single character in the name of an existing file. The following command uses this special character in an argument to the **lp** utility:

```
$ lp memo?
request id is printer_1-456 (4 files)
```

The shell expands the memo? argument and generates a list of the files in the working directory that have names composed of **memo** followed by any single character. The shell passes this list to **lp**. The **lp** utility never "knows" that the shell generated the filenames it was called with. If no filename matches the ambiguous file reference, the Bourne Shell and Korn Shell pass the string itself (memo?) to the command. Depending on how it is set up, the C Shell may display an error message (No match) or pass the string itself.

The following example uses **ls** to display the filenames that memo? does and does not match:

```
$ ls
mem          memo12     memo9      memoalex   newmemo5
memo         memo5      memoa      memos
$ ls memo?
memo5   memo9   memoa   memos
```

The memo? ambiguous file reference does not match **mem, memo, memo12, memoalex,** or **newmemo5**.

You can also use a question mark in the middle of an ambiguous file reference:

```
$ ls
7may4report     may14report     may4report.79   mayqreport
may.report      may4report      may_report      mayreport
$ ls may?report
may.report   may4report   may_report   mayqreport
```

To practice with filename generation, you can use echo as well as ls. The echo utility displays the arguments that the shell passes to it. Try giving the following command:

```
$ echo may?report
may.report    may4report    may_report    mayqreport
```

The shell expands the ambiguous file reference into a list of all files in the working directory that match the string **may?report** and passes this list to echo, as though you had entered the list of filenames as arguments to echo. The echo utility responds to this command by displaying the list of filenames.

The * Special Character

The asterisk performs a function similar to that of the question mark, except that it matches any number of characters, *including zero characters,* in a filename. The following example shows all the files in the current directory and then all the filenames that begin with the string **memo**:

```
$ ls
amemo          memo          memoa          memosally      user.memo
mem            memo.0612     memorandum     sallymemo
$ echo memo*
memo memo.0612 memoa memorandum memosally
```

The ambiguous file reference **memo*** does not match **amemo, mem, sallymemo,** or **user.memo.**

An asterisk does not match a leading period (one that indicates an invisible filename). Consequently, if you want to match filenames that begin with a period, you must explicitly include the period in the ambiguous file reference.

The ls utility also has an option, **–a,** that causes it to display invisible filenames:

```
$ ls -a
.              .aaa          aaa            memo.sally    sally.0612    thurs
..             .profile      memo.0612      report        saturday
$ echo *
aaa memo.0612 memo.sally report sally.0612 saturday thurs
$ echo .*
. .. .aaa .profile
```

The command **echo *** does not display **.** (the working directory), **..** (the parent of the working directory), **.aaa** or **.profile.** The command **echo .*** displays only those four names.

OPTIONAL (Continued)

```
$ ls -a
.                .private      memo.0612    reminder
..               .profile      private      report
$ echo .p*
.private .profile
```

In the final example, .p* does not match **memo.0612, private, reminder,** or
report. The following command causes ls to list **.private** and **.profile** in addition
to the entire contents of the . directory (the working directory) and the .. directory
(the parent of the working directory).

```
$ ls .*
.private    .profile

.:
memo.0612   private     reminder    report

..:
.
.
```

If you establish conventions for naming files, you can take advantage of
ambiguous file references. For example, if you end all your text file filenames
with **.txt,** you can reference that group of files with *.txt. Following this convention, the command below will send all the text files in the working directory to
the printer. The ampersand causes lp to run in the background.

```
$ lp *.txt &
4312
request id is printer_1-457 (5 files)
```

The [ ] Special Characters

A pair of square brackets surrounding a list of characters causes the shell to match
filenames containing the individual characters. Whereas **memo?** matches **memo**
followed by any character, **memo[17a]** is more restrictive—it matches only
memo1, memo7, and **memoa.** The brackets define a *character class* that includes
all the characters within the brackets. The shell expands an argument that
includes a character class definition, substituting each member of the character
class, *one at a time*, in place of the brackets and their contents. The shell passes a
list of matching filenames to the command it is calling.

Each character class definition can replace only a single character within a filename. The brackets and their contents are like a question mark that will substitute only the members of the character class.

The first of the following commands lists the names of all the files in the working directory that begin with **a**, **e**, **i**, **o**, or **u**. The second command displays the contents of the files named **page2.txt**, **page4.txt**, **page6.txt**, and **page8.txt**.

```
$ echo [aeiou]*
.
.
.
$ cat page[2468].txt
.
.
.
```

A hyphen defines a range of characters within a character class definition. For example, [6-9] represents [6789], and [a-z] represents all lowercase letters.

The following command lines show three ways to print the files named **part0**, **part1**, **part2**, **part3**, and **part5**. Each of the command lines calls **lp** with five filenames.

```
$ lp part0 part1 part2 part3 part5
request id is printer_1-457 (5 files)


$ lp part[01235]
request id is printer_1-458 (5 files)


$ lp part[0-35]
request id is printer_1-459 (5 files)
```

The first command line explicitly specifies the five filenames. The second and third command lines use ambiguous file references, incorporating character class definitions. The shell expands the argument on the second command line to include all files that have names beginning with **part** and ending with any of the characters in the character class. The character class is explicitly defined as **0**, **1**, **2**, **3**, and **5**. The third command line also uses a character class definition, except it defines the character class to be all characters in the range from 0-3 and 5.

The following command line will print 36 files, **part0** through **part35**:

```
$ lp part[0-9] part[12][0-9] part3[0-5]
request id is printer_1-460 (36 files)
$
```

The next two examples list the names of some of the files in the working directory. The first lists the files whose names start with a through m. The second lists files whose names end with x, y, or z.

```
$ echo [a-m]*
  .
  .
  .

$ echo *[x-z]
  .
  .
  .
```

SUMMARY

The shell is the UNIX command interpreter. It scans the command line for proper syntax, picking out the command name and any arguments. Many programs use options to modify the effects of a command. Most UNIX utilities identify options by their leading hyphens.

When you give the shell a command, it tries to find an executable program with the same name as the command. If it does, it executes the program. If it does not, it tells you that it cannot find or execute the program.

When the shell executes a command, it assigns a file to the command's *standard input* and *standard output*. By default, the shell causes a command's standard input to come from the terminal keyboard and its standard output to go to the terminal screen. You can instruct the shell to *redirect* a command's standard input or standard output to any reasonable file or device. You can also connect the standard output of one command to the standard input of another using a pipe.

When a command runs in the *foreground*, the shell waits for it to finish before it gives you another prompt and allows you to continue. If you put an ampersand (**&**) at the end of a command line, the shell executes the command in the *background* and gives you another prompt immediately.

The shell interprets special characters on a command line for *filename generation*. It uses a question mark to represent any single character and an asterisk to represent zero or more characters. A reference to a file that includes one of these characters is called an *ambiguous file reference*.

REVIEW EXERCISES

1. What does the shell ordinarily do while a command is executing? What should you do if you do not want to wait for a command to finish before running another command?

2. What command line will redirect the standard output from the **sort** command into a file called **phone_list**? Assume the input file is called **numbers**.

3. Can the **grep** utility be used as a filter? Explain your answer.

4. Describe two ways you can create a file called **book** that contains the contents of two other files, **part1** and **part2**.

5. Rewrite the following sequence of commands using **sort** as a filter:

```
$ sort list > temp
$ lp temp
$ rm temp
```

6. What is a PID number? Why are they useful when you run processes in the background?

7. Assume the following files are in the working directory:

```
$ ls
intro      notesb     ref2      section1   section3   section4b
notesa     ref1       ref3      section2   section4a
```

What command(s) (including wild cards) can you use to:

a. list all files that begin with **section**.

b. list the files **section1**, **section2**, and **section3**.

c. list the **intro** file only.

d. list the files **section1**, **section3**, **ref1**, and **ref3**.

8. Why don't command names and filenames usually have embedded spaces? If you wanted to create a filename containing a space, how would you do it? (This is a thought exercise—it is not a recommended practice.)

9. If you accidentally create a filename with a nonprinting character in it (e.g., a CONTROL character), how can you rename the file?

10. Create a file called **answers** and then give the following command:

```
$ > answers.0188 < answers cat
```

Explain what the command does. What is the more traditional way of accomplishing the same thing? How can the shell recognize that **cat** is the command name (that is, argument zero) even though it does not come first on the command line?

11. Why can't the **noclobber** variable protect you from overwriting an existing file with **cp** or **mv**?

CHAPTER
6

THE vi
EDITOR

This chapter shows how to use the vi editor to change existing text files.
It assumes that you have read the part of Chapter 2 that explains how to
specify your terminal and get started using vi. This chapter goes into
detail about many of the vi commands and explains the use of parameters for customizing vi for your needs. At the end of the chapter is a
quick reference summary of vi commands.

The vi editor is very large and powerful, and only some of its features are described here. Nonetheless, if vi is completely new to you, you may find even the set of commands described here overwhelming. The vi editor provides a variety of different ways to accomplish any specified editing task. A useful strategy when learning vi is to learn a subset of commands that enables you to accomplish basic editing tasks and then to learn other commands that will enable you to do things more quickly and efficiently as you become more comfortable with the editor.

INTRODUCTION TO vi

This section contains historical information on vi, some useful facts about how vi operates, and suggestions on what you can do when you encounter exceptional conditions, such as system crashes or not being able to exit from vi. It also summarizes some of the information on vi that was presented in Chapter 2.

History of vi

The vi editor was developed at the University of California, Berkeley, as part of Berkeley UNIX. Although many systems have supported vi for a long time, it became an official part of AT&T UNIX only with the release of System V.

Before vi was developed, the standard UNIX system editor was ed. The ed editor was line-oriented, which made it difficult to see the context of your editing. Then ex came along—ex was a superset of ed. The most notable advantage that ex had over ed was a display editing facility that allowed users to work with a full screen of text instead of with only a line at a time. While you were using ex, you could use the display editing facility by giving ex the command vi (for visual mode). People used the display editing facility of ex so extensively that the developers of ex made it possible to start the editor so that you were using the display editing facility at once, without having to start ex and give the vi command. Appropriately, they named the new facility vi.

You can still call the visual mode from ex, and you can go back to ex while you are using vi. Give vi a **Q** command to use ex, or give ex a **vi** command to switch to visual mode.

Modes of Operation

The ex editor has five modes of operation:

• ex Command Mode
• ex Input Mode

- vi Command Mode
- vi Input Mode
- vi Last Line Mode

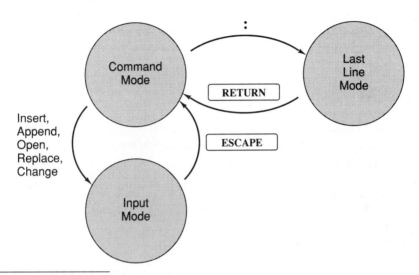

FIGURE 6-1   Modes in vi

While you are using vi, you will mostly use vi Command Mode and Input Mode. On occasion you will use Last Line Mode. While in Command Mode, vi accepts keystrokes as commands, responding to each command as you enter it. In Command Mode, vi does not display the characters you type. In Input Mode, vi accepts keystrokes as text, displaying the text as you enter it. All commands that start with a colon (:) put vi in Last Line Mode. The colon moves the cursor to the bottom line of the screen, where you enter the rest of the command.

In addition to the position of the cursor, there is another important difference between Last Line Mode and Command Mode. When you give a command in Command Mode, you do not have to terminate the command with RETURN. However, you must terminate all Last Line Mode commands with a RETURN (ESCAPE also works).

You will not normally use the ex modes. When this chapter refers to Input and Command Modes, it refers to the vi modes and not to the ex modes.

At the start of an editing session, vi is in Command Mode. There are several commands, such as Insert and Append, that put vi in Input Mode. When you press the ESCAPE key, vi always reverts to Command Mode.

The Change and Replace commands combine Command and Input Modes. The Change command deletes the text you want to change and puts vi in Input Mode so you can insert new text. The Replace command deletes the character(s) you overwrite and inserts the new one(s) you enter. Figure 6-1 shows the modes as well as the methods for changing between them.

Correcting Text as You Insert It

While vi is in Input Mode, you can use the erase and line kill keys to back up over text that you are inserting so you can correct it. You can also use CONTROL-W to back up to the beginning of the word you are entering. Using these techniques, you cannot back up past the beginning of the line you are working on or past the beginning of the text you entered since you most recently put vi into Input Mode.

Command Case

Be certain to observe the case of commands, as this chapter describes them. The same letter serves as two different commands, depending on whether you enter it as an uppercase or lowercase character.

If vi seems to be behaving strangely, check to see if the SHIFT LOCK (or CAPS LOCK) on the terminal is on. Turn it off!

The Work Buffer

The vi editor does all its work in the *Work Buffer*. At the start of an editing session, vi reads the file you are editing from the disk into the Work Buffer. During the editing session, vi makes all changes to this copy of the file. It does not change the disk file until you write the contents of the Work Buffer back to the disk. Normally, when you end an editing session, you command vi to write out the contents of the Work Buffer, which makes the changes to the text final. When you edit a new file, vi does not create the file until it writes the contents of the Work Buffer to the disk, usually at the end of the editing session.

Storing the text you are editing in the Work Buffer has advantages and disadvantages. If you accidentally end an editing session without writing out the contents of the Work Buffer, all your work is lost. However, if you unintentionally make some major changes (such as deleting the entire contents of the Work Buffer), you can end the editing session without implementing the changes. The vi editor will leave the file as it was when you last wrote it out.

If you want to use the vi editor to look at a file but not to change it, you can use the view command:

```
$ view filename
```

This command calls the vi editor with the **–R** (read-only) option. Once you have invoked the editor in this way, it will not let you write the contents of the Work Buffer back to the file on the disk.

Abnormal Termination of an Editing Session

You can end an editing session in one of two ways: Either vi saves the changes you made during the editing session, or it does not save them. Chapter 2 explained that the **ZZ** command saves the contents of the Work Buffer and exits from vi.

You can end an editing session without writing out the contents of the Work Buffer by giving the following command. (The **:** puts vi in Last Line Mode— you must press RETURN to execute the command.)

:q!

When you use this command to end an editing session, vi does not preserve the contents of the Work Buffer—you lose all the work you did since the last time you wrote the Work Buffer to disk. The next time you edit or use the file, it will appear as it did the last time you wrote the Work Buffer to disk. Use the **:q!** command cautiously.

You may run into a situation where you have created or edited a file, and vi will not let you exit. When you give the **ZZ** command, you will see the message No current filename if you forgot to specify a filename when you first called vi. If vi will not let you exit normally, you can use the Write command (**:w**) to name the file and write it to disk before you quit using vi. To write the file, give the following command, substituting the name of the file in place of **filename** (remember to follow the command with a RETURN):

:w filename

After you give the Write command, you can use **:q** to quit. You do not need to use the exclamation point (that is, **q!**) because the exclamation point is necessary only when you have made changes since the last time you wrote the Work Buffer to disk. Refer to page 143 for more information about the Write command.

===

OPTIONAL

It may also be necessary to write a file using **:w filename** if you do not have write permission for the file you are editing. If you give the **ZZ** command and see the message Permission denied or the message File is read only, you do not have write permission for the file. Use the Write command with a temporary filename to write the file to disk under a different filename. If you do not have write permission to the working directory, vi may still not be able to write your file to the disk. Give the command again, using an absolute pathname of a dummy (nonexistent) file in your home directory in place of **filename**. (Alex might give the command **:w /home/alex/temp**.)

===

Recovering Text After a Crash

If the system crashes while you are editing a file with **vi**, you can often recover text that would otherwise be lost. If the system saved a copy of your Work Buffer, it may send you mail telling you so. However, even if you did not get mail when the system was brought up, give the following command to see if the system saved the contents of your Work Buffer:

> **vi –r filename**

If your work was saved, you will be editing a recent copy of your Work Buffer. Use **:w** immediately to save the salvaged copy of the Work Buffer to disk, and then continue editing.

THE DISPLAY

The **vi** editor uses the status line and several special symbols to give information about what is happening during an editing session.

The Status Line

The **vi** editor displays status information on the bottom line—the twenty-fourth line of most terminals. This information includes error messages, information about the deletion or addition of blocks of text, and file status information. In addition, **vi** displays Last Line Mode commands on the status line.

Redrawing the Screen

In some cases, **vi** uses an @ symbol at the left of the screen to replace deleted lines. The **vi** editor does this rather than refreshing the screen so that users, especially those using a UNIX system over slow telephone lines, do not have to wait through unnecessary pauses when text is deleted from the screen. This symbol appears only on the screen and is never written to the Work Buffer or file. If the screen becomes cluttered with these symbols, enter CONTROL-L (some terminals use CONTROL-R) while **vi** is in Command Mode to redraw the screen.

You may also want to redraw the screen if another user writes to you while you are in **vi**. When this happens, the other user's message becomes intermixed with the display of the Work Buffer, and this can be confusing. The other user's message *does not* become part of the Work Buffer—it only affects the display. If this happens when you are in Input Mode, press ESCAPE to get into Command Mode, and then press CONTROL-L (or CONTROL-R) to redraw the screen.

Be sure to read the other user's message before redrawing the screen since redrawing the screen causes the message to disappear. You can write back to the other user while in vi (see page 150) or quit vi and use the write command from the shell.

The Tilde (~) Symbol

If the end of the file is displayed on the screen, vi marks lines that would appear past the end of the file with a tilde (~) at the left of the screen. When you start editing a new file, the vi editor marks every line on the screen, except for the first line, with these symbols.

COMMAND MODE—MOVING THE CURSOR

While vi is in Command Mode, you can position the cursor over any character on the screen. You can also display a different portion of the Work Buffer on the screen. By manipulating the screen and cursor position, you can place the cursor on any character in the Work Buffer.

You can move the cursor forward or backward through the text. As illustrated in Figure 6-2, *forward* always means toward the bottom of the screen and

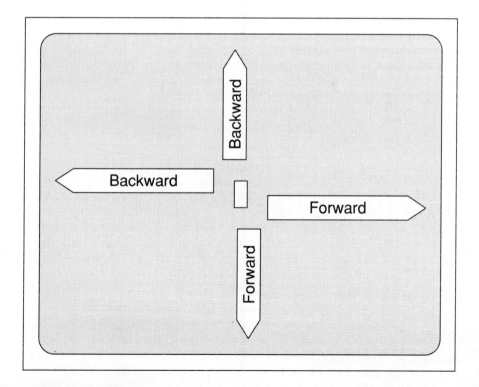

FIGURE 6-2   Forward and Backward

the end of the file. *Backward* means toward the top of the screen and the beginning of the file. When you use a command that moves the cursor forward past the end (right) of a line, the cursor generally moves to the beginning (left) of the next line. When you move it backward past the beginning of a line, it moves to the end of the previous line.

You can move the cursor through the text by any *Unit of Measure* (i.e., character, word, line, sentence, paragraph, or screen.) If you precede a cursor-movement command with a number, called a *Repeat Factor,* the cursor moves that number of units through the text. Refer to the sections at the end of this chapter on "Units of Measure" and "Repeat Factors" for more precise definitions of these terms.

Moving the Cursor by Characters

The SPACE bar moves the cursor forward, one character at a time, toward the right side of the screen. The l (ell) key and the RIGHT ARROW key (see Figure 6-3) do the same thing. The command 7SPACE or 7l moves the cursor seven characters to the right. These keys *cannot* move the cursor past the end of the current line to the beginning of the next.

The h key and the LEFT ARROW key are similar to the l key but work in the opposite direction.

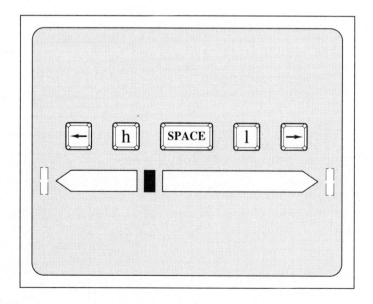

FIGURE 6-3   Moving the Cursor by Characters

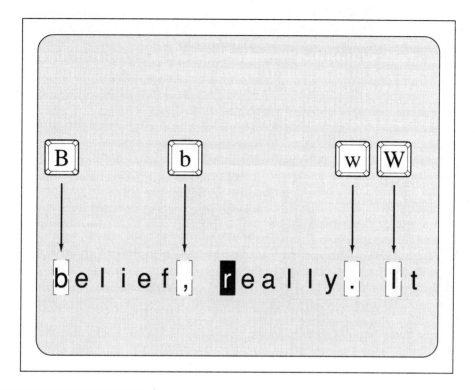

FIGURE 6-4   Moving the Cursor by Words

Moving the Cursor by Words

The **w** key moves the cursor forward to the first letter of the next word (Figure 6-4). Groups of punctuation count as words. This command goes to the next line if that is where the next word is, unless the line ends with a SPACE. The command **15w** moves the cursor to the first character of the fifteenth subsequent word.

The **W** key is similar to the **w** key, except that it moves the cursor by blank delimited words, including punctuation, as it skips forward over words. (See "Blank Delimited Word," page 152.)

The **b** key moves the cursor backward to the first letter of the previous word. The **B** key moves the cursor backward by blank delimited words.

Moving the Cursor by Lines

The RETURN key moves the cursor to the beginning of the next line (Figure 6-5), and the **j** and DOWN ARROW keys move it down one line to the character just below the current character. If there is no character immediately below the current

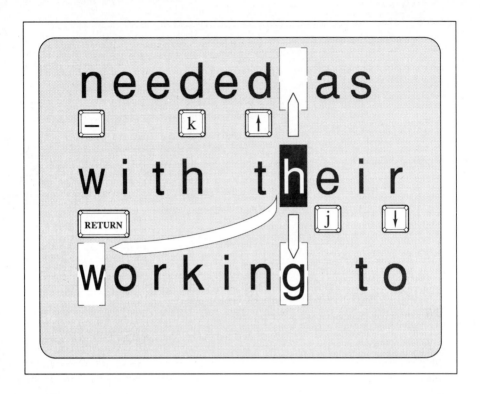

FIGURE 6-5   Moving the Cursor by Lines

character, the cursor moves to the end of the next line. The cursor will not move past the last line of text.

The **k** and UP ARROW keys are similar to the **j** key, but they work in the opposite direction. Also, the minus (–) key is similar to the RETURN key, but it works in the opposite direction.

Moving the Cursor by Sentences and Paragraphs

The) and } keys move the cursor forward to the beginning of the next sentence or paragraph, respectively (Figure 6-6). The (and { keys move the cursor backward to the beginning of the current sentence or paragraph.

Moving the Cursor Within the Screen

The **H** key positions the cursor at the left end of the top, or Home, line of the screen. The **M** key moves the cursor to the Middle line, and **L** moves it to the bottom, or Lower line. See Figure 6-6.

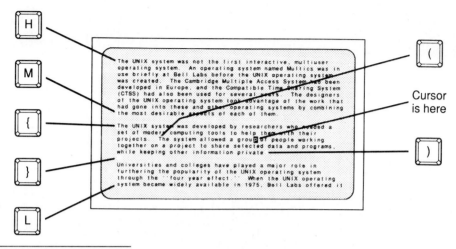

FIGURE 6-6   Moving the Cursor by Sentences, Paragraphs, **H**, **M**, and **L**

Viewing Different Parts of the Work Buffer

The screen displays a portion of the text that is in the Work Buffer. You can display the text preceding or following the text on the screen by *scrolling* the display. You can also display a portion of the Work Buffer based on a line number.

Press CONTROL-D to scroll the screen Down (forward) through the file so that vi displays half a screenful of new text. Use CONTROL-U to scroll the screen Up (backward) the same amount. The CONTROL-F (Forward) or CONTROL-B (Backward) keys display almost a *whole* screenful of new text, leaving a couple of lines from the previous screen for continuity. See Figure 6-7.

When you enter a line number followed by **G** (Goto), vi displays a specific line in the Work Buffer. If you press **G** without a number, vi positions the cursor on the last line in the Work Buffer. Line numbers are implicit; your file does not need to have actual line numbers for you to use this command. Refer to "Line Numbers," page 146, if you want vi to display line numbers.

INPUT MODE

The Insert, Append, Open, Change, and Replace commands put vi in Input Mode. While vi is in Input Mode, you can put new text into the Work Buffer. Always press the ESCAPE key to return vi to Command Mode when you finish entering text. Refer to "Show Mode" in the "Parameters" section (page 146) if you want vi to remind you when it is in Input Mode.

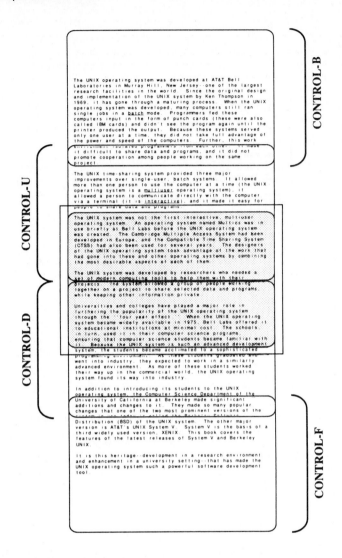

FIGURE 6-7   Moving the Cursor by CONTROL Characters

The Insert Commands

The **i** command puts **vi** in Input Mode and places the text you enter *before* the character the cursor is on (the *current character*). The **I** command places text at the beginning of the current line. See Figure 6-8. Although **i** and **I** commands sometimes overwrite text on the screen, the characters in the Work Buffer are not changed (only the display is affected). The overwritten text will be redisplayed when you press ESCAPE and **vi** returns to Command Mode. Use **i** or **I** to insert a few characters or words into existing text or to insert text in a new file.

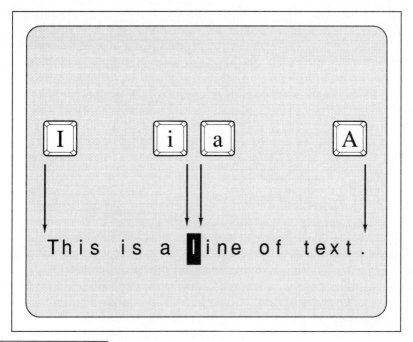

FIGURE 6-8   The **i**, **I**, **a**, and **A** Commands

The Append Commands

The **a** command is similar to the **i** command, except that it places the text you enter *after* the current character (Figure 6-8). The **A** command places the text *after* the last character on the current line.

The Open Commands

The **o** and **O** commands open a blank line within existing text, place the cursor at the beginning of the new (blank) line, and put vi in Input Mode. The **O** command opens a line *above* the current line; **o** opens one below. Use the Open commands when entering several new lines within existing text.

The Replace Commands

The **R** and **r** commands cause the new text you enter to overwrite (replace) existing text. The single character you enter following an **r** command overwrites the current character. After you enter that character, vi automatically returns to Command Mode. You do not need to press the ESCAPE key.

The **R** command causes *all* subsequent characters to overwrite existing text until you press ESCAPE and vi returns to Command Mode.

Caution.   These commands may appear to behave strangely if you replace TAB characters. TAB characters can appear as several SPACES—until you try to replace them. They are actually only one character and will be replaced by a single character. Refer to "Invisible Characters," page 147, for information on how to display TABS as visible characters.

The Quote Command

You can use the Quote command, CONTROL-V, while you are in Input Mode. The Quote command enables you to insert into your text characters that have special meanings to vi. Among these characters are CONTROL-L (or CONTROL-R), which redraws the screen; CONTROL-W, which backs the cursor up a word to the left; and ESCAPE, which ends Input Mode.

To insert one of these characters into your text, type CONTROL-V and then the character. CONTROL-V quotes the single character that follows it. For example, to insert the sequence ESCAPE[2J into a file you are creating in vi, you type the character sequence CONTROL-V ESCAPE[2J. This is the character sequence that clears the screen of a DEC VT-100 terminal. Although you would not ordinarily want to type this sequence into a document, you might want to use it or another ESCAPE sequence in a shell script you are creating in vi. Refer to Chapters 8 and 9 and Appendix A for information about writing shell scripts.

COMMAND MODE—DELETING AND CHANGING TEXT

The Undo Commands

The Undo command, **u**, undoes what you just did. It restores text that you deleted or changed by mistake. The Undo command restores only the most recently deleted text. If you delete a line and then change a word, Undo restores only the changed word—not the deleted line. The **U** command restores the current line to the way it was before you started changing it, even after several changes.

The Delete Character Command

The **x** command deletes the current character. You can precede the **x** command by a Repeat Factor to delete several characters on the current line, starting with the current character. A *Repeat Factor* specifies the number of times a command is performed.

The Delete Command

The **d** command removes text from the Work Buffer. The amount of text that **d** removes depends on the Repeat Factor and the Unit of Measure you enter after the **d**. After the text is deleted, **vi** is still in Command Mode.

Caution.   The command **d** RETURN deletes two lines: the current line and the following one. Use the **dd** command to delete just the current line, or precede **dd** by a Repeat Factor to delete several lines.

A list of some Delete commands follows. Each of the commands, except the last group, deletes *from* the current character.

Delete Command	Action
d0	delete to beginning of line
dw	delete to end of word
d3w	delete to end of third word
db	delete to beginning of word
dW	delete to end of blank delimited word
dB	delete to beginning of blank delimited word
d7B	delete to seventh previous beginning of blank delimited word
d)	delete to end of sentence
d4)	delete to end of fourth sentence
d(	delete to beginning of sentence
d}	delete to end of paragraph
d{	delete to beginning of paragraph
d7{	delete to seventh preceding beginning of paragraph

Delete

Command	Action
dd	delete the current line
5dd	delete five lines starting with the current line
dL	delete through last line on screen
dH	delete through first line on screen
dG	delete through end of Work Buffer
d1G	delete through beginning of Work Buffer

The Change Command

The **c** command replaces existing text with new text. The new text does not have to occupy the same space as the existing text. You can change a word to several words, a line to several lines, or a paragraph to a single character.

The Change command deletes the amount of text specified by the Unit of Measure that follows it and puts vi in Input Mode. When you finish entering the new text and press ESCAPE, the old word, line, sentence, or paragraph is changed to the new one.

When you change less than a line of text, vi does not delete the text immediately. Instead, the **c** command places a dollar sign at the end of the text that it will change and leaves vi in Input Mode. You may appear to overwrite text, but only the text that precedes the dollar sign changes in the Work Buffer. Other text remains in the Work Buffer and will be redisplayed when you press ESCAPE. When you change a line or more, vi deletes the lines as soon as you give the Change command.

A list of some Change commands follows. Each of the commands, except the last group, changes text *from* the current character.

Change

Command	Action
cw	change to end of word
c3w	change to end of third word
cb	change to beginning of word
cW	change to end of blank delimited word
cB	change to beginning of blank delimited word
c7B	change to beginning of seventh previous blank delimited word
c)	change to end of sentence
c4)	change to end of fourth sentence
c(	change to beginning of sentence

	Change **Command**	**Action**
	c}	change to end of paragraph
	c{	change to beginning of paragraph
	c7{	change to beginning of seventh preceding paragraph
	cc	change the current line
	5cc	change five lines starting with the current line

SEARCHING FOR A STRING

The Search Commands

The vi editor will search backward or forward through the Work Buffer to find a specific string of text. To find the next occurrence of a string (forward), press the forward slash (/) key, enter the text you want to find (called the *Search String*), and press RETURN. When you press the slash key, vi displays a slash on the status line. As you enter the string of text, it too is displayed on the status line. When you press RETURN, vi searches for the string. If vi finds the string, it positions the cursor on the first character of the string. If you use a question mark (?) in place of the forward slash, vi searches for the previous occurrence of the string.

The N and n keys repeat the last search without the need for you to enter the Search String again. The n key repeats the original search exactly, and the N key repeats the search in the opposite direction of the original search.

If you need to include a forward slash in a forward search or a question mark in a backward search, you must quote it by preceding it with a backslash (\).

Normally, if you are searching forward and vi does not find the Search String before it gets to the end of the Work Buffer, it will *wrap around* and continue the search at the beginning of the Work Buffer. During a backward search, vi will wrap around from the beginning of the Work Buffer to the end. Also, vi normally performs case-sensitive searches. Refer to "Wrap Scan" (page 147) and "Ignore Case in Searches" (page 147) for information about how to change these search parameters.

Special Characters in Search Strings.   Because the Search String is a regular expression (refer to Appendix B), some characters take on a special meaning within the Search String. The following paragraphs list some of these characters. The first two (^ and $) always have their special meaning, and the rest can have their special meaning turned off. Refer to "Allow Special Characters in Searches," page 147.

The Beginning-of-Line Indicator (^).   When the first character in a Search String is a caret or circumflex, it matches the beginning of a line. The command /^the finds the next line that begins with the string the.

The End-of-Line Indicator ($).   Similarly, a dollar sign matches the end of a line. The command /!$ finds the next line that ends with an exclamation point.

The Any Character Indicator (.).   A period matches *any* character, anywhere in the Search String. The command /l..e finds line, followed, like, included, all memory, or any other word or character string that contains an l followed by any two characters and an e. To search for an actual period, use a backslash to quote the period (\.).

The End-of-Word Indicator (\>).   This pair of characters matches the end of a word. The command /s\> finds the next word that ends with an s. Notice that, whereas backslash (\) is typically used to *turn off* the special meaning of a character, the character sequence \> has a special meaning, and > alone does not.

The Beginning-of-Word Indicator (\<).   This pair of characters matches the beginning of a word. The command /\<The finds the next word that begins with The. The Beginning-of-Word Indicator uses backslash in the same, atypical way as the End-of-Word Indicator.

The Character Class Definition ([]).   Square brackets surrounding two or more characters match any *single* character located between the brackets. The command /dis[ck] finds the next occurrence of *either* disk or disc.

There are two special characters you can use within a character class definition. A caret (^) as the first character following the left bracket defines the character class to be *any but the following characters*. A hyphen between two characters indicates a range of characters. Refer to the examples below.

Command	Result
/and	finds the next occurrence of the string and **Examples:** sand, and, standard, slander, andiron
/\<and\>	finds the next occurrence of the word and **Example:** and
/^The	finds the next line that starts with The **Examples:** The... There...

Command	Result
/^[0–9][0–9])	finds the next line that starts with a two-digit number followed by a right parenthesis **Examples:** 77)... 01)... 15)...
/\<[adr]	finds the next word that starts with an a, d, or r **Examples:** apple, drive, road, argument, right

OPTIONAL

SUBSTITUTING ONE STRING FOR ANOTHER

A Substitute command is a combination of a Search command and a Change command. It searches for a string just as the / command does, allowing the same special characters that the previous section discussed. When it finds a string, the Substitute command changes it. The format of the Substitute command is shown below. As with all commands that begin with a colon, vi executes a Substitute command from the status line.

:[address]s/search-string/replace-string[/g]

The next sections discuss the **address**, **s** command, **search-string**, **replace-string**, and **g** flag.

The Substitute Address

If you do not specify an address, Substitute searches only the current line. If you use a single line number as the address, Substitute searches that line. If the address is two line numbers separated by a comma, Substitute searches those lines and the lines between. Refer to "Line Numbers," page 146, if you want vi to display line numbers.

Within the address, a period represents the current line, and a dollar sign represents the last line in the Work Buffer. In many versions of vi, a percent sign represents the entire Work Buffer. You can perform address arithmetic using plus and minus signs. Some examples of addresses are shown in the following list.

Address	Portion of Work Buffer Addressed
5	line 5
77,100	lines 77 through 100 inclusive
1,.	the beginning of the Work Buffer through the current line
.,$	the current line through the end of the Work Buffer
1,$	the entire Work Buffer
%	the entire Work Buffer (in some versions of vi only)
.,.+10	the current line through the tenth following line (eleven lines in all)

The Search and Replace Strings

An s, indicating that a Substitute command follows, comes after the address. A delimiter, marking the beginning of the Search String, follows the s. Although the examples in this book use a forward slash, you can use any character that is not a letter or number as a delimiter. You must use the same delimiter at the end of the Search String.

Next comes the Search String. It has the same format as the Search String in the / command and can include the same special characters. (The Search String is a regular expression; refer to Appendix B for more information.) Another delimiter marks the end of the Search String and the beginning of the Replace String. The Replace String is the string that will replace the Search String. The only special characters in the Replace String are the ampersand (**&**), which represents the text that was matched by the Search String, and the backslash, which quotes the character following it. Refer to the following examples and Appendix B.

To replace only the *first occurrence* of the Search String on each line within the specified address, press the RETURN or ESCAPE key after you enter the Replace String. If you want a *global* substitute—that is, if you want to replace *all* occurrences of the Search String on all addressed lines—enter a third delimiter (/) and a **g** before you press RETURN or ESCAPE.

Command	Result
:s/bigger/biggest	replaces the string bigger on the current line with biggest **Example:** bigger → biggest

OPTIONAL (Continued)

Command	Result
:1,.s/Ch 1/Ch 2/g	replaces every occurrence of the string Ch 1, before or on the current line, with Ch 2 **Examples:** Ch 1 → Ch 2 Ch 12 → Ch 22
:1,$s/ten/10/g	replaces every occurrence of the string ten by the string 10 **Examples:** ten → 10, often → of10 tenant → 10ant
:1,$s/\<ten\>/10/g	replaces every occurrence of the word ten by the string 10 **Examples:** ten → 10
:.,.+10s/every/each/g	replaces every occurrence of the string every by the string each on the current line through the tenth following line **Examples:** every → each everything → eachthing

MISCELLANEOUS COMMANDS

The Join Command

The Join command, **J**, joins two lines of text. **J** joins the line below the current line to the end of the current line. It inserts a SPACE between what was previously two lines and leaves the cursor on this SPACE. If the current line ends with a period, exclamation point, or question mark, vi inserts two SPACES.

You can always "unjoin" (break) a line into two lines by replacing the SPACE or SPACES where you want to break the line with a RETURN.

The Status Command

The Status command, CONTROL-G, displays the name of the file you are editing, the line number of the current line, the total number of lines in the Work Buffer, and the percent of the Work Buffer preceding the current line.

The . Command

The . (period) command repeats the most recent command that made a change. If, for example, you had just given a **d2w** command (delete the next two words), the . command would delete the next two words. If you had just inserted text, the . command would repeat the insertion of the same text.

This command is useful if you want to change some, but not all, occurrences of a word or phrase in the Work Buffer. Search for the first occurrence of the word (use /), then make the change you want (use **cw**). Following these two commands, you can use **n** to search for the next occurrence of the word and . to make the same change to it. If you do not want to make the change, use **n** again to find the next occurrence.

THE PUT, DELETE, AND YANK COMMANDS

The vi editor has a General-Purpose Buffer and 26 Named Buffers that can hold text during an editing session. These buffers are useful if you want to move or copy a portion of text to another location in the Work Buffer. A combination of the Delete and Put commands removes text from one location in the Work Buffer and places it in another. The Yank and Put commands copy text to another location in the Work Buffer without changing the original text.

The General-Purpose Buffer

The vi editor stores the text that you most recently changed, deleted, or yanked (see page 133) in the General-Purpose Buffer. The Undo command uses the General-Purpose Buffer when it restores text.

The Put Commands.   The Put commands, **P** and **p**, copy text from the General-Purpose Buffer into the Work Buffer.

If you delete or yank characters or words into the General-Purpose Buffer, **P** inserts them before the current *character,* and **p** inserts them after. If you delete or yank lines, sentences, or paragraphs, **P** inserts the contents of the General-Purpose Buffer before the *line* the cursor is on, and **p** inserts it after.

The Put commands do not destroy the contents of the General-Purpose Buffer, so it is possible to place the same text at several points within the file by using one Delete or Yank command and several Put commands.

Because vi has only one General-Purpose Buffer and vi changes the contents of this buffer each time you give a Change, Delete, or Yank command, **you can use only cursor positioning commands between a Delete or Yank command**

and the corresponding Put command. Any other commands change the contents of the General-Purpose Buffer and therefore change the results of the Put command. If you do not plan to use the Put command immediately after a Delete or Yank, you should use a Named Buffer rather than the General-Purpose Buffer (see "The Named Buffers," below).

The Delete Commands.   Any of the Delete commands that were described earlier in this chapter (page 133) automatically places the deleted text in the General-Purpose Buffer. Just as you can use the Undo command to put the deleted text back where it came from, you can use a Put command to put the deleted text at another location in the Work Buffer.

For example, if you delete a word from the middle of a sentence using the **dw** command and then move the cursor to a SPACE between two words and give a **p** command, vi will place the word you just deleted at the new location. Or, if you delete a line using the **dd** command and then move the cursor to the line *below* the line where you want the deleted line to appear and give a **P** command, vi will place the line at the new location.

The Yank Commands.   The Yank commands are identical to the Delete commands, except that they do not delete text from the Work Buffer. The vi editor places a *copy* of the yanked text in the General-Purpose Buffer so that you can use Put to place another copy of it elsewhere in the Work Buffer. Use the Yank command, **y**, just as you use **d**, the Delete command.

Caution.   Just as **d** RETURN deletes two lines, **y** RETURN yanks two lines. Use the **yy** command to yank the current line.

For example, if you yank three lines using a **3yy** command and then move the cursor to the line *above* the line where you want a copy of the yanked lines to appear and give a **p** command, vi will copy the lines to the new location.

OPTIONAL

The Named Buffers

You can use a Named Buffer with any of the Delete, Yank, or Put commands. There are 26 Named Buffers, each named by a letter of the alphabet. Each Named Buffer can store a different block of text so that you can recall each block as needed. Unlike the General-Purpose Buffer, vi does not change the contents of a Named Buffer unless you use a command that specifically overwrites that buffer. The vi editor maintains the contents of the Named Buffers throughout an editing session.

The vi editor stores text in a Named Buffer if you precede a Delete or Yank command with a double quotation mark (") and a buffer name (e.g., "kyy yanks a copy of the current line into buffer k). You can use a Named Buffer in two ways. If you give the name of the buffer as a lowercase letter, vi overwrites the contents of the buffer when it deletes or yanks text into the buffer. If you use an uppercase letter, vi appends the newly deleted or yanked text to the end of the buffer. This feature enables you to collect blocks of text from various sections of a file and then deposit them at one place in the file with a single command. Named Buffers are also useful when you are moving a section of a file and do not want to use Put immediately after the corresponding Delete, and when you want to insert a paragraph, sentence, or phrase repeatedly in a document.

If you have one sentence that you will be using throughout a document, you can yank the sentence into a Named Buffer and put it wherever you need it by using the following procedure. After inserting the first occurrence of the sentence and pressing ESCAPE to return to Command Mode, leave the cursor on the line containing the sentence. (The sentence must appear on a line or lines by itself for this procedure to work.) Then yank the sentence into buffer a by giving a "ayy command (or "a2yy if the sentence takes up two lines). Now, as you are entering text, any time you need the sentence, you can return to Command Mode and give the command "ap to put a copy of the sentence below the line the cursor is on.

This technique provides a quick and easy way to insert text that you use frequently in a document. For example, if you were editing a legal document, you might use a Named Buffer to store the phrase The Plaintiff alleges that the Defendant to save yourself the trouble of typing it in every time you want to use it. Similarly, if you were creating a letter that frequently used a long company name, such as American Telephone and Telegraph Company, you might put it into a Named Buffer.

READING AND WRITING FILES

The vi editor reads a disk file into the Work Buffer when you call vi from the shell. The ZZ command that terminates the editing session writes the contents of the Work Buffer back to the disk file. This section discusses other ways of reading text into the Work Buffer and writing it out.

The Read Command

The Read command reads a file into the Work Buffer. The new file does not overwrite any text in the Work Buffer but is positioned following the single address (or the current line if you do not specify an address). You can use an address of 0 to read the file into the beginning of the Work Buffer. The format of the Read command follows:

>:[address]r [filename]

As with other commands that begin with a colon, when you enter the colon, it appears on the status line. The **filename** is the pathname of the file that you want to read and must be terminated by RETURN. If you omit the **filename**, vi reads the file you are editing from the disk.

The Write Command

The Write command writes part or all of the Work Buffer to a file. You can use an address to write out part of the Work Buffer and a filename to specify a file to receive the text. If you do not use an address or filename, vi writes the entire contents of the Work Buffer to the file you are editing, updating the file on the disk.

During a long editing session, it is a good idea to use the Write command occasionally. Then, if a problem develops, a recent copy of the Work Buffer is safe on the disk. If you use a **:q!** command to exit from vi, the disk file will reflect the version of the Work Buffer at the time you last used the Write command.

The formats of the Write command follow:

>:[address]w[!] [filename]

>:[address]w>> filename

You can use the second format of the Write command to append text to an existing file. The next sections discuss the components of the Write command.

The Address.   If you use an address, it specifies the portion of the Work Buffer that you want vi to write to the disk. The address follows the form of the address that the Substitute command uses. If you do not use an address, vi writes out the entire contents of the Work Buffer.

The w and !.   Because Write can quickly destroy a large amount of work, vi demands that you enter an exclamation point following the **w** as a safeguard against accidentally overwriting a file. The only times you do not need an exclamation point are when you are writing out the entire contents of the Work Buffer to the file being edited (using no address, no filename) and when you are writing part or all of the Work Buffer to a new file. When you are writing part of the file to the file being edited, or when you are overwriting another file, you must use an exclamation point.

The Filename.   The optional filename is the pathname of the file you are writing to. If you do not specify a filename, vi writes to the file you are editing.

IDENTIFYING THE CURRENT FILE

The File command identifies the file you are currently editing in the Work Buffer. The filename the File command identifies is the one the Write command uses if you give a **:w** command (rather than **:w filename**). The format of the File command follows:

> **:f**

The File command displays the filename, the current line number, the number of lines in the Work Buffer, and the percentage of the Work Buffer that is above the current line. The File command also displays [Modified] if the Work Buffer has been changed since the last time it was written to disk. An example of the display produced by the File command follows:

```
" practice"  [Modified]  line 6 of 8  --75%--
```

SETTING PARAMETERS

You can adapt vi to your needs and habits by setting vi parameters. These parameters perform many functions, such as displaying line numbers, automatically inserting RETURNS for you, and establishing nonstandard searches.

You can set parameters in several different ways. You can set them while you are using vi, to establish the environment for the current editing session. Alternatively, you can set the parameters in your **.profile** (Bourne and Korn Shells) or **.login** (C Shell) file or in a startup file that vi uses, **.exrc**. When you set the parameters in any of those three files, each time you use vi, the environment has been established and you can begin editing immediately.

Setting Parameters from vi

To set a parameter while you are using vi, enter a colon (:), the word **set**, a SPACE, and the parameter (see the "Parameters" section, following). The command appears on the status line as you type it and takes effect when you press RETURN.

Setting Parameters in a Startup File

If you are using the Bourne or Korn Shell, you can set vi parameters by putting the following lines in the **.profile** file in your home directory:

>**EXINIT='set parm1 parm2 ...'**
>**export EXINIT**

Replace **parm1** and **parm2** with parameters selected from the list in the next section. **EXINIT** is a variable that vi reads.

If you are using the C Shell, put the following line in the **.login** file in your home directory:

>**setenv EXINIT 'set parm1 parm2'**

Again, replace **parm1** and **parm2** with parameters from the following section.

Instead of setting vi parameters in your **.login** or **.profile** file, you can create a **.exrc** file and set them there. If you set the parameters in a **.exrc** file, use the following format:

>**set parm1 parm2 ...**

When you start vi, it looks for a **.exrc** file in your current directory. If it does not find one there, it looks in your home directory. If you set parameters in your **.profile** or **.login** file, as well as in **.exrc**, the parameters in **.exrc** will take precedence since **.exrc** is executed later than **.profile** and **.login**.

OPTIONAL

Because vi looks for a **.exrc** file in your current directory and then in your home directory, you can use several **.exrc** files to customize your environment for editing different kinds of files. For example, you could set the parameters you like to use for most editing tasks in a **.exrc** file in your home directory. For special editing tasks, such as creating program source code or writing a long article, you could put a **.exrc** file in the directory you use when working on that task. When you start vi from a directory with a **.exrc** file in it, vi will execute the **.exrc** file in that directory. Whenever you start vi from a directory that does not have a **.exrc** file, vi will execute the **.exrc** file in your home directory.

Parameters

This section contains a list of some of the most useful vi parameters. The vi editor displays a complete list of parameters and how they are currently set when you give the command **:set all** followed by a RETURN while using vi.

Line Numbers.   The vi editor does not normally display the line number associated with each line. To display line numbers, set the parameter **number**. To cause line numbers not to be displayed, set the parameter **nonumber**.

Line numbers—whether displayed or not—are not part of the file, are not stored with the file, and are not displayed when the file is printed. They only appear on the screen while you are using vi.

Line Wrap Margin.   The line wrap margin causes vi to break the text that you are inserting at approximately the specified number of characters from the right margin. The vi editor breaks the text by inserting a NEWLINE character at the closest blank delimited word boundary. Setting the line wrap margin is handy if you want all your text lines to be about the same length. It relieves you of the burden of remembering to press RETURN after each line of input.

Set the parameter **wrapmargin=nn**, where **nn** is the number of characters *from the right side of the screen* where you want vi to break the text. This number is not the column width of the text but the distance from the end of the text to the right edge of the screen. Setting the wrap margin to 0 (zero) turns this feature off. By default, vi sets the wrap margin to 0.

Shell.   While you are in vi, you can cause vi to spawn a new shell. You can either create an interactive shell (if you want to run several commands) or run a single command. The **shell** parameter determines what shell vi will invoke. By default, vi sets the **shell** parameter to your login shell. To change it, set the parameter **shell=pathname**, where **pathname** is the full pathname of the shell you want to use.

Show Mode.   The vi editor does not normally give you a visual cue to let you know when it is in Input Mode. On some versions of vi, however, you can set the parameter **showmode** to display INPUT MODE at the lower right of the screen when vi is in Input Mode. Set **noshowmode** to cause vi to not display the message. This parameter is not available on all versions of vi.

Flash.   The vi editor normally causes the terminal to beep when you give an invalid command or press ESCAPE when you are in Command Mode. Setting the parameter **flash** causes the terminal to flash instead of beep. Set **noflash** to cause it to beep. This parameter is not available on all versions of vi.

Ignore Case in Searches.
The vi editor normally performs case-sensitive searches, differentiating between uppercase and lowercase letters. It performs case-insensitive searches when you set the **ignorecase** parameter. Set **noignorecase** to restore case-sensitive searches.

Allow Special Characters in Searches.
Each of the following characters and character pairs normally has a special meaning when you use it within a Search String. Refer to ''Special Characters in Search Strings,'' page 135.

.   \<   \>   [   ]

When you set the **nomagic** parameter, these characters no longer have special meanings. The **magic** parameter gives them back their special meanings.

The ^ and $ characters always have a special meaning within Search Strings, regardless of how you set this parameter.

Invisible Characters.
To cause vi to display TABS as ^I and to mark the end of each line with a $, set the parameter **list**. To display TABS as white space and not mark ends of lines, set **nolist**.

Wrap Scan.
Normally, when a search for the next occurrence of a Search String reaches the end of the Work Buffer, vi continues the search at the beginning of the Work Buffer. The reverse is true of a search for the previous occurrence of a Search String. The **nowrapscan** parameter stops the search at either end of the Work Buffer. Set the **wrapscan** parameter if you want searches to once again wrap around the ends of the Work Buffer.

Automatic Indention.
The automatic indention feature works with the **shiftwidth** parameter to provide a regular set of indentions for programs or tabular material. This feature is normally off. You can turn it on by setting **autoindent** (or **ai**) and turn it off by setting **noautoindent** (or **noai**).

When automatic indention is on and vi is in Input Mode, CONTROL-T moves the cursor from the left margin (or an indention) to the next indention position, RETURN moves the cursor to the left side of the next line under the first character of the previous line, and CONTROL-D backs up over indention positions. The CONTROL-T and CONTROL-D characters function in a manner analogous to TAB and BACKTAB keys, but they function only before text is placed on a line.

Shift Width.   The **shiftwidth** parameter controls the functioning of CONTROL-T and CONTROL-D in Input Mode when automatic indention is on. Set the parameter **shiftwidth=nn**, where **nn** is the spacing of the indention positions. Setting the shift width is similar to setting the TAB stops on a typewriter; however, with **shiftwidth** the distance between TAB stops is always constant.

OPTIONAL

ADVANCED EDITING TECHNIQUES

This section presents several commands that you may find useful once you have become comfortable using vi.

Using Markers

While you are using vi, you can set and use as many as 26 markers. Set a marker by giving the command **ma**, where **a** is any letter from a to z. Once you have set a marker, you can use it in a manner similar to a line number. The vi editor does not preserve markers when you stop editing a file.

You can move the cursor to a marker by preceding the marker name with a single quotation mark. For example, to set marker **t**, position the cursor on the line you want to mark, and give the command **mt**. Unless you reset marker **t** or delete the line it marks, during this editing session you can return to the line you marked with the command ´**t**.

You can delete all text from the current line to marker **r** with the following command:

    d ´ r

You can use markers in addresses of commands in place of line numbers. The following command will replace all occurrences of The with THE on all lines from marker **m** to the current line (marker **m** must precede the current line):

    : ´ m , . s / The / THE / g

Editing Other Files

The following command causes vi to edit the file you specify with **filename**:

    :e[!] [filename]

If you want to save the contents of the Work Buffer, you must write it out (using :w) before you give this command. If you do not want to save the contents of the Work Buffer, vi insists that you use an exclamation point to show that you know that you will lose the work you did since the last time you wrote out the Work Buffer. If you do not supply a **filename**, vi edits the same file you are currently working on.

You can give the command **:e!** to start an editing session over again. This command returns the Work Buffer to the state it was in the last time you wrote it out, or, if you have not written it out, the state it was in when you started editing the file. This is useful when you make mistakes editing a file and decide that it would be easier to start over than to repair the mistakes.

Because this command does not destroy the contents of the Named Buffers, you can store text from one file in a Named Buffer, use a **:e** command to edit a second file, and put text from the Named Buffer in the second file. A **:e** command does destroy the contents of the General-Purpose Buffer.

Executing Shell Commands from vi

You can execute shell commands in several ways while you are using vi. You can create a new, interactive shell by giving the following command and pressing RETURN:

:sh

The **shell** parameter determines what kind of shell is created (usually a Bourne, C, or Korn Shell). By default, **shell** is the same as your login shell.

After you have done what you want to do in the shell, you can return to vi by exiting from the shell (press CONTROL-D or give the command **exit**).

Caution.   When you create a new shell in this manner, you must remember that you are still using vi. A common mistake is to start editing the same file from the new shell, forgetting that vi is already editing the file from a different shell. Because each invocation of vi uses a different Work Buffer, you will overwrite any work you did from the more recent invocation of vi when you finally get around to exiting from the original invocation of vi (assuming that you write the file to disk when you exit).

You can execute a shell command line from vi by giving the following command, replacing **command** with the command line you want to execute. Terminate the command with a RETURN.

:!command

The vi editor will spawn a new shell that will execute the **command**. When the command runs to completion, the newly spawned shell will return control to the editor.

Users frequently use this feature to carry on a dialog with the write command. If Alex gets a message from Jenny while he is in vi, he can use the following command to write back to Jenny. After giving the command, Alex can carry on a dialog with Jenny in the same way he would if he had invoked write from the shell.

```
:!write jenny
```

If Alex has modified the Work Buffer since he last wrote the file to disk, vi will display the following message before starting the write command:

```
[No write since last change]
```

When Alex finishes his dialog with Jenny, he presses CONTROL-D to terminate the write command. Then vi displays the following message:

```
[Hit return to continue]
```

When Alex presses RETURN, he can continue his editing session in vi.

You can execute a command from vi and have vi replace the current line with the output from the command. If you do not want to replace any text, put the cursor on a blank line before giving the command.

```
!!command
```

Nothing will happen when you enter the first exclamation point. When you enter the second one, vi will move the cursor to the status line and allow you to enter the command you want to execute. Because this command puts vi in Last Line Mode, you must end the command with a RETURN.

Finally, you can execute a command from vi with the standard input to the command coming from all or part of the file you are editing and the standard output from the command replacing the input in the file you are editing. You can use this type of command to sort a list in place in a file you are working on.

To specify the block of text that is to become the standard input for the command, move the cursor to one end of the block of text. If you want to specify the whole file, move the cursor to the beginning or end of the file. Then enter an exclamation point followed by a command that would normally move the cursor to the other end of the block of text. For example, if the cursor is at the beginning of the file and you want to specify the whole file, give the command **!G**. If you want to specify the part of the file between the cursor and marker **b**, you will give the command **!ʹb**. After you give the cursor movement command, vi will display an exclamation point on the status line and allow you to give a command.

For example, to sort a list of names in a file, move the cursor to the beginning of the list and set marker **q** with an **mq** command. Then move the cursor to the end of the list and give the following command:

```
!ʹqsort
```

Press RETURN and wait. After a few moments, you will see the sorted list replace the original list on the screen. If the command did not do what you expected, you can undo the change with a **u** command.

UNITS OF MEASURE

Many vi commands operate on a block of text—from a character to many paragraphs. You can specify the size of a block of text with a *Unit of Measure*. You can specify multiple Units of Measure by preceding a Unit of Measure with a number, called a Repeat Factor. This section defines the various Units of Measure.

Character

A character is one character, visible or not, printable or not, including SPACES and TABS.

Examples of Characters

a	q
A	.
TAB	5
SPACE	R
—	>

Word

A word is similar to an ordinary word in the English language. It is a string of one or more characters that is bounded on both sides by any combination of one or more of the following elements: a punctuation mark, SPACE, TAB, numeral, or NEWLINE. In addition, vi considers each group of punctuation marks to be a word.

Text	Word Count
pear	1 word
pear!	2 words
pear!)	2 words
pear!) The	3 words
pear!) "The	4 words
This is a short, concise line (no frills).	11 words

Blank Delimited Word

A blank delimited word is the same as a word, except that it includes adjacent punctuation. Blank delimited words are separated from each other by one or more of the following elements: a SPACE, TAB, or NEWLINE.

Text	Blank Delimited Word Count
pear	1 blank delimited word
pear!	1 blank delimited words
pear!)	1 blank delimited words
pear!) The	2 blank delimited words
pear!) "The	2 blank delimited words
This is a short, concise line (no frills).	8 blank delimited words

Line

A line is a string of characters bounded by NEWLINES. It is not necessarily a single, physical line on the terminal. You can enter a very long single (logical) line that wraps around (continues on the next physical line) several times. It is a good idea, however, to avoid long logical lines by terminating lines with a RETURN before they reach the right side of the terminal screen. Terminating lines in this manner ensures that each physical line contains one logical line and avoids confusion when you edit and format text. Some commands do not *appear* to work properly on physical lines that are longer than the width of the screen. For example, with the cursor on a long logical line that wraps around several physical lines, pressing RETURN once will appear to move the cursor down more than one line.

Sentence

A sentence is an English sentence or the equivalent. A sentence starts at the end of the previous sentence and ends with a period, exclamation point, or question mark, followed by two SPACES or a NEWLINE.

Text	Sentence Count
That's it. This is one sentence.	1 sentence: only 1 SPACE after the first period—NEWLINE after the second period
That's it. This is two sentences.	2 sentences: 2 SPACES after the first period— NEWLINE after the second period
What? Three sentences? One line!	3 sentences: 2 SPACES after the first two question marks—NEWLINE after the exclamation point
This sentence takes up a total of three lines.	1 sentence: NEWLINE after the period

Paragraph

A paragraph is preceded and followed by one or more blank lines. A blank line is composed of two NEWLINE characters in a row.

Text	Paragraph Count
one paragraph	1 paragraph: blank line before and after text
This may appear to be more than one paragraph. Just because there are two indentions does not mean it qualifies as two paragraphs.	1 paragraph: blank line before and after text
Even though in	3 paragraphs: 3 blocks of text separated by blank lines
English this is only one sentence,	
vi considers it to be three paragraphs.	

Screen

The terminal screen is a window that opens onto part of the Work Buffer. You can position this window so that it shows different portions of the Work Buffer.

Repeat Factor

A number that precedes a Unit of Measure is a Repeat Factor. Just as the *5* in *5 inches* causes you to consider *5 inches* as a single unit of measure, a Repeat Factor causes vi to group more than one Unit of Measure and consider it as a single Unit of Measure. For example, the command **w** moves the cursor forward one word. The command **5w** moves the cursor forward five words, and **250w** moves it 250 words. If you do not specify a Repeat Factor, vi assumes that you mean one Unit of Measure.

SUMMARY

This summary of vi includes all the commands covered in this chapter, plus some new ones.

Starting vi

Command	Function
vi *filename*	edit *filename* starting at line 1
vi +*n filename*	edit *filename* starting at line *n*
vi + *filename*	edit *filename* starting at the last line
vi +/*pattern filename*	edit *filename* starting at the first line containing the *pattern*
vi −r *filename*	recover *filename* after a system crash

Moving the Cursor by Units of Measure

You must be in Command Mode to use commands that move the cursor by Units of Measure. They are the Units of Measure that you can use in Change, Delete, and Yank commands. Each of these commands can be preceded with a Repeat Factor.

Command	Moves the Cursor
SPACE, l, or →	space to the right
h or ←	space to the left
w	word to the right
W	blank delimited word to the right
b	word to the left
B	blank delimited word to the left
$	end of line
e	end of word to the right
E	end of blank delimited word to the right
0	beginning of line (cannot be used with a Repeat Factor)
RETURN	beginning of next line
j or ↓	down one line
−	beginning of previous line
k or ↑	up one line
)	end of sentence
(	beginning of sentence
}	end of paragraph
{	beginning of paragraph

Viewing Different Parts of the Work Buffer

Command	Moves the Cursor
CONTROL-D	forward one-half screenful
CONTROL-U	backward one-half screenful
CONTROL-F	forward one screenful
CONTROL-B	backward one screenful
nG	to line n (without n to the last line)
H	to the top of screen
M	to the middle of screen
L	to the bottom of screen

Adding Text

All the following commands (except **r**) leave vi in Input Mode. You must press ESCAPE to return it to Command Mode.

Command	Insert Text
i	before cursor
I	before first nonblank character on line
a	after cursor
A	at end of line
o	open a line below the current line
O	open a line above the current line
r	replace current character (no ESCAPE needed)
R	replace characters, starting with current character (overwrite until ESCAPE)

Deleting and Changing Text

In the following list, M is a Unit of Measure that you can precede with a Repeat Factor. The n is a Repeat Factor.

Command	Effect
*n*x	delete the number of characters specified by *n*, starting with the current character
*n*X	delete *n* characters before the current character, starting with the character preceding the current character
d*M*	delete text specified by *M*
*n*dd	delete the number of lines specified by *n*
D	delete to end of the line

The following commands leave vi in Input Mode. You must press ESCAPE to return it to Command Mode.

Command	Effect
*n*s	substitute the number of characters specified by *n*
c*M*	change text specified by *M*
*n*cc	change the number of lines specified by *n*
C	change to end of line

Searching for a String

In the following list, *rexp* is a regular expression that can be a simple string of characters.

Command	Effect
/*rexp* RETURN	search forward for *rexp*
?*rexp* RETURN	search backward for *rexp*
n	repeat original search exactly
N	repeat original search, opposite direction
/RETURN	repeat original search forward
?RETURN	repeat original search backward

String Substitution

The format of a Substitute command follows:

:[address]s/search-string/replace-string[/g]

address	is one line number or two line numbers separated by a comma. A . represents the current line, $ represents the last line, and % represents the entire file in some versions of vi. You can use a marker in place of a line number.
search-string	is a regular expression that can be a simple string of characters.
replace-string	is the replacement string.
g	indicates a global replacement (more than one replacement per line).

Miscellaneous Commands

Command	Effect
J	join the current line and the following line
.	repeat the most recent command that made a change
:w *file*	write contents of Work Buffer to *file* (to current file if there is no *file*)
:q	quit vi.
ZZ	write contents of Work Buffer to current file and quit vi.
:f or CONTROL-G	display the filename, the status, the current line number, the number of lines in the Work Buffer, and the percent of the Work Buffer preceding the current line
CONTROL-V	insert the next character literally (use in Input Mode)
~	change uppercase to lowercase, and vice versa

Yanking and Putting Text

In the following list, *M* is a Unit of Measure that you can precede with a Repeat Factor. The *n* is a Repeat Factor. You can precede any of these commands with the name of a buffer in the form "*x* where *x* is the name of the buffer (a-z).

Command	Effect
y*M*	yank text specified by *M*
*n*yy	yank the number of lines specified by *n*
Y	yank to end of line
P	put text before or above
p	put text after or below

Advanced Commands

Command	Effect
m*x*	set marker *x*, where *x* is a letter from a to z
ʹ ʹ	move cursor back to its previous location
ʹ*x*	move cursor to marker *x*, where *x* is a letter from a to z
:e! *file*	edit file, discarding changes to current file (use :w first if you want to keep the changes)
:sh	create a shell
:!*command*	create a shell and execute command
!!*command*	create a shell, execute command, place output in file replacing the current line

REVIEW EXERCISES

1. How can you cause vi to enter Input Mode? How can you make it revert to Command Mode?

2. What is the Work Buffer? Name two ways of writing the contents of the Work Buffer to the disk.

3. If you have a file that contains the following paragraph and the cursor is on the second tilde (~), how can you:

   a. move the cursor to the end of the paragraph

   b. move the cursor to the beginning of the word Unfortunately

   c. change the word character to letter

```
The vi editor has a command, tilde (~),
that changes lowercase letters to
uppercase and vice versa.
Unfortunately, the ~ command does
not work with a Unit of Measure or
a Repeat Factor, so you have to change
the case of one character at a time.
```

4. In vi, with the cursor positioned on the first letter of a word, give the command **x** followed by **p**. Explain what happens.

5. What are the differences between the following commands:

   a. **i** and **I**

   b. **a** and **A**

   c. **o** and **O**

   d. **r** and **R**

   e. **u** and **U**

6. What command would you use to search backwards through the Work Buffer for lines that start with the word it?

7. What command will substitute all occurrences of the phrase this week with the phrase next week?

8. Consider the following scenario: You start vi to edit an existing file. You make many changes to the file and then realize that you deleted a critical section of the file early in your editing session. You want to get that section back, but you do not want to lose all the other changes you made. What would you do?

9. Consider the following scenario: Alex puts the following line in his **.login** file:

```
setenv EXINIT ´set number wrapmargin=10 showmode´
```

Then Alex creates a **.exrc** file in the directory **/home/alex/literature** with the following line in it:

```
set nonumber
```

What will the parameter settings be when Alex runs vi while the working directory is **/home/alex/bin**? What will they be when he runs vi from the directory **/home/alex/literature**? What will they be when he edits the file **/home/alex/literature/promo**?

OPTIONAL

10. What commands can you use to take a paragraph from one file and insert it in a second file?

11. Create a file that contains the following list, and then execute commands from within vi to sort the list and display it in two columns. (*Hint:* See the pr command in Part II).

```
Command Mode
Input Mode
Last Line Mode
Work Buffer
General-Purpose Buffer
Named Buffer
Regular Expression
Search String
Replace String
Startup File
Repeat Factor
```

12. How do the Named Buffers differ from the General-Purpose Buffer?

CHAPTER
7

THE nroff
TEXT FORMATTER

This chapter shows how to use the nroff text formatting program to prepare documents. It discusses the theory of filling and justifying lines, describes the structure of an input file, and shows how to use nroff commands. Most of the commands described in this chapter are part of the **mm** macro package. The summary at the end of the chapter covers plain nroff commands, **mm** commands, and the **ms** macro package.

INTRODUCTION TO nroff

Input to nroff is a file of text that you create using an editor such as vi. Output from nroff is paginated, formatted text that you can send to a terminal, printer, or ordinary file. Commands embedded in the input file determine what the output text looks like.

The nroff formatter has default values for all margins, line lengths, indentions, and spacing of text on a page. If your input file contains text without embedded commands, nroff uses these default values to format the output text. You can use as few or as many commands as the complexity of the formatting job requires.

The nroff formatter can accomplish many formatting tasks. Among its capabilities, nroff can

- fill lines
- right-justify lines
- hyphenate words
- center text
- generate footnotes
- automatically number headings
- number pages
- put the date on each page
- put a header on each page
- put a footer on each page
- produce numbered lists

The output from nroff is designed to go to a terminal or line printer. A related formatter, troff, sends its output to a high-resolution output device such as a laser printer or phototypesetter. Because of the higher resolution of these devices, troff gives you much more control over the way the output looks. The troff formatter has commands that change the size and style of type you use. It can also produce special symbols such as em dashes (—). Where nroff underlines type, troff uses *italic* type. You can use all the commands in this chapter with troff—each command may, however, have slightly different effects with troff than with nroff.

Several preprocessors work with either nroff or troff. Two of them, eqn and tbl, are widely used; the eqn preprocessor assists in formatting equations, and tbl formats tables.

Instructing nroff to format a file can be tedious and unnecessarily complex. To make the job easier, nroff allows you to define and use *macros*. A macro is a short command that nroff expands into a longer sequence of commands. But to learn to use this facility to format a document of moderate complexity, you would ordinarily need an in-depth knowledge of nroff.

Because so many people's formatting needs are similar, nroff provides several predefined packages of macros. Using an existing *macro package* can make a job easier, allowing you to concentrate on the content, rather than the format, of a document. Two macro packages are widely used: the **mm** (memorandum) and **ms** (manuscript) macro packages. The **mm** macros are part of System V's Documenter's Workbench. The **ms** macros are typically available only on older versions of AT&T UNIX and on Berkeley UNIX.

This chapter shows how to use nroff with the **mm** (memorandum) and **ms** (manuscript) macro packages. However, the chapter goes into detail only about the **mm** macros. The **ms** macros are described in the Summary. If you plan to use the **ms** macros, you will probably want to read this chapter through the section "Using nroff with a Macro Package" and then skip ahead to the Summary.

THEORY OF FILLING AND JUSTIFYING LINES

The ability to *fill* and *justify* lines is the most important feature of any formatter. It is this process that gives the output text its finished appearance. A filled line of output text is brought as close to the right margin as possible without padding the line with SPACES; a filled and justified line is padded so that it reaches the right margin.

Input File:

```
The ability to fill and justify lines is the
most important
feature of any formatter.
```

Filled Output Text:

```
The ability to fill and
justify lines is the
most important feature
of any formatter.
```

Filled and Justified Output Text:

```
The ability to fill and
justify lines is the
most important feature
of any formatter.
```

Filling a Line

The format of the output text does not depend on the length of lines in the input file. To nroff, the input file is a stream of words. To produce a line of output text, nroff takes words from the input stream and keeps adding them to the output line until it gets to a word that brings the line past the right margin. If nroff can hyphenate and include part of this word on the line, it does. Otherwise it saves this word for the next line of output text. At this point, the line is *filled*. It cannot hold the entire next word, or part of the next word if it was hyphenated, without exceeding the right margin. When each of the output lines is filled, the right edge of the output text is ragged. It is said to have a *ragged right* margin.

Justifying Text

All the lines in justified text come exactly to (are flush with) the right margin. The only exception is the last line of a paragraph, which is never justified. Justified text is said to have a *flush right* margin. If you use the **mm** macros, your text will be filled but not justified (refer to the section "Justification" in this chapter for ways to change this). In contrast, the **ms** macros justify text by default.

Before a line can be justified, it must be filled. To justify text, nroff expands single SPACES between words in the filled line, one at a time, to double, triple, or more SPACES as it brings the right end of the line to the right margin. (Some versions also increase the space between letters or words by fractions of SPACES.)

THE INPUT FILE

You can prepare the input file with an editor such as vi. Each line in the input file contains either an nroff command or text. This section discusses both types of lines.

Command Lines

A line in the input file containing an nroff command begins with a period or a single quotation mark. This chapter does not discuss command lines that begin with a single quotation mark—they are just mentioned here so that you can avoid putting a single quotation mark at the beginning of a line and inadvertently giving nroff a command. A line beginning with a SPACE and a line with nothing on it (a *blank line*) also have special meanings to nroff; refer to the section ''Breaks'' in this chapter.

Because nroff considers a line in the input file that begins with a period, a single quotation mark, or a SPACE to be a command line, regular lines of text cannot begin with any of these characters.

Commands.   Commands follow a period at the beginning of a line in the input file. A command is composed of one or two letters or a number and a letter. Plain nroff commands use lowercase letters; the **mm** and **ms** macro package commands use uppercase letters. The following is a list of sample commands:

Plain nroff Commands	**mm Macro Package Commands**
.bp	.P
.ce	.AL
.fi	.I
.nf	.DS
.nr	.BI

Command Arguments.   Some commands require additional information on the same line with the command. SPACES separate these pieces of information, or arguments, from the command and from each other. You can quote arguments that include SPACES by preceding and following them with double quotation marks (")—nroff will interpret everything between the double quotation marks as a single argument.

There are two kinds of arguments: measurements and text. A measurement gives some information to nroff but is not printed. When text appears after a command, nroff places it in the output text in some special manner.

The following command takes a number as an argument. It centers the next three input lines in the output text. The **3** is a measurement that tells nroff how many lines to center.

```
.ce 3
```

The next command takes text as an argument. It underlines the word that follows it on the same line. The **I** stands for *italic* (nroff underlines the text because it cannot produce italic type). Both the **mm** and **ms** macro packages include this command.

```
.I  important
```

The next command uses both types of arguments. The Head command from the **mm** macro package places a numbered head in the text. The heading level is specified by the first argument, and the body of the head is specified by the second. The second argument contains SPACES; the double quotation marks cause nroff to consider the heading text as a single argument.

```
.H 4 "This is a Level Four Head"
```

If you want to have double quotes within a quoted string, use two pairs of double quotes.

```
.H 3 "The Third ""Word"" is Quoted"
```

Text Lines

All lines in the input file that are not command lines are text lines. The nroff formatter processes these lines into the output text according to the specifications of the command lines.

NUMBER REGISTERS

Because the **mm** and **ms** macros are designed to be used by novices as well as experts, most commands have default values. As an example, the following **mm** command by itself inserts a left-aligned, level-one heading in the output text:

```
.H 1 "INTRODUCTION"
```

However, the heading command has several default features that can be changed. For instance, the heading can be centered rather than left-aligned, and it can be preceded by a page eject (causing the heading to appear at the top of a page). As you become more comfortable with nroff and **mm**, you will probably want to change these features to customize the look of your document.

You can change many defaults using the *number register* command. A *register* is a location in memory that nroff uses to store a number, and the macros use registers to control various aspects of document format. The number register command changes the default values. For example, the following **mm** command causes first-level headings to appear at the top of a page, rather than after text on the current page:

```
.nr Ej 1
```

Typically, when a default value is changed, all subsequent invocations of the feature are affected. For example, once you set the **Ej** register to 1, all subsequent first-level headings are affected, until you change the setting of the **Ej** register again. Because documents often have a uniform style throughout, it is common to change defaults prior to the first line of text in the document and not to change them again. However, most defaults can be changed repeatedly anywhere in the input file.

Just as you can alter the way headings appear using the **.nr** command, you can change paragraph style, vertical spacing, and more. You can change other default characteristics using macros, such as the style of footnotes, and you can change others with plain nroff commands.

USING nroff WITH A MACRO PACKAGE

When you are using a macro package, you have to be careful about including plain nroff commands in the file because the nroff commands may interfere with the macros. However, in a file that is processed by nroff *and* the **mm** macro package, you can use all the regular nroff commands that are described in this chapter. You cannot use both **mm** and ms macros in the same file.

Running nroff

The following command line indicates to nroff that you want to use the **mm** macro package:

```
$ nroff -mm filename
```

The **-mm** is the option that selects the macro package, and the **filename** is the name of the input file you want to format. If you are using **ms** rather than **mm**, you will use the following command line:

```
$ nroff -ms filename
```

Each of these two command lines sends the formatted text to the standard output. Unless you redirect it to a file or send it through a pipe, the text appears on the terminal. You can use the pg utility (or the more utility) to view one screenful of text at a time. (Press RETURN or SPACE to view additional pages after the first.)

```
$ nroff -mm file | pg
```

You can inspect nroff output before sending it to the printer by redirecting it and using either pg or more.

```
$ nroff -mm file > hold
$ pg hold
```

If the output is what you want, you can send it to the printer using lp.

```
$ lp hold
request id is printer_1-540 (1 file)
```

You can also use a pipe to send the output directly to the printer without first inspecting it.

```
$ nroff -mm file | lp
request id is printer_1-541 (standard input)
```

If the output looks strange on your terminal but prints correctly on your printer, or vice versa, you may need to use nroff's **-T** option or the col filter. The **-T** option takes an argument that specifies the type of output device (see page 209). The col filter removes control characters (see page 194).

Choosing a Macro Package

The remainder of this chapter discusses the **mm** macros. If both the **mm** and **ms** macro packages are available on your system, you will probably want to use the **mm** macros. They are more powerful and more flexible than the **ms** macros. The **ms** macros are introduced in the Summary at the end of the chapter. If you plan to use **ms**, you may want to skip ahead to the Summary.

PARAGRAPHS

An nroff paragraph is a block of output text that usually has one or more blank lines above and below it. With the **mm** macros, nroff fills, but does not justify, lines of the paragraph unless you instruct it otherwise (refer to the **.SA** command, page 196).

The nroff formatter provides two types of paragraphs: left block and standard (indented). All the lines in a *left-block* paragraph are flush with the left margin. The first line of a *standard* paragraph is indented, and all the following lines are flush with the left margin.

The format of a Paragraph command is shown below. (The square brackets indicate that the argument they surround is optional.)

.P [type]

If you do not specify **type**, the **.P** command initially produces left-block paragraphs. You can change the default type with the **Pt** register (following).

The **type** controls the type of the paragraph immediately following the command only. It temporarily overrides the default paragraph type. When you specify **type** equal to 0 (zero), nroff produces a left-block paragraph; a 1 produces a standard paragraph.

Input File:

```
.P
This is a left-block paragraph.
When you give a .P command without
an argument and without changing the
value of the Pt register, this is what
you get.
.P 1
This is a standard paragraph.
The first line is indented; the rest
come out to the left margin.
The 1 following the .P command
overrides the default paragraph type
and forces this to be a standard
paragraph.
```

Output Text:

```
This is a left-block paragraph.  When you give a .P command
without an argument and without changing the value of the Pt
register, this is what you get.

     This is a standard paragraph.  The first line is
indented; the rest come out to the left margin.  The 1
following the .P command overrides the default paragraph
type and forces this to be a standard paragraph.
```

The **Pt** (paragraph type) register controls the default paragraph type for all the Paragraph commands that follow it. Initially, the **Pt** register has a value of 0 (zero), causing **.P** commands to yield left-block paragraphs. Using the following command to change the value of **Pt** to 1 causes **.P** commands to produce standard paragraphs:

```
.nr Pt 1
```

Below, nroff produces standard paragraphs without the use of an argument after each **.P** command.

Input File:

```
.nr Pt 1
.P
This is a standard paragraph.
Setting the Pt register to 1 causes
all subsequent .P commands to produce
standard paragraphs.
Now it is necessary to follow a .P command
with a 0 if you want to print a left-block
paragraph.
.P 0
This is a left-block paragraph.
The 0 following the .P command only affects
this paragraph -- the next one is a standard
paragraph by default.
.P
Each .P command from now on (unless you
change the value of the Pt register) produces a
standard paragraph.
```

Output Text:

```
        This is a standard paragraph.  Setting the Pt register
 ·to 1 causes all subsequent .P commands to produce standard
paragraphs.  Now it is necessary to follow a .P command with
a 0 if you want to print a left-block paragraph.

This is a left-block paragraph.  The 0 following the .P
command only affects this paragraph -- the next one is a
standard paragraph by default.

        Each .P command from now on (unless you change the
value of the Pt register) produces a standard paragraph.
```

The **Pi** (paragraph indention) register controls the number of SPACES that precede the first line of indented paragraphs. Initially, **Pi** is set to 5. The following command changes the paragraph indention to 12.

```
.nr  Pi  12
```

If you set **Pi** to 0, standard paragraphs appear to be left-block paragraphs because they are not indented.

LISTS

A list is a set of items, such as words, lines, paragraphs, or sections, each one of which is preceded by a design element, such as a number, dash, word, or phrase. The **mm** macros provide automatically numbered or lettered lists where each item is preceded by the same design element (e.g., a dash) and lists where each item is preceded by a different word or phrase. You can nest lists up to six levels deep.

All lists start with a List-initialization command (**.AL**, **.DL**, **.ML**, or **.VL**) that tells nroff what kind of list follows. A **.LI** (list item) command precedes each item within the list, and a **.LE** (list end) command ends the list.

An example of a simple, automatically numbered list follows.

Input File:

```
.AL
.LI
This is the first list item.
.LI
This is the second list item.
Each item must be preceded by
a .LI command.
.LI
This is the last item in the list.
.LE
```

Output Text:

```
   1 .   This  is  the  first  list  item.

   2 .   This  is  the  second  list  item.   Each  item must  be
         preceded  by  a  .LI  command.

   3 .   This  is  the  last  item  in  the  list.
```

Automatic Lists

The **.AL** (automatic list) command generates lists that are numbered or lettered in a variety of ways (see the preceding and following examples). The format of the command is shown below.

> **.AL** [type] [indention] [separation]

You can select **type** from the following list:

type	Result
1	Arabic numbers (default)
A	uppercase letters
a	lowercase letters
I	uppercase Roman numbers
i	lowercase Roman numbers

The **indention** is the number of SPACES that the text is to be indented. If it is null or missing, nroff uses the value of the **Li** register. The **separation** is 0 (default) for a blank line separating items in the list and 1 for no lines separating items. There is always a blank line before the first item in a list.

To explicitly set an argument to null, use a pair of double quotes. You should explicitly set an argument to null (or fill in the default value of the argument) if you need it as a place holder. For example, if you want to start an alphabetic list with the default type, indention, and a separation of 1, you can use the following command:

> .AL " " " " 1

The following example shows a three-level list. The **Ls** register controls spacing above and below items based on the level of each item. (If you set **Ls** to 1, nroff leaves blank lines only around level-1 items, setting **Ls** to 2 leaves blank lines around level-1 and level-2 items, and so on.) Initially, **Ls** is set to 6, which means that nroff leaves a blank line above and below each item (levels 1-6). The following example sets **Ls** equal to 2, which causes nroff to leave blank lines around level-1 and level-2 list items only.

Input File:

```
.nr Ls 2
.AL I
.LI
This example shows an automatic list that is nested
to three levels.
The first level uses uppercase Roman numerals to
identify list items.
.P
Note that paragraphs can appear inside list items.
.AL
.LI
Each of the second-level list items is preceded by
an Arabic number.
.LI
As with all automatic lists, each List Item (.LI) command
increments the number (or letter) preceding each list item.
.AL a
.LI
This item is at the third level of this list.
.LI
The third-level items are identified by lowercase letters.
.LI
The Ls register was set to 2 before this list was started
so that third-level items would not be separated from each
other by blank lines.
.LE
.LI
Because the Ls register was set to 2, level-1 and level-2
items are still separated from each other by blank lines.
.LE
.LI
Each .LE (list end) command ends a list level.
As each level ends, the previous (higher level) list takes
over.
The next .LE command corresponds to the first .AL command
and ends the entire list.
.LE
```

Output Text:

    I.   This example shows an automatic list that is nested to three levels. The first level uses uppercase Roman numerals to identify list items.

        Note that paragraphs can appear inside list items.

        1.   Each of the second-level list items is preceded by an Arabic number.

        2.   As with all automatic lists, each List Item (.LI) command increments the number (or letter) preceding each list item.

            a.   This item is at the third level of this list.
            b.   The third-level items are identified by lowercase letters.
            c.   The Ls register was set to 2 before this list was started so that third-level items would not be separated from each other by blank lines.

        3.   Because the Ls register was set to 2, level-1 and level-2 items are still separated from each other by blank lines.

   II.   Each .LE (list end) command ends a list level. As each level ends, the previous (higher level) list takes over. The next .LE command corresponds to the first .AL command and ends the entire list.

The Dash List

A dash and a single SPACE precede each element in a dash list. The format of the List-initialization command for a dash list is shown below.

    .DL [indention] [separation]

The **indention** is the number of SPACES that the text is indented. If it is null or missing, nroff uses the value of the **Pi** register (see page 173) so that the text lines up with the first line of an indented paragraph. The **separation** is 0 (default) for a blank line separating items in the list and 1 for no lines separating items. There is always a blank line before the first item in a list.

Input File:

```
This is regular text.
It is here to show the effect of indenting a list.
.DL 15
.LI
This is the first item.
.LI
This is a dash list.
.LI
Each item is indented 15 SPACEs.
.LI
This is the last item.
.LE
```

Output Text:

```
This is regular text.   It is here to show the effect of
indenting a list.

                - This is the first item.

                - This is a dash list.

                - Each item is indented 15 SPACEs.

                - This is the last item.
```

The Marked List

Each item in a marked list begins with a mark that is specified in the List-initialization command. The mark can be more than one character, but you must quote all SPACES within the mark by preceding each with a backslash so that nroff does not expand them. The format for a marked list is shown below.

.ML mark [indention] [separation]

The **mark** is the element that is to appear before each item in the list. The **indention** is the number of SPACES that the text is indented. If it is null or missing, nroff indents the text one SPACE more than the number of characters in the mark. The **separation** is 0 (default) for a blank line separating items in the list and 1 for no lines separating items. There is always a blank line before the first item in a list.

Input File:

```
.ML >
.LI
This is a marked list.
.LI
It uses a greater-than symbol as a mark.
.LI
You can use any mark you like.
.LE

.ML READ\ THIS\ --> 15
.LI
A marked list can use a mark composed of many characters.
.LI
If the mark contains SPACEs, each SPACE must be preceded
by a backslash.
.LI
See the next section ("The Variable-Item List") if you
want to have
a different mark appear before each item.
.LE
```

Output Text:

```
    > This is a marked list.

    > It uses a greater-than symbol as a mark.

    > You can use any mark you like.

      READ THIS --> A marked list can use a mark composed of many
                    characters.

      READ THIS --> If the mark contains SPACEs, each SPACE must
                    be preceded by a backslash.

      READ THIS --> See the next section ("The Variable-Item
                    List") if you want to have a different mark
                    appear before each item.
```

The Variable-Item List

A variable-item list allows you to put a different mark before each item in the list. The text that acts as the mark for a particular item is specified in each List Item command. The format of a variable-item List-initialization command is shown below.

.VL indention [mark-indention] [separation]

The **indention** is the number of SPACES that the text is indented. The **mark-indention** is the number of SPACES that each mark is indented. The default value is 0 (the mark is left-justified). The **separation** is 0 (default) for a blank line separating items in the list and 1 for no lines separating items. There is always a blank line before the first item in a list.

Input File:

```
.VL 15
.LI Useful
Variable lists are useful for many purposes.
.LI Glossaries
They are frequently used for glossaries.
.LI Flexible
You can customize variable lists to suit your needs.
.LI Low\ Overhead
They are also easy to use.
Remember to quote SPACEs within marks by preceding
each with a backslash.
.LE
```

Output Text:

Useful	Variable lists are useful for many purposes.
Glossaries	They are frequently used for glossaries.
Flexible	You can customize variable lists to suit your needs.
Low Overhead	They are also easy to use. Remember to quote SPACEs within marks by preceding each with a backslash.

The List Item Command

The format of the List Item command that must precede each item in a list is shown below.

.LI [mark] [prefix]

The **mark** is the mark for a variable-list list. If you use it with another type of list, it will replace the mark for the current item only. If you include a second argument (the **prefix**), it causes the **mark** to precede the current mark and has the effect of emphasizing it. You can use any character as the **prefix**. Your choice of characters has no effect on the outcome of the list.

Input File:

```
In order to successfully complete the test,
you must follow all the starred instructions.
Instructions that are not starred may or may
not be helpful to you.
.AL
.LI
Use a pencil.
.LI * x
Draw a square.
.LI note
The square does not have to be precise.
Approximate the shape of a square to the
best of your ability using the tools you
have.
.LI
Try not to use the eraser.
.LI * x
Draw a triangle.
.LE
```

Output Text:

```
In order to successfully complete the test, you must follow
all the starred instructions.  Instructions that are not
starred may or may not be helpful to you.

    1.  Use a pencil.

*   2.  Draw a square.

note    The square does not have to be precise.  Approximate
        the shape of a square to the best of your ability
        using the tools you have.

    4.  Try not to use the eraser.

*   5.  Draw a triangle.
```

The List End Command

The List End command must terminate all lists. Its format is as follows:

.LE [separation]

The **separation** is 0 (default) for no blank lines following the list and 1 for a blank line.

UNDERLINED AND BOLD FONTS

The **.I** (italic) command causes nroff to underline text. (If you were using troff, the typesetting version of nroff, the text would be printed in an italic style of type, hence the name of the command.)

You can use the **.I** command with or without arguments. With a single argument, the **.I** command underlines that argument only. Without an argument, it underlines all subsequent text until a **.R** (Roman) command stops the underlining. The following example demonstrates these uses of the **.I** command.

Input File:

```
This is an example of the use of
the .I command.
It
.I will
underline text.
If you want to underline more than a single word,
.I
do not give the .I command an argument.
.R
Use the .R command to return to
text that is not underlined.
```

Output Text:

```
This is an example of the use of the .I command. It will
underline text. If you want to underline more than a single
word, do not give the .I command an argument. Use the .R
command to return to text that is not underlined.
```

With two arguments, the **.I** command underlines the first argument, displaying the second without underlining it and without any intervening SPACES. This is useful when an underlined word is followed immediately by punctuation (e.g., a period or right parenthesis).

The **.RI** (Roman-italic) command allows you to have text immediately preceding and following an underlined word. This command displays its arguments alternating between Roman and underlined text.

Input File:

```
When you give the .I command two
arguments, it underlines the first,
removes the space between the arguments,
and prints the second in a regular (called
.I Roman )
font.

The .RI command alternates between Roman
and underlined
.RI ( italic )
fonts.
```

Output Text:

```
When you give the .I command two arguments, it underlines
the first, removes the space between the arguments, and
prints the second in a regular (called Roman) font.

The .RI command alternates between Roman and underlined
(italic) fonts.
```

The **.B** (bold) command displays text in a bold font. (Some printers are not capable of producing bold type. On these machines, there is no difference between bold and Roman text.)

In a manner similar to the **.RI** command, the following commands alternate between other fonts.

Command	Font
.IB	underlined-bold
.BI	bold-underlined
.IR	underlined-Roman
.RI	Roman-underlined
.RB	Roman-bold
.BR	bold-Roman

HEADINGS

A *heading* (or *head*) is a title within text. Headings are usually set off from the surrounding text by typeface and position. The **mm** macros provide extensive heading capabilities, including automatic generation of heading numbers for up to seven levels of headings, heading formatting, and automatic generation of a table of contents based on headings. As with paragraphs, you can change many aspects of headings by changing the values of registers.

Numbered Headings

A *numbered heading* is a heading that is preceded by a number in the form 2.5.7. A **.H** (heading) command indicates that a numbered heading follows. Each time you use a **.H** command, it automatically increments the number corresponding to the heading level you specify (e.g., if the previous heading number was 2.5.7 and you specified a third-level head, the new heading number would be 2.5.8; if you specified a second-level head, it would be 2.6). The format of a Heading command is shown below.

.H level [heading-text]

The **level** is the desired heading level from 1 through 7, and the **heading-text** is the text of the heading. If the **heading-text** includes any SPACES, you must enclose the text in double quotation marks. See the following example.

By default, nroff prints level-1 and level-2 heads in boldface followed by a single blank line. These two levels are distinguished by the section number that precedes them and the way (by convention) you enter them: level 1 in all uppercase letters and level 2 in lowercase letters with initial capital letters. Level-3 through -7 heads are underlined run-in headings followed by two SPACES. The section numbers that precede each of these five levels distinguish them.

Input File:

```
.H 1  " PARTS"
This example demonstrates how numbered headings work.
It uses a parts list as sample text.
.H 2  " Screws"
By default, level-2 heads are printed in boldface type and
separated from the following text by a single blank line.
.H 3  " Sheet Metal Screws"
Level-3 heads are underlined and run in to the
following text.
.H 3  " Wood Screws"
Each subsequent level-3 head increments the third-level
heading number.
.H 4  " Phillips Head"
Level-4 heads are displayed the same way as level-3 heads.
.H 4  " Slotted Head"
This is a level-4 head.
It increments the fourth-level heading number.
.H 3  " Specially Hardened Screws"
This is another third-level head.
.H 2  " Nails"
This level-2 head increments the second-level
heading number.
```

Output Text:

```
   1.  PARTS

   This example demonstrates how numbered headings work.  It
   uses a parts list as sample text.

   1.1  Screws

   By default, level-2 heads are printed in boldface type and
   separated from the following text by a single blank line.

   1.1.1  Sheet Metal Screws  Level-3 heads are underlined and
   run in to the following text.

   1.1.2  Wood Screws  Each subsequent level-3 head increments
   the third-level heading number.

   1.1.2.1  Phillips Head  Level-4 heads are displayed the same
   way as level-3 heads.

   1.1.2.2  Slotted Head  This is a level-4 head.  It
   increments the fourth-level heading number.

   1.1.3  Specially Hardened Screws  This is another third-
   level head.

   1.2  Nails

   This level-2 head increments the second-level heading
   number.
```

Unnumbered Headings

A **.HU** (heading-unnumbered) command indicates that an unnumbered heading
follows. Unnumbered headings are similar to numbered headings, except they are
not preceded by level numbers. The format of a **.HU** command follows:

.HU heading-text

As with a numbered heading, the **heading-text** is the text of the heading,
enclosed in double quotation marks if it contains SPACES.

Input File:

```
.HU "Unnumbered Heading"
By default, unnumbered headings are level-2 heads.
That is, unnumbered heads adopt the style and format
characteristics of the level-2 heads.
If you change the value of the Hu register, the level of
subsequent unnumbered heads changes to the new value of Hu.
```

Output Text:

Unnumbered Heading

By default, unnumbered headings are level-2 heads. That is, unnumbered heads adopt the style and format characteristics of the level-2 heads. If you change the value of the Hu register, the level of subsequent unnumbered heads changes to the new value of Hu.

By default, unnumbered headings are level–2 heads. If you want unnumbered headings at a different level (for appearance or for the table of contents described later on), you must change the value of the **Hu** register before giving a **.HU** command. The following commands produce a third-level unnumbered heading:

```
.nr Hu 3
.HU "This is a Third-Level Head"
```

Subsequent **.HU** commands will also produce third-level heads until you change the value of the **Hu** register.

OPTIONAL

Changing Heading Format

The following paragraphs explain how to change the format of both numbered and unnumbered headings of various levels. If you are satisfied with the heads produced by the **.HU** and **.H** commands, you can skip this section.

Forcing Heads to the Tops of Pages.   You can force all first-level heads to start at the top of a page by setting the **Ej** (ejection) register to 1.

```
.nr  Ej  1
```

If you set the **Ej** register to a larger number, all headings at that level and lower will begin on a new page (e.g., setting **Ej** to 3 causes level-1, -2, and -3 heads to start new pages).

Breaks After Heads.   By default, level-1 and level-2 heads appear on lines by themselves, and level-3 through -7 heads are run in to the text. A head occurs on a line by itself if it is followed by a *break*. The **Hb** (head-break) register controls which heads have breaks following them. The following command causes only level-5, -6, and -7 heads to run in to the text. It causes a break following all heads at level 4 and lower.

```
.nr  Hb  4
```

Blank Lines After Heads.   By default, level-1 and level-2 heads are followed by single blank lines, and level-3 through -7 heads are not. Actually, the format of level-3 through -7 heads is controlled by the **Hb** register (above); you cannot separate run-in heads from the text by a blank line. But if you set the **Hs** (head-space) register to a value less than the **Hb** register, you can produce three kinds of heads: heads followed by a break and a blank line, heads followed by a break and no blank line, and run-in heads. For example, the following commands will cause level-1, -2, and -3 heads to be followed by a blank line, level-4 and -5 heads to be followed by a break but no blank line, and level-6 and -7 heads to run in to the following text.

```
.nr  Hb  5
.nr  Hs  3
```

Heading Indents.   The **Hi** (heading-indent) register controls the indention of the line of text that follows heads that are followed by breaks. If it is set to 0, the line is left-justified; if it is 1, indention is controlled by the **Pt** (paragraph type) register (see page 171); if it is 2, nroff indents the text to line up with the first word of the heading text.

Centered Heads.   The **Hc** (head-center) register controls which heads are centered. By default, there are no centered heads (**Hc** is equal to 0). If you set **Hc** to

OPTIONAL (Continued)
a value greater than 0, nroff will center all heads at that level and lower, except it will never center run-in heads.

Table of Contents

The **mm** macros can cause nroff to create a table of contents automatically at the end of a document (you have to manually move it to the front, where it belongs). The table of contents lists all headings lower than and including the heading level specified by the **Cl** (contents-level) register along with the appropriate page numbers. The default value for **Cl** is 2; that is, nroff includes all first- and second-level heads in the table of contents. If you want a different value of **Cl**, you must change it at the beginning of the text file, before the first header command. As an example, the following command changes the value of the **Cl** register to 3, causing the table of contents to include first-, second-, and third-level heads.

```
.nr Cl 3
```

A **.TC** command at the *end* of the text file causes nroff to print the table of contents. Without this command, nroff will not print a table of contents.

DISPLAYS

A display is a block of text that nroff normally treats as a *keep*. A keep is an integral unit; nroff does not let a page break occur inside a keep. A display can be a chart, table, or paragraph that must appear intact. You can define a display by placing the appropriate nroff commands before and after the block of text in the input file.

Unless you instruct nroff otherwise, displays are not filled or indented in the output text; nroff preserves the spacing and formatting of the text from the input file.

Headings (**.H** or **.HU** commands) and footnotes (see page 192) must not appear within displays.

Static Displays

When nroff finds a block of text in the input file that you have specified as a static display, it places the text on the current page only if there is room for the entire block. If there is not enough room, nroff starts a new page and places the block of text there. A static display is depicted on the right-hand side of Figure 7-1.

A **.DS** (display-static) command precedes the text of a static display, and a
.DE (display-end) command follows it. The format of a static display is shown
below.

    .DS [position] [fill] [right-position]
    text
    .DE

You can choose the **position** from the following table—it determines how
nroff positions the display. If you do not specify a **position**, nroff positions the
display flush with the left margin.

L   (left) positions the display flush against the left margin (default).

I   (indent) indents the display by the value of the **Si** (static-indent) register, which is initially set to 5.

C   (center) centers each line between the left and right margins.

CB (center block) centers the entire display as a block of text (a single
unit), using the longest line for positioning.

The **fill** controls whether or not nroff fills the text in the display (see page 165
for an explanation of filling text). If you omit this argument, or if you specify it
as N (nofill), nroff does not fill the text. If it is an F (fill), nroff fills the text.

The **right-position** is the number of characters that you want the right margin
indented. This value has no effect when the display is not being filled.

Two registers affect the format of static displays. The **Si** (static-indent) register controls the number of spaces that nroff indents an indented static display.
The **Ds** register controls spacing before and after the display; if you set it to 0
(zero), no blank line will appear before or after the display.

═══

OPTIONAL

Floating Displays

A floating display is similar to a static display; it is a block of text that nroff
keeps on one page. However, if there is no room for a floating display on the
current page, nroff sets aside the display and finishes filling the page with the text
from the input file that follows the display. When the page is full, nroff places
the display at the top of the next page and then continues with the text from the
previous page. Refer to the left-hand side of Figure 7-1.

The placement of a floating display "floats" with respect to the output text.
A floating display is useful for displaying a table or chart that is not context-
sensitive when you do not want a blank space at the bottom of a page.

The format of a floating display is shown on page 192.

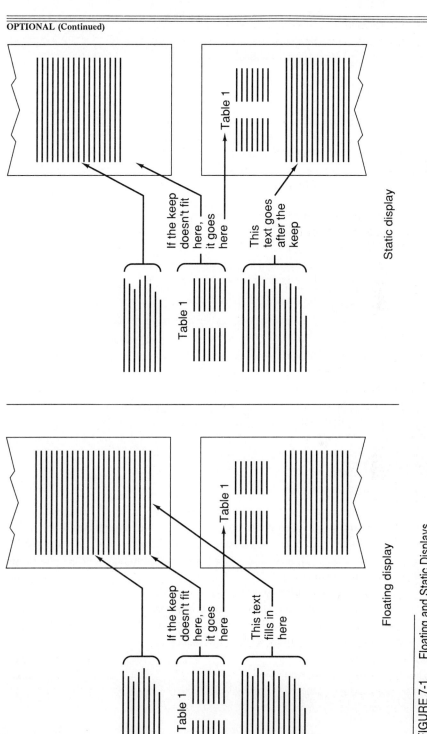

FIGURE 7-1   Floating and Static Displays

.DF [position] [fill] [right-position]
text
.DE

The **De** and **Df** registers affect the format of floating displays.

When set to 1 (one), the **De** (display-eject) register causes nroff to eject the current page after a floating display so that any following text appears on the next page and only one floating display appears on a page. The initial value of **De** is 0 (zero), which causes nroff not to take any special action after a display.

The **Df** (display-float) register causes nroff to float floating displays in different manners. It can take any of the values from the following table:

0   output floating displays at the end of the document

1   output floating displays on the page they occur or at the end of the document if there is not room on the page

2   output only one floating display at the top of a new page

3   output only one floating display on the page it occurs or at the top of the next page if there is not room on the current page

4   output all floating displays starting at the top of a new page—more than one display per page is allowed

5   output floating displays on the page they occur or at the top of the next page if there is no room on the current page (default)

FOOTNOTES

You must embed footnotes in the input text immediately after you reference them. The nroff formatter places a footnote at the bottom of the page it occurs on in the output file unless there is not enough room, in which case it moves it (or part of it) to the next page. If you like, nroff can sequentially number footnotes throughout the document.

The nroff formatter processes footnotes in Fill Mode. It does not permit other footnotes, headings, or displays within a footnote.

There are two kinds of footnotes available under the **mm** macros: *automatically numbered* footnotes and *labeled* footnotes.

The nroff formatter sequentially numbers automatically numbered footnotes throughout the document. This scheme is useful if you add and delete footnotes frequently because it automatically compensates for these footnotes by renumbering the remaining footnotes.

Labeled footnotes are more conventional. You specify a label for each footnote: an asterisk, a number, or whatever you like.

The format of an automatically numbered footnote follows:

```
text\*F
.FS
footnote
.FE
text
```

You must put the *F in your input file as shown. The **mm** macros will cause nroff to replace the *F with the proper footnote number. If footnote numbers do not appear as superscripts on your printer, you may want to use square brackets ([]) around footnote numbers (see the example on page 199).

The format of a labeled footnote is shown below.

```
text**
.FS **
footnote
.FE
text
```

The ** is the label. You can replace it with any string of characters you like. You must put the label in two places: (1) at the end of the text, just before the footnote; and (2) immediately following the .FS macro that starts the footnote.

OPTIONAL

If you do not like the default footnote style, you can use the **.FD** command to change the footnote style. It has the following format:

.FD [format] [renumber]

The **format** is a number from 0 through 11 from the following table:

OPTIONAL (Continued)

Format	Hyphen	Adjust	Indent	Label
0	no	yes	yes	left
1	yes	yes	yes	left
2	no	no	yes	left
3	yes	no	yes	left
4	no	yes	no	left
5	yes	yes	no	left
6	no	no	no	left
7	yes	no	no	left
8	no	yes	yes	right
9	yes	yes	yes	right
10	no	no	yes	right
11	yes	no	yes	right

The **renumber** can be set to 1 to cause automatically numbered footnotes to start over again with number 1 following each first-level head.

Figure 7-2 on page 200 contains examples of footnotes.

When you review on your terminal an output file that contains footnotes, you may notice some odd-looking characters—for example, ^]—around the footnote labels. These are control characters that cause the numbers to be superscripted when you print a hard copy, assuming your printer supports superscripts and is set up properly. When you want to view the file on your terminal, you can remove the control characters by piping the nroff output through the col utility. The following nroff output is piped through col and then pg, so that it will be displayed one screenful at a time:

```
$ nroff -mm file | col | pg
```

The **−T** option to nroff may also improve the readability of an output file displayed on your terminal (see page 209).

RUNNING TITLES

There are two categories of running titles: *headers* and *footers*. Headers (sometimes called *running heads*) appear at the top of all pages, all even-numbered, or all odd-numbered pages. You can have three headers in use at one time (page header, even header, and odd header). In the same manner, footers appear at the bottoms of pages.

The **mm** macros provide three-part titles for headers and footers. For example, a **.PH** (page-header) command takes the following format:

.PH ″ ′ **left**′ **center**′ **right**′ ″

The **left** is a string that nroff left-justifies at the top of each page. In a similar manner, **center** and **right** represent strings that are centered and right-justified.

The initial value of the page header is the page number, centered between hyphens. The values of the odd header, even header, and footers are initially blank lines.

The following table lists all of the header and footer commands:

Title Command	What It Stands For	Where nroff Puts the Title
.PH	page header	top of every page
.EH	even header	top of even-numbered pages
.OH	odd header	top of odd-numbered pages
.PF	page footer	bottom of every page
.EF	even footer	bottom of even-numbered pages
.OF	odd footer	bottom of odd-numbered pages

Page Numbers and the Date

You can cause the page number not to appear at the top of pages by changing the value of the center portion of the page header. An easy way to do this is to set the page header to a null string, as follows:

    .PH " "

You can also cause the page number to appear in a different position on the page by incorporating the **P** (page-number) register in a title. The page number is generated by placing the following sequence of characters within a title:

```
\ \ \ \nP
```

The first of the following commands removes the page number from the center-top of each page and places the title of the work flush left at the top of all pages. The second and third commands position the page number at the bottom-left of even-numbered pages and the bottom-right of odd-numbered pages.

```
.PH  " ′The Story of My Life′′ "
.EF  " ′\\\\nP′′ "
.OF  " ′′′\\\\nP′ "
```

The current date is stored in the **DT** (date) string. The following command causes nroff to display the date, centered at the bottom of every page:

```
.PF  " ′′\\\\*(DT′′ "
```

TEXT AND PAGE LAYOUT

This section explains how to justify text, skip pages, and skip lines. The next two sections ("Using Plain nroff Commands with **mm** Macros" and "Setting Parameters from the Command Line") discuss other commands that affect the appearance of the output text.

Justification

By default, text produced by the **mm** macros is not right-justified (see page 165). You can turn on justification by giving the following command:

```
.SA  1
```

You can turn it off again with the same command and an argument of 0.

```
.SA  0
```

Input File:

```
This text demonstrates the default mm
macro style -- the text is not
right-justified.
The text is filled but is not, however,
brought out to the right margin.
Look at the difference between this and the
following text.

.SA 1
You can use an .SA 1 command to
cause nroff to justify text.
This command causes nroff to produce an
even right margin (i.e., the text is
right-justified).
Some people like this style.
However, many people think that a ragged
right margin makes text easier to read.

.SA 0
An .SA 0 command causes nroff to revert
to its initial style, ragged right
margins.
```

Output Text:

```
This text demonstrates the default mm macro style -- the
text is not right-justified.  The text is filled but is not,
however, brought out to the right margin.  Look at the
difference between this and the following text.

You can use an .SA 1 command to cause nroff to justify text.
This command causes  nroff to produce an even right margin
(i.e., the text is right-justified).  Some people like  this
style.  However,  many  people  think  that  a ragged right
margin makes text easier to read.

An .SA 0 command causes nroff to revert to its initial
style, ragged right margins.
```

Skipping Lines

The **.SP** (space) command leaves the number of blank lines that you give it as an argument. The following example shows how to use **.SP**.

Input File:

```
This example demonstrates the use of
the .SP command.
.SP 3
There are three blank lines above this line.
```

Output Text:

```
This example demonstrates the use of the .SP command.


There are three blank lines above this line.
```

It is frequently simpler to just leave blank lines in the input file rather than give a **.SP** command to create one or two blank lines.

Skipping Pages

When used without an argument, the **.SK** (skip page) command skips to the top of the next page. With an argument, **.SK** leaves the number of blank pages that you give it as an argument. The nroff formatter still displays titles (headers and footers) on the blank pages. The following command leaves two blank pages:

```
.SK 2
```

The **.SK** command is useful when you want to leave blank pages in order to add manually produced figures to a document.

Skipping to the Top of an Odd-Numbered Page.   The **.OP** (odd-page) command skips to the top of the next odd-numbered page. You can use this command to make sure that a chapter starts on an odd-numbered page.

Input File:

```
.PH " "
.EH " ´ \\\\nP´ ´TITLE´ "
.OH " ´TITLE´ ´ \\\\nP´ "
.PF " ´ ´ \\\\*(DT´ ´ "
.nr Pt 1
.nr Pi 10
.P
This sample illustrates some of the page layout features
of the mm macros.
It also demonstrates footnotes[.\*F]
.FS
This is an example of an automatically numbered footnote.
.FE
and various paragraph features.
.P
The first command[\*F]
.FS
The .PH command at the beginning of this example.
.FE
removes the default page header[\*F]
.FS
The default page header is the page number enclosed
in hyphens.
.FE
by replacing it with a null string.
The even- and odd-page headers do not displace the page
header because the mm macros display them on the line
below the page header.*
.FS *
You can take advantage of two lines of page headers on
each page.
(As you can see from this footnote, you can mix
labeled and automatically numbered footnotes in an
input file.)
.FE
.P
Setting the Pt register to 1 causes .P commands to yield
standard (indented) paragraphs.
The Pi register controls the amount of indention.
In this example it´s set to 10 spaces.
```

TITLE   1

        This sample illustrates some of the page layout
features of the mm macros. It also demonstrates
footnotes[1] and various paragraph features.

        The first command[2] removes the default page
header[3] by replacing it with a null string. The even- and
odd-page headers do not displace the page header because the
mm macros display them on the line below the page header.*

        Setting the Pt register to 1 causes .P commands to
yield standard (indented) paragraphs. The Pi register
controls the amount of indention. In this example it's set
to 10 spaces.
.
.

----

1. This is an example of an automatically numbered
    footnote.

2. The .PH command at the beginning of this example.

3. The default page header is the page number enclosed in
    hyphens.

 * You can take advantage of two lines of page headers on
    each page. (As you can see from this footnote, you can
    mix labeled and automatically numbered footnotes in an
    input file.)

                        May 24, 1990

FIGURE 7-2   Output Text: A Sample Page

USING PLAIN nroff COMMANDS WITH mm MACROS

In general, you should not mix plain nroff commands with **mm** macros because
they may change the way the macros work. However, you may find the following
plain nroff commands useful. They should not alter the functioning of the **mm**
macros.

Breaks

This section covers plain nroff commands that end (or break) lines. When you command nroff to end a line, it stops filling the line and does not justify it. What happens afterward depends on the command you use.

The End-line Command.   The simplest End-line command is the **.br** (break) plain nroff command. It does nothing except end (or break) a line. Subsequent text begins on the next line.

Input File:

```
This is an example of the simplest
kind of break, or End-line, command.
nroff can be halfway through filling
a line, but when you give a
.br
Break command, it ends the line it
was filling and continues on the
next line.
```

Output Text:

```
This is an example of the simplest kind of break, or End-
line, command.  nroff can be halfway through filling a line,
but when you give a
Break command, it ends the line it was filling and continues
on the next line.
```

The Implicit End-line Command.   Any line in the input file that begins with a SPACE automatically ends the current line of output text. The new line begins with a SPACE. If you begin a line in the input file with five SPACES, the new line in the output text will begin with five SPACES. This feature allows you to indent a paragraph without an explicit command.

The implicit End-line command is of limited use, but it is important to understand how it works so that you do not use it unintentionally.

Input File:

```
This is an example of how a line of
input text, beginning with a SPACE,
 causes the line to end
and a new line to start.
     If you start a line of input text
with five SPACEs, the output line starts
with five SPACEs.
```

Output Text:

```
This is an example of how a line of input text, beginning
with a SPACE,
 causes the line to end and a new line to start.
     If you start a line of input text with five SPACEs, the
output line starts with five SPACEs.
```

Blank Lines.   A blank line in the input file causes a break in the output text. After the break, the nroff formatter copies one or more blank lines from the input file to the output text.

The **mm** macros try not to leave blank lines at the top of a page of output text—refer to page 207, ''Leaving Blank Lines at the Top of a Page,'' if you need blank lines at the top of a page.

Centering Lines.   The .ce (center) plain nroff command centers one or more following input lines of text. Without an argument, this command centers the input line that follows it. With an argument, the **.ce** command centers the number of input lines its argument specifies.

Input File:

```
This example demonstrates two ways to use the .ce command.
Without an argument, the command
.ce
centers
only the line that follows it.
You can use an argument to specify the number of lines you
want centered.
.ce 3
This line is centered,
as is this line,
and this one.
This line is not centered; it is part
of the text that follows the centered lines.
```

Output Text:

```
This example demonstrates two ways to use the .ce command.
Without an argument, the command
                          centers
only the line that follows it.  You can use an argument to
specify the number of lines you want centered.
                   This line is centered,
                      as is this line,
                       and this one.
This line is not centered; it is part of the text that
follows the centered lines.
```

Filling Lines

The **.nf** (nofill) plain **nroff** command causes **nroff** *not* to fill (see page 165) output lines of text. The output lines are exactly the same as the input lines. The initial condition, filling lines of text, can be restored with the **.fi** (fill) plain **nroff** command.

The two commands—.**nf** and .**fi**—are typically used around sections of an input file that are not prose, such as a person's address or a poem. In those sections, line breaks must occur in specified places, and justifying is not appropriate.

Double-Spacing

You can double- (or triple-) space output text by using the .**ls** (line-spacing) plain nroff command. The following command specifies double-spaced output text:

```
. l s   2
```

An argument of 3 specifies triple-spacing, and a 1 restores the initial condition of single-spacing.

Tab Settings

Tabs in nroff are similar to tabs on a typewriter: They define horizontal positions for columns of information. Once you set tab positions, they remain in effect until you change them or until the end of the document. If you do not set tabs, nroff uses its default tab positions (every eight characters, starting at the current indent or left margin).

The .**ta** command clears all previous tab positions and sets new tab positions as its arguments specify. Without any arguments, .**ta** clears all tab positions. After you establish the tab positions you want to use, a TAB character (CONTROL-I) causes the following text to appear in the next tab position to the right.

The following example demonstrates what happens when there are no more tab positions on a line. The word *demonstrate* takes up more than one column, forcing the next word (*the*) over to what would be the next column, if there was one. Because there is not another column, the TAB in the input text has no effect, and the word following the TAB appears immediately after the preceding word. In the following .**ta** command, **i** stands for inches. You can also use **n** for characters.

Temporary Indentions

The .**ti** (temporary-indent) command causes nroff to indent the next line of output text. An argument to the command specifies the amount of indention. The line after the indented line comes back to the current margin.

Input File:

```
This example demonstrates the use of tabs.
After setting three tab positions, nroff
produces four aligned columns
of words.
You will generally want to produce tabular
material in Nofill Mode.

.ta 1i 2i 3i
This TAB example TAB demonstrates TAB the
use TAB of TAB tabs. TAB After
setting TAB three TAB tab TAB positions,
nroff TAB produces TAB four TAB aligned
columns TAB of TAB words.
```

Output Text:

```
This example demonstrates the use of tabs.  After setting
three tab positions, nroff produces four aligned columns of
words.  You will generally want to produce tabular material
in Nofill Mode.

This        example      demonstrates  the
use         of           tabs.         After
setting     three        tab           positions,
nroff       produces     four          aligned
columns     of           words.
```

The following command sets a temporary indent of seven characters to the right of the current indent. The **+** adds the 7 to the current indent; without it, nroff would set the temporary indent absolutely to seven characters from the left margin (page offset). The **n** stands for characters; you can also use **i** for inches.

```
.ti  +7n
```

Input File:

```
This example demonstrates the use of the Temporary
Indent command.

.ti +1i
All the text following the first
line comes back to the left margin
because the .ti command affects only one line.
```

Output Text:

```
This example demonstrates the use of the Temporary Indent
command.

        All the text following the first line comes back
to the left margin because the .ti command affects only one
line.
```

Comments

A comment in an input file is a note that nroff ignores and does not send to the output text. You can use comments to leave notes in a file for yourself or some-one else—items you want to add to the file, references you want to check, or markers so you can easily find where you stopped reading or editing.

A \" precedes a comment, and the end of a line ends a comment. If you want a line that has nothing but a comment on it, place a period before the comment indicator. Refer to the following example.

Input File:

```
This is input text.\"Check to see if this comment appears
.\" in the output text.
This is some more input text.
It follows a comment.
```

Output Text:

```
This is input text.  This is some more input text.  It
follows a comment.
```

Leaving Blank Lines at the Top of a Page

The nroff formatter has a special mechanism to prevent it from leaving blank lines at the top of a page. This mechanism keeps the blank lines that precede headings from appearing at the top of a page. The result is that text always starts at the same position on each page.

Sometime you may want blank lines at the top of a page. Give an **.rs** (restore spacing) command and then skip the number of lines you want with an **.SP** command, or simply leave the blank lines in the input file.

Input File:

```
.rs
.SP 5
This is the first line of text.
```

Output Text:

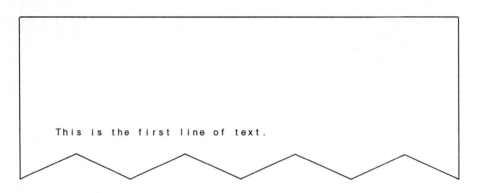

```
This  is  the  first  line  of  text.
```

OPTIONAL

Switching the Source File

The **.so** (source) command causes the nroff formatter to take its input from another file before continuing with the current file. An argument to **.so** specifies the file that nroff will switch to. The following example tells nroff to take its input temporarily from the file **/home/alex/doc/ltr.macros**:

```
.so  /home/alex/doc/ltr.macros
```

The **.so** command enables you to put different parts of a document in different files. Although you can also do this by specifying the files in order on the nroff command line, **.so** provides more flexibility. You can use **.so** to switch to another input file when you are in the middle of the original file; then the switched-to file may use **.so** to switch to another file; and so forth.

One common use of **.so** is to switch from a file containing the text of a document to a file that contains **mm** and nroff commands. The commands in the file specified by .so set up format characteristics of the document, and the .so typically occurs near the top of the document file. Users often create several files that set up the formats (e.g., line width, page headers and footers, line spacing) for different kinds of documents. For example, Alex might have one file that contains commands suitable for a business letter (such as **ltr.macros** above), another one for memos, and a third for monthly reports. Then when he begins working on a business letter, for example, he uses the **.so** command to cause nroff to process the appropriate file to establish format characteristics at the beginning of his letter.

SETTING PARAMETERS FROM THE COMMAND LINE

You can set several important parameters that control the output text from the command line when you call nroff with the **mm** macro package.

Page Length

The **mm** macros store the page length in the **L** (length) register. The default value is 66 lines (11 inches). If you want to change the page length, you must do so from the command line. The −rL84 in the following command line changes the page length to 14 inches (84 lines). The command line formats the **report** file and sends the output to the printer. The **&** causes the entire process to run in the background.

```
$ nroff −mm −rL84 report | lp &
1324
request id is printer_1-542 (standard input)
```

Page Offset

The **mm** macros store the page offset in the **O** (offset) register. The default value is 9 characters ($^3/_4$ of an inch) from the left edge of the screen or page. You can change the page offset from the command line. The following command line changes the offset to 18 characters:

```
$ nroff −mm −rO18 report
```

Page Width

The **mm** macros store the initial line length in the **W** (width) register. The default value is 72 characters (6 inches). You can change the line length from the command line. The following command line changes the line length to 60 characters:

```
$ nroff −mm −rW60 report
```

Output Terminal Type

Sometimes it is necessary to use the terminal type (−**T**) option to tell nroff the type of terminal or printer you plan to send the output to. This information enables nroff to make certain features of the output (such as bold characters and underlining) suitable for the device it will be displayed or printed on. Typically, the terminal type you use to display the output on your terminal screen will be different from the terminal type you use for a document that will be sent to the printer. The following command formats **report** for a printer:

```
$ nroff -Tlp -mm report | lp &
```

If your nroff output looks strange when you display it on your terminal or print a hard copy, ask the system administrator what terminal type you should use. If the **-T** option does not solve the problem, try using the col filter (see page 194).

Outputting Selected Pages

You can control which pages of output text nroff outputs with the **-o** (output) option on the command line. Follow the **-o** with the numbers of the pages you want to see. Separate page numbers with commas for single pages or with hyphens for ranges of pages. A hyphen before the first page number displays all pages from the beginning of the document through that page. A hyphen following the last page number in the list prints the last pages of the document. The following command prints pages 5, 10, 15 through 20, and 35 through the end of the output text from the file **report**:

```
$ nroff -mm -o5,10,15-20,35- report | lp
request id is printer_1-543 (standard input)
```

SUMMARY

This summary describes the commands covered in this chapter and introduces some additional ones. First, the summary describes plain nroff commands. These commands work with or without a macro package. Following the plain commands, the summary reviews **mm** macro package commands. Finally, it introduces commands for the **ms** macro package. Although you can use selected plain nroff commands with either macro package, you cannot mix commands from the **ms** and **mm** macro packages.

Plain nroff Commands

Each command must start at the beginning of a line in the input file. A command line starts with a SPACE, a single quotation mark, or a period.

Breaks

Command	Break Line and ...
.br	break line, nothing else
.sp *n*	leave *n* blank lines
.ce *n*	center next *n* lines (one line if *n* is missing)
.bp	begin new page

Margins

Command	Effect
.na	do not justify lines
.ad b	justify lines
.nf	do not fill lines
.fi	fill lines
.in[±]*x*i	adjust left margin to the right (+) or left (−) *x* inches (if no ±, set indent absolutely to *x* inches)
.ti[±]*x*i	for the next line only, adjust left margin as above
.po[±]*x*i	adjust page offset as above (not with **mm** macros)

Headings

Command	Effect
.tl ′*left*′ *center*′ *right*′	produce a three-part heading; replace *left, center,* and *right* with the text of the title to appear at the left, center, and right of the page

Changing Dimensions

Command **Effect**

.ls *x*   replace *x* with 1, 2, or 3 to single-, double-, or triple-space text

.ll[±]*x*i   adjust line length to the right (+) or left (−) *x* inches (if no ±, set length absolutely to *x* inches)

Hyphenation

Command **Effect**

.nh   turn off hyphenation

.hy   turn on hyphenation

Number Registers   The **mm** (and **ms**) macros take advantage of this plain nroff command to set parameters for macro commands.

Command **Effect**

.nr *x n*   set register *x* to value *n* (register names can be one or two characters long)

Switch Source File

Command **Effect**

.so *file*   switch input file to *file*

The mm Macro Commands

As the beginning of this chapter explains, **mm** macro commands use number registers to alter the way commands work. You set a number register as explained in the "Number Registers" section (see page 168).

Paragraphs

Command	Effect
.P [*type*]	set *type* to 0 for a left-block paragraph or to 1 for a standard (indented) paragraph

Registers

Pt	establishes the default paragraph type: 0 for left-block (initial value) or 1 for standard
Pi	establishes the indention of the first line of standard paragraphs (initially 5 spaces)

Lists

Command: .AL [*type*] [*indention*] [*separation*]
Effect: start automatic list; choose *type* from: 1, A, a, I, or i

Command: .DL [*indention*] [*separation*]
Effect: start dash list

Command: .ML *mark* [*indention*] [*separation*]
Effect: start marked list; *mark* is the element used to mark list items

Command: .VL *indention* [*mark-indention*] [*separation*]
Effect: start variable-item list; set marks for each list item with **.LI**

Command: .LI [*mark*] [*prefix*]
Effect: start new list item

Command: .LE [*separation*]
Effect: end list

Registers

Li	text indention if *indention* is not supplied (automatic list)
Pi	text indention if *indention* is not supplied (dash list)
Ls	spacing above and below items based on item level

Fonts

Command	Effect
.R	print the argument in a Roman (regular) font; without an argument, print all subsequent text in a Roman font
.B	as above, bold font
.I	as above, underlined font
.BI	alternate bold and underlined fonts for each argument
.BR	alternate bold and Roman fonts for each argument
.IB	alternate underlined and bold fonts for each argument
.IR	alternate underlined and Roman fonts for each argument
.RB	alternate Roman and bold fonts for each argument
.RI	alternate Roman and underlined fonts for each argument

Headings

Command: .H *level* [*heading-text*]
Effect: produce a numbered heading; specify a number (1-7) for *level*

Command: .HU *heading-text*
Effect: produce an unnumbered heading

Registers

Hu	level of subsequent unnumbered heads
Ej	level of heads that are forced to the tops of new pages
Hb	level of heads that appear followed by line breaks
Hc	level of centered heads
Hi	indent of text following heads that are followed by line breaks:

0   left-justified
1   indention controlled by **Pt** register
2   line up with first word of head

All running headers and footers (at the tops and bottoms of pages) have the following format:

.PH **"′ left′ center′ right′ "**

Substitute the text you want for any or all of **left, center,** and **right**. You can use the following macros in place of **.PH** above:

Command   Effect

.EF   even footer appears at the bottom of even-
      numbered pages

.EH   even header appears at the top of even-
      numbered pages

.OF   odd footer appears at the bottom of odd-
      numbered pages

.OH   odd header appears at the top of odd-
      numbered pages

.PF   page footer appears at the bottom of every
      page

.PH   page header appears at the top of every page

Footnotes and Displays

Command: .FS
Effect: start footnote

Command: .FE
Effect: end footnote

Command: .FD [*format*] [*renumber*]
Effect: set footnote style—see page 193

Command: .DS [*position*] [*fill*] [*right-position*]
Effect: start static display; choose *position* from the
following list:
L   flush left
I   indent according to **Si** register
C   center each line
CB   center display as a block
set *fill* to N (No Fill) or F (Fill); and set
right-position to the number of characters
the display will be indented from the right
margin (use with Fill only)

Command: .DF [*position*] [*fill*] [*right-position*]
Effect: start floating display (see **.DS** above)

Command: .DE
Effect: end display

Registers
Si   controls indent when *position* is I
Ds   set to 0 for no space above and below
display, 1 for space
De   set to 1 to eject page after a floating display
Df   set floating display characteristics (see page
192)

Miscellaneous Commands

Command   **Effect**

.SA *x*   turn on ($x = 1$) or turn off ($x = 0$) justification
.SP *x*   leave *x* blank lines
.SK *x*   skip *x* pages
.OP   skip to the top of an odd-numbered page
.TC   print table of contents (put at end of input
file)

Register
Cl   specify heading levels to be included in table
of contents (must appear before first heading in input file)

Command Line Parameters   You must set the registers described in this section as command line options. They are shown the way you must enter them on
the command line.

Option	Effect
–rL*xx*	set the page length to *xx* lines
–rO*xx*	set the page offset to *xx* characters
–rW*xx*	set the page width to *xx* characters
–T*terminal-type*	set the output device type to *terminal-type*

The ms Macro Commands

Paragraphs

Command	Effect
.PP	start standard paragraph, first line indented
.LP	start left-block paragraph, all lines flush left
.IP [*mark*] [*indention*]	start indented paragraph with hanging mark; without mark, indent paragraph
.QP	start block quote

Margins

Command	Effect
.RS	move left margin 5 spaces to the right
.RE	move left margin 5 spaces to the left

Headings

Command	Effect
.SH	following text is an underlined section heading
.NH [*x*]	following text is a numbered, underlined section heading at level *x;* without *x,* the current level is used
.ND	no date
.ds LH *left-header*	sets left header for all pages but the first
.ds CH *center-header*	sets center header for all pages but the first
.ds RH *right-header*	sets the right header for all pages but the first
.ds LF *left-footer*	sets the left footer for all pages
.ds CF *center-footer*	sets the center footer for all pages
.ds RF *right-footer*	sets the right footer for all pages

Keeps, Footnotes, and Displays

Command	Effect
.KS	start standard keep (A *keep* is a block of text nroff keeps on one page)
.KF	start floating keep
.KE	end any keep
.FS	start footnote
.FE	end footnote
.DS	[*position*] start standard display with keep; choose *position* from the following list:
	L flush left
	C centered
.ID	start standard display with no keep
.LD	start flush left display with no keep
.CD	start centered display with no keep

Underlining

Command	Effect
.I [*text*]	underline *text;* without an argument, underline all subsequent text
.R	print all subsequent text in Roman (regular) font (turns off underlining)

Changing Dimensions

Register	Effect
VS xp	establishes vertical spacing: set x to 12 for single spacing, 24 for double, or 36 for triple
PD xp	establishes the number of blank lines before paragraphs: set x to 12 for a single line, 24 for two lines, or 36 for three lines
LL xi	set line length to x inches
FL xi	set footnote length to x inches

Register	Effect
Pl *x*n	set paragraph indention to *x* characters
Ql *x*n	set block quote paragraph indention to *x* characters
HM *x*i	set header margin to *x* inches
FM *x*i	set footer margin to *x* inches

REVIEW EXERCISES

These exercises assume you are using nroff with the **mm** macro package.

1. What does it mean for a text formatter like nroff to fill lines? What does filled and justified text look like?

2. How can you get nroff to produce standard paragraphs throughout a document? How can you cause it to produce a single standard paragraph in a document filled with left-block paragraphs?

3. Create a document and use the automatic list command to create the following embedded lists. Blank lines should separate the list items.

```
 I.    Meat
 II.   Vegetables
 III.     Fruit
            A. Oranges
            B. Lemons
                    a. Meyer Lemons
                    b. Eureka Lemons
            C. Grapefruit
            D. Strawberries
            E. Apples
```

Format the document using nroff and **mm** to demonstrate that the formatted output has the desired characteristics.

4. Using the **.I** command, how would you produce the following output:

a. e.g., *Tuesday*)

b. It happened at noon (*yesterday*)!

c. Have you read *The Wall Street Journal* lately?

5. Create a document and insert the list items in Exercise 3 as first-, second-, and third-level heads. All heads should appear on lines by themselves, and the level-1 and level-2 heads should be followed by single blank lines.

6. To the document you created for Exercise 5, add a command that will cause nroff to print a table of contents.

7. Create a document that contains the following text and automatically numbered footnote.

```
The .RL command produces a reference list.[1] It is used in
the same way other lists are used—items are identified
by .LI and the list ends with .LE.  The reference list
occurs in the document wherever you insert it.  Each item
in a reference list is marked by a number enclosed in
square brackets.
    .

    .

----------

    1. Reference lists are often used for bibliographies.
```

Set up the footnote style so that the footnote will be hyphenated, adjusted, and indented and the label will be right-justified.

8. What set of page header and footer commands will create a document with the following characteristics:

a. The title ''Introduction'' centered at the top of each page.

b. On even-numbered pages, the page number at the bottom-left and the date at the bottom-right.

c. On odd-numbered pages, the page number at the bottom-right and the date at the bottom-left.

9. How can you leave four blank pages in the middle of a document?

10. What command line will format a file called **daily_report** using the **mm** macros and sending only pages 10, 13, and 19-21 to the printer?

CHAPTER

8

THE BOURNE SHELL

The Bourne Shell is both a command interpreter and a high-level programming language. As a command interpreter, it processes commands that you enter in response to its prompt. When you use the Bourne Shell as a programming language, it processes groups of commands stored in files called *shell scripts*. This chapter expands on the interactive features introduced in Chapter 5, explains how to create and run shell scripts, and explores aspects of shell programming, such as variables and flow control commands. Although this chapter is primarily about the Bourne Shell, most of it also applies to the Korn Shell. The theoretical portions of this chapter and the sections "Creating a Simple Shell Script" and "Command Separation and Grouping" apply to the C Shell as well as the Korn Shell. Appendix A describes the unique features of the Korn Shell, and Chapter 9 describes the C Shell.

This chapter starts by describing some fundamentals of using the shell. The first section, "Creating a Simple Shell Script," describes the basics of writing and running simple shell scripts. The following two sections—"Command Separation and Grouping" and "Redirecting the Standard Error"—provide information that you will find useful whether you are writing shell scripts or just using the shell interactively. The rest of the chapter explains concepts and commands, such as subshells, variables, and control structures, that you will need to write more sophisticated shell scripts.

Because many users prefer the Bourne Shell's programming language to the C Shell's, and because it is the basis of the Korn Shell programming language, this chapter describes Bourne Shell programming in detail. In the section on flow control commands, simple examples that illustrate the concepts are followed by more complicated examples in sections marked OPTIONAL. The more complex scripts illustrate traditional shell programming practices and introduce some UNIX utilities often used in scripts. If shell programming is new to you, you may want to skip these sections the first time you read the chapter. Return to them later when you feel comfortable with the basic concepts.

If you are not interested in mastering shell programming right now, you may want to skip the "Processes," "Variables," and "Flow Control Commands" sections of the chapter. However, you should read the "Keyword Shell Variables" section (page 241). The keyword shell variables control important characteristics of the shell environment when you are using the shell either interactively as a command interpreter or as a programming language.

CREATING A SIMPLE SHELL SCRIPT

A *shell script* is a file that contains commands to be executed by the shell. The commands in a shell script can be any commands you can enter in response to a shell prompt. For example, a command in a shell script might invoke a UNIX utility, a compiled program you have written, or another shell script. Like commands you give on the command line, a command in a shell script can use ambiguous file references and can have its input or output redirected from a file or sent through a pipe. (You can also use pipes and redirection with the input and output of the script itself.) In addition to the commands you would ordinarily use on the command line, there are a group of commands, the *flow control commands*, that were designed specifically for use in shell scripts. The flow control commands enable you to alter the order of execution of commands in a script as you would alter the order of execution of statements in a typical structured programming language.

The easiest way to run a shell script is to give its filename on the command line. The shell then interprets and executes the commands in the script, one after another. Thus, by using a shell script you can initiate simply and quickly a complex series of tasks or a repetitive procedure.

Making a File Executable

In order to execute a shell script by giving its name as a command, you must have permission to read and execute the file that contains the script. Execute permission tells the shell and the system that the owner, group, or public has permission to execute the file. It also implies that the content of the file is executable.

When you initially create a shell script using an editor such as vi, the file will typically not have its execute permission set. The example below shows a file, **whoson**, that is a shell script containing three command lines. When you initially create a file like **whoson**, you cannot execute it by giving its name as a command because you do not have execute permission.

```
$ cat whoson
date
echo Users Currently Logged In
who


$ whoson
whoson: execute permission denied
```

The shell does not recognize **whoson** as an executable file and issues an error message when you try to execute it.

As shown in Chapter 4, the chmod utility changes the access privileges associated with a file. Below, ls with the –l option displays the access permissions of **whoson** before and after chmod gives the owner execute permission.

```
$ ls -l whoson
-rw-r--r-- 1 alex    pubs        42   Jun 15 10:55 whoson
$ chmod u+x whoson
$ ls -l whoson
-rwxr--r-- 1 alex    pubs        42   Jun 15 10:55 whoson


$ whoson
Fri Jun 15 10:59:40 PDT 1990
Users Currently Logged In
alex        console Jun 15 08:26
jenny       tty02   Jun 15 10:04
hls         tty06   Jun 15 08:51
```

The first ls displays a hyphen as the fourth character, indicating that the owner does not have permission to execute the file. Then chmod uses two arguments to give the owner execute access permission. The **u+x** causes chmod to add (**+**) execute access permission (**x**) for the owner (**u**). (The **u** stands for *user*, although it actually refers to the owner of the file, who may or may not be the user of the file at any given time.) The second argument is the name of the file.

The second **ls** shows an **x** in the fourth position, indicating that the owner now has execute permission.

If other users are going to execute the file, you must also change group and/or public access privileges. For more information on access permissions, refer to "Access Permissions" in Chapter 4 and to **ls** and **chmod** in Part II.

Finally, the shell executes the file when its name is given as a command. If you try typing **whoson** in response to a shell prompt and you get an error message such as **whoson: Command not found.**, your login shell is not set up to search for executable files in the working directory. Try giving the command below.

```
$  ./whoson
```

The **./** explicitly tells the shell to look for an executable file in the working directory. To change your environment so that the shell will search the working directory, refer to the **PATH** variable on page 242.

Now you know how to write and execute your own simple shell scripts. Shell scripts are convenient tools for running complex commands and series of commands that are run frequently. The next two sections of the chapter, "Command Separation and Grouping" and "Redirecting the Standard Error," describe features that are useful when you are running commands either on a command line or from within a script. The following section, "Processes," explains the relationships between commands, shell scripts, and UNIX system processes. It describes how a shell script is invoked and run and describes the environment in which it is run.

COMMAND SEPARATION AND GROUPING

When you give the shell commands interactively or write a shell script, you must separate commands from one another. This section reviews the ways you can do this that were covered in Chapter 5 and introduces a few new ones.

The NEWLINE and ; Characters

The NEWLINE character is a unique command separator because it initiates execution of the command preceding it. You have seen this throughout this book each time you press the RETURN key at the end of a command line.

The semicolon (;) is a command separator that *does not* initiate execution of a command and *does not* change any aspect of how the command functions. You can execute a series of commands sequentially by entering them on a single command line and separating each from the next by a ;. To initiate execution of the sequence of commands, you must terminate the command line with a RETURN.

```
$  a  ;  b  ;  c
```

If **a**, **b**, and **c** are commands, the preceding command line yields the same results as the following three command lines:

```
$  a
$  b
$  c
```

Although the white space around the semicolons in the example above makes the command line easier to read, it is not necessary. None of the command separators needs to be surrounded by SPACES or TABS.

The \ Character

When you are typing a long command line and you reach the right side of your display screen, you can use a backslash (\) character to continue the command on the next line. The backslash quotes the NEWLINE character that follows it so that the shell does not treat it as a command terminator.

The | and & Characters

Other command separators are the pipe symbol (|) and the background task symbol (**&**). These command separators *do not* start execution of a command but *do* change some aspect of how the command functions. They alter where the input or output comes from or goes to, or they determine whether the shell executes the task in the background or foreground.

The following command line initiates a job that comprises three tasks. The shell directs the output from task **a** to task **b** and directs **b**'s output to **c**. Because the shell runs the entire job in the foreground, you do not get a prompt back until task **c** runs to completion.

```
$  a  |  b  |  c
```

The next command line executes tasks **a** and **b** in the background and task **c** in the foreground. The shell displays the process identification numbers (PIDs) for the processes running in the background. You get a prompt back as soon as **c** finishes.

```
$  a  &  b  &  c
14271
14272
```

The following command line executes all three tasks as background jobs. You get a prompt immediately.

```
$ a & b & c &
14290
14291
14292
```

You can use a pipe to send the output from one subtask to the next and run the whole job as a background task. Again, the prompt comes back immediately.

```
$ a | b | c &
14302
```

═══

OPTIONAL

You can see a demonstration of sequential and concurrent processes run in both the foreground and background. Create a group of executable files named **a**, **b**, **c**, and **d**. Have each file echo its name over and over as file **a** (below) does. The **\c** causes echo to suppress the NEWLINE it ordinarily prints. (Your version of echo may use an option, **-n**, instead of **\c**.)

```
$ cat a
echo " aaaaaaaaaaaaaaaaaaaaaaaaaa\c "
echo " aaaaaaaaaaaaaaaaaaaaaaaaaa\c "
echo " aaaaaaaaaaaaaaaaaaaaaaaaaa\c "
echo " aaaaaaaaaaaaaaaaaaaaaaaaaa\c "
echo " aaaaaaaaaaaaaaaaaaaaaaaaaa\c "
```

Execute the files sequentially and concurrently, using the example command lines from this section. When you execute two of these shell scripts sequentially, their output follows one another. When you execute two of them concurrently, their output is interspersed as control is passed back and forth between the tasks. The results will not always be identical because the UNIX system schedules jobs slightly differently each time they run. Two sample runs are shown here:

```
$ a&b&c&
14717
14718
14719
$ aaaaaaaaaaaaaaaaaaaaaaaaaaaaaaccccccccccccccccccccccccccccccccccc
ccccccccccccccccccccccccccccccccccccccccccccccccccccccccccccccccccc
cccccccccccccccccccccccccccccaaaaaaaaaaaaaaaaaaaaaaaaaaaaaaaaaaaaaa
aaaaaaaaaaaaaaaaaaaaaaaaaaaaaaaaaaaaaaaaaaaaaaaaaaaaaaaaaaaaaaaaaaaa
aaaaaaaaaaaabbbbbbbbbbbbbbbbbbbbbbbbbbbbbbbbbbbbbbbbbbbbbbbbbbbbbbbbb
bbbbbbbbbbbbbbbbbbbbbbbbbbbbbbbbbbbbbbbbbbbbbbbbbbbbbbbbbbbbbbbbbbbbbb
bbbbbbbbbbbbbbbbbbb
```

OPTIONAL (Continued)
```
$  a&b&c&
14738
14739
14740
$  ccccccccccccccccccccccccccccccccccccccccccccccccccccccccc
ccccccccccccccccccccccccccccccccccccccccccccccccccccccccccccc
ccccccbbbbbbbbbbbbbbbbbbbbbbbbbbbbbbbbbbbbbbbbbbbbbbbbbbbbaaa
aaaaaaaaaaaaaaaaaaaaaaaaaaaaaaaaaaaaaaaaaaaaaaaaaaaaaaaaaaaaa
aaaaaaaaaaaaaaaaaaaaaaaaaaaaaaaaaaaaaaaaaaaaaaaaaaaaaaaaaaaaa
aabbbbbbbbbbbbbbbbbbbbbbbbbbbbbbbbbbbbbbbbbbbbbbbbbbbbbbbbbbbb
bbbbbbbbbbbbbbbbbbb
```

Command Grouping

You can use parentheses to group commands. The shell creates a new shell, a *subshell*, for each group, treating each group of commands as a job and forking processes as needed to execute the commands.

The command line below executes commands **a** and **b** sequentially in the background while executing **c** in the foreground. The shell prompt returns when **c** finishes execution.

```
$  (a  ;  b)  &  c
15007
```

This example differs from the earlier example **a & b & c** because tasks **a** and **b** are initiated not concurrently but sequentially.

Similarly, the following command line executes **a** and **b** sequentially in the background and, at the same time, executes **c** and **d** sequentially in the background. The prompt returns immediately.

```
$  (a  ;  b)  &  (c  ;  d)  &
15020
15021
```

In the following shell script, the second pair of parentheses create a subshell to run the commands following the pipe. Because of the parentheses, the output of the first **tar** command is available for the second **tar** command, despite the intervening **cd** command. Without the parentheses, the output of the first **tar** would be sent to **cd** and lost, because **cd** does not accept input from its standard input. The **$1** and **$2** are shell variables that represent the first and second command line arguments (see page 246). The first pair of parentheses, which create a subshell to run the first two commands, are necessary so that users can call **cpdir** with relative pathnames. Without these parentheses, the first **cd** command would change the working directory of the script (and, consequently, the working direc-

---

OPTIONAL (Continued)

tory of the second cd command), whereas with the parentheses only the working directory of the subshell changes.

```
$ cat cpdir
( cd $1 ; tar cf - . ) | ( cd $2 ; tar xvf - )
$ cpdir /home/alex/sources /home/alex/memo/biblio
```

The preceding command line copies the files and subdirectories included in the **/home/alex/sources** directory to the **/home/alex/memo/biblio** directory. This shell script can save a lot of time and effort when you are reorganizing your directory structure on older releases of System V. Under UNIX System V Release 4, you can use the –r option to cp instead. (Refer to cp in Part II. For information about the tar utility, see tar in Part II).

Refer to the "Processes" section on page 231 for more information about subshells.

NEW TO UNIX SYSTEM V Release 4

JOB CONTROL

Using job control, you can move commands from the foreground to the background and vice versa, stop commands temporarily, and get a list of the current commands. The Berkeley UNIX C Shell has supported job control for many years, though job control features were often not implemented in the C Shell on computers running System V. System V Release 4 includes a new utility called jsh that includes C Shell job control features but is otherwise identical to the Bourne Shell (sh). In the example below, the Shell does not recognize the jobs command. If you start up the Job Shell, the jobs command is recognized but prints no messages because you have no jobs currently running.

```
$ jobs
jobs: not found
$ jsh
$ jobs
$
```

See page 305 for a complete description of job control features. The Korn Shell also supports job control in the same manner as the C Shell and Job Shell.

If your default login shell is not the Job Shell but you would like to use job control features regularly, ask your system administrator to set up jsh as your login shell.

REDIRECTING THE STANDARD ERROR

Chapter 5 described the concept of standard output and explained how to redirect a command's standard output. In addition to the standard output, commands can send their output to another place: the *standard error*. A command can send error messages to standard error to keep them from getting mixed up with the information it sends to its standard output. Just as with the standard output, unless you redirect it, the shell sends a command's standard error output to the terminal. Unless you redirect one or the other, you will not know the difference between the output a command sends to its standard output and the output it sends to its standard error.

The following examples demonstrate how to redirect the standard output and the standard error to different files or to the same file. When you call cat with the name of a file that does not exist and the name of a file that does exist, it sends an error message to the standard error and copies the file to the standard output. Unless you redirect them, both messages appear on the terminal.

```
$ cat y
This is y.
$ cat x y
cat: cannot open x
This is y.
```

When you redirect the standard output of a command using the greater than symbol, the error output is not affected—it still appears on the terminal.

```
$ cat x y > hold
cat: cannot open x
$ cat hold
This is y.
```

Similarly, when you send the standard output through a pipe, the error output is not affected. In the example below, the standard output of cat is sent through a pipe to the tr (translate) command, which is used to convert lowercase characters to uppercase. The text that cat sends to the standard error is not translated because it goes directly to the terminal rather than through the pipe.

```
$ cat x y | tr "[a-z]" "[A-Z]"
cat: cannot open x
THIS IS Y.
```

The following example redirects the standard output and the error output to different files. The notation **2>** tells the shell where to redirect the error output.

The **1>** is the same as **>** and tells the shell where to redirect the standard output. You can use **>** in place of **1>**.

```
$ cat x y 1> hold1 2> hold2
$ cat hold1
This is y.
$ cat hold2
cat: cannot open x
```

Next, **1>** redirects the standard output to **hold**. Then **2>&1** declares file descriptor 2 to be a duplicate of file descriptor 1. The result is that both the standard output and the standard error are redirected to **hold**.

```
$ cat x y 1> hold 2>&1
$ cat hold
cat: cannot open x
This is y.
```

In the above example, **1> hold** precedes **2>&1**. If they had been listed in the opposite order, the standard error would have been redirected to be a duplicate of the standard output before the standard output was redirected to **hold**. In that case only the standard output would have been redirected.

The next example declares file descriptor 2 to be a duplicate of file descriptor 1 and sends file descriptor 1 through a pipe to the **tr** command.

```
$ cat x y 2>&1 | tr "[a-z]" "[A-Z]"
CAT: CANNOT OPEN X
THIS IS Y.
```

You can also use **1>&2** to redirect the standard output of a command to the standard error. This technique is often used in shell scripts to send error messages to the standard error. In the following script, the standard output of the first **echo** command is redirected to the standard error:

```
$ cat message_demo
echo This is an error message. 1>&2
echo This is not an error message.
```

If you use **message_demo** and you do not redirect the standard output or the standard error of the script, the output of both **echo** commands will appear on your terminal. However, if you redirect the standard output, error messages like the one above will still go to your terminal. Refer to links on page 257 for an example of a script that uses **1>&2** to redirect the output of **echo** to the standard error to display error messages.

You can also use the **exec** command to redirect the standard input, standard output, and standard error of a shell script from within the script (see page 283).

PROCESSES

A *process* is the execution of a command by the UNIX system. The shell that starts up when you log in is a command, or a process, like any other. Whenever you give the name of a UNIX utility on the command line, a process is initiated. When you run a shell script, another shell process is started, and additional processes are created for each command in the script. Depending on how you invoke the shell script, the script will be run either by a new shell or by a subshell of the current shell.

Process Structure

Like the file structure, the process structure is hierarchical. It has parents, children, and even a *root*. A parent process *forks* a child process, which in turn can fork other processes. *Fork* is the name of an operating system routine that creates a new process. (You can also use the term *spawns;* the words are interchangeable.) One of the first things the UNIX operating system does to begin execution when a machine is started up is to start a single process—process identification (PID) number 1. This process holds the same position in the process structure as the root directory does in the file structure. It is the ancestor of all processes that each user works with. On older versions of System V, it forked a getty process for each terminal, which waited until a user started to log in. The action of logging in transformed the getty process into a login process and finally into the user's shell process. On System V Release 4, a single process, ttymon, monitors all lines and starts up the appropriate login process.

Executing a Command

When you give the shell a command, it usually forks (or spawns) a child process to execute the command. While the child process is executing the command, the parent process *sleeps*. While a process is sleeping, it does not use any computer time; it remains inactive, waiting to wake up. When the child process finishes executing the command, it dies. The parent process (which is running the shell) wakes up and prompts you for another command.

When you request that the shell run a process in the background (by ending a command with an &), the shell forks a child process without going to sleep and without waiting for the child process to run to completion. The parent process, executing the shell, reports the PID number of the child and prompts you for another command. The child process runs in the background, independent of its parent.

Although the shell forks a process for most of the commands you give it, some commands are built into the shell, and consequently the shell does not need to fork a process to run them. For a complete list of the built-in commands refer to page 289.

Within a given process, such as your login shell or a subshell, you can declare, initialize, read, and change variables. But, by default, a variable is local to a process. When a process forks a child process, the parent does not automatically pass the value of a variable to the child. You can make the value of a variable available to child processes by using the **export** command. Refer to page 237 for information about the **export** command.

Process Identification

The UNIX system assigns a unique process identification (PID) number at the inception of each process. As long as a process is in existence, it keeps the same PID number. During one session, the same process is always executing the login shell. When you fork a new process—for example, when you use an editor—the new (child) process has a different PID number from its parent process. When you return to the login shell, you will find it is still being executed by the same process and has the same PID number as when you logged in.

The interaction below shows that the process running the shell forked (is the parent of) the process running **ps**. When you call **ps** with the –l option, it displays a long listing of information about each process. The line of the **ps** display with **sh** in the COMD column refers to the process running the shell. The column headed by PID lists the process ID number. The column headed PPID lists the PID number of the *parent* of each of the processes. From the PID and PPID columns, you can see that the process running the shell (PID 14137) is the parent of the process running **ps** (PID 14166): The parent PID number of **ps** is the same as the PID number of the shell. (See **ps** in Part II for a complete description of all the columns the –l option displays.)

```
$ ps -l
F S UID   PID  PPID  C PRI  NI  ADDR  SZ WCHAN TTY    TIME COMD
1 S 107 14137     1  0  30  20   59a  10  e2b6 tty14  0:06 sh
1 R 107 14166 14137 97  20  20   5e7  11       tty14  0:02 ps
```

When you give another **ps** –l command, you can see that the shell is still being run by the same process but that it forked another process to run **ps**.

```
$ ps -l
F S UID   PID  PPID  C PRI  NI  ADDR  SZ WCHAN TTY    TIME COMD
1 S 107 14137     1  0  30  20   4e4  10  e2b6 tty14  0:07 sh
1 R 107 14208 14137 91  20  20   3ae  11       tty14  0:02 ps
```

The section "PID Numbers" (page 249) describes two shell variables, $$ and $!, that report on process identification numbers.

Invoking a Shell Script

With the exception of the commands that are built into the shell, whenever you give the shell a command on the command line, the shell forks, which creates a duplicate of the shell process (that is, a subshell). The new process attempts to *exec*, or execute, the command. Like fork, exec is a routine executed by the operating system. If the command is an executable program (such as a C program), the exec will succeed, and the system will execute the command as part of the current process. If the command is a shell script, however, the exec will fail. When the exec fails, the command is assumed to be a shell script, and the subshell will run the commands in the script. Unlike your login shell, which expects input from the command line, the subshell takes its input from a file, the shell script.

You can save the shell the trouble of trying and failing with the initial exec by using the sh command to exec a shell to run the script directly. In the following example, sh creates a new shell that takes its input from the file called **whoson**:

```
$ sh whoson
```

Because the sh command expects to read a file containing commands, you do not need execute permission for **whoson**. (However, you do need read permission.) Note that although sh takes its input from a file, its standard input, standard output, and standard error are still connected to the terminal.

Although using sh to invoke a shell script is more direct from the operating system's point of view, users typically prefer to make the file executable and run the script by typing its name on the command line. It is easier just to type the name, and it is consistent with the way other kinds of programs are invoked (so users do not need to know whether they are running a shell script or another kind of program).

On some implementations of System V, you can put a special sequence of characters on the first line of a shell script to indicate to the operating system that it is a script. Because the operating system checks the initial characters of a program before attempting to exec it, these characters save the system from making an unsuccessful attempt. They also tell the system whether to invoke the Bourne, C, or Korn Shell to run the script.

If the first two characters of a script are #!, the system interprets the characters that follow as the pathname of a shell. The following example specifies that the current script should be run by the Bourne Shell:

```
$ cat bourne_script
#!/usr/bin/sh
echo This is a Bourne Shell script.
```

If the first character of a script is a pound sign and the second character is *not* an exclamation point, the system uses the C Shell to run the script.

When a pound sign occurs in a location in a script other than the first character position, the shell script interprets it as indicating the beginning of a comment. The shell ignores everything between a pound sign and the next NEWLINE character.

VARIABLES

The shell has variables you create and assign values to, as well as variables that are set by the shell itself. In this chapter the variables you can name and assign values to are referred to as *user-created variables*. You can change the values of these variables at any time, and you can make them *readonly*, so that they cannot subsequently be changed. You can also *export* them, so that they will be accessible to shells you may fork during the current login session. All variables, even those whose values are numbers, are stored as strings of characters.

Those variables that are set by the shell are referred to as shell variables. Some of the shell variables are called *keyword variables*, or *keyword parameters*, because their short, mnemonic names have special meanings to the shell. When you start a shell (by logging in, for example), the shell inherits several keyword variables from the environment. Among these variables are **HOME**, which identifies your home directory, and **PATH**, which determines what directories the shell looks in when you give it a command. Other keyword variables are created by the shell and initialized with default values when it is started up, whereas others do not exist until you set them. Although the shell automatically assigns values to the keyword variables, you can change them at any time. Normally, you would set them in your **.profile** file if they need to be changed at all.

Another group of shell variables do not have distinct names and values. You can reference these variables with special, two-character labels (such as $? and $#). The values of these variables reflect different aspects of your ongoing interaction with the shell. For example, whenever a command is given on the command line, each argument on the command line becomes the value of one of these special shell variables. These variables enable you to create shell scripts that use command line arguments. Because you cannot assign values to these variables as you can to the others, they are referred to in this chapter as *readonly shell variables*. (However, you can change some of these variables using the set command—see page 247.)

The following sections describe user-created variables, keyword shell variables, and readonly shell variables.

User-Created Variables

You can declare any sequence of letters and digits as the name of a variable, as long as the first character is a letter. The first line in the example below declares the variable named **person** and initializes it with the value **alex**. When you assign a value to a variable, **you must not precede or follow the equal sign with a** SPACE or TAB.

Since the echo command copies its arguments to the standard output, you can use it to display the values of variables.

```
$ person=alex
$ echo person
person
$ echo $person
alex
```

The second line shows that **person** does not represent **alex**. The string per-son is echoed as person. The shell only substitutes the value of a variable when you precede the name of the variable with a dollar sign ($). The command **echo $person** displays the value of the variable **person**. It does not display $person because the shell does not pass $person to echo as an argument. Because of the leading $ the shell recognizes that $person is the name of a variable, *substitutes* the value of the variable, and passes that value to echo. The echo command displays the value of the variable, not its name, never knowing that you called it with a variable. The final command (above) displays the value of the variable **person**.

You can prevent the shell from substituting the value of a variable by quoting the leading $. Double quotation marks will not prevent the substitution; however, single quotation marks or the backslash (\) character will.

```
$ echo $person
alex
$ echo "$person"
alex
$ echo ' $person '
$person
$ echo \$person
$person
```

Since double quotation marks do not prevent variable substitution but do turn off the special meanings of most other characters, they are useful both when you

are assigning values to variables and when you use those values. In order to
assign a value that contains SPACES or TABS to a variable, use double quotation
marks around the value.

```
$ person="alex and jenny"
$ echo $person
alex and jenny
```

When you reference a variable that contains TABS or multiple adjacent SPACES, you
should also use quotation marks to preserve the spacing. If you do not quote the
variable, echo interprets each string of nonblank characters in the value as a
separate argument, and it puts a single space between them when it copies them to
the standard output.

```
$ person="alex    and    jenny"
$ echo "$person"
alex    and    jenny
$ echo $person
alex and jenny
```

Although the shell does not interpret special characters such as * and ? as
special when they occur in the value of a variable, it does interpret them as special when you reference the variable. Consequently, they should also be quoted.

```
$ memo=alex*
$ echo "$memo"
alex*
$ echo $memo
alex.report alex.summary
$ ls
alex.report
alex.summary
```

The example above shows that when **$memo** is not quoted, the shell matches the
value **alex*** to two files in the working directory, **alex.report** and **alex.summary**.
When the variable is quoted, echo displays **alex***.

Removing Variables.   A variable exists as long as the shell in which it was
created exists. To remove the value of a variable, set it to null.

```
$ person=
$ echo $person

$
```

You can remove a variable with the unset command. For example, to remove the **person** variable, you would give the following command:

```
$ unset person
```

The readonly Command.

You can use the readonly command to ensure that the value of a variable cannot be changed. The next example declares the variable **person** to be readonly. You must assign a value to a variable *before* you declare it to be readonly; you cannot change its value after the declaration. When you attempt to change the value of a readonly variable, the shell displays an error message.

```
$ person=jenny
$ echo $person
jenny
$ readonly person
$ person=helen
person: is read only
```

If you use the readonly command without an argument, it displays a list of all user-created readonly variables. If the user had made any keyword shell variables readonly, they would also be displayed. The readonly command does not display the special readonly shell variables (e.g., $?, $#).

```
$ readonly
readonly person
```

The export Command.

Variables are ordinarily local to the process in which they are declared. Consequently, a shell script does not have access to variables you declared in your login shell unless you take actions to make the variables available. The most commonly used method for making variables available to child processes is with the export command.

Once you use the export command with a variable name as an argument, the shell places the value of the variable in the calling environment of child processes. This *call by value* gives each child process a copy of the variable for its own use.

Below, the **extest1** shell script assigns a value of american to the variable named **cheese**. Then it displays its filename (**extest1**) and the value of **cheese**. The **extest1** script then calls **subtest**, which attempts to display the same information. Then **subtest** declares a **cheese** variable and displays its value. When **subtest** finishes, it returns control to the parent process executing **extest1**, which again displays the value of the original **cheese** variable.

```
$ cat extest1
cheese=american
echo "extest1 1: $cheese"
subtest
echo "extest1 2: $cheese"
$ cat subtest
echo "subtest 1: $cheese"
cheese=swiss
echo "subtest 2: $cheese"
$ extest1
extest1 1: american
subtest 1:
subtest 2: swiss
extest1 2: american
```

The **subtest** script never receives the value of **cheese** from **extest1**, and **extest1** never loses the value. When a process attempts to display the value of a variable that has not been declared, as is the case with **subtest**, it displays nothing—the value of an undeclared variable is that of a null string.

The following script, **extest2**, is the same as **extest1** except that it uses the export command to make **cheese** available to the **subtest** script:

```
$ cat extest2
export cheese
cheese=american
echo "extest2 1: $cheese"
subtest
echo "extest2 2: $cheese"
$ extest2
extest2 1: american
subtest 1: american
subtest 2: swiss
extest2 2: american
```

Here, the child process inherits the value of **cheese** as american and, after displaying this value, changes *its copy* to swiss. When control is returned to the parent, the parent's copy of **cheese** still retains its original value, american.

The read Command.   As you begin writing shell scripts, you will soon realize that one of the most common uses of user-created variables is for storing information that the script prompts the user for. Using the read command, your scripts can accept input from the user and store the input in variables you create. The read command reads one line from the standard input and assigns the line to one or more variables. The following script shows how read works:

```
$ cat read1
echo "Go ahead: \c"
read firstline
echo "You entered: $firstline"
$ read1
Go ahead: This is a line.
You entered: This is a line.
```

The first line of the **read1** script uses echo to prompt you to enter a line of text. The \c suppresses the NEWLINE following the string that echo displays. When you use a character like \ that has a special meaning to both the shell and to the echo command, you must quote it so that the shell passes it along unchanged to echo. In the example above, the entire text string is quoted.

The second line in the example above reads the text into the variable **firstline**. The third line verifies the action of the read command by displaying the value of **firstline**. The variable is quoted (along with the text string) in this example because you, as the script writer, cannot anticipate what characters the user might answer in response to the prompt. For example, consider what would happen if the variable were not quoted and the user entered * in response to the prompt.

```
$ read1_no_quote
Go ahead: *
You entered: read1 script.1
$ ls
read1     script.1
```

As the ls command demonstrates, the shell expanded the asterisk into a list of all the files in the working directory. When the variable **$filename** is surrounded by double quotation marks, the asterisk is not expanded by the shell. Thus, the **read1** script shown above behaves correctly.

```
$ read1
Go ahead: *
You entered: *
```

Of course, if you want the shell to use the special meanings of the special characters, you should not use quotes.

The **read2** script shown below prompts for a command line and reads it into the variable **command**. The script then executes the command line by placing **$command** on a line by itself. (Note that the $ in front of **command** is *not* a shell prompt.) When the shell executes the script, it replaces the variable with its value and executes the command line as part of the script.

```
$ cat read2
echo "Enter a command: \c"
read command
$command
echo Thanks
```

Below, **read2** reads a command line that calls the echo command. The shell executes the command and then displays Thanks. In the next example, **read2** reads a command line that executes the who utility.

```
$ read2
Enter a command: echo Please display this message.
Please display this message.
Thanks
$ read2
Enter a command: who
alex        tty11           Jun 15 07:50
scott       tty7            Jun 15 11:54
Thanks
```

In the following example, the **read3** script reads values into three variables. The read command assigns one word (that is, one sequence of nonblank characters) to each variable.

```
$ cat read3
echo "Enter something: \c"
read word1 word2 word3
echo "Word 1 is: $word1"
echo "Word 2 is: $word2"
echo "Word 3 is: $word3"
$ read3
Enter something: this is something
Word 1 is: this
Word 2 is: is
Word 3 is: something
```

If you enter more words than read has variables, read assigns one word to each variable, with all the left-over words going to the last variable. Actually, **read1** and **read2** both assigned the first word and all the left-over words to the one variable they each had to work with.

Below, read accepts five words into three variables. It assigns the first word to the first variable, the second word to the second variable, and the third through fifth words to the third variable.

```
$ read3
Enter something: this is something else, really.
Word 1 is:   this
Word 2 is:   is
Word 3 is:   something else, really.
```

Command Substitution.   A second common use of user-created variables is to store the output of a command. When you enclose a command between two backquotes, or grave accent marks (`), the shell replaces the command, including the accent marks, with the output of the command. This process is referred to as *command substitution.*

The following shell script assigns the output of the **pwd** utility to the variable **dir** and displays a message containing this variable:

```
$ cat dir
dir=`pwd`
echo "You are using the $dir directory."
$ dir
You are using the /home/jenny directory.
```

Although this example illustrates how to use backquotes to assign the output of a command to a variable, it is not a realistic example. You can more easily display the output of pwd in the output of echo without using a variable.

```
$ cat dir2
echo You are using the `pwd` directory.
$ dir2
You are using the /home/jenny directory.
```

Refer to the **dateset** script (page 248), the **links** script (page 257), and the **safedit** script (page 276) for more examples of the use of backquotes to assign values to variables.

Keyword Shell Variables

Most of the keyword variables are either inherited by the shell when it is started up or declared and initialized by the shell at that time. You can assign new values to these variables from the command line or from the **.profile** file in your home directory.

Typically, users want these variables to apply to their login shell as well as to any other shells or subshells they might create. Consequently, these variables must be exported. They can be exported before or after they are set. Traditionally they are exported after they are set.

HOME.   By default, your home directory is your working directory when you first log in. The system administrator determines your home directory when you establish your account and stores this information in the **/etc/passwd** file. When you log in, the shell inherits the pathname of your home directory and assigns it to the variable **HOME**.

When you give a **cd** command without an argument, cd makes the directory whose name is stored in **HOME** the working directory.

```
$ echo $HOME
/home/jenny
$ cd
$ pwd
/home/jenny
```

The example above shows the value of the **HOME** variable and the effect of the cd utility. After you execute cd without an argument, the pathname of the working directory is the same as the value of **HOME**.

PATH.   When you give the shell an absolute or relative pathname that is not just a simple filename as a command, it looks in the specified directory for an executable file with the appropriate filename. If the executable file does not have the exact pathname that you specify, the shell reports that it cannot find (or execute) the program. Alternatively, if you give the shell a simple filename as a command, it searches through certain directories for the program you want to execute. The shell looks in several directories for a file that has the same name as the command and that you have execute permission for. The **PATH** shell variable controls this search path.

When you log in, the shell assigns a default value to the **PATH** variable. On System V, the default specifies that the shell search the **/usr/bin** and **/usr/sbin** directories. The **/usr/bin** and **/usr/sbin** directories are the standard directories for storing utilities. If the shell does not find the file in any of these directories, it reports that it cannot find (or execute) the command.

The **PATH** variable specifies the directories in the order the shell is to search them. Each must be separated from the next by a colon. The following command causes the search for an executable file to start with **/usr/bin**, followed by **/usr/sbin**. If the shell fails to find the file in those directories, it looks in **/home/jenny/bin** and then in the working directory (specified by a trailing colon). For security reasons it is a good idea to search the standard directories before the working directory. The export command below makes the new value of **PATH** accessible to subshells and other shells you may invoke during the login session.

```
$ PATH=/usr/bin:/usr/sbin:/home/jenny/bin:
$ export PATH
```

Since UNIX traditionally stores executable files in directories called **bin**, users also typically put their executables in their own **bin** directories. If you put your own **bin** directory in your **PATH** as Jenny has, the shell will look there for any commands that it cannot find in the standard directories.

MAIL.   The **MAIL** variable contains the name of the file that your mail is stored in. Normally, the absolute pathname of this file is **/var/mail/name**, or **/var/spool/mail/name**, where **name** is your login name.

The **MAILPATH** variable contains a list of filenames separated by colons. If this variable is set, the shell informs you when any one of the files is modified (e.g., when mail arrives). You can follow any of the filenames in the list with a percent sign (%) followed by a message. The message will replace the you have mail message when you get mail while you are logged in.

The **MAILCHECK** variable specifies how often, in seconds, the shell checks for new mail. The default is 600 seconds (10 minutes). If you set this variable to zero, the shell will check before each prompt.

PS1.   The shell prompt lets you know that the shell is waiting for you to give it a command. The Bourne Shell prompt used in the examples throughout this book is a $ followed by a SPACE. Your prompt may differ. The shell stores the prompt as a string in the **PS1** variable. When you change the value of this variable, the appearance of your prompt changes.

If you are working on more than one machine, it can be helpful to incorporate a machine name in your prompt. The following example shows how to change the prompt to the machine name *bravo* followed by a colon and a SPACE.

```
$ PS1="bravo:  "
bravo: echo test
test
bravo:
```

Refer to page 288 for a shell function that causes the prompt to display the name of the working directory.

PS2.   Prompt string 2 is a secondary prompt that the shell stores in **PS2**. On the first line of the following example, an unclosed quoted string follows an **echo** command. The shell assumes that the command is not finished and, on the second line, gives the default secondary prompt (>). This prompt indicates that the shell is waiting for the user to continue the command line. The shell waits until it receives the quotation mark that closes the string and then executes the command.

```
$ echo "demonstration of prompt string
> 2"
demonstration of prompt string
2
$ PS2="secondary prompt:  "
$ echo "this demonstrates
secondary prompt: prompt string 2"
this demonstrates
prompt string 2
$
```

The second command above changes the secondary prompt to secondary prompt: followed by a SPACE. A multiline echo command demonstrates the new prompt.

IFS.   You can always use a SPACE or TAB to separate fields on the command line. When you assign **IFS** (internal-field separator) the value of another character, you can also use this character to separate fields.

The following example demonstrates how setting **IFS** can affect interpretation of a command line:

```
$ cat a:b:c:d
cat: cannot open a:b:c:d
$ IFS=:
$ cat a:b:c:d
cat: cannot open a
cat: cannot open b
cat: cannot open c
cat: cannot open d
```

The first time cat is called, the shell interprets the string a:b:c:d as a single argument, and cat reports that it cannot open the file **a:b:c:d**. After **IFS** is set to : the shell interprets the same string as four separate arguments.

There are a variety of side effects of changing the **IFS** variable, so change it cautiously.

CDPATH.   The **CDPATH** variable affects the operation of the cd command. It takes on the value of a list of absolute pathnames (similar to the **PATH** variable) and is usually set in the **.profile** file with command lines such as the following:

```
$ CDPATH=:$HOME:$HOME/literature
$ export CDPATH
```

If **CDPATH** is not set, when you specify a simple filename as an argument to cd, cd always searches the working directory for a subdirectory with the same name as the argument. If the subdirectory does not exist, cd issues an error message. If **CDPATH** is set, cd searches for an appropriately named subdirectory in one of the directories in the **CDPATH** list. If it finds one, that directory becomes the working directory. Since users typically want cd to search the working directory first, **CDPATH** usually starts with a colon.

TZ.   The **TZ** variable describes what time zone your login session will operate in. It is usually set by the system administrator. The format for setting the **TZ** variable is shown below.

TZ=zzzX[ddd]

The **zzz** is the three-letter name of the local time zone, **X** is the number of hours that the local time zone differs from Greenwich Mean Time (GMT), and **ddd** is the three-letter name of the local daylight saving time zone.

The following command sets the **TZ** variable for California:

```
$ TZ=PST8PDT
$ export TZ
```

Running .profile with the . Command.   After you edit your **.profile** file to change the values of keyword shell variables, you do not have to wait until the next time you log in to put the changes into effect. You can run **.profile** with the . (dot) command. Using the . command is similar to running a shell script, except that the . command runs the script as part of the current process. Consequently, when you use . to run a script from your login shell, changes you make to the variables from within the script affect the login shell. If you ran **.profile** as a regular shell script, the new variables would be in effect only in the subshell running the script.

The **.profile** file below sets the **TERM, PATH, PS1,** and **CDPATH** variables as well as setting the line kill character to CONTROL-U. The . command puts the new values into effect.

```
$ cat .profile
TERM=vt100
PATH=/usr/bin:/usr/sbin:/home/alex/bin:
PS1="alex:  "
CDPATH=:$HOME
export TERM PATH PS1 CDPATH
stty kill '^u'
$ . .profile
alex:
```

Readonly Shell Variables

Name of the Calling Program.   The shell stores in the variable $0 the name of the command that you use to call a program. It is variable number zero because it appears before the first argument on the command line.

```
$ cat abc
echo The name of the command used
echo to execute this shell script was $0
$ abc
The name of the command used
to execute this shell script was abc
```

This shell script uses echo to verify the name of the script you are executing. The **abc** file must be executable (use chmod), and your **PATH** must be set up to search the working directory in order for this example to work.

Command Line Arguments.   The shell stores the first nine command line arguments in the variables **$1, $2, ..., $9** (often called *positional parameters*). Although the other arguments are not thrown away, they must be promoted to one of the first nine positions before you can access them using one of these variables (see the **shift** command on page 247). These variables appear in this, the "Readonly Shell Variables" section, because you cannot assign them values using an equal sign. You can, however, use the **set** command (page 247) to assign new values to them.

```
$ cat display_5args
echo The first five command line
echo arguments are $1 $2 $3 $4 $5
$ display_5args jenny alex helen
The first five command line
arguments are jenny alex helen
```

The **display_5args** script displays the first five command line arguments. The variables representing arguments that were not present on the command line, **$4** and **$5**, have a null value.

The variable **$*** represents all the command line arguments (not just the first nine), as the **display_all** program demonstrates:

```
$ cat display_all
echo $*
$ display_all a b c d e f g h i j k l m n o p
a b c d e f g h i j k l m n o p
```

The **$@** variable is the same as **$*** except when they are enclosed in double quotation marks. Using **"$*"** puts a single pair of double quotation marks around the entire set of arguments; using **"$@"** quotes the arguments individually. This makes **$@** more useful than **$*** in shell scripts, as the **whos** script on page 264 demonstrates.

The variable **$#** contains the number of arguments on the command line. This string variable represents a decimal number. You can use the **expr** utility to perform computations involving this number, and you can use **test** to perform logical tests on it. There is more information on **expr** and **test** in the "Flow Control Commands" section of this chapter and in Part II.

```
$ cat num_args
echo "This shell script was called
with $# arguments."
$ num_args helen alex jenny
This shell script was called
with 3 arguments.
```

In the preceding example, the **echo** command echoes a quoted string that spans two lines. Because the newline is quoted, the shell passes the entire string that is between the quotation marks—including the newline—to echo as an argument.

The shift Command.

The shift command promotes each of the command line arguments. The second argument (which was represented by **$2**) becomes the first (now represented by **$1**), the third becomes the second, the fourth becomes the third, and so forth.

Using the command line argument variables (**$1-$9**), you can access only the first nine command line arguments from a shell script. The shift command gives you access to the tenth command line argument by making it the ninth, and it makes the first unavailable. Successive shift commands make additional arguments available. There is, however, no ''unshift'' command to bring back arguments that are no longer available.

```
$ cat demo_shift
echo "arg1= $1     arg2= $2     arg3= $3"
shift
echo "arg1= $1     arg2= $2     arg3= $3"
shift
echo "arg1= $1     arg2= $2     arg3= $3"
shift
echo "arg1= $1     arg2= $2     arg3= $3"
shift
$ demo_shift alice helen jenny
arg1= alice     arg2= helen     arg3= jenny
arg1= helen     arg2= jenny     arg3=
arg1= jenny     arg2=     arg3=
arg1=     arg2=     arg3=
demo_shift: cannot shift
```

This example calls the **demo_shift** program with three arguments. Double quotation marks were used around the arguments to echo to preserve the spacing of the output display. The program displays the arguments and shifts them repeatedly, until there are no more arguments to shift. The shell displays an error message when the script executes shift after it has run out of variables.

The set Command.

When you call set with one or more arguments, it sets the values of the command line argument variables (**$1-$9**) to its arguments. The following script uses set to set the first three command line argument variables:

```
$ cat set_it
set this is it
echo $3 $2 $1
$ set_it
it is this
```

You can use command substitution (see page 241) with **set** to cause it to use the standard output of another command as its arguments.

The script below shows how to use the **date** utility and the **set** command to provide the date in a useful format. The first command shows the output from **date**. Then **cat** displays the **dateset** script. The first command in the script uses backquotes to set the command line argument variables to the output of **date**. Subsequent commands display the values of variables **$1, $2, $3,** and **$4**. The final command displays the date in a format that you can use in a letter or report. You can also use the **format** argument to **date** to modify the format of its output. Refer to **date** in Part II.

```
$ date
Fri Jun 15 23:04:09 PDT 1990
$ cat dateset
set `date`
echo $*
echo
echo "Argument 1: $1"
echo "Argument 2: $2"
echo "Argument 3: $3"
echo "Argument 4: $4"
echo
echo $2 $3, $6
$ dateset
Fri Jun 15 23:04:13 PDT 1990

Argument 1: Fri
Argument 2: Jun
Argument 3: 15
Argument 4: 23:04:13

Jun 15, 1990
```

Without any arguments, **set** displays a list of the variables that are set. Note that **set** displays user-created variables (e.g., **person=alex**) as well as shell keyword variables.

```
$ set
HOME=/home/alex
IFS=

LOGNAME=alex
MAIL=/var/mail/alex
PATH=/usr/bin:/usr/sbin:/home/alex/bin:
PS1=$
PS2=>
SHELL=/usr/bin/sh
TERM=vt100
person=alex
```

PID Numbers.   The shell stores the PID number of the process that is executing it in the $$ variable. In the following interaction, echo displays the value of this variable, and the ps utility confirms its value. Both commands show that the shell has a PID of 14137.

```
$ echo $$
14137
$ ps
    PID   TTY        TIME  COMMAND
  14137  tty14      0:06  sh
  14565  tty14      0:02  ps
```

Because the echo command is built into the Bourne Shell on System V, the echo command above does not cause the shell to create another process. However, the results are the same whether echo is a built-in command or not, because the shell substitutes the value of $$ *before* it forks a new process to run a command. The next example shows that the shell substitutes the value of $$ *before* it forks a new process. The shell substitutes the value of $$ and passes that value to cp as a prefix for a new filename. This technique is useful for creating unique filenames when the meaningfulness of the names does not matter—it is often used in shell scripts for creating names of temporary files.

```
$ echo $$
14137
$ cp memo $$.memo
$ ls
14137.memo  memo
```

The example below demonstrates that the shell creates a new shell process when it runs a shell script. The example uses the **id2** script, which displays the PID of the process running the subshell that runs **id2**.

```
$ cat id2
echo $0 PID = $$
$ echo $$
14137
$ id2
id2 PID = 15253
$ echo $$
14137
```

The first echo in the example displays the PID of the login shell. Then **id2** displays its name ($0) and the PID of the subshell. Finally, the last echo shows that the current process is the login shell again.

The $! variable has the value of the PID number of the last process that you ran in the background. The following example executes ps as a background task and then uses echo to display the value of $!:

```
$ ps &
15309
$     PID  TTY       TIME COMMAND
  14137  tty14    0:07 sh
  15309  tty14    0:02 ps
echo $!
15309
$
```

Although the prompt in this example appears to be out of sequence, it is not. The shell displays a prompt after displaying the PID number of a background process. The output from the background process follows the prompt. The **echo** command is given in response to the prompt, although the command does not appear to follow the prompt immediately. You can press RETURN if you want to see another prompt before issuing a command.

Exit Status.   When a process stops executing for any reason, it returns an *exit status* to its parent process. The exit status is also referred to as a *condition code* or *return code*. The shell stores the exit status of the last command in the $? variable.

By convention, a nonzero exit status represents a false value and means that the command failed. A zero is true and means that the command was successful.

You can specify the exit status that a shell script will return by using an exit command, followed by a number, to terminate the script. If you do not use exit with a number to terminate a script, the exit status of the script will be the exit status of the last command the script ran. The following example shows that the number specifies the exit status:

```
$ cat es
echo This program returns an exit
echo status of 7.
exit 7
$ es
This program returns an exit
status of 7.
$ echo $?
7
$ echo $?
0
```

The **es** shell script displays a message and then terminates execution with an exit command that returns an exit status of 7. Then echo displays the value of the exit status of **es**. The second echo displays the value of the exit status of the first echo. The value is zero because the first echo was successful.

FLOW CONTROL COMMANDS

The *flow control commands* alter the order of execution of commands within a shell script. They include control structures—simple two-way branch If statements, multiple branch Case statements, and For, While, and Until statements. In addition, the shell provides Here documents, which redirect the standard input to a command in a script from within the script itself; the **exec** command, which transfers control to another command or script; and the **trap** command, which specifies commands to be executed when a script terminates prematurely.

If Then

The format of the If Then control structure follows. The **bold** words in the format description are the items you supply to cause the structure to have the desired effect. The other words are the keywords the shell uses to identify the control structure.

> if **test-command**
>   then
>   **commands**
> fi

As seen in Figure 8-1, the If statement tests the status that the **test-command** returns and transfers control based on this status. When you spell *if* backward, it's *fi;* the Fi statement marks the end of the If structure.

The following script prompts you and reads in two words. Then it uses an If structure to evaluate the result returned by the **test** command when it compares the two words. The **test** command returns a status of *true,* if the two words are the same, and *false,* if they are not. Double quotation marks are used around $word1 and $word2 so that **test** will work properly if the user enters a string that contains a SPACE or another special character.

```
$ cat if1
echo "word 1: \c"
read word1
echo "word 2: \c"
read word2
```

```
if  test  " $word1 "  =  " $word2 "
     then
          echo Match
fi
echo End of program.
$ if1
word1: peach
word2: peach
Match
End of program.
```

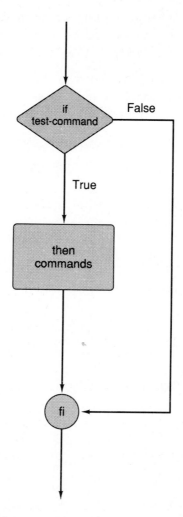

FIGURE 8-1   If Then Flowchart

The If statement executes the statements immediately following it if *its* argument (that is, everything following the keyword If up to a NEWLINE or semicolon) returns a *true* exit status. The test utility returns a *true* status if its first and third arguments have the relationship specified by its second argument. If this command returns a *true* status (= 0), the shell executes the commands between the Then and Fi statements. If the command returns a *false* status (not = 0), the shell passes control to the statement after Fi without executing the statements between Then and Fi. The effect of this If statement is to display Match if the two words match. It always displays End of program.

The next program uses an If structure at the beginning of a script to check that the user supplied at least one argument on the command line. The effect of this If statement is to display a message and exit from the script if the user did not supply an argument.

```
$ cat chkargs
if test $# = 0
    then
            echo You must supply at least one argument.
            exit
fi
echo Program running.
$ chkargs
You must supply at least one argument.
$ chkargs abc
Program running.
```

A test like the one in **chkargs** is a key component of any script that requires arguments. To prevent the user from receiving meaningless or confusing information from the script, it should always check to see whether the user has supplied the appropriate arguments. Sometimes the script will simply test to see whether arguments exist (as in **chkargs**), whereas other scripts will need to test for a specific number of arguments or specific kinds of arguments (readable files, for example). Refer to test in Part II for more information on the kinds of tests the test command will perform.

The following example is another version of **chkargs** that checks for arguments in a way that is more traditional for UNIX shell scripts. First, the example uses the square bracket ([]) synonym for test. Rather than using the word test in your scripts, you can surround the arguments to test with square brackets, as shown. The square brackets must be surrounded by white space (that is, SPACES or TABS).

```
$ cat chkargs
if [ $# = 0 ]
   then
        echo Usage: chkargs argument... 1>&2
        exit 1
fi
echo Program running.
exit 0
$ chkargs
Usage: chkargs arguments
$ chkargs abc
Program running.
```

Second, the error message is a *usage message* that uses a standard notation to specify the arguments the script takes. Usage messages similar to the one in **chkargs** are provided by many UNIX utilities. When you call a command with the wrong number or kinds of arguments, you will often see a usage message. (Try giving the **cp** command without any arguments.) The notation is similar to the notation used in the ''Format'' descriptions for the utilities in Part II. The **...** following **argument** indicates that there may be more than one instance of **argument**.

Third, the usage message is redirected to the standard error.

Fourth, after presenting the usage message, **chkargs** exits with an exit status of 1, indicating that an error occurred. The **exit** command at the end of the script causes **chkargs** to exit with a 0 exit status.

If Then Else

The introduction of the Else statement turns the If structure into the two-way branch shown in Figure 8-2. The format of the If Then Else control structure follows:

> if **test-command**
>   then
>   **commands**
>   else
>   **commands**
> fi

If the **test-command** returns a *true* status, the If structure executes the commands between the Then and Else statements and then diverts control to Fi, and the shell continues with the next command in the script. If the **test-command** returns a *false* status, it executes the commands following the Else statement.

The following script builds on the **chkargs** script. When you call **out** with arguments that are names of files, it displays the files on the terminal. If the first argument is a **–v**, **out** uses pg to display the files. (You may need to use more rather than pg if you try running this script.)

After determining that it was called with at least one argument, **out** tests its first argument to see if it is not **–v**. If the test is true (if the first argument is not **–v**), the script uses cat to display the files. If the test is false (if the first argument is **–v**), **out** shifts the arguments to get rid of the **–v** and displays the files using pg.

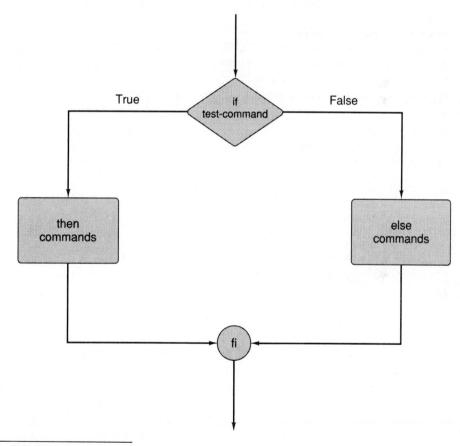

FIGURE 8-2   If Then Else Flowchart

```
$ cat out
if [ $# = 0 ]
    then
          echo "Usage: out [-v] filenames" 1>&2
          exit 1
fi
if [ "$1" != "-v" ]
    then
          cat -- "$@"
    else
          shift
          pg "$@"
fi
```

OPTIONAL

In **out**, the -- argument to **cat** tells the **cat** utility that no more options follow on the command line. This argument prevents **cat** from interpreting a filename that begins with - as an option. Although many UNIX commands recognize the -- option, the **pg** utility does not, so there is no easy way to prevent **pg** from interpreting a filename argument as an option.

If Then Elif

The format of the If Then Elif control structure follows:

> if **test-command**
>   then
>   **commands**
>   elif **test-command**
>   then
>   **commands**
>   else
>   **commands**
> fi

The Elif statement combines the Else and If statements and allows you to construct a nested set of If Then Else structures (Figure 8-3).

The example below shows an If Then Elif control structure. This shell script compares three words. In the first If statement it uses an AND operator (-a) as an argument to **test**. The **test** command returns a *true* status only if the first and the second logical comparisons are true (that is, if **word1** matches **word2**, and **word2** matches **word3**). If **test** returns a *true* status, the program executes the command following the next Then statement and passes control to Fi, and the script terminates.

If the three words are not the same, the structure passes control to the first Elif, which begins a series of tests to see whether any pair of words is the same. As the nesting continues, if any one of the If statements is satisfied, the structure passes control to the next Then statement and subsequently to the statement after Fi. Each time an Elif statement is not satisfied, the structure passes control to the next Elif statement.

```
$ cat if3
echo "word 1: \c"
read word1
echo "word 2: \c"
read word2
echo "word 3: \c"
read word3
if [ "$word1" = "$word2" -a "$word2" = "$word3" ]
    then
        echo "Match: words 1, 2, & 3"
    elif [ "$word1" = "$word2" ]
        then
            echo "Match: words 1 & 2"
    elif [ "$word1" = "$word3" ]
        then
            echo "Match: words 1 & 3"
    elif [ "$word2" = "$word3" ]
        then
            echo "Match: words 2 & 3"
    else
        echo No match
fi
```

The **if3** script uses double quotation marks around the arguments to echo that contain **&** to prevent the shell from interpreting **&** as a special character.

===

OPTIONAL

The following script, **links,** demonstrates the If Then and If Then Elif control structures. The **links** script finds links to a file specified as the first argument to **links.** When you run **links,** you can specify a second argument, which is the directory in which **links** will begin searching for links. The **links** script searches that directory and all of its subdirectories. If you do not specify a directory on the command line, **links** begins its search at the working directory.

OPTIONAL (Continued)

```
$ cat links
:
# identify links to a file
# Usage: links file [directory]

if [ $# = 0 ]
    then
        echo "Usage: links file [directory]"   1>&2
        exit 1
fi
if [ -d "$1" ]
    then
        echo "Usage: links file [directory]" 1>&2
        exit 1
    else
        file="$1"
fi
if [ $# = 1 ]
    then
        directory="."
    elif [ -d "$2" ]
        then
            directory="$2"
    else
        echo "Usage: links file [directory]" 1>&2
        exit 1
fi

# Check for existence of file:
ls "$file" 2> /dev/null | grep "$file" > /dev/null
if [ $? != 0 ]
    then
        echo "links: $file not found" 1>&2
        exit 1
fi

# Check link count on file:
set -- `ls -l "$file"`
linkcnt=$2
if [ $linkcnt = 1 ]
    then
        echo "links: no other links to $file" 1>&2
        exit 0
fi

# Get the inode of the given file:
set `ls -i "$file"`
inode=$1

# Find and print the files with that inode number:
echo "links: using find to search for links..." 1>&2
find "$directory" -inum $inode -print
```

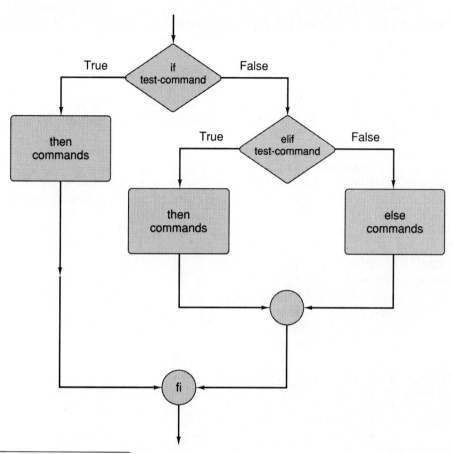

FIGURE 8-3   If Then Elif Flowchart

In the example below, Alex uses **links** while he is in his home directory to search for links to a file called **letter** in the working directory. The **links** script reports that **/home/alex/letter** and **/home/jenny/draft** are links to the same file.

```
$ links letter /home
links: using find to search for links...
/home/alex/letter
/home/jenny/draft
```

In addition to the If Then Elif control structure, **links** introduces other features that are commonly used by experienced shell programmers. The following discussion describes **links** section by section.

The second and third lines of **links** are comments—the shell ignores the text that follows pound signs up to the next NEWLINE character. The first two comments in **links** briefly identify what the file does and how to use it. The square brackets around the **directory** argument in the usage statement indicate that the **directory** argument is optional. Because a pound sign as the first character of a script has a special status on some systems (see page 233), the comments do not begin on the first line. The first line contains only a colon (:), which is the null command. (All it does is return a 0 exit status.) In this script, the colon is just a place holder—it occupies the first character position so that a pound sign does not occur there.

The first If statement in **links** tests to see whether **links** was called with any arguments. If **links** was not called with any arguments, **links** sends a usage message to the standard error and exits with a status of 1. The double quotation marks around the usage message prevent the shell from interpreting the square brackets as special characters.

The second If statement verifies that **$1** is not a directory. If it is a directory, **links** presents a usage message and exits. If it is not a directory, **links** saves the value of **$1** in the **file** variable because later in the script the **set** command resets the command line arguments. If the value of **$1** were not saved before the **set** command, it would be lost.

The next section of **links** is an If Then Elif statement. The first **test-command** determines whether the user specified a single argument on the command line. If the **test-command** returns 0 (true), the user-created variable named **directory** is assigned the value of the working directory (.). If the **test-command** returns a false value, the Elif statement is executed. The Elif statement tests to see whether the second argument is a directory (the **–d** argument to **test** returns a *true* value if the file exists and is a directory). If it is a directory, the **directory** variable is set equal to the second command line argument, **$2**. If **$2** is not a directory, **links** displays a usage message to the standard error and exits with a status of 1.

The next section of **links** verifies that **$file** is the name of an existing file. This is an important section of the script because it would be pointless for **links** to spend time looking for links to a nonexistent file. Unfortunately, the **test** command on System V does not provide a simple way to determine that a file exists without also determining whether it has other characteristics that do not matter to **links**. Consequently, the **links** script uses a roundabout technique for verifying the existence of the file. The **links** script uses **ls** to list the name of **$file** and sends the standard output through a pipe to the **grep** command, which searches for the string **$file**. If **$file** exists, the standard output of **ls** contains the name of the file. If **$file** does not exist, **ls** sends a message to its standard error and nothing to its standard output. The standard error output of **ls** and the standard output of **grep** are redirected to **/dev/null**. The **/dev/null** file is a special file, the "bit bucket," which is guaranteed to be empty. Users commonly redirect unwanted output to **/dev/null**, effectively throwing the output away. In this case, the output of **grep** is redirected there because **links** only uses the exit status of **grep**. The exit status of **grep** is 0 if **grep** found the string it was searching for, and 1 otherwise. If **grep** returns a nonzero exit status, an error message is displayed. This message uses the standard format for error messages from shell scripts—the script name followed by a colon and the message.

Next **links** uses **set** and **ls –l** to check the number of links **$file** has. The **set** command uses command substitution to set the readonly shell variables **$1** to **$9** to the output of **ls –l**. In the output of **ls –l**, the second field is the link count, so the user-created variable **linkcnt** is set equal to **$2**. The **––** is used with the **set** command to prevent it from interpreting as an option the first argument **ls –l** produces (the first argument is the access permissions for the file, and it is likely to begin with –). The If statement checks whether **$linkcnt** is equal to 1; if it is, **links** presents a message and exits. Although this message is not, strictly speaking, an error message, it is redirected to the standard error. The way **links** has been written, all informational messages are sent to the standard error. Only the final product of **links**, the pathnames of links to the specified file, is sent to the standard output. Because the standard output contains only the pathnames of links, users can easily send it through a pipe to a filter.

If the link count is greater than one, **links** goes on to identify the inode for **$file**. As Chapter 4 explained (page 87), comparing the inodes associated with filenames is a good way to determine whether the filenames are links to the same file. The **links** script uses **set** again to set the readonly shell variables to the output of **ls –i**. The first argument to **set** will be the inode number for the file, so the user-created variable named **inode** is set to the value of **$1**.

Finally, **links** uses the **find** utility to search for filenames having inodes that match **$inode**. The **find** utility searches for files that meet the criteria specified by its arguments. The **find** utility begins its search with the directory specified by its first argument (**$directory**, in this case), and it searches all subdirectories. The other arguments to **find** specify that files having inodes matching **$inode** should be printed on the standard output. Because files in different file systems may have the same inode number (yet they are not linked), **$directory** should be in the same file system as **$file** for accurate results. Refer to pages 82 and 384 for more information about file systems and links. Refer to Part II for more information about **find**.

The **echo** above the **find** command in **links**, which tells the user that **find** is running, is included because **find** is slow. Because **links** does not include a final exit statement, the exit status of **links** will be that of the last command it runs, **find**.

When you are writing a script like **links**, it is easy to make mistakes. While you are debugging it, you can use the shell's **–x** option, which causes the shell to echo each command it runs. This trace of a script's execution can give you a lot of information about where bugs are. To run a script with the **–x** option, use a command such as the following:

```
$ sh -x links
```

You can also set the shell's **-x** option by putting the following **set** command at the top of the script.

```
set -x
```

For In

The For In structure has the following format:

for **loop-index** in **argument-list**
do
    commands
done

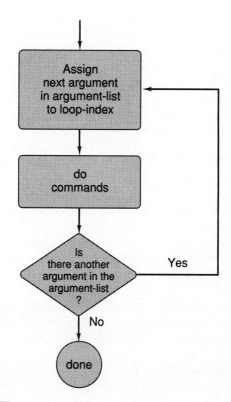

FIGURE 8-4   For In Flowchart

This structure (Figure 8-4) assigns the value of the first argument in the **argument-list** to the **loop-index** and executes the **commands** between the Do and Done statements. The Do and Done statements mark the beginning and end of the For loop.

After the structure passes control to the Done statement, it assigns the value of the second argument in the **argument-list** to the **loop-index** and repeats the **commands**. The structure repeats the **commands** between the Do and Done statements—once for each of the arguments in the **argument-list**. When the structure exhausts the **argument-list,** it passes control to the Done statement, and the shell continues with the next command in the script.

The For In structure shown below assigns apples to the user-created variable **fruit** and then displays the value of **fruit,** which is apples. Next, it assigns oranges to **fruit** and repeats the process. When it exhausts the argument list, the structure transfers control to the statement following Done, which displays a message.

```
$ cat fruit
for fruit in apples oranges pears bananas
do
      echo $fruit
done
echo Task complete.


$ fruit
apples
oranges
pears
bananas
Task complete.
```

For

The For structure has the following format:

    for **loop-index**
    do
        commands
    done

In the For structure, the **loop-index** automatically takes on the value of each of the command line parameters, one at a time. It performs a series of commands involving each parameter in turn.

The shell script below shows a For structure displaying each of the command line arguments. The first line of the shell script, for args, implies for args in "$@", where the shell expands "$@" into a quoted list of command line arguments. The balance of the script corresponds to the For In structure.

```
$ cat for_test
for args
do
      echo $args
done


$ for_test candy gum chocolate
candy
gum
chocolate
```

OPTIONAL

The script below, **whos**, demonstrates the usefulness of the implied "$@" in the For structure. You can give **whos** one or more **id**s for users as arguments (e.g., a user's name or login), and **whos** will display information about the users. The information **whos** displays is taken from the first and fifth fields in the **/etc/passwd** file. The first field always contains a user's login, and the fifth field typically contains the user's name. You can use a login as an argument to **whos** to identify the user's name or use a name as an argument in order to identify the login. The **whos** script is similar to the finger utility, although **whos** provides less information.

```
$ cat whos
:
# adapted from finger.sh by Lee Sailer
# UNIX/WORLD, III:11, p. 67, Fig. 2

if [ $# = 0 ]
    then
        echo "Usage: whos id..." 1>&2
        exit 1
fi

for i
do
    awk -F: '{print $1, $5}' /etc/passwd | grep -i "$i"
done
```

Following, **whos** identifies the user whose login is chas and the user whose name is Marilou Smith.

```
$ whos chas "Marilou Smith"
chas Charles Casey
msmith Marilou Smith
```

The **whos** script uses a For statement to loop through the command line arguments. The implied use of *"$@"* in the For loop has particular utility in this script because it causes the For loop to treat an argument containing a space as a single argument. For instance, in the example above, the user quoted **Marilou Smith**, which causes the shell to pass it to the script as a single argument. Then the implied *"$@"* in the For statement causes the shell to regenerate the quoted argument *"Marilou Smith"* so that it is again treated as a single argument.

For each command line argument, **whos** searches for the **id** in the **/etc/passwd** file. Inside the For loop, the **awk** utility extracts the first ($1) and fifth ($5) fields from the lines in **/etc/passwd** (which contain the user's login and information about the user, respectively). The $1 and $5 are arguments that the **awk** command sets and uses—they are included within single quotes and are not interpreted at all by the shell. (Do not confuse them with the readonly shell variables that correspond to the command line arguments.) The first and fifth fields are piped to the **grep** utility. The **grep** utility searches for $i, (which has taken on the value of a command line argument) in its input. The **–i** option causes **grep** to ignore case as it searches. It prints out each line in its input that contains the current argument.

Because the **whos** script gets its information from the **/etc/passwd** file, the information it displays will only be as informative as the information in **/etc/passwd**. For more information about **awk** and **grep**, refer to **awk** and **grep** in Part II. For more information about **/etc/passwd**, refer to Chapter 11.

While

The While structure (see Figure 8-5) has the following format:

> while **test-command**
> do
>   **commands**
> done

As long as the **test-command** returns a *true* exit status, the structure continues to execute the series of **commands** delimited by the Do and Done statements. Before each loop through the **commands**, the structure executes the **test-**

command. When the exit status of the **test-command** is *false,* the structure passes control to the Done statement, and the shell continues with the next command in the script.

The shell script shown below first initializes the variable **number** to the character value of zero—shell variables can take on only values of character strings. The **test** utility, represented by [and], then determines if the value of the variable **number** is less than 10. The **count** script calls **test,** using –lt to perform a *numerical* test. [You must use **–ne** (not equal), **–eq** (equal), **–gt** (greater than), **–ge** (greater than or equal), **–lt** (less than), or **–le** (less than or equal) for numerical comparisons, and = (equal) or != (not equal) for string comparisons.] The **test** utility has an exit status of *true* as long as **number** is less than 10. As long as **test** returns *true,* the structure executes the commands between the Do and Done statements.

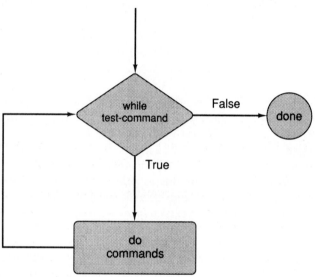

FIGURE 8-5   While Flowchart

The first command following Do displays the string represented by **number.** The next command uses the **expr** utility to increment the value of **number** by one. Here, **expr** converts its arguments to numbers, adds them, converts the result to characters, and echoes them to the standard output. The backquotes cause the command that they enclose to be replaced by the output of the command. This value is then assigned to the variable **number**. The first time through the loop, **number** has a value of zero, so expr converts the strings 0 and 1 to numbers, adds them, and converts the result back to a string (1). The shell then assigns this value to the **number** variable. The Done statement closes the loop and returns control to the While statement to start the loop over again. The final echo command causes **count** to send a NEWLINE to the standard output, so that the next prompt occurs in the leftmost column on the display (rather than immediately following 9).

```
$ cat count
number=0
while [ "$number" -lt 10 ]
do
    echo "$number\c"
    number=`expr $number + 1`
done
echo
$ count
0123456789
$
```

OPTIONAL

The next shell script, **spell_check**, shows another use of a While structure. You can use **spell_check** to find the incorrect spellings in a file. It uses the spell utility, which checks your file against a dictionary of correctly spelled words. The spell utility sends a list of the words that are not in its dictionary to the standard output. This script goes a step further, enabling you to identify a list of words that should be considered correct spellings and removing those words from the output of spell. This script is useful for removing words that you use frequently, such as names and technical terms, that are not in a standard dictionary.

The spell utility also provides an option that enables you to do what the **spell_check** script does.

The **spell_check** script requires two filename arguments: the first file contains your list of correctly spelled words, and the second file is the file that is to be checked. The first If statement verifies that the user specified two arguments, and the next two If statements verify that both arguments are readable files. (With the **−r** operator, test determines whether a file is readable, and the exclamation point negates the sense of the following operator.)

```
$ cat spell_check
:
# remove correct spellings from spell output

if [ $# != 2 ]
    then
        echo "Usage: spell_check file1 file2" 1>&2
        echo "file1: list of correct spellings" 1>&2
        echo "file2: file to be checked" 1>&2
        exit 1
fi

if [ ! -r "$1" ]
    then
        echo "spell_check: $1 is not readable" 1>&2
        exit 1
fi

if [ ! -r "$2" ]
    then
        echo "spell_check: $2 is not readable" 1>&2
        exit 1
fi

spell "$2" |
while read line
do
    grep "^$line\$" "$1" > /dev/null
    if [ $? != 0 ]
        then
            echo $line
    fi
done
```

The **spell_check** script sends the output from spell through a pipe to the standard input of the While command, and the While structure reads one line at a time from its standard input. The **test-command** (that is, **read line**) returns a *true* exit status as long as it receives a line from the standard input. Inside the While loop, grep determines whether the line that was read is in the list of correctly spelled words. The pattern grep searches for (the value of the **line** variable) is preceded and followed by special characters that specify the beginning and end of a line (^ and $, respectively). These special characters are used so that grep will find a match only if the $line variable matches an entire line in the file of correctly spelled words. (Otherwise, grep would match a string such as **tomo** in the output of spell if the file of correctly spelled words contained the word **tomorrow**.) The output of grep is redirected to **/dev/null**, because it is not needed (output that is redirected to **/dev/null** disappears). Then the If statement checks the exit status of grep, which is 0 only if a matching line was found. If the exit status is *not* 0, the word was *not* in the file of correctly spelled words, and echo displays it on the standard output. Once the While structure detects the End Of File, the **test-command** returns a *false* exit status, control is passed out of the While structure, and the script terminates.

Before you use **spell_check**, you should create a file of correct spellings containing words that you use frequently but that are not in a standard dictionary. For example, if you work for a company called **Blankenship and Klimowski, Attorneys,** you would put **Blankenship** and **Klimowski** into the file. The following example shows how **spell_check** checks the spelling in a file called **memo** and removes **Blankenship** and **Klimowski** from the output list of incorrectly spelled words.

```
$ spell memo
Blankenship
Klimowski
targat
hte
$ cat word_list
Blankenship
Klimowski
$ spell_check word_list memo
targat
hte
```

Refer to Part II for more information about spell.

Until

The Until and While structures are very similar. They differ only in the sense of the test at the top of the loop. Figure 8-6 shows that Until continues to loop *until* the **test-command** returns a *true* exit status. The While structure loops *while* the **test-command** continues to return a *true* or nonerror condition. The Until structure is shown below.

```
until test-command
do
    commands
done
```

The following script demonstrates an Until structure that includes a read command. When the user enters the correct string of characters, the **test-command** is satisfied, and the structure passes control out of the loop.

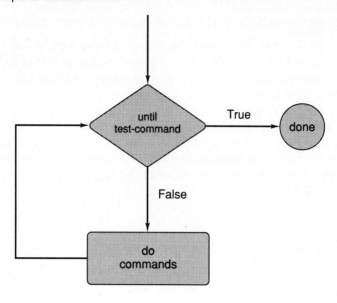

FIGURE 8-6   Until Flowchart

```
$ cat until1
secretname=jenny
name=noname
echo Try to guess the secret name!
echo
until [ "$name" = "$secretname" ]
do
      echo "Your guess: \c"
      read name
done
echo Very good.
$ until1
Try to guess the secret name!

Your guess: helen
Your guess: barbara
Your guess: jenny
Very good.
```

OPTIONAL

The **locktty** script below is similar to the lock command on Berkeley UNIX. It prompts the user for a key (or password), and then it uses an Until control structure to ''lock'' the terminal. The Until statement causes the system to ignore any characters typed at the keyboard until the user types in the original key, which unlocks the terminal. The **locktty** script can keep people from using your

---

OPTIONAL (Continued)

terminal while you are away from it for short periods of time. It saves you from
having to log out if you are concerned about other users using your login.

```
$ cat locktty
:
# adapted from lock.sh by Howard G. Port and
# Evelyn Siwakowsky
# UNIX/WORLD, III:4, p. 74, Fig. 3

trap '' 1 2 3 24
stty -echo
echo "Key: \c"
read key_1
echo
echo "Again: \c"
read key_2
echo
key_3=
if [ "$key_1" = "$key_2" ]
    then
            tput clear
            until [ "$key_3" = "$key_2" ]
            do
                    read key_3
            done
      else
            echo "locktty: keys do not match" 1>&2
fi
stty echo
```

The **trap** command at the beginning of the **locktty** script stops a user from
being able to terminate the script by sending it a signal (e.g., by pressing the interrupt key, which is usually DEL or CONTROL-C). Trapping signal 24 means that,
under System V Release 4, no one can use CONTROL-Z (job control, a stop from a
tty) to defeat the lock. The **stty –echo** command causes the terminal not to echo
characters typed at the keyboard to the screen. This prevents the keys (or passwords) the user types in from appearing on the screen. After turning off echoing,
the script prompts the user for a key, reads the key into the user-created variable
key_1, and then prompts the user to enter the same key again and saves it in the
user-created variable **key_2.** The statement **key_3=** creates a variable with a null
value. If **key_1** and **key_2** match, **locktty** clears the screen (with the **tput** command) and starts an Until loop. The Until loop keeps attempting to read from the
terminal and assigning the input to the **key_3** variable. Once the user types in a
string that matches one of the original keys (**key_2**), the Until loop terminates,
and echoing is turned back on.

For more information about **stty,** refer to **stty** in Part II. The **trap** command
is described on page 284.

The Break and Continue Commands

You can interrupt a For, While, or Until loop with a Break or Continue command. Break transfers control to the statement after the Done statement, terminating execution of the loop. Continue transfers control to the Done statement, which continues execution of the loop.

Case

The Case structure is shown below.

```
case test-string in
    pattern-1)
        commands-1
        ;;
    pattern-2)
        commands-2
        ;;
    pattern-3)
        commands-3
        ;;
        .

        .

esac
```

Figure 8-7 shows that the Case structure provides a multiple branch decision mechanism. The path that the structure chooses depends on a match between the **test-string** and one of the **patterns**.

The following Case structure uses the value of the character that the user enters as the test string. This value is represented by **letter**. If the test string has a value of A, the structure executes the command following A). If the test string has a value of B or C, the structure executes the appropriate command. The asterisk indicates *any string of characters* and serves as a catchall, in case there is no match. The second sample execution of **case1** shows the user entering a lowercase b. Because b does not match the uppercase B in the Case statement, the program tells you there is no match.

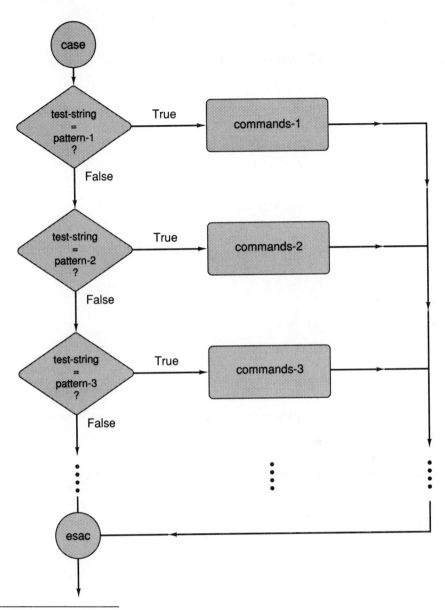

FIGURE 8-7   Case Flowchart

```
$ cat case1
echo "Enter A, B, or C: \c"
read letter
case "$letter" in
    A)
          echo You entered A
          ;;
    B)
          echo You entered B
          ;;
    C)
          echo You entered C
          ;;
     *)
          echo You did not enter A, B, or C
          ;;
esac


$ case1
Enter A, B, or C: B
You entered B
$ case1
Enter A, B, or C: b
You did not enter A, B, or C
```

The pattern in the Case structure is analogous to that of an ambiguous file reference. You can use the following special characters and strings:

* An asterisk matches any string of characters. You can use it for the default case.

? A question mark matches any single character.

[...] Square brackets define a character class. Any characters enclosed within square brackets are tried, one at a time, in an attempt to match a single character. A hyphen between two characters specifies a range of characters.

| A vertical bar separates alternate choices that will satisfy a particular branch of the Case structure.

The next program is a variation of the previous one. This script accepts uppercase and lowercase letters.

```
$ cat case2
echo "Enter A, B, or C: \c"
read letter
case "$letter" in
    a|A)
        echo You entered A
        ;;
    b|B)
        echo You entered B
        ;;
    c|C)
        echo You entered C
        ;;
    *)
        echo You did not enter A, B, or C
        ;;
esac
$ case2
Enter A, B, or C: b
You entered B
```

The following example shows how the Case structure can be used to create a menu. The menu in the script **command_menu** uses the echo command to present menu items and prompt the user for a selection. The Case structure executes the appropriate utility, depending on the user's selection.

```
$ cat command_menu
:
# menu interface to simple commands

echo "\n        COMMAND MENU\n"
echo "   a.  Current date and time"
echo "   b.  Users currently logged in"
echo "   c.  Name of the working directory"
echo "   d.  Contents of the working directory\n"
echo "Enter a, b, c, or d:   \c"
read answer
echo
```

OPTIONAL (Continued)

```
case " $answer " in
    a)
            date
            ;;
    b)
            who
            ;;
    c)
            pwd
            ;;
    d)
            ls  -C
            ;;
    *)
            echo "Your selection, $answer, is not available."
            ;;
esac
echo
$ command_menu
```

```
        COMMAND MENU

    a.  Current date and time
    b.  Users currently logged in
    c.  Name of the working directory
    d.  Contents of the working directory

Enter a, b, c, or d: a

Fri Jun 15 14:11:57 PDT 1990
```

The Case control structure is also frequently used in scripts for taking different actions, depending on how many command line arguments the script was called with. The script below, **safedit**, uses a Case structure that branches based on the number of command line arguments ($#). The **safedit** script saves a backup copy of a file you are editing with **vi**.

```
$ cat safedit
:
# adapted from safedit.sh by Evan Kaminer
# UNIX/WORLD, IV:11, p. 129, Listing 2

PATH=/usr/bin:/usr/sbin
script=`basename $0`
```

OPTIONAL (Continued)

```
case $# in
    0)
        vi
        exit 0
        ;;
    1)
        if [ ! -f "$1" ]
            then
                vi "$1"
                exit 0
        fi
        if [ ! -r "$1" -o ! -w "$1" ]
            then
                echo "$script: check permissions" \
" on $1" 1>&2
                exit 1
            else
                editfile=$1
        fi
        if [ ! -w "." ]
            then
                echo "$script: backup cannot be" \
" created in the working directory" 1>&2
                exit 1
        fi
        ;;
    *)
        echo "Usage: $script [file-to-edit]" 1>&2
        exit 1
        ;;
esac
tempfile=/tmp/$$.$script
cp $editfile $tempfile
if vi $editfile
    then
        mv $tempfile bak.`basename $editfile`
        echo "$script: backup file created"
    else
        mv $tempfile editerr
        echo "$script: edit error--copy of original" \
" file is in editerr" 1>&2
fi
```

If the user calls **safedit** without any arguments, the Case structure executes its first branch and calls vi without a filename argument. Because an existing file is not being edited, **safedit** does not create a backup file. (See the **:w** command on page 143 for an explanation of how to exit from vi when you have called it without a filename.) If the user calls **safedit** with one argument, the commands in the second branch of the Case structure are run, and **safedit** verifies that **$1** is the name of a file for which the user has read and write permission or that the file specified by **$1** does not yet exist. The **safedit** script also verifies that the user has write permission for the working directory. If the user calls **safedit** with more than one argument, the third branch of the Case structure presents a usage message and exits with a status of 1.

In addition to the use of a Case structure for branching based on the number of command line arguments, the **safedit** script introduces several other features that are commonly used in shell scripts. First, at the beginning of the script the **PATH** variable is set to search **/usr/bin** and **/usr/sbin**. This ensures that the commands executed by the script will be the standard utilities (which are kept in **/usr/bin** and **/usr/sbin**). By setting **PATH** inside a script, you can avoid the problems that might occur if users have set up **PATH** to search their own directories first and they have scripts or programs with the same names as utilities the script uses.

NEW TO UNIX SYSTEM V Release 4

If it is installed on your system, the **/usr/ucb** directory contains commands from the BSD or XENIX compatibility package. These packages include commands that were not merged into the standard set of UNIX System V Release 4 utilities. A command in this directory with the same name as a standard UNIX command (e.g., echo) usually has some different options or features. If you prefer to use the commands provided in a compatibility package, you should set the **PATH** variable to search **/usr/ucb** first.

Second, the following line creates a variable called **script** and assigns the simple filename of the script to it.

```
script=`basename $0`
```

The basename command sends the simple filename component of its argument to the standard output, which is assigned to the variable called **script** using command substitution. If Alex calls the script with any one of the following commands, the output of basename will always be the simple filename **safedit**:

```
$ /home/alex/bin/safedit memo

$ ./safedit memo

$ safedit memo
```

After the **script** variable is set to the simple filename of the script, the **script** variable is used in place of the filename in usage and error messages. By using a variable that is derived from the command that invoked the script rather than a filename that has been typed directly into the script, you can create links to the script or rename it, and the usage and error messages will still provide accurate information.

A third significant feature of **safedit** is the use of the **$$** variable in a temporary filename. The statement below the Esac statement creates and assigns a value to the **tempfile** variable. This variable contains the name of a temporary file that is stored in the **/tmp** directory (as are many temporary files). The temporary filename begins with the PID of the current shell and ends with the name of the script. The PID is used because it ensures that the filename will be unique, and **safedit** will not attempt to overwrite an existing file (as might happen if two people were using **safedit** at the same time and not using unique filenames). The name of the script is appended so that, should the file be left in **/tmp** for some reason, you or the system administrator will be able to figure out where it came from. The PID is used in front of **$script** in the filename, rather than after it, because of the 14-character limit on filenames on some file systems on System V. Since the PID is what ensures the uniqueness of the filename, it is placed first so that it will not be truncated. (If the **$script** component is truncated, the filename will still be unique.) For the same reason, when a backup file is created inside the If control structure a few lines down in the script, the filename is composed of the string **bak.** followed by the name of the file being edited. If **bak** were used as a suffix rather than a prefix and the original filename were 14 characters, the **.bak** might be lost, and the original file would be overwritten. The basename command extracts the simple filename of **$editfile** before it is prefixed with **bak.**.

Fourth, **safedit** uses an unusual **test-command** in the If structure, **vi $editfile**. The **test-command** calls vi to edit **$editfile**. When the user finishes editing the file and exits from vi, vi returns an exit code that is the basis for branching by the If control structure. If the editing session completed successfully, vi returns a 0, and the statements following the Then statement are executed. If vi does not terminate normally (as would occur if the user used a kill command from another terminal to kill the vi process), vi returns a nonzero exit status, and the statements following Else are executed.

The Here Document

A Here document allows you to redirect input to a shell script from within the shell script itself. It is called a Here document because it is *here*, immediately accessible in the shell script, instead of *there*, in another file.

The following script, **birthday**, contains a Here document. The two *less than* symbols on the first line indicate to the shell that a Here document follows. One or more characters that delimit the Here document follow the *less than* symbols—this example uses plus signs. Whereas the first delimiter can occur adjacent to the *less than* symbols, the second delimiter must occur on a line by itself. The shell sends everything between the two delimiters to the process as its standard input. In the following example, it is as though you had redirected the standard input to grep from a file, except that the file is embedded in the shell script. Just as the shell does not treat special characters that occur in the standard input of a shell script as special, so also the special characters that occur between the delimiters in a Here document are not considered special.

```
$ cat birthday
grep -i "$1" <<+
Alex      June 22
Barbara   February 3
Darlene   May 8
Helen     March 13
Jenny     January 23
Nancy     June 26
+
$ birthday Jenny
Jenny     January 23
$ birthday June
Alex      June 22
Nancy     June 26
```

When you run **birthday**, it lists all the lines in the Here document that contain the argument you called it with. In the preceding example, the first time **birthday** is run, it displays Jenny's birthday because it is called with an argument of **Jenny**. The second run displays all the birthdays in June.

===
OPTIONAL

The next script, **bundle**, includes a clever use of a Here document.* The **bundle** script is an elegant example of a type of script that is often called **shar** (for *sh*ell *ar*chive). The **bundle** script creats a file that contains several other files that can easily be recreated.

---

*Brian W. Kernighan and Rob Pike, *The UNIX Programming Environment,* (c) 1984, p. 98. Reprinted by permission of Prentice Hall, Inc., Englewood Cliffs, NJ.

Creating a single file like this is useful when you want to send several files through electronic mail. Although the tar utility can also be used to combine files, tar puts CONTROL and null characters into the resulting file that mailx and mail cannot handle. (See Part II for more information about tar.) If your system makes a special interpretation of the first character of a script (see page 233), add a top line to **bundle** containing a colon (:).

```
$ cat bundle
# bundle:  group files into distribution package

echo '# To unbundle, sh this file'
for i
do
    echo "echo $i 1>&2"
    echo "cat >$i <<'End of $i' "
    cat $i
    echo "End of $i"
done
```

As the example below shows, the output that **bundle** creates is a shell script, which is redirected to a file called **bothfiles**. It contains the contents of each file given as an argument to **bundle** (**file1** and **file2** in this case) inside a Here document. To extract the original files from **bothfiles**, the user simply runs it. Before each Here document is a cat command that causes the Here document to be written to a new file when **bothfiles** is run.

```
$ cat file1
This is a file.
It contains two lines.
$ cat file2
This is another file.
It contains
three lines.
$ bundle file1 file2 > bothfiles
$ cat bothfiles
# To unbundle, sh this file
echo file1 1>&2
cat >file1 <<'End of file1'
This is a file.
It contains two lines.
End of file1
echo file2 1>&2
cat >file2 <<'End of file2'
This is another file.
It contains
three lines.
End of file2
```

Below, **file1** and **file2** are removed before **bothfiles** is run. The **bothfiles** script echoes the names of the files it creates as it creates them. Finally, the ls command shows that **bothfiles** has recreated **file1** and **file2**.

```
$ rm file1 file2
$ sh bothfiles
file1
file2
$ ls
bothfiles
file1
file2
```

The exec Command

The exec command is a shell built-in command that has two primary purposes: to run a command without creating a new process and to redirect the standard input, standard output, or standard error of a shell script from within the script.

When the shell executes a command that is not built into the shell, it typically creates a new process. The new process inherits environment variables from its parent process, but not the local variables of its parent. In contrast, when you run a command using exec, exec executes the new command in place of (overlays) the current process. Consequently, the environment, including local variables, of the original process is available to the new command.

Insofar as exec runs a command in the environment of the original process, it is similar to the . (dot) command (see page 245). However, unlike the . command, which can only run scripts, exec can run both scripts and compiled programs. Also, whereas the . command returns control to the original script when it finishes running, exec does not.

The format of the exec command follows:

exec command arguments

Because no new process is created when you run a command using exec, the command runs more quickly. However, since exec does not return control to the original program, the exec command can be used only with the last command that you want to run in a script. The following script shows that control is not returned to the script:

```
$ cat exec_demo
who
exec date
echo This echo command is never executed.
$ exec_demo
barbara   console Jun 14 07:15
chas       tty05   Jun 14 06:33
Thu Jun 14 08:20:51 PDT 1990
```

The next example is a modified version of the **out** script (see page 256). It uses exec to execute the final command the script runs. Since the original out script runs either cat or pg and then terminates, the new version of **out** uses exec with both cat and pg.

```
$ cat out
if [ $# = 0 ]
    then
            echo "Usage: out [-v] filenames" 1>&2
            exit 1
fi
if [ "$1" != "-v" ]
    then
            exec cat -- "$@"
    else
            shift
            exec pg "$@"
fi
```

The second major use of exec is to redirect the standard input, standard output, or standard error of a script. From inside a shell script, you can use exec to redirect the input to or output from the script. After a command such as the following, all the input to a script is redirected to come from the file called **infile**:

```
exec < infile
```

Similarly, the following command redirects the standard output and the standard error to **outfile** and **errfile**, respectively:

```
exec > outfile 2> errfile
```

When a script prompts the user for input, it is useful to redirect the output from within the script to go to the terminal, in cases when the user is likely to have redirected the output from the script. When redirecting the output in a script, you can use **/dev/tty** as a synonym for the user's terminal. The **/dev/tty** device is a pseudonym the system maintains for the terminal the user is logged in on. The pseudonym enables you to refer to the user's terminal without knowing which device it is. (The actual device appears in the second column of the output of who.) By redirecting the output from a script to **/dev/tty**, you can ensure that prompts will go to the user's terminal, regardless of whether the user redirected the output from the script. The following command redirects to the terminal the output from a script that contains it:

```
exec > /dev/tty
```

Using exec to redirect the output to **/dev/tty** has one disadvantage—all subsequent output is redirected, unless you use exec again in the script. If you do not want to redirect the output from all subsequent commands in a script, you can redirect the individual echo commands that display prompts.

```
echo "Please enter your name:\c " > /dev/tty
```

Recent versions of System V allow you also to redirect the input to read to come from **/dev/tty**.

```
read name < /dev/tty
```

On earlier versions of System V you cannot redirect the input to the read command.

The trap Command

You can use the **trap** command to trap a *signal*. A signal is a report to a process about a condition. The UNIX system uses signals to report interrupts generated by the user (e.g., by pressing the interrupt key) as well as bad system calls, broken pipes, illegal instructions, and other conditions. Using the trap command you can direct the actions a script will take when it receives a signal.

This discussion covers the five signals that are significant when you work with shell scripts. The following table lists the signals, the signal numbers that systems often ascribe to them, and the conditions that usually generate each signal. The signal numbers may be different on your system—check the file called **/usr/include/sys/signal.h**, or ask your system administrator.

Signal	Number	Generating Conditions
hang up	1	disconnect phone line
terminal interrupt	2	pressing the interrupt key (usually DEL or CONTROL-C)
quit	3	pressing CONTROL-| or CONTROL-\
kill	9	the kill command with the –9 option (cannot be trapped)
software termination	15	default of the kill command
stop	24	pressing the job control stop key (usually CONTROL-Z)

When a script traps a signal, it takes whatever action you specify. It can remove files or finish any other processing as needed, display a message, terminate execution immediately, or ignore the signal. If you do not use a trap command in a script, any of the above signals can terminate it while it is running in the foreground. Because the kill signal cannot be trapped, you can always use kill –9 to terminate a script (or any other process). Refer to kill in Part II.

The format of a trap command is shown below.

trap [′ commands′] signal-numbers

The **signal-numbers** are the numbers of the signals that the trap command will catch. One or more **signal-numbers** must be present. The **commands** part is optional. If it is not present, the command resets the trap to its initial condition, which is to exit from the script. If the **commands** part is present, the shell executes the **commands** when it catches one of the signals. After executing the **commands**, the shell resumes executing the script where it left off. If you want trap to prevent a script from exiting when it receives a signal, but not to explicitly run any commands, you can use trap with a null (empty) **command**. The following command traps signal number 15, and the script continues:

```
$ trap ′ ′ 15
```

The following script demonstrates the use of the trap command to trap signal number 2. It returns an exit status of 1.

```
$ cat inter
trap 'echo PROGRAM INTERRUPTED; exit 1' 2
while :
do
    echo Program running.
done
```

The first line of **inter** sets up a trap for signal number 2. When the signal is caught, the shell executes the two commands between the single quotation marks in the trap command. The echo command displays the message PROGRAM INTERRUPTED. Then exit terminates this shell, and the parent shell displays a prompt. If the exit command were not there, the shell would return control to the While loop after displaying the message. The While loop repeats continuously until the script receives a signal because the : command always returns a *true* exit status.

The trap command is frequently used in shell scripts to remove temporary files when a script is terminated prematurely. If a script has created temporary files and then terminated before it removes them, they will be left around, cluttering up the **/tmp** file system.

The following shell script, **addbanner**, uses two trap commands to remove a temporary file. Together, the two trap commands remove a temporary file when the script terminates normally or due to a hangup, software interrupt, quit, or software termination signal.

```
$ cat addbanner
:
script=`basename $0`

if [ ! -r "$HOME/banner" ]
    then
        echo "$script: need readable $HOME/banner" \
        "file" 1>&2
        exit 1
fi

trap 'exit 1' 1 2 3 15
trap 'rm /tmp/$$.$script 2> /dev/null ' 0

for file
do
    if [ -r "$file" -a -w "$file" ]
        then
            cat $HOME/banner $file > /tmp/$$.$script
            cp /tmp/$$.$script $file
            echo "$script: banner added to $file" 1>&2
        else
            echo "$script: need read and write" \
            "permission for $file" 1>&2
    fi
done
```

When it is called with one or more filename arguments, **addbanner** loops through the files adding a header to the top of each. This script is useful when you use a standard format at the top of your documents, such as a standard layout for memos, or when you want to add a standard header to shell scripts. The header is kept in a file called **banner** in the user's home directory. The **HOME** shell variable is used to indicate the user's home directory so that **addbanner** can be used by several users without modification. If Alex uses **/home/alex** in place of **$HOME** and he then gives the script to Jenny, she will either have to change it or **addbanner** will use Alex's **banner** file when Jenny runs **addbanner**.

The first **trap** command in **addbanner** causes it to exit with a status of 1 when it receives a hangup, software interrupt, or software termination signal. The second **trap** command uses a 0 in place of **signal-number**, which causes **trap** to execute its command argument *whenever* the script exits due to an **exit** command or due to reaching its end. Together, these two **trap** commands remove a temporary file whether the script terminates either normally or prematurely. The standard error output of the second **trap** command is sent to **/dev/null** for cases in which the **trap** attempts to remove a nonexistent temporary file. In those cases, **rm** sends an error message to the standard error output. Because the standard error output is redirected to **/dev/null**, the user will not see the message.

FUNCTIONS

UNIX System V Release 2 introduced *shell functions*. A shell function is similar to a shell script, in that it stores a series of commands for execution at a later time. However, because the shell stores a function in the computer's main memory instead of in a file, you can access it more quickly than you can a script. Also, the shell preprocesses (parses) a function so that it starts up more quickly than a script. Finally, the shell executes a shell function in the same shell that called it.

Users typically declare shell functions either in their **.profile** file or in scripts they want to use the functions in; or they enter the functions in directly from the command line. You can remove functions with the **unset** command. The shell will not keep functions once you log out.

The format you use to declare a shell function is shown below.

```
function-name ()
{
    commands
}
```

The **function-name** is the name you use to call the function. The **commands** is the list of commands the function executes when you call it. These **commands** can include anything you can include in a shell script.

The next example shows how to create a simple function that displays the date, a header, and a list of the people who are using the system. This function runs the same commands as the **whoson** script described on page 223.

```
$ whoson ()
{
    date
    echo Users Currently Logged In
    who
}
$ whoson
Thu Jun 14 09:51:09 PDT 1990
Users Currently Logged In
hls         console Jun 14 08:59
alex        tty20   Jun 14 09:33
jenny       tty24   Jun 14 09:23
```

If you want to have the **whoson** function always available without having to enter it each time you log in, put its definition in your **.profile** file. After adding **whoson** to your **.profile** file, run **.profile** using the **.** (dot) command to put the changes into effect immediately. For more information about **.profile**, see page 74.

```
$ cat .profile
TERM=vt100
export TERM
stty kill '^u'
whoson ()
{
    date
    echo Users Currently Logged In
    who
}
$ . .profile
```

The next function changes your prompt to include the name of the new working directory when you change directories. After you define this function in your **.profile** file and run **.profile**, you can change directories using the **go** command, and the new directory will be displayed as part of your prompt.

```
$ cat .profile
    .
    .
# adapted from go by S. D. Andarmani
# UNIX/WORLD, III:5, p. 77, Fig. 6
```

```
go ()
{
    cd $1
    PS1 = " [ `pwd` ]   "
}
```

```
$  . .profile
$ pwd
/home/alex
$ go literature
[/home/alex/literature] go
[/home/alex]
```

SUMMARY

The shell is both a *command interpreter* and a *programming language.* As a command interpreter, the shell executes commands you enter in response to its prompt. When you use it as a programming language, the shell executes commands from files called *shell scripts.*

You can declare shell scripts to be functions so that they are immediately available and the shell can execute them more quickly. Job control features are available if you run jsh instead of sh.

The shell executes commands by means of processes. Each process has a unique process identification (PID) number. When you give the shell a command, it generally *forks* a new process that executes the command. The shell has some commands that are built in. It does not fork a new process to execute these commands. The following built-in commands are available on both System V and Berkeley UNIX.

Built-in Command	Action
:	null command
.	execute a program or shell script as part of the current process
`pgm`	replace with the output of the **pgm** command
break	exit from For, While, or Until loop
bg	move a command to the background (jsh only)
cd	change working directory
continue	start with next iteration of For, While, or Until loop
echo	display arguments
eval	scan and evaluate the command line
exec	execute a program in place of the current process

Built-in Command	Action
exit	exit from current shell (usually the same as CONTROL-D)
export	place the value of a variable in the calling environment
fg	move a command to the foreground (jsh only)
getopts	parse arguments to a shell script
hash	remember the location of a command in the search path
jobs	list the current commands (jsh only)
newgrp	change the user's group
pwd	print the name of the working directory
read	read a line from the standard input
readonly	declare a variable to be readonly
return	exit from a function
set	set shell flags or command line argument variables; without an argument, display a list of all variables
shift	promote each command line argument
stop	stop a background job (jsh only)
test	compare arguments
times	display times for the current shell and its children
trap	trap a signal
type	display how each argument would be interpreted as a command
ulimit	limit the size of files written by the shell
umask	file-creation mask
unset	remove a variable or function
wait	wait for a background process to terminate

You can execute a shell script (or a compiled program) by giving yourself execute permission for the file (using chmod) and using the name of the file as a command. If you precede the filename of a shell script with an **sh** command, you do not need execute permission.

The shell allows you to define *variables*. When you give the shell a command, it examines the command line for words that begin with unquoted dollar signs. It assumes that these words are variables and substitutes a value for each of them. You can declare and initialize a variable by assigning a value to it. On System V, you can remove a variable declaration by using the unset command.

The shell also defines some variables. The readonly variables are preceded by dollar signs because you can only reference them in this manner—you cannot assign values to them.

Variable	Contents
CDPATH	list of directories for the shell to check when you give a **cd** command
HOME	pathname of your home directory
IFS	internal-field separator
MAIL	file where the system stores your mail
MAILCHECK	specifies how often the shell checks your mailbox
MAILPATH	list of other potential mailboxes
PATH	search path for commands
PS1	prompt string 1
PS2	prompt string 2
SHELL	identifies the name of the invoked shell
$0	name of the calling program
$n	value of the nth command line argument (can be changed by **set**)
$*	all of the command line arguments (can be changed by **set**)
$@	all of the command line arguments (can be changed by **set**)
$#	count of the command line arguments
$$	PID number of the current process
$!	PID number of the most recent background task
$?	exit status of the last task that was executed

The shell provides the following *control structures* so you can alter the flow of control within a shell script:

if then fi
if then else fi
if then elif else fi
for in do done
for do done
while do done
until do done
case in esac

Some of the special characters the shell recognizes follow:

Special Character	Function
NEWLINE	initiates execution of a command
;	separates commands
( )	groups commands for execution by a sub-shell or identifies a function
&	executes a command in the background
|	pipe
>	redirects standard output
>>	appends standard output
<	redirects standard input
<<	Here document
*	any string of characters in an ambiguous file reference
?	any single character in an ambiguous file reference
\	quotes the following character
'	quotes a string, preventing all substitutions
`	performs command substitution
"	quotes a string, allowing variable and command substitution
[ ]	character class in an ambiguous file reference
$	references a variable
.	executes a command (only at the beginning of a line)
#	begins a comment
{ }	command grouping (used to surround the contents of a function)
:	null command, returns true exit status

REVIEW EXERCISES

1. Set up your **PATH** variable so that it searches the following directories in order:

   a. **/usr/bin**

   b. **/usr/sbin**

   c. **/usr/lbin**

   d. your own **bin** directory

   e. the working directory

If there is a file called **whereis** in **/usr/lbin** and also one in your own **bin**, which one will be executed when you type **whereis** on the command line? (Assume you have execute permission for both of the files.)

2. If your **PATH** variable is not set to search the working directory, how can you execute a program located there?

3. Explain what happens when you give the following commands:

```
$ person=jenny
$ echo $´person´
$ echo $\person
```

What does this imply about the order in which the shell processes the command line?

4. Write a shell script that displays the first 12 command line arguments, one argument per line.

5. Name two ways you can identify the PID of your login shell.

6. The following shell script adds entries to a file called **journal** in your home directory. It can help you keep track of phone conversations and meetings.

```
$ cat journal
:
# journal: add journal entries to the file
# $HOME/journal

file=$HOME/journal
date >> $file
echo "Enter name of person or group:   \c"
read person
echo "$person" >> $file
echo >> $file
cat >> $file
echo "----------------------------------" >> $file
echo >> $file
```

Add commands to **journal** to verify that the user has write permission for a file called **journal** in the user's home directory, if such a file exists. The script should take appropriate actions if a **journal** file exists and the user does not have write permission. Verify that the modified script works.

What did you have to do to the script in order to be able to execute it? Why does it use read the first time it accepts input from the terminal and the cat utility the second time?

7. What are the two ways you can execute a shell script when you do not have execute access permission? Can you execute a shell script if you do not have read access permission?

8. Type in the following shell scripts and run them:

```
$ cat report_dir
old_dir=`pwd`
echo "Current working directory:  " $old_dir
go_home
echo "Current working directory:  " `pwd`

$ cat go_home
cd
echo "New working directory:  " `pwd`
echo "Last working directory:  " $old_dir
```

What is wrong? Change them so that they work correctly.

9. Explain the behavior of the following shell script:

```
$ cat quote_demo
twoliner="This is line 1.
This is line 2."
echo "$twoliner\n"
echo $twoliner
```

10. Enhance the **spell_check** script (page 267) so that you can specify a list of words that you want to add to the output of **spell**. You can use a list of words like this to cull usages you do not want in your documents. For example, if you decide you want to use **disk** rather than **disc** in your documents, you can add **disc** to the list of words and **spell_check** will complain if you use **disc** in a document.

11. Modify the **locktty** script (page 270) to accept an optional argument, **banner**. The **locktty** script should display the string **banner** on the user's screen while the terminal is locked. Use the **banner** command to display the string. The **banner** command displays its arguments to the standard output.

    You can use the **banner** argument to display a message such as "back at 1," "see Jenny," or "at lunch" while the terminal is locked.

12. Write a shell function that defines **ls** to be the same as **/usr/bin/ls –F**. Once you have the **ls** function defined, how can you run the **ls** utility without the **–F** option?

    It is typically not a good idea to redefine the names of standard UNIX utilities such as **ls**. Why not? List all the reasons you can think of.

CHAPTER
9

THE
C SHELL

The C Shell performs the same function as the Bourne, Job, and Korn Shells—it provides an interface between you and the UNIX operating system. It is an interactive command interpreter as well as a high-level programming language. At any one time you will be using either the Bourne Shell, the Job Shell, the Korn Shell, or the C Shell, although it is possible to switch back and forth between them. This chapter contrasts the C Shell with the Bourne Shell, paying particular attention to those facets of the C Shell that are absent from the Bourne Shell. Although Chapter 8 is not specifically about the C Shell, it discusses many important concepts that are common to both shells and provides a good background for this chapter. The unique features of the Korn Shell are described in Appendix A.

The C Shell originated on Berkeley UNIX and is first officially included in System V with Release 4, although many manufacturers have provided the C Shell in their implementations of earlier releases of System V. When the C Shell is provided on a machine that runs an older version of System V, some of the features may be missing. Most notably, the C Shell's job control may not be provided. Also, the newer features of the C Shell, such as filename completion and directory stack manipulation, are often missing.

You can customize the C Shell to make it more tolerant of mistakes and easier to use. By setting the proper shell variables, you can have the C Shell warn you when you appear to be accidentally logging out or overwriting a file. The alias mechanism makes it easy to change the names of existing commands and create new ones. The history mechanism allows you to edit and rerun previous command lines. Also, C Shell variables are much more versatile than those of the Bourne Shell. The C Shell processes arrays of numbers and strings and evaluates logical and numerical expressions.

Because of aliases, history, and other features, you may want to use the C Shell as your login shell. At the same time, you may find the Bourne Shell easier to use as a programming language.

ENTERING AND LEAVING THE C SHELL

If your version of UNIX has the C Shell and you are not already using it, you can execute the C Shell by giving the command **csh**. If you are not sure which shell you are using, use the ps utility to find out. It will show that you are running csh (the C Shell), sh (the Bourne Shell), or ksh (the Korn Shell).

If you want to use the C Shell as a matter of course, the system administrator can set up the **/etc/passwd** file so that you are using the C Shell immediately when you log in. On some systems, you can give a **chsh csh** (change to C Shell) command to effect the same change. Use **chsh sh** if you want to go back to using the Bourne Shell.

You can run Bourne, C, and Korn Shell scripts while using any one of the shells as a command interpreter. Several methods have been provided for selecting the shell that will run a script. Refer to page 322, "C Shell Scripts."

There are several ways to leave a C Shell. The way that you use is dependent on two factors: whether the shell variable **ignoreeof** is set and whether you are using the shell that you logged in on or another shell that you created after you logged in. If you are not sure how to exit from a C Shell, press CONTROL-D. You will either exit or receive instructions on how to exit. If you have not set **ignoreeof** and it has not been set for you in one of your startup files (see page 323), you can exit from any shell using CONTROL-D (the same procedure you use to exit from the Bourne Shell).

If **ignoreeof** is set, CONTROL-D will not work. The **ignoreeof** variable causes the shell to display a message telling you how to exit. You can always exit from a C Shell by giving an **exit** command. A **logout** command allows you to exit only from the login shell. More information on **ignoreeof** can be found on page 320.

HISTORY

The history mechanism maintains a list of recently used command lines, also called *events,* and it provides a shorthand for reexecuting any of the events in the list. The shorthand also enables you to execute variations on previous commands and to reuse arguments from them. The shorthand makes it easy to replicate complicated commands and arguments that you used earlier in the login session and to enter a series of commands that differ from one another in minor ways. The history list is also useful as a record of what you have done. It can be helpful when you have made mistakes and are not sure what you did or when you want to keep a record of a procedure that involved a series of commands.

The **history** variable (page 319) determines the number of events preserved in this list. Typically, you will want to preserve about 100 events. If you attempt to preserve too many events, you may run out of memory.

The C Shell assigns a sequential *event number* to each of your command lines. If you wish, the C Shell can display this number as part of its prompt (see page 319). Many of the examples in this chapter show numbered prompts. The history mechanism preserves events whether or not you use a numbered prompt.

Give the following command manually, or place it in your **.cshrc** startup file, to establish a history list of the 100 most recent events:

```
% set history = 100
```

The following command causes the C Shell to save the 20 most recent events across login sessions:

```
% set savehist = 20
```

After you set **savehist,** you can log out and log in again, and the events from the first login session will still be available in your history list.

Give the command **history** to display the events in the history list. When you first set the **history** variable, the history list will just record the events back to the command line you used to set it.

```
32 % history
    23  ls -l
    24  cat temp
    25  rm temp
    26  vi memo
    27  lp memo
    28  vi memo
    29  lp memo
    30  mail jenny < memo
    31  rm memo
    32  history
```

As you run commands and your history list becomes longer, it will run off the top of the screen when you use the history command. Pipe the output of history through more (or pg) to browse through it, or use the tail command to look at the end of it. (Refer to tail on page 61 or in Part II).

Reexecuting Events

You can reexecute any event in the history list. Even if there is no history list, you can always reexecute the previous event. There are three ways to reference an event: by its absolute event number, by its number relative to the current event, or by the text it contains.

All references to events begin with an exclamation point. One or more characters follow the exclamation point to specify an event.

Reexecuting the Previous Event.   You can always reexecute the previous event by giving the command !!. In the following example, event 4 reexecutes event 3.

```
3 % ls -l text
-rw-rw-r-- 1 alex    pubs         5   Jun 14 12:51 text
4 % !!
ls -l text
-rw-rw-r-- 1 alex    pubs         5   Jun 14 12:51 text
```

When you use the history mechanism to reexecute an event, the C Shell displays the command it is executing, as the example above shows.

Using Event Numbers.   A number following an exclamation point refers to an event. If that event is in the history list, the C Shell executes it. A negative number following an exclamation point references an event relative to the current event (e.g., !-3 refers to the third preceding event). Both of the following commands reexecute event 3:

```
7 % !3
ls -l text
-rw-rw-r-- 1 alex    pubs         5   Jun 14 12:51 text
8 % !-5
ls -l text
-rw-rw-r-- 1 alex    pubs         5   Jun 14 12:51 text
```

Using Event Text.   When a string of text follows an exclamation point, the C Shell searches for and executes the most recent event that *began* with that string.

If you enclose the string between question marks, the C Shell executes the most recent event *containing* that string. The final question mark is optional if a RETURN would immediately follow it.

```
53 % history
    48 cat letter
    49 cat memo
    50 lp memo
    51 mail jenny < memo
    52 ls -l
    53 history
54 % !l
ls -l
 .
 .
 .
55 % !lp
lp memo
56 % !?letter?
cat letter
 .
 .
 .
```

OPTIONAL

Words Within Events

You can select any word or series of words from an event. The words are numbered starting with 0, representing the first command on the line, and continuing with 1, representing the first word following the command, through n, representing the last word on the line.

To specify a particular word from a previous event, follow the event specification (such as !14) with a colon and the number of the word in the previous event. (Use !14:3 to specify the third word from event 14.) You can specify a range of words by separating two word numbers with a hyphen. The first word following the command (word number one) can be specified by a caret (^), and the last word, by a dollar sign.

```
72 % echo apple grape orange pear
apple grape orange pear
73 % echo !72:2
echo grape
grape
```

```
74 % echo !72:^
echo apple
apple
75 % !72:0 !72:$
echo pear
pear
76 % echo !72:2-4
echo grape orange pear
grape orange pear
77 % !72:0-$
echo apple grape orange pear
apple grape orange pear
```

As the next example shows, !$ refers to the last word of the previous event. You can use this shorthand to edit, for example, a file you just displayed with cat.

```
% cat report.718
   .
   .
% vi !$
vi report.718
   .
   .
```

If an event contains a single command, the word numbers correspond to the argument numbers. If an event contains more than one command, this correspondence is not true for commands after the first. Event 78, below, contains two commands, separated by a semicolon so that the shell executes them sequentially. The semicolon is word number five.

```
78 % !72 ; echo helen jenny barbara
echo apple grape orange pear ; echo helen jenny barbara
apple grape orange pear
helen jenny barbara
79 % echo !78:7
echo helen
helen
80 % echo !78:4-7
echo pear ; echo helen
pear
helen
```

Modifying Previous Events

On occasion, you may want to reexecute an event, changing some aspect of it. Perhaps you entered a complex command line with a typo or incorrect pathname.

Or you may want to reexecute a command, specifying a different argument. You can modify an event, or a word of an event, by following the event or word specifier with a colon and a modifier. The following example shows the substitute modifier correcting a typo in the previous event.

```
145 % car /home/jenny/memo.0507 /home/alex/letter.0507
car: Command not found.
146 % !!:s/car/cat
cat /home/jenny/memo.0507 /home/alex/letter.0507
.
.
```

As a special case, you can use an abbreviated form of the substitute modifier, shown here, to change the most recent event.

```
% ^old^new
```

produces the same results as

```
% !!:s/old/new
```

Thus, event 146 could have been entered as

```
146 % ^car^cat
cat /home/jenny/memo.0507 /home/alex/letter.0507
.
.
```

Following is a list of modifiers.

Modifier	Mnemonic	Effect
h	head	remove the last element of a pathname
r	root	remove the filename extension
t	tail	remove all elements of a pathname except the last
&	repeat	repeat the previous substitution
p	print	do not execute the modified event
q	quote	quote the modifications so that no further modifications take place
[g]s/old/new/	substitute	substitute **new** for **old**

The s modifier substitutes the first occurrence of the old string with the new one. Placing a **g** before the **s** (**gs/old/new/**) causes a global substitution, replacing all occurrences of the old string. The **/** is the delimiter in these examples, but you can use any character that is not in either the **old** or the **new** string. The final delimiter is optional if a RETURN would immediately follow it. Like the vi Substitute command, the history mechanism replaces an ampersand (**&**) in the new string with the old string. The shell replaces a null old string (**s//new/**) with the previous old string or string within a command that you searched for with **?string?**.

The following examples demonstrate the use of history modifiers:

```
66 % echo /home/jenny/letter.0406 /home/jenny/memo.prv
/home/jenny/letter.0406 /home/jenny/memo.prv
67 % !!:h
echo /home/jenny /home/jenny/memo.prv
/home/jenny /home/jenny/memo.prv
68 % echo !66:2:h
echo /home/jenny
/home/jenny
69 % echo !66:2:t
echo memo.prv
memo.prv
70 % echo !66:1:r
echo /home/jenny/letter
/home/jenny/letter
71 % echo !66:1:p
echo /home/jenny/letter.0406
```

Event 66 displays two filenames. Event 67 recalls the previous event, modified by **h**. Because the command did not specify a word from the event, it modified word 1 and recalled the entire previous event. Events 68 through 70 recall and modify specific words from event 66. In these cases, only the specified words are recalled. Event 71 uses the **p** modifier to display, but not execute, the resulting command.

ALIAS

The alias command performs a string substitution on the command line according to your specifications. The C Shell alias mechanism allows you to define new commands. The format of an alias command is shown below.

alias [entered-command [executed-command]]

The **entered-command** is the command that you enter in response to the C Shell prompt. The **executed-command** is the string that alias substitutes for the **entered-command**.

The following example shows how to use alias. The alias command in event 6 causes the C Shell to substitute ls −l every time you give an **ll** command. Event 7 demonstrates this substitution.

```
5 % ls
one       three   two
6 % alias ll ls −l
7 % ll
total 3
−rwxrw−r−− 1 jenny pubs       17   Mar   5 11:36 one
−rw−rw−r−− 1 jenny pubs       42   Mar   5 11:14 three
−rwxrw−r−− 1 jenny pubs       11   Mar   5 11:35 two
```

Instead of using **ll** as an alias, you can use **ls**; however, this is not recommended. If you do use it, scripts that you run will also use the alias, which may cause them to malfunction. However, if you do use **ls** rather than **ll**, you can avoid the alias substitution (on the command line only) by placing \ in front of **ls**.

```
8 % alias ls ls −l
9 % ls three
−rw−rw−r−−  1 jenny   pubs  42 Mar   5 11:14 three
10 % \ls three
three
```

You can use alias to create short names for commands that you use often. For example, if you use the more utility frequently, you could use alias to substitute more when you give the command **m**.

```
10 % alias m more
11 % m aldus.brief
  .
  .
```

You can also use alias to protect yourself from mistakes. The example below uses an alias to substitute the interactive version of the mv utility when you give the command **mi**. The interactive option to mv causes it to prompt you for verification when the move would overwrite an existing file.

```
12 % alias mi mv −i
13 % mi aldus.brief.2 aldus.brief
remove aldus.brief? y
```

Finally, you can use alias to create new commands. If your system does not have the head utility, you can use the alias below to create your own. The sed command below prints out ten lines of a file and quits. This is similar to what the head utility does. Refer to Chapter 3 for more information about head, and to Part II for information about sed.

```
14 % alias head sed 10q
15 % head aldus.brief
.
.
.
```

When you give an alias command without any arguments (event 16), the C Shell displays a list of all the aliases. When given with one argument (event 17), the alias for that argument is displayed. An unalias command (event 18) removes an alias from the list of aliases.

```
16 % alias
head     sed 10q
ll       ls -l
m        more
mi       mv -i
17 % alias head
sed 10q
18 % unalias head
19 % alias
ll       ls -i
m        more
mi       mv -i
```

==

OPTIONAL

Implementation of alias

When you enter a command line, the C Shell breaks it into commands. Next, the C Shell substitutes an alias for each command that has an alias. After it makes these substitutions, the C Shell substitutes aliases over and over again until there are no aliases left. The alias command flags a self-referencing alias to prevent an infinite loop.

```
82 % alias a b
83 % alias b c
84 % alias c echo finished
85 % alias
a        b
b        c
c        (echo finished)
86 % a
finished
```

OPTIONAL (Continued)

Events 82, 83, and 84 define a series of aliases that reference each other; event 85 uses alias without any arguments to display all the aliases. The C Shell executes event 86 as follows:

1. a is replaced by its alias b.

2. b is replaced by its alias c.

3. c is replaced by its alias echo finished.

4. There are no further aliases, so the shell executes the echo command.

Argument Substitution

The alias command substitutes command line arguments using the same scheme as the history mechanism, with a single exclamation point representing the current event. Modifiers are the same as those used by history (page 301). The exclamation points are quoted in the following example so that the shell does not interpret them but passes them on to alias:

```
21 % alias last echo \!:$
22 % last this is just a test
test
23 % alias fn2 echo \!:2:t
24 % fn2 /home/jenny/test /home/alex/temp /home/barbara/new
temp
```

Event 21 defines an alias for **last** that echoes the last argument. Event 23 defines an alias for **fn2** that echoes the simple filename, or tail, of the second argument on the command line.

JOB CONTROL

Using the C Shell's job control, you can move commands from the foreground to the background and vice versa, stop commands temporarily, and get a list of the current jobs.

When you give a command to the C Shell, it assigns the command a job number. You can then use the job number to work with the command. In the following example, the C Shell lists the job number and PID number of each command run in the background. The jobs command lists the current jobs.

```
86 % nroff -mm glossary > glossary.out &
[1] 26025
87 % date &
[2] 26028
Fri Jun 17 16:56:11 PDT 1990
[2]    Done                    date
88 % find /usr -name ace -print > findout &
[2] 26041
89 % jobs
[1]   - Running    nroff -mm glossary > glossary.out
[2]   + Running    find /usr -name ace -print > findout
```

In this example, the jobs command lists the first job, an nroff command, as job 1. The date command does not appear in the jobs list because it completed before jobs was run. Since the date command also completed before find was run, the find command became job 2.

To move a job that is running in the background into the foreground, use the fg command with the job number as an argument. When specifying the job, precede the job number with a percent sign. The following example moves job 2 into the foreground:

```
90 % fg %2
```

You can also refer to a job by following the percent sign with a unique string that identifies the first few characters of the command. Instead of the above command, for example, you could have used **fg %find** or **fg %f** since either one uniquely identifies job 2. If you precede the string with a question mark, it will match a job that contains the string anywhere within the command. If there is only one job running in the background, an fg command without any arguments will bring it to the foreground.

To put the job into the background, press CONTROL-Z to stop the job. Then use the bg command to start the job running in the background.

```
91 % bg
```

When a job is running in the background, you can use the stop command to stop it. Then use bg or fg to restart it.

If a background job attempts to read from the terminal, the C Shell will stop it. When this happens you must move the job into the foreground so that it can read from the terminal.

Although background jobs are ordinarily allowed to send output to the terminal, you can cause the C Shell to stop a job if it attempts to write to the terminal. Give the command **stty tostop** if you want background commands to stop when they attempt to write to the terminal.

The C Shell notifies you whenever a job *changes state*. Specifically, it notifies you when a job starts, stops, completes, or moves from the foreground to the background, or vice versa. By default, the C Shell displays the notice after your next prompt so that the notice does not disrupt your work. If you set the **notify** variable, the C Shell will notify you immediately about any job that changes state (see "Shell Variables That Act as Switches," page 320). If you do not set the **notify** variable, you can still cause the C Shell to notify you immediately about specific commands. The notify command causes the C Shell to display a notice about a specific job immediately after a change in state. Without an argument, notify reports on the current job. With a job as an argument, it reports on the specified job. Both of the following commands will cause the shell to notify you when job 2 changes state:

```
92 % notify %2

93 % notify %find
```

The C Shell also warns you if you try to leave a shell while there are stopped jobs. After the warning, if you then use the jobs command to review the list of jobs, or if you immediately try to leave the C Shell again, you will be allowed to leave and your jobs will be terminated.

REDIRECTING THE STANDARD ERROR

Under the C Shell, you can combine and redirect the standard output and the standard error (see page 229) using a *greater than* symbol followed by an ampersand.

```
14 % cat x
x: No such file or directory
15 % cat y
This is y.
16 % cat x y >& hold
17 % cat hold
x: No such file or directory
This is y.
```

It is useful to combine and redirect output when you want to run a slow command in the background and do not want its output cluttering up your terminal screen. For example, because the find utility often takes a while to complete, it is a good idea to run it in the background.

The next command finds all the files anywhere in the file system hierarchy that are called **bibliography**. It runs in the background and sends its output to a file called **findout**. Because the find utility sends to its error output a report of directories that you do not have permission to search, you will have a record in the **findout** file of any files called **bibliography** that are found, as well as a record of the directories that could not be searched.

```
18 % find / -name bibliography -print >& findout &
```

While you are running in the background a command that has its output redirect d
to a file, you can look at the output by using the tail utility with the –f option.
The –f option causes tail to display new lines as they are written to the file.

```
19 % tail −f findout
```

To terminate the tail command, press the interrupt key (usually DEL or CONTROL-C).
Refer to Part II for more information about find and tail.

FILENAME GENERATION

The C Shell generates filenames the same way the Bourne Shell does, with an
added feature. Refer to Chapter 5 for an introduction to filename generation.

The C Shell uses the tilde (~) as a special character for filename generation.
By itself, ~ expands into the pathname of your home directory. When you follow
the tilde with the login name of a user, the C Shell expands it into the pathname
of the home directory of that user. The following example shows how to copy the
file named **idea.txt** into Helen's home directory (Helen's login name is hls):

```
152 % cp idea.txt ~hls
```

You can turn off the filename-expansion feature of the C Shell by setting the
noglob variable. When **noglob** is set, the shell treats ***, ?, [ ],** and ~ as regular
characters.

FILENAME COMPLETION

The version of the C Shell that is included with System V Release 4 completes
filenames and user names after you specify unique prefixes. Filename completion
is similar to filename generation, but the goal of filename completion is always to
select a single file. Together, they make it practical to use long, descriptive
filenames.

To enable the filename completion feature, set the **filec** variable. Refer to the
"Variables" section for more information about the set command and **filec**.

```
41 % set filec
```

To use filename completion when you are typing in a filename on the command line, type in enough of the name to uniquely identify the file in the directory, and then press ESCAPE. The C Shell will fill in the name. The following

example shows the user typing the command **cat trig1A**, pressing ESCAPE, and the system filling in the rest of the filename of the file that begins with the string **trig1A**:

```
42 % cat trig1A → ESCAPE → cat trig1A.302488
```

If two or more filenames match the prefix, the C Shell fills in the filenames to the point where the ambiguity occurs and causes the terminal to beep. (Some terminals flash instead of beeping.)

```
43 % ls h*
help.hist       help.text       help.trig01
44 % cat h → ESCAPE → cat help. (BEEP)
```

You can fill in enough characters to resolve the ambiguity and then press ESCAPE again. Alternatively, you can press CONTROL-D and the C Shell will present a list of matching filenames.

```
45 % cat help → CONTROL-D → cat help
                           help.text
                           help.hist
                           help.trig01
```

The C Shell will then redraw the command line you have typed so you can disambiguate the filename (and press ESCAPE again) or finish typing the rest of the name.

The ESCAPE and CONTROL-D keys can also be used with the tilde (~) to expand user names. If you type in ~ and a unique prefix for a user name, you can then press ESCAPE and the shell will complete it. If you press CONTROL-D, the shell presents a list of alternatives.

```
46 % mail ~all → ESCAPE → mail allen
47 % mail ~al → CONTROL-D → mail ~al (BEEP)
                           alex
                           allen
```

DIRECTORY STACK MANIPULATION

The C Shell has the ability to store a list of directories you are using, and it enables you to move among them simply and easily. The list is referred to as a *stack*. You can think of it as a stack of phonograph records, where you typically add records to and remove records from the top of the stack.

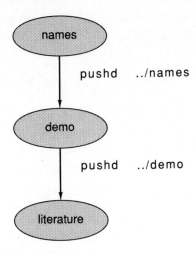

FIGURE 9-1   Creating a Directory Stack

You can display the contents of the stack using the dirs command. If you call dirs when the stack is empty, dirs puts the working directory on the top of the stack.

```
53 % dirs
~/literature
```

The dirs command uses the tilde to represent the user's home directory. In this and the following examples, the directory structure shown in Figure 4-6 is assumed.

To change directories and add the new directory to the top of the stack, use the pushd (push directory) command. The pushd command also displays the contents of the stack. The following example is illustrated in Figure 9-1:

```
54 % pushd ../demo
~/demo ~/literature
55 % pwd
/home/alex/demo
56 % pushd ../names
~/names ~/demo ~/literature
57 % pwd
/home/alex/names
```

When you use pushd without an argument, it changes the working directory to the second directory on the stack and makes it the top directory on the stack. This action is shown in Figure 9-2.

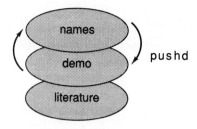

FIGURE 9-2   Using pushd to Change Directories

```
58 % pushd
~/demo  ~/names  ~/literature
59 % pwd
/home/alex/demo
```

Using pushd in this way, you can easily move back and forth between two directories. To access another directory in the stack, call pushd with a numeric argument (preceded by a plus sign). The directories in the stack are numbered starting with the top directory, which is number 0. The following pushd command changes the working directory to **literature** and moves it to the top of the stack:

```
60 % pushd +2
~/literature  ~/demo  ~/names
61 % pwd
/home/alex/literature
```

To remove a directory from the stack, use the popd (pop directory) command. As Figure 9-3 shows, without an argument, popd removes the top directory from the stack and changes the working directory to the new top directory.

```
64 % popd
~/demo  ~/names
65 % pwd
/home/alex/demo
```

To remove a directory other than the top one from the stack, use popd with a numeric argument, preceded by a plus sign. If you remove a directory other than directory number 0 on the stack, this command does not change the working directory.

```
66 % popd +1
~/demo
67 % pwd
/home/alex/demo
```

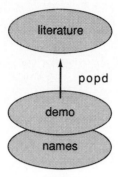

FIGURE 9-3   Using popd to Remove a Directory from the Stack

VARIABLES

The C Shell, like the Bourne Shell, uses only string variables. The C Shell can, however, work with these variables as numbers. You must use the expr command to perform arithmetic operations on numbers in the Bourne Shell. The arithmetic functions of expr, and more, are built into the C Shell.

This section uses the term *numeric variable* to describe a string variable that contains a number that the C Shell uses in arithmetic or logical-arithmetic computations. However, no true numeric variables exist.

A C Shell variable name consists of 1 to 20 characters, which can be letters, digits, and underscores (_). The first character of a variable name cannot be a digit.

Variable Substitution

Three commands declare and manipulate variables: set, @, and setenv. The set command assumes that a variable is a nonnumeric string variable. The @ command works only with numeric variables. Both set and @ declare local variables. The setenv command declares a variable *and* places it in the calling environment of all child processes. Using setenv is similar to using export in the Bourne Shell (see page 237 for a discussion of local and environment variables).

Once the value—or merely the existence—of a variable has been established, the C Shell substitutes the value of that variable when it sees the variable on a command line or in a shell script. The C Shell, like the Bourne Shell, recognizes a word that begins with a dollar sign as a variable. If you quote the dollar sign by preceding it with a backslash (\$), the shell will not perform the substitution. When a variable is within double quotation marks, the substitution occurs even if you quote the dollar sign. If the variable is within single quotation marks, the substitution will not occur, regardless of whether or not you quote the dollar sign.

String Variables

The C Shell treats string variables similarly to the way the Bourne Shell does. The major difference is in their declaration and assignment. The C Shell uses an explicit command, set (or setenv), to declare and/or assign a value to a string variable.

```
1 % set name = fred
2 % echo $name
fred
3 % set
argv      ()
home      /home/jenny
name      fred
shell     /usr/bin/csh
status    0
```

Event 1 declares the variable **name** and assigns the string fred to it. Unlike the Bourne Shell, the C Shell allows SPACES around the equal sign. (They are not required with set; however, they are required with setenv.) Event 2 displays this value. When you give a set command without any arguments, it displays a list of all the declared variables and their values. When you give a set command with only the name of a variable and no value, it sets the variable to a null string. Refer to events 4 and 5, below. Events 6 and 7 show that the unset command removes a variable from the list of declared variables.

```
4 % set name
5 % echo $name
6 % unset name
7 % set
argv      ()
home      /home/jenny
shell     /usr/bin/csh
status    0
```

Arrays of String Variables

Before you can access individual elements of an array, you must declare the entire array. To declare an array, you need to assign a value to each element of the array.

```
8 % set colors = (red green blue orange yellow)
9 % echo $colors
red green blue orange yellow
10 % echo $colors[3]
blue
11 % echo $colors[2-4]
green blue orange
```

```
12 % set shapes = ( '  '  '  '  '  '  '  '  '  ' )
13 % echo $shapes
14 % set shapes[4] = square
15 % echo $shapes[4]
square
```

Event 8 declares the array of string variables named **colors** to have five elements and assigns values to each of these elements. If you do not know the
values of the elements at the time you declare an array, you can declare an array
containing the necessary number of null elements. See event 12.

You can reference an entire array by preceding its name with a dollar sign
(event 9). A number in square brackets following a reference to the array refers
to an element of the array (events 10, 14, and 15). Two numbers in square brackets, separated by a hyphen, refer to two or more adjacent elements of the array
(event 11). See "Special Forms of User Variables," page 317, for more information on arrays.

Numeric Variables

The @ command assigns a value to a numeric variable. You can declare single
numeric variables with the @ command, just as you can use the **set** command to
declare nonnumeric variables. If you give @ a nonnumeric argument, it displays
an Expression syntax. error message.

Many of the expressions that the @ command can evaluate and the operators
it recognizes are derived from the C programming language. The format of a
declaration or assignment using the @ command is shown below.

> @ **variable-name operator expression**

The **variable-name** is the name of the variable that you are declaring or
assigning a value to. The **operator** is one of the C assignment operators: =, +=,
-=, *=, /=, or %=. (See page 418 for an explanation of these operators.) The
expression is an arithmetic expression that can include most C operators; refer to
"Expressions," the subsection that follows. You can use parentheses within the
expression for clarity or to change the order of evaluation. Parentheses must surround parts of the expression that contain any of the following characters: <, >,
&, or | .

Expressions.   An expression can be composed of constants, variables, and the
following operators (listed in order of decreasing precedence):

Parentheses

   ()   change the order of evaluation

Unary Operators

-    unary minus
~   one's complement
!   logical negation

Arithmetic Operators

%   remainder
/   divide
*   multiply
-    subtract
+   add

Shift Operators

>>   right shift
<<   left shift

Relational Operators

>   greater than
<   less than
>=   greater than or equal to
<=   less than or equal to
!=   not equal to (compare strings)
==   equal to (compare strings)

Bitwise Operators

&   AND
^   exclusive OR
| inclusive OR

Logical Operators

&&   AND
|| OR

Expressions follow these rules:

1. The shell considers a number that begins with a 0 (zero) to be an octal number.
2. The shell evaluates a missing or null argument as 0.
3. All results are decimal numbers.
4. Except for != and ==, the operators act on numeric arguments.
5. You must separate each element of an expression from adjacent elements by a SPACE, unless the adjacent element is an &, | , <, >, (, or).

There is also a group of expressions that involve files rather than numeric variables or strings. These expressions are described on page 325.

```
216 % @ count = 0
217 % echo $count
0
218 % @ count = ( 5 + 2 )
219 % echo $count
7
220 % @ result = ( $count < 5 )
221 % echo $result
0
222 % @ count += 5
223 % echo $count
12
224 % @ count++
225 % echo $count
13
```

Event 216 declares the variable **count** and assigns a value of 0 to it. Event 218 shows the result of an arithmetic operation being assigned to a variable. Event 220 uses @ to assign the result of a logical operation involving a constant and a variable to **result**. The value of the operation is false (= 0) because the variable **count** is not less than 5. Event 222 is a compressed form of the following assignment statement:

```
% @ count = ( $count + 5 )
```

Event 224 uses a postfix operator to increment **count** by 1.

Arrays of Numeric Variables.   You must use the **set** command to declare an array of numeric variables before you can use the @ command to assign values to the elements of the array. The **set** command can assign any values to the elements of a numeric array, including zeros, other numbers, and null strings.

Assigning a value to an element of a numeric array is similar to assigning a value to a simple numeric variable. The only difference is that you must specify the element, or index, of the array. The format is shown below.

@ variable-name[index] operator expression

The **index** specifies the element of the array that is being addressed. The first element has an index of 1. The **index** must be either a numeric constant or a variable. It cannot be an expression. In the preceding format, the square brackets around **index** are part of the format and do not indicate **index** is optional.

```
226 % set ages = (0 0 0 0 0)
227 % @ ages[2] = 15
228 % @ ages[3] = ($ages[2] + 4)
229 % echo $ages[3]
19
230 % echo $ages
0 15 19 0 0
```

Elements of a numeric array behave as though they were simple numeric variables. The difference is that you must use set to declare a numeric array. Event 226 above declares an array with five elements, each having a value of 0. Events 227 and 228 assign values to elements of the array, and event 229 displays the value of one of the elements. Event 230 displays all the elements of the array.

Braces

You can use braces to distinguish a variable from surrounding text without the use of a separator (e.g., a SPACE).

```
100 % set prefix = Alex
101 % echo $prefix is short for $prefix{ander}.
Alex is short for Alexander.
```

Without braces in this example, **prefix** would have to be separated from ander with a SPACE so that the shell would recognize **prefix** as a variable. This change would cause Alexander to become Alex ander.

Special Forms of User Variables

A special variable in the following format stores the number of elements in an array:

$#variable-name

You can determine whether a variable has been declared or not by testing a variable of the next format:

$?variable-name

This variable has a value of 1 if **variable-name** has been declared. Otherwise it has a value of 0.

```
205 % set days = (mon tues wed thurs fri)
206 % echo $#days
5
207 % echo $?days
1
208 % unset days
209 % echo $?days
0
```

Event 206 displays the number of elements in the **days** array that was set in event 205. Event 207 shows that **days** has been declared because **$?days** echoes as 1 (= true). Events 208 and 209 show what happens when **days** is unset.

Shell Variables

This section lists the shell variables that are either set by the shell, inherited by the shell from the environment, or set by the user and used by the shell. The section is divided into two parts. The first contains variables that take on significant values (e.g., the PID number of a background process). The second part lists variables that act as switches—*on* if they are declared, *off* if they are not).

Many of these variables are most often set from within one of the C Shell's two startup files: **.login** or **.cshrc**. Refer to page 323 for more information about **.login** and **.cshrc**.

Shell Variables That Take On Values

$argv   This shell variable contains the command line arguments from the command that the shell invoked. For example, **argv[0]** contains the name of the calling program, and **argv[1]** contains the first command line argument. You can change any element of this array except **argv[0]**. Use **argv[*]** to reference all the arguments together. You can abbreviate references to **argv** as $* (short for $argv[*]) and $n (short for $argv[n]).

$#argv The shell sets this variable to the number of elements in **argv**, excluding the element **argv[0]**.

$cdpath The **cdpath** variable affects the operation of cd in the same way the Bourne Shell's **CDPATH** variable does (see page 244). It takes on the value of a list of absolute pathnames (similar to the **PATH** variable) and is usually set in the **.login** file with a command line such as the following:

```
set cdpath = (/home/jenny /home/jenny/letters)
```

When you call cd with a simple filename, it searches the working directory for a subdirectory with that name. If one is not found, cd searches the directories listed in **cdpath** for the subdirectory.

$cwd The shell sets this variable to the name of the working directory. When you access a directory through a symbolic link, the C Shell sets **cwd** to the name of the symbolic link. Refer to page 88 for more information about symbolic links.

$history This variable controls the size of your history list. As a rule of thumb, its value should be kept around 100. If you assign too large a value, the shell can run out of memory. Refer to "History," page 297.

$HOME This variable is the same as the **HOME** variable in the Bourne Shell. It has the value of the pathname of the home directory of the user. The cd command refers to this variable, as does the filename expansion of ~ (see "Filename Generation," page 308).

$PATH This variable is the same as the **PATH** variable in the Bourne Shell. If it is not set, you can execute a file only if you specify its full pathname. You can set your **PATH** variable with a command such as the following:

```
% setenv PATH (/usr/bin /usr/sbin /home/alex/bin .)
```

$prompt This variable is similar to the **PS1** variable in the Bourne Shell. If it is not set, the prompt will be %, or # for the system administrator (Superuser). The shell expands an exclamation point in the prompt string to the current event number. (Just as the shell replaces a variable in a shell script with its value, the shell replaces an exclamation point in the prompt string with the current event number.) Following is a typical command line from a **.cshrc** file that sets the value of **prompt**:

```
set prompt = ' ! % '
```

You must quote the exclamation point so the shell does not expand it before assigning it to the variable **prompt**.

$savehist   This variable specifies the number of commands that will be saved from the history list when you log out. These events are saved in a file called **.history** in your home directory. The shell uses them as the initial history list when you log in again so that your history continues across login sessions.

$shell   This variable contains the pathname of the shell.

$status   This variable contains the exit status returned by the last command.

$$ As in the Bourne Shell, this variable contains the PID number of the current shell.

Shell Variables That Act as Switches

The following shell variables act as switches; their values are not significant. If the variable has been declared, the shell takes the specified action. If not, the action is not taken or is negated. You can set these variables in your **.cshrc** file, in a shell script, or from the command line.

$echo   When you call the C Shell with the **–x** option, it sets the **echo** variable. You can also set **echo** using a **set** command. In either case, when you declare **echo**, the C Shell displays each command before it executes that command.

$filec   The **filec** variable enables the filename completion feature. Filename completion is a new feature of the C Shell that complements the filename generation facility. When **filec** is set, you can a enter a partial filename on the command line and then press ESCAPE to cause the shell to complete it, or press CONTROL-D to list all the filenames that match the prefix you entered. Refer to page 308 for more information about filename completion.

$ignoreeof   When you set the **ignoreeof** variable, you cannot exit from the shell using CONTROL-D, so you cannot accidentally log out. When this variable is declared, you must use **exit** or **logout** to leave a shell.

$noclobber   The **noclobber** variable prevents you from accidentally overwriting a file when you redirect output. It also prevents you from creating a file when you attempt to append output to a nonexistent file. To override **noclobber,** add an exclamation point to the symbol you use for redirecting or appending output (that is, >! and >>!).

When you do *not* declare **noclobber,** these command lines have the following effects.

Command Line	Effect
x > fileout	Redirects the standard output from process **x** to **fileout.** Overwrites **fileout** if it exists.
x >> fileout	Redirects the standard output from process **x** to **fileout.** Appends new output to the end of **fileout** if it exists. Creates **fileout** if it does not exist.

When you declare **noclobber,** the command lines have different effects.

Command Line	Effect
x > fileout	Redirects the standard output from process **x** to **fileout.** The C Shell displays an error message if **fileout** exists and it does not overwrite the file.
x >> fileout	Redirects the standard output from process **x** to **fileout.** Appends new output to the end of **fileout** if it exists. The C Shell displays an error message if **fileout** does not exist. It does not create the file.

$noglob   When you declare **noglob,** the C Shell will not expand ambiguous filenames. You can use *, ?, ~, and [ ] on the command line or in a shell script without quoting them.

$nonomatch   When you declare **nonomatch,** the C Shell passes an ambiguous file reference that does not match a filename to the command that is being called. The shell does not expand the file reference. When you do not declare **nonomatch,** the C Shell generates a No match. error message and does not execute the command.

```
35 % cat questions?
No match.
36 % set nonomatch
37 % cat questions?
cat: cannot open questions?
```

$notify   When the **notify** variable is set, the C Shell will send a message to your terminal whenever one of your background commands completes. Ordinarily, the C Shell will notify you about a job completion immediately before the next prompt. Refer to "Job Control," page 305.

$verbose   The C Shell declares the **verbose** variable when you call it with the –v option. You can also declare it using the set command. In either case, **verbose** causes the C Shell to display each command after a history substitution. (Refer to "History," page 297.)

C SHELL SCRIPTS

Just as the Bourne Shell can execute a file of Bourne Shell commands, so also the C Shell can execute a file of C Shell commands. The concepts of writing and executing scripts in the two shells are similar. However, the methods of declaring and assigning values to variables and the syntax of control structures are different.

Executing a C Shell Script

You can run Bourne, C, and Korn Shell scripts while using any one of the shells as a command interpreter. There are several different methods for selecting the shell a script will be run by. On some implementations of System V, one way you can cause a script to be run by the C Shell is to put a pound sign (#) as the first character of the first line. However, if the first character of the script is a pound sign and the second character is an exclamation point, on some systems the following characters are interpreted as the name of a shell to be used to run the script. If the line below is used as the first line of a script, the script will be run under the C Shell.

```
#!/usr/bin/csh
```

If you run a script by explicitly invoking a particular shell, it will be run by that shell regardless of what is on its first line. In the following example, the script **reminder** will be run by the C Shell.

```
75 % csh reminder
```

Refer to "Invoking a Shell Script" on page 233 for more information about ways to select a shell to run a script.

Automatically Executed Shell Scripts

The Bourne Shell automatically executes one file (the **.profile** file in your home directory) when you log in. The C Shell executes three files at different times during a session.

.login   When you log in and start a session, the C Shell executes the contents of the **.login** file that is located in your home directory. This file should contain commands that you want to execute once, at the beginning of each session. The environment is established from this shell script. You can use setenv to declare environment variables here. You can also declare the type of terminal that you are using in your **.login** file. A sample **.login** file follows:

```
76 % cat .login
setenv TERM vt100
stty erase '^X' kill '^U' -lcase -tabs
echo "This is who's on the machine:"
who
```

This file establishes the type of terminal that you are using by setting the **TERM** variable. In this case, the Termcap or Terminfo name for the terminal is vt100. The sample **.login** file then executes the stty utility, displays a message, and executes the who utility so that you know who else is using the machine. More information about the setenv command can be found in "Variables," starting on page 312.

.cshrc   The C Shell executes the **.cshrc** file that is located in your home directory each time you invoke a new C Shell, such as when you log in or execute a C Shell script. You can use this file to establish variables and parameters that are local to a specific shell. Each time you create a new shell, the C Shell reinitializes these variables for the new shell. A sample **.cshrc** file follows:

```
77 % cat .cshrc
set noclobber
set ignoreeof
set history = 100
set prompt = " \! % "
set PATH = (/usr/bin /usr/sbin /home/jenny/bin .)
alias h history
alias ll ls -l
```

This sample **.cshrc** file sets several shell variables and establishes two aliases.

.logout   The C Shell executes the **.logout** file in your home directory when you log off the system—normally when you finish your session.

Below is a sample **.logout** file that displays a reminder. The sleep command ensures that echo has time to display the message before the system logs you out (for dial-up lines).

```
78 % cat .logout
echo Remember to turn on call
echo forwarding before you go home.
sleep 10
```

CONTROL STRUCTURES

The C Shell uses many of the same control structures as the Bourne Shell. In each case the syntax is different, but the effects are the same. This section summarizes the differences between the control structures in the two shells. A more complete discussion of control structures can be found in Chapter 8.

If

The format of the If control structure is as follows:

   if (**expression**) **simple-command**

The If control structure works only with simple commands, not pipes or lists of commands. You can use the If Then control structure (page 326) to execute more complex commands.

```
79 % cat if_1
# routine to show the use of a simple If
# control structure
#
if ($#argv == 0) echo "if_1: there are no arguments"
```

This program checks to see if it was called without any arguments. If the expression (enclosed in parentheses) evaluates to *true*—that is, if there were zero arguments on the command line—the If structure displays a message to that effect.

In addition to the logical expressions listed on page 315, you can use expressions that return a value based on the status of a file. The format of this type of expression is shown below:

–n filename

where **n** is from the following list.

n	Meaning
d	The file is a directory file.
e	The file exists.
f	The file is an ordinary file.
o	The user owns the file.
r	The user has read access to the file.
w	The user has write access to the file.
x	The user has execute access to the file.
z	The file is 0 bytes long.

If the specified file does not exist or is not accessible, the C Shell evaluates the expression as 0. Otherwise, if the result of the test is true, the expression has a value of 1; if it is false, the expression has a value of 0.

Goto

The format of a Goto statement is as follows:

goto **label**

A Goto statement transfers control to the statement beginning with **label**:. The following example demonstrates the use of Goto:

```
80 % cat goto_1
#
# test for 2 arguments
#
if ($#argv == 2) goto goodargs
echo "Usage: goto_1 arg1 arg2"
exit 1
goodargs:
.
.
```

The message the **goto_1** script presents is a standard usage message. Refer to page 254 for more information about usage messages.

Interrupt Handling

The Onintr statement transfers control when you interrupt a shell script. The format of an Onintr statement is shown below.

onintr **label**

When you press the interrupt key during execution of a shell script, the shell transfers control to the statement beginning with label:.

This statement allows you to terminate a script gracefully when it is interrupted. You can use it to ensure that, when it is interrupted, a shell script removes temporary files before returning control to the shell.

The following script demonstrates Onintr. It loops continuously until you press the interrupt key, at which time it displays a message and returns control to the shell.

```
81 % cat onintr_1
# demonstration of onintr
onintr close
while (1 == 1)
      echo Program is running.
      sleep 2
end
close:
echo End of program.
```

If the script created temporary files, it might use Onintr to remove them.

```
close:
rm -f /tmp/$$*
```

The ambiguous file reference **/tmp/$$*** matches all files in **/tmp** that begin with the PID of the current shell. Refer to page 249 for a description of this technique for naming temporary files.

If Then Else

The three forms of the If Then Else control structure are as follows:

Form 1:

```
if (expression) then
    commands
endif
```

Form 2:

```
if (expression) then
    commands
else
    commands
endif
```

Form 3:

```
if (expression) then
    commands
else if (expression) then
    commands

    .
    .
    .

else
    commands
endif
```

The first form is an extension of the simple If structure; it executes more complex **commands** or a series of **commands** if the **expression** is true. This form is still a one-way branch.

The second form is a two-way branch. If the **expression** is true, the structure executes the first set of **commands**. If it is false, the set of **commands** following Else is executed.

The third form is similar to the If Then Elif structure of the Bourne Shell. It performs tests until it finds an **expression** that is true and then executes the corresponding **commands**.

```
82 % cat if_else_1
# routine to categorize the first
# command line argument
#
set class
set number = $argv[1]
#
if ($number < 0) then
    @ class = 0
else if (0 <= $number && $number < 100) then
    @ class = 1
else if (100 <= $number && $number < 200) then
    @ class = 2
else
    @ class = 3
endif
#
echo The number $number is in class ${class}.
```

This example program assigns a value of 0, 1, 2, or 3 to the variable **class**, based on the value of the first command line argument. The variable **class** is declared at the beginning of the program for clarity; you do not need to declare it before its first use. Again, for clarity, the script assigns the value of the first command line argument to **number**. The first If statement tests to see if **number** is less than 0. If it is, the script assigns 0 to **class**. If it is not, the second If tests to see if the number is between 0 and 100. The && is a logical AND, yielding a value of *true* if the expression on each side is true. If the number is between 0 and 100, 1 is assigned to **class**. A similar test determines whether the number is between 100 and 200. If it is not, the final Else assigns 3 to **class**. Endif closes the If control structure.

The final statement uses braces ({}) to isolate the variable **class** from the following period. Again, the braces isolate the period for clarity; the shell does not consider a punctuation mark as part of a variable name. The braces would be required if you wanted other characters to follow immediately after the variable.

Foreach

The Foreach structure parallels the For In structure of the Bourne Shell. Its format is as follows:

> foreach **loop-index** (**argument-list**)
>   **commands**
> end

This structure loops through the **commands**. The first time through the loop, the structure assigns the value of the first argument in the **argument-list** to the **loop-index**. When control reaches the End statement, the shell assigns the value of the next argument from the **argument-list** to the **loop-index** and executes the commands again. The shell repeats this procedure until it exhausts the **argument-list**.

The following C Shell script uses a Foreach structure to loop through the files in the working directory containing a specified string of characters in their filename and to change the string. For example, it can be used to change the string **memo** in filenames to **letter**. The filenames **memo.1, dailymemo,** and **memories** would be changed to **letter.1, dailyletter,** and **letterries**. This script requires two arguments: the string to be changed and the new string. The **argument-list** of the Foreach structure uses a regular expression to loop through all filenames that contain the first argument. For each filename that matches the regular expression, the mv utility changes the filename. The sed utility substitutes the first argument for the second argument in the filename. The **$1** and **$2** are abbreviated forms of **$argv[1]** and **$argv[2]**. (Refer to Part II for more information about sed.)

```
83 % cat rename
# Usage:  rename arg1 arg2
#         changes the string arg1 in the names of files
#         in the working directory to the string arg2
#
if ($#argv != 2) goto usage

foreach i ( *$1* )
    mv $i `echo $i | sed -n s/$1/$2/p`
end

usage:
echo "Usage: rename arg1 arg2"
exit 1
```

═══

OPTIONAL

The next script uses a Foreach loop to assign the command line arguments to the elements of an array.

```
84 % cat foreach_1
# routine to zero-fill argv to 20 arguments
#
set buffer = (0 0 0 0 0 0 0 0 0 0 0 0 0 0 0 0 0 0 0 0)
set count = 1
#
if ($#argv > 20) goto toomany
#
    foreach argument ($argv[*])
        set buffer[$count] = $argument
        @ count++
    end
```

OPTIONAL (Continued)
```
#
# REPLACE argtest ON THE NEXT LINE WITH
# THE PROGRAM YOU WANT TO CALL.
exec argtest $buffer[*]
exit 0
#
toomany:
echo "Usage: foreach_1 [up to 20 arguments]"
exit 1
```

This script calls another program named **argtest** with a command line guaranteed to contain 20 arguments. If **foreach_1** is called with fewer than 20 arguments, it fills the command line with zeros to complete the 20 arguments for **argtest**. More than 20 arguments cause it to display a usage message.

The Foreach structure loops through the commands one time for each of the command line arguments. Each time through the loop, it assigns the value of the next argument from the command line to the variable **argument**. Then it assigns each of these values to an element of the array **buffer**. The variable **count** maintains the index for the **buffer** array. A postfix operator increments **count** using the @ command (@ **count++**). An exec command (see page 282) calls **argtest** so that a new process is not initiated. (Once **argtest** is called, the process running this routine is no longer needed, so there is no need for a new process.)

Break and Continue

You can interrupt a Foreach loop with a Break or Continue statement. These statements execute the remaining commands on the line before they transfer control. Break transfers control to the statement after the End statement, terminating execution of the loop. Continue transfers control to the End statement, which continues execution of the loop.

While

The format of the While structure is shown below.

> while (**expression**)
>   **commands**
> end

This structure continues to loop through the **commands** *while* the **expression** is true. If the **expression** is false the first time it is evaluated, the structure never executes the **commands**. You can use Break and Continue statements in a While structure; refer to the previous discussion.

```
85 % cat while_1
# Demonstration of a While control structure.
# This routine sums the numbers between 1 and
# n, n being the first argument on the command
# line.
#
set limit = $argv[1]
set index = 1
set sum = 0
#
    while ($index <= $limit)
         @ sum += $index
         @ index++
    end
#
echo The sum is $sum
```

This program computes the sum of all the integers up to and including n, where n is the first argument on the command line. The **+=** operator assigns the value of **sum + index** to **sum**.

Switch

The Switch structure is analogous to the Case structure of the Bourne Shell.

switch (**test-string**)

    case **pattern**:
        commands
    breaksw

    case **pattern**:
        commands
    breaksw

    .

    .

    default:
        commands
    breaksw

endsw

The **breaksw** statement causes execution to continue after the **endsw** statement. Refer to the discussion of the Case statement in Chapter 8 for a discussion of special characters you can use within the patterns.

```
86 % cat switch_1
# Demonstration of a Switch control structure.
# This routine tests the first command line argument
# for yes or no, any combination of upper and lower-
# case characters.
#
# test that argv[1] exists
if ($#argv == 0) then
    echo "Usage: switch_1 [yes|no]"
    exit 1
else
# argv[1] exists, set up switch based on its value
    switch ($argv[1])
    #
    # case of YES
        case [yY][eE][sS]:
        echo Argument one is yes.
        breaksw
    #
    # case of NO
        case [nN][oO]:
        echo Argument one is no.
        breaksw
    #
    # default case
        default:
        echo Argument one is neither yes nor no.
        breaksw
    endsw
endif
```

Reading User Input

Some implementations of the C Shell use a **set** command to read a line from the terminal and assign it to a variable.

The following portion of a shell script prompts the user and reads a line of input into the variable **input_line**:

```
echo "Input the next condition: "
set input_line = $<
```

If your version does not have this feature, you can use the **head** utility to read user input.

```
echo "Input the next condition: "
set input_line = `head -1`
```

Here, **head –1** displays the first line it receives from its standard input. The backquotes cause the shell to execute the command in place, replacing the command they enclose with the output from the command. See page 241 for more information on command substitution.

BUILT-IN COMMANDS

Built-in commands are part of (built into) the C Shell.

When you give a simple filename as a command, the shell searches the directory structure for the program you want, using the **PATH** variable as a guide. When it finds the program, the shell forks a new process to execute it.

The shell executes a built-in command as part of the calling process. It does not fork a new process to execute the command. It does not need to search the directory structure for the command program because the program is immediately available to the shell. The following list describes many of the built-in commands.

@.   This command is similar to the **set** command, but it can evaluate expressions. See "Numeric Variables," page 314.

alias.   This command creates and displays aliases. See "Alias," page 302.

alloc.   This command displays a report of the amount of used and free memory.

bg.   This command moves jobs into the background. See "Job Control," page 305.

cd (or chdir).   This command changes working directories. Refer to the **cd** utility in Part II for more information.

dirs.   This command displays the directory stack. See "Directory Stack Manipulation," page 309.

echo.   This command displays its arguments. On System V, echo uses \c to suppress the NEWLINE it usually displays. Refer to echo in Part II for more information.

eval.   This command scans and evaluates the command line. When you put eval in front of a command, the command is scanned twice by the shell before it is executed. This is useful when you have a command that is generated as a result of command or variable substitution. Because of the order in which the shell processes a command line, it is sometimes necessary to repeat the scan in order to achieve the desired result.

exec.   This command is similar to the exec command of the Bourne Shell. The exec command overlays the program that is currently being executed with another program in the same shell. The original program is lost. Refer to the exec command in Chapter 8 for more information; also refer to source later in this section.

exit.   You can use this command to exit from a C Shell. When you follow it with an argument that is a number, the number is the exit status that the shell returns to its parent process. Refer to the **status** variable, page 320.

fg.   This command moves jobs into the foreground. See ''Job Control,'' page 305.

glob.   This command is like the echo command, except it does not display spaces between its arguments and does not follow its display with a NEWLINE.

hashstat.   This command reports on the efficiency of the C Shell's *hash* mechanism. The C Shell uses the hash mechanism to speed the process of searching through the directories in your search path.

history.   This command displays the history list of commands. See ''History,'' page 297.

jobs.   This command identifies the current jobs, or commands. See ''Job Control,'' page 305.

kill.   This command terminates jobs or processes. See kill in Part II.

limit.   This command limits the computer resources that can be used by the current process and any processes it creates. You can put limits on the number of seconds the process can use the central processing unit (CPU), the size of files that can be created, and so forth.

login.   This command, which you can follow with a user name, logs in a user.

logout.   This command ends a session if you are using your original (login) shell.

nice.   This command can be used to lower the processing priority of a command or a shell. It is useful if you want to run a command that makes large demands on the central processing unit of the computer but you do not need the output of the command right away. If you are the Superuser, you can use nice to raise the processing priority of a command.

nohup.   This command allows you to log off while processes are running in the background without terminating the processes. Some systems are set up to do this automatically. Refer to nohup in Part II.

notify.   This command causes the shell to notify you immediately when the status of one of your jobs changes. Refer to "Job Control," page 305.

popd.   This command removes a directory from the directory stack. See "Directory Stack Manipulation," page 309.

pushd.   This command changes the current working directory and places the new directory at the top of the directory stack. See "Directory Stack Manipulation," page 309.

rehash.   This command is used to recreate the internal tables used by the C Shell's hash mechanism. Whenever a new C Shell is invoked, the hash mechanism creates a sorted list of all commands available to the user. You should use the rehash command after you add a command to one of the directories in the search path to cause the shell to recreate the sorted list of commands. If you don't, the C Shell may not be able to find the new command.

repeat.   This command takes two arguments: a count and simple command (no pipes or lists of commands). It repeats the command the number of times specified by the count.

set.   This command declares, initializes, and displays the values of local variables. See "Variables," page 312.

setenv.   This command declares and initializes the values of environment variables. See "Variables," page 312. Many systems include a printenv or env command that displays the values of environment variables.

shift.   This command is analogous to the Bourne Shell shift command (page 247). Without an argument, shift promotes the indexes of the **argv[*]** array. You can use it with an argument to perform the same operation on another array.

source.   The source command causes the current C Shell to execute a shell script given as its argument. It is similar to the . command in the Bourne Shell. The source command expects a C Shell script, so no leading pound sign is required in the script. The current shell executes source so that the script can contain commands, such as set, that affect the current shell. After you make changes to the **.cshrc** or **.login** file, you can use source to execute it from within the login shell in order to put the changes into effect.

stop.   This command stops a job that is running in the background. See "Job Control," page 305.

suspend.   This command stops the current shell. It is similar to CONTROL-Z, which stops jobs running in the foreground.

time.   The time command executes the command that you give it as an argument. It displays the elapsed time, the system time, and the execution time for the command. Without an argument, time displays the times for the current shell and its children.

umask.   This command can be used to identify or change the access permissions that are assigned to files you create. Refer to umask in Part II for more information.

unalias.   This command removes an alias. See "Alias," page 302.

OPTIONAL (Continued)

unhash.   This command turns off the hash mechanism. Refer to the hashstat and **rehash** built-ins.

unlimit.   This command removes limits on the current process. See **limit**, page 335.

unset.   This command removes a variable declaration. See ''Variables,'' page 312.

unsetenv.   This command removes an environment variable declaration. See ''Variables,'' page 312.

wait.   This command causes the shell to wait for all child processes to terminate, as does the Bourne Shell's **wait** command. When you give a **wait** command in response to a C Shell prompt, the C Shell will not display a prompt and will not accept a command until all background processes have finished execution. If you interrupt it with the interrupt key, **wait** displays a list of outstanding processes before returning control to the shell.

Control Structures

The control structures listed below are also built-in commands. They allow you to alter the flow of control in C Shell scripts. Refer to ''Control Structures,'' beginning on page 324.

break
continue
foreach end
goto
if
if then endif
if then else endif
onintr
switch case breaksw default endsw
while end

SUMMARY

The C Shell, like the Bourne Shell, is both a command interpreter and a programming language. It was developed at the University of California at Berkeley and has most of the facilities of the Bourne Shell, plus some others.

Among its most important features, the C Shell:

- Protects against overwriting files and accidentally logging off
- Maintains a history of recent commands
- Provides an alias mechanism for altering commands
- Provides job control
- Provides filename completion
- Provides directory stack manipulation
- Executes specific files when you log in, log out, and fork a new shell
- Evaluates logical and numerical expressions
- Processes arrays of variables representing numbers and strings
- Uses control structures to control execution within a shell script

The C Shell is available in System V Release 4 and on many machines that run older versions of System V. However, the C Shell that is provided with older releases of System V is often missing such features as job control, filename completion, and directory stack manipulation.

REVIEW EXERCISES

1. How can you review a list of the commands you executed recently? How can you reexecute the last event?

2. Assume the following is your history list:

```
37    mailx alex
38    cd /home/jenny/correspondence/business/cheese_co
39    more letter.0321
40    vi letter.0321
41    cp letter.0321 letter.0325
42    grep hansen letter.0325
43    vi letter.0325
44    lp letter*
45    cd ../milk_co
46    pwd
47    vi wilson.0321 wilson.0329
```

Using the history mechanism, what commands can you use to:

a. send mail to Alex

b. use vi to edit a file called **wilson.0329**

c. print a hard copy of **wilson.0329**

d. rename **wilson.0321** to **wilson.0322**

3. How can you identify all the aliases currently in effect?

4. What statement can you put in your **.cshrc** file to prevent yourself from accidentally overwriting a file when you redirect output? How can you override this feature? What statement can you put in your **.cshrc** file to prevent the C Shell from expanding ambiguous filenames?

5. What lines do you need to change in the Bourne Shell script **command_menu** in Chapter 8 (page 275) to make it a C Shell script? Make the changes and verify that it works.

6. Put the following line in your **.login** file. If there is another line in your **.login** file that sets the **prompt** variable, put a # in front of it to make it into a comment for the time being.

```
set prompt = " \! `pwd`> "
```

Put the next line into your **.cshrc** file.

```
alias go 'chdir \!:1; set prompt = " \! `pwd`> " '
```

Together these two lines in your **.login** and **.cshrc** files will include the name of the working directory in your prompt if you use the command **go** to change directories. For example, if Alex is in his **letter** directory and the current event number is 27, his prompt will be:

```
27 /home/alex/letter>
```

Verify that these statements work. Why do you need a statement in your **.login** file as well as one in your **.cshrc** file? (This exercise assumes that the C Shell is your login shell.)

7. Users often find rm (and even **rm –i**) too unforgiving because it removes files irrevocably. Create an alias that will move your files into a temporary directory (such as **$HOME/.trash**) when you give the command **delete**. Create a second alias called **undelete** that will move a file from the temporary directory into the working directory. Finally, put the following lines in your **.logout** file to remove any files that you deleted during the login session:

```
/usr/bin/rm -f $home/.trash/* >& /dev/null
```

What happens if there are no files in the **.trash** directory?

8. Assume the working directory contains the following files:

```
adams.ltr.03
adams.brief
adams.ltr.07
abelson.09
abelson.brief
anthony.073
anthony.brief
azevedo.99
```

What will happen if you press ESCAPE after typing the following commands?

a. **more adams.l**

b. **cat a**

c. **ls ant**

d. **file az**

What will happen if you press CONTROL-D after typing these commands?

a. **ls ab**

b. **more A**

9. What does the following command do?

```
137 % pushd ~/literature
```

10. If you start a command in the foreground and later decide that it should run in the background, what should you do? How can you prevent a command from sending output to the terminal once you have moved it into the background?

CHAPTER

10

PROGRAMMING
TOOLS

The UNIX system provides an exceptional programming environment. Because the operating system was written mostly in C by highly talented programmers who had their own needs in mind, UNIX provides an ideal environment for programming in C. Operating system services are readily accessible to the C programmer in the form of function libraries and system calls. In addition, there are a variety of tools for making the development and maintenance of programs easier.

   This chapter describes how to use the C compiler as well as two of the most useful software development tools, the make utility and System V's Source Code Control System (SCCS). The make utility helps you keep track of which modules of a program have been updated, and it helps to ensure that when you compile a program you use the latest versions of all program modules. The Source Code Control System tracks the versions of files involved in a project.

PROGRAMMING IN C

One of the main reasons the UNIX system provides an excellent C programming environment is that C programs can easily access the services of the operating system. The system calls—the routines that make operating system services available to programmers—are written in C, like most of the rest of the operating system. The system calls provide services such as creating files, reading from and writing to files, collecting information about files, allocating memory, and sending signals to processes. When you write a C program, you can use the system calls in the same way you use ordinary C program modules, or *functions,* that you have written.

A variety of *libraries* of functions have been developed to support programming in C on UNIX. The libraries are collections of related functions that you can use just as you use your own functions and the system calls. Many of the library functions access basic operating system services through the system calls, providing the services in ways that are more suited to typical programming tasks. Other library functions serve special purposes (e.g., the math library functions).

This chapter describes the processes of writing and compiling a C program. However, it will not teach you to program in C. If you want to learn C, consult one of the many available texts.

Writing a C Program

You must use an editor, such as vi, to write a C program. When you create a C program file, add .c as an extension to the filename. The C compiler expects C source files to end in .c.

Typing in the source code for a program is similar to typing in a memo or shell script—the editor does not know whether your file is a C program, a shell script, or an ordinary text document. You are responsible for making the contents of the file structurally and syntactically suitable for the C compiler to process.

Figure 10-1 illustrates the structure of a simple C program. The first two lines of the program are comments that describe what the program does. The string /* identifies the beginning of the comment, and the string */ identifies the end—the C compiler ignores all the characters between them. Because a comment can span two or more lines, the */ at the end of the first line and the /* at the beginning of the second are not necessary—they were included in **tabs.c** for clarity. As the comment explains, the program reads its standard input, coverts TAB characters into the appropriate number of spaces, and writes the transformed input to the standard output. Like many UNIX utilities, this program is a filter.

Preprocessor directives follow the comments at the top of the program; these are instructions for the C preprocessor. During the initial phase of compilation, the C preprocessor expands the directives, making the program ready for the later stages of the compilation process.

```
$ cat tabs.c
/* convert tabs in standard input to spaces     */ ┐
/* in standard output while maintaining columns */ ┘  Comments

#include    <stdio.h>      ┐  Preprocessor Directives
#define     TABSIZE     8  ┘

main()
{
int c;            /* character read from stdin   */
int posn = 0;     /* column position of character */
int inc;          /* column increment to tab stop */

while ((c = getchar()) != EOF)
    switch(c)
        {
        case '\t':                    /* c is a tab */
            inc = findstop(posn);
            posn += inc;
            for ( ; inc > 0; inc--)
                putchar(' ');
            break;
        case '\n':                  /* c is a newline */
            putchar(c);
            posn = 0;
            break;
        default:              /* c is anything else */
            putchar(c);
            posn++;
            break;
        }
}

/* compute size of increment to next tab stop    */

findstop(col)
int col;     /* column position of tab character */
{
return (TABSIZE - (col % TABSIZE));
}
```

FIGURE 10-1   A Simple C Program

You can use the **#define** preprocessor directive to define *symbolic constants* and *macros*. Symbolic constants are names that you can use in your programs in place of constant values. For example, **tabs.c** uses a **#define** preprocessor directive to associate the symbolic constant, **TABSIZE**, with the constant 8. **TAB-SIZE** is used in the program in place of the constant 8 as the distance between TAB stops. By convention, the names of symbolic constants are composed of all uppercase letters.

By defining symbolic names for constant values, you can make your program easier to read and easier to modify. If you later decide to change a constant, you need only change the preprocessor directive rather than changing the value everywhere it occurs in your program. If you replace the **#define** directive for **TAB-SIZE** in Figure 10-1 with the following directive, the program will place TAB stops every four columns rather than every eight:

```
#define      TABSIZE    4
```

You can also use **#define** statements to define macros, which are similar to short functions. The following macro determines whether a character is a digit:

```
#define      numeric(n)      (n >= '0' && n <= '9')
```

You can use the macro **numeric(n)** in your code in the same way you use functions. However, macros are not really functions—the C preprocessor replaces macros with C code rather than with function calls.

When several symbolic constant and macro definitions are used in different modules of a program, they are typically collected together in a single file called a *header file* (or an *include file*). Although the C compiler does not put constraints on the names of header files, by convention they end in **.h**. The name of the header file is then listed in an **#include** preprocessor directive in each program source file that uses any of the symbolic constants or macros. The program in Figure 10-1 uses **getchar** and **putchar**, which are macros defined in **stdio.h** on many systems. The **stdio.h** header file defines a variety of general-purpose macros and is used by many system calls and C library functions.

The angle brackets (< and >) that surround **stdio.h** in **tabs.c** instruct the C preprocessor to look for the header file in a standard directory (**/usr/include** on most systems). If you want to include a header file from another directory, use double quotes and specify the absolute pathname of the file. The following example includes a header file from one of Alex's directories:

```
#include "/home/alex/cprogs/ledg.h"
```

Although you can call most C functions anything you want, each program must have exactly one function named **main**. The main function is the control module—your program begins execution with the main function. Typically, **main** will call other functions in turn, which may call yet other functions, and so forth. By putting different operations into separate functions, you can make a program easier to read and maintain. The program in Figure 10-1 uses a function **findstop** to compute the distance to the next TAB stop. Although this single statement could easily have been included in the main function, isolating it in a separate function draws attention to a key computation.

Functions can also make both development and maintenance of the program more efficient. By putting a frequently used code segment into a function, you avoid entering the same code over and over again into the program. Later when you want to make changes to the code, you only need to change it once.

If your program is long and involves several functions, you may want to split it into two or more files. A C program can be split into any number of different files; however, each function must be wholly contained within a file. You should put **#define** preprocessor directives into a header file and include the header file in any source file that uses the directives. Each source filename must have a **.c** extension.

Compiling a Program

To compile **tabs.c**, give the following command:

```
$ cc tabs.c
```

The cc utility calls the C preprocessor, the C compiler, the assembler, and the link editor. The four components of the compilation process are shown in Figure 10-2.

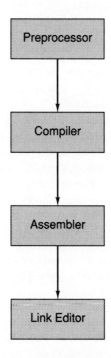

FIGURE 10-2   Components of the Compilation Process

The C preprocessor expands symbolic constant and macro definitions and also includes header files. The compilation phase creates assembly language code corresponding to the instructions in the source file. Then the assembler creates machine-readable object code. One object file is created for each source file. Each object file has the same name as the source file, with the exception that the **.c** extension is replaced with a **.o**. In the example on page 345, a single object file would be created, **tabs.o**. However, after the C compiler successfully completes all phases of the compilation process for a program contained in a single source file, it creates the executable file and then removes the **.o** file. If you successfully compile **tabs.c**, you will not see the **.o** file.

During the final phase of the compilation process, the link editor searches specified libraries for functions your program uses and combines object modules for those functions with your program's object modules. By default, the C compiler searches the standard C library, **libc.a**, which contains functions that handle input and output and provides many other general-purpose capabilities. If you want the link editor to search other libraries, you must use the **–l** option to specify the libraries on the command line. Unlike most options to UNIX system utilities, the **–l** option does not come before all filenames on the command line—it comes after all the filenames of all modules that it applies to. In the next example, the C compiler searches the math library, **libm.a**:

```
$ cc calc.c -lm
```

As you can see from the example, the **–l** option uses abbreviations for library names, appending the letter following **–l** to **lib** and adding a **.a** extension. The **m** in the example above stands for **libm.a**.

As the last step of the compilation process, by default the link editor creates an executable file named **a.out**. If there is only one object file, cc removes the object file after it successfully creates the executable. In the next example, there are several object files, and cc does not remove them. The **–O** option causes cc to use the C compiler optimizer. The optimizer makes object code more efficient so that the executable program runs more quickly.

```
$ cc -O ledger.c acctspay.c acctsrec.c
$ ls
a.out          acctspay.o  acctsrec.o  ledger.o
acctspay.c  acctsrec.c  ledger.c
```

You can use the executable **a.out** in the same way you use shell scripts and other programs—by typing its name on the command line. The program in Figure 10-1 expects to read from its standard input, so once you have created the executable, **a.out**, you can use a command such as the following to run it:

```
$ a.out < mymemo
```

If you want to save the **a.out** file, you should change the name to a more descriptive one. Otherwise, you might accidentally overwrite it during a later compilation.

```
$ mv a.out tabs
```

To save the trouble of renaming **a.out** files, you can specify the name of the executable file when you use CC. If you use the **-o** option, the C compiler will give the executable the name of your choice rather than **a.out**. In the next example, the executable is called **accounting**:

```
$ cc -o accounting ledger.c acctspay.c acctsrec.c
```

Assuming the executable file does not read from its standard input or require arguments, you can run it with the following command:

```
$ accounting
```

If you want to compile some but not all of the modules of a program, you can use the **-c** option to CC, which suppresses the link editing phase. The **-c** option is useful because it does not treat unresolved external references as errors; this capability enables you to compile and debug the syntax of the modules of a program as you create them. Once you have compiled and debugged all the modules, you can run CC again with the object files as arguments to produce an executable program. In the next example, CC produces three object files but no executable:

```
$ cc -c ledger.c acctspay.c acctsrec.c
$ ls
acctspay.c  acctspay.o  acctsrec.c  acctsrec.o  ledger.c    ledger.o
```

If you then run CC again using the object files, CC will produce the executable. Because the C compiler recognizes the filename extension **.o**, it recognizes that the files only need to be linked. You can also include both **.c** and **.o** files on a single command line, as in this example:

```
$ cc -o accounting ledger.o acctspay.c acctsrec.o
```

The C compiler recognizes that the **.c** file needs to be preprocessed and compiled, whereas the **.o** files do not. The C compiler also accepts assembly language files ending in **.s**, and it treats them appropriately (that is, CC assembles and links them). This feature makes it easy to modify and recompile a program.

With large programs that have many different modules, the ability to compile modules separately and link them with previously compiled modules can save time. The make utility provides an automated method for figuring out what program modules need to be recompiled (see page 349). For more information about the C compiler, refer to cc in Part II.

Debugging C Programs

The C compiler is liberal about the kinds of constructs it allows in programs. Like many other UNIX utilities, cc seems to be based on the philosophy that the user *means* what he or she says (or types) and that no news is good news. The C compiler allows almost anything that is logically possible according to the definition of the language. Although this approach gives the programmer a great deal of flexibility and control, it can make debugging difficult.

The UNIX system provides several tools to make debugging easier. The C program verifier, lint, is one of the most useful. It checks programs for potential bugs and portability problems. Unlike the C compiler, lint is very strict. It detects and reports on a wide variety of problems and potential problems, including variables that are used before they are set, arguments to functions that are not used, and functions that use return values that were never returned. Although you are free to ignore lint's warnings and go ahead and compile your program, a warning typically means that the program has a bug or a nonportable construct or that you have violated a standard of good programming. Paying attention to lint's warnings is a good way to debug your programs and to hone your programming skills.

The UNIX system also provides a debugger for tackling problems that evade lint and the C compiler. System V's debugger is called sdb (symbolic debugger). The sdb utility is a high-level debugger—it enables you to analyze the execution of a program in terms of C language statements. It also provides a lower-level view for analyzing the execution of a program in terms of the machine instructions.

The sdb utility enables you to monitor and control the execution of a program. You can step through a program on a line-by-line basis while you examine the state of the execution environment. It also allows you to examine *core* files. When a serious error occurs during the execution of a program, the operating system displays a message such as Segmentation violation −− Core dumped and creates a core file containing information about the state of the program and the system when the failure occurred. Using sdb you can identify the line in the program where the error occurred, the values of variables at that point, and so forth. Because core files tend to be large and take up valuable disk space, be sure to remove them after you are done.

If you want to use the debugger with a program, you should use the −g option when you compile the program. The −g option causes cc to generate additional information that is used by the debugger. Refer to the documentation that comes with your system for information about how to use sdb.

THE make UTILITY

When you have a large program with many source and header files, the files typi-cally depend on one another in complex ways. When you change a file that other files depend on, you *must* recompile all dependent files. For example, you might have several source files, all of which use a single header file. When you make a change to the header file, each of the source files must be recompiled. The header file might depend on other header files, and so forth. These sorts of dependency relationships are shown in Figure 10-3. (Each arrow in Figure 10-3 points from a file to another file that depends on it.)

When you are working on a large program, it can be difficult, time consum-ing, and tedious to determine which modules need to be recompiled due to their dependency relationships. The make utility automates this process.

In its simplest use, make looks at *dependency lines* in a file named **makefile** in the working directory. The dependency lines indicate relationships among files, specifying a *target file* that depends on one or more *prerequisite* files. If you have modified any of the prerequisite files more recently than its target file, make updates the target file based on *construction commands* that follow the depen-dency line. The make utility normally stops if it encounters an error during the construction process.

A simple **makefile** has the following format:

target: **prerequisite-list**
TAB   **construction-commands**

The dependency line is composed of the **target** and the **prerequisite-list,** separated by a colon. The **construction-commands** line must start with a TAB and must follow the dependency line.

The **target** is the name of the file that depends on the files in the **prerequisite-list**. The **construction-commands** are regular commands to the shell that construct (usually compile and/or link) the target file. The make utility executes the **construction-commands** when the modification time of one or more of the files in the **prerequisite-list** is more recent than that of the target file.

The example below shows the dependency line and construction commands for the file called **form** in Figure 10-3. It depends on its prerequisites, **size.o** and **length.o**. An appropriate CC command constructs the **target**.

```
form: size.o length.o
      cc -o form size.o length.o
```

Each of the prerequisites on one dependency line can be a target on another dependency line. For example, both **size.o** and **length.o** are targets on other dependency lines. Although the example in Figure 10-3 is simple, the nesting of

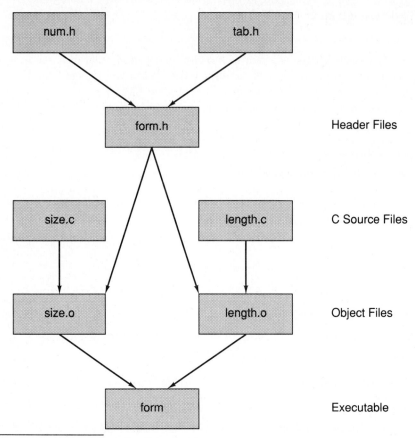

FIGURE 10-3   Dependency Graph for the Target **form**

dependency specifications can create a complex hierarchy that specifies relation-ships among many files.

The following **makefile** corresponds to the complete dependency graph shown in Figure 10-3. The executable file **form** depends on two object files, and the object files each depend on their respective source files and a header file, **form.h**. In turn, **form.h** depends on two other header files.

```
$ cat makefile
form: size.o length.o
        cc -o form size.o length.o
size.o: size.c form.h
        cc -c size.c
```

```
length.o:  length.c  form.h
       cc  -c  length.c

form.h:  num.h  table.h
     cat  num.h  table.h  >  form.h
```

The last line illustrates the fact that you can put any Bourne Shell command on a construction line. (However, creating a header file by catenating two other header files is not something you see done often.) Because **makefiles** are processed by the Bourne Shell, the command line should be one that you could input in response to a Bourne Shell prompt.

Implied Dependencies

You can rely on *implied* dependencies and construction commands to make your job of writing a **makefile** easier. If you do not include a dependency line for an object file, make assumes that it depends on a compiler or assembler source code file. Thus, if a prerequisite for a target file is **xxx.o**, and there is no construction command following a dependency line for the **xxx.o** target, make looks for one of the following files in the working directory. If it finds an appropriate source file, make provides a default construction command line that calls the proper compiler or the assembler to create the object file.

Filename	Type of File
xxx.c	C source code
xxx.r	RATFOR source code
xxx.f	FORTRAN source code
xxx.y	YACC source code
xxx.l	Lex source code
xxx.s	assembler source code

RATFOR and FORTRAN are standard programming languages, and YACC and Lex are UNIX tools for creating command languages.

The next example shows a **makefile** that keeps a file named **compute** up-to-date. The first three lines (each beginning with a pound sign, #) are comment lines. Because make ignores lines that begin with pound signs, you can use pound signs to set off comments. The first dependency line shows that **compute** depends on two object files: **compute.o** and **calc.o**. The corresponding construction line gives the command make needs to produce **compute**. The next dependency line shows that **compute.o** not only depends on its C source file but also on a header file, **compute.h**. The construction line for **compute.o** uses the C compiler optimizer (–O option). The final dependency and construction lines are not required. In their absence, make would infer that **calc.o** was dependent on **calc.c** and would produce the command line needed for the compilation.

```
$ cat makefile
#
# makefile for compute
#

compute: compute.o calc.o
        cc -o compute compute.o calc.o

compute.o: compute.c compute.h
        cc -c -O compute.c

calc.o: calc.c
        cc -c calc.c
```

Following are some sample executions of make, based on the previous **makefile**. As the ls command below shows, **compute.o**, **calc.o**, and **compute** are not up-to-date. Consequently, the make command runs the construction commands that recreate them.

```
$ ls -l
total 22
-rw-rw----  1 alex   pubs      179 Jun 21 18:20 calc.c
-rw-rw----  1 alex   pubs      354 Jun 21 16:02 calc.o
-rwxrwx---  1 alex   pubs     6337 Jun 21 16:04 compute
-rw-rw----  1 alex   pubs      780 Jun 21 18:20 compute.c
-rw-rw----  1 alex   pubs       49 Jun 21 16:04 compute.h
-rw-rw----  1 alex   pubs      880 Jun 21 16:04 compute.o
-rw-rw----  1 alex   pubs      311 Jun 21 15:56 makefile
$ make
        cc -c -O compute.c
        cc -c calc.c
        cc -o compute compute.o calc.o
```

If you run make once and then run it again without making any changes to the prerequisite files, make indicates that the program is up-to-date by not executing any commands.

```
$ make
'compute' is up to date.
```

The following example uses the touch utility to change the modification time of a prerequisite file. This simulation shows what would happen if you were to make a change to the file. The make utility executes only the commands necessary to make the out-of-date targets up-to-date.

```
$ touch calc.c
$ make
        cc -c calc.c
        cc -o compute compute.o calc.o
```

In the next example, touch changes the modification time of **compute.h**. The make utility recreates **compute.o** because it depends on **compute.h**, and make recreates the executable because it depends on **compute.o**.

```
$ touch compute.h
$ make
        cc -c -O compute.c
        cc -o compute compute.o calc.o
```

As these examples illustrate, touch is useful when you want to fool make into recompiling programs or into *not* recompiling them. You can use it to update the modification times of all the source files so that make considers that nothing is up-to-date. The make utility will then recompile everything. Alternatively, you can use touch or the –t option to make to touch all relevant files so that make considers everything to be up-to-date. This is useful if the modification times of files have changed, yet the files are all up-to-date. (For example, this situation occurs when you copy a complete set of files from one directory to another.) If you want to see what make *would* do if you ran it, run make with the –n option.

OPTIONAL

Macros

The make utility has a macro facility that enables you to create and use macros within a **makefile**. The format of a macro definition is shown below.

ID = list

Replace **ID** with an identifying name, and replace **list** with a list of filenames. After this macro definition, $(**ID**) represents **list** in the **makefile**.

By default, make invokes the C compiler without any options (except the –c option when it is appropriate to compile but not to link a file). You can use the **CFLAGS** macro definition, as shown below, to cause make to call the C compiler with specific options. Replace **options** with the options you want to use.

CFLAGS = options

The following **makefile** uses macros, implied dependencies, and construc-
tions:

```
#
# makefile: report, print, printf, printh
#

CFLAGS  = -O
FILES = in.c out.c ratio.c process.c tally.c
OBJECTS = in.o out.o ratio.o process.o tally.o
HEADERS = names.h companies.h conventions.h

report: $(OBJECTS)
        cc -o report $(OBJECTS)

ratio.o: $(HEADERS)

process.o: $(HEADERS)

tally.o: $(HEADERS)

print:
        pr $(FILES) $(HEADERS) | lp

printf:
        pr $(FILES) | lp

printh:
        pr $(HEADERS) | lp
```

Following the comment lines, the **makefile** uses **CFLAGS** to make sure that
make always selects the C optimizer (**-O** option) when it invokes the C compiler
as the result of an implied construction. (Whenever you put a construction line in
a **makefile**, the construction line overrides **CFLAGS** and any other implied construction lines.) Following **CFLAGS**, the **makefile** defines the **FILES**,
OBJECTS, and **HEADERS** macros. Each of these macros defines a list of files.

The first dependency line shows that **report** depends on the list of files that
OBJECTS defines. The corresponding construction line links the **OBJECTS** and
creates an executable file named **report**.

The next three dependency lines show that three object files depend on the
list of files that **HEADERS** defines. There are no construction lines, so when it is
necessary, make looks for a source code file corresponding to each of the object
files and compiles it. These three dependency lines ensure that the object files are
recompiled if any of the header files is changed.

You can combine several targets on one dependency line, so these three
dependency lines could have been combined into one line, as follows:

```
ratio.o process.o tally.o:  $(HEADERS)
```

The final three dependency lines send source and header files to the printer. They have nothing to do with compiling the **report** file. None of these targets (**print, printf,** and **printh**) depends on anything. When you call one of these targets from the command line, make executes the construction line following it. As an example, the following command prints all the source files that **FILES** defines:

```
$ make printf
```

THE SOURCE CODE CONTROL SYSTEM

When you work on a project involving many files that evolve over long periods of time, it can be hard to keep track of the versions of the files, especially if several people are making updates. This problem occurs particularly in large software development projects. Source code and documentation files change frequently as you fix bugs, enhance programs, and release new versions of the software. It becomes even more complex when there is more than one active version of each file. Frequently, customers are using one version of a file while a newer version is being modified. You can easily lose track of the versions and accidentally undo changes that were already made or duplicate earlier work.

To help avoid these kinds of problems, UNIX System V provides utilities for managing and tracking changes to files. These utilities comprise the Source Code Control System, or SCCS. SCCS can be used to control changes to files. Although it can be used on any text file, SCCS is most often used to manage source code and software documentation.

SCCS can control who is allowed to update files. For each update, it records who made the changes and includes notes about why the changes were made. Because SCCS stores the original version of a file as well as changes to the file as they are made, it is possible to regenerate any version of a file. By saving the changes that are made to a file rather than a complete new version, SCCS conserves disk space; however, SCCS files themselves consume a lot of space because of all the information they store about each update. Whether SCCS actually saves disk space or not depends on the sizes of the files and the nature of the changes that are made to them.

This section provides an overview of SCCS. The SCCS utilities are described in more detail in Part II, where they are listed under their individual names.

Evolution of an SCCS File

When you change an SCCS file and record the changes in SCCS, the set of changes is referred to as a *delta*. Each delta has an associated version number, or SCCS Identification String (called SID), consisting of either two or four components. The first two, which are always used, are the *release* and *level* numbers. When an SCCS file is initially created, by default SCCS assigns a release number of 1 and a level number of 1, which corresponds to Version 1.1 (or delta 1.1). Also by default, SCCS assigns subsequent version numbers of 1.2, 1.3, and so on. However, you have control over the version numbers and can skip level numbers or change the release number. You should ordinarily only change the release number when the file has undergone a major revision.

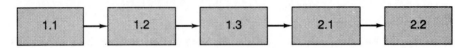

FIGURE 10-4   The History of an SCCS File

Usually, files undergo a sequential development, where each delta includes all previous deltas. This kind of development is depicted in Figure 10-4. However, there are cases when changes are made to an intermediate version of a file. For example, if you were working on the source code file shown in Figure 10-4, and you had to make an emergency bug fix to Version 2.1 to deliver to customers prior to delivering Version 2.2, you would want to record a delta that reflected that fix but that excluded the changes involved in Version 2.2. In that case you would create the *branch* delta shown in Figure 10-5.

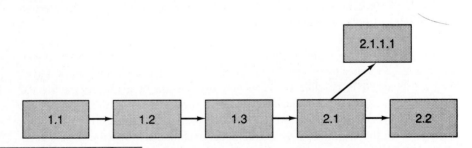

FIGURE 10-5   A Branch in the Evolution of an SCCS File

It is possible that you would work on the two deltas to Version 2.1 concurrently or that you would work on one while someone else worked on the other. However, because SCCS was designed to avoid the problems of coordination that occur when changes are made independently on the same file, SCCS normally prohibits concurrent deltas to the same version. Although you ordinarily would not want to, you can override this restriction if necessary.

Unlike the earlier, sequentially applied deltas, the branch delta in Figure 10-5 has four components to its version number: *release, level, branch*, and *sequence number*. Version 2.1.1.1 is the first delta to the first branch on Release 2, Level 1. Successive deltas on that branch would be 2.1.1.2, 2.1.1.3, and so forth. Successive branches on Version 2.1 would start with deltas 2.1.2.1, 2.1.3.1, and so forth.

The evolution of an SCCS file can become complicated when there are many branch deltas. When you record changes to a file, try to keep the evolution of the versions as simple as you can. You should make a delta to a file only when you are sure that the changes you have made are complete. For example, when you are fixing a collection of bugs in a file, you should fix each one and completely test it before recording the changes in a delta. This technique saves you from having deltas that reflect incomplete, transitional stages in the history of a file.

Creating an SCCS File

The admin utility is one of the most important SCCS utilities—you can use it to create SCCS files as well as to change characteristics of existing SCCS files. If you have a Bourne Shell script called **blitz**, you can use admin to create an SCCS encoded version.

The admin command in Figure 10-6 creates the initial version of the SCCS encoded file **s.blitz**, Version 1.1. This file includes the contents of the file **blitz** as well as the control information SCCS adds. The statement admin presents, No id keywords (cm7), is a warning message. The string in parentheses, cm7, is a code for a help message. If you give the command help followed by the code, the help utility will produce an explanation of the message.

```
$ help cm7
cm7 :
"No id keywords"
No SCCS identification keywords were substituted for.
You may not have any keywords in the file,
in which case you can ignore this warning.
   .
   .
```

As the help utility explains, the message in Figure 10-6 indicates that there are no SCCS keywords in the encoded file. Keywords are SCCS codes you can use to insert information about the SCCS file into the text retrieved from the encoded file. For example, you can use keywords to identify the SCCS filename, the version number, and the date and time the text was retrieved from the encoded file.

```
$ cat blitz
:
# A script that noisily but cautiously
# empties the working directory

echo "The working directory is ` pwd ` "
echo "Delete all files in ` pwd ` ? \c"
read answer
case $answer in
        y|Y|[yY]es)
                    echo "OUCH!!  BANG!!  SPLAT!!"
                    rm *
                    echo "We got ´ em boss!"
                    ;;
           *)       echo "Files remain untouched"
                    ;;
esac
$ admin -iblitz s.blitz
No id keywords (cm7)
```

FIGURE 10-6   Contents of the **blitz** File

One SCCS keyword inserts a string [@(#)] in a file that the what command recognizes. The what command is an SCCS utility that sends to the standard output the text that follows the string @(#). Many standard UNIX utilities include these strings to identify the version number of the program. For example, you can use what to identify the version of the Korn Shell on a system.

```
$ what /usr/bin/ksh
/usr/bin/ksh:
          Version 11/16/88d
          /usr/bin/ksh.sl 1.1 4.0 08/07/90 27563 AT&T-SF
```

Because keywords are not used in the examples in this book, you can ignore the warning message when it occurs in the examples.

Although you can call the admin utility with many other arguments, in the form shown in Figure 10-6 its format is:

admin -iname filename

The **name** is the name of the file SCCS will encode. The **filename** is the name of the SCCS encoded file, and it must start with an s. prefix.

After you use admin to create an SCCS encoded file, you should move the original file to a backup directory. If you leave the original file in the working directory, SCCS will not allow you to retrieve the file from the encoded version while you are in that directory.

Retrieving an SCCS File

You should not edit an SCCS encoded file such as **s.blitz**—editing the file would defeat the purpose of using SCCS. Use the **get** utility with the **−e** option to create an unencoded, editable version of the file. The **−e** option indicates to SCCS that you intend to make a delta. In other words, it indicates to SCCS that you plan to make changes and record the changes in SCCS. If you call the **get** utility without the **−e** option, SCCS will create an unencoded version of the file that is not editable. The following command recreates the file **blitz** for editing:

```
$ get −e s.blitz
1.1
new delta 1.2
16 lines
```

The **get** command displays the version number of the retrieved delta, the version number that will be applied when the new changes are recorded in SCCS, and the number of lines in the file. If you forget to move the original **blitz** file to another directory after you create **s.blitz**, **get** will display the following error message. (Again, you can give the command **help ge4** to find out more about the error message.)

```
ERROR [s.blitz]: writable `blitz' exists (ge4)
```

By default, the **get** command retrieves the most recent delta to the file. In the case of the file **s.blitz**, that delta is Version 1.1. You can also use **get** with the **−r** option to retrieve a specific delta or to change the number of the new delta.

```
$ get −e −r2 s.blitz
1.1
new delta 2.1
16 lines
```

Because there are no existing versions with a release number of 2, this command retrieves the latest delta prior to Release 2, and it changes the new version number to 2.1. If versions with a release number of 2 already existed, this command would have retrieved the most recent one.

If you retrieve a version that is earlier than the most recent version, SCCS will create a branch delta. For example, if a version number higher than 1.2 exists for **s.blitz**, retrieving Version 1.2 creates a branch delta.

```
$ get -e -r1.2 s.blitz
1.2
new delta 1.2.1.1
16 lines
```

It is easiest to keep track of the evolution of your SCCS files if only one get is active for a specific file at a time. However, SCCS allows you to simultaneously update different versions of a file as long as you put the retrieved files in different directories. If you try to retrieve a version while the working directory contains a previously retrieved version that is editable, SCCS displays an error message.

By default, SCCS prevents you from simultaneously working on two deltas to the same version of a file. If you want to have more than one get active against a single version of a file, you must use the admin utility to add the j flag to the SCCS file (SCCS distinguishes between *options,* which are used on the command line, and *flags,* which are added to a file as control information). Refer to admin in Part II for more information.

Recording Changes to an SCCS File

After you have edited the retrieved file and are ready to record the changes in SCCS, use the delta utility to record your changes. The user who retrieves a file must be the one who gives the delta command. Consequently, you can use delta only if you were the one who executed the corresponding get.

```
$ delta s.blitz
comments?
```

The delta utility prompts you for comments. In response, enter the reason for the changes. Assuming you had changed the echo commands inside the Case control structure in **blitz** as shown in Figure 10-7, you might enter the comment shown. Most versions of SCCS use a NEWLINE to terminate a comment, so to continue a comment from one line to the next, you must escape the NEWLINE character (that is, precede the NEWLINE with a backslash). Other versions of SCCS expect comments to span multiple lines, and they terminate a comment when you use CONTROL-D on a line by itself. If your version of SCCS uses CONTROL-D to terminate a comment, do not escape the NEWLINES that occur within comments.

After you enter a comment, delta displays a warning message followed by the version number and a summary of the changes that were made to the file.

If you make a delta and later decide to remove it, you can use the rmdel utility to delete it. The following command removes Version 1.2 of **s.blitz**:

```
$ rmdel -r1.2 s.blitz
```

```
$ cat blitz
:
# A script that cautiously
# empties the working directory

echo "The working directory is ` pwd ` "
echo "Delete all files in ` pwd ` ? \c"
read answer
case "$answer" in
        y|Y|[yY]es)
                        echo "Files being removed"
                        rm *
                        echo "Done"
                        ;;
        *)              echo "Files remain untouched"
                        ;;
esac
$ delta s.blitz
comments? frivolous statements replaced \
with serious ones
No id keywords (cm7)
1.2
3 inserted
3 deleted
13 unchanged
```

FIGURE 10-7   Modified **blitz** File

The rmdel utility removes only the latest version or the latest version on a branch. After using rmdel to remove the latest version, you can remove the next most recent version, and so forth.

Although you would not want to edit it, you can look at an SCCS encoded file to get a better idea of how SCCS works. The file **s.blitz** is shown in Figure 10-8. To look at an encoded file, use cat with the −v option and pipe the output through pg or more. The −v option causes cat to display visible representations of nonprinting characters. The characters ^A at the start of some lines represent CONTROL-A, which SCCS uses to identify lines that contain control information.

Obtaining the History of an SCCS File

The prs utility prints information about the history of an SCCS file. Although you can call prs with a variety of arguments that specify what information it

```
$ cat -v s.blitz | pg
^Ah48993
^As 00003/00003/00013
^Ad D 1.2 90/06/21 10:38:25 alex 2 1
^Ac frivolous statements replaced
^Ac with serious ones
^Ae
^As 00016/00000/00000
^Ad D 1.1 90/06/21 10:35:34 alex 1 0
^Ac date and time created 90/06/21 10:35:34 by alex
^Ae
^Au
^AU
^At
^AT
^AI 1
:
^AD 2
# A script that noisily but cautiously
^AE 2
^AI 2
# A script that cautiously
^AE 2
# empties the working directory

echo "The working directory is `pwd`"
echo "Delete all files in `pwd`? \c"
read answer
case $answer in
        y|Y|[yY]es)
^AD 2
                echo "OUCH!!  BANG!!  SPLAT!!"
^AE 2
^AI 2
                echo "Files being removed"
^AE 2
                rm *
^AD 2
                echo "We got 'em boss!"
^AE 2
^AI 2
                echo "Done"
^AE 2
                ;;
        *)      echo "Files remain untouched"
                ;;
esac
^AE 1
```

FIGURE 10-8   Contents of an Encoded SCCS File

```
$ prs s.blitz
s.blitz:

D 1.2 90/06/21 10:38:25 alex 2 1 00003/00003/00013
MRs:
COMMENTS:
frivolous statements replaced
with serious ones

D 1.1 90/06/21 10:35:34 alex 1 0 00016/00000/00000
MRs:
COMMENTS:
date and time created 90/06/21 10:35:34 by alex
```

FIGURE 10-9   The prs Utility

reports and the format of the report, when it is called without any arguments, **prs** prints summary information about all deltas.

Figure 10-9 shows the following information about each delta: the date and time of creation, the user who made the delta, the sequence number of the delta and its predecessor, and the number of lines inserted, deleted, and unchanged. After the MRs: label would be a list of any modification request (MR) numbers for the delta. A *modification request* is a bug report against a program or software document. There is no information after the modification request prompt in Figure 10-9 because the examples do not use MR numbers. If you use the **v** flag and the **-m** option with **admin**, **delta** prompts you for MR numbers each time you use it. See **admin** in Part II for more information.

Restricting Access to SCCS Files

You can use the **admin** utility to establish a list of users who are allowed to make deltas to an SCCS file. By default, the list of users who can make changes to a file is empty, which means that anyone can make a delta. The following command gives permission to Alex and Jenny and implicitly denies permission to everyone else. After this command is executed, only Alex and Jenny will be able to make deltas:

```
$ admin -aalex -ajenny s.blitz
```

The **-e** (erase) flag removes a user from the list, denying him or her permission to make deltas. The following command removes Jenny from the list of authorized users.

```
$ admin -ejenny s.blitz
```

In addition to allowing you to restrict access to a list of users, SCCS allows you to *lock* releases of a file so that no one can change them. The following command uses the **-f** option to set the l flag to lock Release 1 of **s.blitz**:

```
$ admin -fl1 s.blitz
```

After executing this command, if you try to retrieve a Release 1 delta for editing, get will give you an error message. Use the following command to lock all releases of the **s.blitz** file:

```
$ admin -fla s.blitz
```

SUMMARY

The operating system interface to C programs and a variety of software development tools make the UNIX system well suited to programming in C. The C libraries provide general-purpose C functions that make operating system services and other functionality available to C programmers. The standard C library, **libc**, is always accessible to C programs, and you can use other libraries by including them in an option to the cc command.

You can write a C program using a text editor, such as vi. C programs always have a function called **main** and often have several other functions. You can use preprocessor directives to define symbolic constants and macros and to instruct the preprocessor to include header files.

When you use the cc command, it first calls the C preprocessor, followed by the C compiler and the assembler. The compiler creates assembly language code, which the assembler uses to create object modules. Finally, the link editor combines the object modules into an executable file. You can use the C program verifier, lint, and a debugger (sdb) to aid in the process of debugging a program.

The make utility uses a file named **makefile** that documents the relationships among files. You can use it to keep track of which modules of a program are out-of-date and to compile files in order to keep all modules up-to-date.

The Source Code Control System, SCCS, comprises several utility programs that track changes to files involved in large software projects. SCCS stores the original files as well as each set of changes that was made to the originals so that you can regenerate any version of a file at any time. SCCS also documents the history of a file by recording who made each delta and when and why they made it.

REVIEW EXERCISES

1. How would you instruct the C preprocessor to include the header file **/usr/include/math.h** in your C program? How would you instruct it to include **/home/alex/headers/declar.h**?

2. What function does every C program have? Why should you split large programs into several functions?

3. What command could you use to compile **prog.c** and **func.c** into an executable called **cprog**?

4. In the **makefile** below, identify:

   a. targets

   b. construction commands

   c. prerequisites

   d. macros

```
$ cat makefile
COBJECTS = menu.o users.o resellers.o prospects.o
HFILES = menu.h

leads: $(COBJECTS)
        cc -o leads $(COBJECTS)

menu.o users.o resellers.o prospects.o: $(HFILES)
```

5. If you are using the **makefile** in the previous exercise, what will happen if you give the following command?

```
$ make
```

6. After compiling leads (refer to the **makefile** above), if you change **users.c** and run make again, what will make do?

7. Write a **makefile** that reflects the following relationships:

   a. The C source files **transactions.c** and **reports.c** are compiled to produce an executable, **accts**.

   b. **transactions.c** and **reports.c** include a header file **accts.h**.

   c. The header file **accts.h** is composed of two other header files: **trans.h** and **reps.h**.

8. Add the necessary dependency and construction lines to the **makefile** for **compute** (see page 352) to format an nroff document, **compute.n,** that describes the **compute** program and includes the program source code. (*Hint:* Refer to the **.so** command in Chapter 7 for ideas about how to include the program source file in the nroff file.)

9. What command can you use to create an SCCS encoded version of a file called **answers**? What command can you use to retrieve an editable version of **answers**?

10. How can you restrict the SCCS encoded file **s.answers** so that:

    a. only barbara and hls can make changes

    b. no one can make changes to Release 2

11. If you retrieve Version 4.1 of the file **s.answers** for editing and then attempt to retrieve the same version again, what will SCCS do? Why is SCCS set up this way?

CHAPTER

11

SYSTEM ADMINISTRATION

The system administrator is responsible for setting up new users, installing and removing terminals, making sure there is enough space on the disk, backing up files, bringing up and shutting down the system, helping users when they have problems, and taking care of other computer housekeeping tasks.

Because UNIX is so flexible, and because it runs on so many different machines, this chapter cannot discuss every system configuration or every action you will have to take as a system administrator. This chapter complements the administration section of the manual that came with your computer.

The chapter assumes you are familiar with the following terms. Refer to the Glossary, page 673, for definitions.

- block
- daemon
- device filename
- device
- environment
- file system
- fork
- kernel
- login shell

- mount (a device)
- process
- restricted shell
- root file system
- run level
- signal
- spawn
- system console

UNIX System V Release 4 includes a file system structure that is very different from earlier releases of System V. The new organization makes it easier for other computers running compatible software to share certain files that are identical on many systems, such as utilities and manual pages. At the same time each system must maintain private areas for files that are different on all systems, such as databases, system log files, and spooling areas.

This chapter describes the location of files, utilities, and directories in System V Release 4. If you are working with an earlier release of System V, you may find that the pathnames are different on your system. For example, utilities that are in **/sbin** and **/usr/sbin** on System V Release 4 might be found in **/etc** or **/bin** on earlier releases of System V. The **/var** directory did not exist in standard releases of System V prior to Release 4; instead, subdirectories of **/var** were located in the **/usr** directory.

THE SYSTEM ADMINISTRATOR AND THE SUPERUSER

Usually one person is designated as the system administrator. On large systems this can be a full-time job. Frequently on smaller systems a user of the system is assigned to do system administration in addition to his or her other work.

When you are logged in as the system administrator, you have certain system-wide powers that are beyond those of ordinary users.

- Some commands, such as commands that halt the system, can be executed only by the system administrator.

- Read, write, and execute file access permissions do not affect the system administrator. The system administrator can search any directory and create a file in or remove a file from any directory. The system administrator can also read from, write to, or execute any file.

* Some restrictions and safeguards that are built into some commands do not apply to the system administrator. For example, the system administrator can change any user's password without knowing the old password.

Because the system administrator has powers that can affect the security of any user's files as well as the security of the entire system, there is a special login name and password for the user who can log in on the system to perform these functions. The login name is generally *root*. Although you can set up a UNIX system with any name in place of root, it is not advisable to do so. Many programs depend on this name being *root*. There is also a special term for the user who has logged in as *root;* this user is called the *Superuser.*

Because of the extensive powers of destruction you have when you are the Superuser, it is a good idea to become the Superuser only when needed. If you are just doing your ordinary day-to-day work, log in as yourself. That way you will not erase someone else's files or bring down the machine by mistake.

There are three ways to become the Superuser:

1. When you bring up the system, if it comes up in single-user mode (see page 373), you are automatically logged in as the Superuser.

2. Once the system is up and running in multiuser mode (page 374), you can log in as *root,* and if you supply the proper password, you will be the Superuser.

3. You can give an **su** (substitute user) command while you are logged in as yourself, and, with the proper password, you will have the privileges of the Superuser. To be sure that you are using the system's official version of **su** (and not one planted on your system by someone trying to break in), you should always specify **su**'s absolute pathname (that is, **/usr/bin/su**) when you use it.

Once you have given an **su** command to become the Superuser, you return to your normal status by terminating the shell (by pressing CONTROL-D or giving an **exit** command). To remind you of your special powers, the shell normally displays a different prompt (usually #) while you are logged in as the Superuser.

The /usr/sbin Directory

Many of the commands you will use as the Superuser are typically kept in the **/usr/sbin** directory. They are kept there (rather than in **/usr/bin**) to lessen the chance that a user other than the Superuser will try to use one by mistake. You can execute these commands by giving their full pathnames on the command line (e.g., **/usr/sbin/mkfs**) *or* by including the **/usr/sbin** directory in your **PATH** when you are logged in as the Superuser. The following line in the **/.profile** file will put **/usr/sbin** in your **PATH** when you log in as *root* using either the Bourne or Korn Shell:

```
PATH=/usr/sbin:$PATH
```

If your Superuser login uses the C Shell, also put the next line in the **/.login** file. You need to set the **PATH** variable in both **.login** and **.profile** because in certain cases (such as when you initially start up the system) the Superuser login uses the Bourne Shell, regardless of whether it is set up to use the C Shell.

```
setenv PATH /usr/sbin:$PATH
```

SYSTEM ADMINISTRATION MENU INTERFACE

System V Release 2 introduced a utility called **sysadm** to help simplify the task of system administration by providing a menu interface for common tasks. You will probably find it easier to set up and control your system if you take advantage of the menu interface. In System V Release 4, **sysadm** has been updated and expanded to include at least 12 activities.

Backup Scheduling, Setup, and Control.   This menu includes items that allow you to set parameters that control backups, to schedule and run backups, and to review information about completed backups.

Diagnosing System Errors.   Tasks on this menu allow you to review information on disk errors and to seek advice on repairing the errors.

File System Creation, Checking, and Mounting.   From this menu you can create new file systems as well as identify and check the integrity of existing file systems. You can control the availability of files by mounting and unmounting file systems. You can also review information about disk usage, including space utilization and file sizes and ages.

Machine Configuration, Display, and Powerdown.   Tasks on this menu allow you to examine the system configuration, set up parameters used during the booting process, and shut down the system to run further diagnostics, reboot, or shut off the power.

Network Services Administration.   This menu includes items that help you to configure your system to run the uucp utilities as well as local area network utilities. It will also help you set up the remote file system packages for NFS and RFS.

Port Access Services and Monitors.   Tasks on this menu allow you to set up and change settings for terminal lines as well as programs that establish network services and serial line connections.

Printer Configuration and Services.   From this menu you can add and configure printers, start and stop the printing service, and monitor and adjust printer job queues.

Restore from Backup Data.   This menu includes items to allow you to restore lost files or file systems.

Software Installation and Removal.   Tasks on this menu allow you to install or remove additional software packages as well as to identify which packages have been installed and to check their integrity.

Storage Device Operations and Definitions.   This menu allows you to describe the characteristics of the disk and tape devices on your system in a format that will be used by system software.

System Name, Date/Time, and Initial Password Setup.   You can set up your system's name, specify the correct date and time, and assign passwords for various administrative accounts using this menu.

User Login and Group Administration.   Use this menu to add, change, and delete user accounts on your system.

DETAILED DESCRIPTION OF SYSTEM OPERATION

This section covers the following topics:

- booting the system
- single-user mode and maintenance
- the transition from single-user to multiuser mode
- multiuser mode
- logging in
- bringing the system down
- crashes

It covers these topics so that you understand the basics of how the system functions and can make intelligent decisions as a system administrator. It does not cover every aspect of system administration to the depth necessary to set up or modify all system functions. It provides a guide to bringing a system up and keeping it running on a day-to-day basis. Refer to your system manual for procedures specific to your machine.

Subsequent sections of this chapter and Part II of this book describe many of the system administration files and utilities in detail.

Bringing Up (Booting) the System

Booting a system is the process of reading the UNIX system kernel into the system memory and starting it running. (The kernel is the heart of the UNIX system and is usually stored in **/stand/unix** on System V Release 4 or in **/unix** on earlier releases.)

Some systems come up automatically, whereas others require you to enter information at the system console before they get started. As the last step of the boot procedure, the UNIX operating system runs the init program as process number 1. The init program is the first genuine process to run after booting, and it becomes the parent of all the login shells that will eventually run on the system.

On System V, the init process has several *run levels,* although you will typically only use two: **s**, or single-user, and **2**, or multiuser. What init does at each run level is controlled by a file called **/etc/inittab**. The init program is responsible for running the **rc** shell scripts that perform various startup and maintenance functions. On older versions of System V, init also forked a getty process for each line that someone could log in on. In System V Release 4, one process called ttymon monitors all lines on the system and starts up the appropriate login process when it detects activity on a line.

One entry in the **/etc/inittab** file, the **initdefault** entry, determines whether the system usually comes up in single-user or multiuser mode. This entry specifies the initial run level (single-user or multiuser). Usually, System V comes up in single-user mode with only the system console operational and only the root file system mounted (that is, accessible). The root file system is the base on which all other file systems are mounted, and it is never dismounted.

When you are ready to put the system into multiuser mode, you can call init to change the run level so that the system is in multiuser mode.

The **rc**, or *run command,* scripts on System V handle tasks that need to be taken care of when you first bring the system up and subsequently when the system goes from single-user to multiuser mode. The run command scripts are shell scripts that have the letters **rc** in their filenames; they are located in the **/sbin** directory. Different manufacturers put different commands in these scripts so that they can have different effects. Typically, on booting up the system, the **/sbin/brc** and **/sbin/bcheckrc** scripts check the file systems and ask you to enter the date and time. When the system goes from single-user to multiuser mode, the **/sbin/rc2** script mounts the necessary file systems. The **/sbin/rc0** and **/sbin/rc1** scripts are run when you bring the system down to single-user mode. Each of the run command scripts **rc0, rc1,** and **rc2** reads and executes commands in a specific directory. To customize the **rc** scripts, you can add shell scripts to those directories or remove existing shell scripts from them.

Single-User Mode.   When your system is in single-user mode, only the system console is enabled; however, you can still run programs from the console as you would from any terminal in multiuser mode. The only difference is that not all file systems may be mounted. You will not be able to access files on file systems that are not mounted.

When you change a file while in single-user mode, the modified file is not written out automatically to the hard disk. To cause the system to write out any changes you have made, type the sync command periodically while in single-user mode as well as right before going into multiuser mode.

Maintenance.   With the system in single-user mode, you can perform maintenance that requires file systems unmounted or just a quiet system (no one except you using it, so that no user programs interfere with disk maintenance and backup programs).

Backing Up Files.   Although you can back up files while other people are using the system, it is better if you back them up while users are not using the files; the files will not be changing, and you will be assured of accurate copies of all the files.

Checking File System Integrity.   The fsck (file system check) utility verifies the integrity of a file system and, if possible, repairs any problems it finds. A file system (except the root) must not be mounted while fsck is checking it.

If you do not specify a device when you run fsck, fsck will check all devices listed in a certain file. On System V Release 4 the file is called **/etc/vfstab** (virtual file system table). On earlier releases of System V, the file was called **/etc/checklist** and contained the information in a different format.

Because many file system repairs destroy data, fsck asks you before making each repair. Two options cause fsck to run without asking you questions. The –y option assumes a *yes* response to all questions, and a –n assumes *no*.

Always run fsck on a file system before it is mounted. The fsck utility should be run on *all* file systems before the UNIX system is brought up in multiuser mode after it has been down for any reason. Many **rc** scripts run fsck on all file systems that will be mounted (frequently with the –y option and using **vfstab** to specify the files to be checked). Refer to fsck in Part II for more information.

Going Multiuser.   After you have determined that all is well with all file systems, you can bring the operating system up to multiuser mode.

An entry in the **inittab** file determines which run level number represents the multiuser state. On most systems, giving the command

```
# init 2
```

in response to the Superuser prompt (when the system is in single-user mode) brings the system up to multiuser mode. Once the system is in multiuser mode, you will see a login: prompt. The **inittab** file controls which terminals and dial-in lines become active. The init process selects all lines in the **inittab** file that specify run level 2. It also calls the **/sbin/rc2** file to mount the appropriate file systems.

Multiuser Mode

Multiuser mode is the normal state for a UNIX system. All appropriate file systems are mounted, and users can log in from all connected terminals and dial-in lines.

Logging In.   When you bring a system up in multiuser mode, the Service Access Controller (sac) starts up the appropriate port monitors, such as ttymon, to monitor the lines on which users can log in. (For more information on the Service Access Facility and ttymon, consult the documentation supplied with your system.) The ttymon process displays a login: prompt on a terminal and waits for someone to try to log in. When you enter your login name, ttymon establishes the characteristics of your terminal and then overlays itself with a login process and passes to the login process whatever you entered in response to the login: prompt. The login program consults the **/etc/passwd** file to see if there is a password associated with the login name you entered. If there is, login prompts you for a password; if not, it continues without requiring a password. If your login name requires a password, login verifies the password you enter by checking the **/etc/passwd** (older System V) or **/etc/shadow** (System V Release 4) file. If either your login name or password is not correct, login displays Login incorrect. and prompts you to log in again.

If the login name and password are correct, login consults the **/etc/passwd** file to initialize your user and group IDs, establish your home directory, and determine what shell you will be working with.

The login utility assigns values to the **HOME, PATH, LOGNAME, SHELL,** and **MAIL** variables. The login command looks in the **/etc/group** file to identify all the groups the user belongs to (refer to the discussion on page 377 for more information). When login has finished its work, it overlays itself with a shell. The variables are inherited by your login shell.

If your login shell is the Bourne, Job, or Korn Shell, it assigns values to the **IFS, MAILCHECK, PS1,** and **PS2** shell variables (Chapter 8 covers these variables) and then executes the commands in the **/etc/profile** shell script. Exactly what this script does is system-dependent. It usually displays the contents of the

/etc/motd (message of the day) file on the terminal, lets you know if you have any mail, runs the **news** utility, and sets the file creation mask **umask** (see Part II).

After executing the commands in **/etc/profile**, the Bourne, Job, or Korn Shell reads and executes the commands from the **.profile** shell script in your home directory. Because the shell executes a user's **.profile** script *after* the **/etc/profile** script, a sophisticated user can override any variables or conventions that were established by the system. A new user can remain uninvolved in these complications.

If the user's login shell is the C Shell, it sets several shell variables and then reads and executes the commands in the user's **.login** and **.cshrc** files.

Running a Program and Logging Out.   When you see a shell prompt, you can execute a program or log off the system.

When you log out, the process running the shell dies, and the operating system signals **init** that one of its children has died. When **init** receives one of these signals, it takes action based on the contents of the **/etc/inittab** file; in the case of a process controlling a line for a terminal, it informs **ttymon** that the line is free for another user.

Bringing the System Down

A program named **/usr/sbin/shutdown** performs all the tasks involved in bringing the system down. Use this script to bring the system down; refer to your system manual for more information. The next section describes the steps you can use to perform the key steps of **shutdown** manually.

Going to Single-User Mode.   Because going from multiuser to single-user mode can affect other users, you must be the Superuser to make this change. Make sure you give other users enough warning before going to single-user mode; otherwise they may lose whatever they were working on.

Although it is not recommended, you can use the following procedure in place of **shutdown**:

1. Log in as *root* or use **su** to become the Superuser.
2. Use **wall** (write all) to warn everyone who is using the system. Then, use **killall** to terminate all user processes except yours.
3. Give the command **sync** three times in a row. The **sync** utility forces the system to write out the contents of all disk buffers, thereby ensuring that the data on the disk is up-to-date. Because **sync** returns a prompt *before* it has completed, giving the command three times or more is one way you can be confident that at least the first one has time to complete.

4. Use **umount** to unmount all mounted devices. (You can use **mount** without an argument to see what devices are mounted.)

5. Give the command **init s** to bring the system down to single-user mode.

Turning the Power Off.   Once the system is in single-user mode, shutting it down is quite straightforward. If you have run any programs since you brought it down to single-user mode, you must run **sync** again (do it several times) before turning the power off or resetting the system. Consult your system manual for details on your system.

The only time you will not use **sync** before turning the power off or resetting the system is after using **fsck** to repair the root file system. Refer to **fsck** in Part II for details.

Crashes

A *crash* is the system stopping when you do not intend it to. After a crash, the operating system must be brought up carefully to minimize possible damage to the file systems. Frequently, there will be no damage or minimal damage to the file systems.

Although the file systems are frequently checked automatically during the boot process, you may have to check them manually, depending on how your system is set up and how you initiated the boot process. To check the file systems manually after a crash, boot the system so it is in single-user mode. **DO NOT** mount any devices other than the root (which the UNIX system mounts automatically). Run **fsck** on the root immediately, repairing the root as suggested by **fsck**. If you repair the root file system, reboot the system immediately *without* running **sync**. Then run **fsck** on all the other file systems *before* mounting them. Repair them as needed. Make note of any ordinary files or directories that you repair (and can identify), and inform their owners that they may not be complete or correct. Look in the **lost+found** directory in each file system for missing files. Refer to **fsck** in Part II for more information.

If files are not correct or are missing altogether, you may have to recreate them from a backup copy of the file system. Refer to "Backing Up Files," page 387, for more information.

OPTIONAL

IMPORTANT FILES AND DIRECTORIES

Many files are important to the administration of the system. This section details the most common of these (in alphabetical order). Refer also to page 80, "Important Standard Directories and Files."

/dev/null   Any output you redirect to this file will disappear. You can send error messages from shell scripts here when you do not want the user to see them.

If you redirect input from this file, it will appear as a null (empty) file. You can create an empty file named **nothing** by giving the following command. You can also use this technique to truncate an existing file to zero length without changing its permissions.

```
$ cat /dev/null > nothing
```

/etc/cron.d   By default, users cannot use the **at** or **crontab** utilities to schedule jobs in advance. The **/etc/cron.d** directory includes files named **at.allow** and **cron.allow** that list the login names of users who are permitted to use these utilities. Files called **at.deny** and **cron.deny** in this directory specify users who are not permitted to use the corresponding utilities. If you wish to allow everyone to use them, create empty **at.deny** and **cron.deny** files (and do not create **at.allow** or **cron.allow** files).

/etc/group   Groups allow users to share files or programs without allowing all system users access to them. This scheme is useful if several users are working with files that are not public information.

An entry in the **/etc/group** file has the four fields shown below. If an entry is too long to fit on one line, end the line with a backslash (\), which will quote the following RETURN, and continue the entry on the next line.

group-name:password:group-ID:login-name-list

The **group-name** is from one to six characters, the first being alphabetic and none being uppercase. The **password** is an optional encrypted password. Because there is no good way to enter a password into the **group** file, group passwords are not very useful and should be avoided. The **group-ID** is a number between 0 and 65,535, with 0-99 being reserved. The **login-name-list** is a comma-separated list of users who belong to that group. A sample entry in a **group** file is shown below. The group is named **pubs**, has no password, and has a group ID of 141.

```
pubs::141:alex,jenny,scott,hls,barbara
```

The **/etc/group** file does not define groups. Groups come into existence when a user is assigned a group ID number in the **/etc/passwd** file. The **/etc/group** file associates a name with each group.

Although the **/etc/group** file has the same structure on System V Release 4 and earlier versions of System V, groups are used differently on System V Release 4.

NEW TO UNIX SYSTEM V Release 4

Each user has a primary group, which is the group that user is assigned in the **/etc/passwd** file. In addition, you may belong to other groups, depending on what **login-name-lists** you are included on in the **/etc/group** file. In effect, you simultaneously belong to both your primary group and to any groups you are assigned to in **/etc/group**. When you attempt to access a file you do not own, the operating system checks to see whether you are a member of the group that has access to the file. If you are, your access permissions are controlled by the group access permissions for the file. If you are not a member of the group that has access to the file, you are subject to the public access permissions for the file.

When you create a new file, it is assigned to the group that is associated with the directory the file is being written into, assuming that you belong to the group. If you do not belong to the group that has access to the directory, the file is assigned to your primary group.

On older releases of System V, you need to use the newgrp to change your group ID number to another group, assuming you are listed in the **login-name-list** of that group. The newgrp command takes an argument, which is the name of the group you want to change to. (You can always use newgrp without an argument to change your group ID back to what it was when you first logged in.)

/etc/mnttab   The *mount table* file contains a list of all currently mounted devices and is called **/etc/mnttab**. When you call mount without any arguments, mount consults this table and displays a list of mounted devices. On most systems, this file is not an ASCII text file—you cannot edit it with a text editor. (In any case, you *should not* edit it.)

The operating system maintains its own internal mount table, which may, on occasion, differ from this file. The surest way to bring the **mnttab** file in line with the operating system's mount table is to bring the system down and reboot it. Each time you (or an **rc** script) call mount or umount, these programs make the necessary changes to **mnttab**.

/etc/motd   The **/etc/motd** file contains the message of the day. The **/etc/profile** script usually uses cat to display this file each time someone logs in. The file should not be too long because users tend to see the message many times. Being subjected to a long message of the day can also be tedious for users who communicate with the system over slow dial-up lines.

/etc/passwd   Each entry in the **passwd** file occupies a line, has seven fields, and describes one user to the system. Colons separate each field from the adjacent fields.

login-name:dummy-password:user-ID:group-ID:info:directory:program

The **login-name** is the user's login name—the name the user enters in response to the login: prompt. The **dummy password** is a new feature introduced in System V Release 4. The value of the dummy password is the character **x**. Older versions of System V included an encrypted password in this field; beginning with System V Release 4, the encrypted password is stored in a file called **/etc/shadow**. See page 381 for a description of the **/etc/shadow** file.

The **user-ID** is a user ID number from 0 to 65,535, with 0 indicating the Superuser, and 0-99 reserved by convention. The **group-ID** identifies the user as a member of a group. It is a number between 0 and 65,535, with 0-99 being reserved, and 1 being the default. The **info** is information that various programs, such as accounting programs, use to further identify the user. Normally, it contains at least the user's name.

The **directory** is the absolute pathname of the user's home directory. The **program** is the program that will run after the user logs in. If **program** is not present, **/usr/bin/sh** is assumed. You can put **/usr/bin/csh** here to log in to the C Shell, or **/usr/bin/jsh** to log in to the Job Shell, or **/usr/bin/ksh** to log in to the Korn Shell. The restricted shell, a limited version of the Bourne Shell that prevents full access to the system, is identified as **/usr/bin/rsh**.

A brief sample **passwd** file is shown below. The **guest** login runs the restricted shell. The **info** field stores names.

```
# cat /etc/passwd
root:x:0:1::/:/usr/bin/sh
bill:x:102:100:Bill Hanley:/home/bill:/usr/bin/csh
roy:x:104:100:Roy Wong:/home/roy:/usr/bin/ksh
alex:x:106:100:Alex Watson:/home/alex:/usr/bin/sh
jenny:x:107:100:Jenny Chen:/home/jenny:/usr/bin/sh
guest:x:110:110::/tmp/guest:/usr/bin/rsh
```

The program specified in the right-hand field of each line in the **passwd** file is usually a shell, but as shown below, it can be any program. The following line in the **passwd** file will create a "user" whose only purpose is to execute the who utility:

```
who:x:1000:1000:execute who:/usr:/usr/bin/who
```

Using **who** as a login name causes the system to log you in, execute the who utility, and log you out. This entry in the **passwd** file does not provide a shell—there is no way for you to stay logged in after who is finished executing.

/etc/profile   A login shell is the first shell you work with when you log in on a system. If your login shell is the Bourne, Job, or Korn Shell, the first thing it does is to execute the commands in this file in the same environment as the shell. (For more information on executing a shell script in this manner, refer to the discussion of the . (dot) command on page 245.) This file allows the system

administrator to establish system-wide environment parameters that can be over-
ridden by individual users. Using this file, you can set shell variables, execute
utilities, and take care of other housekeeping tasks. It is not executed by the C
Shell.

Following is an example of an **/etc/profile** file that displays the message of
the day (the **/etc/motd** file), sets the file creation mask, and displays all the recent
news items:

```
# cat /etc/profile
cat /etc/motd
umask 022
news
```

.profile   The Bourne, Job, and Korn Shells execute the commands in this file in
the same environment as the shell each time a user logs in. This file *must* be
located in a user's home directory. (Each user has a different **.profile** file.) It
usually specifies a terminal type (for vi and other programs), runs stty to establish
terminal characteristics desired by the user, and performs other housekeeping
functions when a user logs in.

A typical **.profile** file specifying a vt100 terminal and CONTROL-H as the erase
key is as follows:

```
$ cat .profile
TERM=vt100
export TERM
stty erase '^h'
```

If you log in from more than one type of terminal, you may want to construct
a more elaborate routine, such as the following one, that asks you for the terminal
type each time you log in:

```
$ cat .profile
echo "Terminal type: \c"
read TERM
export TERM
stty erase '^h'
```

.login   This file performs the same function as the **.profile** file in the user's home
directory, but it is used by the C Shell. Because the C Shell does not execute
/etc/profile, users are responsible for using **.login** to set up their own environments and display the system-wide news.

The Run Command Files   The init program executes a run command, or **rc**, file
each time it changes state or run level. The run command scripts perform tasks

OPTIONAL (Continued)

such as mounting file systems (when the system goes multiuser), removing temporary files (after the file systems are mounted) and unmounting file systems (when the system is returned to single-user mode). On System V Release 4 the run command scripts are called **/sbin/brc**, **/sbin/bcheckrc**, **/sbin/rc0**, **/sbin/rc1**, **/sbin/rc2**, and **/sbin/rc3**.

/etc/shadow   Each entry in the shadow password file contains nine fields, separated by colons:

login-name:password:last-mod:min:max:warn:inactive:expire:flag

The **login-name** is the user's login name—the name the user enters in response to the login: prompt. The **password** is an encrypted password that the passwd utility puts into this file. If unauthorized access is not a problem, the password field can initially be null (::). When the user logs in, he or she can run passwd to select a password. Otherwise, you can run passwd while you are the Superuser to assign a password to the user.

The **last-mod** field is a number that indicates when the password was last modified. The **min** value is the minimum number of days that must elapse before the password can be changed; **max** is the maximum number of days before the password must be changed. The value of **warn** specifies how much advance warning (in days) to give the user before the password expires. The account will be invalidated if the number of days between login sessions exceeds the number of days specified in the **inactive** field. The account will also be invalid as of the date specified in the **expire** field. The last field in an entry, **flag**, is reserved for future use.

The shadow password file should not be publicly readable (or writable) in order to make it more difficult for someone to break into your system by identifying accounts without passwords or by using specialized programs that try to match encrypted passwords.

/etc/vfstab or /etc/checklist   The file that contains a list of device filenames that fsck checks by default is called **/etc/vfstab** on System V Release 4, and **/etc/checklist** on older releases of System V. This list should be the same as the list of devices that the run command (**rc**) script mounts when you bring the system up to multiuser mode. Sample files are as follows.

```
# cat /etc/vfstab
/dev/root        /dev/rroot        /        s5   1   yes   -
/dev/dsk/0s3     /dev/rdsk/0s3     /usr     s5   1   yes   -
/dev/dsk/0s4     /dev/rdsk/0s4     /home    s5   1   yes   -
/dev/dsk/0s10    /dev/rdsk/0s10    /stand   bfs  1   yes   -
/dev/dsk/0s13    /dev/rdsk/0s13    /tmp     s5   1   yes   -
```

OPTIONAL (Continued)

The /etc/vfstab file includes seven fields separated by spaces. They specify:

- the block device name (see page 386)
- the character device name that fsck should check (see page 386)
- the mount directory of the file system
- the file system type
- a number used by fsck to decide whether to check the file system
- whether the file system should be mounted automatically
- options, such as whether the file system is mounted for reading and writing (default) or just for reading

If there is no entry for a particular field, a hyphen serves as a placeholder.

Older releases of System V do not use the /etc/vfstab file; instead, fsck checks a file called /etc/checklist to determine which file systems need to be checked.

```
# cat /etc/checklist
/dev/dsk/0s0
/dev/dsk/0s1
```

/stand/unix or /unix   This file contains the UNIX system kernel that is loaded when you boot the system. On System V Release 4 it is located in /stand/unix; on earlier releases it is called /unix.

/usr/sbin/shutdown   Use this program to bring the system down properly—refer to your system manual for more information. On some systems the /usr/sbin/shutdown file is a shell script; on others it is a C program. If you do not have this file, refer to the section of this chapter ''Bringing the System Down.''

/var/news   The /var/news directory has files that contain items of interest to system users. For users whose login shells are the Job, Korn, or Bourne Shells, either the /etc/profile or .profile script usually calls news each time a user logs in. The news utility displays all the items in the /var/news directory that the user has not seen yet. If the user's login shell is the C Shell, the .login script usually calls news.

TYPES OF FILES

System V Release 4 supports several types of files: ordinary, directory, block special, character special, fifo special, sockets, and symbolic links. Ordinary files hold user data; directories hold directory information. Special files represent routines in the kernel that provide access to some feature of the operating system. Block and character special files represent device drivers that let you communicate with peripheral devices such as terminals, printers, and disk drives. Fifo (*first in, first out*) special files, also called *named pipes*, allow unrelated programs to exchange information. System V Release 4 also includes support for *sockets* and *symbolic links*. Sockets allow unrelated processes on the same or different computers to exchange information. One type of socket, UNIX domain sockets, are special files. Symbolic links allow you to link files that are in different file systems. (Plain links, or *hard links*, work only within a single file system.)

Ordinary Versus Directory Files

An *ordinary* file stores user data, such as textual information and programs.

A *directory* is a disk file with a standard format that stores a list of names of ordinary files and other directories. It relates each of these filenames to an *inode number*. An inode number identifies the *inode* for a file, which is a data structure that defines the file's existence. Inodes contain critical information such as who the owner of the file is and where it is located on disk.

When you move (mv) a file, you change the filename portion of the directory entry that is associated with the inode that describes the file. You do not create a new inode.

When you make an additional hard link (ln) to a file, you create another reference (an additional filename) to the inode that describes the file. You do not create a new inode.

When you remove (rm) a file, you remove the entry in the directory that describes the file. When you remove the last link to a file (the inode keeps track of the number of links), the operating system puts all the blocks the inode pointed to back in the *free list* (the list of blocks on the disk that are available for use).

Every directory always has at least two entries (. and ..). The . entry is a link to the directory itself. The .. entry is a link to the parent directory. In the case of the root directory, where there is no parent, the .. entry is a link to the root directory itself. Ordinary users cannot create hard links to directories.

Symbolic Links

Because each file system has a separate set of inodes, you can create hard links to a file only from within the file system in which the file resides. To get around this limitation, System V Release 4 has symbolic links. Files that are linked by a symbolic link do not share an inode, so you can create a symbolic link to a file from within any file system. You can also create a symbolic link to a directory. Refer to Chapter 4 for more information about symbolic links.

Special Files

By convention, special files appear in the **/dev** directory. Each special file represents a device: You read from and write to the file to read from and write to the device it represents. (Fifo special files represent pipes: You read from and write to the file to read from and write to the pipe. Similarly, you read from and write to a socket special file to read from and write to the socket.) Although you will not normally read directly from and write directly to device files, the kernel and many UNIX system utilities do.

System V Release 2 added several subdirectories to the **/dev** directory. The **/dev/dsk** and **/dev/rdsk** subdirectories contain entries that represent hard-disk drives. The **/dev/mt** and **/dev/rmt** subdirectories contain entries that represent magnetic tape drives. Prior to Release 2, all the device files in these directories were located directly in **/dev**.

The following example shows part of the display an **ls –l** command produces for the **/dev** directory on System V:

```
#  ls  -l  /dev
total  4
crw--w--w-  2  root     system   8,    1 May   4 18:36 console
drwxrwxr-x  1  root     root         762 May   4 15:05 dsk
crw--w--w-  1  daemon   system   9,    0 May   4 11:16 lp
drwxrwxr-x  1  root     root         672 May   4 15:07 mt
crw-rw-rw-  1  bin      system   6,    2 May   2 16:40 null
drwxrwxr-x  1  root     root         762 May   4 15:05 rdsk
drwxrwxr-x  1  root     root         672 May   4 15:07 rmt
brw-rw-rw-  1  root     system   0,    1 Sep  22 12:31 swap
crw-rw-rw-  1  root     system   8,    0 Apr  24 11:19 tty00
crw-rw-rw-  1  root     system   8,    2 Nov  21 21:10 tty02
crw-rw-rw-  1  alex     system   8,    3 May   5 11:32 tty03
crw-rw-rw-  1  root     system   8,    4 May   4 18:04 tty04
```

The first character of each line is a **b**, **c**, **d**, **l**, **p**, or **s** for block, character, directory, symbolic link, pipe, or socket (see below). The next nine characters represent the permissions for the file, followed by the number of hard links and the names of the owner and group. Where the number of bytes in a file would appear for an ordinary or directory file, a device file shows its *major* and *minor* *device numbers* separated by a comma (see below). The rest of the line is the same as any other **ls –l** listing.

Fifo Special Files.   Unless you are writing sophisticated programs, you will not be working with fifo special files (called named pipes).

The term *fifo* stands for *first in, first out*—the way any pipe works. The first information that you put in one end is the first information that comes out the other end. When you use a pipe on a command line to send the output of a program to the printer, the printer prints the information in the same order that the program produced it.

The UNIX system has had pipes for many generations. System V is the first version to use named pipes. Without named pipes, only processes that were children of the same ancestor could exchange information using pipes. Using named pipes, *any* two processes can exchange information. One program writes to a fifo special file. Another program reads from the same file. The programs do not have to run at the same time or be aware of each other's activity. The operating system handles all buffering and information storage.

NEW TO UNIX SYSTEM V Release 4

Sockets.   Like fifo special files, sockets allow processes that are not running at the same time and that are not the children of the same ancestor to exchange information. Sockets are the central mechanism of the interprocess communication facility that is the basis of the networking facility on System V Release 4. When you use networking utilities, pairs of cooperating sockets manage the communication between the processes on your computer and the remote computer. Sockets form the basis of utilities such as **rlogin** (remote login) and **rcp** (remote copy).

Major and Minor Device Numbers.   A *major device number* represents a class of hardware devices: a terminal, printer, tape drive, disk drive, and so on. In the preceding list of the **/dev** directory, all the terminals have a major device number of 8, and the printer (**lp**) is 9.

A *minor device number* represents a particular piece of hardware within a class. Although all the terminals are grouped together by their major device number (8), each has a different minor device number (tty00 is 0, tty02 is 2, and so on). This setup allows one piece of software (the device driver) to service all similar hardware while being able to distinguish among different physical units.

Block and Character Devices.

This section makes distinctions based on typical device drivers. Because the distinctions are based on device drivers, and because device drivers can be changed to suit a particular purpose, the distinctions in this section will not pertain to every system.

A *block device* is an I/O (input/output) device that is characterized by

- the ability to perform random access reads
- a specific block size
- handling only single blocks of data at a time
- accepting only transactions that involve whole blocks of data
- being able to have a file system mounted on it
- having the kernel buffer its input and output
- appearing to the operating system as a series of blocks numbered from 0 through $n - 1$, where n is the number of blocks on the device

The standard block devices on a UNIX system are disk and tape drives.

A *character device* is any device that is not a block device. Some examples of character devices are printers, terminals, and modems.

The device driver for a character device determines how a program reads from and writes to the device. For example, the device driver for a terminal allows a program to read the information you type on the terminal in two ways. A program can read single characters from a terminal in *raw* mode (that is, without the driver doing any interpretation of the characters). This mode has nothing to do with the *raw device* described in the following section. Alternatively, a program can read a line at a time. When a program reads a line at a time, the driver handles the erase and kill characters so that the program never sees typing mistakes and corrections. In this case the program reads everything from the beginning of a line to the RETURN that ends a line; the number of characters in a line can vary.

Raw Block Devices.

Device driver programs for block devices usually have two entry points so that they can be used in two ways: as block devices *or* as character devices. The character device form of a block device is called a *raw* device. Raw tape devices are usually located in the **/dev/rmt** directory, and raw disk devices are in **/dev/rdsk**. A raw device is characterized by

- direct I/O (no buffering through the kernel)
- a one-to-one correspondence between system calls and hardware requests
- device-dependent restrictions on I/O

An example of the use of a raw device is writing a tape with tar. If you use tar and specify a block tape device (e.g., **/dev/mt/1m**), tar will write only one block (usually 1024 bytes) to the tape at a time. Even if you specify a blocking factor (using the **–b** option), tar will write only one block at a time. Following each write, the device driver leaves an inter-record gap on the tape. The inter-record gap can be as long as the record. Thus, half the tape can be filled with gaps.

Using the raw tape device (e.g., **/dev/rmt/1m**), tar will write as many blocks as you specify each time it writes to the tape. If you specify a blocking factor of 20, you will be able to fit almost twice as much information on the tape as when using the block device.

Streams.   A new character processing subsystem, *streams*, was introduced with System V Release 3. The streams subsystem provides a connection between a user's process and a device driver, composed of one or more character processing modules. The streams character handling system is designed to be simpler, more modular, and more efficient and to provide better support for networking than the traditional approach provides.

Streams devices can coexist with traditional devices on a system. As a user, you will typically not be aware of whether input and output are handled by a traditional character device driver or by a streams device.

DAY-TO-DAY SYSTEM ADMINISTRATION FUNCTIONS

In addition to bringing up and shutting down the system, you have other responsibilities as the system administrator. This section covers the most important of these responsibilities.

Backing Up Files

One of the most neglected tasks of the system administrator is making backup copies of files on a regular basis. The backup copies are vital in two instances: when the system malfunctions and files are lost and when a user (or the system administrator) deletes a file by accident.

You must back up the file systems on a regular basis. Backup files are usually kept on floppy disks or magnetic tape, as determined by your system. Exactly how often you should back up which files depends on your system and needs. The criterion is, "If the system crashes, how much work are you willing to lose?" Ideally, you would back up all the files on the system every few minutes so that you would never lose more than a few minutes of work.

The trade-off is, "How often are you willing to back up the files?". The backup procedure typically slows down the machine for other users, takes a certain amount of your time, and requires that you have and store the media (tape or disk) that you keep the backup on.

The more people using the machine, the more often you should back up the file systems. A common schedule might have you perform a partial backup one or two times a day and a full backup one or two times a week.

A *partial* backup makes copies of the files that have been created or modified since the last backup. A *full* backup makes copies of all files, regardless of when they were created or accessed.

Several utilities are designed to make backup copies of files; this book discusses the cpio (copy archives in and out) utility that you can use in conjunction with find. The find utility locates files based on criteria you specify—for example, the last time the file was modified. The cpio utility makes a copy of ordinary files that you or find specifies. Specifics on cpio and find are in Part II of this book. You can also use the tar utility discussed in Part II to back up files.

OPTIONAL

Using the find and cpio Utilities.

The following sample command line recursively backs up all subdirectories and ordinary files within the **/usr** directory. The backup device is **/dev/rmt/1m**; the device you should use depends on your system configuration. The example shows the Superuser prompt because the person executing the command must be logged in as Superuser in order to be able to look through all the directories in **/usr** and read the necessary files.

```
# find /usr -print | cpio -oB /dev/rmt/1m
```

The **bkup** shell script (following) is a variation of the preceding command. The **-print** option of find writes a list of filenames to the standard output; cpio reads the standard output of find for the list of filenames to back up. (The Bourne shell allows you to end a line with a pipe without quoting the following NEWLINE—it expects to see the command that will receive the output from the pipe on the next line.) The cpio utility copies the files to its standard output, which is directed to the tape drive **/dev/rmt/1m**. At the same time, the **-v** (verbose) option causes cpio to send a list of the filenames to standard error, which is saved in a temporary file. The last line in the temporary file will be a count of the number of blocks written by cpio. If you know the typical value for the block count from day to day, when you check this number you may be more likely to notice when something goes wrong and the backup is incomplete. The pr utility sends this list to the printer using lp (with the **-s** option, lp suppresses the request id... message). The last command removes the temporary file, which is no longer needed.

OPTIONAL (Continued)

```
# cat bkup
find /usr -print |
cpio -oBv 1> /dev/rmt/1m 2> /tmp/$$.cpio
pr /tmp/$$.cpio | lp -s
rm /tmp/$$.cpio
```

The next example demonstrates a partial backup. It finds and copies to tape all files on the entire system (/) that have been modified within the last two days (**-mtime -2**). Again, a list of files is sent to the printer.

```
# cat bkup2
find / -mtime -2 -print |
cpio -oBv 1> /dev/rmt/1m 2> /tmp/$$.cpio
pr /tmp/$$.cpio | lp -s
rm /tmp/$$.cpio
```

Restoring from a Backup File.   The cpio utility can restore a single file, a list of files, or an entire file system. The following command restores the **/usr** directory from **/dev/rmt/1m**, assuming that only **/usr** was written to **/dev/rmt/1m**:

```
# cpio -id < /dev/rmt/1m
```

If several directories had been saved on the tape on **/dev/rmt/1m**, the following command would extract only **/usr**:

```
# cpio -id /usr < /dev/rmt/1m
```

When you restore files, cpio will not overwrite a newer version of a file with an older version, unless you include the **-u** option.

If you use a relative pathname rather than an absolute pathname with find when you create a cpio tape, you can put the files in a different directory when you extract them. Use cd to change directories to the new directory, and run the cpio command to extract the files from there.

Adding and Removing Users

More than a login name is required for a user to be able to log in and use the system. A user must have the necessary files, directories, permissions, and, optionally, a password in order to log in. Minimally, a user must have an entry in the **/etc/passwd** file and a home directory.

Adding a New User.   System V Release 4 includes a new utility called useradd that makes it easier to add new user accounts to your system. On earlier releases of System V, some manufacturers provided shell scripts (such as /etc/adduser) for adding new users. If your system has one of these scripts, use it. Otherwise, the following description explains how to add a new user to the system.

The first item a new user requires is an entry in the /etc/passwd file. While you are logged in as the Superuser, use vi or another editor to add an entry.

Below is a sample entry in the /etc/passwd file; refer to page 378 for more information. Do *not* use a group or user ID less than 100.

```
alex:x:106:100:Alex Watson:/home/alex:/bin/sh
```

You could have created the same entry using the useradd utility as follows:

```
# useradd -m -g 100 -c "Alex Watson" alex
```

By default, useradd will assign the next highest unused user ID to the new account and specify the Bourne Shell as the user's login shell. The options specified in the above example cause useradd to create the user's home directory (in /home by default), specify the user's group ID, and indicate the user's full name as a comment field.

To give the user a password, use the passwd utility with the user's login name as an argument. Because you are logged in as the Superuser, passwd does not ask you for the old password, even if there is one. Because of this special treatment, you can give users a new password when they forget their old one. The password will be encrypted and stored in the shadow password file, /etc/shadow.

```
# passwd alex
Changing password for alex.
New password:
Type new password again:
```

Now use mkdir to create the user's home directory you specified in the passwd file and use chown to make the user the owner of the new directory. Use chgrp to associate the new directory with the owner's primary group. Finally, use chmod to establish the desired access privileges. The following example sets up the directory so that anyone besides the owner can scan through and read files in the home directory, but they cannot change files or write to the directory:

```
# mkdir  /home/alex
# chown alex /home/alex
# chgrp pubs /home/alex
# chmod 755 /home/alex
```

To test the new setup, log in as the new user and create an appropriate .**profile** or .**login** file in the new user's home directory. (You may have to manually assign a value to and export the **TERM** shell variable if you want to use **vi** to create this file—see page 34.) It is a common practice to have a default .**login** or .**profile** file that is copied into each new user's home directory. System V Release 4 includes a standard directory, **/etc/skel**, where such default files can be stored. If you use the useradd utility to create a new account and specify **–k /etc/skel** as an option, the default files in **/etc/skel** will be automatically copied to the new user's home directory.

Removing a User.   If appropriate, make a backup copy of all the files belonging to a user before deleting them.

NEW TO UNIX SYSTEM V Release 4

System V Release 4 includes a utility called userdel that makes it easier to delete old user accounts from your system. The following command will remove **alex**'s account, his home directory, and all his files.

```
# userdel -r alex
```

To turn off a user's account temporarily, you can use the usermod utility to change the expiration date for the account. The following command line will prevent **alex** from logging in because it specifies that his account expired in the past (December 31, 1989).

```
# usermod -e "12/31/89" alex
```

If the userdel utility is not available on your system, you can remove a user by removing the user's entry in the **passwd** and **shadow** files and removing all the user's files and directories.

If you just want to prevent a user from logging in temporarily and the system is not on a network, you can change the user's password. In some networked environments, just changing a user's password will not prevent the user from logging in—you need to remove the user's entry in the **passwd** file.

Checking Your Mail

Remember to log in as *root* periodically to see if there is any mail for the system administrator. Users frequently use electronic mail to communicate with the system administrator.

You will not receive reminders about mail that arrives for *root* if you always use the su command to perform system administration tasks. However, after using su to become *root,* you can give the **mailx –u root** command to look at the Superuser's mail.

Scheduling Routine Tasks

It is a good practice to schedule certain routine tasks to run automatically. For example, you may want to remove old core files once a week, summarize accounting data daily, and rotate system log files monthly. The cron utility is designed to run commands at regularly scheduled times. Using the crontab utility, a user may submit a list of commands in a format that can be read and executed by cron. Refer to crontab in Part II for more information.

PROBLEMS

It is your responsibility as the system administrator to keep the system secure and running smoothly. If a user is having a problem, it usually falls to the administrator to help the user get back on the right track. This section presents some suggestions on ways to keep users happy and the system functioning at its peak.

When a User Cannot Log In

If a user cannot log in on the system, follow these steps to determine where the problem is.

Determine if just that one user has a problem, just that one user's terminal has a problem, or if the problem is more widespread.

If just that user has a problem, it may be that the user does not know how to log in. The user's terminal will respond when you press RETURN, and you will be able to log in as yourself. Make sure the user has a valid login name and password; then show the user how to log in.

If just that one user's terminal has a problem, other users will be using the system, but that user's terminal will not respond when you press RETURN. Try pressing the BREAK and RETURN keys alternately to reestablish the proper baud rate. Make sure the terminal is set for a legal baud rate. Try pressing the following keys:

CONTROL-Q   This key "unsticks" the terminal if someone pressed CONTROL-S.

interrupt	This key stops a runaway process that has hung up the terminal. The interrupt key is usually DEL or CONTROL-C.
ESCAPE	This key can help if the user is in Input Mode in vi.
CONTROL-L	This key redraws the screen if the user was using vi.
CONTROL-R	This key is an alternate for CONTROL-L.

Check the terminal cable from where it plugs into the terminal to where it plugs into the computer. Check the /etc/inittab entry for that line. Finally, try turning the terminal off and then turning it back on again.

If the problem appears to be widespread, check to see if you can log in from the system console. If you can, make sure the system is in multiuser mode. If you cannot, the system may have crashed—reboot it.

Keeping a Machine Log

A machine log that includes the following information may be helpful in finding and fixing problems with the system. Note the time and date for each entry in the log. Avoid the temptation of keeping the log *only* on the computer, because it will be most useful to you at times when the machine is down.

hardware modifications	Keep track of *all* modifications to the hardware—even those installed by factory representatives.
system software modifications	Keep track of any modification that anyone makes to the operating system software, whether it's a patch or a new version of a program.
hardware malfunctions	Keep as accurate a list as possible of any problems with the system. Make note of any error messages or numbers that the system displays on the system console and what users were doing when the problem occurred.
user complaints	Make a list of all reasonable complaints made by knowledgeable users (e.g., machine is abnormally slow).

Keeping the System Secure

No system with dial-in lines or public access to terminals is absolutely secure. You can make your system as secure as possible by changing the Superuser pass-

word frequently and choosing passwords that are hard to guess. Do not tell anyone who does not *absolutely* need to know what the Superuser password is. You
can also encourage system users to choose difficult passwords and to change them
periodically.

A password that is hard to guess is one that someone else would not be likely
to think that you would have chosen. Do not use words from the dictionary,
names of relatives, pets, or friends, or backward spellings of words. A good strategy is to choose a couple of short words, include some punctuation (e.g., put a
SPACE between them), and replace a couple of the letters in the words with
numbers. Remember that only the first eight characters of a password are
significant.

Make sure that no one (except the Superuser) can write to files containing
programs that are owned by root and run in the set user ID mode (e.g., **mailx**,
mail, and **su**). Also make sure that users do not transfer programs that run in the
set user ID mode and are owned by root onto the system by means of mounting
tapes or disks. These programs can be used to disable system security. Refer to
chmod in Part II for more information about the set user ID mode.

Monitoring Disk Usage

Disk space is usually a precious commodity. Sooner or later, you will probably
start to run out of it. Do not fill up a disk—the UNIX operating system runs best
with at least 5 to 30 percent of the disk space free in each file system. The
minimum amount of free space you should maintain on each file system is
machine-dependent. Using more than the maximum optimal disk space in a file
system degrades system performance. If there is no space on a file system, you
cannot write to it at all.

System V provides several programs that you can use to determine who is
using how much disk space on what file systems. Refer to the du and df utilities
and the **–size** option of the find utility in Part II. System V Release 4 provides
these utilities as well as the disk quota system, which is described below.

The *only* ways to increase the amount of free space on a file system are to
delete files and condense directories. This section contains some ideas on ways to
maintain a file system so that it does not get overloaded.

Growing Files.   Some files, such as log files and temporary files, grow automatically over time. Core dump files take up space and are rarely needed. Also,
occasionally users create processes that accidentally generate huge files. As the
system administrator, you must review these files periodically so that they do not
get out of hand.

If a file system is running out of space quickly (e.g., over the period of an

OPTIONAL (Continued)

hour rather than weeks or months), the first thing to do is to figure out why it is running out of space. Use the **ps –ef** command to determine whether a user has created a runaway process that is creating a huge file. In evaluating the output of **ps**, look for a process that has used a large amount of CPU time. If such a process is running and creating a large file, the file will continue to grow as you free up space. If you remove the huge file, the space it occupied will not be freed until the process terminates, so you need to kill the process. Try to contact the user running the process and ask the user to kill it. If you cannot contact the user, log in as root and kill the process. Refer to kill in Part II for more information.

If no single process is consuming the disk space, but rather it has been used up gradually, you should locate unneeded files and delete them. You can archive them using cpio or tar before you delete them.

You can safely remove any files named **core** that have not been accessed for several days. The following command performs this function:

```
# find / –name core –atime +3 –exec rm {} \;
```

Look through the **/tmp** and **/var/tmp** directories for old temporary files and remove them. The **/usr/lib/spell/spellhist** file keeps track of all the misspelled words that spell finds—make sure it does not get too big. Keep track of disk usage in **/var/mail**, **/var/spool**, **/var/adm**, and **/var/news**.

NEW TO UNIX SYSTEM V Release 4

Disk Quota System.   System V Release 4 includes a disk quota system for limiting the disk space and number of files owned by individual users. You can choose to limit each user's disk space or the number of files each user can own or both. For each resource that is limited, there are actually two limits. The lower limit, or *quota*, can be exceeded by the user although a warning is presented each time the user logs in when he or she is above the quota. After a certain number of warnings (set by the system administrator), the system will behave as if the user has reached the upper limit. Once the upper limit is reached or the user has received the specified number of warnings, the user will not be allowed to create any more files or use any more disk space. The user's only recourse at that point is to remove some files.

Users can review their usage and limits with the quota command. The Superuser can use quota to obtain information about any user.

To set up the disk quota system, you may have to reconfigure the system. The system configuration process is beyond the scope of this book. Refer to the system administration manuals that came with your system.

Once you have reconfigured the system, you must decide which file systems to limit and how to allocate space among users. Typically, only file systems that

NEW TO UNIX SYSTEM V Release 4 (Continued)

contain users' home directories, such as **/home**, are limited. Use the edquota command to set the quotas, and then quotaon to start the quota system. You will probably want to put the quotaon command into the appropriate run command script so that the quota system will be enabled when you bring the system up (see page 380). The quota system is automatically disabled when the file systems are dismounted.

OPTIONAL

Removing Unused Space from a Directory.
A directory on a standard System V file system (type **s5** in System V Release 4) should not contain more than 320 entries—file system indirection makes large directories inefficient. The following command lists names of directories larger than 5K bytes (320 entries):

```
# find / -type d -size +5 -print
```

The point at which a directory on a type **ufs** file system becomes inefficient varies, depending on the length of the filenames it contains. The same principle applies—you should keep your directories relatively small.

If you find a directory that is too large, you can usually break it into several smaller directories by moving its contents into new directories. Make sure you remove the original directory once you have moved its contents.

Because UNIX files do not shrink, removing a file from a directory will not shrink the directory, even though it will make more space on the disk. To remove unused space and make a directory smaller, you must copy all the files into a new directory and remove the original directory.

The following procedure removes unused directory space. First, remove all unneeded files from the large directory. Then, following the sample below, make a smaller copy of the directory. The sample procedure removes unused space from a directory named **/home/alex/large**. The directory **/home/alex/hold** holds the directory while it is being processed. The **cpdir** script copies all the files from the old directory to the new one. (Refer to page 228 for more information about **cpdir**. On System V Release 4, you can use **cp −r** instead.) Make sure that, after creating the new directory, you set its access privileges to that of the original directory. After you complete the procedure, you can use the new directory just as you did the old.

```
# mv /home/alex/large /home/alex/hold
# mkdir /home/alex/large
# cpdir /home/alex/hold /home/alex/large
# rm -rf /home/alex/hold
```

GETTING INFORMATION TO USERS

As the system administrator, one of your primary responsibilities is communicating with the system users. You need to make announcements such as when the system will be down for maintenance, when a class on some new software will be held, and how users can access the new system printer. You can even start to fill the role of a small local newspaper, letting users know about new employees, births, the company picnic, and so on.

Different items you want to communicate will have different priorities. Information about the company picnic in two months is not as time-sensitive as the fact that you are bringing the system down in five minutes. To meet these differing needs, the UNIX operating system provides different ways of communicating. The most common methods are described and contrasted below. All of these methods are generally available to everyone, except for **motd** (the message of the day), which is typically reserved for the Superuser.

wall.   The wall (write all) utility is most effective for communicating immediately with everyone who is logged in. It works in the same way as write, but it sends a message to everyone who is logged in. Use it if you are about to bring the system down or you are in another crisis situation. Users who are not logged in will not get the message.

Use wall while you are the Superuser *only* in crisis situations—it will interrupt anything anyone is doing.

write.   Use the write utility to communicate with any individual user who is logged in. You might use it to ask a user to stop running a program that is bogging down the system. Users can also use write to ask you, for example, to mount a tape or restore a file.

mailx.   The mailx and mail utilities are useful for communicating less urgent information to one or more system users. When you send mail, you have to be willing to wait for each user to read the mail. The mail utilities are useful for reminding users that they are forgetting to log out, bills are past due, or they are using too much disk space.

Users can easily make permanent records of messages they receive via mailx, as opposed to messages received via write, so that they can keep track of important details. It would be appropriate to use mailx or mail to inform users about a new, complex procedure—each user could keep a copy of the information for reference.

Message of the Day.   All users see the message of the day each time they log in. You can edit the **/etc/motd** file to change the message. The message of the day can alert users to upcoming periodic maintenance, new system features, or a change in procedures.

news.   The **news** utility displays news: meeting announcements, new hardware or software on the system, new employees, parties, and so on.

SUMMARY

The system administrator is responsible for backing up files, adding and removing users, helping users who have problems logging in, and keeping track of disk usage and system security.

This chapter explains many of the files and programs you will have to work with to maintain a UNIX system. Much of the work you do as the system administrator requires you to log in as the Superuser. The login name for the Superuser is *root*. When you are logged in as the Superuser, you have extensive system-wide powers that you do not normally have. You can read from and write to any file and execute programs that ordinary users are not permitted to execute.

A series of programs and files control how the system appears at any given time. Many of the files you work with as the system administrator are located in the **/etc** directory.

When you bring up the system, it is frequently in single-user mode. In this mode, only the system console is functional, and not all the file systems are mounted. When the system is in single-user mode, you can back up files and use **fsck** to check the integrity of file systems before you mount them. The **init** utility brings the system to its normal multiuser state.

With the system running in multiuser mode, you can still perform many administration tasks, such as adding users and terminals.

REVIEW EXERCISES

1. If you have a directory that contains 500 entries and you remove 200 of them, why will there still be a problem with the size of the directory? What can you do about it?

2. What option should you use with **fsck** if you just want to review the status of your file systems without making any changes to them? How does **fsck** determine what devices to check if you do not specify one on the command line?

3. How does single-user mode differ from multiuser mode?

4. If Alex belongs to five groups—inhouse, pubs, sys, other, and supers—how would his group memberships be represented? Assume that inhouse is his primary group. How would Alex create a file that belongs to the group pubs?

5. How can you identify the user ID of another user on your system? What is the user ID of root?

6. How can you redirect the output of the find command so that whatever it sends to the standard error disappears?

7. How many inodes does a file have? What happens when you add a hard link to a file? What happens when you add a symbolic link?

8. What are the differences between a raw device and a block device?

9. Develop a strategy for coming up with a password that an intruder would not be likely to guess but that you will be able to remember.

10. How would you communicate each of the following messages?

   a. The system is coming down tomorrow at 6:00 in the evening for periodic maintenance.

   b. The system is coming down in five minutes.

   c. Jenny's jobs are slowing the system down drastically, and she should postpone them.

   d. Alex's wife just had a baby girl.

11. How would you restrict access to a tape drive on your system so that only certain users could read and write tapes?

12. When fsck puts files in a **lost+found** directory, it has lost the directory information for the files (and thus has lost the names of the files). Each file is given a new name, which is the same as the inode number for the file:

```
$ ls -l lost+found
-rw-r--r-- 1 alex   pubs   110 Jun 10 10:55 51262
```

What can you do to identify these files and restore them?

THE UNIX UTILITY PROGRAMS

Following is a list of the utilities grouped by function. Although most of these are true utilities (that is, programs), others are commands that are built into the shells.

Utilities That Display and Manipulate Files

awk	search for and process patterns in a file (page 414)
cat	join or display files (page 443)
comm	compare sorted files (page 455)
cp	copy files (page 457)
cpio	store and retrieve files in an archive format (page 459)
diff	display the differences between two files (page 470)
find	find files (page 486)
grep	search for a pattern in files (page 502)
head	display the beginning of a file (page 506)
ln	make a link to a file (page 510)
lp	print files (page 512)
ls	display information about files (page 515)
mkdir	make a directory (page 532)
more	display a file one screenful at a time (page 533)
mv	move (rename) a file (page a536)
od	dump a file (page 542)
pg	display a file one screenful at a time (page 544)
pr	paginate a file (page 548)
rcp	copy files to or from a remote computer (page 559)
rm	remove a file (page 563)
rmdir	remove a directory (page 567)
sed	stream editor (noninteractive) (page 570)
sort	sort and/or merge files (page 588)
spell	check a file for spelling errors (page 598)
tail	display the last part of a file (page 605)
tar	store or retrieve files from an archive file (page 608)
uniq	display lines of a file that are unique (page 622)
wc	display counts of lines, words, and characters (page 625)

Communication Utilities

mailx	send or receive electronic mail (page 522)

mesg   enable/disable reception of messages (page 531)

news   display system-wide news (page 539)

write   send a message to another user (page 629)

Utilities That Display and Alter Status

cd   change to another working directory (page 447)

chgrp   change the group that is associated with a file (page 449)

chmod   change the access mode of a file (page 450)

chown   change the owner of a file (page 454)

date   display or set the time and date (page 464)

df   display the amount of available disk space (page 469)

du   display information on disk usage (page 477)

file   display file classification (page 485)

kill   terminate a process (page 508)

newgrp   temporarily change the group identification of a user (page 538)

nice   change the priority of a command (page 540)

nohup   run a command that will keep running after you log out (page 541)

ps   display process status (page 555)

ruptime   display status of computers attached to a network (page 568)

rwho   display names of users on computers attached to a network (page 569)

sleep   process that sleeps for a specified interval (page 587)

stty   display or set terminal parameters (page 600)

umask   set file-creation permissions mask (page 621)

who   display names of users (page 627)

Utilities That Are Programming Tools

cc   C compiler (page 445)

make   keep a set of programs current (page 529)

touch   update a file's modification time (page 616)

Source Code Control System Utilities

admin   create or change the characteristics of an SCCS file (page 407)

delta   record changes in an SCCS file (page 466)

get   retrieve an SCCS file (page 498)

prs   print the history of an SCCS file (page 551)

rmdel   remove a delta from an SCCS file (page 565)

Miscellaneous Utilities

at   execute a shell script at a specified time (page 411)

cal   display a calendar (page 440)

calendar   present reminders (page 442)

crontab   schedule a command to run at a regularly specified time (page 462)

echo   display a message (page 479)

expr   evaluate an expression (page 481)

fsck   check and repair a file system (page 493)

rlogin log in on a remote computer (page 561)

shl   call the shell layer manager (page 583)

tee   copy the standard input to the standard output and to one or more files (page 611)

test   evaluate an expression (page 612)

tr   replaced specified characters (page 618)

tty   display the terminal pathname (page 620)

The following sample command shows the format that is used throughout Part II. Each section of this sample command explains what you can expect to find following each heading within each section in Part II.

These descriptions of the commands are similar to the descriptions in the user's reference manual that comes with your UNIX system; however, most users find the descriptions in this book easier to read and understand. These descriptions emphasize the most useful features of the commands and often leave out the more obscure features. For information about the less commonly used features, refer to the manuals that come with your system. If you are running a version of System V that is older than Release 4, some of the features described here for a particular command may not be available to you.

sample command

This section gives the name of the command, followed by a brief description.

Format

sample_command [options] arguments

This section includes syntax descriptions like the one above that show you how to run the command. Options and arguments enclosed in square brackets ([]) are not required.

Hyphenated words listed as arguments to a command identify single arguments (e.g., **source-file**) or groups of similar arguments (e.g., **directory-list**). As an example, **file-list** means a list of one or more files.

Summary

Unless stated otherwise, the output from a command goes to its standard output. The ''Standard Input and Standard Output'' section on page 99 explains how to redirect output so that it goes to a file other than the terminal.

The statement that a command ''takes its input from files you specify on the command line or from its standard input'' indicates that the command is a member of the class of UNIX commands that takes input from files specified on the command line or, if you do not specify a filename, from its standard input. It also means that the command can receive input redirected from a file or sent through a pipe. See page 107.

Arguments

This section describes the arguments that you use when you run the command. The argument itself, as shown in the preceding ''Format'' section, is printed in **bold type**.

Options

The ''Options'' section lists the common options that you can use with the command. Unless specified otherwise, you must precede all options with a hyphen. Most commands accept a single hyphen before multiple options. See page 95.

Notes

You will find miscellaneous notes, some important and others merely interesting, in this section.

Examples

This section contains examples of how to use the command. It is tutorial and is more casual than the preceding sections of the command description.

admin

Create an SCCS file or change the characteristics of an SCCS file.

Format

admin [options] –iname filename
admin [options] –n file-list
admin [options] file-list

Summary

The admin utility is part of SCCS (Source Code Control System—refer to page 355 for more information). The admin utility creates and changes characteristics of SCCS files.

Use the first format shown above to create an SCCS-encoded version of an existing file, or use the second format to create one or more new SCCS-encoded files that are not based on existing files. The third format changes characteristics of SCCS files.

Arguments

In the first format, **filename** is the name that will be given to the newly encoded SCCS file. Like the names of all SCCS files, the **filename** must begin with the characters **s.**. In the second format shown, **file-list** is a list of SCCS filenames to be assigned to the newly created files. Each of the files in the **file-list** must also begin with **s.**. The first format creates a single SCCS-encoded file based on an existing file. The second format creates any number of new SCCS-encoded files based on null deltas.

The **file-list** in the third format is a list of existing SCCS files. If a directory is included in **file-list**, admin includes in **file-list** all of the SCCS-encoded files in the directory.

Options

–iname   **initialize**   The admin utility uses the file called **name** as the initial delta for a new SCCS file.

–n   **new**   This option causes SCCS to create a new SCCS-encoded file. When it is used without the –i option, admin creates a new SCCS file based on a null delta. When you use the –i option, you do not need to use **–n**. (It is redundant.)

admin

-rx   **release**   This option identifies the version number admin will associate with an initial delta. Replace **x** with the version number (see page 356 for an explanation of version numbers). If you specify only the release component of the version number, SCCS inserts the delta into the first level of the release. For example, if you use **-r3**, SCCS inserts the delta into Version 3.1. If the release is not specified on the command line, admin inserts the initial delta into Version 1.1. The **-r** option can be used only when **-i** is also used.

-fflag[value]   This option inserts a **flag** in the SCCS file. Flags override default characteristics of SCCS files. Any number of flags may be specified on a single command line. See the next section for information about flags and their values.

-dflag   **delete**   This option removes a **flag** from an SCCS file. Multiple **-d** options can be used on a single command line to remove multiple flags. See the next section for information about flags.

-ycomment   The **-y** option causes admin to insert **comment** as the comment for the initial delta in a new SCCS file. Replace **comment** with the text of your comment. You must surround your comment with quotation marks if it contains spaces. If you do not use **-y** when creating an initial delta, SCCS inserts a standard comment, including the date and time of creation and the login of the user who created it. You can use **-y** only when creating an initial delta. (Otherwise, admin ignores it.)

-mmrlist   The **mrlist** is a list of the modification requests that are the reason for an initial delta. Replace **mrlist** with a comma-separated list of modification request numbers. The **-m** option can be used only if the **v** flag is set, and only on an initial delta. Refer to the next section for an explanation of flags.

-alogin   **authorize**   This option adds **login** to the list of users who are allowed to make deltas to the files. Replace **login** with the user's login name. Before any users are added to the list of authorized users, the list is assumed to be empty, and any user can make a delta. You can use any number of **-a** options on a command line. If a numerical group ID is used in place of **login**, all the users belonging to the group can make deltas to the file. If a **login** is preceded by an exclamation point, **!login**, the user will be denied permission to make deltas.

-e login   **erase**   Once you have used the –a option to add a user to the list of authorized users, you can remove that user with **–e**. Like the **–a** option, you can use **–e** with a numerical group ID in place of **login**, and you can use **–e** several times on a command line.

Flags

The admin utility can insert flags in SCCS files to change default characteristics of the files. Each **flag** must be preceded by the **–f** option on the command line.

llist   **lock**   This flag identifies releases that users are not allowed to make deltas against. The **list** may include a single release number, several release numbers separated by commas, or **a,** which locks all releases.

v   **verbose**   This flag causes the delta utility to prompt you for modification request numbers in addition to comments.

b   **branch**   This flag allows you to create branch deltas for the highest-numbered trunk delta. To make these branches, you must use the **–b** option with the get utility. You can always make branch deltas for trunk deltas that have successors on the trunk (that is, regardless of whether the **b** flag is set).

j   **joint edit**   This flag allows multiple concurrent updates to the same version of an SCCS file. This flag is rarely used because one of the purposes of SCCS is to prevent different people from making changes to the same file at the same time. If this flag is not set, once you have used get with the **–e** option on a version of an SCCS file, you must use delta to record the changes before anyone can again use get with the **–e** option on that version.

Examples

The following command creates a new SCCS-encoded file called **s.menu1** that includes the file **menu1** as its first delta.

```
$ admin -imenu1 s.menu1
No id keywords (cm7)
```

The message admin displays, No id keywords, indicates that there are no SCCS keywords in the new file. When keywords are included in an SCCS file, information about the SCCS file is inserted in the corresponding text file retrieved by get.

Keywords are beyond the scope of this book—you can ignore the warning message when it occurs in the examples.

The next command creates three new SCCS-encoded files. These files are not created from existing files, and, consequently, the initial version of each is empty.

```
$ admin -n s.menu_mon s.menu_tues s.menu_wed
```

The next example locks Release 2 of the SCCS-encoded file **s.menus_march**. It also adds alex and barbara to the list of users who are authorized to make deltas. Of course, alex and barbara cannot make deltas to Release 2.

```
$ admin -fl2 -aalex -abarbara s.menus_march
```

Any time after you execute the above command, you can remove barbara from the list with the following command. This command also uses the **-d** option to remove the lock on Release 2.

```
$ admin -dl2 -ebarbara s.mcnus_march
```

at

Execute a shell script at a time you specify.

Format

> **at [–m] time [date] [+ increment]**
> **at [–l | –r] [job-list]**
> **atq**

Summary

The **at** utility causes the operating system to execute commands it receives from its standard input. It executes them as a shell script in the working directory at the time you specify.

When the operating system executes commands using **at**, it uses electronic mail to send you the standard output and standard error output of the resulting process. You can redirect the output to avoid getting mail.

The **atq** utility provides a list of **at** jobs you have queued. It is similar to **at** with the –l option.

Arguments

In the first format shown above, **time** is the time of day you want **at** to execute the job. You can specify the **time** as a one-, two-, or four-digit number. One- and two-digit numbers specify an hour, and four-digit numbers specify an hour and minute. The **at** utility assumes a 24-hour clock unless you place **am**, **pm**, **midnight**, or **noon** immediately after the number, in which case, **at** uses a 12-hour clock. You can use the word **now** in place of **time**; however, if you do you must also specify a **date** or an **increment** (that is, the command **at now** is not valid, but the command **at now saturday** is).

The **date** is the day of the week or date of the month on which you want **at** to execute the job. If you do not specify a day, **at** executes the job today if the hour you specify in **time** is greater than the current hour. If the hour is less than the current hour, **at** executes the job tomorrow.

To specify a day of the week, you can spell it out or abbreviate it to three letters. You can also use the days **today** and **tomorrow**.

Use the name of a month followed by the number of the day in the month to specify a date. You can follow the month and day number with a year.

The **increment** is a number followed by one of the following (plural or singular is allowed): **minutes, hours, days, weeks, months,** or **years**. The **at** utility adds the **increment** to the **time** (and **date**) you specify. In place of **increment**, you can use the word **next** (e.g., to specify **next week, next month,** or **next year**).

In the second format shown above, **job-list** is a list of one or more job numbers for **at** jobs. You can identify job numbers using the –l option to **at**.

Options

The **–l** and **–r** options are not for use when you initiate a job with **at**. You can use them only to determine the status of a job or to a cancel job.

-l   **list**   This option displays a list of all jobs that you have submitted with **at**. The **job-list** is a list of one or more job numbers of the jobs you want **at** to list. If you do not include a **job-list, at** lists all your jobs.

-m   **mail**   If you use this option, **at** sends you mail after the job is run. The mail contains the standard error output if there was any; otherwise, it contains a short message informing you that no errors occurred. Without this option, **at** does not provide any confirmation that the job was run (except for mailing you any output that is not redirected to a file).

-r   **remove**   This option cancels jobs that you previously submitted with **at**. The **job-list** argument is a list of one or more job numbers of the jobs you want to cancel. If you do not remember the job number, use the **–l** option to list your jobs and their numbers.

Notes

The shell saves the environment variables and the working directory that are in effect at the time you submit an **at** job so that they are available when it executes the commands.

The system administrator must put your login name in the file named **/etc/cron.d/at.allow** for you to be able to use **at**.

Examples

You can use either of the following techniques to paginate and print **long_file** at two o'clock tomorrow morning. The first example executes the command directly from the command line, and the second example uses a file containing the necessary command (**pr_tonight**) and executes it using **at**. If you execute the command directly from the command line, you must signal the end of the list of commands by pressing CONTROL-D at the beginning of a line.

The line that begins with job contains the job number and the time **at** will execute the job.

```
$ at 2am
pr long_file | lp
CONTROL-D
job 474285600.a at Fri Jul 6 02:00:00   1990
$ cat pr_tonight
pr long_file | lp
$ at 2am < pr_tonight
job 474285601.a at Fri Jul 6 02:00:00   1990
```

If you give an **at** –l command following the two preceding commands, **at** displays a list of jobs in its queue.

```
$ at -l
user = alex          474285600.a      Fri Jul 6 02:00:00    1990
user = alex          474285601.a      Fri Jul 6 02:00:00    1990
```

The following command removes one of the jobs from the queue.

```
$ at -r 474285600.a
$ at -l
474285601.a      at Fri Jul 6 02:00:00    1990
```

The next example executes **cmdfile** at 3:30 P.M. (1530 hours) a week from next Wednesday.

```
$ at 1530 wed +1 week < cmdfile
job 474852600.a at Wed Jul 18 15:30:00 1990
```

The final example executes an nroff job at 7 P.M. on Friday. It creates an intermediate file and redirects the error output and prints the file.

```
$ at 7pm Friday
nroff -mm report > report.out 2> report.err
lp report.out
CONTROL-D
job 474346800.a at Fri Jul 6 19:00:00 1990
```

awk

Search for and process a pattern in a file.

Format

> **awk [–Fc] –f program-file [file-list]**
> **awk program [file-list]**

Summary

The **awk** utility is a pattern-scanning and processing language. It searches one or more files to see if they contain lines that match specified patterns and then performs actions, such as writing the line to the standard output or incrementing a counter, each time it finds a match.

You can use **awk** to generate reports or filter text. It works equally well with numbers and text; when you mix the two, **awk** will almost always come up with the right answer.

The authors of **awk** (Alfred V. Aho, Peter J. Weinberger, and Brian W. Kernighan) designed it to be easy to use and, to this end, they sacrificed execution speed.

The **awk** utility takes many of its constructs from the C programming language. It includes the following features:

- flexible format
- conditional execution
- looping statements
- numeric variables
- string variables
- regular expressions
- C's printf

The **awk** utility takes its input from files you specify on the command line or from its standard input.

Arguments

The first format uses a **program-file**, which is the pathname of a file containing an **awk** program. See "Description," below.

The second format uses a **program**, which is an **awk** program included on the command line. This format allows you to write simple, short **awk** programs without having to create a separate **program-file**. To prevent the shell from interpreting the awk commands as shell commands, it is a good idea to enclose the **program** in single quotation marks.

The **file-list** contains pathnames of the ordinary files that awk processes. These are the input files.

Options

If you do not use the **–f** option, awk uses the first command line argument as its program.

–f **program-file**   **file**   This option causes awk to read its program from the **program-file** given as the first command line argument.

–F*c*   **field**   This option specifies an input field separator, **c**, to be used in place of the default separators (SPACE and TAB). The field separator can be any single character.

Notes

See page 438 for examples of awk error messages.

Description

An awk program consists of one or more program lines containing a **pattern** and/or **action** in the following format:

pattern { action }

The **pattern** selects lines from the input file. The awk utility performs the **action** on all lines that the **pattern** selects. You must enclose the **action** within braces so that awk can differentiate it from the **pattern**. If a program line does not contain a **pattern**, awk selects all lines in the input file. If a program line does not contain an **action**, awk copies the selected lines to its standard output.

To start, awk compares the first line in the input file (from the **file-list**) with each **pattern** in the **program-file** or **program**. If a **pattern** selects the line (if there is a match), awk takes the **action** associated with the **pattern**. If the line is not selected, awk takes no action. When awk has completed its comparisons for the first line of the input file, it repeats the process for the next line of input. It continues this process, comparing subsequent lines in the input file, until it has read the entire **file-list**.

If several **patterns** select the same line, awk takes the **actions** associated with each of the **patterns** in the order they appear. It is therefore possible for awk to send a single line from the input file to its standard output more than once.

Patterns

You can use a regular expression (refer to Appendix B), enclosed within slashes, as a pattern. The ~ operator tests to see if a field or variable matches a regular expression. The !~ operator tests for no match.

You can process arithmetic and character relational expressions with the following relational operators.

Operator	Meaning
<	less than
<=	less than or equal to
==	equal to
!=	not equal to
>=	greater than or equal to
>	greater than

You can combine any of the patterns described above using the Boolean operators || (OR) or && (AND).

The comma is the range operator. If you separate two patterns with a comma on a single awk program line, awk selects a range of lines beginning with the first line that contains the first pattern. The last line awk selects is the next subsequent line that contains the second pattern. After awk finds the second pattern, it starts the process over by looking for the first pattern again.

Two unique patterns, **BEGIN** and **END**, allow you to execute commands before awk starts its processing and after it finishes. The awk utility executes the actions associated with the **BEGIN** pattern before, and with the **END** pattern after, it processes all the files in the **file-list**.

Actions

The action portion of an awk command causes awk to take action when it matches a pattern. If you do not specify an action, awk performs the default action, which is the Print command (explicitly represented as {print}). This action copies the record (normally a line—see "Variables" below) from the input file to awk's standard output.

You can follow a Print command with arguments, causing awk to print just the arguments you specify. The arguments can be variables or string constants. Using awk, you can send the output from a Print command to a file (>), append it to a file (>>), or pipe it to the input of another program (|).

Unless you separate items in a Print command with commas, awk catenates them. Commas cause awk to separate the items with the output field separator (normally a SPACE—see "Variables" below).

You can include several actions on one line within a set of braces by separating them with semicolons.

Comments

The awk utility disregards anything on a program line following a pound sign (#). You can document an awk program by preceding comments with this symbol.

Variables

You declare and initialize user variables when you use them (that is, you do not have to declare them *before* you use them). In addition, awk maintains program variables for your use. You can use both user and program variables in the pattern *and* in the action portion of an awk program. Following is a list of program variables.

Variable	Represents
NR	record number of current record
$0	the current record (as a single variable)
NF	number of fields in the current record
$1-$n	fields in the current record
FS	input field separator (default: SPACE or TAB)
OFS	output field separator (default: SPACE)
RS	input record separator (default: NEWLINE)
ORS	output record separator (default: NEWLINE)
FILENAME	name of the current input file

The input and output record separators are, by default, NEWLINE characters. Thus, awk takes each line in the input file to be a separate record and appends a NEWLINE to the end of each record that it sends to its standard output. The input field separators are, by default, SPACES and TABS. The output field separator is a SPACE. You can change the value of any of the separators at any time by assigning a new value to its associated variable. Also, the input field separator can be set on the command line using the –F option.

Functions

The functions that awk provides for manipulating numbers and strings follow.

Name	Function
length(str)	returns the number of characters in **str**; if you do not supply an argument, it returns the number of characters in the current input record
int(num)	returns the integer portion of **num**

index(str1,str2)   returns the index of **str2** in **str1** or 0 if **str2** is not present

split(str,arr,del)   places elements of **str,** delimited by **del,** in the array **arr[1]...arr[n]**; returns the number of elements in the array

sprintf(fmt,args)   formats **args** according to **fmt** and returns the formatted string; mimics the C programming language function of the same name

substr(str,pos,len)   returns a substring of **str** that begins at **pos** and is **len** characters long

Operators

The following awk arithmetic operators are from the C programming language.

*   multiplies the expression preceding the operator by the expression following it

/   divides the expression preceding the operator by the expression following it

%   takes the remainder after dividing the expression preceding the operator by the expression following it

\+   adds the expression preceding the operator and the expression following it

−   subtracts the expression following the operator from the expression preceding it

=   assigns the value of the expression following the operator to the variable preceding it

++   increments the variable preceding the operator

−−   decrements the variable preceding the operator

+=   adds the expression following the operator to the variable preceding it and assigns the result to the variable preceding the operator

−=   subtracts the expression following the operator from the variable preceding it and assigns the result to the variable preceding the operator

*=   multiplies the variable preceding the operator by the expression following it and assigns the result to the variable preceding the operator

/=   divides the variable preceding the operator by the expression following it and assigns the result to the variable preceding the operator

%=   takes the remainder, after dividing the variable preceding the operator by the expression following it, and assigns the result to the variable preceding the operator

Associative Arrays

An associative array is one of awk's most powerful features. An associative array uses strings as its indexes. Using an associative array, you can mimic a traditional array by using numeric strings as indexes.

You assign a value to an element of an associative array just as you would assign a value to any other awk variable. The format is shown below.

    array[string] = value

The **array** is the name of the array, **string** is the index of the element of the array you are assigning a value to, and **value** is the value you are assigning to the element of the array.

There is a special For structure you can use with an awk array. The format is:

    for (elem in array) action

The **elem** is a variable that takes on the values of each of the elements in the array as the For structure loops through them, **array** is the name of the array, and **action** is the action that awk takes for each element in the array. You can use the **elem** variable in this **action**.

The "Examples" section contains programs that use associative arrays.

Printf

You can use the Printf command in place of Print to control the format of the output that awk generates. The awk version of Printf is similar to that of the C language. A Printf command takes the following format:

    printf "control-string" arg1, arg2, ..., argn

The **control-string** determines how Printf will format **arg1-n**. The **arg1-n** can be variables or other expressions. Within the **control-string**, you can use \n to indicate a NEWLINE and \t to indicate a TAB.

The **control-string** contains conversion specifications, one for each argument (**arg1-n**). A conversion specification has the following format:

% [–][x[.y]]conv

The – causes Printf to left justify the argument. The **x** is the minimum field width, and the **.y** is the number of places to the right of a decimal point in a number. The **conv** is a letter from the following list.

conv	Conversion
d	decimal
e	exponential notation
f	floating-point number
g	use **f** or **e**, whichever is shorter
o	unsigned octal
s	string of characters
x	unsigned hexadecimal

Refer to the following "Examples" section for examples of how to use Printf.

Examples

A simple **awk** program is shown below.

```
{ print }
```

This program consists of one program line that is an action. It uses no pattern. Because the pattern is missing, **awk** selects all lines in the input file. Without any arguments, the Print command prints each selected line in its entirety. This program copies the input file to its standard output.

The following program has a pattern part without an explicit action.

```
/jenny/
```

In this case, **awk** selects all lines from the input file that contain the string **jenny**. When you do not specify an action, **awk** assumes the action to be Print. This program copies all the lines in the input file that contain **jenny** to its standard output.

The following examples work with the **cars** data file. From left to right, the columns in the file contain each car's make, model, year of manufacture, mileage, and price. All white space in this file is composed of single TABS (there are no SPACES in the file).

```
$ cat cars
plym     fury      77      73      2500
chevy    nova      79      60      3000
ford     mustang   65      45      10000
volvo    gl        78      102     9850
ford     ltd       83      15      10500
chevy    nova      80      50      3500
fiat     600       65      115     450
honda    accord    81      30      6000
ford     thundbd   84      10      17000
toyota   tercel    82      180     750
chevy    impala    65      85      1550
ford     bronco    83      25      9500
```

The first example below selects all lines that contain the string chevy. The slashes indicate that chevy is a regular expression. This example has no action part.

Although neither awk nor shell syntax requires single quotation marks on the command line, it is a good idea to use them because they prevent many problems. If the awk program you create on the command line includes SPACES or any special characters that the shell will interpret, you must quote them. Always enclosing the program in single quotation marks is the easiest way of making sure you have quoted any characters that need to be quoted.

```
$ awk '/chevy/' cars
chevy    nova      79      60      3000
chevy    nova      80      50      3500
chevy    impala    65      85      1550
```

The next example selects all lines from the file (it has no pattern part). The braces enclose the action part—you must always use braces to delimit the action part so awk can distinguish the pattern part from the action part. This example prints the third field ($3), a SPACE (indicated by the comma), and the first field ($1) of each selected line.

```
$ awk '{print $3, $1}' cars
77 plym
79 chevy
65 ford
78 volvo
83 ford
80 chevy
65 fiat
81 honda
84 ford
82 toyota
65 chevy
83 ford
```

The next example includes both a pattern and an action part. It selects all lines that contain the string chevy and prints the third and first fields from the lines it selects.

```
$ awk  ' /chevy/ {print $3, $1} '  cars
79 chevy
80 chevy
65 chevy
```

The next example selects lines that contain a match for the regular expression h. Because there is no explicit action, it prints all the lines it selects.

```
$ awk  ' /h/ '  cars
chevy    nova     79        60        3000
chevy    nova     80        50        3500
honda    accord   81        30        6000
ford     thundbd  84        10        17000
chevy    impala   65        85        1550
```

The next pattern uses the matches operator (~) to select all lines that contain the letter h in the first field.

```
$ awk  ' $1 ~ /h/ '  cars
chevy    nova     79        60        3000
chevy    nova     80        50        3500
honda    accord   81        30        6000
chevy    impala   65        85        1550
```

The caret (^) in a regular expression forces a match at the beginning of the line or, in this case, the beginning of the first field.

```
$ awk  ' $1 ~ /^h/ '  cars
honda    accord   81        30        6000
```

A pair of brackets surrounds a character class definition (refer to Appendix B, ''Regular Expressions''). Below, awk selects all lines that have a second field that begins with t or m. Then it prints the third and second fields, a dollar sign, and the fifth field.

```
$ awk  ' $2 ~ /^[tm]/ {print $3, $2, "$" $5} '  cars
65 mustang $10000
84 thundbd $17000
82 tercel $750
```

The next example shows three roles that a dollar sign can play in an awk program. A dollar sign followed by a number forms the name of a field. Within a regular expression, a dollar sign forces a match at the end of a line or field (5$).

And, within a string, you can use a dollar sign as itself.

```
$ awk ' $3 ~ /5$/ {print $3, $1, "$" $5} ' cars
65 ford $10000
65 fiat $450
65 chevy $1550
```

Below, the equals relational operator (==) causes awk to perform a numeric comparison between the third field in each line and the number 65. The awk command takes the default action, Print, on each line that matches.

```
$ awk ' $3 == 65 ' cars
ford      mustang 65       45        10000
fiat      600     65       115       450
chevy     impala  65       85        1550
```

The next example finds all cars priced at or under $3000.

```
$ awk ' $5 <= 3000 ' cars
plym      fury    77       73        2500
chevy     nova    79       60        3000
fiat      600     65       115       450
toyota    tercel  82       180       750
chevy     impala  65       85        1550
```

When you use double quotation marks, awk performs textual comparisons, using the ASCII collating sequence as the basis of the comparison. Below, awk shows that the *strings* 450 and 750 fall in the range that lies between the *strings* 2000 and 9000.

```
$ awk ' $5 >= "2000" && $5 < "9000" ' cars
plym      fury    77       73        2500
chevy     nova    79       60        3000
chevy     nova    80       50        3500
fiat      600     65       115       450
honda     accord  81       30        6000
toyota    tercel  82       180       750
```

When you need a numeric comparison, do not use quotation marks. The next example gives the correct results. It is the same as the previous example but omits the double quotation marks.

```
$ awk ' $5 >= 2000 && $5 < 9000 ' cars
plym      fury    77       73        2500
chevy     nova    79       60        3000
chevy     nova    80       50        3500
honda     accord  81       30        6000
```

Next, the range operator (,) selects a group of lines. The first line it selects is the one specified by the pattern before the comma. The last line is the one selected by the pattern after the comma. If there is no line that matches the pattern after the comma, **awk** selects every line up to the end of the file. The example selects all lines starting with the line that contains volvo and concluding with the line that contains fiat.

```
$ awk  ′/volvo/ , /fiat/ ′ cars
volvo    gl        78       102     9850
ford     ltd       83       15      10500
chevy    nova      80       50      3500
fiat     600       65       115     450
```

After the range operator finds its first group of lines, it starts the process over, looking for a line that matches the pattern before the comma. In the following example, **awk** finds three groups of lines that fall between chevy and ford. Although the fifth line in the file contains ford, **awk** does not select it because, when it is processing the fifth line, it is searching for chevy.

```
$ awk  ′/chevy/ , /ford/ ′ cars
chevy    nova      79       60      3000
ford     mustang   65       45      10000
chevy    nova      80       50      3500
fiat     600       65       115     450
honda    accord    81       30      6000
ford     thundbd   84       10      17000
chevy    impala    65       85      1550
ford     bronco    83       25      9500
```

When you are writing a longer **awk** program, it is convenient to put the program in a file and reference the file on the command line. Use the **-f** option followed by the name of the file containing the **awk** program.

Following is an **awk** program that has two actions and uses the **BEGIN** pattern. The **awk** utility performs the action associated with **BEGIN** before it processes any of the lines of the data file. The **pr_header awk** program uses **BEGIN** to print a header.

The second action, { print }, has no pattern part and prints all the lines in the file.

```
$ cat pr_header
BEGIN     {print "Make      Model     Year      Miles     Price"}
          {print}

$ awk -f pr_header cars
Make      Model     Year      Miles     Price
plym      fury      77        73        2500
chevy     nova      79        60        3000
```

```
ford      mustang  65        45        10000
volvo     gl       78        102       9850
ford      ltd      83        15        10500
chevy     nova     80        50        3500
fiat      600      65        115       450
honda     accord   81        30        6000
ford      thundbd  84        10        17000
toyota    tercel   82        180       750
chevy     impala   65        85        1550
ford      bronco   83        25        9500
```

In the previous and following examples, the white space in the headers is composed of single TABS so that the titles line up with the columns of data.

```
$ cat pr_header2
BEGIN   {
print "Make       Model     Year    Miles     Price"
print "----------------------------------------------"
}
            {print}
```

```
$ awk -f pr_header2 cars
Make      Model    Year     Miles    Price
-------------------------------------------
plym      fury     77       73       2500
chevy     nova     79       60       3000
ford      mustang  65       45       10000
volvo     gl       78       102      9850
ford      ltd      83       15       10500
chevy     nova     80       50       3500
fiat      600      65       115      450
honda     accord   81       30       6000
ford      thundbd  84       10       17000
toyota    tercel   82       180      750
chevy     impala   65       85       1550
ford      bronco   83       25       9500
```

When you call the **length** function without an argument, it returns the number of characters in the current line, including field separators. The $0 variable always contains the value of the current line. In the next example, awk prepends the length to each line, and then a pipe sends the output from awk to sort so that the lines of the **cars** file appear in order of length. Because the formatting of the report depends on TABS, including three extra characters at the beginning of each line throws off the format of the last line. A remedy for this situation will be covered shortly.

```
$ awk '{print length, $0}' cars | sort
19 fiat 600      65        115       450
20 ford ltd      83        15        10500
20 plym fury     77        73        2500
20 volvo gl      78        102       9850
21 chevy nova    79        60        3000
21 chevy nova    80        50        3500
22 ford  bronco  83        25        9500
23 chevy impala  65        85        1550
23 honda accord  81        30        6000
24 ford  mustang 65        45        10000
24 ford  thundbd 84        10        17000
24 toyota        tercel    82        180       750
```

The **NR** variable contains the record (line) number of the current line. The following pattern selects all lines that contain more than 23 characters. The action prints the line number of all the selected lines.

```
$ awk 'length > 23 {print NR}' cars
3
9
10
```

You can combine the range operator (,) and the **NR** variable to display a group of lines of a file based on their line numbers. The next example displays lines 2 through 4.

```
$ awk 'NR == 2 , NR == 4' cars
chevy    nova    79      60      3000
ford     mustang 65      45      10000
volvo    gl      78      102     9850
```

The **END** pattern works in a manner similar to the **BEGIN** pattern, except awk takes the actions associated with it after it has processed the last of its input lines. The following report displays information only after it has processed the entire data file. The NR variable retains its value after awk has finished processing the data file so an action associated with an **END** pattern can use it.

```
$ awk 'END {print NR, "cars for sale."}' cars
12 cars for sale.
```

The next example uses If commands to change the values of some of the first fields. As long as awk does not make any changes to a record, it leaves the entire record, including separators, intact. Once it makes a change to a record, it changes all separators in that record to the default. The default output field separator is a SPACE.

```
$ cat separ_demo
        {
        if ($1 ~ /ply/)   $1 = "plymouth"
        if ($1 ~ /chev/)  $1 = "chevrolet"
        print
        }

$ awk -f separ_demo cars
plymouth fury 77 73 2500
chevrolet nova 79 60 3000
ford      mustang  65        45        10000
volvo     gl       78        102       9850
ford      ltd      83        15        10500
chevrolet nova 80 50 3500
fiat      600      65        115       450
honda     accord   81        30        6000
ford      thundbd  84        10        17000
toyota    tercel   82        180       750
chevrolet impala 65 85 1550
ford      bronco   83        25        9500
```

You can change the default value of the output field separator by assigning a value to the **OFS** variable. There is one TAB character between the quotation marks in the following example.

This fix improves the appearance of the report but does not properly line up the columns.

```
$ cat ofs_demo
BEGIN   {OFS = " "}
        {
        if ($1 ~ /ply/)   $1 = "plymouth"
        if ($1 ~ /chev/)  $1 = "chevrolet"
        print
        }

$ awk -f ofs_demo cars
plymouth fury      77       73       2500
chevrolet          nova     79       60       3000
ford      mustang  65       45       10000
volvo     gl       78       102      9850
ford      ltd      83       15       10500
chevrolet          nova     80       50       3500
fiat      600      65       115      450
honda     accord   81       30       6000
ford      thundbd  84       10       17000
toyota    tercel   82       180      750
chevrolet          impala   65       85       1550
ford      bronco   83       25       9500
```

You can use Printf to refine the output format (refer to page 419). (The following example uses a backslash at the end of a program line to mask the following NEWLINE from awk. You can use this technique to continue a long line over one or more lines without affecting the outcome of the program.)

```
$ cat printf_demo
BEGIN {
  print "                                        Miles"
  print "Make        Model        Year        (000)        Price"
  print "-----------------------------------------------------------"
      }
      {
  if ($1 ~ /ply/)  $1 = "plymouth"
  if ($1 ~ /chev/) $1 = "chevrolet"
          printf "%-10s %-8s     19%2d    %5d        $ %8.2f\n",\
          $1, $2, $3, $4, $5
          }
```

```
$ awk -f printf_demo cars
                            Miles
Make          Model        Year     (000)              Price
------------------------------------------------------------
plymouth      fury         1977       73      $   2500.00
chevrolet     nova         1979       60      $   3000.00
ford          mustang      1965       45      $  10000.00
volvo         gl           1978      102      $   9850.00
ford          ltd          1983       15      $  10500.00
chevrolet     nova         1980       50      $   3500.00
fiat          600          1965      115      $    450.00
honda         accord       1981       30      $   6000.00
ford          thundbd      1984       10      $  17000.00
toyota        tercel       1982      180      $    750.00
chevrolet     impala       1965       85      $   1550.00
ford          bronco       1983       25      $   9500.00
```

The next example creates two new files, one with all the lines that contain chevy and the other with lines containing ford.

```
$ cat redirect_out
/chevy/           {print > "chevfile"}
/ford/            {print > "fordfile"}
END               {print "done."}
$ awk -f redirect_out cars
done.
$ cat chevfile
chevy     nova     `79        60        3000
chevy     nova     80         50        3500
chevy     impala   65         85        1550
```

The **summary** program produces a summary report on all cars and newer cars. The first two lines of declarations are not required; awk automatically declares and initializes variables as you use them. After awk reads all the input data, it computes and displays averages.

```
$ cat summary
BEGIN    {
         yearsum = 0 ; costsum = 0
         newcostsum = 0 ; newcount = 0
         }
         {
         yearsum += $3
         costsum += $5
         }
$3 > 80  {newcostsum += $5 ; newcount ++}
END      {
         printf "Average age of cars is %3.1f years\n",\
                90 - (yearsum/NR)
         printf "Average cost of cars is $%7.2f\n",\
                costsum/NR
         printf "Average cost of newer cars is $%7.2f\n",\
                newcostsum/newcount
         }

$ awk -f summary cars
Average age of cars is 13.2 years
Average cost of cars is $6216.67
Average cost of newer cars is $8750.00
```

Following, grep shows the format of a line from the **passwd** file that the next example uses.

```
$ grep 'sobell' /etc/passwd
mark:x:107:100:ext 112:/home/mark:/bin/csh
```

The next example demonstrates a technique for finding the largest number in a field. Because it works with the **passwd** file, which delimits fields with colons (:), it changes the input field separator (**FS**) before reading any data. (Alternatively, the **–F** option could be used on the command line to change the input field separator.) This example reads the **passwd** file and determines the next available user ID number (field 3). The numbers do not have to be in order in the **passwd** file for this program to work.

The pattern causes awk to select records that contain a user ID number greater than any previous user ID number that it has processed. Each time it selects a record, it assigns the value of the new user ID number to the **saveit** variable. Then awk uses the new value of **saveit** to test the user ID of all subsequent records.

Finally, awk adds 1 to the value of **saveit** and displays the result.

```
$ cat find_uid
BEGIN               {FS = ":"
                    saveit = 0}
$3 > saveit         {saveit = $3}
END                 {print "Next UID is " saveit + 1}

$ awk -f find_uid /etc/passwd
Next available UID is 192
```

The next example shows another report based on the **cars** file. This report uses nested If Else statements to substitute values based on the contents of the price field. The program has no pattern part—it processes every record.

```
$ cat price_range
{
if ($5 <= 5000) $5 = "inexpensive"
else if ($5 > 5000 && $5 < 10000) $5 = "please ask"
else if ($5 >= 10000) $5 = "expensive"
printf "%-10s %-8s    19%2d    %5d    %-12s\n",\
        $1, $2, $3, $4, $5
}

$ awk -f price_range cars
plym        fury        1977        73      inexpensive
chevy       nova        1979        60      inexpensive
ford        mustang     1965        45      expensive
volvo       gl          1978        102     please ask
ford        ltd         1983        15      expensive
chevy       nova        1980        50      inexpensive
fiat        600         1965        115     inexpensive
honda       accord      1981        30      please ask
ford        thundbd     1984        10      expensive
toyota      tercel      1982        180     inexpensive
chevy       impala      1965        85      inexpensive
ford        bronco      1983        25      please ask
```

Below, the **manuf** associative array uses the contents of the first field of each record in the **cars** file as an index. The array is composed of the elements **manuf[plym]**, **manuf[chevy]**, **manuf[ford]**, and so on. The **++** C language operator increments the variable that it follows.

The action following the **END** pattern is the special For structure that loops through the elements of an associative array. A pipe sends the output through **sort** to produce an alphabetical list of cars and the quantities in stock.

```
$ cat manuf
awk '              {manuf[$1]++}
END       {for (name in manuf) print name, manuf[name]}
' cars |
sort

$ manuf
chevy 3
fiat 1
ford 4
honda 1
plym 1
toyota 1
volvo 1
```

The **manuf.sh** program is a more complete shell script that includes error checking. This script lists and counts the contents of a column in a file, with both the column number and the name of the file specified on the command line.

The first awk action (the one that starts with {count) uses the shell variable **$1** in the middle of the awk program to specify an array index. The single quotation marks cause the shell to substitute the value of the first command line argument in place of **$1**, so that **$1** is interpreted before the awk command is invoked. The leading dollar sign (the one before the first single quotation mark) causes awk to interpret what the shell substitutes as a field number. Refer to Chapter 8 for more information on shell scripts.

```
$ cat manuf.sh
if [ $# != 2 ]
    then
          echo "Usage: manuf.sh field file"
          exit 1
fi
awk < $2 '
          {count[$'$1']++}
END       {for (item in count) printf "%-20s%-20s\n",\
                   item, count[item]}' |
sort

$ manuf.sh
Usage: manuf.sh field file
$ manuf.sh 1 cars
chevy                3
fiat                 1
ford                 4
honda                1
plym                 1
toyota               1
volvo                1
```

```
$ manuf.sh 3 cars
65                  3
77                  1
78                  1
79                  1
80                  1
81                  1
82                  1
83                  2
84                  1
```

The **word_usage** script displays a word usage list for a file you specify on the command line. The deroff utility removes nroff and troff commands from a file and, with the –w option, lists the words one to a line. The sort utility orders the file with the most frequently used words at the top of the list. It sorts groups of words that are used the same number of times in alphabetical order. Refer to sort in Part II for more information.

```
$ cat word_usage
deroff -w $* |
awk            '
               {count[$1]++}
END            {for (item in count) printf "%-15s%3s\n",\
                       item, count[item]}' |
sort +1nr +0f -1

$ word_usage textfile
the               42
file              29
fsck              27
system            22
you               22
to                21
it                17
SIZE              14
and               13
MODE              13
  .
  .
```

Below is a similar program in a different format. The style mimics that of a C program and may be easier to read and work with for more complex awk programs.

```
$ cat word_count
deroff -w $* |
awk ' {
    count[$1]++
}
END {
    for (item in count)
        {
        if (count[item] > 4)
            {
            printf "%-15s%3s\n", item, count[item]
            }
        }
} ' |
sort +1nr +0f -1
```

The tail utility displays the last ten lines of output, illustrating that words occurring fewer than five times are not listed.

```
$ word_count textfile | tail
directories      5
if               5
information      5
INODE            5
more             5
no               5
on               5
response         5
this             5
will             5
```

The next example shows one way to put a date on a report. The first line of input to the awk program comes from date. The awk program reads this line as record number 1 (NR == 1) and processes it accordingly. It processes all subsequent records with the action associated with the next pattern (NR > 1).

```
$ cat report
if (test $# = 0) then
    echo "You must supply a filename."
    exit
fi
(date; cat $*) |
awk '
NR == 1    {print "Report for", $1, $2, $3 ", " $6}
NR >  1    {print $5 "    " $1}'
```

awk

```
$ report cars
Report for Mon Jul 9, 1990
2500     plym
3000     chevy
10000    ford
9850     volvo
10500    ford
3500     chevy
450      fiat
6000     honda
17000    ford
750      toyota
1550     chevy
9500     ford
```

The next example uses the **numbers** file and sums each of the columns in a file you specify on the command line. It performs error checking, discarding fields that contain nonnumeric entries. It also displays a grand total for the file.

```
$ cat numbers
10        20        30.3      40.5
20        30        45.7      66.1
30        xyz       50        70
40        75        107.2     55.6
50        20        30.3      40.5
60        30        45.O      66.1
70        1134.7    50        70
80        75        107.2     55.6
90        176       30.3      40.5
100       1027.45   45.7      66.1
110       123       50        57a.5
120       75        107.2     55.6
```

```
$ cat tally
awk '    BEGIN {
              ORS = ""
              }
NR == 1       {
       nfields = NF
       }
       {
       if ($0 ~ /[^0-9. \t]/)
              {
              print "\nRecord " NR " skipped:\n\t"
              print $0 "\n"
              next
              }
```

```
        else
            {
            for (count = 1; count <= nfields; count++)
                {
                printf "%10.2f", $count > "tally.out"
                sum[count] += $count
                gtotal += $count
                }
            print "\n" > "tally.out"
            }
        }
END    {
        for (count = 1; count <= nfields; count++)
            {
            print "    -------" > "tally.out"
            }
        print "\n" > "tally.out"
        for (count = 1; count <= nfields; count++)
            {
            printf "%10.2f", sum[count] > "tally.out"
            }
        print "\n\n          Grand Total " gtotal "\n" > "tally.out"
} ´ < numbers
```

```
$ tally
Record 3 skipped:
          30        xyz        50        70

Record 6 skipped:
          60        30        45.O        66.1

Record 11 skipped:
          110        123        50        57a.5

$ cat tally.out
      10.00      20.00      30.30      40.50
      20.00      30.00      45.70      66.10
      40.00      75.00     107.20      55.60
      50.00      20.00      30.30      40.50
      70.00    1134.70      50.00      70.00
      80.00      75.00     107.20      55.60
      90.00     176.00      30.30      40.50
     100.00    1027.45      45.70      66.10
     120.00      75.00     107.20      55.60
     -------    -------    -------    -------
     580.00    2633.15     553.90     490.50

          Grand Total 4257.55
```

The next awk example reads the **passwd** file. It lists users who do not have passwords and users who have duplicate user ID numbers. (The pwck utility will also perform these checks, as well as a few more.)

```
$ cat /etc/passwd
bill::102:100:ext 123:/home/bill:/bin/sh
roy:x:104:100:ext 475:/home/roy:/bin/sh
tom:x:105:100:ext 476:/home/tom:/bin/sh
lynn:x:166:100:ext 500:/home/lynn:/bin/sh
mark:x:107:100:ext 112:/home/mark:/bin/csh
sales:x:108:100:ext 102:/m/market:/bin/sh
anne:x:109:100:ext 355:/home/anne:/bin/sh
toni::164:100:ext 357:/home/toni:/bin/sh
ginny:x:115:100:ext 109:/home/ginny:/bin/sh
chuck:x:116:100:ext 146:/home/chuck:/bin/sh
neil:x:164:100:ext 159:/home/neil:/bin/sh
rmi:x:118:100:ext 178:/home/rmi:/bin/sh
vern:x:119:100:ext 201:/home/vern:/bin/sh
bob:x:120:100:ext 227:/home/bob:/bin/sh
janet:x:122:100:ext 229:/home/janet:/bin/sh
maggie:x:124:100:ext 244:/home/maggie:/bin/sh
dan::126:100::/home/dan:/bin/sh
dave:x:108:100:ext 427:/home/dave:/bin/sh
mary:x:129:100:ext 303:/home/mary:/bin/sh


$ cat passwd_check
awk < /etc/passwd ' BEGIN{
    uid[void] = "" # tell awk that uid is an array
    }
    {       # no pattern indicates process all records
    dup = 0       # initialize duplicate flag
    split($0, field, ":") # split into fields delimited by ":"
    if (field[2] == "")   # check for null password field
        {
        if (field[5] == "")# check for null info field
            {
            print field[1] " has no password."
            }
        else
            {
            print field[1] " ("field[5]") has no password."
            }
        }
    for (name in uid) # loop through uid array
        {
        if (uid[name] == field[3])# check for 2nd use of UID
            {
            print field[1] " has the same UID as "\
                name " : UID = " uid[name]
            dup = 1  # set duplicate flag
            }
        }
    if (!dup)   # same as: if (dup == 0)
            # assign UID and login name to uid array
        {
        uid[field[1]] = field[3]
        }
}'
```

```
$ passwd_check
bill (ext 123) has no password.
toni (ext 357) has no password.
neil has the same UID as toni : UID = 164
dan has no password.
dave has the same UID as sales : UID = 108
```

The final example shows a complete interactive shell script that uses awk to generate a report.

```
$ cat list_cars
trap 'rm -f $$.tem > /dev/null;echo $0 aborted.;exit 1' 1 2 15
echo "Price range (e.g., 5000 7500): \c"
read lowrange hirange

echo '
                                    Miles
Make          Model          Year    (000)         Price
-----------------------------------------------------' > $$.tem
awk < cars '
$5 >= '$lowrange' && $5 <= '$hirange' {
        if ($1 ~ /ply/)  $1 = "plymouth"
        if ($1 ~ /chev/) $1 = "chevrolet"
        printf "%-10s %-8s    19%2d    %5d    $ %8.2f\n",\
            $1, $2, $3, $4, $5
        }' | sort -n +5 >> $$.tem
cat $$.tem
rm $$.tem
```

```
$ list_cars
Price range (e.g., 5000 7500): 3000 8000

                                  Miles
Make          Model          Year    (000)            Price
-----------------------------------------------------
chevrolet     nova           1979     60       $   3000.00
chevrolet     nova           1980     50       $   3500.00
honda         accord         1981     30       $   6000.00
```

```
$ list_cars
Price range (e.g., 5000 7500): 0 2000

                                  Miles
Make          Model          Year    (000)            Price
-----------------------------------------------------
fiat          600            1965    115       $    450.00
toyota        tercel         1982    180       $    750.00
chevrolet     impala         1965     85       $   1550.00
```

```
$ list_cars
Price range (e.g., 5000 7500): 15000 100000

                                  Miles
Make          Model      Year    (000)       Price
-----------------------------------------------------
ford          thundbd    1984      10    $ 17000.00
```

Error Messages

The following examples show some of the more common causes of awk's infamous error messages (and nonmessages).

The first example leaves the single quotation marks off the command line, so the shell interprets $3 and $1 as shell variables. Another problem is that, because there are no single quotation marks, the shell passes awk four arguments instead of two.

```
$ awk {print $3, $1} cars
awk: syntax error near line 1
awk: illegal statement near line 1
```

The next command line includes a typo that awk does not catch (prinnt). Instead of issuing an error message, awk just does not do anything useful.

```
$ awk ´$3 >= 83 {prinnt $1}´ cars
```

The next example has no braces around the action.

```
$ awk ´/chevy/ print $3, $1´ cars
awk: syntax error near line 1
awk: bailing out near line 1
```

There is no problem with the next example—awk did just what you asked it to. (None of the lines in the file contained a z).

```
$ awk ´/z/´ cars
```

The following program contains a useless action (the Print command is probably missing).

```
$ awk ´{$3}´ cars
awk: illegal statement 56250
  record number 1
```

The next example shows another improper action, but this time awk did not issue an error message.

```
$ awk ´{$3 " made by " $1}´ cars
```

Following is a format that awk did not particularly care for. This example needs a backslash after the first Print command to quote the following NEWLINE.

```
$ cat print_cars
BEGIN                   {print
"Make     Model     Year     Miles     Price"}
                        {print}

$ awk -f print_cars cars
awk: illegal statement 57422
```

You must use double quotation marks, not single quotation marks, to delimit strings.

```
$ awk ´$3 ~ /5$/ {print $3, $1, ´$´ $5}´ cars
awk: trying to access field 10000
 record number 3
```

cal

Display a calendar.

Format

> **cal [month] year**
> **cal**

Summary

The cal utility displays a calendar for a month or year.

Arguments

The arguments specify the month and year cal displays a calendar for. The **month** is a decimal integer from 1 to 12, and the **year** is a decimal integer. If you do not specify any arguments, cal displays a calendar for the current month.

Options

There are no options.

Notes

Do not abbreviate the year. The year 90 does not represent the same year as 1990.

Examples

The following command displays a calendar for August 1990.

```
$ cal 8 1990
   August 1990
 S  M Tu  W Th  F  S
             1  2  3  4
 5  6  7  8  9 10 11
12 13 14 15 16 17 18
19 20 21 22 23 24 25
26 27 28 29 30 31
```

The next command displays a calendar for all of 1949.

$ cal 1949

1949

```
          Jan                     Feb                     Mar
 S  M Tu  W Th  F  S      S  M Tu  W Th  F  S      S  M Tu  W Th  F  S
                   1               1  2  3  4  5               1  2  3  4  5
 2  3  4  5  6  7  8      6  7  8  9 10 11 12      6  7  8  9 10 11 12
 9 10 11 12 13 14 15     13 14 15 16 17 18 19     13 14 15 16 17 18 19
16 17 18 19 20 21 22     20 21 22 23 24 25 26     20 21 22 23 24 25 26
23 24 25 26 27 28 29     27 28                    27 28 29 30 31
30 31
          Apr                     May                     Jun
 S  M Tu  W Th  F  S      S  M Tu  W Th  F  S      S  M Tu  W Th  F  S
                1  2      1  2  3  4  5  6  7               1  2  3  4
 3  4  5  6  7  8  9      8  9 10 11 12 13 14      5  6  7  8  9 10 11
10 11 12 13 14 15 16     15 16 17 18 19 20 21     12 13 14 15 16 17 18
17 18 19 20 21 22 23     22 23 24 25 26 27 28     19 20 21 22 23 24 25
24 25 26 27 28 29 30     29 30 31                 26 27 28 29 30
          Jul                     Aug                     Sep
 S  M Tu  W Th  F  S      S  M Tu  W Th  F  S      S  M Tu  W Th  F  S
                1  2         1  2  3  4  5  6               1  2  3
 3  4  5  6  7  8  9      7  8  9 10 11 12 13      4  5  6  7  8  9 10
10 11 12 13 14 15 16     14 15 16 17 18 19 20     11 12 13 14 15 16 17
17 18 19 20 21 22 23     21 22 23 24 25 26 27     18 19 20 21 22 23 24
24 25 26 27 28 29 30     28 29 30 31              25 26 27 28 29 30
31
          Oct                     Nov                     Dec
 S  M Tu  W Th  F  S      S  M Tu  W Th  F  S      S  M Tu  W Th  F  S
                   1         1  2  3  4  5               1  2  3
 2  3  4  5  6  7  8      6  7  8  9 10 11 12      4  5  6  7  8  9 10
 9 10 11 12 13 14 15     13 14 15 16 17 18 19     11 12 13 14 15 16 17
16 17 18 19 20 21 22     20 21 22 23 24 25 26     18 19 20 21 22 23 24
23 24 25 26 27 28 29     27 28 29 30              25 26 27 28 29 30 31
30 31
```

cal

calendar

Present reminders.

Format

calendar

Summary

The UNIX system provides calendar as a service. If your system is set up to run calendar automatically, it will send you mail (typically once a day). The mail will contain lines from a file called **calendar** in your home directory that contain that day's or the next day's date. You can also use the calendar command to display these lines from your **calendar** file.

Options and Arguments

There are no options or arguments.

Notes

During the weekend, the *next day* goes through Monday.

The **calendar** file *must* be in your home directory and must have read access permission for everyone. The dates can appear anywhere on the line in the file, in various formats, but must show the month preceding the day of the month.

When you execute calendar, or have your **.profile** or **.login** file execute it, calendar displays any lines in the **calendar** file that contain that day's or the next day's date.

The calendar utility ignores a year as part of the date.

Example

The following example of a **calendar** file shows some of the ways you can express the date. If you place this file in your home directory, each of the three lines will be sent to you by mail on the date you specify and one day previous to it.

```
$ cat calendar
This line will be displayed on 7/20
Jul 28: remember to call Frank
On July 30 five years ago...
```

cat

Join or display files.

Format

    cat [options] [file-list]

Summary

The cat utility joins files end to end. It takes its input from files you specify on the command line or from its standard input. You can use cat to display the contents of one or more text files on the terminal.

Arguments

The **file-list** is composed of pathnames of one or more files that cat displays. You can use a hyphen in place of a filename to cause cat to read its standard input [e.g., **cat a – b** gets its input from file **a**, its standard input (terminated by a CONTROL-D if you enter it at the keyboard), and then file **b**].

Options

-e   **end of line**   This option marks the ends of lines with dollar signs. In order for this option to work, you must use it with the **–v** option.

-s   **silent**   This option causes cat not to display a message when it cannot find a file.

-t   **tabs**   This option marks TABS with ^Is. In order for this option to work, you must use it with the **–v** option.

-u   **unbuffered**   This option causes cat not to buffer output.

-v   **visual**   This option causes cat to display nonprinting characters other than TABS, NEWLINES, and FORM-FEEDS. It also allows the **–t** and **–e** options to function.

Notes

Use the od utility (see page 542) to display the contents of a file that does not contain text (e.g., an executable program file).

    The name cat is derived from one of the functions of this utility, *catenate*, which means to join together sequentially, or end to end.

Caution.   Despite cat's warning message, the shell destroys the input file (**letter**) before invoking cat.

```
$ cat memo letter > letter
cat: input letter is output
```

If you are using the C Shell or the Korn Shell, you can prevent problems of this sort by setting the **noclobber** variable.

Examples

The following command line displays on the terminal the contents of the text file named **memo**.

```
$ cat memo
.
.
```

The next example catenates three files and redirects the output to a file named **all**.

```
$ cat page1 letter memo > all
```

You can use cat to create short text files without using an editor. Enter the command line shown below, type the text that you want in the file, and then press CONTROL-D on a line by itself. The cat utility takes its input from its standard input (the terminal), and the shell redirects its standard output (a copy of the input) to the file you specify. The CONTROL-D signals the end of file and causes cat to return control to the shell. (Also see page 100.)

```
$ cat > new_file
.
.
(text)
.
.
CONTROL-D
```

Below, a pipe sends the output from who to the standard input of cat. The cat utility creates the **output** file that contains the contents of the **header** file, the output of who, and finally, **footer**. The hyphen on the command line causes cat to read its standard input after reading **header** and before reading **footer**.

```
$ who | cat header - footer > output
```

cc

C compiler

Format

    cc [options] file-list [–larg]

Summary

Based on the command line options, **cc** compiles, assembles, and loads C language source files. It can also assemble and load assembly language source files or merely load object files.

    The **cc** utility uses the following naming conventions:

- A filename extension of **.c** indicates a C language source program.
- A filename extension of **.s** indicates an assembly language source program.
- A filename extension of **.o** indicates an object program.

    The **cc** utility takes its input from files you specify on the command line. Unless you use the **–o** option, **cc** stores the executable program it produces in **a.out**.

Arguments

The **file-list** contains the pathnames of the files that **cc** is to compile, assemble, and/or load.

Options

Without any options, **cc** accepts C language source files, assembly language source files, and object files that follow the naming conventions outlined above. It compiles, assembles, and loads these files as appropriate, producing an executable file named **a.out**. The **cc** utility puts the object code in files with the same base filename as their source but with a filename extension of **.o**. If you compile, assemble, and load a single C source file with one **cc** command, **cc** deletes the object file.

    –c   **compile** This option causes **cc** not to load object files. The **cc** utility compiles and/or assembles source files and leaves the corresponding object code in files with filename extensions of **.o**.

–o **file**   **output** This option causes **cc** to place the executable program in **file** instead of **a.out**. You can use any filename in place of **file**.

    –O   **optimize** This option optimizes C source program compilation.

-S   **compile only**   With this option, cc compiles only C source files. The cc utility compiles C files and leaves the corresponding assembly language source code in files with filename extensions of **.s**.

-g   This option causes cc to include additional information that is used by the debugger.

-larg   **search library**   With this option, cc searches both the /lib/lib**arg**.a and the /usr/lib/lib**arg**.a libraries and loads any required functions. You must replace **arg** with the name of the library you want to search. For example, the **–lm** option normally loads the standard math library.

   The position of this option is significant; it generally needs to go at the end of the command line. The loader uses the library only to resolve undefined symbols from modules that *precede* the library option on the command line.

Examples

The first example compiles, assembles, and loads a single C program, **compute.c**. The executable output is put in **a.out**. The cc utility deletes the object file.

```
$ cc compute.c
```

The next example compiles the same program using the C optimizer (**–O** option). It assembles and then loads the optimized code. The **–o** option causes cc to put the executable output in **compute**.

```
$ cc –O –o compute compute.c
```

Next, a C source file, an assembly language file, and an object file are compiled, assembled, and loaded. The executable output goes to **progo**.

```
$ cc –o progo procom.c profast.s proout.o
```

Finally, cc searches the standard math library stored in **/lib/libm.a** when it is loading the **himath** program. It places the executable output in **a.out**.

```
$ cc himath.c –lm
```

cd

Change to another working directory.

Format

cd [directory]

Summary

When you call cd and specify a directory, that directory becomes the working directory. If you do not specify a directory on the command line, cd makes your home directory the working directory.

Argument

The **directory** is the pathname of the directory that you want to become the working directory.

Options

There are no options.

Notes

The cd program is not really a utility but a built-in command in the Bourne Shell, the C Shell, and the Korn Shell. Refer to the discussion of the **HOME** shell variable in Chapters 8 and 9. Chapter 4 contains a discussion of cd.

Each of the three shells has a variable, **CDPATH** (**cdpath** in the C Shell), that affects the operation of cd. The **CDPATH** variable contains a list of directories cd will search in addition to the working directory. If **CDPATH** is not set, cd searches only the working directory. If it is set, cd searches each of the directories in **CDPATH**'s directory list. Refer to page 244 for more information about **CDPATH** or page 319 for more information about **cdpath**.

The Korn Shell built-in cd command has some features in addition to those common to all three shells. Refer to Appendix A.

Examples

The following command makes your home directory become the working directory.

```
$ cd
```

The next command makes the **/home/alex/literature** directory the working directory. The pwd utility verifies the change.

```
$ cd /home/alex/literature
$ pwd
/home/alex/literature
```

Next, cd makes a subdirectory of the working directory the new working directory.

```
$ cd memos
$ pwd
/home/alex/literature/memos
```

Finally, cd uses the **..** reference to the parent of the working directory to make the parent the new working directory.

```
$ cd ..
```

chgrp

Change the group that is associated with a file.

Format

chgrp [options] group file-list

Summary

The chgrp utility changes the group that is associated with a file.

Arguments

The **group** is the name or numeric group ID of the new group. The **file-list** is a list of pathnames of the files whose group association you want to change.

Options

–R   **recursive**   When you include directories in **file-list,** this option causes chgrp to descend the directory hierarchy, setting the specified group ID on all files encountered.

Notes

Only the owner of a file or the Superuser can change the group association of a file.

Example

The following command changes the group that the **manuals** file is associated with. The new group is pubs.

```
$ chgrp pubs manuals
```

chmod

Change the access mode of a file.

Format

> chmod [options] who[operation][permission] file-list
> chmod [options] mode file-list

Summary

The **chmod** utility changes the ways in which a file can be accessed by the owner of the file, the group to which the file belongs, and/or all other users. Only the owner of a file or the Superuser can change the access mode, or permissions, of a file.

You can specify the new access mode absolutely or symbolically.

Arguments

Arguments give **chmod** information about which files are to have their modes changed in what ways.

Symbolic

The **chmod** utility changes the access permission for the class of user specified by **who**. The class of user is designated by one or more of the following letters:

> u   **user**   owner of the file
> g   **group**   group to which the owner belongs
> o   **other**   all other users
> a   **all**   can be used in place of **u**, **g**, and **o** above

The **operation** to be performed is defined by the following list:

> +   add permission for the specified user class
> -   remove permission for the specified user class
> =   set permission for the specified user—reset all other permissions for that user class

The access **permission** is defined by the following list:

> r   read permission
> w   write permission

x	execute permission
s	set user ID or set group ID (depending on the **who** argument) to that of the owner of the file while the file is being executed
t	set the sticky bit (only the Superuser can set the sticky bit, and it can only be used with **u**)—see page 683

Absolute

In place of the symbolic method of changing the access permissions for a file, you can use an octal number to represent the mode. Construct the number by ORing the appropriate values from the following table. (To OR two octal numbers from the following table, you can just add them. Refer to the second table following for examples.)

Number	Meaning
4000	set user ID when the program is executed
2000	set group ID when the program is executed
1000	sticky bit
0400	owner can read the file
0200	owner can write to the file
0100	owner can execute the file
0040	group can read the file
0020	group can write to the file
0010	group can execute the file
0004	others can read the file
0002	others can write to the file
0001	others can execute the file

The following table lists some typical modes.

Mode	Meaning
0777	owner, group, and public can read, write, and execute file
0755	owner can read, write, and execute; group and public can read and execute file
0644	owner can read and write; group and public can read file
0711	owner can read, write, and execute; group and public can execute file

Options

-R   **recursive** When you include directories in the **file-list,** this option causes chmod to descend the directory hierarchy, setting the specified modes on all files encountered.

Notes

You can use the ls utility (with the –l option) to display file access privileges (page 515).

Chapter 4 contains a discussion of file access privileges.

When you are using symbolic arguments, the only time you can omit the **permission** from the command line is when the **operation** is **=**. This omission takes away all permissions.

Examples

The following examples show how to use the chmod utility to change permissions on a file named **temp.** The initial access mode of **temp** is shown by ls.

```
$ ls -l temp
-rw-rw-r-- 1 alex    pubs       57   Jul 12 16:47 temp
```

The command line below removes all access permissions for the group and all other users so that only the owner has access to the file. When you do not follow an equal sign with a permission, chmod removes all permissions for the specified user class. The ls utility verifies the change.

```
$ chmod go= temp
$ ls -l temp
-rw------- 1 alex    pubs       57   Jul 12 16:47 temp
```

The next command changes the access modes for all users (owner, group, and all others) to read and write. Now anyone can read from or write to the file. Again, ls verifies the change.

```
$ chmod a=rw temp
$ ls -l temp
-rw-rw-rw- 1 alex    pubs       57   Jul 12 16:47 temp
```

Using an absolute argument, the **a=rw** becomes **666.** The next command performs the same function as the previous **chmod** command.

```
$ chmod 666 temp
```

The following command removes the write access privilege for all other users. This change means that members of the pubs group can still read from and write to the file, but other users can only read from the file.

```
$ chmod o-w temp
$ ls -l temp
-rw-rw-r-- 1 alex    pubs        57  Jul 12 16:47 temp
```

The command that yields the same result using an absolute argument is shown below.

```
$ chmod 664 temp
```

The final command adds execute access privilege for all users. If **temp** is a shell script or other executable file, all users can now execute it.

```
$ chmod a+x temp
$ ls -l temp
-rwxrwxr-x 1 alex    pubs        57  Jul 12 16:47 temp
```

Again, the absolute command that yields the same result:

```
$ chmod 775 temp
```

chown

Change the owner of a file.

Format

chown owner file-list

Summary

The chown utility changes the owner of a file.

Arguments

The **owner** is the name or numeric user ID of the new owner. The **file-list** is a list of pathnames of the files whose ownership you want to change.

Options

–R **recursive** When you include directories in the **file-list,** this option causes chown to descend the directory hierarchy, setting the specified ownership on all files encountered.

Notes

Only the owner of a file or the Superuser can change the ownership of a file.

Examples

The following command changes the owner of the **chapter1** file in the **manuals** directory. The new owner is jenny.

```
$ chown jenny manuals/chapter1
```

The command below makes alex the owner of all files in the **/home/alex/literature** directory and in all of its subdirectories.

```
# chown -R alex /home/alex/literature
```

comm

Compare sorted files.

Format

comm [options] file1 file2

Summary

The comm utility displays a line-by-line comparison of two sorted files. (If the files have not been sorted, comm will not work properly.) The display is in three columns. The first column lists all lines found only in **file1,** the second column lists lines found only in **file2,** and the third lists those common to both files. Lines in the second column are preceded by one TAB and those in the third column are preceded by two TABS.

Input comes from the files you specify on the command line. (Refer to "Arguments" below for an exception.)

Arguments

The **file1** and **file2** are pathnames of the files that comm compares. You can use a hyphen in place of either **file1** or **file2** (but not both) to cause comm to use its standard input.

Options

You can use the options **–1, –2,** and **–3** individually or in combination.

–1 comm does not display column 1 (does not display lines it finds only in **file1**).

–2 comm does not display column 2 (does not display lines it finds only in **file2**).

–3 comm does not display column 3 (does not display lines it finds in both files).

Examples

The following examples use two files, **c** and **d,** that are in the working directory. The contents of these files are shown below. As with all input to comm, the files are in sorted order. Refer to the **sort** utility for information on sorting files.

File c   **File d**

bbbbb   aaaaa
ccccc   ddddd
ddddd   eeeee
eeeee   ggggg
fffff   hhhhh

The first command (below) calls comm without any options, so it displays three columns. The first column lists those lines found only in file **c**, the second column lists those found in **d**, and the third lists the lines found in both **c** and **d**.

```
$ comm c d
            aaaaa
bbbbb
ccccc
                    ddddd
                    eeeee
fffff
            ggggg
            hhhhh
```

The next example shows the use of options to prevent comm from displaying columns 1 and 2. The result is column 3, a list of the lines common to files **c** and **d**.

```
$ comm −12 c d
ddddd
eeeee
```

cp

Copy one or more files.

Format

    cp [options] source-file destination-file
    cp [options] source-file-list destination-directory

Summary

The cp utility copies one or more ordinary files, including text and executable program files. It has two modes of operation: The first copies one file to another, and the second copies one or more files to a directory.

Arguments

The **source-file** is the pathname of the ordinary file that cp is going to copy. The **destination-file** is the pathname that cp will assign to the resulting copy of the file.

    The **source-file-list** is one or more pathnames of ordinary files that cp is going to copy. When you use the **–r** option, the **source-file-list** can also contain directories. The **destination-directory** is the pathname of the directory that cp places the resulting copied files in.

    When you specify a **destination-directory**, cp gives each of the copied files the same simple filename as its **source-file**. If, for example, you copy the text file **/home/jenny/memo.416** to the **/home/jenny/archives** directory, the copy will also have the simple filename **memo.416**, but the new pathname that cp gives it will be **/home/jenny/archives/memo.416**.

Options

  –i   **interactive** This option causes cp to prompt the user whenever the copy will overwrite an existing file. After you enter **y**, cp will continue. If you enter anything other than **y**, cp will not make the copy.

  –p   **preserve** This option causes cp to set the modification times and file access permissions of each copy to match those of the **source-file**. Without the **–p** option, cp uses the current file creation mask to modify the access permissions (Refer to umask on page 621 for a description of the file creation mask).

−r   **recursive**   You can use this option when the destination is a directory. If any of the files in the **source-file-list** is a directory, the **−r** option will cause cp to copy the contents of that directory and any of its subdirectories into the **destination-directory**. The subdirectories themselves are copied as well as the files they contain.

Notes

If the **destination-file** exists before you execute cp, cp overwrites the file, destroying the contents but leaving the access privileges and owner associated with the file as they were.

If the **destination-file** does not exist, cp uses the access privileges for the **source-file**. The user becomes the owner of the **destination-file**, and the user's group becomes the group associated with the **destination-file**.

Examples

The first command makes a copy of the file **letter** in the working directory. The name of the copy is **letter.sav**.

```
$ cp letter letter.sav
```

The next command copies all the files with filenames ending in **.c** into the **archives** directory, a subdirectory of the working directory. Each copied file retains its simple filename but has a new absolute pathname.

```
$ cp *.c archives
```

The next example copies **memo** from the **/home/jenny** directory to the working directory.

```
$ cp /home/jenny/memo .
```

The final command copies two files named **memo** and **letter** into another directory. The copies have the same simple filenames as the source files (**memo** and **letter**) but have different absolute pathnames. The absolute pathnames of the copied files are **/home/jenny/memo** and **/home/jenny/letter**.

```
$ cp memo letter /home/jenny
```

cpio

Store and retrieve files in an archive format.

Format

cpio –o[options]
cpio –i[options] [patterns]
cpio –p[options] directory

Summary

The cpio utility has three functions. It copies one or more files into a single archive file, retrieves specified files from an archive file it previously created, and copies directories. If you specify a tape or other removable media file, you can use cpio to create backup copies of files, to transport files to other, compatible systems, and to create archives.

Arguments

The **patterns** specify the files you want to retrieve with the –i option. The patterns take the same form as ambiguous file references for the shell, with ?, *, and [ ] matching the slash that separates files in a pathname.

If you do not specify a pattern, cpio copies all the files.

The **directory** specifies the directory that is to receive the files that the –p option copies.

Options

The cpio utility has three major options and several other options that you can use with the major options. You can use only one major option at a time.

Major Options

–o   **out**   This option causes cpio to read its standard input to obtain a list of pathnames of ordinary files. It combines these files, together with header information, into a single archive file that it copies to its standard output.

–i   **in**   This option causes cpio to read its standard input, which cpio must have previously produced with a –o option. It selectively extracts files from its input, based on the patterns you give as arguments.

    Files that you stored using relative pathnames will appear in the working directory or a subdirectory. Files stored with absolute pathnames will appear as specified by their absolute pathnames.

-p   **pass**   This option causes cpio to read its standard input to obtain a list of pathnames of ordinary files. It copies these files to the directory you give as an argument. This option is useful for copying directories and their contents.

Other Options

-a   **access time**   cpio resets the access times of input files after copying them.

-B   **block**   This option blocks data written to or read from a raw magnetic tape device at 5120 bytes/record (do not use with the **-p** option). Without **-B**, the data blocks are 512 bytes each.

-c   **compatible**   This option causes cpio to write header information in ASCII so that other (incompatible) machines can read the file. Without **-c**, only machines of the same type can read the archive properly.

-d   **directory**   cpio creates directories when needed as it is copying files (do not use with the **-o** option).

-f   This option copies all files not specified by the patterns (**-i** option only).

-k   This option causes cpio to try to skip over any corrupted data it encounters, extracting as much good data from the archive as possible. This option is valuable if the archive has been damaged by a disk or tape error (for use only with the **-i** option).

-l   **link**   When possible, this option links files instead of copying them (for use only with the **-p** option).

-m   **modification time**   This option keeps the original modification times of ordinary files. If you use find with the **-depth** option to send files to cpio, cpio also preserves the original modification times of directories.

-r   **rename**   This option allows you to rename files as cpio copies them. Before it copies each file, cpio prompts you with the name of the file—you respond with the new name. If you just press RETURN, cpio will not copy the file.

-t   **table of contents**   This option displays a list of filenames without copying them. When you use this option with the **-v** option, cpio displays file access permissions, ownership, and access time along with the name of each file.

-u   **unconditional**   This option copies older files over newer ones with the same name—without this option, cpio will not overwrite these newer files.

-v   **verbose**   This option displays a list of files that cpio is copying.

Examples

The following example copies all the files in the working directory to the tape on **/dev/rmt/0m**. It does not copy the contents of subdirectories because ls does not supply the pathnames of files in subdirectories. When it finishes, cpio displays the number of 512 byte blocks it copied.

```
$ ls | cpio -o > /dev/rmt/0m
7 blocks
```

The next example copies all the files in the working directory *and* all subdirectories. The **–depth** argument causes find to list all entries in a directory before listing the directory itself. The **–m** option causes cpio to preserve the original modification times of files. Because the **–depth** argument to find is used, cpio can also preserve the original modification times of directories. The **–B** option blocks the tape at 5120 bytes/record.

```
$ find . -depth -print | cpio -oB > /dev/rmt/0m
30 blocks
```

Next, cpio copies all of Alex's home directory and all subdirectories to the floppy disk on device **/dev/ifdsk00** (do not use the **–B** option on any media other than tape).

```
$ find /home/alex -print | cpio -o > /dev/ifdsk00
293 blocks
```

The next command reads back the files that the previous command wrote to the disk. Because cpio will not overwrite newer files with older ones, the following command will not overwrite any files that have been updated since the previous **cpio** command. You can use the **–u** option to overwrite newer files.

```
$ cpio -i < /dev/ifdsk00
```

The final example displays the table of contents for an archive file.

```
$ cpio -itv < /dev/ifdsk00
```

crontab

Specify jobs to run at regularly scheduled times.

Format

    crontab [filename]
    crontab [options] [user-name]

Summary

The crontab utility allows you to submit a list of jobs that the system will run for you at the times you specify. The commands are stored in files that are referred to as **crontab** files. The system utility called cron reads the **crontab** files and runs the commands. If a command line in your **crontab** file does not redirect its output, the standard output and error output will be mailed to you.

Arguments

In the first format, **filename** is the name of a file that contains the **crontab** commands. If you do not specify a **filename** for crontab to read, it will read commands from the standard input as you type them; end with CONTROL-D.

The **user-name** in the second format can be specified by the Superuser to change the **crontab** file for a particular user.

Options

-e   **edit**   This option runs a text editor on your **crontab** file, enabling you to add, change, or delete entries.

-l   **list**   This option displays the contents of your **crontab** file.

-r   **remove**   This option removes your **crontab** file.

Notes

Each **crontab** entry begins with five fields that specify when the command should run (minute, hour, day of the month, month of the year, and day of the week). If an asterisk appears in a field instead of a number, cron interprets that as a wild card for all possible values.

The system administrator determines which users should be allowed to use the crontab utility. By default, users cannot use the crontab utility to schedule jobs in advance. The **/etc/cron.d** directory includes a file called **cron.allow** that lists the login names of users who are permitted to use crontab. A file called **cron.deny** in this directory specifies users who are not permitted to use crontab. To allow everyone to use crontab, create an empty **cron.deny** file (and do not create a **cron.allow** file).

Examples

In the example below, the root user sets up a command to be run by cron every Saturday (day 6) morning at 2:05 A.M. that will remove all **core** files on the system that have not been accessed in the previous five days.

```
# crontab
5 2 * * 6        /usr/bin/find / -name core -atime +5 -exec rm {} \;
CONTROL-D
```

To add an entry to your **crontab** file, run the crontab utility with the -e (edit) option. The crontab utility supplied with earlier versions of System V may not support the -e option. In that case, you need to make a copy of your existing **crontab** file, edit it, and then resubmit it as in the example below. The -l (list) option displays a copy of your **crontab** file.

```
# crontab -l > newcron
# cat newcron
5 2 * * 6        /usr/bin/find / -name core -atime +5 -exec rm {} \;
# vi newcron
.
.
.
# crontab newcron
# crontab -l
5 2 * * 6        /usr/bin/find / -name core -atime +5 -exec rm {} \;
17 4 * * *       /usr/sbin/pwck
```

In this example, the root user added an entry to run the pwck utility (which checks the password file for errors) every morning at 4:17 A.M.. Since the output of pwck was not redirected, it will be mailed to the root user automatically.

date

Display or set the time and date.

Format

date [option] [+format]
date [option] newdate

Summary

The date utility displays the time and date. The Superuser can use it to change the time and date.

Arguments

When the Superuser specifies a **newdate**, the system changes the system clock to reflect the new date. The **newdate** argument has the following format:

nnddhhmm[cc[yy]

The **nn** is the number of the month (01-12), **dd** is the day of the month (01-31), **hh** is the hour based on a 24-hour clock (00-23), and **mm** is the minutes (00-59). The last four digits are optional; if you do not specify a year, date assumes the year has not changed. The optional **cc** specifies the first two digits of the year (the value of the century minus one), and **yy** specifies the last two digits of the year.

You can use the **+format** argument to specify the format of the output of date. Following the **+** sign, you can specify a format string consisting of **field descriptors** and text. The **field descriptors** are preceded by percent signs, and each one is replaced by its value in the output. Following is a list of the **field descriptors**.

Field Descriptor	Meaning
a	abbreviated weekday—Sun to Sat
d	day of the month—01 to 31
D	date in mm/dd/yy format
h	abbreviated month—Jan to Dec
H	hour—00 to 23
j	day of the year—001 to 366
m	month of the year—01 to 12
M	minutes—00 to 59

Field Descriptor	Meaning
r	time in A.M./P.M. notation
y	last two digits of the year—00 to 99
S	seconds—00 to 59
T	time in HH:MM:SS format
w	day of the week—0 to 7 (Sunday = 0)
n	NEWLINE character
t	TAB character
Y	year in 4-digit format

Any character in a format string that is not either a percent sign (%) or a field descriptor is assumed to be ordinary text and is copied to the output. You can use ordinary text to add punctuation to the date and to add labels (e.g., you can put the word **DATE:** in front of the date). You should surround the format argument in single quotes if it contains spaces or other characters that have a special meaning to the shell.

Options

–u   **universal**   This option displays or sets the date in Greenwich Mean Time (universal time). The system operates in GMT, and date converts it to and from the local standard time and daylight saving time.

Examples

The first example below shows how to set the date for 3:36 P.M. on July 12.

```
# date 07121536
Thu Jul 12 15:36 PDT 1990
```

The next example shows the **format** argument. It causes date to display the date in a commonly used format.

```
$ date ´ +%h %d, 19%y ´
Jul 12, 1990
```

delta

Record changes in an SCCS-encoded file.

Format

> delta [options] file-list

Summary

The delta utility is part of SCCS (the Source Code Control System; see page 355 for more information). The delta utility records in SCCS the changes made to a file previously retrieved by using the get utility with the –e option.

Arguments

The **file-list** is a list of SCCS-encoded files, which all start with **s.**. If the list includes directory names, all files that begin with **s.** in the named directory are added to **file-list**. Any files in **file-list** that do not begin with **s.** or that are unreadable are ignored.

Options

-p   **print**   This option causes delta to run the diff command to compare the versions of the file before and after the delta is performed. The results of the diff are displayed on the standard output.

-m[**mrlist**]   **modification requests**   If the **v** flag has been set with the admin utility, this option can be used to input a list of modification requests. They will be used as the reason for the delta. You cannot use this option if the **v** flag has not been set. If the **–m** option is not used and the **v** flag has been set, the prompt **MRs?** will appear on the user's terminal if it is the standard input. Any input that precedes an unescaped RETURN will be used as modification request numbers. You can enter a null list of modification requests either by using the **–m** option with no **mrlist** or by pressing RETURN after the **MRs?** prompt.

-y[**comments**]   This option allows you to enter text that will be used as the reason for making the delta. If you do not use the **–y** option and the standard input is a terminal, delta will prompt you for comments. Whether you use the **–y** option or **delta** presents the **comments?** prompt, you can have a null comment. To create a null comment, do not enter anything after the **–y** option, or press RETURN after the **comments?** prompt.

–rversion-number   **release** This option is used only when the same person has two or more outstanding **gets** on the same SCCS file. The **–r** option identifies the **get** that the current **delta** corresponds to. You can specify the version number that was used for the **get** or the version number that will be used for the **delta**.

Examples

These examples illustrate the use of the **delta** utility after **get** has been used with the **–e** option to retrieve the highest trunk delta.

In the first example, the **v** flag is set on **s.memo**. In the subsequent **delta**, the user is prompted for a list of modification requests. The user inputs a list of numbers followed by RETURN.

```
$ admin -fv s.memo
$ delta s.memo
MRs? 19539 74A 13704
comments?
.
.
```

In the next example, the **–m** option is used to enter the same list of modification requests.

```
$ delta -m "19539 74A 13704" s.memo
comments? changes based on reviews
.
.
```

Below, the user enters comments directly on the command line following the **–y** option.

```
$ delta -y "changes based on reviews" s.memo
MRs?
.
.
```

The final example illustrates what happens when you have multiple **gets** outstanding on different versions of a file.

```
$ delta s.memo
.
.
ERROR [s.memo]: missing -r argument (de1)
```

You must use the **-r** option to identify the version associated with the delta.

```
$ delta -r2.2 s.memo
.
.
```

df

Display the amount of available disk space.

Format

df [options] [file-system-list]

Summary

The **df** (disk free) utility reports how much free space is left on any mounted device or directory in terms of blocks (there is usually 1 kilobyte, or 1024 bytes, per block).

Arguments

When you call **df** without an argument, it reports on the free space on each of the currently mounted devices.

The **file-system-list** is an optional list of one or more pathnames that specify the file systems you want a report on. The **df** utility permits you to refer to a mounted file system by its device pathname *or* by the pathname of the directory it is mounted on.

Options

−t   **total**   This option causes **df** to display the number of blocks that are in use as well as the number of free blocks.

Example

Below, **df** displays information about the two mounted file systems on a machine.

```
$ df
/       (/dev/dsk/c1d0s0):   2742 blocks    818 files
/usr    (/dev/dsk/c1d0s2):   7138 blocks   3077 files
```

diff

Display the differences between two files.

Format

> **diff [options] file1 file2**
> **diff [options] file1 directory**
> **diff [options] directory file2**
> **diff [options] directory1 directory2**

Summary

The diff utility displays the differences between two files on a line-by-line basis. It displays the differences as instructions that you can use to edit one of the files to make it the same as the other.

When the arguments to diff are two filenames, diff compares the specified files. When the arguments are a file and a directory, diff compares the file with a file in the specified directory that has the same filename. When the arguments to diff are two directories, diff compares all the pairs of files in the two directories that have the same filenames.

Arguments

The **file1** and **file2** are pathnames of the files that diff works on. When the **directory** argument is used in place of **file2**, diff looks for a file in **directory** with the same name as **file1**. Similarly, when the directory argument is used in place of **file1**, diff looks for a file in **directory** with the same name as **file2**. You can use a hyphen in place of **file1** or **file2** to cause diff to use its standard input. When two directory arguments are specified, diff compares all files in **directory1** with files in **directory2** that have the same names.

Options

-b   **blanks** This option causes diff to ignore blanks (SPACES and TABS) at the ends of lines and to consider other strings of blanks equal.

-c   **context** This option causes diff to display the sections of the two files that differ, including the three lines before and the three lines following each line that differs. Each line that is missing from **file2** is preceded by –; each line that is added to **file2** is preceded by +; and lines that have different versions in the two files are marked with !. When lines that differ are within three lines of each other, they are grouped together in the output.

-C[n]   **context**   This option is similar to the **–c** option; the value of **n** determines the number of lines of context that diff displays.

-e   **ed**   This option creates a script for the ed editor that will edit **file1** to make it the same as **file2** and displays it on the standard output. You must add **w** (write) and **q** (quit) instructions to the end of the script if you are going to redirect input to ed from the script.

When you use **–e**, diff displays the changes in reverse order—changes to the end of the file are listed before changes to the top. This prevents early changes from affecting later changes when the script is used as input to ed. If ed made changes to the top of the file first, the changes might affect later changes to the end of the file. For example, if a line near the top were deleted, subsequent line numbers in the script would be wrong.

Description

When you use diff without any options, it produces a series of lines containing Add (**a**), Delete (**d**), and Change (**c**) instructions. Each of these lines is followed by the lines from the file that you need to add, delete, or change. A *less than* symbol (<) precedes lines from **file1**. A *greater than* symbol (>) precedes lines from **file2**. The diff output is in the format shown below. A pair of line numbers separated by a comma represents a range of lines; diff uses a single line number to represent a single line.

Instruction	Meaning (to change file1 to file2)
`line1 a line2,line3` `> lines from file2`	append lines from **file2** after line1 in **file1**
`line1,line2 d line3` `< lines from file1`	delete line1 through line2 from **file1**

`line1,line2 c line3,line4`
`< lines from file1`
`---`
`> lines from file2`
	change line1 through line2 in **file1** to lines from **file2**

The diff utility assumes that you are going to convert **file1** to **file2**. The line numbers to the left of each of the **a**, **c**, or **d** instructions always pertain to **file1**; numbers to the right of the instructions apply to **file2**. To convert **file1** to **file2**, ignore the line numbers to the right of the instructions. (To convert **file2** to **file1**, run diff again, reversing the order of the arguments.)

Examples

The first example shows how diff displays the differences between two short, similar files.

```
$ cat m
aaaaa
bbbbb
ccccc
$ cat n
aaaaa
ccccc
$ diff m n
2d1
< bbbbb
```

The difference between files **m** and **n** is that the second line from file **m** (bbbbb) is missing from file **n**. The first line that diff displays (2d1) indicates that you need to delete the second line from file 1 (**m**) to make it the same as file 2 (**n**). Ignore the numbers following the letters on the instruction lines. (They would apply if you were converting **file2** to **file1**.) The next line diff displays starts with a *less than* symbol (<), indicating that this line of text is from **file1**. In this example you do not need this information—all you need to know is the line number so that you can delete the line.

The next example uses the same **m** file and a new file, **p**, to demonstrate diff issuing an **a** (append) instruction.

```
$ cat p
aaaaa
bbbbb
rrrrr
ccccc
$ diff m p
2a3
> rrrrr
```

In the preceding example, diff issued the instruction 2a3 to indicate that you must append a line to file **m**, after line 2, to make it the same as file **p**. The second line that diff displayed indicates that the line is from file **p** (the line begins with >, indicating **file2**). In this example you need the information on this line; the appended line must contain the text rrrrr.

The next example uses **m** again, this time with file **r**, to show how diff indicates a line that needs to be changed.

```
$ cat r
aaaaa
qqqqq
ccccc
$ diff m r
2c2
< bbbbb
---
> qqqqq
```

The difference between the two files is in line 2: File **m** contains bbbbb, and file **r** contains qqqqq. Above, diff displays 2c2 to indicate that you need to change line 2. After indicating that a change is needed, diff shows that you must change line 2 in file **m** (bbbbb) to line 2 in file **r** (qqqqq) to make the files the same. The three hyphens indicate the end of the text in file **m** that needs to be changed and the start of the text in file **r** that is to replace it.

Next, a *group* of lines in file **m** needs to be changed to make it the same as file **t**.

```
$ cat t
aaaaa
lllll
hhhhh
nnnnn
$ diff m t
2,3c2,4
< bbbbb
< ccccc
---
> lllll
> hhhhh
> nnnnn
```

Above, diff indicates that you need to change lines 2 through 3 (2,3) in file **m** from bbbbb and ccccc to lllll, hhhhh, and nnnnn.

The next set of examples demonstrates how to use diff to keep track of versions of a file that is repeatedly updated, without maintaining a library of each version in its entirety. This is similar in concept to what SCCS does. With the −e option, diff creates a script for the ed editor that can recreate the second file from the first. If you keep a copy of the original file and the ed script that diff creates each time you update the file, you can recreate any version of the file. Because these scripts are usually shorter than the files they are relating, the scripts can help conserve disk space.

In these examples, **menu1** is the original file. When it needs to be updated, it is copied to **menu2** and the changes are made to the copy of the file. The resulting files are shown below.

diff

```
$ cat menu1
BREAKFAST
        scrambled eggs
        toast
        orange juice

LUNCH
        hamburger on roll
        small salad
        milk shake

DINNER
        sirloin steak
        peas
        potato
        vanilla ice cream


$ cat menu2
BREAKFAST
        poached eggs
        toast
        orange juice

LUNCH
        hamburger on roll
        French fries
        milk shake

DINNER
        chef's salad
        fruit
        cheese
```

Below, diff with the −e option produces an ed script that details the changes between the two versions of the file. The first command line redirects the output from diff to **2changes**; cat displays the resulting file. The ed Change Mode is invoked by the **c** command. In this mode, the lines that you specify in the command are replaced by the text that you enter following the command. A period instructs ed to terminate the Change Mode and return to the Command Mode.

```
$ diff −e menu1 menu2 > 2changes
$ cat 2changes
12,15c
        chef's salad
        fruit
        cheese
.
8c
        French fries
.
2c
        poached eggs
.
```

The only commands missing from the ed script that diff creates are Write (**w**) and Quit (**q**). In the following example, cat appends these to **2changes**. (You can also use an editor to add the commands to the file.)

```
$ cat >> 2changes
w
q
CONTROL-D
```

The next example repeats the process when the file is updated for the second time. The file is copied (to **menu3**), the changes are made to the copy, and the original (**menu2** in this case) and the edited copy are processed by diff. The cat utility displays the ed script after the necessary commands have been added to it.

```
$ cat menu3
BREAKFAST
        poached eggs
        toast
        grapefruit juice

LUNCH
        tuna sandwich
        French fries

DINNER
        pot luck


$ diff -e menu2 menu3 > 3changes
$ cat >> 3changes
w
q
CONTROL-D

$ cat 3changes
12,14c
        pot luck
.
9d
7c
        tuna sandwich
.
4c
        grapefruit juice
.
w
q
```

The **menu2** and **menu3** files are no longer needed; diff can recreate them from **menu1**, **2changes**, and **3changes**. The process of recreating a file follows. First, copy the original file to a file that will become the updated file. (If you make changes to the original file, you may not be able to go back and recreate one of the intermediate files.)

```
$ cp menu1 recreate
```

Next, use **ed** to edit the copy of the original file (**recreate**) with input from **2changes**. The **ed** editor displays the number of characters it reads and writes. After it has been edited with **2changes**, the file is the same as the original **menu2**.

```
$ ed recreate < 2changes
214
189
$ cat recreate
BREAKFAST
        poached eggs
        toast
        orange juice

LUNCH
        hamburger on roll
        French fries
        milk shake

DINNER
        chef's salad
        fruit
        cheese
```

If you just want **menu2**, you can stop at this point. By editing the recreated **menu2** (now **recreate**) with input from **3changes**, the example below recreates **menu3**.

```
$ ed recreate < 3changes
189
139
$ cat recreate
BREAKFAST
        poached eggs
        toast
        grapefruit juice

LUNCH
        tuna sandwich
        French fries

DINNER
        pot luck
```

du

Display information on disk usage.

Format

du [options] [directory-list] [file-list]

Summary

The du (disk usage) utility reports how much space is used by a directory (along with all its subdirectories and files) or a file. It displays the number of blocks (usually 1024 bytes each) that are occupied by the directory or file.

Arguments

Without an argument, du displays information only about the working directory and its subdirectories.

The **directory-list** specifies the directories you want information about. If you use the **–a** or **–s** option, you can also include the names of ordinary files in **file-list**.

Options

Without any options, du displays information only for each directory you specify, or about the working directory and its subdirectories if you do not specify any arguments.

–a **all** This option displays information for each file in **file-list** and for each file in the directories in **directory-list**.

–r **report** This option causes du to report on directories it cannot open and files it cannot read. Without this option, du does not report this information.

–s **summary** This option displays summary information for each of the directories and files you specify.

Examples

Below, du displays size information about subdirectories in the working directory. The last line contains the grand total for the working directory and its subdirectories.

```
$ du
127         ./brown
5           ./memo
.
.
.
1493        .
```

Next, du displays only the grand total for the working directory.

```
$ du -s
1493        .
```

The last example displays the total size of all the files in /usr that the user can read (du skips files that are not readable).

```
$ du -s /usr
11472  /usr
```

echo

Display a message.

Format

echo message

Summary

The echo command copies its arguments, followed by a NEWLINE, to its standard output.

Arguments

The **message** is one or more arguments. These arguments can include quoted strings, ambiguous file references, and shell variables. A SPACE separates each argument from the others. The shell recognizes unquoted special characters in the arguments (e.g., the shell expands an asterisk into a list of filenames in the working directory).

You can terminate the **message** with a \c to prevent echo from displaying the NEWLINE that normally ends a **message**. To prevent the shell from interpreting the backslash as a special character, you must quote it. The "Examples" section shows the three ways you can quote the \c.

Options

There are no options.

Notes

You can use echo to send messages to the terminal from a shell script (refer to Chapter 8). For other uses of echo, refer to the discussion of echo at the end of Chapter 5.

Beginning with System V Release 2, echo was built into the Bourne Shell. The Korn Shell provides both echo and the print command, which is similar to echo but has more features.

Examples

The second through fourth examples following show three ways to quote a \c and prevent echo from appending a NEWLINE to the end of the message.

echo

```
$ echo 'Today is Friday.'
Today is Friday.

$ echo 'There is no newline after this.\c'
There is no newline after this.$

$ echo "There is no newline after this.\c"
There is no newline after this.$

$ echo There is no newline after this.\\c
There is no newline after this.$

$ echo 'This is a
> multiline
> echo command.'
This is a
multiline
echo command.
```

expr

Evaluate an expression.

Format

expr expression

Summary

The expr utility evaluates an expression and displays the result. It evaluates character strings that represent either numeric or nonnumeric values. Operators are used with the strings to form expressions.

Arguments

The **expression** is composed of strings with operators in between. Each string and operator constitute a distinct argument that you must separate from other arguments with a SPACE. Operators that have special meanings to the shell (e.g., the multiplication operator, *) must be quoted.

The following list of expr operators is in order of decreasing precedence. You can change the order of evaluation by using parentheses.

: **comparison**
This operator compares two strings, starting with the first character in each string and ending with the last character in the second string. The second string is a regular expression. If there is a match, it displays the number of characters in the second string. If there is no match, it displays a zero.

* **multiplication**
/ **division**
% **remainder**
These operators work only on strings that contain the numerals 0 through 9 and optionally a leading minus sign. They convert the strings to integer numbers, perform the specified arithmetic operation on numbers, and convert the result back to a string before displaying it.

+ **addition**
– **subtraction**
These operators function in the same manner as those described above.

expr

<   **less than**
<=   **less than or equal to**
=   **equal to**
!=   **not equal to**
>=   **greater than or equal to**
>   **greater than**

These relational operators work on both numeric and nonnumeric arguments. If one or both of the arguments is nonnumeric, the comparison is nonnumeric, using the machine collating sequence (usually ASCII). If both arguments are numeric, the comparison is numeric. The expr utility displays a 1 (one) if the comparison is true and a 0 (zero) if it is false.

&   **AND**

The AND operator evaluates both of its arguments. If neither is 0 or a null string, it displays the value of the first argument. Otherwise, it displays a 0. You must quote this operator.

| **OR**

This operator evaluates the first argument. If it is neither 0 nor a null string, it displays the value of the first argument. Otherwise, it displays the value of the second argument. You must quote this operator.

Options

There are no options.

Notes

The expr utility returns an exit status of 0 (zero) if the expression is neither a null string nor the number 0, a status of 1 if the expression is null or 0, and a status of 2 if the expression is invalid.

The expr utility is useful in Bourne Shell scripts. Because the C and Korn Shells have the equivalent of expr built in, C and Korn Shell scripts do not normally use expr.

Although expr and this discussion distinguish between numeric and nonnumeric arguments, all arguments to expr are actually nonnumeric (character strings). When applicable, expr attempts to convert an argument to a number (e.g., when using the + operator). If a string contains characters other than 0 through 9 with an optional leading minus sign, expr cannot convert it. Specifically, if a string contains a plus sign or a decimal point, expr considers it to be nonnumeric.

Examples

The following examples show command lines that call expr to evaluate constants.

You can also use expr to evaluate variables in a shell script. In the fourth example, expr displays an error message because of the illegal decimal point in 5.3.

```
$ expr 17 + 40
57
$ expr 10 - 24
-14
$ expr -17 + 20
3
$ expr 5.3 \* 4
expr: non-numeric argument
```

The multiplication (*), division (/), and remainder (%) operators provide additional arithmetic power, as the examples below show. You must quote the multiplication operator (precede it with a backslash) so that the shell does not treat it as a special character (an ambiguous file reference). Note that you cannot put quotation marks around the entire expression because each string and operator must be a separate argument.

```
$ expr 5 \* 4
20
$ expr 21 / 7
3
$ expr 23 % 7
2
```

The next two examples show how you can use parentheses to change the order of evaluation. You must quote each parenthesis and surround the backslash/parenthesis combination with SPACES.

```
$ expr 2 \* 3 + 4
10
$ expr 2 \* \( 3 + 4 \)
14
```

You can use relational operators to determine the relationship between numeric or nonnumeric arguments. The command below uses expr to compare two strings to see if they are equal. The expr utility displays a 0 when the relationship is false, and a 1 when it is true.

```
$ expr fred = mark
0
$ expr mark = mark
1
```

Relational operators, which you must also quote, can establish order between numeric or nonnumeric arguments. Again, if a relationship is true, expr displays a 1.

expr

```
$ expr fred \> mark
0
$ expr fred \< mark
1
$ expr 5 \< 7
1
```

The next command compares 5 with m. When one of the arguments expr is comparing with a relational operator is nonnumeric, expr considers the other to be nonnumeric. In this case, because m is nonnumeric, expr treats 5 as a non-numeric argument. The comparison is between the ASCII (on most machines) values of m and 5. The ASCII value of m is 109, and 5 is 53, so expr evaluates the relationship as true.

```
$ expr 5 \< m
1
```

The next example shows the matching operator determining that the four characters in the second string match four characters in the first string. The expr utility displays a 4.

```
$ expr abcdefghijkl : abcd
4
```

The & operator displays a 0 if one or both of its arguments are 0 or a null string. Otherwise, it displays the first argument.

```
$ expr ' ' \& book
0
$ expr magazine \& book
magazine
$ expr 5 \& 0
0
$ expr 5 \& 6
5
```

The | operator displays the first argument if it is not 0 or a null string. Other-wise, it displays the second argument.

```
$ expr ' ' \| book
book
$ expr magazine \| book
magazine
$ expr 5 \| 0
5
$ expr 0 \| 5
5
$ expr 5 \| 6
5
```

file

Display file classification.

Format

file [option] [file-list]

Summary

The file utility classifies files according to their contents.

Arguments

The **file-list** contains the pathnames of one or more files that file classifies. You can specify any kind of file, including ordinary, directory, and special files, in the **file-list**.

Options

–f **file** file This option causes file to take the names of files to be examined from **file** rather than from the command line.

Notes

The file utility works by examining the first part of a file, looking for keywords and special numbers (referred to as *magic numbers*) that the linker and other programs use. It also examines the access permissions associated with the file. The results of file are not always correct.

Examples

Some examples of file identification follow.

```
$ file memo proc new
memo:              English text
proc:              commands text
new:               empty
```

A few of the classifications that file displays follow.

```
English text       directory
ascii text         empty
c program text     executable
commands text      sccs
data
```

find

Find files.

Format

find directory-list expression

Summary

The find utility selects files that are located in specified directories and are described by an expression. It does not generate any output without an explicit instruction to do so.

Arguments

The **directory-list** contains the pathnames of one or more directories that find is to search. When find searches a directory, it searches all subdirectories, to all levels.

The **expression** contains one or more criteria, as described in ''Criteria,'' below. The find utility tests each of the files in each of the directories in the **directory-list** to see if it meets the criteria described by the **expression**.

A SPACE separating two criteria is a logical AND operator: The file must meet *both* criteria to be selected. A **-o** separating the criteria is a logical OR operator: The file must meet one or the other (or both) of the criteria to be selected.

You can negate any criterion by preceding it with an exclamation point. The find utility evaluates criteria from left to right unless you group them using parentheses.

Within the **expression** you must quote special characters so that the shell does not interpret them but passes them to the find utility. Special characters that you may frequently use with find are parentheses, square brackets, question marks, and asterisks.

Each element within the **expression** is a separate argument. You must separate arguments from each other with SPACES. There must be a SPACE on both sides of each parenthesis, exclamation point, criterion, or other element. When you use a backslash to quote a special character, the SPACES go on each side of the pair of characters (e.g., " \[").

Options

There are no options.

Criteria

Following is a list of criteria that you can use within the **expression**. As used in this list, ±n is a decimal integer that can be expressed as **+n** (meaning more than n), **−n** (meaning less than **n**), or **n** (meaning exactly **n**).

-name **filename**   The file being evaluated meets this criterion if **filename** matches its name. You can use ambiguous file references but must quote them.

-type **filetype**   The file being evaluated meets this criterion if its file type is the specified **filetype**. You can select a file type from the following list.

filetype	Description
b	block special file
c	character special file
d	directory file
f	ordinary file
p	fifo (named pipe)
l	symbolic link

-links ±n   The file being evaluated meets this criterion if it has the number of links specified by ±n.

-user **name**   The file being evaluated meets this criterion if it belongs to the user with the login name, **name**. You can use a numeric user ID in place of **name**.

-group **name**   The file being evaluated meets this criterion if it belongs to the group with the group name, **name**. You can use a numeric group ID in place of **name**.

-inum **n**   The file being evaluated meets this criterion if its inode number is **n**.

-size ±n[c]   The file being evaluated meets this criterion if it is the size specified by ±n, measured in blocks. Follow **n** with the letter **c** to measure files in characters.

-atime ±n   The file being evaluated meets this criterion if it was last accessed the number of days ago specified by ±n. When you use this option, find changes the access times of directories it searches.

-mtime ±n   The file being evaluated meets this criterion if it was last modified the number of days ago specified by ±n.

-newer **filename**   The file being evaluated meets this criterion if it was modified more recently than **filename**.

-print   The file being evaluated always meets this action criterion. When evaluation of the **expression** reaches this criterion, find displays the pathname of the file it is evaluating. If this is the only criterion in the **expression**, find displays the names of all the files in the **directory-list**. If this criterion appears with other criteria, find displays the name only if the preceding criteria are met. Refer to "Discussion" and "Notes," following.

-exec **command \;**   The file being evaluated meets this action criterion if the **command** returns a zero (true value) as an exit status. You must terminate the **command** with a quoted semicolon. A pair of braces ({}) within the **command** represents the filename of the file being evaluated.

You can use the **-exec** action criterion at the end of a group of other criteria to execute the **command** if the preceding criteria are met. Refer to the following "Discussion."

-ok **command \;**   This action criterion is the same as **-exec**, except that it displays each of the **command**s to be executed, enclosed in angle brackets. The find utility executes the **command** only if it receives a **y** from its standard input.

-depth   The file being evaluated always meets this action criterion. It causes find to take action on entries in a directory before it acts on the directory itself. When you use find to send files to the cpio utility, the **-depth** criterion enables cpio to preserve modification times of directories (assuming you use the **-m** option to cpio).

-mount   The file being evaluated always meets this action criterion. It causes find not to search directories in file systems other than the one in which the current **directory** (from the **directory-list** argument) resides.

-nouser   The file being evaluated meets this criterion if it belongs to a user who is not in the **/etc/passwd** file (that is, the user ID associated with the file does not correspond to a known user of the system).

-nogroup   The file being evaluated meets this criterion if it belongs to a group that is not listed in the **/etc/group** file.

-local   The file being evaluated meets this criterion if it resides on a local file system (not a file system mounted remotely over the network).

-follow   When this criterion is specified and find encounters a symbolic link pointing to a directory file, it will follow the link.

Discussion

Assume that **x** and **y** are criteria. The following command line never tests to see if the file meets criterion **y** if it does not meet criterion **x**. Because the criteria are separated by a SPACE (the logical AND operator), once find determines that criterion **x** is not met, the file cannot meet the criteria, so find does not continue testing. You can read the expression as "(test to see) if the file meets criterion **x** *and* (SPACE means *and*) criterion **y**."

find dir x y

The next command line tests the file against criterion **y** if criterion **x** is not met. The file can still meet the criteria, so find continues the evaluation. It is read as "(test to see) if criterion **x** *or* criterion **y** is met." If the file meets criterion **x**, find does not evaluate criterion **y**, as there is no need.

find dir x –o y

Certain "criteria" do not select files but cause find to take action. The action is triggered when find evaluates one of these *action criteria*. Therefore, the position of an action criterion on the command line, and not the result of its evaluation, determines whether find takes the action.

The **–print** action criterion causes find to display the pathname of the file it is testing. The following command line displays the names of all files in the **dir** directory (and all subdirectories) that meet criterion **x**.

find dir x –print

The following command line displays the names of *all* the files in the **dir** directory (whether they meet criterion **x** or not).

find dir –print x

Notes

You must explicitly instruct find to display filenames if you want it to do so. Unless you include the **–print** criterion or its equivalent on the command line, find does its work silently. Refer to the first example below.

You can use the **–a** operator between criteria for clarity. This operator is a logical AND operator, just as the SPACE is.

Examples

The following command line finds all the files in the working directory, and all subdirectories, that have filenames that begin with a. The command uses a period to designate the working directory and quotes the ambiguous file reference. The command does not instruct find to do anything with these files—not even display their names. This is not a useful example, but it demonstrates a common problem when using find.

```
$ find . –name ´ a* ´
```

The next command line finds *and displays the filenames of* all the files in the working directory, and all subdirectories, that have filenames that begin with a.

```
$ find . –name ´ a* ´  –print
.
.
```

The following command line sends a list of selected filenames to the cpio utility, which writes them to tape. The first part of the command line ends with a pipe symbol, so the shell expects another command to follow and prints a secondary prompt (>) before accepting the rest of the command line. You can read this find command as, "find, in the root directory and all subdirectories (/), all files that are ordinary files (**–type f**) that have been modified within the past day (**–mtime –1**), with the exception of files whose names are suffixed with .o (**! –name** ´ *.o´)." (An object file carries a .o suffix and usually does not need to be preserved, as it can be recreated from the corresponding program source code.)

```
$ find / –type f –mtime –1 ! –name ´ *.o ´  –print |
> cpio –oB > /dev/rmt/0m
```

The command line below finds, displays the filenames of, and deletes all the files in the working directory, and all subdirectories, that are named **core** and

unk. The parentheses, and the semicolon following **–exec,** are quoted so that the shell does not treat them as special characters. SPACES separate the quoted parentheses from other elements on the command line. You can read this find command as, "find, in the working directory and all subdirectories (.), all files that are named **core** (**–name core**) *or* (**–o**) are named **junk** (**–name junk**) [if a file meets these criteria, continue with] *and* (SPACE) print (**–print**) the name of the file *and* (SPACE) delete the file (**–exec rm {}**)."

```
$ find . \( -name core -o -name junk \) -print -exec rm {} \;
.
.
```

The shell script below uses find with the grep command to identify the names of files that contain a particular string. This script enables you to look for a file when you remember its contents but cannot remember what its filename is. The **finder** script below locates files in the current directory and all subdirectories that contain the string specified on the command line.

```
$ cat finder
find . -exec grep -l "$1" {} \;
$ finder "Executive Meeting"
./january/memo.0102
./april/memo.0415
```

When **finder** is called with the string "Executive Meeting", it locates two files containing that string, **./january/memo.0102** and **./april/memo.0415**. The period (.) in the pathnames represents the current directory (that is, **january** and **april** are subdirectories of the current directory).

The next command finds all files in two user directories that are larger than 100 blocks (**–size +100**) and have only been accessed more than five days ago— that is, have not been accessed within the past five days (**–atime +5**). This **find** command then asks whether you want to delete the file (**–ok rm {}**). You must respond to each of these queries with a **y** (for *yes*) or **n** (for *no*). The rm command works only if you have execute and write access permission to the directory.

```
$ find /home/alex /home/barbara -size +100 -atime +5 -ok rm {} \;
< rm ... /home/alex/notes >?    y
< rm ... /home/alex/letter >?    n
.
.
```

In this example, **/home/alex/memos** is a symbolic link to the directory named **/home/jenny/memos**. When the **–follow** option is used with find, the symbolic link is followed and the contents of that directory are found.

```
$ ls -l /home/alex
lrwxrwxrwx  1 alex    pubs      17 Aug 19 17:07 memos -> /home/jenny/memos
-rw-r--r--  1 alex    pubs    5119 Aug 19 17:08 report
$ find /home/alex -print
/home/alex
/home/alex/memos
/home/alex/report
/home/alex/.profile
$ find /home/alex -follow -print
/home/alex
/home/alex/memos
/home/alex/memos/memo.817
/home/alex/memos/memo.710
/home/alex/report
/home/alex/.profile
```

fsck

Check and repair a file system.

Format

/etc/fsck [options] [file-systems-list]

Summary

The fsck utility verifies the integrity of a file system and reports on any problems it finds. For each problem it finds, fsck asks you if you want it to attempt to fix the problem or ignore it. If you repair the problem, you may lose some data; however, that is often the most reasonable alternative.

The fsck utility should be run only by the system administrator, who must be logged in as the Superuser. When fsck is run on a file system, the file system should not be mounted. The root file system, which cannot be unmounted, must be quiescent. The best way to ensure quiescence is to bring the system down to single-user mode.

Arguments

The **file-systems-list** is an optional list of file systems you want fsck to check. If you do not specify a list, it checks the file systems listed in the **/etc/vfstab** file (System V Release 4) or the **/etc/checklist** (older versions of System V).

Except for the root, you should always check the raw device representing the file system. This device is usually the one whose simple filename begins with **r**.

Options

Without any options, fsck checks the file systems in the **file-systems-list** (or in **/etc/vfstab**). When a file system is consistent, you will see a report such as the following:

```
/dev/dsk/c1d0s0
File system: root Volume: 10.a

** Phase 1 - Check Blocks and Sizes
** Phase 2 - Check Pathnames
** Phase 3 - Check Connectivity
** Phase 4 - Check Reference Count
** Phase 5 - Check Free List
** Phase 6 - Salvage Free List
xxx files yyy blocks zzz free
```

If fsck finds problems with a file system, it reports on each of them, giving you the choice of having it either repair or ignore the problem.

-y   **yes**   fsck assumes a *yes* response to all questions and makes any necessary repairs to the file system. If the file system is corrupt, you can lose files by using **-y** to respond *yes* automatically to all of fsck's questions.

-n   **no**   fsck assumes a *no* response to all questions and only reports on problems. It does not make any repairs.

-F **fstype**   System V Release 4 includes support for different types of file systems, each of which may have unique characteristics that fsck should check. The file system type for a particular filesystem is specified in the fourth field of its entry in the **/etc/vfstab** file, and fsck will use that information unless you specify the **fstype** with this option. Typical values for **fstype** are **s5** (the traditional System V filesystem) and **ufs** (a version of the Berkeley ''Fast File System'').

The following options are valid on the **s5** file system type.

-s   This option causes fsck to reconstruct a new free list and rewrite the superblock unconditionally. The *free list* is a list of pointers that describe disk blocks that are available to store data. The *superblock* contains housekeeping information, such as the number of inodes in the file system and free list information. It is an index into the rest of the file system.

-S   This option is the same as **-s** except that it will not reconstruct the free list if there are any problems with the file system.

-q   **quiet**   This option checks and repairs the file system without as much reporting. If necessary, it will automatically fix counts in the super-block and salvage the free list.

-D   **directory**   This option checks for bad blocks in directories.

-f   **fast**   This option runs only Phases 1, 5, and, if necessary, 6 of fsck.

The following options are valid on the **ufs** file system type. Note that a **ufs**-specific option must be preceded by the special **-o** option to be recognized properly by fsck.

-o -b=**block#**   This option causes fsck to use the block specified by **block#** as the superblock of the file system.

-o -p   **preen**   This option causes **fsck** to supply a **y** response to questions about minor inconsistencies and an **n** response to all other questions. This option is often used when **fsck** is run by the run command scripts during the boot process.

Notes

If you are repairing a file system, you must run **fsck** on the unmounted file system. If you are repairing the root file system, run **fsck** while the system is in single-user mode and no other user processes are running. After repairing root, you must bring the system down immediately, without running **sync**, and reboot it.

Although it is technically feasible to repair files that are damaged and that **fsck** says you should remove, it is usually not practical. The best insurance against significant loss of data is frequent backups. Refer to Chapter 11 for more information on backing up the system.

If you do not have write permission to the file system **fsck** is checking, **fsck** will report problems but not give you an opportunity to fix them.

When **fsck** encounters a file that has lost its link to its filename, **fsck** asks you whether you want to reconnect it. If you choose to fix the problem, the file is put in a directory called **lost+found**, and it is given its inode number as a name. In order for **fsck** to restore files in this way, there should be a **lost+found** directory in the root directory of each file system. For example, if your file systems are **/**, **/usr**, and **/tmp**, you should have the following **lost+found** directories: **/lost+found**, **/usr/lost+found**, and **/tmp/lost+found**. Each of the **lost+found** directories must be slotted. To put *slots* in a directory, add many files to the directory (e.g., 50) and then remove them. This procedure creates unused entries in the directory that **fsck** can use to store the inode numbers for files that have lost their links.

Messages

This section explains **fsck**'s standard messages. It does not explain every message that **fsck** produces. In general, **fsck** suggests the most logical way of dealing with a problem in the file structure. Unless you have information that suggests another response, respond to its prompts with *yes*. Use the system backup tapes or disks to restore any data that is lost as a result of this process.

Phase 1 – Check Blocks and Sizes.   Phase 1 checks inode information.

Phase 1B – Rescan for More Dups.   When **fsck** finds a duplicate block in Phase 1, it repeats its search. A *duplicate block* is a block that is claimed to be part of two different files.

Phase 2 – Check Pathnames.   In Phase 2, fsck checks for directories that pointed to bad inodes it found in Phase 1.

Phase 3 – Check Connectivity.   Phase 3 looks for unreferenced directories and a nonexistent or full **lost+found** directory.

Phase 4 – Check Reference Counts.   Phase 4 checks for unreferenced files, a nonexistent or full **lost+found** directory, bad link counts, bad blocks, duplicate blocks, and incorrect inode counts.

Phase 5 – Check Free List.   Phase 5 checks the free block list for bad blocks, bad counts, duplicate blocks, and unused blocks.

Phase 6 – Salvage Free List.   If Phase 5 found problems, Phase 6 fixes them.

Cleanup.   Once fsck has repaired the file system, it informs you about the status of the file system and tells you what you must do.

*****File System Was Modified*****.   The fsck utility displays this message if it has repaired the file system.

On a standard **s5** file system, fsck will display messages such as the following when it has finished checking the file system.

xxx files yyy blocks zzz free.   This message lets you know how many files (**xxx**) are using how many blocks (**yyy**), and how many blocks are free (**zzz**) for your use.

*****Boot UNIX (No Sync!)*****.   The fsck utility displays this message when it has modified a mounted file system (including the root). If you see this message, you must reboot the system immediately, without using sync. Refer to page 375 for more information.

After checking a **ufs** file system, fsck will display messages such as the following.

vvv files, www used, xxx free (yyy frags, zzz blocks).   A file system block on a **ufs** file system can hold up to 8192 bytes of information. Each **ufs** file system block is broken into *fragments,* or parts, so that when a file needs only a portion of a block, the remainder of the block can be made available for allocation to other files. This message lets you know how many files (**vvv**) are using how many fragment-sized blocks (**www**), and how many fragment-sized blocks are free in the file system. The numbers in parentheses break the free count into **yyy** free fragments and **zzz** free full-sized blocks.

fsck

get

Create an unencoded version of an SCCS file.

Format

get [options] file-list

Summary

The get utility is part of SCCS (the Source Code Control System; see page 355 for more information). The get utility retrieves files from their SCCS-encoded versions. The retrieved files are given the same names as their encoded counterparts, except the leading s. is removed. The options determine characteristics of the retrieved files.

Arguments

The file-list is a list of SCCS-encoded files, which all start with s.. If the list includes directory names, all files that begin with s. in the named directory are added to file-list. Any files in file-list that do not begin with s. or that are unreadable are ignored. The get utility will not create an unencoded version of a file if a file with the same name exists in the current directory.

Options

Without any options, get retrieves the most recent version of the SCCS file. The file will not be editable. To create an editable version of an SCCS file, you must use the −e option.

−e   **edit** Use this option to indicate to SCCS that you intend to edit the retrieved file and then to use delta to create a new SCCS-encoded version. The version of the encoded file that get will retrieve depends on the other options you use. If you do not use options to specify characteristics of the retrieved file, the most recent version of the encoded file will be retrieved. Once you have used get with the −e option on a particular version, you cannot use it again on the same version until after you have used delta to complete the first cycle of editing, unless you have set the j flag (see admin on page 407). You can always use get with the −e option on another version of the file; however, you must give the command from a different directory. If you try to use get with the −e option twice in the same directory, the second get will fail because a writable file with the unencoded filename already exists in that directory.

-rversion-number   **release**   This option identifies a particular version of the SCCS-encoded file to be retrieved. If the **-e** option is used with **-r**, **-r** also determines the version number of the associated delta. The version number specified with the **-r** option may include up to four components: release, level, branch, and sequence number. The version retrieved depends on the version number components you specify with the **-r** option and on what versions already exist. Similarly, if you use **-e**, the version number of the created delta depends both on the number you specify and on what versions already exist. See "Version Numbers," below, for further information.

    -b   **branch**   This option can be used with the **-e** option to create a branch delta for a trunk delta that has no successors on the trunk. To use the **-b** option, you must have set the **b** flag using the admin utility. If the **b** flag has not been set or if the retrieved delta has a successor delta, the **-b** option will be ignored.

  -cdate-time   **cutoff**   This option causes deltas made after **date-time** to be excluded from the retrieved file. The **date-time** argument has the format:

    YY[MM[DD[HH[MM[SS]]]]]

The brackets indicate that all components of **date-time** may be omitted except **YY**, starting from the right. The maximum possible values will be substituted for any omitted values (e.g., 59 is used if **SS** is omitted). The two-digit components may be separated by any number of nonnumeric characters. For example, a colon (**:**) may be used between the components (e.g., 90:02:26:03:36).

    -k   **keyword**   You can use this option to recreate an editable file if you accidentally remove or ruin a file that you previously retrieved with get. The keywords in the new copy will be preserved, so they will not be lost when you finish editing the file and run delta.

Version Numbers

Following is a summary of how the get utility identifies what version to retrieve when you use the **-r** option and what version number to assign to the new delta. For each type of version number that you can specify with the **-r** option, and each set of conditions, the list describes the version that will be retrieved and the delta that will be created.

The summary describes the cases when the **−b** option is not in use. When you use the **−b** option, a new branch is always created.

The following descriptions refer to *trunk deltas* and *branch deltas*. Trunk deltas have two-component version numbers (release.level), whereas branch version numbers have four components (release.level.branch.sequence).

get

Component Specified:	Release

Condition:	Release specified is the highest existing release.
Version retrieved:	Highest existing level in the specified release.
Delta created:	Next level for the specified release.

Condition:	Release number is higher than the highest existing release.
Version retrieved:	Highest existing level in the highest existing release.
Delta created:	First level of the specified release number.

Condition:	Release number is less than the highest existing release, and release number is nonexistent.
Version retrieved:	Highest existing level in the highest release that is less than the specified release.
Delta created:	A new branch for the retrieved delta.

Condition:	Release number is less than the highest existing release, and release number exists.
Version retrieved:	Highest existing trunk delta in the specified release.
Delta created:	A new branch for the retrieved delta.

Component Specified:	Release.Level

Condition:	No trunk successor exists.
Version retrieved:	Specified trunk delta.
Delta created:	Next trunk delta (that is, level + 1)

Condition:	Trunk successor exists.
Version retrieved:	Specified trunk delta (i.e., release.level).
Delta created:	New branch for the retrieved trunk delta.

Component Specified:	Release.Level.Branch

Version retrieved:	Highest sequence number on the specified branch
Delta created:	Next sequence number on the specified branch.

Component Specified:	Release.Level.Branch.Sequence
Condition:	Branch corresponds to highest existing branch for the specified release.level.
Version retrieved:	Specified release.level.branch.sequence.
Delta created:	Next sequence number.
Condition:	Branch number is less than the highest existing branch.
Version retrieved:	Specified release.level.branch.sequence.
Delta created:	New branch for the specified release.level.

Examples

The first command retrieves the highest numbered trunk delta. This file will not be editable.

```
$ get s.thesis
3.1
.
.
```

The next command includes in the retrieved file only deltas created on or before 2 P.M. (1400 hours) on March 5, 1990.

```
$ get -c90:03:05:14:00:00 s.thesis
.
.
```

The following command retrieves the highest numbered trunk delta for editing. The new delta will have the same release number and the next level number.

```
$ get -e s.thesis
3.1
new delta 3.2
.
.
```

Below, the highest existing trunk delta will be retrieved (because the specified release, 4, is higher than any existing release). The new delta will be Version 4.1.

```
$ get -e -r4 s.thesis
3.1
new delta 4.1
.
.
```

grep

Search for a pattern in files.

Format

grep [options] pattern [file-list]

Summary

The grep utility searches one or more files, line by line, for a **pattern**. The **pattern** can be a simple string or another form of a regular expression (see Appendix B for more information on regular expressions). The grep utility takes various actions, specified by options, each time it finds a line that contains a match for the **pattern**.

The grep utility takes its input from files you specify on the command line or from its standard input.

Arguments

The **pattern** is a regular expression as defined in Appendix B. You must quote regular expressions that contain special characters, SPACES, or TABS. An easy way to quote these characters is to enclose the entire expression within single quotation marks.

The **file-list** contains pathnames of ordinary text files that grep searches.

Options

If you do not specify any options, grep sends lines that contain a match for **pattern** to its standard output. If you specify more than one file on the command line, grep precedes each line that it displays with the name of the file that it came from and a colon.

   -c   **count** This option causes grep to display only the number of lines in each file that contain a match.

   -i   **ignore case** This option causes lowercase letters in the pattern to match uppercase letters in the file, and vice versa. Use this option when searching for a word that may be at the beginning of a sentence (that is, may or may not start with an uppercase letter).

   -l   **list** The grep utility displays only the name of each file that contains one or more matches. It displays each filename only once, even if the file contains more than one match.

-n   **number**   The **grep** utility precedes each line by its line number in the file. The file does not need to contain line numbers—this number represents the number of lines in the file up to and including the displayed line.

-v   **reverse sense of test**   This option causes lines *not* containing a match to satisfy the search. When you use this option by itself, **grep** displays all lines that do not contain a match for the **pattern**.

Notes

The **grep** utility returns an exit status of 0 if it finds a match, 1 if it does not find a match, and 2 if the file is not accessible or there is a syntax error.

Two utilities perform functions similar to that of **grep**. The **egrep** utility can be faster than **grep** but may also use more memory. It allows you to use *full regular expressions,* which include a wider set of special characters than do ordinary regular expressions (refer to page 661). The **fgrep** utility is fast and compact, but it can process only simple strings, not regular expressions.

Examples

The following examples assume that the working directory contains three files: **testa, testb,** and **testc.** The contents of each file are shown below.

File testa	File testb	File testc
aaabb	aaaaa	AAAAA
bbbcc	bbbbb	BBBBB
ff–ff	ccccc	CCCCC
cccdd	ddddd	DDDDD
dddaa		

The **grep** utility can search for a pattern that is a simple string of characters. The following command line searches **testa** for, and displays each line containing, the string **bb.**

```
$ grep bb testa
aaabb
bbbcc
```

The **–v** option reverses the sense of the test. The example below displays all the lines *without* **bb.**

```
$ grep –v bb testa
ff–ff
cccdd
dddaa
```

The **–n** option displays the line number of each displayed line.

```
$ grep -n bb testa
1:aaabb
2:bbbcc
```

The **grep** utility can search through more than one file. Below, **grep** searches through each file in the working directory. (The ambiguous file reference * matches all filenames.) The name of the file containing the string precedes each line of output.

```
$ grep bb *
testa:aaabb
testa:bbbcc
testb:bbbbb
```

The search that **grep** performs is case-sensitive. Because the previous examples specified lowercase **bb**, **grep** did not find the uppercase string, BBBBB, in **testc**. The **–i** option causes both uppercase *and* lowercase letters to match either case of letter in the pattern.

```
$ grep -i bb *
testa:aaabb
testa:bbbcc
testb:bbbbb
testc:BBBBB
$ grep -i BB *
testa:aaabb
testa:bbbcc
testb:bbbbb
testc:BBBBB
```

The **–c** option displays the name of each file, followed by the number of lines in the file that contain a match.

```
$ grep -c bb *
testa:2
testb:1
testc:0
```

The following command line displays lines from the file **text2** that contain a string of characters starting with **st**, followed by zero or more characters (.* represents zero or more characters in a regular expression—see Appendix B), and ending in **ing**.

```
$ grep 'st.*ing' text2
.
.
```

The ^ regular expression can be used alone to match every line in a file. Together with the **–n** option, it can be used to display the lines in a file, preceded by their line numbers.

```
$ grep -n '^' testa
1:aaabb
2:bbbcc
3:ff-ff
4:cccdd
5:dddaa
```

The final command line calls the vi editor with a list of files in the working directory that contain the string **Sampson**. The backquotes (see page 241) cause the shell to execute the grep command in place and supply vi with a list of filenames that you want to edit. (The single quotation marks are not necessary in this example, but they are required if the string you are searching for contains special characters or SPACES. It is generally a good habit to quote the pattern so that the shell does not interpret any special characters it may contain.)

```
$ vi `grep -l 'Sampson' *`
.
.
```

head

Display the beginning (head) of a file.

Format

head [–number] [file-list]

Summary

The **head** utility displays the beginning of a file. It takes its input from one or more files you specify on the command line or from its standard input.

Arguments

Without a **number**, **head** displays the first ten lines of a file. The **file-list** contains pathnames of the files that **head** displays. If you specify more than one file, **head** will print the filename of each file before it displays the first few lines. If you do not specify any files, **head** takes its input from its standard input.

Options

There are no options.

Examples

The examples are based on the following **lines** file:

```
$ cat lines
line one
line two
line three
line four
line five
line six
line seven
line eight
line nine
line ten
line eleven
```

First, **head** displays the first ten lines of the **lines** file (no arguments).

```
$ head lines
line one
line two
line three
line four
line five
line six
line seven
line eight
line nine
line ten
```

The next example displays the first three lines (**–3**) of the file.

```
$ head –3 lines
line one
line two
line three
```

kill

Terminate a process.

Format

kill [option] PID-list

Summary

The kill utility terminates one or more processes by sending them signals. By default, kill sends software termination signals (signal number 15), although an option allows you to send a different signal. The process must belong to the user executing kill, unless the user is the Superuser. The kill utility displays a message when it terminates a process.

Arguments

The **PID-list** contains process identification (PID) numbers of processes kill is to terminate.

Options

You can specify a signal number (0-15), preceded by a hyphen, as an option before the **PID-list** to cause kill to send the signal you specify to the process.

Notes

The shell displays the PID number of a background process when you initiate the process. You can also use the ps utility to determine PID numbers.

If the software termination signal does not terminate the process, try using a kill signal (signal number 9). A process can choose to ignore any signal except signal number 9.

The kill command is built into both the C, Job, and Korn Shells. When you are using one of those shells, you can use job identifiers in place of the **PID-list**. Job identifiers consist of a percent sign (%) followed by either a job number or a string that uniquely identifies the job. The built-in versions of kill also allow you to specify signals by name rather than number. You can use the **kill −l** command to list the signal names.

To terminate all processes that the current login process initiated and have the operating system log you out, give the command **kill −9 0**.

Caution. If you run this command while you are logged in as Superuser, you will bring the system down.

If you do not specify a signal number when you use kill with process number 0, kill terminates all processes that you are running in the background.

Examples

The first example shows a command line executing the file **compute** as a background process and the kill utility terminating it.

```
$ compute &
17542
$ kill 17542
```

The next example shows the ps utility determining the PID number of the background process running a program named **xprog** and the kill utility terminating **xprog** with a signal number 9.

```
$ ps
   PID   TTY      TIME COMMAND
 22921   tty11    0:10 sh
 23714   tty11    0:00 xprog
 23715   tty11    0:03 ps
$ kill -9 23714
23714 Killed
```

You can run the following command to terminate all your jobs and log yourself out:

```
$ kill -9 0

login:
```

You should not run this command if you are logged in as Superuser.

ln

Make a link to a file.

Format

ln [options] existing-file new-link
ln [options] existing-file-list directory

Summary

By default, ln makes *hard links*. A hard link to a file is indistinguishable from the original filename. You can refer to the file either by its original filename or by the name given to it by the ln command, and in either case the effects will be the same. All hard links to a file must be in the same file system as the original file.

When you are using ln, you can use the first format shown above to create a link between an existing file and a new filename. You can use the second format to link existing files into a different directory. The new links will have the same simple filenames as the original files but different full pathnames.

You can use ln to create *symbolic links* as well as hard links. Unlike a hard link, a symbolic link can exist in a different file system from the linked-to file. Also, a symbolic link can connect to a directory. Refer to Chapter 4 for more information about symbolic links.

Arguments

The **existing-file** is the pathname of the file you want to make a link to. The **new-link** is the pathname of the new link. When you are making a symbolic link, the **existing-file** may be a directory; otherwise, it cannot be a directory.

Using the second format, the **existing-file-list** contains the pathnames of the ordinary files you want to make links to. The ln utility establishes the new links so that they appear in the **directory**. The simple filenames of the entries in the **directory** are the same as the simple filenames of the files in the **existing-file-list**.

Options

–f   **force**   This option causes ln to complete a link regardless of file access permissions. Refer to "Notes" below.

–s   **symbolic link**   This option causes ln to create a symbolic link. When you use this option, the **existing-file** and **new-link** may be directories.

Notes

A hard link is an entry in a directory that points to a file. The operating system makes the first link to a file when you create the file using an editor, a program, or redirected output. You can make additional links using ln and remove links with rm. The ls utility, with the –l option, shows you how many links a file has. Refer to the end of Chapter 4 for a discussion of links.

If the **new-link** is the name of an existing file and you do not have write access permission to it, ln displays your access permission and waits for a response (unless you used the –f option).

You can use symbolic links to link across file systems and to create links to directories. When you use the ls –l command to list information about a symbolic link, ls displays –> and the name of the linked-to file after the name of the link.

Examples

The first command makes a link between **memo2** in the **/home/alex/literature** directory and the working directory. The file appears as **memo2** (the simple filename of the existing file) in the working directory.

```
$  ln  /home/alex/literature/memo2  .
```

The next command makes a link to the same file. This time, the file appears as **new_memo** in the working directory.

```
$  ln  /home/alex/literature/memo2  new_memo
```

The command below makes a link so that the file appears in another user's directory. You must have write and execute access permission to the other user's directory for this command to work. If you own the file, you can use chmod to give the other user write access permission to the file.

```
$  ln  /home/alex/literature/memo2  /home/jenny/new_memo
```

The next command makes a symbolic link to an existing file, **memo3**, in the directory **/home/alex/literature**. The symbolic link is in a different file system, **/tmp**. The ls –l command shows the linked-to filename.

```
$  pwd
/home/alex/literature
$  ln  -s  memo3  /tmp/memo
$  ls  -l  /tmp/memo
lrwxrwxrwx 1 alex   5  Jul 13 11:44 /tmp/memo  -> memo3
```

lp

Print files.

Format

> lp [options] [file-list]
> lpstat
> cancel job-number

Summary

The lp utility places one or more files in the line printer queue. It provides orderly access to the printer for several users or processes. You can use the cancel utility to remove files from the queue, and the lpstat utility to check the status of files in the queue. Refer to "Notes" below.

The lp utility takes its input from files you specify on the command line or from its standard input. It sends a unique identification number to its standard output and the specified files to the printer. You can use the identification number with the cancel utility to cancel the specified job.

Arguments

The **file-list** is a list of one or more pathnames of ordinary text files that lp prints.

The **job-number** argument to cancel is the identifier that lp assigns to the job. It is displayed when you submit a job to lp and when you run lpstat.

Options

Check with the system administrator about installation-dependent options.

-c   **copy file**   The lp utility copies a file before placing it in the printer queue so that it cannot be changed. If you do not use this option, the printed copy will reflect any changes you make before it is printed.

-d **printer**   **destination**   The lp utility sends your file to the destination **printer**. If you do not use this option to specify a printer, lp will use the printer named by the **LPDEST** variable in your shell environment or the system's default printer (if **LPDEST** is not set).

-m   **mail**   The lp utility uses the mail utility to report when the file has finished printing.

-nx **number of copies** This option causes lp to print **x** copies. Replace **x** with a number.

-s **suppress** This option causes lp to suppress the **request**id message you would otherwise get when you submit a print job.

-w **write** The lp utility uses the write utility to report when the file has finished printing. If you are not logged in, lp uses mail.

Notes

The lpstat utility displays the status of jobs in the printer queue. Without any options or arguments, lpstat displays the status of all printing jobs you started with lp.

The cancel utility aborts a job that you started with lp. You must call it with an argument, the job identification number of the job you want to cancel.

The next section includes examples showing typical uses of lpstat and cancel. Refer to the manual that comes with your UNIX system for a complete list of the options and arguments to lpstat and cancel.

Examples

The following command line prints the file named **memo2**. The message following the command is from lp. It tells you the job number (printer_1-496) in case you want to use cancel to cancel the job.

```
$ lp memo2
request id is printer_1-496 (1 file)
```

Below, a pipe sends the output of the ls utility to the printer.

```
$ ls | lp
request id is printer_1-497 (standard input)
```

Next, nroff (with the **mm** macro package) formats **report7** and sends it to the printer using a pipe and lp. The job runs in the background.

```
$ nroff -mm report7 | lp &
12345
12346
request id is printer_1-498 (standard input)
```

The next examples use two different methods to paginate and send the **memo** file to the printer. Refer to the pr utility for more information.

```
$ cat memo | pr | lp
request id is printer_1-499 (standard input)
$ pr memo | lp
request id is printer_1-500 (standard input)
```

The example below shows that job printer_1-500 is waiting to be printed. It was submitted by Alex at 11:59 A.M. on July 13.

```
$ lpstat
printer_1-500        alex           5721    Jul 13 11:59
```

The following command cancels printing job number 500 on printer_1.

```
$ cancel printer_1-500
```

ls

Display information about one or more files.

Format

ls [options] [file-list]

Summary

The ls utility displays information about one or more files. It lists the information alphabetically by filename unless you use an option to change the order.

Arguments

When you do not use an argument, ls displays the names of the files in the working directory. If you do not use the **–a** option, ls does not list files whose filenames begin with **..**

The **file-list** contains one or more pathnames of files. You can use the pathname of any ordinary, directory, or device file. These pathnames can include ambiguous file references.

When you specify a directory, ls displays the contents of the directory. The ls utility displays the name of the directory only when it is needed to avoid ambiguity (that is, when ls is displaying the contents of more than one directory, it displays the names of the directories to indicate which files you can find in which directory). If you specify an ordinary file, ls displays information about just that file.

Options

The options determine the type of information ls displays, how it displays it, and the order it displays the information in.

When you do not use an option, ls displays a short listing, containing only the names of files.

-a   **all entries**   Without a **file-list** (no arguments on the command line), this option displays information about all the files in the working directory, including invisible files (those with filenames that begin with a period). When you do not use this option, ls does not list information about invisible files, unless you list the name of an invisible file in **file-list**.

In a similar manner, when you use this option with a **file-list** that includes an appropriate ambiguous file reference, ls displays information about invisible files. (The * ambiguous file reference does not match a leading period in a filename—see page 114.)

-c   **creation time**   This option causes ls to sort files by the time the inode for
the file was last changed.

-C   **columns**   This option lists files in vertically sorted columns. When output
is going to the terminal, –C is the default on System V Release 4.

-d   **directory**   This option displays the names of directories without displaying
their contents. When you give this option without an argument, ls displays
information about the working directory. This option displays ordinary files
normally.

-F   This option displays a slash after each directory, an asterisk after each executable file, and an *at* sign (@) after symbolic links.

-g   **group only**   This option generates the same display as the –l option, except
it does not include the owner column.

-i   **inode**   This option displays the inode number of each file. With the –l
option, this option displays the inode number in column 1 and shifts each of
the other items over one column to the right.

-l   **long**   This option displays several columns of information about each file.
The –l option displays the seven columns shown in Figure II-1. The first
column, which contains 11 characters, is divided as follows.

> The first character describes the type of file:
>
> -   indicates an ordinary file
> b   indicates a block device file
> c   indicates a character device file
> d   indicates a directory
> p   indicates a fifo (named pipe)
> l   indicates a symbolic link

Refer to Chapters 4 and 11 for more information on types of files.
The next nine characters represent all the access permissions
associated with the file. These nine characters are divided into three
sets of three characters each.
The first three characters represent the owner's access permissions. If the owner has read access permission to the file, an **r**
appears in the first character position. If the owner is not permitted to
read the file, a hyphen appears in this position. The next two positions represent the owner's write and execute access permissions. A
w appears in the second position if the owner is permitted to write to
the file, and an **x** appears in the third position if the owner is permit-

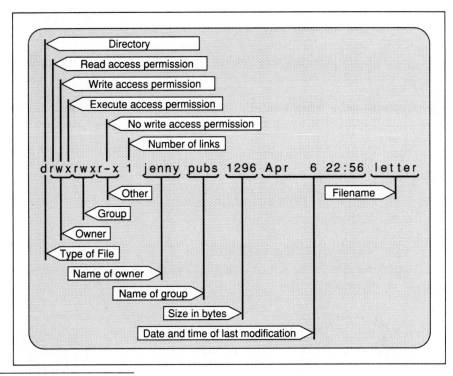

FIGURE Part II-1   ls –l

ted to execute the file. An **s** in the third position indicates that the file has set user ID permission and execute permission. An **S** indicates set user ID without execute permission. A hyphen indicates the owner does not have the access permission associated with the character position.

In a similar manner, the second and third sets of three characters represent the access permissions of the user's group and other users. An **s** in the third position of the second set of characters indicates that the file has set group ID permission with execute permission, and an **S** indicates set group ID without execute permission.

The last character is **t** if the sticky bit is set with execute permission, and **T** if it is set without execute permission.

Refer to chmod for information on changing access permissions.

The second column indicates the number of hard links to the file. Refer to Chapter 4 for more information on links.

The third and fourth columns display the name of the owner of the file and the name of the group the file belongs to.

The fifth column indicates the size of the file in bytes or, if information about a device file is being displayed, the major and minor device numbers.

In the case of a directory, this number is the size of the actual directory file, not the size of the files that are entries within the directory. (Use du to display the size of all the files in a directory.)

The last three columns display the date and time the file was last modified and the filename.

-L   **symbolic link**   When you use this option, ls lists information about the file referenced by each symbolic link rather than information about the link itself.

-o   **owner only**   This option generates the same display as the –l option, except it does not include the group column.

-p   **indicate directories**   This option puts a slash after the names of directories.

-q   **question marks**   This option displays nonprinting characters in a filename as question marks.

-r   **reverse**   This option displays the list of filenames in reverse alphabetical order or, when you use it with the –t or –u options, in reverse time order (least recently modified or accessed first).

-R   **recursive**   This option recursively lists subdirectories.

-s   **size**   This option displays the size of each file in (usually 1024-byte) blocks. The size precedes the filename. With the –l option, this option displays the size in column 1 and shifts each of the other items over one column to the right.

-t   **time modified**   This option displays the list of filenames in order by the time of last modification. It displays first the files that were modified most recently.

-u   **time accessed**   When you use this option with the –t option, it sorts by the last time each file was accessed. When you use it with –l, it displays access times rather than modification times.

-x   This option lists files in horizontally sorted columns.

-1   **one column**   This option causes ls to list one filename per line. This is the default when output is not sent to the terminal.

Notes

Refer to page 112 for examples of using ls with ambiguous file references.

Examples

All the following examples assume that the user does not change to another working directory.

The first command line shows the ls utility with only the −x option and no arguments. You see an alphabetical list of the names of the files in the working directory. The −x option puts the list in columns sorted horizontally.

```
$ ls −x
bin            c            calendar
execute        letters      shell
```

The −F option appends a slash (/) to files that are directories, an asterisk to files that are executable, and an *at* sign (@) after symbolic links.

```
$ ls −Fx
bin/           c/           calendar
execute*       letters/     shell@
```

Next, the −l (long) option displays a long list. The files are still in alphabetical order.

```
$ ls −l
total 8
drwxrwxr−x   2 jenny  pubs     80  May 20 09:17  bin
drwxrwxr−x   2 jenny  pubs    144  Mar 26 11:59  c
−rw−rw−r−−   1 jenny  pubs    104  May 28 11:44  calendar
−rwxrw−r−−   1 jenny  pubs     85  May  6 08:27  execute
drwxrwxr−x   2 jenny  pubs     32  Oct  6 22:56  letters
drwxrwxr−x  16 jenny  pubs   1296  Jun  6 17:33  shell
```

The −a (all) option lists all files, including invisible ones. Note that the list is printed in columns sorted vertically (default).

```
$ ls −a
.              .profile     c            execute      shell
..             bin          calendar     letters
```

Combining the −a and −l options displays a long listing of all the files, including invisible files, in the working directory. This list is still in alphabetical order.

```
$ ls -al
total 12
drwxrwxr-x   6 jenny  pubs     480 Jun  6 17:42 .
drwxrwx---  26 root   system   816 Jun  6 14:45 ..
-rw-rw-r--   1 jenny  pubs     161 Jun  6 17:15 .profile
drwxrwxr-x   2 jenny  pubs      80 May 20 09:17 bin
drwxrwxr-x   2 jenny  pubs     144 Mar 26 11:59 c
-rw-rw-r--   1 jenny  pubs     104 May 28 11:44 calendar
-rwxrw-r--   1 jenny  pubs      85 May  6 08:27 execute
drwxrwxr-x   2 jenny  pubs      32 Oct  6 22:56 letters
drwxrwxr-x  16 jenny  pubs    1296 Jun  6 17:33 shell
```

If you add the **–r** (reverse order) option to the command line, ls produces a list in reverse alphabetical order.

```
$ ls -ral
total 12
drwxrwxr-x  16 jenny  pubs    1296 Jun  6 17:33 shell
drwxrwxr-x   2 jenny  pubs      32 Oct  6 22:56 letters
-rwxrw-r--   1 jenny  pubs      85 May  6 08:27 execute
-rw-rw-r--   1 jenny  pubs     104 May 28 11:44 calendar
drwxrwxr-x   2 jenny  pubs     144 Mar 26 11:59 c
drwxrwxr-x   2 jenny  pubs      80 May 20 09:17 bin
-rw-rw-r--   1 jenny  pubs     161 Jun  6 17:15 .profile
drwxrwx---  26 root   system   816 Jun  6 14:45 ..
drwxrwxr-x   6 jenny  pubs     480 Jun  6 17:42 .
```

Use the **–t** and **–l** options to list files so that the most recently modified file appears at the top of the list.

```
$ ls -tl
total 8
drwxrwxr-x  16 jenny  pubs    1296 Jun  6 17:33 shell
-rw-rw-r--   1 jenny  pubs     104 May 28 11:44 calendar
drwxrwxr-x   2 jenny  pubs      80 May 20 09:17 bin
-rwxrw-r--   1 jenny  pubs      85 May  6 08:27 execute
drwxrwxr-x   2 jenny  pubs     144 Mar 26 11:59 c
drwxrwxr-x   2 jenny  pubs      32 Oct  6 22:56 letters
```

Together the **–r** and **–t** options cause ls to list files with the file you modified least recently at the top of the list.

```
$ ls -trl
total 8
drwxrwxr-x   2 jenny  pubs      32 Oct  6 22:56 letters
drwxrwxr-x   2 jenny  pubs     144 Mar 26 11:59 c
-rwxrw-r--   1 jenny  pubs      85 May  6 08:27 execute
drwxrwxr-x   2 jenny  pubs      80 May 20 09:17 bin
-rw-rw-r--   1 jenny  pubs     104 May 28 11:44 calendar
drwxrwxr-x  16 jenny  pubs    1296 Jun  6 17:33 shell
```

The next example shows ls with a directory filename as an argument. The ls
utility lists the contents of the directory in alphabetical order.

```
$  ls  bin
c           e              lsdir
```

The –l option gives a long listing of the contents of the directory.

```
$  ls  -l  bin
total  3
-rwxrw-r-x  1  jenny  pubs        48    Apr   6  21:38  c
-rwxrw-r--  1  jenny  pubs       156    Apr   6  21:40  e
-rwxrw-r--  1  jenny `pubs       136    May   7  16:48  lsdir
```

To display information about the directory file itself, use the **–d** (directory)
option. This option causes ls to list information only about the directory.

```
$  ls  -dl  bin
drwxrwxr-x  2  jenny  pubs        80  May  20  09:17  bin
```

mailx

Send or receive electronic mail.

Format

mailx [–s subject] user-list
mailx [options]

Summary

The mailx utility sends and receives electronic mail. The mailx utility is based on Berkeley UNIX mail (System V has an earlier, simpler electronic mail utility that is also called mail).

When you use mailx to send someone a message, mailx puts the message in that user's mailbox, which is typically a file named **/var/mail/login-name**, where **login-name** is the login name of the user you are sending the message to. When you use mailx to read messages that other people have sent you, mailx normally reads from your mailbox and then stores the messages after you read them in a file named **mbox** in your home directory .

The way mailx appears and functions depends to a large extent on the mailx *environment.* When you call mailx, it establishes an environment that is based on variables that are set in two files: the **/usr/share/lib/mailx/mailx.rc** file and a **.mailrc** file in your home directory. The system administrator sets up the first file. You can change any aspects of your mailx environment that the administrator has set up by setting variables in your **.mailrc** file. Or, if you are satisfied with the administrator's choices, you do not need to have a **.mailrc** file at all.

Options

-f [**filename**]   This option causes mailx to read messages from **filename** instead of from your system mailbox. If you do not specify a filename, mailx reads the **mbox** file in your home directory.

-H   This option displays a list of message headers without giving you the opportunity to read the messages.

-s **subject**   When you are sending messages, this option sets the subject field to **subject**.

Arguments

Without any arguments, mailx displays any messages that are waiting for you.

With one or more arguments, mailx sends messages. The **user-list** is a list of the users you are sending messages to.

Sending Messages

You send a message by giving the command **mailx** followed by the login names of the people you want to send messages to. Depending on how its environment variables are set, mailx may prompt you for a subject. If it does, enter a line of information in response to the prompt. This line will appear as the header when the recipients read the message. After entering the subject, mailx is in the Input Mode, and you can enter the text of your message. The mailx utility does not prompt you for the text.

You can run mailx commands while mailx is in the Input Mode. All Input Mode commands start with a tilde (~). They are called *tilde escapes* because they temporarily allow you to escape from the Input Mode so that you can give a command. The tilde must appear as the first character on a line.

The following list describes some of the more important tilde escapes.

~! **command**   Allows you to give a shell command while you are composing a message. Replace **command** with a shell command line.

~?   Displays a list of all tilde escapes.

~b **name-list**   **blind**   Sends blind carbon copies (bcc) to the users in the **name-list**. The people who receive blind carbon copies are not listed on the copy of the message that goes to the addressee; the people who receive regular carbon copies (cc) are listed—see **c**, following.

~c **name-list**   **carbon copy**   Sends carbon copies (cc) to the users in the **name-list**.

~h   **header**   Causes mailx to prompt you for the subject, to, cc, and bcc fields. Each prompt includes the field as it exists; you can use the erase and line kill keys to back up and edit the fields.

~m **msg-list**   **message**   Reads the messages specified by the **msg-list** into the message you are composing, placing a TAB at the beginning of each line. (Refer to "Reading Messages," following, for a description of **msg-list**.) You can use ~m only when you are sending a message while reading your messages (see the **m** and **r** commands, also in "Reading Messages").

~p   **print**   Displays the entire message you are currently composing.

mailx

~q   **quit**   Quits, saving the message you are composing in the file **dead.letter** in your home directory.

~r **filename**   **read**   Reads **filename** into the message you are composing.

~s **subject**   **subject**   Sets the subject field for the message you are composing to **subject**.

~t **name-list**   **to**   Adds the users in the **name-list** to the list of people who will receive the message.

~v   **vi**   Calls the vi editor so that you can edit the message you are composing.

~x   **exit**   Exits without saving the message you are composing.

Reading Messages

When you have mail you want to read, call mailx without any arguments. The mailx utility will display a list of headers of messages waiting for you. Each line of the display will have the following format:

[>] status message-# from-name date lines/characters [subject]

The > indicates that the message is the current message. The **status** is **N** if the message is new, or **U** (for unread) if the message is not new (that is, you have seen its header before) but you have not read it yet. The **message-#** is the sequential number of the message in your mailbox. The **from-name** is the name of the person who sent you the message. The **date** and **lines/characters** are the date the message was sent and its size. The **subject** is the optional subject field for the message.

After the list of headers, mailx displays its prompt, usually a question mark. The mailx utility is in Command Mode, waiting for you to give it a command. The easiest way to read your messages is to press RETURN. After each message, mailx will prompt you. Keep pressing RETURN to read each message in turn.

Pressing RETURN is a shorthand technique for printing the next message. Generally, you will give mailx commands to manipulate and respond to your messages.

In the following summary of commands, **msg-list** is a message number, a range of message numbers (use a hyphen to indicate a range: a–b), or the login name of a user. If you do not specify a **msg-list** where one is called for, mailx responds as though you had specified the current message. The *current message* is the message that is preceded by a > in the header list.

Most of the following commands can appear in your **.mailrc** file; however, it usually makes sense to use only **alias** and **set** there.

!command	Allows you to run a shell command while you are reading messages. Replace **command** with a shell command line.
| command	Pipe the current message through a shell **command** line.
?	Displays a list of all mailx commands.
alias a-name name-list	Declares that **a-name** (alias name) represents all the login names in the **name-list**. When you want to send a message to everyone in the **name-list**, all you need to do is send a message to **a-name**. The mailx utility automatically expands **a-name** into the **name-list**. This command usually appears in a **.mailrc** file.
d msg-list	**delete** Deletes the messages in the **msg-list** from your mailbox.
x	**exit** Exits from mailx without changing your mailbox. If you deleted any messages during this session with mailx, they are not removed from your mailbox.
h	**header** Displays a list of headers. Refer to the **z** command if you want to scroll the list of headers.
m name	**mail** Sends a message to **name**. Using this command is similar to calling mailx with **name** from the command line.
p msg-list	**print** Displays the messages in the **msg-list**.
pr msg-list	**preserve** Preserves messages in the **msg-list** in your mailbox. Use this command after you have read a message but do not want to remove it from your mailbox. Refer to the **q** command.
q	**quit** Exits from mailx, saving in your **mbox** file messages that you read and did not delete and leaving messages that you have not read in your mailbox. You can use the **pr** command to force mailx to leave a message in your mailbox even though you have read it.
r message	**reply** Replies to a message. This command copies the subject line of the **message** and addresses a reply

mailx

message to the person who sent you the **message**. Everyone who got a copy of the original **message** also gets a copy of the new message. The **r** command puts mailx in Input Mode so you can compose a message.

R message   **reply**   Replies to a message. This command is like the **r** command, except it sends a reply only to the person who sent you the message.

s msg-list filename   **save**   Saves a message in a file. Without any arguments, this command saves the current message in your **mbox** file. If you specify only a **msg-list**, it saves in your **mbox** file the messages you specify. If you specify a **filename**, it saves your messages in that file. When you use the **q** command after saving a message, mailx will not save the message in your mailbox or **mbox** file (unless you used the **s** command without a **filename**).

set   See the introduction to the following section, "The mailx Environment" for a description of this command. Although you can give the **set** command in response to a mailx prompt, it is typically used in **.mailrc** files.

t msg-list   Displays the messages in the **msg-list**.

top msg-list   Displays the top few lines of the specified messages.

u msg-list   **undelete**   Restores the specified messages. You can restore a deleted message only if you have not quit from mailx since you deleted the message.

v msg-list   **vi**   Edits the specified messages with vi.

z±   Scrolls the list of headers (see the **h** command) forward (+) or backward (–).

The mailx Environment

You can set up the mailx environment by setting variables in the **.mailrc** file in your home directory using the mailx **set** command. The **set** command has the following format:

set name[=value]

The **name** is the name of the mailx variable that you are setting, and the **value** is the optional value you are assigning to the variable. The **value** may be either a string or a number. If you use **set** without a value, mailx assigns the variable a null value (the values of some mailx variables are not relevant; it is only important that they are set).

Following is a list of some of the more important mailx variables:

askcc   Set this variable if you want mailx to prompt you for names of people to receive "carbon" copies of messages you send. By default, mailx sets the **noaskcc** variable.

asksub   Set this variable if you want mailx to prompt you for a subject. By default, mailx sets this variable.

crt=**number**   Set this variable if you want mailx to pipe long messages through pg or more. Specify the number of lines on your screen with **number**. If you are using a standard ASCII terminal, set **number** to 24. The mailx utility will use pg by default; if you prefer to use more, set the value of **PAGER** to more in your **.mailrc** file.

ignore   Set this variable if you want mailx to ignore interrupts while you are composing and sending messages. Setting **ignore** can make your job easier if you are working over a noisy telephone line. By default, mailx sets the **noignore** variable.

record=**filename**   When you set this variable, mailx puts a copy of all your outgoing messages in the file you specify with **filename**.

Notes

By default, the Bourne Shell checks every ten minutes for new mail. If mail has arrived, it presents a message before the next prompt. You can change the frequency of the checks by setting the **MAILCHECK** variable in your shell environment (see page 243).

System V Release 4 includes a vacation utility that can send a response to anyone who sends you a message while you are on vacation (see your system documentation for more information on vacation).

Examples

The following example shows Alex reading his messages with mailx. After calling mailx and seeing that he has two messages, he gives the command **t 2** (just **2** is enough) followed by a RETURN to display the second message. After displaying the message, mailx displays a prompt, and Alex deletes the message with a **d** command.

```
$ mailx
mailx version 4.0  Type ? for help.
"/var/mail/alex": 2 messages 2 new
>  N  1 jenny    Thu Jul 12 15:01 16/363 our meeting
   N  2 hls      Thu Jul 12 20:01 10/241 your trip
? t 2
(text of message 2)
.
.
.
? d
```

After reading his second message, Alex tries to read his first message by pressing RETURN. The mailx utility tells him he is at the end of his mailbox (At EOF), so he gives the command **t 1** (or just **1**) followed by a RETURN to view his first piece of mail. After reading it, he chooses to send a copy of it to the printer by typing **| lp**. Finally, he decides he did not really want to delete his second message and that he wants to read both messages again later, so he exits from mailx with an **x** command, leaving both messages in his mailbox.

```
? RETURN
At EOF
? t 1
(text of message 1)
.
.
? | lp
request id is printer_1-501 (standard input)
? x
$
```

make

Keep a set of programs current.

Format

make [options] [target-files]

Summary

The make utility keeps a set of executable programs current, based on differences in the modification times of the programs and the source files that each is dependent on. The executable programs, or **target-files**, are dependent on one or more **prerequisite** files. The relationships between **target-files** and **prerequisites** are specified on *dependency lines* in a **makefile**. **Construction commands** follow the dependency line, specifying how make can update the **target-files**. Refer to Chapter 10 for more information about **makefiles**.

Arguments

The **target-files** refer to targets on dependency lines in **makefile**. If you do not specify a **target-file,** make updates the target on the first dependency line in **makefile**.

Options

If you do not use the **–f** option, make takes its input from a file named **makefile** or **Makefile** in the working directory. Below, this file is referred to as **makefile**.

-f **file**   **input file**   This option causes make to use **file** as input in place of **makefile**. You can use any filename in place of **file**.

-n   **no execution**   This option causes make to display the commands it would execute to bring the **target-files** up to date, but not actually to execute the commands.

-t   **touch**   This option updates modification times of target files but does not execute any construction commands. Refer to the touch utility.

Examples

The first example causes make to bring the **target-file** called **analysis** up-to-date by issuing the three cc commands shown below. It uses a file called **makefile** or **Makefile** in the working directory.

```
$ make analysis
cc -c analy.c
cc -c stats.c
cc -o analysis analy.o stats.o
```

The example below also updates **analysis**, but it uses a **makefile** called **analysis.mk** in the working directory.

```
$ make -f analysis.mk analysis
'analysis' is up to date.
```

The following example lists the commands make would execute to bring the **target-file** called **credit** up-to-date. It does not actually execute the commands.

```
$ make -n credit
cc -c -O credit.c
cc -c -O accounts.c
cc -c -O terms.c
cc -o credit credit.c accounts.c terms.c
```

The next example uses the **-t** option to update the modification time of the **target-file** called **credit**. After you use the **-t** option, make thinks that **credit** is up-to-date.

```
$ make -t credit
$ make credit
'credit' is up to date.
```

mesg

Enable/disable reception of messages.

Format

mesg [y/n]

Summary

The mesg utility enables or disables reception of messages sent by someone using the write utility. When you call mesg without an argument, it tells you whether messages are enabled or disabled.

Arguments

The n (no) disables reception of messages, and the y (yes) enables reception.

Options

There are no options.

Notes

On most systems, when you first log in, messages are enabled. The nroff and pr utilities automatically disable messages while they are sending output to the terminal.

Examples

The following example demonstrates how to disable messages.

```
$ mesg n
```

The next example calls mesg without an option and verifies that you disabled messages.

```
$ mesg
is n
```

mkdir

Make a directory.

Format

mkdir [options] directory-list

Summary

The mkdir utility creates one or more directories.

Arguments

The **directory-list** contains one or more pathnames of directories that mkdir creates.

Options

-p   **parent**   If the parent directory of the directory you are creating does not already exist, it will be created by mkdir if you use the **–p** option.

Notes

You must have permission to write to and to search (execute permission) the parent directory of the directory you are creating. The mkdir utility creates directories that contain the standard invisible entries . (representing the directory itself) and .. (representing the parent directory).

Examples

The following command creates a directory named **accounts** as a subdirectory of the working directory, and a directory named **prospective** as a subdirectory of **accounts**.

```
$ mkdir -p accounts/prospective
```

Below, without changing working directories, the same user creates another subdirectory within the **accounts** directory.

```
$ mkdir accounts/existing
```

Finally, the user changes the working directory to the **accounts** directory and creates one more subdirectory.

```
$ cd accounts
$ mkdir closed
```

more

Display a file, one screenful at a time.

Format

> **more [options] [file-list]**
> **page [options] [file-list]**

Summary

The **more** utility allows you to view a text file at a terminal. It is similar to **cat** but pauses each time it fills the screen. In response to the **more** prompt, you can press the SPACE bar to view another screenful, or use any of the other **more** commands to skip forward or backward in the file, display the current line number, invoke the **vi** editor, or display a list of the available commands. The **more** commands are described below. If you use the **page** command rather than **more**, the screen will be cleared before each screenful is printed, so that it will not appear to scroll.

The number followed by a percent sign that **more** displays as part of its prompt represents the portion of the file that it has already displayed.

This utility takes its input from files you specify on the command line or from its standard input.

Arguments

The **file-list** is the list of files that you want to view. If you do not specify any files in **file-list,** **more** reads from its standard input.

Options

-n **number of lines** This option specifies the number of lines **more** will display in a screenful. Replace **n** with the number of lines your terminal screen displays. If you do not use this option, **more** uses the **TERM** variable and the information in **/etc/termcap** to determine the size of the screen.

-d **display** This option causes **more** to display an explanatory message after each screenful (Press space to continue, ´q´ to quit.) and to display a message after the user enters an illegal command (Press ´h´ for instructions). This makes **more** easier for beginners to use.

more

    -s   **squeeze** This option causes more to present multiple, adjacent blank lines as a single blank line. When you use more to display paginated text, such as nroff output, this option cuts out page headers and footers.

    +n   This option causes more to start displaying the file at line number **n**.

  +/pattern   This option causes more to start displaying the file two lines above the line containing **pattern**.

Notes

You can set the options to more either from the command line when you call more or by setting a variable called **MORE**. For example, to use more with the **-d** option, you can use the following commands from the Bourne Shell.

```
$ MORE=-d; export MORE
```

Bourne and Korn Shell users typically set **MORE** from their **.profile** file, and C Shell users set it from their **.cshrc** file. Once you have set the **MORE** variable, more will be invoked with the specified option each time it is called. The **MORE** variable applies whether you invoke more from the command line or whether another utility (like man or mailx) calls it.

Commands

Whenever more pauses, you may use any of the following commands. The *n* is an optional numeric argument. It defaults to 1. You do not need to follow these commands with RETURN.

Command	Effect
*n*SPACE	Displays *n* more lines; without *n*, it displays the next screenful.
d	Displays half a screenful.
*n*f	Skips *n* screenfuls and displays a screenful.
*n*b	Skips back *n* screenfuls and displays a screenful.
q or :q	Exits from more.
=	Displays the current line number.
v	Starts up the vi editor on the current file, at the current line.

h   Displays a list of all the **more** commands.

n/rexp   Searches for the *n*th occurrence of the regular expression *rexp*. The *n* is optional.

*n*n   Searches for the *n*th occurrence of the last regular expression entered.

!command   Invokes a shell and runs *command*.

n:n   Skips to the *n*th next file listed on the command line.

n:p   Skips to the *n*th previous file listed on the command line.

:f   Displays the current filename and line number.

.   Repeats the previous command.

RETURN   Displays the next line.

Examples

The following command line displays the file **letter**. To view more of **letter**, the user presses the SPACE bar in response to the **more** prompt.

```
$ more letter
.
.
--More--(71%) SPACE
.
.
$
```

Instead of pressing SPACE, the user could have pressed **h** to display a list of the **more** commands, could have pressed **v** to cause **more** to invoke the **vi** editor on the current line, or could have given any one of the other **more** commands.

In the next example, **more** starts displaying **letter** two lines above the line containing the word **receive**.

```
$ more +/receive letter
When we last spoke (January 14, 1991), I agreed that
we would ship your order within one week of
the date we receive it into our warehouse.
.
.
.
--More--(92%) SPACE
.
.
```

mv

Move (rename) a file.

Format

mv [options] existing-file new-filename
mv [options] existing-file-list directory
mv [options] existing-directory new-directory

Summary

The mv utility moves, or renames, one or more files. It has three formats. The first renames a single file with a new filename you supply. The second renames one or more files so that they appear in a specified directory. The third renames a directory.

The mv utility physically moves the file if it is not possible to rename it (that is, if you move it from one file system to another).

Options

-f **force** This option causes mv to complete a move regardless of file access permissions. Refer to ''Notes,'' below.

-i **interactive** This option causes mv to prompt you if a move would overwrite an existing file. If you respond **y** or **yes**, the move proceeds; otherwise, the file is not moved.

Arguments

In the first form of mv, the **existing-file** is a pathname that specifies the ordinary file that you want to rename. The **new-filename** is the new pathname of the file.

In the second form, the **existing-file-list** contains the pathnames of the files that you want to rename, and the **directory** specifies the new parent directory for the files. The files you rename will have the same simple filenames as the simple filenames of each of the files in the **existing-file-list** but new absolute pathnames.

The third form renames the **existing-directory** with the **new-directory** name. This form works only when the **new-directory** does not already exist.

Notes

The UNIX system implements mv as ln and rm. When you execute the mv utility, it first makes a link (ln) to the **new-file** and then deletes (rm) the **existing-file**. If the **new-file** already exists, mv deletes it before creating the link.

As with rm, you must have write and execute access permission to the parent directory of the **existing-file**, but you do not need read or write access permission to the file itself. If the move will overwrite an existing file that you do not have write permission for, mv displays the access permission and waits for a response. If you enter **y** or **yes**, mv renames the file; otherwise it does not. If you use the **–f** option, mv will not prompt you for a response—it will go ahead and overwrite the file.

If the **existing-file** and the **new-file** or **directory** are on different file systems, the UNIX system implements mv as cp and rm. In this case, mv actually moves the file instead of just renaming it. After a file is moved, the user who moved the file becomes the owner of the file.

The mv utility will not move a file onto itself.

Examples

The first command line renames **letter**, a file in the working directory, as **letter.1201**.

```
$ mv letter letter.1201
```

The next command line renames the file so that it appears, with the same simple filename, in the **/usr/archives** directory.

```
$ mv letter.1201 /usr/archives
```

The next example renames all the files in the working directory with filenames that begin with **memo** so they appear in the **/usr/backup** directory.

```
$ mv memo* /usr/backup
```

newgrp

Temporarily change the group identification of a user.

Format

newgrp [group]

Summary

The newgrp command forks a new shell. While you are using the new shell, you have the privileges of a member of the group you named on the command line (that is, you can access files a member of the group can access). In order to use newgrp to change your group identification, you must be listed in the /etc/group file as a member of the **group**. Refer to page 377 for more information on this file.

Arguments

When you call newgrp with an argument, it changes your group identification to the **group** you specify. Without an argument, it changes your group identification back to the group specified in the /etc/passwd file.

Options

There are no options.

Notes

If you want to determine which group you are currently associated with, create a file and use ls with the –l option to display the group the file is associated with. The file will be associated with the group you are associated with.

Examples

Following, Alex creates three files, using newgrp first to change to the *pubs* group and then using it without an argument to change back to his login group, *other*. The ls utility displays the different groups he is associated with.

```
$ cat /dev/null > test1
$ newgrp pubs
$ cat /dev/null > test2
$ newgrp
$ cat /dev/null > test3
$ ls -l test?
-rw-r--r-- 1 alex  other    0  Jul 20 21:40 test1
-rw-r--r-- 1 alex  pubs     0  Jul 20 21:40 test2
-rw-r--r-- 1 alex  other    0  Jul 20 21:41 test3
```

news

Display news.

Format

news [options] [items]

Summary

The news utility displays news items from the **/var/news** directory.

Arguments

The **items** are the names of news items that news will print. The names of news items are the filenames of files in the **/var/news** directory, and they are the names displayed by the **–n** option.

Options

Without any options, news displays all files from the **news** directory that were modified more recently than the file **.news_time** in your home directory. Then it updates the modification time of the **.news_time** file. The effect is that, without any options, news displays all news files that you have not seen.

-a   **all**   This option displays all news items.

-n   **names**   This option displays the names of items that news would print if you were to call it without any options.

-s   This option displays the number of items that news would print if you were to call it without any options.

Notes

You can press the interrupt key (usually DEL) once to stop a news item from printing, or twice to exit from news.

nice

Change the priority of a command.

Format

nice [option] command-line

Summary

The nice utility executes a command line at a different priority than the command line would otherwise have. You can specify a decrement in the range of 1–19, which decreases the priority of the command. The Superuser can use nice to increase the priority of a command by using a negative decrement.

The C Shell has a built-in nice command that has a different syntax. Refer to "Notes," below.

Arguments

The **command-line** is the command line you want to execute at a different priority.

Options

Without any options, nice defaults to a decrement of 10 (the absence of an option is equivalent to a **−10** option). You specify a decrement as a number preceded by a hyphen (to give a job the lowest priority possible, use an option of **−19**).

When you log in as the Superuser, you can specify a negative decrement as a number preceded by two hyphens (e.g., **−−12**). A negative decrement increases the priority of a command.

Notes

When you are using the C Shell's built-in nice command, a plus sign followed by a number decreases the priority of a process (e.g., **+12**). The Superuser can increase the priority of a process by using a hyphen followed by a number (e.g., **−12**).

Example

The following command executes nroff in the background at the lowest possible priority.

```
$ nice −19 nroff −mm chapter1 > chapter1.out &
24135
```

nohup

Run a command that will keep running after you log out.

Format

nohup command-line

Summary

The nohup utility executes a command line so that the command will keep running after you log out. Normally when you log out, the system kills all processes you have started.

The C Shell has a built-in nohup command. Refer to "Notes," below.

Arguments

The **command-line** is the command line you want to execute.

Options

There are no options.

Notes

If you do not redirect the output from a process that you execute with nohup, both the standard output *and* standard error output are sent to the file named **nohup.out** in the working directory. If you do not have write permission to the working directory, nohup opens a **nohup.out** file in your home directory.

Unlike the nohup utility, the C Shell's nohup command does not send output to the **nohup.out** file. The C Shell also automatically keeps commands that you run in the background running after you log out.

Example

The following command executes nroff in the background using nohup.

```
$ nohup nroff -mm memo > memo.out &
14235
```

od

Dump the contents of a file.

Format

od [options] [file]

Summary

The **od** utility dumps the contents of a file. It is useful for viewing executable (object) files and text files with embedded nonprinting characters.

This utility takes its input from the file you specify on the command line or from its standard input.

Arguments

The **file** is the pathname of the file that od displays. If you do not specify a **file** argument, od reads from its standard input.

Options

If you do not specify an option, the dump is in octal.

-c   **character**   This option produces a character dump. The od utility displays certain nonprinting characters as printing characters preceded by a backslash. It displays as three-digit octal numbers any nonprinting characters that are not in the following list.

Symbol	Character
\0	null
\b	BACKSPACE
\f	FORM-FEED
\n	NEWLINE
\r	RETURN
\t	TAB

-d   **decimal**   This option produces a decimal dump.

-o   **octal**   This option produces an octal dump. This is the default.

-x   **hexadecimal**   This option produces a hexadecimal dump.

Notes

The name od is short for octal dump.

Example

The example below shows the **sample** file displayed by cat and od with a −c
option. The numbers to the left of the characters in the dump are the octal byte
numbers of the first character on each line. The last number displayed is the octal
byte number of the last byte in the file.

```
$ cat sample
This is a sample file.

It includes TABs:        , and NEWLINEs.
Here's what a dumped number looks like: 755.
$ od −c sample
0000000 T h i s     i s     a     s a m p l e
0000020     f i l e . \n \n I t     i n c l u
0000040 d e s     T A B s : \t ,     a n d
0000060 N E W L I N E s . \n H e r e ' s
0000100     w h a t     a     d u m p e d     n
0000120 u m b e r     l o o k s     l i k e
0000140 :     7 5 5 . \n \0
0000147
```

pg

Display a file, one screenful at a time.

Format

pg [options] [file-list]

Summary

The pg utility displays a text file on a terminal a screenful at a time. It is similar to cat but pauses each time it fills the screen. In response to the pg prompt, you can press RETURN to view another screenful, press the interrupt key (usually DEL) to terminate the program, or give one of the commands discussed below.

This utility takes its input from files you specify on the command line or from its standard input.

Arguments

The **file-list** is the list of files that you want to view. If no files are specified, pg reads from its standard input.

Options

The options allow you to configure pg to your needs and liking.

-c **clear** This option homes the cursor and clears the screen before displaying each screenful.

-e **end** This option causes pg *not* to pause at the end of each file.

-f **force** This option keeps pg from splitting long lines. It is useful for displaying files that contain lines with nonprinting characters. (When a line contains many nonprinting characters and they are displayed, the line may be more than twice its original length.) These characters appear in files to cause the terminal to underline or display characters in reverse video.

+**line** This option causes pg to start displaying the file at the specified **line**. Replace **line** with the line number you want to start with.

-n **no newline** This option causes **pg** commands to take effect as soon as you enter them without waiting for you to press RETURN.

+/**pattern**/   This option causes **pg** to start displaying the file at the first line that contains the string or matches the **pattern**. Replace **pattern** with the string or other regular expression you want to match.

–p**prompt**   This option causes **pg** to use the prompt you specify in place of its default prompt (:). Replace **prompt** with the prompt you want **pg** to use. If you include the string %d in the **prompt, pg** will replace it with the number of the page it is displaying each time it issues the prompt.

–s   **standout**   This option causes **pg** to display all its messages and prompts in standout mode. Standout mode is usually reverse video and is dependent on the Terminfo name you use to describe your terminal.

–**lines**   This option causes **pg** to use the screen size you specify. Replace **lines** with the number of lines you want **pg** to use as a screen size. If you do not use this option, **pg** uses one fewer line than the height of the screen.

Notes

Also refer to the more utility described on page 533.

Commands

While you are viewing a file, you can give **pg** commands that affect what it displays next or how it displays it. Always give a command in response to the **pg** prompt [a colon (:) unless you change it with the –**p** option], and terminate it with a RETURN (unless you use the –**n** option). The **pg** utility displays a list of available commands when you give the command **h**.

Searching for a Pattern

You can search forward or backward for a pattern using one of the following command formats:

[**n**]/**pattern**/[**tmb**]
[**n**]?**pattern**?[**tmb**]

The **n** is an optional number that searches for the **n**th occurrence of the pattern. If you do not specify **n, pg** searches for the first occurrence. The / delimiter causes **pg** to search forward, and ? causes it to search backward. [Some terminals cannot handle question marks properly, so **pg** allows you to use carets (^) in place of the question marks.]

The **pattern** is a string or other regular expression that you are searching for. Refer to Appendix B for more information on regular expressions.

The optional character that follows the final delimiter (**/** or **?**) indicates where you want pg to position the pattern on the screen. Normally, pg positions the pattern at the top of the screen (**t**). You can select the middle (**m**) or bottom (**b**) of the screen if you prefer. Once you select a position, pg uses that position until you specify a new position.

Displaying Text by Its Position in the File

In response to the pg prompt, you can display a portion of the file based on its location in reference to the beginning of the file or to the portion of the file you are currently viewing.

You can precede each of the following commands with an address. The pg utility interprets an address that you precede with a plus or minus sign as a relative address—an address that is relative to the portion of the file you are currently viewing. A plus indicates forward, toward the end of the file, and a minus indicates backward, toward the beginning of the file. Without a sign, pg assumes the address specifies a distance from the beginning of the file. The address is in units of lines or pages, as is appropriate to the command.

SPACE   A SPACE displays the next page. You can enter a number of pages as an address before the SPACE command. (Unless you use the **−n** option, you must terminate this, and all commands, with a RETURN.)

l   **lines**   With a relative address, an l scrolls the screen the number of lines you specify (the default is one line). With an absolute address, l causes pg to display the line you specify at the top of the screen.

d   **down**   A **d** or CONTROL-D command scrolls the screen by one-half screenful.

Displaying Other Files

Use the following commands when you have specified more than one file on the command line and you want to view a file other than the one you are currently looking at.

n   **next**   Give the command **n** to view the next file. Precede the **n** with a number, **i**, to view the ith subsequent file.

p   **previous**   Use the **p** command like the **n** command to view the previous file from the **file-list**.

Example

The following example shows pg displaying **memo**. The user just presses RETURN in response to pg's prompts. In the final prompt, the EOF stands for *end of file*.

```
$  pg  memo
 .
 .
: RETURN
 .
 .
: RETURN
 .
 .
( EOF ) : RETURN
```

pr

Paginate a file for printing.

Format

pr [options] [file-list]

Summary

The pr utility breaks files into pages, usually in preparation for printing. Each page has a header with the name of the file, date, time, and page number.

The pr utility takes its input from files you specify on the command line or from its standard input. The output from pr goes to its standard output and is frequently redirected by a pipe to the lp utility for printing.

Arguments

The **file-list** contains the pathnames of ordinary text files you want pr to paginate. If you do not specify any files, pr reads its standard input.

Options

You can embed options within the **file-list**. An embedded option affects only files following it on the command line.

+page   This option causes pr to begin its output with the specified **page**. Note that this option begins with a *plus sign*, not a hyphen. Replace **page** with the page number you want to start with.

−columns   This option causes pr to display its output in the number of **columns** specified. Replace **columns** with the number of columns you want.

−d   **double-space**   This option causes pr to double-space its output.

−h header   **header**   The pr utility displays the **header** at the top of each page in place of the filename. If the header contains SPACES, you must enclose it within quotation marks. Replace **header** with the header you want pr to use.

−llines   **length**   This option changes the page length from the standard 66 lines to **lines**. Replace **lines** with the number of lines per page you want.

-m   **multiple columns**   This option displays all specified files simultaneously in multiple columns.

-n[ck]   **number**   This option causes pr to number the lines of the file. Both the **c** and **k** arguments are optional. The **c** is a character that is appended to the number to separate the number from the contents of the file. If **c** is not specified, TAB is used. The **k** argument specifies the number of digits in each line number. By default, **k** is five.

-sx   **separate**   This option separates columns with the single character **x** instead of SPACES. Replace **x** with the delimiter you want to use. If you do not specify **x**, pr uses TABS as separation characters.

-t   **no header or trailer**   This option causes pr not to display its five-line page header and trailer. The header that pr normally displays includes the name of the file, the date, time, and page number. The trailer is five blank lines.

-wn   **width**   This option changes the page width from its standard 72 columns to **n** columns. Replace **n** with the number of columns you want. This option is effective only with multi-column output (that is, the **–m** and **–n** options.)

Notes

When you use the **–columns** option to display the output in multiple columns, pr displays the same number of lines in each column (with the possible exception of the last column).

The write utility cannot send messages to your terminal while you are running pr with its output going to the terminal. Disabling messages prevents another user from sending you a message and disrupting pr's output to your screen.

Examples

The first command line shows pr paginating a file named **memo** and sending its output through a pipe to lp for printing.

```
$ pr memo | lp
request id is printer_1-501 (standard input)
```

Next, **memo** is sent to the printer again, this time with a special heading at the top of each page. The job is run in the background.

```
$ pr -h 'MEMO RE: BOOK' memo | lp &
request id is printer_1-502 (standard input)
23456
23457
```

Below, pr displays the **memo** file on the terminal, without any header, start-ing with page 3.

```
$ pr -t +3 memo
.
.
```

The final command displays the output from ls in six columns on the screen. This command line is useful if you are using an older version of System V that does not support the −C (column) option of ls.

```
$ ls | pr -6 -t
.
.
```

prs

Print a summary of the history of an SCCS file.

Format

prs [options] file-list

Summary

The prs utility is part of SCCS (Source Code Control System; see page 355 for more information). The prs utility prints a summary of one or more deltas to an SCCS file. If you do not give prs any options, it prints a standard summary of every delta in the history of a file. With options, prs prints a summary only of selected deltas. You can also use a data specification with the **–d** option to select the information that will be displayed about each delta and to select the format in which it will be displayed.

Arguments

The **file-list** is a list of SCCS-encoded files, which all start with **s.**. If the list includes directory names, all files that begin with **s.** in the named directory are added to **file-list**. The prs utility reports on all files listed in **file-list**. Any files in **file-list** that do not begin with **s.** or that are unreadable are ignored.

Options

–d**data-specification**

This option specifies the data that will be included in the display and the format of the display. You can put labels into the display by including text in the data specification. Refer to "Data Specifications" for more information.

–r[**version-number**]

release   This option selects the delta you want information about. If you use **–r** without a version number, prs prints information about the most recent delta.

–c**date-time**

cutoff   This option can be used together with either **–e** or **–l** to select all the deltas made either before or after a cutoff date-time. The **date-time** argument has the format:

YY[MM[DD[HH[MM[SS]]]]]

The brackets indicate that all components of **date-time** may be omitted except **YY**, starting from the right. The maximum possible values will be substituted for any omitted values (e.g., 59 is used if **SS** is omitted). The two-digit components may be separated by any number of nonnumeric characters. For example, colon (:) may be used between the components (e.g., 90:02:26:03:36). If the –c option is used, either –e or –l must also be used.

–e   **earlier**   When used with –r, this option causes prs to print information about all the deltas created earlier than the specified delta as well as about the specified delta. When used with –c, it causes prs to print information about all deltas created prior to the specified **date-time**.

–l   **later**   When used with –r, this option causes prs to print information about all the deltas created later than the specified delta, as well as about the specified delta. When used with –c, it causes prs to print information about all deltas created after the specified **date-time**.

–a   **all**   This option causes prs to print information about deltas that have been removed as well as about existing deltas. Without this option, only existing deltas are reported on.

Data Specifications

You can use the following keywords after the –d option to tell prs what information to display and how to display it. In the data specification following –d, you can use \t to specify a TAB, or \n to specify a NEWLINE. Text in the data specification that is not a keyword is printed in the output as it appears in the data specification. A typical data specification includes several keywords separated by SPACES, TABS, or NEWLINES. The following specification is a default specification prs uses if you do not include a specification on the command line:

```
" : D t : \ t : DL : \ nMR s : \ n : MR : COMMENTS : \ n : C : "
```

The strings MRs: and COMMENTS: are labels, and the \t and \n represent TAB and NEWLINE, respectively. All the other characters inside the double quotation marks are keywords. The following table lists the most useful keywords.

Keyword	Explanation
:DT:	delta type (D for delta, R for removed delta)
:DL:	number of lines inserted, deleted, and unchanged
:I:	version number (SCCS Identification String)
:D:	date delta was created
:T:	time delta was created
:P:	creator of the delta
:DS:	sequence number of the delta
:DP:	sequence number of the preceding delta
:MR:	modification request numbers for the delta
:C:	comments for the delta
:Dt:	the same as :DT :I: :D: :T: :P: :DS: :DP:

Examples

The first example prints standard information about every delta that has been made to the SCCS-encoded file **s.dissertation**.

```
$ prs s.dissertation
s.dissertation:

D 1.3 90/07/22 14:10:45 alex 3 2      00018/00005/04046
MRs:
COMMENTS:
edits

D 1.2 90/07/21 11:07:32 alex 2 1      00080/00000/04051
MRs:
COMMENTS:
added abstract for chapter 4

D 1.1 90/07/20 14:06:14 alex 1 0      04051/00000/00000
MRs:
COMMENTS:
date and time created 90/07/20 14:06:14 by alex
```

The next example prints information only about Version 1.3.

```
$ prs -r1.3 s.dissertation
s.dissertation:

D 1.3 90/07/22 14:10:45 alex 3 2      00018/00005/04046
MRs:
COMMENTS:
edits
```

Below, the comments are printed out for each delta that was created prior to 1:00 P.M. on July 22, 1990.

```
$ prs -d":C:" -c90:07:22:12 -e s.dissertation
added abstract for chapter 4

date and time created 90/07/20 14:06:14 by alex
```

The next command prints out the following information for the most recent delta: the type of the delta, the date and time of creation, and the creator of the delta. Spaces are used to separate the data items.

```
$ prs -d":DT: :D: :T: :P:" s.dissertation
D 90/07/22 14:10:45 alex
```

ps

Display process status.

Format

ps [options]

Summary

The **ps** utility displays status information about active processes.

When you run **ps** without any options, it displays the statuses of all active processes that your terminal controls. You will see four columns, each with one of the following headings:

> PID   **process ID**   This column lists the process ID number of the process.

> TTY   **terminal**   This column lists the number of the terminal that controls the process.

> TIME   This column lists the number of seconds the process has been running.

> COMMAND   This column lists the command name with which the process was called. Use the **–f** option to display the entire command line.

Arguments

There are no arguments.

Options

> –a   **all**   This option displays status information for all processes that any terminal controls.

> –e   **everything**   This option displays status information for all processes.

> –f   **full**   This option displays a subset of the columns that the **–l** option displays, with the addition of the STIME column, which lists the time the process started. It displays the full command line in the COMMAND column.

ps

-g **group**   This option prints the statuses of *process group* leaders in addition to other active processes. Your login shell is a process group leader, as are getty processes running on terminals no one is logged in on.

-l **long**   This option displays a complete status report comprising 14 columns. Each heading is listed below.

F   **flags**   This column lists the flags associated with the process.

S   **state**   This column lists the state of the process.

UID   **user ID**   This is the user ID number of the owner of the process.

PID   **process ID**   This column lists the process ID number of the process.

PPID   **parent PID**   This is the process ID number of the parent process.

C   **central processor utilization**   The system uses this number for scheduling processes.

PRI   **priority**   This is the priority of the process. The higher the number, the lower the priority of the process.

NI   **nice**   This number is established by the nice utility and the operating system. It is used in computing the priority of the process.

ADDR   **address**   This number is the memory or disk address of the process.

SZ   **size**   This number is the size, in blocks, of the core image of the process.

WCHAN   **wait channel**   This column is blank for running processes. If the process is waiting or sleeping, this is the event it is waiting for.

TTY   **terminal**   This column lists the number of the terminal that controls the process.

TIME   This column lists the number of seconds the process has been running.

COMD   This column lists the command name with which the process was called. Use the **–f** option to display the entire command line.

-u **name**   **user**   This option causes **ps** to display status information about the user **name**. Replace **name** with the login name of the user you want information about.

Notes

Because of the way **ps** obtains the command line, the COMD (or COMMAND) column may not be accurate.

Examples

The first example shows the **ps** utility, without any options, displaying the user's active processes. The first process is the shell (**sh**), and the second is the process executing the **ps** utility.

```
$ ps
   PID   TTY      TIME COMMAND
 24059  tty11    0:05 sh
 24259  tty11    0:02 ps
```

With the **–l** (long) option, **ps** displays more information about each of the processes.

```
$ ps -l
F S UID    PID  PPID  C PRI  NI   ADDR  SZ  WCHAN  TTY      TIME COMD
1 S 108 24059     1  0  30  20   146  16  11502  tty11   0:05 sh
1 R 108 24260 24059 78  54  20   371  24         tty11   0:03 ps
```

The next sequence of commands shows how to use **ps** to determine the process number of a process running in the background and how to terminate that process using the **kill** command. In this case, it is not necessary to use **ps** because the shell displays the process number of the background processes. The **ps** utility verifies the PID number.

The first command executes **nroff** in the background. The shell displays the PID number of the process followed by a prompt.

```
$ nroff -mm memo > memo.out &
24264
$
```

Next, **ps** confirms the PID number of the background task. If you did not already know this number, using **ps** would be the only way to find it out.

```
$ ps
   PID   TTY        TIME  COMMAND
 24059   tty11      0:05  sh
 24264   tty11      0:05  nroff
 24267   tty11      0:03  ps
```

Finally, the kill command terminates the process. Refer to the kill utility for more information.

```
$ kill 24264
24264 Terminated
```

rcp

Copy one or more files to or from a remote computer.

Format

> **rcp** [options] **source-file destination-file**
> **rcp** [options] **source-file-list destination-directory**

Summary

The **rcp** utility copies one or more ordinary files, including text and executable program files, between two computers that can communicate over a network. Like the **cp** utility, it has two modes of operation: The first copies one file to another, and the second copies one or more files to a directory.

Arguments

The **source-file** is the pathname of the ordinary file that **rcp** is going to copy. To copy a file *from* a remote computer, precede the file's pathname with the name of the remote computer system followed by a colon (:). The **destination-file** is the pathname that **rcp** will assign to the resulting copy of the file. To copy a file *to* a remote computer, precede the file's pathname with the name of the remote computer system followed by a colon (:).

The **source-file-list** is one or more pathnames of ordinary files that **rcp** is going to copy. When you use the **–r** option, the **source-file-list** can also contain directories. To copy files *from* a remote computer, precede each file's pathname with the name of the remote computer system followed by a colon (:). The **destination-directory** is the pathname of the directory in which **rcp** places the resulting copied files. To copy files *to* a remote computer, precede the directory's pathname with the name of the remote computer system followed by a colon (:).

Options

-p **preserve** This option causes **rcp** to set the modification times and file access permissions of each copy to match those of the **source-file**. Without the **–p** option, **rcp** uses the current file creation mask to modify the access permissions (Refer to **umask** on page 621 for a description of the file creation mask).

-r **recursive** You can use this option when the destination is a directory. If any of the files in the **source-file-list** is a directory, the **–r** option will cause **rcp** to copy the contents of that directory and any of its subdirectories into the **destination-directory**. The subdirectories themselves are copied, as well as the files they contain.

Notes

You must have a login account on the remote computer to be able to copy files to or from it using rcp. If you use a shell wildcard (such as *) in a remote filename, you must quote the pathname so that the wildcard will be interpreted on the remote computer (and not by the local shell). As with cp, if the **destination-file** exists before you execute rcp, rcp overwrites the file.

Examples

The first example copies all the files with filenames ending in **.c** into the **archives** directory on the remote computer named *bravo*. Since the full pathname of of the **archives** directory is not specified, rcp assumes that it is a subdirectory of the user's home directory on *bravo*. The copied files each retain their simple filenames.

```
$ rcp *.c bravo:archives
```

The next example copies **memo** from the **/home/jenny** directory on *bravo* to the working directory on the local computer.

```
$ rcp bravo:/home/jenny/memo  .
```

The next command copies two files named **memo.new** and **letter** to jenny's home directory on the remote computer *bravo*. The absolute pathnames of the copied files on *bravo* are **/home/jenny/memo.new** and **/home/jenny/letter**.

```
$ rcp memo.new letter bravo:/home/jenny
```

The final command copies all the files in jenny's **reports** directory on *bravo* to the **oldreports** directory on the local computer, preserving the original modification dates and file access permissions on the copies.

```
$ rcp -p 'bravo:reports/*' oldreports
```

rlogin

Log in on a remote computer.

Format

   rlogin [option] remote-computer

Summary

The rlogin utility establishes a login session on a remote computer, over a network.

Arguments

The **remote-computer** is the name of a computer that your system can reach over a network.

Options

–l **user-name**   **login**   This option causes rlogin to log you in on the remote computer as the user specified by **user-name** rather than as yourself.

Notes

If the name of your local computer is specified in a file called **/etc/hosts.equiv** on the remote computer, the remote computer will not prompt you to enter your password. Computer systems listed in the **/etc/hosts.equiv** file are considered equally secure.

   An alternative way to specify a trusted relationship is on a per-user basis. Each user's home directory can contain a file called **.rhosts** that contains a list of trusted remote systems and users.

Examples

The following example illustrates the use of rlogin. On the local system, Alex's login name is **alex,** but on the remote computer *bravo* his login name is **awatson.** The remote system prompts alex to enter a password because he is logging in using a different user name than the one he uses on the local system.

```
$ who am i
alex          tty6            Sep 14 13:26
$ rlogin -l awatson bravo
Password:
```

If the local computer is named *hurrah,* a **.rhosts** file on *bravo* like the one below will allow the user alex to log in as the user awatson without entering a password.

```
$ cat /home/alex/.rhosts
hurrah alex
```

rm

Remove a file (delete a link).

Format

rm [options] file-list

Summary

The rm utility removes links to one or more files. It can be used to remove both hard links and symbolic links. When you remove the last hard link, you can no longer access the file, and the system releases the space the file occupied on the disk for use by another file (that is, the file is deleted). Refer to Chapter 4 for more information about hard links and symbolic links.

To delete a file, you must have execute and write access permission to the parent directory of the file, but you do not need read or write access permission to the file itself. If you are running rm from a terminal (that is, rm's standard input is coming from a terminal) and you do not have write access permission to the file, rm displays your access permission and waits for you to respond. If you enter **y** or **yes**, rm deletes the file; otherwise it does not. If its standard input is not coming from the terminal, rm deletes the file without question.

Arguments

The **file-list** contains the list of files that rm deletes. The list can include ambiguous file references. Because you can remove a large number of files with a single command, use rm cautiously, especially when you are using an ambiguous file reference. If you are in doubt as to the effect of an rm command with an ambiguous file reference, use the echo utility with the same file reference first to evaluate the list of files the reference generates.

Options

-f   **force**   This option causes rm to remove files for which you do not have write access permission, without asking for your consent.

-i   **interactive**   This option causes rm to ask you before removing each file. If you use the **-r** option with this option, rm also asks you before examining each directory.

-r   **recursive**   This option causes rm to delete the contents of the specified directory, including all its subdirectories, and the directory itself. Use this option cautiously.

Notes

The sections on the ln utility in Part II and Chapter 4 contain discussions about removing links.

Refer to the rmdir utility in Part II if you need to remove an empty directory.

When you want to remove a file that begins with a hyphen, you must prevent rm from interpreting the filename as an option. A good strategy is to use the full pathname of the file.

Examples

The following command lines delete files, both in the working directory and in another directory.

```
$  rm  memo
$  rm  letter  memo1  memo2
$  rm  /home/jenny/temp
```

The next example asks the user before removing each file in the working directory and its subdirectories. This command is useful for removing filenames that contain special characters, especially SPACES, TABS, and NEWLINES. (You should never create filenames containing these characters on purpose, but it may happen accidentally.)

```
$  rm  -ir  .
```

rmdel

Remove a delta from an SCCS file.

Format

rmdel −rversion-number file-list

Summary

The rmdel utility is part of SCCS (Source Code Control System; see page 355 for more information). The rmdel utility removes changes that were previously recorded in an SCCS file using delta. The rmdel utility will not remove a delta if there is an outstanding get (that is, a get for which the corresponding delta has not been done) on the specified delta. Also, rmdel will not remove a delta if it has a successor (that is, rmdel will only remove the newest delta on the trunk or on a branch).

To use rmdel you must be the owner of the SCCS file and the directory it is in, or be the one who created the delta.

Arguments

The **file-list** is a list of SCCS-encoded files, which all start with **s.**. If the list includes directory names, all files that begin with **s.** in the named directory are added to **file-list**. The rmdel utility removes the specified delta from all files in **file-list**. Any files in **file-list** that do not begin with **s.** or that are unreadable are ignored.

Options

−rversion-number   **release**   This option is mandatory. Use it to specify the full version number of the delta you want to remove. If the delta is a trunk delta, the version number contains two components (release.level). If it is a branch delta, it contains four components (release.level.branch.sequence).

Examples

The following command is applied to an SCCS file called **s.memo**. These deltas to the **s.memo** file exist:

rmdel

```
1 . 1
1 . 2
2 . 1
2 . 1 . 1 . 1
2 . 2
2 . 2 . 1 . 1
2 . 2 . 1 . 2
3 . 1
```

The only deltas that can be removed using rmdel are 3.1 (the only trunk delta with no successors) and 2.1.1.1 and 2.2.1.2. To use rmdel to remove branch delta 2.1.1.1, give the following command:

```
$  rmdel  -r2.1.1.1  s.memo
```

rmdir

Remove a directory.

Format

rmdir directory-list

Summary

The rmdir utility deletes empty directories from the file system by removing links to those directories.

Arguments

The **directory-list** contains pathnames of empty directories that rmdir removes.

Options

There are no options.

Notes

Refer to the rm utility with the **–r** option if you need to remove directories that are not empty, together with their contents.

Examples

The following command line deletes the empty **literature** directory from the working directory.

```
$ rmdir literature
```

The next command line removes the **letters** directory using an absolute pathname.

```
$ rmdir /home/jenny/letters
```

ruptime

Display status of computers attached to a network.

Format

ruptime [option]

Summary

The ruptime utility displays status information about computers attached to a network. By default, ruptime counts only those users who have used their terminals in the past hour.

Arguments

There are no arguments.

Options

-a **all** This option causes ruptime to count all users who are currently logged in, even if they have been idle for more than one hour.

Notes

The information displayed by ruptime is broadcast on the network by the rwhod utility, which is typically started by a run command script when the system reboots. The rwhod utility can create a lot of traffic on the network and may not be running at your site. If ruptime displays a message such as **no hosts!?!**, rwhod is not running.

Examples

The following example illustrates the use of ruptime. The computer name appears in column one. Column two reports the status of the system, followed by the amount of time the system has been up (or down). The number of users logged in on the system appears in the third column. The last column reports the load factor for each machine. From left to right, the load factors indicate the number of processes that have been run in the last minute, the last five minutes, and the last 15 minutes. In this example, the computer *bravo* has been up and running for the past 21 days, 19 hours, and 40 minutes.

```
$ ruptime -a
bravo          up  21+19:40,    1 users,  load 0.12, 0.00, 0.03
hurrah         up  17+16:25,    2 users,  load 1.32, 1.93, 1.16
sobell       down   1+23:34
```

rwho

Display names of users on computers attached to a network.

Format

rwho [option]

Summary

The rwho utility displays the names of users currently logged in on computers attached to a network, together with their terminal device numbers, the times they logged in, and how much time has passed since they typed on their keyboards. By default, rwho displays only the names of users who have used their terminals in the past hour.

Arguments

There are no arguments.

Options

-a   **all**   This option causes rwho to display the names of all users who are currently logged in, even if they have been idle for more than one hour.

Notes

The information displayed by rwho is broadcast on the network by the rwhod utility, which is typically started by a run command script when the system reboots. The rwhod utility can create a lot of traffic on the network and may not be running at your site. If rwho displays no information, it is likely that rwhod is not running.

Examples

The following example illustrates the use of rwho. The user name appears in column one, followed by the name of the computer and the terminal line and the time at which the user logged in. If the fourth column is blank, the user is actively typing at the terminal; otherwise, the fourth column indicates how many hours and minutes have passed since the user last typed on the keyboard.

```
$ rwho -a
awatson    bravo:tty01     Sep 14 10:19
barbara    hurrah:tty01    Sep 13 10:54    2:33
jenny      hurrah:tty02    Sep 14 14:24     :01
```

sed

Edit a file (noninteractively).

Format

> **sed [–n] –f script-file [file-list]**
> **sed [–n] script [file-list]**

Summary

The **sed** utility is a batch (noninteractive) editor. The **sed** commands are usually stored in a **script-file** (as in the first format shown above), although you can give simple **sed** commands from the command line (as in the second format). By default, **sed** copies lines from the **file-list** to its standard output, editing the lines in the process. It selects lines to be edited by position within the file (line number) or context (pattern matching).

The **sed** utility takes its input from files you specify on the command line or from its standard input. Unless you direct output from a **sed** script elsewhere, it goes to its standard output.

Arguments

The **script-file** is the pathname of a file containing a **sed** script (see "Description," following).

The **script** is a **sed** script, included on the command line. This format allows you to write simple, short **sed** scripts without creating a separate script file.

The **file-list** contains pathnames of the ordinary files that **sed** processes. These are the input files. If you do not specify any files, **sed** takes its input from the standard input.

Options

If you do not use the **–f** option, **sed** uses the first command line argument as its script.

- –f **file** This option causes **sed** to read its script from the **script-file** given as the first command line argument.

- –n **no print** **sed** does not copy lines to its standard output except as specified by the Print (**p**) instruction or flag.

Description

A sed script consists of one or more lines in the following format:

[address[,address]] instruction [argument-list]

The **addresses** are optional. If you omit the **address**, sed processes all lines from the input file. The **addresses** select the line(s) the **instruction** part of the command operates on. The **instruction** is the editing instruction that modifies the text. The number and kinds of arguments in the **argument-list** depend on the instruction.

The sed utility processes an input file as follows:

1. sed reads one line from the input file (**file-list**).
2. sed reads the first command from the **script-file** (or command line), and, if the address selects the input line, sed acts on the input line as the instruction specifies.
3. sed reads the next command from the **script-file**. If the address selects the input line, sed acts on the input line (as possibly modified by the previous instruction) as the new instruction specifies.
4. sed repeats step 3 until it has executed all of the commands in the **script-file**.
5. If there is another line in the input file, sed starts over again with step 1; otherwise it is finished.

Addresses

A line number is an address that selects a line. As a special case, the line number $ represents the last line of the last file in the **file-list**.

A regular expression (refer to Appendix B) is an address that selects the lines that contain a string that the expression matches. Slashes must delimit a regular expression used as an address.

Except as noted, zero, one, or two addresses (either line numbers or regular expressions) can precede an instruction. If you do not use an address, sed selects all lines, causing the instruction to act on every input line. One address causes the instruction to act on each input line that the address selects. Two addresses cause the instruction to act on groups of lines. The first address selects the first line in the first group. The second address selects the next subsequent line that it matches; this line is the last line in the first group. After sed selects the last line in a group, it starts the selection process over again, looking for the next subsequent line that the first address matches. This line is the first line in the next group. The sed utility continues this process until it has finished going through the file.

Instructions

d   **delete**   The Delete instruction causes **sed** not to write out the lines it selects. It also causes **sed** not to finish processing the lines. After **sed** executes a Delete instruction, it reads the next input line from the **file-list** and begins over again with the first command in the **script-file**.

n   **next**   The Next instruction reads the next input line from the **file-list**. It writes out the currently selected line, if appropriate, and starts processing the new line with the *next* command in the **script-file**.

a   **append**   The Append instruction appends one or more lines to the currently selected line. If you do not precede the Append command with an address, it appends to each input line from the **file-list**. You cannot precede an Append instruction with two addresses. An Append command has the following format:

[address] a\
text \
text \
.
.
.
text

You must end each line of appended text, except the last, with a backslash. (The backslash quotes the following NEWLINE.) The appended text concludes with a line that does not end with a backslash. The **sed** utility *always* writes out appended text, regardless of whether you set the –**n** flag on the command line. It even writes out the text if you delete the line to which you appended the text.

i   **insert**   The Insert instruction is identical to the Append instruction, except that it places the new text *before* the selected line.

c   **change**   The Change instruction is similar to Append and Insert, except that it changes the selected lines so that they contain the new text. You can use this command with two addresses. If you specify an address range, Change replaces the entire range of lines with a single occurrence of the new text.

s   **substitute**   The Substitute instruction is akin to that of **vi**. It has the following format:

[address[,address]] s/pattern/replacement-string/[g][p][w file]

The **pattern** is a regular expression that is delimited by any character (other than a SPACE or NEWLINE); however, slash (/) is traditionally used. The **replacement-string** starts immediately following the second delimiter and must be terminated by the same delimiter. The final (third) delimiter is required. The **replacement-string** can contain an ampersand (**&**), which sed replaces with the matched **pattern**. Unless you use the **g** flag, the Substitute instruction replaces only the first occurrence of the **pattern** on each selected line.

g   **global flag**   This flag causes the Substitute instruction to replace all nonoverlapping occurrences of the **pattern** on the selected lines.

p   **print flag**   This flag causes sed to send all lines on which it makes substitutions to its standard output. This flag overrides the **–n** option on the command line.

w   **write flag**   This flag is similar to the **p** flag, except that it sends the output to a specified file. A single SPACE and the name of a file must follow the Write flag.

p   **print**   The Print instruction writes the selected lines to the standard output. It writes the lines immediately and does not reflect the effects of subsequent instructions. This instruction overrides the **–n** option on the command line.

w   **write**   This instruction is similar to the **p** instruction, except that it sends the output to a specified file. A single SPACE and the name of a file must follow the Write instruction.

r   **read**   The Read instruction reads the contents of the specified file and appends it to the selected line. You cannot precede a Read instruction with two addresses. A single SPACE and the name of a file must follow a Read instruction.

q   **quit**   The Quit instruction causes sed to stop processing.

Control Structures

!   **NOT**   The NOT structure causes sed to apply the following instruction, located on the same line, to each of the lines *not* selected by the address portion of the command.

{ }   **group instructions**   When you enclose a group of instructions within a pair of braces, a single address (or address pair) selects the lines on which the group of instructions operates.

Notes

The name **sed** stands for stream editor.

Examples

The following examples use the input file **new**.

```
$ cat new
Line one.
The second line.
The third.
This is line four.
Five.
This is the sixth sentence.
This is line seven.
Eighth and last.
```

Unless you instruct it not to, **sed** copies all lines, selected or not, to its standard output. When you use the **–n** option on the command line, **sed** copies only specified lines.

The command line below displays all the lines in the **new** file that contain the word **line** (all lowercase). The command uses the address **/line/**, a regular expression. The **sed** utility selects each of the lines that contains a match for that pattern. The Print **(p)** instruction displays each of the selected lines.

```
$ sed '/line/ p' new
Line one.
The second line.
The second line.
The third.
This is line four.
This is line four.
Five.
This is the sixth sentence.
This is line seven.
This is line seven.
Eighth and last.
```

The preceding command does not use the **–n** option, so it displays all the lines in the input file at least once. It displays the selected lines an additional time because of the Print instruction.

The following command uses the **–n** option so that **sed** displays only the selected lines.

```
$ sed -n ' /line/ p '  new
The second line.
This is line four.
This is line seven.
```

Below, sed copies part of a file based on line numbers. The Print instruction selects and displays lines 3 through 6.

```
$ sed -n ' 3,6 p '  new
The third.
This is line four.
Five.
This is the sixth sentence.
```

The command line below uses the Quit instruction to cause sed to display only the top of a file. This enables you to look at the top of a file in the same way the head command does. This sed command is a handy substitute for head, if you do not have head on your system. Below, sed displays the first five lines of **new**.

```
$ sed ' 5 q '
Line one.
The second line.
The third.
This is line four.
Five.
```

When you need to give sed more complex or lengthy commands, you can use a script file. The following script file (**print3_6**) and command line perform the same function as the command line in the second preceding example.

```
$ cat print3_6
3,6 p

$ sed -n -f print3_6 new
The third.
This is line four.
Five.
This is the sixth sentence.
```

The sed script **append_demo** (below) demonstrates the Append instruction. The command in the script file selects line 2 and appends a NEWLINE and the text AFTER. to the selected line. Because the command line does not include the **-n** option, sed copies all the lines from the input file **new**.

```
$ cat append_demo
2 a\
AFTER.

$ sed -f append_demo new
Line one.
The second line.
AFTER.
The third.
This is line four.
Five.
This is the sixth sentence.
This is line seven.
Eighth and last.
```

The **insert_demo** script selects all the lines containing the string This and inserts a NEWLINE and the text BEFORE. before the selected lines.

```
$ cat insert_demo
/This/ i\
BEFORE.

$ sed -f insert_demo new
Line one.
The second line.
The third.
BEFORE.
This is line four.
Five.
BEFORE.
This is the sixth sentence.
BEFORE.
This is line seven.
Eighth and last.
```

The next example demonstrates a Change instruction with an address range. When you give a Change instruction a range of lines, it does not change each line within the range but changes the block of text to a single occurrence of the new text.

```
$ cat change_demo
2,4 c\
SED WILL INSERT THESE\
THREE LINES IN PLACE\
OF THE SELECTED LINES.
```

```
$ sed -f change_demo new
Line one.
SED WILL INSERT THESE
THREE LINES IN PLACE
OF THE SELECTED LINES.
Five.
This is the sixth sentence.
This is line seven.
Eighth and last.
```

The next example demonstrates a Substitute command. The **sed** utility selects all lines because the command has no address. It replaces the first occurrence on each line of the string line with sentence and displays the resulting line. The **p** flag displays each line where a substitution occurs. The command line calls **sed** with the −n option so that **sed** displays only the lines that the script explicitly requests it to display.

```
$ cat subs_demo
s/line/sentence/p

$ sed -n -f subs_demo new
The second sentence.
This is sentence four.
This is sentence seven.
```

The next example is similar to the preceding one, except a **w** flag and filename (**temp**) at the end of the Substitute command cause **sed** to create the file **temp**. The command line does not include a −n option, so it displays all lines, including those **sed** changes. The cat utility displays the contents of the file **temp**. The word Line (starting with an uppercase L) is not changed.

```
$ cat write_demo1
s/line/sentence/gw temp

$ sed -f write_demo1 new
Line one.
The second sentence.
The third.
This is sentence four.
Five.
This is the sixth sentence.
This is sentence seven.
Eighth and last.

$ cat temp
The second sentence.
This is sentence four.
This is sentence seven.
```

Following is a Bourne shell script named **sub** that will change all occurrences
of **REPORT** to **report**, **FILE** to **file**, and **PROCESS** to **process** in a group of
files. The **for** structure loops through the list of files supplied on the command
line. (See page 263 for more information on the **for** structure.) As it processes
each file, **sub** displays the filename before running sed on the file. This script
uses a multi-line embedded sed command—as long as the newlines within the
command are quoted (they are between single quotation marks), sed accepts the
multi-line command as though it appeared on a single command line. Each substitute command includes a **g** (global) flag to take care of the case where one of
the strings occurs more than one time on a line.

```
$ cat sub
for file
do
        echo $file
        mv $file $$.subhld
        sed ´s/REPORT/report/g
            s/FILE/file/g
            s/PROCESS/process/g´  $$.subhld > $file
done
rm $$.subhld

$ sub file1 file2 file3
file1
file2
file3
```

Below, sed uses the Write command to copy part of a file to another file
(**temp2**). The line numbers **2** and **4**, separated by a comma, select the range of
lines sed is to copy. This script does not alter the lines.

```
$ cat write_demo2
2,4 w temp2

$ sed −n −f write_demo2 new

$ cat temp2
The second line.
The third.
This is line four.
```

The script **write_demo3** is very similar to **write_demo2**, except that it precedes the Write command with the NOT operator (!), causing sed to write to the
file the lines *not* selected by the address.

```
$ cat write_demo3
2,4 !w temp3

$ sed -n -f write_demo3 new

$ cat temp3
Line one.
Five.
This is the sixth sentence.
This is line seven.
Eighth and last.
```

Below, **next_demo1** demonstrates the Next instruction. When sed processes the selected line (line 3), it immediately starts processing the next line, without printing line 3. Thus, it does not display line 3.

```
$ cat next_demo1
3 n
p

$ sed -n -f next_demo1 new
Line one.
The second line.
This is line four.
Five.
This is the sixth sentence.
This is line seven.
Eighth and last.
```

The next example uses a textual address. The sixth line contains the string **the,** so the Next command causes sed not to display it.

```
$ cat next_demo2
/the/ n
p

$ sed -n -f next_demo2 new
Line one.
The second line.
The third.
This is line four.
Five.
This is line seven.
Eighth and last.
```

The next set of examples uses the file **compound.in** to demonstrate how sed instructions work together.

```
$ cat compound.in
1. The words on this page...
2. The words on this page...
3. The words on this page...
4. The words on this page...
```

The first example that uses **compound.in** instructs sed to substitute the string words with text on lines 1, 2, and 3, and the string text with TEXT on lines 2, 3, and 4. It also selects and deletes line 3. The result is text on line 1, TEXT on line 2, no line 3, and words on line 4. The sed utility made two substitutions on lines 2 and 3: It substituted text for words and TEXT for text. Then it deleted line 3.

```
$ cat compound
1,3 s/words/text/
2,4 s/text/TEXT/
3 d

$ sed -f compound compound.in
1. The text on this page...
2. The TEXT on this page...
4. The words on this page...
```

The next example shows that the ordering of instructions within a sed script is critical. After line 2 of the script substitutes the string TEXT in place of text, the third line displays all of the lines that contain TEXT. The Print instruction would have displayed no lines, or different lines, if it had been one line before or after its present location.

```
$ cat compound2
1,3 s/words/text/g
2,4 s/text/TEXT/g
/TEXT/ p
3 d

$ sed -f compound2 compound.in
1. The text on this page...
2. The TEXT on this page...
2. The TEXT on this page...
3. The TEXT on this page...
4. The words on this page...
```

Below, **compound3** appends two lines to line 2. The sed utility displays all the lines from the file once because no -n option appears on the command line. The Print instruction at the end of the script file displays line 3 an additional time.

```
$ cat compound3
2 a\
This is line 2a.\
This is line 2b.
3 p

$ sed -f compound3 compound.in
1. The words on this page...
2. The words on this page...
This is line 2a.
This is line 2b.
3. The words on this page...
3. The words on this page...
4. The words on this page...
```

The next example shows that sed always displays appended text. Here line 2 is deleted, but the Append instruction still displays the two lines that were appended to it. Appended lines are displayed even if you use the -n option on the command line.

```
$ cat compound4
2 a\
This is line 2a.\
This is line 2b.
2 d

$ sed -f compound4 compound.in
1. The words on this page...
This is line 2a.
This is line 2b.
3. The words on this page...
4. The words on this page...
```

The final examples use regular expressions in addresses. The regular expression in the command below (^.) matches one character at the beginning of a line (that is, it matches every line that is not empty). The replacement string (between the second and third slashes) contains a TAB character followed by an ampersand (&). The ampersand takes on the value of whatever the regular expression matched. This type of substitution is useful for indenting a file to create a left margin. See Appendix B for more information on regular expressions.

```
$ sed 's/^./    &/' new
        Line one.
        The second line.
        The third.
.
.
```

You may want to put the above **sed** command into a shell script so that you will
not have to remember it (and retype it) every time you want to indent a file.

```
$ cat indent
sed 's/^./    &/' $*
$ chmod u+x indent
$ indent new
        Line one.
        The second line.
        The third.
.
.
```

Generally, when you create a **sed** command that you think you may want to
use again, it is a good idea to put it into a shell script or a **script-file** to save yourself the effort of trying to reconstruct it.

In the following shell script, the regular expression (two SPACES followed by
a *) matches one or more spaces at the end of a line. It removes trailing spaces at
the end of a line, which is useful for cleaning up files that you created using **vi**.
In **vi** it is easy to create lines that end in a space accidentally, and some **vi** commands do not work correctly on a line that ends in a space.

```
$ cat cleanup
sed 's/  *$//' $*
```

shl

Invoke the shell layer manager.

Format

shl

Summary

UNIX System V Release 2 introduced a form of *job control* to AT&T UNIX (Berkeley UNIX has had job control for quite a while). Job control allows you, from a single terminal, to control up to seven shells at once. These shells, called *layers,* can each be running a different program at the same time. The *current* layer is the one that receives the characters you enter on the keyboard. There can be zero or one current layers at any given time. Using the job-control commands, you can make any layer the current layer, create new layers, delete layers, and list layers.

A different method of job control is also available on System V Release 4 to users of the C Shell and Job Shell. See page 305.

Arguments

There are no arguments.

Options

There are no options.

Description

When you give an **shl** (shell layer) command, the shell layer manager takes over and issues its prompt, which is >>>. To create a new layer, give the **create** command, optionally followed by the name of the layer you want to create. If you do not name the layer, shl will name it **(1)**. You can refer to it as just **1**. If you create additional unnamed layers, shl will name them **(2)** through **(7)**. When you create a layer, you will see the shell prompt, which shl sets to the name of the layer. Use the new shell as you would any shell—give it commands to edit files, compile programs, send mail, and so on. When you want to create a new layer, press CONTROL-Z and you will see the shell layer manager prompt.

You can give the shell layer manager another **create** command to create another layer, a **layers** command to display a list of layers, a **resume** command followed by the name of a layer to make that layer the current layer, a **delete** command followed by the name of a layer to remove a layer, or a **quit** command to stop using the shell layer manager.

In addition, you can give a **block** command to block output from a layer. Blocking output causes a program to stop execution when it it is not the current layer and it tries to send output to the terminal. When you make the blocked layer the current layer, execution resumes and you can view the output. Blocking output prevents programs that are running in layers other than the current layer from flooding the terminal with output while you are working on something else. The **unblock** command reverses the effects of the **block** command.

Commands

Any time after you have logged in, you can start using the shell layer manager. Give the command **shl** in response to the shell prompt. The shell layer manager will display its prompt.

You can abbreviate any of the following commands to as few letters as you wish, as long as it is still unique. In the following list, **name** is the name of a layer, and **name-list** is a list of names of one or more layers separated by SPACES. You can use up to eight characters in a name, but you cannot use the names **(1)** through **(7)** as these are the names shl uses when you create a new layer and do not supply a name.

block **name-list**   Suspend execution of a layer in the **name-list** when it attempts to display output on the terminal and it is not the current layer. Resume execution when it becomes the current layer. See "unblock," below. Refer to the **loblk** argument in the stty section of Part II for a description of another method of blocking output.

create [**name**]   Create a new layer (shell) with the name **name**. If you do not specify a name, shl uses a number from 1 to 7 enclosed in parentheses as the name. You can refer to a numbered shell with its number alone, without the parentheses.

delete **name-list**   Delete all the layers in the **name-list**. Send each process a SIGHUP (that is, hang up) signal.

help   Display a list of commands.

layers [–l] [**name-list**]   List information about the named layers or all layers if there is not a **name-list**. The –l option displays a listing similar to that displayed by ps.

quit   Exit from the shell layer manager. Send each process
in each layer a SIGHUP signal.

resume [**name**]   Make the named layer the current layer. If there is no
name, make the last current layer the new current
layer. If you use a name, you can omit the command
(e.g., **name** has the same effect as **resume name**).

toggle   Make the layer that was the current layer before the
last current layer the new current layer.

unblock **name-list**   Reverse the effects of a **block** command.

Examples

Below, Jenny calls the shell layer manager and gives a Create command (**c**) to
create a layer. Because she did not specify a name for the layer, the shell layer
manager gives it the default name for layer 1, (**1**). Once layer 1 displays its
prompt, (1), Jenny calls mailx. After starting to enter a message to send to Alex,
Jenny presses CONTROL-Z to call the shell layer manager and creates a new layer so
she can check on a directory name she needs to include in her note to Alex.

```
$ shl

>>> c

(1) mailx alex
The file you asked me for in the CONTROL-Z >>> c

(2) ls
.
.
```

After Jenny creates layer 2, she gives an **ls** command (above). Before returning to the note she is still sending Alex, she calls vi to edit a file named **reminder**
(below).

While she is still using vi in layer 2, Jenny presses CONTROL-Z to return to the
shell layer manager. (If you lose track of which layer is running what, you can
give an **l –l** command in response to the shell layer manager prompt to display a
list of active layers and what processes each is running.) After the shell layer
manager displays its prompt, Jenny gives the command **1** to return to layer 1.
The shell layer manager displays resuming 1, and she is back in the middle of
using mailx. She finishes her message to Alex and enters a period to exit from
mailx.

shl

```
( 2 )  v i  r e m i n d e r
    .
    .
CONTROL-Z  > > >  1
r e s u m i n g  1
 d i r e c t o r y  n a m e d  / h o m e / j e n n y / l i t e r a t u r e .

         J e n n y
    .
( 1 )
```

When Jenny gets the prompt for layer 1, she returns to the shell layer manager, deletes layer 1 (**d 1**), and goes back to layer 2 where she was using vi. She presses CONTROL-L (some terminals use CONTROL-R) to refresh the screen, finishes editing her file, and exits from vi.

Finally, Jenny goes back to the shell layer manager, deletes layer 2, checks that there are no active layers (l), and returns to her regular shell with a **q** command.

```
( 1 )  CONTROL-Z  > > > d  1
> > >  2
r e s u m i n g  2
CONTROL-L
    .
    .
( 2 )  CONTROL-Z  > > > d  2
> > >  l
> > >  q
$
```

sleep

Create a process that sleeps for a specified interval.

Format

sleep time

Summary

The **sleep** utility causes the process executing it to go to sleep for the time you specify.

Arguments

The **time** is the length of time, in seconds, that the process will sleep.

Options

There are no options.

Examples

You can use **sleep** from the command line to execute a command after a period of time. The example below executes a process in the background that reminds you to make a phone call in 20 minutes (1200 seconds).

```
$ (sleep 1200; echo 'Remember to make call.') &
2145
```

You can also use **sleep** within a shell script to execute a command at regular intervals. The following **per** shell script executes a program named **update** every 90 seconds.

```
$ cat per
while :
do
    update
    sleep 90
done
```

If you execute a shell script such as **per** in the background, you can only terminate it using the **kill** utility.

sort

Sort and/or merge files.

Format

sort [options] [field-specifier-list] [file-list]

Summary

The **sort** utility sorts and/or merges one or more text files in sequence. When you use the **–n** option, **sort** performs a numeric sort.

The **sort** utility takes its input from files you specify on the command line or from its standard input. Unless you use the **–o** option, output from **sort** goes to its standard output.

Arguments

The **field-specifier-list** specifies one or more sort fields within each line. The **sort** utility uses the sort fields to sort the lines from the **file-list**. The **file-list** contains pathnames of one or more ordinary files that contain the text to be sorted. The **sort** utility sorts and merges the files unless you use the **–m** option, in which case **sort** only merges the files.

Options

If you do not specify an option, **sort** orders the file in the machine collating (usually ASCII) sequence. You can embed options within the **field-specifier-list** by following a field specifier with an option without a leading hyphen—see "Description," later in this section.

-b **ignore leading blanks** Blanks (TAB and SPACE characters) are normally field delimiters in the input file. Unless you use this option, **sort** *also* considers leading blanks to be part of the field they precede. This option causes **sort** to consider multiple blanks as single field delimiters with no intrinsic value, so **sort** does not consider these characters in sort comparisons.

-c **check only** This option checks to see that the file is properly sorted. The **sort** utility does not display anything if everything is in order. It displays a message if the file is not in sorted order and returns an exit status of 1.

-d **dictionary order** This option ignores all characters that are not alphanumeric characters or blanks. Specifically, **sort** does not consider punctuation and CONTROL characters.

-f   **fold lowercase into uppercase**   This option considers all lowercase letters to be uppercase letters. Use this option when you are sorting a file that contains both uppercase and lowercase text.

-i   **ignore**   This option ignores nonprinting characters when you perform a nonnumeric sort.

-m   **merge**   This option assumes that multiple input files are in sorted order and merges them without verifying that they are sorted.

-M   **month**   This option compares fields that contain the names of months. It uses the first three nonblank characters in the field, shifts them to uppercase, and sorts in the order JAN, FEB, ..., DEC. It puts invalid entries first in the sorted list.

-n   **numeric sort**   When you use this option, minus signs and decimal points take on their arithmetic meaning and the **-b** option is implied. The sort utility does not order lines or order sort fields in the machine collating sequence but in arithmetic order.

-o filename   **output filename**   The **filename** is the name of the output file. The sort utility sends its output to this file instead of to its standard output. Replace **filename** with a filename of your choice—it can be the same as one of the names in the **file-list**.

-r   **reverse**   This option reverses the sense of the sort (e.g., **z** precedes **a**).

-tx   **set tab character**   When you use this option, replace the **x** with the character that is the field delimiter in the input file. This character replaces SPACES, which become regular (nondelimiting) characters.

-u   **unique**   This option outputs repeated lines only once. The sort utility outputs lines that are not repeated as it would without this option.

-ymem   This option allows you to specify the amount of memory that sort will use, within system limits. Replace **mem** with the number of kilobytes of memory that you want sort to use. If you omit **mem**, sort will use the maximum amount of memory that the system allows. Replace **mem** with 0 to use the minimum amount of memory possible. When sort runs out of memory, it uses temporary files.

-zrec   This option allows you to specify the maximum line length when you are merging files. Do not use it if you are sorting files. Replace **rec** with the number of bytes in the longest record you are merging. If you do not specify this option, sort may terminate abnormally if it encounters a long line.

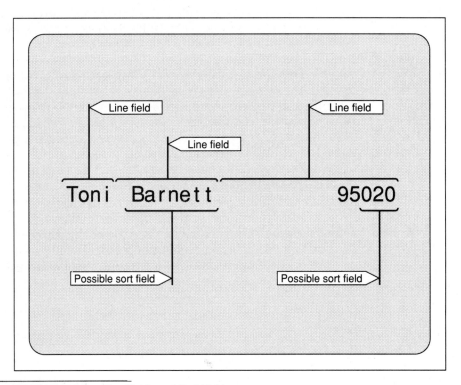

FIGURE Part II-2   Line Fields and Sort Fields

Description

In the following description, a *line field* is a sequence of characters on a line in an input file. These sequences are bounded by blanks or by a blank and the beginning or end of the line. You use line fields to define a sort field.

A *sort field* is a sequence of characters that sort uses to put lines in order. The description of a sort field is based on line fields. A sort field can contain part or all of one or more line fields. Refer to Figure II-2.

The **field-specifier-list** contains pairs of pointers that define subsections of each line (sort fields) for comparison. If you omit the second pointer from a pair, sort assumes the end of the line. A pointer is in the form ±**f.c.** The first of each pair of pointers begins with a plus sign, and the second begins with a hyphen.

You can make a pointer (**f.c**) point to any character on a line. The **f** is the number of line fields you want to *skip*, counting from the beginning of the line. The **c** is the number of characters you want to *skip*, counting from the end of the last line field you skipped with **f**.

The **–b** option causes sort to count multiple leading blanks as a *single* line field delimiter character. If you do not use this option, sort considers each leading blank to be a character in the sort field and includes it in the sort comparison.

You can specify options that pertain only to a given sort field by immediately following the field specifier by one of the options **b, d, f, i, n,** or **r**. In this case, you must *not* precede the options with a hyphen.

If you specify more than one sort field, sort examines them in the order you specify them on the command line. If the first sort field of two lines is the same, sort examines the second sort field. If these are again the same, sort looks at the third field. This process continues for all the sort fields you specify. If all the sort fields are the same, sort examines the entire line.

If you do not use any options or arguments, the sort is based on entire lines.

Examples

The following examples assume that a file named **list**, shown below, is in the working directory. Each line of the file contains three fields: first name, last name, and ZIP code. All the blanks are SPACES, not TABS.

```
$ cat list
Tom Winstrom          94201
Janet Dempsey         94111
Alice MacLeod         94114
David Mack            94114
Toni Barnett          95020
Jack Cooper           94072
Richard MacDonald     95510
```

The first example demonstrates sort without any options or arguments other than a filename. Below, sort sorts the file on a line-by-line basis. If the first characters on two lines are the same, sort looks at the second characters to determine the proper sorted order. If the second characters are the same, sort looks at the third characters. This process continues until sort finds a character that differs between the lines. If the lines are identical, it does not matter which one sort puts first. The sort command in this example needs to examine only the first three letters (at most) of each line. The sort utility displays a list that is in alphabetical order by first name.

```
$ sort list
Alice MacLeod            94114
David Mack               94114
Jack Cooper              94072
Janet Dempsey            94111
Richard MacDonald        95510
Tom Winstrom             94201
Toni Barnett             95020
```

You can instruct sort to skip any number of line fields and characters on a line before beginning its comparison. Blanks normally separate one line field from another. The next example sorts the same list by last name, the second line field. The **+1** argument indicates that sort is to *skip one line field* before beginning its comparison. It skips the first-name field. Because there is no second pointer, the sort field extends to the end of the line. Now the list is almost in last-name order, but there is a problem with Mac.

```
$ sort +1 list
Toni Barnett             95020
Jack Cooper              94072
Janet Dempsey            94111
Richard MacDonald        95510
Alice MacLeod            94114
David Mack               94114
Tom Winstrom             94201
```

In the example above, MacLeod comes before Mack. After finding the sort fields of these two lines the same through the third letter (Mac), sort put L before k because it arranges lines in the order of ASCII character codes. In this ordering, uppercase letters come before lowercase, and therefore L comes before k.

The **–f** option makes sort treat uppercase and lowercase letters as equals and thus fixes the problem with MacLeod and Mack.

```
$ sort -f +1 list
Toni Barnett             95020
Jack Cooper              94072
Janet Dempsey            94111
Richard MacDonald        95510
David Mack               94114
Alice MacLeod            94114
Tom Winstrom             94201
```

The next example attempts to sort list on the third line field, the ZIP code. Below, sort does not put the numbers in order but puts the shortest name first in the sorted list and the longest name last. With the argument of **+2**, sort *skips* two line fields and counts the SPACES after the second line field (last name) as part of the sort field. The ASCII value of a SPACE character is less than that of any other printable character, so sort puts the ZIP code that is preceded by the greatest number of SPACES first and the ZIP code that is preceded by the fewest SPACES last.

```
$ sort +2 list
David Mack              94114
Jack Cooper             94072
Tom Winstrom            94201
Toni Barnett            95020
Janet Dempsey           94111
Alice MacLeod           94114
Richard MacDonald       95510
```

The **–b** option causes sort to ignore leading SPACES. With the **–b** option, the ZIP codes come out in the proper order (below). When sort determines that MacLeod and Mack have the same ZIP codes, it compares the entire lines. The Mack/MacLeod problem crops up again because there is no **–f** option.

```
$ sort –b +2 list
Jack Cooper             94072
Janet Dempsey           94111
Alice MacLeod           94114
David Mack              94114
Tom Winstrom            94201
Toni Barnett            95020
Richard MacDonald       95510
```

The next example shows a **sort** command that not only skips line fields but skips characters as well. The **+2.3** causes sort to skip two line fields and then skip three characters before starting its comparisons. The sort field is, and the following list is sorted in order of, the last two digits in the ZIP code.

The example takes advantage of the fact that if you use two options with sort, you can include them both after a single hyphen. The **–f** option does not fix the MacLeod and Mack problem because sort never compares last names. When it determines that the last two digits of MacLeod and Mack's ZIP codes are the same, it compares the entire lines, starting with the first names. These two lines are in first-name order. The issue of preventing sort from comparing entire lines is covered shortly.

```
$ sort –fb +2.3 list
Tom Winstrom            94201
Richard MacDonald       95510
Janet Dempsey           94111
Alice MacLeod           94114
David Mack              94114
Toni Barnett            95020
Jack Cooper             94072
```

The next set of examples uses the **cars** data file. From left to right, the columns in the file contain each car's make, model, year of manufacture, mileage, and price.

```
$ cat cars
plym      fury      77      73      2500
chevy     nova      79      60      3000
ford      mustang   65      45      10000
volvo     gl        78      102     9850
ford      ltd       83      15      10500
chevy     nova      80      50      3500
fiat      600       65      115     450
honda     accord    81      30      6000
ford      thundbd   84      10      17000
toyota    tercel    82      180     750
chevy     impala    65      85      1550
ford      bronco    83      25      9500
```

Without any options, **sort** displays a sorted copy of the file.

```
$ sort cars
chevy     impala    65      85      1550
chevy     nova      79      60      3000
chevy     nova      80      50      3500
fiat      600       65      115     450
ford      bronco    83      25      9500
ford      ltd       83      15      10500
ford      mustang   65      45      10000
ford      thundbd   84      10      17000
honda     accord    81      30      6000
plym      fury      77      73      2500
toyota    tercel    82      180     750
volvo     gl        78      102     9850
```

A **+0** sort field specifier indicates a sort from the beginning of the line (skip zero fields). Unless you specify otherwise, a sort field extends to the end of the line.

The following example shows one problem to avoid when you are using **sort**. In this example, the objective is to sort by manufacturer and then by price within manufacturer. The command line instructs **sort** to sort on the entire line (**+0**) and then make a second pass, sorting on the fifth field all lines whose first-pass sort fields were the same (**+4**). Because no two lines are the same, **sort** makes only one pass, sorting on each entire line. (If two lines differed only in the fifth field, they would be sorted properly on the first pass anyway, so the second pass would be unnecessary.) Look at the lines with the **ltd** and **mustang**. They are sorted by the second field rather than the fifth, demonstrating that **sort** never made a second pass and never sorted by the fifth field.

```
$ sort +0 +4 cars
chevy     impala    65      85      1550
chevy     nova      79      60      3000
chevy     nova      80      50      3500
fiat      600       65      115     450
ford      bronco    83      25      9500
```

```
ford      ltd       83      15      10500
ford      mustang   65      45      10000
ford      thundbd   84      10      17000
honda     accord    81      30      6000
plym      fury      77      73      2500
toyota    tercel    82      180     750
volvo     gl        78      102     9850
```

The next example forces the first-pass sort to stop just before the second field by defining the end of the first sort field (−1). Now the ltd and mustang are properly sorted by price. But look at the bronco. It is less expensive than the other Fords, but sort has it positioned as the most expensive one. The sort utility put the list in ASCII collating sequence order, not numeric order: 9500 comes after 10000 because 9 comes after 1.

```
$ sort +0 −1 +4 cars
chevy     impala    65      85      1550
chevy     nova      79      60      3000
chevy     nova      80      50      3500
fiat      600       65      115     450
ford      mustang   65      45      10000
ford      ltd       83      15      10500
ford      thundbd   84      10      17000
ford      bronco    83      25      9500
honda     accord    81      30      6000
plym      fury      77      73      2500
toyota    tercel    82      180     750
volvo     gl        78      102     9850
```

The −n (numeric) option on the second pass puts the list in the proper order.

```
$ sort +0 −1 +4n cars
chevy     impala    65      85      1550
chevy     nova      79      60      3000
chevy     nova      80      50      3500
fiat      600       65      115     450
ford      bronco    83      25      9500
ford      mustang   65      45      10000
ford      ltd       83      15      10500
ford      thundbd   84      10      17000
honda     accord    81      30      6000
plym      fury      77      73      2500
toyota    tercel    82      180     750
volvo     gl        78      102     9850
```

The next example again shows that, unless you instruct it otherwise, sort orders a file starting with the field you specify and continuing to the end of the line. It does not make a second pass unless two of the first sort fields are the same. Although this example sorts the cars by years, it does not sort the cars by manufacturer within years.

```
$ sort +2 +0 cars
fiat     600       65       115      450
ford     mustang   65       45       10000
chevy    impala    65       85       1550
plym     fury      77       73       2500
volvo    gl        78       102      9850
chevy    nova      79       60       3000
chevy    nova      80       50       3500
honda    accord    81       30       6000
toyota   tercel    82       180      750
ford     ltd       83       15       10500
ford     bronco    83       25       9500
ford     thundbd   84       10       17000
```

Specifying an end to the sort field for the first pass allows sort to perform its secondary sort properly.

```
$ sort +2 -3 +0 cars
chevy    impala    65       85       1550
fiat     600       65       115      450
ford     mustang   65       45       10000
plym     fury      77       73       2500
volvo    gl        78       102      9850
chevy    nova      79       60       3000
chevy    nova      80       50       3500
honda    accord    81       30       6000
toyota   tercel    82       180      750
ford     bronco    83       25       9500
ford     ltd       83       15       10500
ford     thundbd   84       10       17000
```

The next examples demonstrate an important sorting technique: putting a list in alphabetical order, merging upper- and lowercase entries, and eliminating duplicates.

```
$ cat short
Pear
Pear
apple
pear
Apple
```

A plain sort:

```
$ sort short
Apple
Pear
Pear
apple
pear
```

A folded sort is a good start, but it does not eliminate duplicates.

```
$ sort -f short
Apple
apple
Pear
Pear
pear
```

The **-u** (unique) option eliminates duplicates but causes all the uppercase entries to come first.

```
$ sort -u short
Apple
Pear
apple
pear
```

When you attempt to use both **-u** and **-f**, the lowercase entries get lost.

```
$ sort -uf short
Apple
Pear
```

Two passes are the answer. Both passes are unique sorts, and the first folds uppercase letters onto lowercase ones.

```
$ sort -u +0f +0 short
Apple
apple
Pear
pear
```

spell

Check a file for spelling errors.

Format

spell [options] [+local-file] [file-list]

Summary

The spell utility checks the words in a file against a dictionary file. It displays a list of words that it cannot either find in the dictionary or derive from one of the words in the dictionary. This utility takes its input from files you list on the command line or from its standard input. You can also customize spell's dictionary.

Arguments

The **file-list** is a list of files that spell checks. If you specify more than one file, spell generates one list of words for all the files.

The **+local-file** is a file containing a sorted list of words, one word per line. The spell utility removes the words in **local-file** from its output. The **local-file** supplements the standard dictionary with additional words that are correctly spelled. It is useful for removing proper names and technical terms from the output of spell.

Options

-v   This option displays all words that are not literally in the dictionary. As the example on the next page shows, it gives a proposed derivation for any word spell would normally accept.

-b   **British**   This option accepts British spellings.

Notes

The spell utility is not a foolproof way of finding spelling errors. It also does not check for misused but properly spelled words (e.g., *read* instead of *red*).

Examples

The following examples use spell to check the spelling in the **check** file. The −v option causes spell to display all words that are not actually in its dictionary.

```
$ cat check
Here's a sampel document that is tobe
used with th Spell utilitey.
It obviously needs proofing quite badly.

$ spell check
sampel
th
tobe
utilitey

$ spell -v check
sampel
th
tobe
utilitey
+ly       badly
+'s       Here's
+s        needs
+ly       obviously
+ing      proofing
+d        used
```

stty

Display or set terminal parameters.

Format

stty [options] [arguments]

Summary

Without any arguments, stty displays certain parameters affecting the operation of the terminal. For a complete list of these parameters and an explanation of each, see the following "Arguments" section. The arguments establish or change the parameter(s) you specify.

Options

Without an option or argument, stty displays a summary report that includes only a few of its parameters.

-a   **all**   This option reports on all parameters.

-g   **generate**   This option generates a report of the current settings in a format you can use as arguments to another stty command.

Arguments

The arguments to stty specify which terminal parameters stty is to alter. You can turn on each of the parameters that is preceded by an optional hyphen (indicated in the following list as [-]) by specifying the parameter without the hyphen. You can turn it off by specifying it with the hyphen. Unless specified otherwise, this section describes the parameters in their *on* states.

Modes of Data Transmission

[-]raw   The normal state is **-raw**. When the system reads input in its raw form, it does not interpret the following special characters: erase (usually CONTROL-H or #), line kill (usually CONTROL-U or @), interrupt execution (DEL or CONTROL-C), and EOF (CONTROL-D). In addition, it does not use parity bits. With typical UNIX system humor, you can specify **-raw** as **cooked**.

[-]parenb   Parity enable. When you specify **-parenb**, the system does not use or expect a parity bit when communicating with the terminal.

[-]parodd   Select odd parity. (**–parodd** selects even parity.)

[-]cstopb   Use two stop bits. (**–cstopb** specifies one stop bit.)

Treatment of Characters

[-]nl   Only accept a NEWLINE character as a line terminator. With **–nl** in effect, the system accepts a RETURN character from the terminal as a NEWLINE while it sends a RETURN followed by a LINEFEED to the terminal in place of a NEWLINE.

[-]echo   Echo characters as they are typed (full duplex operation). If a terminal is half duplex and displays two characters for each one it should display, turn the echo parameter off (**–echo**).

[-]lcase   For uppercase only terminals, translate all uppercase characters into lowercase as they are entered. (Also **[–]LCASE.**)

[-]tabs   Transmit each TAB character to the terminal as a TAB character. When **tabs** is turned off (**–tabs**), the system translates each TAB character into the appropriate number of SPACES and transmits these SPACES to the terminal. (Also **[–]tab3.**)

You can use the tabs utility to set the TAB stops on your terminal. By default, they occur every eight columns. Refer to the manuals that come with your system.

Data Line Specifications

[-]hup   Disconnect telephone line when user logs out.

0   Disconnect telephone line immediately.

110 300 600 1200 1800 2400 4800 9600 19200 38400   Set the terminal baud rate to one of these numbers.

Job-Control Parameters

The shell layer manager uses the following parameters. Refer to shl on page 583 for more information on the shell layer manager (shl) and job control.

swtch **x**   Set the character you use to switch control from a layer (shell) to the shell layer manager. By default, **x** is null. When **x** is null, stty sets

stty

swtch to CONTROL-Z. Replace **x** with the character you want to use in place of CONTROL-Z. See "erase" in the following section for conventions you can use to specify CONTROL characters.

[-]loblk   Block output from the layer that you set this parameter in. With this parameter set, the system will suspend output to the terminal until the layer is the current (interactive) layer. Setting **loblk** is the same as giving the shl **block** command. Use **-loblk** (default) to allow the system to send output to the terminal even if the layer is not the current layer.

Job control in the C Shell and Job Shell uses the following parameter.

[-]tostop   Stops background jobs if they attempt to send output to the terminal (**-tostop** allows background jobs to send output to the terminal).

Special Keys

ek   Set the erase and line kill keys to their default values: # and @.

erase **x**   Set the erase key to **x**. To indicate a CONTROL character, precede the **x** with a caret and enclose both characters within single quotation marks (e.g., use ´^H´ for CONTROL-H). Use ´^?´ for DEL and ´^-´ for undefined.

kill **x**   Set the line kill key to **x**. See "erase," above, for conventions.

intr **x**   Set the interrupt key to **x**. See "erase," above, for conventions.

sane   Use this argument to set the terminal parameters to usually acceptable values. The **sane** argument is useful when several stty parameters have changed, making it difficult to use the terminal even to run stty to set things right. If **sane** does not appear to work, try entering CONTROL-J **sane** CONTROL-J.

werase **x**   Set the word erase key to **x**. See "erase," above, for conventions.

Transmission Delays

You can specify any one of each of these sets of parameters. Except for 0 (zero), the numbers following the letters do not have special significance but represent a different amount of delay following the transmission of the character (higher numbers correspond to longer delays). Zero always means no delay.

cr0 cr1 cr2 cr3	Set delay following a RETURN.
nl0 nl1	Set delay following a NEWLINE.
tab0 tab1 tab2 tab3	Set delay following a TAB.
ff0 ff1	Set delay following a FORM-FEED.
bs0 bs1	Set delay following a BACKSPACE.
vt0 vt1	Set delay following a vertical tab.

Notes

The **stty** utility affects the terminal attached to its standard input. You can view or change the characteristics of a terminal other than the one you are using by redirecting the input to **stty**. Refer to the following command format.

stty [arguments] < /dev/ttyxx

The **ttyxx** is the filename of the target terminal. You can change the characteristics of a terminal only if you own its device file or if you are Superuser.

Examples

The first example shows **stty** without any arguments, displaying several terminal operation parameters. (Your system may display more or different parameters.) The character following the **erase** = is the erase key, and the one following **kill** = is the line kill key. The **stty** display always encloses these keys in single quotation marks. A ^ preceding a character indicates a CONTROL key. The example shows the erase key set to CONTROL-H and the line kill key set to CONTROL-U.

If **stty** does not display the erase character, it is set to its default, #. If you do not see a kill character, it is set to its default, @.

```
$ stty
speed 1200 baud
erase = '^h'; kill = '^u'
-parenb -nl echo
```

Next, the **ek** argument returns the erase and line kill keys to their default values.

```
$ stty ek
```

The next display verifies the change. The stty utility does not display either the erase character or the line kill character, indicating that they are both set to their default values.

```
$ stty
speed 1200 baud
-parenb -nl echo
```

The next example sets the erase key to CONTROL-H. A ^ followed by an **h** represents the CONTROL character. You can enter either a lower- or uppercase letter.

```
$ stty erase ´ ^h ´
$ stty
speed 1200 baud
erase = ´^H´; kill = ´@´
-parenb -nl echo
```

Below, stty sets the line kill key to CONTROL-X.

```
$ stty kill ´ ^x ´
$ stty
speed 1200 baud
erase = ´^H´; kill = ´^X´
-parenb -nl echo
```

Below, stty turns off TABS so the appropriate number of SPACES is sent to the terminal in place of a TAB. Use this command if a terminal does not automatically expand TABS.

```
$ stty -tabs
```

If you log in and everything that appears on the terminal is in uppercase letters, give the following command and then check the CAPS LOCK key. If it is set, turn it off.

```
$ STTY -LCASE
```

Turn on **lcase** if the terminal you are using cannot display lowercase characters.

tail

Display the last part (tail) of a file.

Format

tail [±[number]options] [file]

Summary

The tail utility displays the last part of a file. It takes its input from the file you specify on the command line or from its standard input.

Arguments

Without a **number** or **option**, tail displays the last ten lines of a file.

If a plus sign precedes the **option**, tail displays blocks, characters, or lines counting from the beginning of the file. If a hyphen precedes the **option**, tail counts from the end of the file. If a **number** precedes the **option**, that value is used in place of ten.

Options

Without any options, tail counts by lines. The options below must follow immediately after the **number** and not be preceded by a hyphen or a SPACE. If **number** is omitted, tail uses a default value of ten.

b **blocks** This option causes tail to count by blocks.

c **characters** This option causes tail to count by characters.

l **lines** This option causes tail to count by lines (default).

f **follow** After copying the last line of the file, tail enters an endless loop. It waits and copies additional lines from the file if the file grows. This is useful for tracking the progress of a process that is running in the background and sending its output to a file. The tail utility continues to wait indefinitely, so you must use the interrupt key or kill command to terminate it.

r **reverse** Display lines in the reverse order.

Examples

The examples are based on the following **lines** file:

tail

```
$ cat lines
line one
line two
line three
line four
line five
line six
line seven
line eight
line nine
line ten
line eleven
```

First, tail displays the last ten lines of the **lines** file (no options).

```
$ tail lines
line two
line three
line four
line five
line six
line seven
line eight
line nine
line ten
line eleven
```

The next example displays the last three lines (**–3,** no option) of the file.

```
$ tail -3 lines
line nine
line ten
line eleven
```

The example below displays the file, starting at line eight (**+8,** no option).

```
$ tail +8 lines
line eight
line nine
line ten
line eleven
```

The next example displays the last six characters in the file (**–6c**). Only five characters are evident (**leven**); the sixth is a NEWLINE.

```
$ tail -6c lines
leven
```

The example below displays the last four lines in the file in reverse order (**–4r**).

```
$ tail −4r lines
line eleven
line ten
line nine
line eight
```

The final example demonstrates the −f option. Below, tail tracks the output of a make command, which is being sent to the file **accounts.out**.

```
$ make accounts > accounts.out &
$ tail −f accounts.out
        cc −c trans.c
        cc −c reports.c
    .
    .
DELETE
$
```

In the example above, using tail with −f has the same effect as running make in the foreground and letting its output go to the terminal; however, using tail has some advantages. First, the output of make is saved in a file. (The output would not be saved if you simply let it go to the terminal.) Also, if you decide to do something else while make is running and you do not have job control, you can kill tail, and the terminal will be free for you to use while make continues in the background. When you are running a large job, such as compiling a large program, you can use tail with the −f option to check on its progress periodically.

tar

Store or retrieve files from an archive file.

Format

tar key[options] [file-list]

Summary

The tar (tape archive) utility can create, add to, list, and retrieve files from an archive file. The archive file is usually stored on tape.

Key

Use only one of the following keys to indicate what type of action you want tar to take. You can modify the action of the key by following it with one or more options. The key and options do not require a leading hyphen.

r   **write**   tar writes the **file-list** to the end of the tape. It leaves existing files intact.

x   **extract**   tar reads the **file-list** from the tape. Without a **file-list**, it reads all the files from the tape. The tar utility attempts to keep the owner, modification time, and access privileges the same as the original file. If tar reads the same file more than once, the later versions of the file overwrite previous versions.

t   **table of contents**   With a **file-list**, tar displays the name of each of the files in the **file-list** each time it occurs on the tape. Without a **file-list**, tar displays the name of each of the files on the tape.

u   **update**   The tar utility adds the files from the **file-list** if they are not already on the tape *or* if they have been modified since they were last written to the tape. Because of the checking it does, this option is slow.

c   **create**   tar creates a new tape, destroying any files that were previously written to the tape. This key implies the **r** key and, after creating a new tape, functions in the same way as **r**, writing the **file-list** to the tape.

Options

You can specify one or more options following the key. The key and options do not require a leading hyphen.

0-7   Use a number from 0 through 7 to indicate a drive other than the default, which is system-dependent (usually 1). If you are using a version of System V newer than Release 2, follow the drive number with **l**, **m**, or **h**, depending on whether the drive is low, medium, or high density.

v   **verbose**   This option lists each file as tar reads or writes it. With the **t** key, this option causes tar to display additional information about each file.

w   **query**   This option asks you for confirmation before reading or writing each file. Respond with **y** if you want tar to take the action. Any other response causes tar not to take the action.

f   **file**   This option causes tar to write to or read from the next argument instead of the tape drive that the system is set up for tar to use. If you give a hyphen as an argument, tar uses the standard input or output.

b   **block**   This option causes tar to use the next argument as a blocking factor for writing a tape. If you do not specify a blocking factor, tar assumes a blocking factor of 1. The largest blocking factor you can use is 20. This option is effective only when you are writing to a raw device. The tar utility automatically determines the blocking factor when it reads a tape. Do not use this option if you will want to update the tape or if you are creating a disk file.

l   **links**   This option causes tar to display messages if it cannot resolve all the links to files it is copying.

L   This option causes tar to follow symbolic links and to include the linked-to files as if they were normal files and directories.

m   **modification time**   When you use this option, tar does not maintain the original modification times of files it is extracting. Instead, it sets the modification time to the time of extraction.

Arguments

If you use the **f** and/or **b** options, the first one or two arguments must correspond to the options you use. Following these arguments (if they are present) is the **file-list** that lists the filenames of the files you want to write out or read in.

You can use ambiguous file references when you write files but not when you read them.

The name of a directory file within the **file-list** references all files and subdirectories within that directory.

Notes

If you write a file using a simple filename, the file will appear in the working directory when you read it back. If you write a file using a relative pathname, it will appear with that relative pathname, starting from the working directory when you read it back. If you use an absolute pathname to write a file, tar reads it back in with the same pathname.

As you read and write files, tar attempts to preserve links between files. Unless you use the l option, tar does not inform you when it fails to maintain a link.

Examples

The following example makes a copy of the **/home/alex** directory, and all files and subdirectories within that directory, on the standard tar tape. The **v** option causes the command to list all the files it writes to the tape as it proceeds. This command erases anything that was already on the tape.

```
$ tar cv /home/alex
a /home/alex/letter 5 blocks
a /home/alex/memo 11 blocks
a /home/alex/notes 27 blocks
.
.
```

In the next example, the same directory is saved on the tape on device **/dev/rmt1** with a blocking factor of 10. Without the **v** option, tar does not display the list of files it is writing to tape. This command runs in the background and displays its only message after the shell issues a new prompt.

```
$ tar cbf 10 /dev/rmt1 /home/alex &
3452
$ blocking factor = 10
```

The next command displays the table of contents of the tape on device **/dev/rmt1**.

```
$ tar tvf /dev/rmt1
Tar: blocksize = 10
rw-rw-rw-201/0     4720   Jul 25 6:59 1990 /home/alex/letter
rw-rw-rw-201/0    10420   Jul 25 6:59 1990 /home/alex/memo
rw-rw-rw-201/0    27471   Jul 25 6:59 1990 /home/alex/notes
.
.
```

tee

Copy the standard input to the standard output and one or more files.

Format

tee [options] file-list

Summary

The **tee** utility copies its standard input to its standard output *and* to one or more files you specify on the command line.

Arguments

The **file-list** contains the pathnames of files that receive output from **tee**.

Options

Without any options, **tee** overwrites the output files if they exist and responds to interrupts.

-a   **append**   This option causes **tee** to append output to files (not overwrite them).

-i   **ignore interrupts**   With this option, **tee** does not respond to interrupts.

Example

In the following example, a pipe sends the output from make to **tee**, which copies it to its standard output and the file **accounts.out**. The copy that goes to its standard output appears on the screen. The cat utility displays the copy that was sent to the file.

```
$ make accounts | tee accounts.out
        cc -c trans.c
        cc -c reports.c
  .
  .
  .
$ cat accounts.out
        cc -c trans.c
        cc -c reports.c
  .
  .
  .
```

Refer to page 607 for a similar example that uses **tail -f** rather than **tee**.

test

Evaluate an expression.

Format

test expression
[expression]

Summary

The **test** command evaluates an expression and returns a condition code indicating that the expression is either true (= 0) or false (not = 0).

As the second format above shows, instead of using the word **test** when you use the **test** command, you can use square brackets around the expression ([]).

Arguments

The **expression** contains one or more criteria (see the following list) that **test** evaluates. A **–a** separating two criteria is a logical AND operator: Both criteria must be true for **test** to return a condition code of *true*. A **–o** is a logical OR operator. When **–o** separates two criteria, one or the other (or both) of the criteria must be true in order for **test** to return a condition code of *true*.

You can negate any criterion by preceding it with an exclamation point (!). You can group criteria with parentheses. If there are no parentheses, **–a** takes precedence over **–o**, and **test** evaluates operators of equal precedence from left to right.

Within the **expression**, you must quote special characters, such as parentheses, so that the shell does not interpret them but passes them on to **test**.

Because each element (such as a criterion, string, or variable) within the **expression** is a separate argument, you must separate each element from other elements with a SPACE.

Following is a list of criteria you can use within the **expression**.

Criteria

string   This criterion is true if the **string** is not a null string.

–n string   This criterion is true if the **string** has a length greater than zero.

–z string   This criterion is true if the **string** has a length of zero.

string1 = string2   This criterion is true if **string1** is equal to **string2**.

string1 != string2   This criterion is true if **string1** is not equal to **string2**.

int1 relop **int2**   This criterion is true if integer **int1** has the specified algebraic relationship to integer **int2**. The **relop** is a relational operator from the following list.

Relop	Description
-gt	greater than
-ge	greater than or equal to
-eq	equal to
-ne	not equal to
-le	less than or equal to
-lt	less than

-b filename   This criterion is true if the file named **filename** exists and is a block special file.

-c filename   This criterion is true if the file named **filename** exists and is a character special file.

-d filename   This criterion is true if the file named **filename** exists and is a directory.

-f filename   This criterion is true if the file named **filename** exists and is an ordinary file.

-g filename   This criterion is true if the file named **filename** exists and its set group ID bit is set.

-h filename   This criterion is true if the file named **filename** exists and is a symbolic link.

-k filename   This criterion is true if the file named **filename** exists and its sticky bit is set.

-p filename   This criterion is true if the file named **filename** exists and is a named pipe.

-r filename   This criterion is true if the file named **filename** exists and you have read access permission to it.

-s filename   This criterion is true if the file named **filename** exists and contains information (has a size greater than 0 bytes).

-t **file-descriptor**   This criterion is true if the open file with the file descriptor number **file-descriptor** is associated with a terminal. If you do not specify a **file-descriptor**, test assumes number 1 (standard output). The **file-descriptor** for standard input is 0 and for standard error is 2.

-u **filename**   This criterion is true if the file named **filename** exists and its set user ID bit is set.

-w **filename**   This criterion is true if the file named **filename** exists and you have write access permission to it.

-x **filename**   This criterion is true if the file named **filename** exists and you have execute access permission to it.

Notes

The test command is built into the Bourne, Job, and Korn Shells.

Examples

The following examples show how to use the test utility in Bourne Shell scripts. Although test will work from a command line, it is more commonly used in shell scripts to test input or verify access to a file.

The first two examples show incomplete shell scripts. They are not complete because they do not test for upper- as well as lowercase input or inappropriate responses and do not acknowledge more than one response.

The first example prompts the user, reads a line of input into the user variable **user_input**, and uses test to see if the user variable **user_input** matches the quoted string yes. Refer to Chapter 8 for more information on variables, read, and If.

```
$ cat user_in
echo "Input yes or no: \c"
read user_input
if [ "$user_input" = yes ]
    then
        echo You input yes.
fi
```

The next example prompts the user for a filename and then uses test to see if the user has read access permission (-r) for the file *and* (-a) if the file contains information (-s).

test

```
$ cat validate
echo "Enter filename: \c"
read filename
if [ -r "$filename" -a -s "$filename" ]
    then
        echo File $filename exists and contains information.
        echo You have read access permission to the file.
fi
```

Without a number, the –t criterion assumes a value of 1 for the file descriptor and causes **test** to determine whether the process running **test** is sending output to a terminal. The **test** utility returns a value of *true* (**0**) if the process is sending its output to a terminal. Following is a listing of the shell script **term** that runs **test**.

```
$ cat term
test -t
echo "This program is (=0) or is not (=1)
sending its output to a terminal:" $?
```

First, **term** is run with the output going to the terminal; that is, the output is not redirected to a file. The **test** utility returns a 0. The shell stores this value in the shell variable that records the condition code of the last process, **$?**. The **echo** utility displays this value.

```
$ term
This program is (=0) or is not (=1)
sending its output to a terminal: 0
```

The next example runs **term** and redirects the output to a file. The listing of the file **temp** shows that **test** returned a 1, indicating that its output was not going to a terminal.

```
$ term > temp
$ cat temp
This program is (=0) or is not (=1)
sending its output to a terminal: 1
```

touch

Update a file's modification time.

Format

touch [options] [time] file-list

Summary

The touch utility updates the time a file was last accessed and the time it was last modified, allowing you to specify the new access and modification times. This utility is frequently used with the make utility.

Arguments

The **file-list** contains the pathnames of the files touch is to update.

You can use the **time** argument to specify the new date and time. The **time** has the following format:

nnddhhmm[yy]

The **nn** is the number of the month (01-12), **dd** is the day of the month (01-31), **hh** is the hour based on a 24-hour clock (00-23), **mm** is the minutes (00-59), and **yy** is optional and specifies the last two digits of the year. If you do not specify a year, touch assumes the year has not changed. If you do not specify a **time**, touch uses the current time.

Options

When you do not specify the –c option, touch creates the file if it does not exist.

–c   **no create**   Do not create the file if it does not already exist.

When you do not specify the **–a** or **–m** option, touch updates both the access and modification times.

–a   **access time**   When you use this option, touch updates the access time only, leaving the modification time unchanged.

–m   **modification time**   This option causes touch to update the modification time only, leaving the access time unchanged.

Examples

The following examples demonstrate how touch functions. The first commands show touch updating an existing file. The ls utility with the –l option displays the modification time of the file. The last three command lines show touch creating a file.

```
$ ls -l program.c
-rw-r--r-- 1 jenny pubs      136   Nov   7 16:48 program.c
$ touch program.c
$ ls -l program.c
-rw-r--r-- 1 jenny pubs      136   Jul 25 16:33 program.c
$ ls -l read.c
read.c not found
$ touch read.c
$ ls -l read.c
-rw-r--r-- 1 jenny pubs        0   Jul 25 16:35 read.c
```

tr

Replace specified characters.

Format

tr [option] [string1 [string2]]

Summary

The **tr** utility reads its standard input and translates each character in **string1** to the corresponding character in **string2**.

Arguments

The **tr** utility is typically used with two arguments, **string1** and **string2**. The position of each character in the two strings is important; **tr** replaces each character from **string1** with the corresponding character in **string2**.

With one argument, **string1,** and an option (see below), **tr** can be used to delete the characters specified in **string1**.

With no arguments, **tr** simply copies its standard input to its standard output.

Options

-d   **delete**   This option causes **tr** to delete characters that match those specified in **string1**.

-s   **squeeze**   This option causes **tr** to reduce sequences of multiple identical characters in **string2** to single occurrences.

Examples

You can specify a range of characters by hyphenating them and enclosing them in square brackets. The two command lines in the following example produce the same result.

```
$ echo abcdef | tr 'abcdef' 'xyzabc'
xyzabc
$ echo abcdef | tr '[a-c][d-f]' '[x-z][a-c]'
xyzabc
```

The next example demonstrates a popular method for disguising text, often called "rotate 13" (because it replaces the first letter of the alphabet with the 13th, the second with the 14th, and so forth).

```
$ echo The punchline of the joke is ... |
> tr '[A-M][N-Z][a-m][n-z]' '[N-Z][A-M][n-z][a-m]'
Gur chapuyvar bs gur wbxr vf ...
```

To make the text intelligible again, reverse the order of the arguments to tr.

```
$ echo Gur chapuyvar bs gur wbxr vf ... |
> tr '[N-Z][A-M][n-z][a-m]' '[A-M][N-Z][a-m][n-z]'
The punchline of the joke is ...
```

The **-d** option causes tr to delete selected characters.

```
$ echo If you can read this, you can spot the missing vowels! |
> tr -d 'aeiou'
If y cn rd ths, y cn spt th mssng vwls!
```

In the following example tr is used to replace characters and reduce pairs of identical characters to single characters.

```
$ echo tennessee | tr -s 'tnse' 'srne'
serene
```

tty

Display the terminal pathname.

Format

tty [option]

Summary

The tty utility displays the pathname of its standard input file if it is a terminal. The exit status of tty is 0 if the standard input file is a terminal, and 1 if it is not.

Arguments

There are no arguments.

Options

-s   **silent** This option causes tty not to print anything. The exit status of tty is still set, however.

Notes

If its standard input is not a terminal, tty displays not a tty.

Example

The following example illustrates the use of tty.

```
$ tty
/dev/tty11
$ echo $?
0
$ tty < memo
not a tty
$ echo $?
1
```

umask

Establish file-creation permissions mask.

Format

umask [mask]

Summary

The umask command specifies a mask that the system uses to set up access permissions when you create a file.

Arguments

The **mask** is a three-digit octal number, with each digit corresponding to permissions for the owner of the file, members of the group the file is associated with, and everyone else. When you create a file, the system subtracts these numbers from the numbers corresponding to the access permissions the system would otherwise assign to the file. The result is three octal numbers that specify the access permissions for the file. (Refer to the chmod utility in Part II for a complete description and examples of these numbers.)

Without any arguments, umask displays the file-creation permissions **mask**.

Options

There are no options.

Notes

A umask command generally appears in a **.profile** or **.login** file. The umask command is built into the Bourne, C, and Korn Shells.

Example

The following command sets the file-creation permissions mask to **066**. The command has the effect of removing read and write permission for members of the group the file is associated with and everyone else. It leaves the owner's permissions as the system specifies. If the system would otherwise create a file with a permission value of **777** (read, write, and execute access for owner, group, and everyone else), it will now create the file with **711** (all permissions for the owner and only execute permission for group and everyone else).

```
$ umask 066
```

uniq

Display lines of a file that are unique.

Format

uniq [options] [−fields] [+characters] [input-file] [output-file]

Summary

The uniq utility displays a file, removing all but one copy of successive repeated lines. If the file has been sorted (refer to the sort utility), uniq ensures that no two lines that it displays are the same.

The uniq utility takes its input from a file you specify on the command line or from its standard input. Unless you specify the output file on the command line, uniq sends its output to its standard output.

Arguments

In the following description, a *field* is any sequence of characters not containing white space (any combination of SPACES and TABS). Fields are bounded by white space or the beginning or end of a line.

The **−fields** is a number preceded by a hyphen and causes uniq to ignore the first specified number of blank-separated fields of each line. When you use this argument, uniq bases its comparison on the remainder of the line.

The **+characters** is a number preceded by a plus sign and causes uniq to ignore the first specified number of characters of each line. If you also use **−fields**, uniq ignores the number of characters you specify after the end of the last field that it ignores. The **+characters** does *not* ignore blanks following the last ignored field. You must take these blanks into account when you specify the number of characters to ignore.

You can specify the **input-file** on the command line. If you do not specify it, uniq uses its standard input.

You can specify the **output-file** on the command line. If you do not specify it, uniq uses its standard output.

Options

−c   **count**   This option causes uniq to precede each line with the number of occurrences of the line in the input file.

−d   **duplicate lines**   This option causes uniq to display only lines that are repeated.

−u   **unique lines**   This option causes uniq to display only lines that are *not* repeated.

Examples

These examples assume the file named **test** in the working directory contains the following text.

```
$ cat test
boy took bat home
boy took bat home
girl took bat home
dog brought hat home
dog brought hat home
dog brought hat home
```

Without any options, uniq removes all but one copy of successive repeated lines.

```
$ uniq test
boy took bat home
girl took bat home
dog brought hat home
```

The **–c** option displays the number of consecutive occurrences of each line in the file.

```
$ uniq -c test
   2 boy took bat home
   1 girl took bat home
   3 dog brought hat home
```

The **–d** option displays only lines that are consecutively repeated in the file.

```
$ uniq -d test
boy took bat home
dog brought hat home
```

The **–u** option displays only lines that are *not* consecutively repeated in the file.

```
$ uniq -u test
girl took bat home
```

Below, the **–fields** argument (**–1**) skips the first field in each line, causing the lines that begin with boy and the one that begins with girl to appear to be consecutive repeated lines. The uniq utility displays only one occurrence of these lines.

```
$ uniq -1 test
boy took bat home
dog brought hat home
```

The final example uses both the **–fields** and **+characters** arguments (–2 and +2) to first skip two fields and then skip two characters. The two characters this command skips include the SPACE that separates the second and third fields and the first character of the third field. Ignoring these characters, all the lines appear to be consecutive repeated lines containing the string at home. The uniq utility displays only the first of these lines.

```
$ uniq -2 +2 test
boy took bat home
```

wc

Display the number of lines, words, and characters in a file.

Format

wc [options] file-list

Summary

The wc utility displays the number of lines, words, and characters contained in one or more files. If you specify more than one file on the command line, wc displays totals for each file and totals for the group of files.

The wc utility takes its input from files you specify on the command line or from its standard input.

Arguments

The **file-list** contains the pathnames of one or more files that wc analyzes.

Options

-c   **characters**   This option causes wc to display only the number of characters in the file.

-l   **lines**   This option causes wc to display only the number of lines (that is, NEWLINE characters) in the file.

-w   **words**   This option causes wc to display only the number of words in the file.

Notes

A word is a sequence of characters bounded by SPACES, TABS, NEWLINES, or a combination of these.

Examples

The following command line displays an analysis of the file named **memo**. The numbers represent the number of lines, words, and characters in the file.

```
$ wc memo
      5          31          146 memo
```

The next command displays the number of lines and words in three files. The line at the bottom, with the word total in the right column, contains the sum of each column.

```
$ wc -lw memo1 memo2 memo3
        10      62 memo1
        12      74 memo2
        12      68 memo3
        34     204 total
```

who

Display names of users.

Format

who [options]
who am i

Summary

The who utility displays the names of users currently logged in, together with their terminal device numbers, the times they logged in, and other information.

Arguments

When given the two arguments **am i**, who displays the login name of the user who is logged in at the terminal the command is given on, the terminal device number, and the time the user logged in.

Options

–b   **boot**   This option displays the time that the system was last booted.

–H   **header**   This option precedes the output from who with a header.

–l   **login**   This option lists the lines that are waiting for users to log in.

–q   **quick**   This option displays the number of users logged in on the system.

–s   **standard**   This option displays the same list who displays when you do not use any options.

–t   **time**   This option displays the time that the system clock was last changed.

–T   This option is the same as **–u**, but it also includes the **state** field. A + in the **state** field indicates that anyone can write to the terminal, and a – indicates that only the Superuser can write to the terminal. A **?** indicates that the line is bad.

–u   **users**   This option gives a complete listing of users who are logged in.

Description

The format of a line that who displays is shown below.

name [state] line time [activity] [PID] [comment] [exit]

The **name** is the login name of the user. The **state** is the state of the terminal (see the **–T** option). The **line** is the device number associated with the line on which the user is logged in. The **time** is the date and time the user logged in. The **activity** is the length of time since the terminal was last used. A period indicates that the terminal was used within the last minute, and an entry of **old** indicates that the terminal has not been used for at least 24 hours. The **PID** is the process ID number of the user's login shell. The **comment** is the comment field associated with the line as found in the **/etc/inittab** file. The **exit** field contains the termination and exit values of any process that died and was not respawned by init. Refer to Chapter 11 for a discussion of init.

Notes

The finger utility, included with System V Release 4, provides information similar to the information who provides. By default, the finger utility displays information about each user currently logged in, including the user's login name, full name, terminal name, how long the terminal has been idle, and the time the user logged in. The finger utility can also be used over a network to display information about users on a remote system. For more information about finger, refer to the manuals that come with your system.

Examples

The following examples demonstrate the use of the who utility.

```
$ who
jenny         tty01     Jul  25  11:01
alex          tty11     Jul  25  18:11

$ who  am  i
alex          tty11     Jul  25  18:11


$ who  -uH
NAME          LINE      TIME                    IDLE      PID    COMMENTS
jenny         tty01     Jul  25  11:01          .         1003
alex          tty11     Jul  25  18:11          .         1427
```

write

Send a message to another user.

Format

write destination-user [tty-name]

Summary

You and another user can use **write** to establish two-way communication. Both of you must execute the **write** utility, each specifying the other user's login name as the **destination-user**. The **write** utility then copies text, on a line-by-line basis, from each terminal to the other.

When you execute the **write** utility, a message appears on the **destination-user**'s terminal indicating that you are about to transmit a message.

When you want to stop communicating with the other user, press CONTROL-D once at the start of a line to return to the shell. The other user must do the same.

Arguments

The **destination-user** is the login name of the user you are sending a message to. The **tty-name** can be used as a second argument, after the user name, to resolve ambiguities if the **destination-user** is logged in on more than one terminal.

Options

There are no options.

Notes

It may be helpful to set up a protocol for carrying on communication when you use **write**. Try ending each message with **o** for "over" and ending the transmission with **oo** for "over and out." This gives each user time to think and enter a complete message without the other user wondering whether the first user is finished.

While you are using **write**, any line beginning with an exclamation point causes **write** to pass the line, without the exclamation point, to the shell for execution. The other user does not see the command line or the shell output.

Each user controls permission to write to that user's terminal. Refer to the **mesg** utility.

Another utility, talk, is included with System V Release 4. It allows you to have a two-way conversation with another user if you both have display terminals. The talk utility divides the users' screens into two windows and displays the statements of the two users in different windows on both screens. Both users can type simultaneously. Users generally find it easier to hold a conversation with talk than with write. The talk utility can also be used to communicate with a user on a remote system over a network. For more information about talk, refer to the manuals that come with your system.

Example

Refer to Chapter 3 for a tutorial example of write.

APPENDIX

A

INTRODUCTION TO THE KORN SHELL

The Korn Shell includes features of the two earlier shells, the Bourne Shell and the C Shell. It provides both a programming language like the Bourne Shell and many of the interactive features of the C Shell. The Korn Shell implements the hallmark features of the C Shell that make it popular as an interactive command interpreter—aliases, job control, and the history mechanism. It also introduces several new user interface features, including command-line editing.

Because the Korn Shell is designed so that scripts written for the Bourne Shell will run under it without modification, the Korn Shell includes nearly all the features of the Bourne Shell. In addition, the Korn Shell provides report formatting capabilities and several other features that improve its usefulness as a programming language. Also, scripts typically run more quickly under the Korn Shell than under the Bourne Shell because more commands are built in.

This appendix describes the unique characteristics of the Korn Shell. It supplements Chapter 8, "The Bourne Shell," and Chapter 9, "The C Shell." Because job control under the Korn Shell is virtually identical to job control under the C Shell, it is not described here (refer to "Job Control" in Chapter 9). This appendix introduces the most interesting features of the Korn Shell so that you can start using them.

ENTERING AND LEAVING THE KORN SHELL

If you want to use the Korn Shell as your login shell, your system administrator can set up the **/etc/passwd** file so that you will be using the Korn Shell whenever you log in.

If you do not want to log directly into the Korn Shell, use the command **ksh** to start a Korn Shell after you log in.

A dollar sign ($) is the default prompt for the Korn Shell. To change your prompt, set the **PS1** variable. An exclamation point in the value of the **PS1** variable will cause the Korn Shell to include the current command number in the prompt. Because the Korn Shell has a history mechanism and you can access previous commands by event number, it is useful to display the event number in the prompt. The syntax used in setting Korn Shell variables is the same as the syntax the Bourne Shell uses.

```
$ PS1=' ! $ '
2 $
```

The Korn Shell provides a convenient mechanism for including the working directory in your prompt—the Korn Shell automatically sets the **PWD** variable to the pathname of the working directory. The Korn Shell evaluates the **PS1** variable each time it presents the prompt, so if you include the **PWD** variable in the prompt, it will identify the working directory.

Give the following command to set your prompt to display the pathname of the working directory as well as the event number:

```
$ PS1=' ! $PWD> '
2 /home/alex/literature>
```

You must surround the value of **PS1** with single quotation marks to prevent the Korn Shell from substituting the value of the **PWD** variable when you initially set **PS1**. If you use double quotation marks instead of single quotation marks, the Korn Shell will replace $PWD with its value when you initially set the prompt, and consequently the prompt will not change when you change directories.

To leave the Korn Shell, type **exit** or CONTROL-D.

RUNNING KORN SHELL SCRIPTS

To execute a Korn Shell script, give a command such as the following:

```
3 $ ksh script_name
```

This command will work whether or not you are interacting with the Korn Shell when you execute it. The following command works if you are using the Korn Shell as your command interpreter, assuming you have execute permission for a file called **script_name**:

```
4 $ script_name
```

On some systems, another way to ensure that a script will be run by the Korn Shell is to put the following statement on the first line of the script:

```
#!/usr/bin/ksh
```

If the Korn Shell on your system is located in a directory other than **/usr/bin**, you will need to use the appropriate pathname in place of **/usr/bin/ksh**.

COMMAND-LINE EDITING

The Korn Shell allows you to edit the current command line. If you make a mistake, you do not need to back up to the point of the mistake and reenter the command from there or press the line kill key and start over. You can use one of the built-in editors to edit the command line. You can also access and edit previous command lines stored in your history file. Refer to "History" below.

The Korn Shell provides two built-in editors: one is similar to vi, and the second is similar to an editor called emacs. Depending on how the Korn Shell was set up on your system, you may be able to use one, both, or neither of the editors. Only the built-in vi editor is described in this appendix.

To set up your environment so that you can use the built-in vi editor, use the set command below. The −o option enables you to set Korn Shell options, and +o unsets them.

```
9 $ set −o vi
```

Alternatively, you can set the **VISUAL** or the **EDITOR** variable to the pathname of vi. If you set both variables, **VISUAL** will take precedence over **EDITOR**.

```
9 $ VISUAL=/usr/bin/vi
```

```
9 $ EDITOR=/usr/bin/vi
```

After you give one of the three commands above, when you are entering Korn Shell commands you will be in Input Mode. It will not seem any different than entering commands with the Bourne Shell. When you press RETURN to end a command line, the Korn Shell executes the command as usual.

The difference comes when you make a mistake on a command line. If you press ESCAPE to enter Command Mode, you can use most vi commands that you would normally use to edit a line of text. You can use cursor positioning commands, such as the LEFT ARROW and RIGHT ARROW keys (or **h** and **l**). You can also modify the command line using commands such as **x** (delete character), **r** (replace character), and **C** (change to end of line). To return to Input Mode, you can use an Insert (**i**, **I**), Append (**a**, **A**), or Replace command (**R**). You do not have to return to Input Mode to run the command—just press RETURN.

In Command Mode, you can also use several commands that are not included in the vi utility. For example, you can type an equal sign (=) while the cursor is on a word, and the built-in vi editor will list the pathnames that would match the current word if an asterisk were appended to it. Here, the = command is used to expand the word **tab**:

```
10 $ cat tab → = → cat tab
                 1) table
                 2) tab5
```

If you use an asterisk (*) instead of the equal sign, the built-in vi editor appends an asterisk to the current word and generates a list of filenames:

```
10 $ cat tab → * → cat table tab5
```

After it fills in the filenames, the built-in vi editor goes into Input Mode. If no filenames match, the built-in vi editor will cause your terminal to beep (some terminals flash instead of beep).

After making corrections to the command line, press RETURN to execute the command. RETURN causes the Korn Shell to execute the command regardless of whether you are in Command Mode or Input Mode and regardless of where the cursor is on the command line. At the next prompt, you will be back in Input Mode.

The built-in vi editor commands are listed in the Summary at the end of this appendix.

HISTORY

The Korn Shell, like the C Shell, keeps a history of recently executed commands. However, the Korn Shell commands you use to access the history list are different from the C Shell commands. You can select, edit, and reexecute any command in the history list from the current or a previous login session.

If it is set, the **HISTSIZE** variable determines the number of commands that are saved in the history list. If it is not set, 128 commands are saved. The **HIST-FILE** variable identifies the file the list is stored in. If **HISTFILE** is not set, the history file will be kept in a file called **.sh_history** in your home directory.

Some versions of the Korn Shell keep incrementing the event number from one login session to the next. Consequently, the event numbers eventually become very large. To cause the history mechanism to start over with number 1, remove the history file. The next time you log in, the first prompt will be event 1, and so forth. Of course, one drawback of this approach is that events from previous sessions are no longer available in the history file.

To access and edit any of the commands in your history file, you can use either the built-in vi editor, the built-in emacs editor, or the built-in command fc. This section describes the built-in vi editor and the fc command.

Using the Built-In vi Editor on Previous Commands

When you are using the built-in vi editor and are in Command Mode, you can access previous commands using several vi commands that move the cursor up and down. It is as if you are using vi with a screen that has only one line on it—if you use a command to move up one line, that line will appear on your screen. If you use the **k** command to move up one line, you will access the previous command. Then, if you use the **j** command to move down one line, you will be back to the original command.

You can search through the history list to find the most recent command that contains a specific string of text. Press the forward slash (**/**) key followed by a *Search String* to find the most recent command containing a string that matches the Search String. Use a question mark (**?**) in place of the forward slash to access the next command containing the string. The forward slash and question mark search in the opposite directions of the corresponding commands in the vi utility. Also, unlike the Search Strings the vi utility uses, these Search Strings cannot contain regular expressions.

To access an event in the history list by event number, enter the number followed by a **G**. Use **G** without a number to access the oldest command available in the history list. (This is the opposite of what **G** does in the vi utility.)

Once the command you want to reexecute is on the command line, you can edit it or press RETURN to execute it.

Using the fc Command

The built-in command fc (fix command) enables you to display the history file as well as to edit and reexecute previous commands. It provides many of the same capabilities as the built-in editors.

Viewing the History List.   When it is called with the –l option, fc displays commands from the history file on the standard output. By default, **fc –l** lists the 16 most recent commands in a numbered list.

```
28 $ fc -l
13       vi memo.0490
14       lp memo.0490
15       mv memo.0490 memo.041190
16       cd
17       view calendar
18       cd correspondence
19       vi letter.adams01
20       spell letter.adams01
21       nroff letter.adams01 > adams.out
22       more adams.out
23       lp adams.out
24       rm adams.out
25       cd ../memos
26       ls
27       rm *0486
28       fc -l
```

Because the Korn Shell sets up a system-wide alias, **history,** for the **fc –l** command, you can also use the **history** command to print the history list.

The **fc** command can take one or two arguments when it is used with the **–l** option. The arguments specify a part of the history list to be displayed. The format of this command is shown below.

fc –l first [last]

The **fc** command lists commands beginning with the most recent event that matches the **first** argument. The argument can be either the number of the event, the first few characters of the command line, or a negative number (which is taken to be the *n*th previous command). The next command displays the history list beginning with event 17.

```
29 $ fc -l 17
17       view calendar
18       cd correspondence
19       vi letter.adams01
20       spell letter.adams01
21       nroff letter.adams01 > adams.out
22       more adams.out
23       lp adams.out
24       rm adams.out
25       cd ../memos
26       ls
27       rm *0486
28       fc -l
29       fc -l 17
```

If you give fc a second argument, it prints out all commands from the most recent event that matches the first argument to the most recent event that matches the second. The following command lists the most recent event that began with the string view through the most recent command line that began with the letters sp:

```
30 $ fc -l view sp
17      view calendar
18      cd correspondence
19      vi letter.adams01
20      spell letter.adams01
```

To list a single command from the history file, use the same identifier for the first and second arguments. The following command lists event 17:

```
31 $ fc -l 17 17
17      view calendar
```

Editing and Reexecuting Previous Commands.   You can use the fc command to edit and reexecute previous commands. The format of this usage of fc is shown below.

fc [–e editor] [first [last]]

When you call fc with the –e option followed by the name of an editor, fc will call up the editor with commands in the Work Buffer. Without **first** and **last**, fc defaults to the most recent command. The next example invokes the vi editor to edit the most recent command:

```
32 $ fc -e vi
```

The fc command does not use the Korn Shell's built-in vi editor—it uses the vi utility described in Chapter 6. If you set the **FCEDIT** variable, you do not need to use the –e option to specify an editor on the command line.

```
33 $ FCEDIT=/usr/bin/vi
34 $ export FCEDIT
35 $ fc
```

If you call fc with a single argument, it will invoke the editor to allow you to work on the specified command. The next example starts vi with command 21 in the Work Buffer. When you exit from vi, the Korn Shell automatically executes the command.

```
36 $ fc 21
```

Again, you can identify commands with numbers or by specifying the first few characters of the command name. The next example calls the editor to work on the most recent event that begins with the letters **vi** through event number 22:

```
37 $ fc vi 22
```

When you use the editor to change a series of commands, or when you call the editor to work on one command and then add other commands, the Korn Shell treats the entire set of commands as one event. That is, if you edit a series of commands (as shown above) and execute them, they will be listed as a single new event in the history list.

Reexecuting Previous Commands Without Calling the Editor.   You can reexecute previous commands without going into the editor. If you call fc with – as the name of the editor, it skips the editing phase and reexecutes the command. The following example reexecutes event 23:

```
38 $ fc −e − 23
lp adams.out
```

The Korn Shell sets up a system-wide alias, **r**, that you can use instead of the above command. The following example has the same effect as the one above:

```
39 $ r 23
lp adams.out
```

When you use either one of the two previous examples, you can tell the fc command to substitute one string for another. The next example substitutes the string **john** for the string **adams** in event 20:

```
40 $ r adams=john 20
spell letter.john01
```

You can use a positive or negative number or a string as an event identifier. Without the event identifier, **r** performs the substitution on the previous event.

TILDE (~) SUBSTITUTION

The Korn Shell provides the tilde expansion feature of the C Shell, but with some added capabilities. As you can with the C Shell, you can use the tilde (~) by itself on the command line to represent your home directory. Also, you can use ~ followed by a user's login name to represent the home directory of that user.

The additional capabilities are provided by ~+ and ~-. The ~+ string expands to the pathname of the working directory, and ~- expands to the pathname of the previous working directory.

ALIASES

The Korn Shell provides aliases that are similar to C Shell aliases, although Korn Shell aliases have a different syntax, some additional features, and they do not allow arguments. Use a Korn Shell function if you need to use arguments. Refer to the description of Bourne Shell functions in Chapter 8. (Korn Shell functions are very similar to Bourne Shell functions.)

The format of the alias command used for establishing an alias is shown below.

alias [–x] name=command

The **x** option causes alias to export the alias so that it will be accessible to child processes. Even exported aliases are not available after you log out and then log in again, so users typically establish aliases in one of the Korn Shell startup files. Refer to "Startup Files," below.

The next example creates an exported alias for a chmod command:

```
53 $ alias -x xp=´ chmod +x ´
54 $ xp script_name
```

You can use the **–t** option to alias to create a *tracked alias* as shown here:

alias –t name

Tracked aliases are to the Korn Shell what the hashing mechanism is to the C Shell. After you set up a tracked alias for a command, the next time you invoke the command, alias will substitute the full pathname for the command. On subsequent executions of the command, the shell uses the full pathname, which is more efficient since it avoids a path search. Later, if you change the **PATH** variable, all tracked aliases will become undefined. Then the next time you use each alias, its pathname will be reestablished.

The built-in command **set** has an option, **trackall**, that causes the Korn Shell to create a tracked alias for each command that you enter. Users typically use this option rather than setting up tracked aliases for individual commands.

```
55 $ set -o trackall
```

When you call it with no arguments, the Korn Shell's alias lists all the aliases that are currently set, as the C Shell alias command does. Also, you can use the first of the following commands to list all exported aliases, or use the second command to list all tracked aliases:

```
56 $ alias -x
 .
 .
 .
57 $ alias -t
 .
 .
 .
```

To remove an alias, use the unalias command followed by the alias name. The following example removes the alias **delete**:

```
58 $ unalias delete
```

STARTUP FILES

The Korn Shell uses all the environment variables used by the Bourne Shell as well as several others. These variables establish characteristics of your environment, such as what editor you will use for command-line editing and what editor the fc command will use. These variables should be set up, along with commands that establish other characteristics of the Korn Shell environment, in one of the Korn Shell's startup files.

Like the Bourne Shell, the Korn Shell reads and executes **/etc/profile** and the **.profile** file in your home directory when you log in. The Korn Shell can also execute another file whenever a new shell begins execution. This file will be run only if the **ENV** variable has been set to its filename and it is a readable file. Users typically name this file **.kshrc** because it is analogous to the C Shell's **.cshrc** file.

How you use the startup files depends on whether the Korn Shell is your login shell. If it is your login shell, you can use the **.profile** file to set up Korn Shell variables. Be sure to use the export command to make the variables available to child processes. In your **.profile** file you should also establish your erase and line kill keys and set up the same variables you would set up for the Bourne Shell—**CDPATH, PATH, PS1, PS2, TERM**, and so forth—unless these are set in **/etc/profile**. The Korn Shell uses the **COLUMNS** variable, which corresponds to the number of columns on your screen, rather than **TERM**. By default it is set to 80; you should set it if the number of columns on your screen is not 80. Even though the Korn Shell does not use **TERM**, you should still set it because many utilities, such as vi, use it.

You should set options to the **set** command and define aliases and functions in the file specified by **ENV**. You can define functions in the same way you define Bourne Shell functions. You can also export functions, just as you can export aliases, to make them accessible to child processes. To export a function, use a command such as the following. The **typeset** command is described on page 642.

```
76 $ typeset -xf function-name
```

If the Korn Shell is not your login shell, you should set the variables that are specific to the Korn Shell in the file specified by **ENV** rather than in **.profile** since the Korn Shell will not execute **.profile** when you invoke it. However, you must set and export the **ENV** variable in either the **.login** or **.profile** file, depending on whether your login shell is the Bourne Shell or the C Shell. This variable tells the Korn Shell what file to execute whenever a Korn Shell is executed. Use the file specified by **ENV** to set the rest of the Korn Shell variables and define aliases, functions, and options to the **set** command.

When you start up the Korn Shell, it inherits the environment variables that were set by the previous shell. You need to reset variables such as **SHELL** and **PS1** that should have different values while you are using the Korn Shell. Set and export them in the file specified by **ENV**.

Following is a list of variables you should set in one of the startup files:

COLUMNS   This variable identifies the number of columns on your screen. Its default value is 80.

ENV   This variable identifies the file that will be executed each time a new shell is started up.

FCEDIT   This variable identifies the editor that the **fc** command uses.

HISTFILE   This variable identifies the file used to store the history list. If **HISTFILE** is not set, the Korn Shell uses **.sh_history** in the user's home directory.

HISTSIZE   This variable identifies the number of commands that the Korn Shell keeps in the history list. If **HISTSIZE** is not set, the Korn Shell keeps 128 commands.

VISUAL   This variable determines what editor will be used for command-line editing. It must end in the characters **vi**, **emacs**, or **gmacs**. If it is not set, the Korn Shell uses the value of the **EDITOR** variable.

Sample **.profile** and **.kshrc** files follow:

```
77 $ cat .profile
CDPATH=:$HOME
ENV=$HOME/.kshrc
FCEDIT=/usr/bin/vi
HISTFILE=$HOME/.ksh_hist
HISTSIZE=100
PATH=/usr/bin:/usr/sbin:$HOME/bin:
PS1='! $PWD> '
SHELL=/usr/bin/ksh
TERM=vt100
VISUAL=/usr/bin/vi
TZ=PST8PDT
export CDPATH ENV FCEDIT HISTSIZE HISTFILE
export PATH PS1 SHELL TERM VISUAL TZ
stty -parity erase ^H kill ^U

78 $ cat .kshrc
set -o trackall
alias -x more=m
alias -x history=h
```

BUILT-IN COMMANDS

Besides the built-in commands alias and fc, the Korn Shell has all the built-ins the Bourne Shell provides as well as several others. This section describes the most useful of these commands.

The typeset Command

You can use the typeset command to assign attributes to Korn Shell variables. Two of these attributes, readonly and export, are available with the Bourne Shell. Other Korn Shell attributes determine how the variable is represented internally and the way it is printed. If you do not assign any attributes to a variable, it will have the characteristics of a plain Bourne Shell variable. This section describes the attributes that are most generally useful.

Several of the attributes control the way data is printed. Two options to typeset, **-u** and **-l**, set the **uppercase** and **lowercase** attributes, respectively. The following command converts the value of the variable called **name** to uppercase:

```
81 $ typeset -u name
82 $ name="Barbara Jackson"
83 $ print $name
BARBARA JACKSON
```

The print command here is a Korn Shell built-in that you can use in place of echo. The print command supports the features that echo has on both System V and Berkeley UNIX. To suppress the trailing NEWLINE that echo ordinarily prints, you can use either a trailing \c or the –n option with the print command.

Three of the attributes are for field justification—one removes leading blanks and left-justifies (–L), another adds leading blanks and right-justifies (–R), and a third right-justifies and fills with leading zeros (–Z). If one of these options is followed by a number, the number is interpreted as the length of the variable string. The next example left-justifies the value of the variable **last** in a field of ten characters:

```
84 $ typeset –L10 last
85 $ last=Winterbotham
86 $ print $last
Winterboth
```

As this example demonstrates, values will be truncated if they are longer than the specified length of the variable. If you do not specify the length using typeset, the length will be set based on the length of the first value assigned to the variable.

The following Korn Shell script, **print_report**, uses the typeset command to format and print a report. Refer to Chapter 8 for a description of the While control structure.

```
87 $ cat print_report
typeset –uL10 last
typeset –uL8 first
typeset –R10 amount
typeset –L4 space
IFS="     "
space=" "

cat $1 |
while read last first amount
do
     print "$last $space $first $amount"
done
```

The **print_report** script reads one line at a time from a data file. The data file is assumed to contain three fields separated by tabs, which are read into three variables: **last, first,** and **amount.** Because the typeset command set attributes of the variables, **last** is truncated to ten characters and converted to uppercase, **first** is truncated to eight characters and converted to uppercase, and **amount** is right-justified. When the variables are printed out they have those characteristics. The **print_report** script also uses a null variable, **space,** to separate the fields for the first and last names. Here, **print_report** creates a report using the information in a file called **data:**

```
88 $ cat data
Last Name          First    Amount

Everett Elliott 30
Hansen   Richard 40
Hernandez        Jose      450
Taylor-Smith     Susan     90
Valenzuela       Maria     300
Washington       Tom       150

89 $ print_report data
LAST  NAME         FIRST             AMOUNT

EVERETT            ELLIOTT              30
HANSEN             RICHARD              40
HERNANDEZ          JOSE                450
TAYLOR-SMI         SUSAN                90
VALENZUELA         MARIA               300
WASHINGTON         TOM                 150
```

Another option to the **typeset** command, **–i**, creates an integer variable. If you follow **–i** with a number between 2 and 36, the number is taken as the base. Without a number following **–i**, base 10 is used. The following example creates an integer variable called **int** in base 2:

```
94 $ typeset –i2 int
95 $ int=7
96 $ print $int
2#111
```

The **2#** indicates the base of the number.

The cd Command

The Korn Shell's **cd** command has two special features. First, you can use a dash (–) in place of the directory name, and **cd** will make the previous working directory the current working directory. The – is useful when you are working with files in two directories or when you are working in one directory and temporarily go to another directory and then want to return to the original directory.

The second special feature of **cd** allows you to use two arguments:

cd old new

The **cd** command replaces the string **old** in the current pathname with the string **new** and changes the working directory to the new pathname.

```
97 $ pwd
/home/alex/literature
98 $ cd alex jenny
/home/jenny/literature
```

The let Command

The let command enables you to do integer arithmetic. It evaluates expressions that contain constants, shell variables, and operators. The format of the let command follows:

let expressions

Recent versions of the Korn Shell recognize all the operators that can be used in @ command expressions. These operators include the basic arithmetic operators—addition (+), subtraction (–), multiplication (*), division (/), and remainder (%)—as well as several comparison operators (<, >, <=, >=), logical operators, and shift operators. In addition, you can use parentheses to override the precedence of the operators, as you can with the @ command. The complete list of operators is given on page 315.

Variables used in arithmetic expressions do not need to have the integer attribute set; however, the arithmetic will be evaluated more quickly if they do. (Refer to "The typeset Command" above.) Constants are assumed to be in base 10 unless you specify an alternate base. They have the following format:

[base#]n

The optional **base** is a decimal number between 2 and 36, and **n** is a number in that base. For example, **16#100** is 100 in base 16 (256 in base 10). The Korn Shell truncates anything following a decimal point.

Because each expression is interpreted as a single word by the Korn Shell, if you put SPACES in the expression, then you must quote the expression. You must also quote it if it contains characters that have special meaning to the shell.

For convenience, the Korn Shell provides an alternative syntax for arithmetic expressions. Instead of using the word **let**, you can surround a command with two pairs of parentheses, and it will be treated as a quoted arithmetic expression.

Each of the following examples is a valid use of the let command:

```
101 $ let total=4392+706 sub=998-203
102 $ let answer="5 * 92 + 8 * 37"
103 $ let var="5 * (92 + 8) * 37"
104 $ ((var = 9 % 4))
```

You can use **let** as the **test-command** in If, While, and Until control structures in shell scripts. The **let** command returns a 0, or *true,* exit status if the last
expression evaluated is nonzero; otherwise, it returns a 1, or *false,* exit status.

The next example uses the relational operator **==** to compare two variables.
The **guess_divisors** script prompts the user for a number and a potential divisor of
that number. The script uses the modulo (or remainder) operator to identify the
remainder when the first number is divided by the second number. If the
remainder is 0, the **test-command** evaluates to *true,* and the Korn Shell executes
the first part of the If construct. Otherwise, the Korn Shell executes the commands following Else. When a variable is referenced inside a **let** command, the $
that usually precedes the variable name is not necessary.

```
105 $ cat guess_divisors
print "Dividend: \c"
read dividend
print "Pick a divisor: \c"
read divisor

let remainder=dividend%divisor

if (( remainder == 0 ))
    then
        print Right, $divisor is a divisor of $dividend
    else
        print Sorry, $divisor is not a divisor of \
        $dividend
fi

106 $ guess_divisor
Dividend:   41
Pick a divisor:   15
Sorry, 15 is not a divisor of 41
```

Integer variables and the **let** command are particularly useful when you are
using the Korn Shell's array variables. If you use a subscript with any variable,
the variable becomes an array. You do not have to declare the variable to be an
array or initialize all its elements (as you do with the C Shell). You can use any
arithmetic expression that evaluates to an integer between 0 and 511 (or greater,
depending on your system) as a subscript. When you reference an array variable
without a subscript, the Korn Shell interprets it as meaning element 0.

The following example creates an array called **ran** with ten elements (having
index values of 0-9), each of which contains a random number between 0 and 99.
It then prints out each element of the array.

```
107 $ cat ran_array
RANDOM=$$
integer i=0
while (( i < 10 ))
do
    (( ran[i] = RANDOM % 100 ))
    print ${ran[$i]}
    i=i+1
done
```

The first line of **ran_array** initializes the shell variable **RANDOM** to the current process identification number ($$). **RANDOM** is unique among the shell variables: It generates a random integer each time it is referenced. The While loop assigns a random number to ten elements of the user-created array **ran**. Using the % operator, the value of **RANDOM** is divided by 100, and the remainder is taken, which ensures that the value of each element of **ran** will be between 0 and 99. The print command displays the value of each element. When you reference an array variable and it is not part of a let command, you must surround it with braces, as the print command shows.

The Select Control Structure

The Select control structure provides a simple method for creating menus. When you use Select in a Korn Shell script, it sends menu items to the standard error and prompts the user for a selection. The Select control structure has the following format:

```
select identifier in word ...
do
    commands
done
```

Typically, the **word**s are the names of menu items. Select presents each **word** preceded by a menu number and then prompts the user for input. The prompt is controlled by the **PS3** variable, and it defaults to #? if it is not set. If the user enters a number corresponding to one of the menu items, the Korn Shell sets **identifier** to the **word** that corresponds to the number. If the user presses RETURN without typing anything, the menu and the prompt are presented again. If the user enters something other than one of the menu selections, the **identifier** is set to null. The user's input is saved in the shell variable called **REPLY** so that, if the user enters an invalid response, you can access that response in the **REPLY** variable.

When using the Select control structure to create a menu, you should usually use a Case statement in place of **commands**. The next example shows a menu that executes simple UNIX commands:

```
111 $ cat select_menu
print "\n\tCOMMAND MENU\n"

PS3="Enter your selection: "

select choice in "Date and Time"  "Users Logged In" \
        "Working Directory" \
        "Files" "Exit Menu"
do
    case $choice in
        "Date and Time")
            date
            ;;
        "Users Logged In")
            who
            ;;
        "Working Directory")
            pwd
            ;;
        "Files")
            ls
            ;;
        "Exit Menu")
            exit
            ;;
        *)
            print "select_menu: $REPLY is not a" \
            "valid choice."
    esac
done



112 $ select_menu

        COMMAND MENU

1) Date and Time
2) Users Logged In
3) Working Directory
4) Files
5) Exit Menu
Enter your selection: 1
Thu Jun 28 12:58:11 PDT 1990
Enter your selection: 3
/home/alex/literature
Enter your selection: 5
113 $
```

SUMMARY

The Korn Shell implements nearly all the features of the Bourne Shell as well as versions of the most useful interactive features of the C Shell. The Korn Shell provides two built-in command-line editors: a vi-like editor and an emacs-like editor. When you use the built-in vi editor, as you enter commands in response to a Korn Shell prompt, you are in Input Mode. You can press ESCAPE to enter Command Mode. Pressing RETURN executes your command and returns you to Input Mode. You can access previous commands either using a built-in editor or using the built-in command fc.

The Korn Shell's built-in alias command is very similar to the C Shell's. However, the Korn Shell allows you to export aliases and to create tracked aliases, which the C Shell does not allow. (The C Shell uses hashing rather than tracked aliases.) Also, the Korn Shell's aliases cannot take arguments, whereas the C Shell's can. The Korn Shell also allows you to export functions.

The Korn Shell provides several built-in commands in addition to those provided by the Bourne Shell. The typeset command enables you to assign attributes to variables that are useful for formatting the variables to be printed out in reports, among other things. You can do integer arithmetic using let, a command similar to the C Shell's @ command, and you can create array variables. The Select control structure provides a simple method for creating menus in shell scripts.

The Built-In vi Editor

This summary describes commands you can use with the built-in vi editor.

Positioning the Cursor

Command	Moves the Cursor
SPACE or l	space to the right
h	space to the left
w	word to the right
W	blank delimited word to the right
b	word to the left
B	blank delimited word to the left
$	end of line
e	end of word to the right
E	end of blank delimited word to the right
0	beginning of line
^	first nonblank on line

Adding Text

All the following commands (except **r**) leave the Korn Shell in Input Mode. You must press ESCAPE to return to Command Mode.

Command	Insert Text
i	before cursor
I	before first nonblank character on line
a	after cursor
A	at end of line
r	replace current character (no ESCAPE needed)
R	replace characters, starting with current character (overwrite until ESCAPE)

Deleting and Changing Text

In the following list, n is a Repeat Factor.

Command	Effect
nx	delete the number of characters specified by n, starting with the current character
nX	delete the number of characters specified by n, starting with the character following the current character
D	delete to end of line
dd	delete current command
C	change to end of line

History Commands

In the following list, *string* is a simple string of characters.

Command	Effect
j or +	get next command
k or −	get previous command
nG	get command number n
/*string* RETURN	search backward for *string* (less recent)
?*string* RETURN	search forward for *string* (more recent)
n	repeat original search exactly
N	repeat original search, opposite direction
#	inserts the current command as a comment in the history list
nv	calls vi to edit command n (without n, it calls vi to edit the current line)

Miscellaneous Commands

Command	Effect
=	list pathnames that match the current word
*	perform filename generation
u	undo most recent change
U	restore current command line to its previous state
~	change the case of the current character
n.	repeat the last command *n* times

REGULAR EXPRESSIONS

A regular expression defines a set of one or more strings of characters. Several of the UNIX utilities, including ed, vi, grep, awk, and sed, use regular expressions to search for and replace strings.

A simple string of characters is a regular expression that defines one string of characters: itself. A more complex regular expression uses letters, numbers, and special characters to define many different strings of characters. A regular expression is said to *match* any string it defines.

This appendix describes the regular expressions used by **ed**, **vi**, **grep**, **awk**, and **sed**. The regular expressions used in ambiguous file references with the shell are somewhat different. They are described in Chapter 5.

CHARACTERS

As used in this appendix, a *character* is any character *except* a NEWLINE. Most characters represent themselves within a regular expression. A *special character* is one that does not represent itself. If you need to use a special character to represent itself, see the section of this appendix "Quoting Special Characters."

DELIMITERS

A character, called a *delimiter*, usually marks the beginning and end of a regular expression. The delimiter is always a special character for the regular expression it delimits (that is, it does not represent itself but marks the beginning and end of the expression). You can use any character as a delimiter, as long as you use the same character at both ends of the regular expression. For simplicity, all the regular expressions in this appendix use a forward slash as a delimiter. In some unambiguous cases, the second delimiter is not required. For example, you can sometimes omit the second delimiter when it would be followed immediately by a RETURN. Delimiters are not used with any of the **grep** family of utilities (**grep**, **egrep**, and **fgrep**).

SIMPLE STRINGS

The most basic regular expression is a simple string that contains no special characters except the delimiters. A simple string matches only itself.

In the following examples, the strings that are matched are underlined.

Regular Expression	Meaning	Examples
/ring/	matches ring	ring, spring, ringing, stringing

Regular Expression	Meaning	Examples
/Thursday/	matches Thursday	Thursday, Thursday's
/or not/	matches or not	or not, poor nothing

SPECIAL CHARACTERS

You can use special characters within a regular expression to cause it to match more than one string.

Period

A period (.) matches any character.

Regular Expression	Meaning	Examples
/ .alk/	matches all strings that contain a SPACE followed by any character followed by alk	will talk, may balk
/.ing/	matches all strings with any character preceding ing	singing, ping, before inglenook

Square Brackets

Square brackets ([]) define a *character class* that matches any single character within the brackets. If the first character following the left square bracket is a caret (^), the square brackets define a character class that matches any single character not within the brackets. You can use a hyphen to indicate a range of characters. Within a character class definition, backslashes, asterisks, and dollar signs (all described in the following sections) lose their special meanings. A right square bracket (appearing as a member of the character class) can appear only as the first character following the left square bracket, and a caret is special only if it is the first character following the left bracket.

Regular Expression	Meaning	Examples
/[bB]ill/	defines the character class containing b and B—matches a member of the character class followed by ill	<u>bill</u>, <u>Bill</u>, <u>bill</u>ed
/t[aeiou].k/	matches t followed by a lowercase vowel, any character, and a k	<u>talk</u>ative, s<u>tink</u>, <u>teak</u>, <u>tank</u>er
/number [6-9]/	matches number followed by a SPACE and a member of the character class	<u>number 6</u>0, <u>number 8</u>:, get <u>number 9</u>
/[^a–zA–Z]/	matches any character that is not a letter	<u>1</u>, <u>7</u>, <u>@</u>, <u>,</u>, <u>}</u>, Stop<u>!</u>

Asterisk

An asterisk can follow a regular expression that represents a single character. The asterisk represents *zero* or more occurrences of a match of the regular expression. An asterisk following a period matches any string of characters. (A period matches any character, and an asterisk matches zero or more occurrences of the preceding regular expression.) A character class definition followed by an asterisk matches any string of characters that are members of the character class.

A regular expression that includes a special character always matches the longest possible string starting as far toward the beginning (left) of the line as possible.

Regular Expression	Meaning	Examples
/ab*c/	matches a followed by zero or more b's followed by a c	<u>ac</u>, <u>abc</u>, <u>abbc</u>, debbca<u>abbbc</u>

Regular Expression	Meaning	Examples
/ab.*c/	matches **ab** followed by zero or more other characters followed by **c**	abc, abxc, ab45c, xab 756.345 x cat
/t.*ing/	matches **t** followed by zero or more characters followed by **ing**	thing, ting, I thought of going
/[a–zA–Z]*/	matches a string composed only of letters and SPACES	1. any string without numbers or punctuation!
/(.*)/	matches as long a string as possible between (and)	Get (this) and (that);
/([^)]*)/	matches the shortest string possible that starts with (and ends with)	(this), a (this and that)

Caret and Dollar Sign

A regular expression that begins with a caret (^) can match a string only at the beginning of a line. In a similar manner, a dollar sign at the end of a regular expression matches the end of a line.

Regular Expression	Meaning	Examples
/^T/	matches a **T** at the beginning of a line	This line... That Time... In Time
/^+[0–9]/	matches a plus sign followed by a number at the beginning of a line	+5 +45.72 +759 Keep this...
/:$/	matches a colon that ends a line	...below:

Quoting Special Characters

You can quote any special character (but not a digit or a parenthesis) by preceding it with a backslash. Quoting a special character makes it represent itself.

Regular Expression	Meaning	Examples
/end\./	matches all strings that contain end followed by a period	The end., send. pretend.mail
/\\/	matches a single backslash	\
/*/	matches an asterisk	*.c, an asterisk (*)
/\[5\]/	matches the string [5]	it was five [5]
/and\/or/	matches and/or	and/or

RULES

The following rules govern the application of regular expressions.

Longest Match Possible

As stated previously, a regular expression always matches the longest possible string starting as far toward the beginning of the line as possible. For example, given the following string:

    This (rug) is not what it once was (a long time ago), is it?

The
expression: /Th.*is/
matches: This (rug) is not what it once was (a long time ago), is

and: /(.*)/
matches: (rug) is not what it once was (a long time ago)

however: /([^)]*)/
matches: (rug)

Given the following string:

singing songs, singing more and more

The
expression: /s.*ing/
matches: singing songs, singing

and: /s.*ing song/
matches: singing song

Empty Regular Expressions

An empty regular expression always represents the last regular expression that you used. For example, if you give vi the following Substitute command:

    :s/mike/robert/

and then you want to make the same substitution again, you can use the command:

    :s//robert/

Alternatively, you can use the following commands to search for the string mike and then make the substitution:

    /mike/
    s//robert/

The empty regular expression (//) represents the last regular expression you used (/mike/).

BRACKETING EXPRESSIONS

You can use quoted parentheses, \(and \), to *bracket* a regular expression. The string that the bracketed regular expression matches can subsequently be used, as explained in "Quoted Digits," below. A regular expression does not attempt to match quoted parentheses. Thus, a regular expression enclosed within quoted parentheses matches what the same regular expression without the parentheses would match.

The expression: /\(rexp\)/
matches: what /rexp/ would match

and: /a\(b*\)c/
matches: what /ab*c/ would match

You can nest quoted parentheses. The following expression consists of two bracketed expressions, one within the other.

  / \ ([a–z] \ ([A–Z] * \ ) x \ ) /

It matches:

  3 t dMNOR x I u

The bracketed expressions are identified only by the opening \(, so there is no ambiguity in identifying them.

THE REPLACEMENT STRING

The **vi** and **sed** editors use regular expressions as Search Strings within Substitute commands. You can use two special characters, ampersands (**&**) and quoted digits (**\x**), to represent the matched strings within the corresponding Replacement String.

Ampersands

Within a Replacement String, an ampersand (**&**) takes on the value of the string that the Search String (regular expression) matched.

For example, the following **vi** Substitute command surrounds a string of one or more numbers with NN. The ampersand in the Replacement String matches whatever string of numbers the regular expression (Search String) matched.

  : s / [0–9] [0–9] * / NN&NN /

Two character class definitions are required because the regular expression [0–9]* matches *zero* or more occurrences of a digit, and *any* character string is zero or more occurrences of a digit.

Quoted Digits

Within the regular expression itself, a quoted digit (**\x**) takes on the value of the string that the bracketed regular expression beginning with the *x*th \(matched.

Within a Replacement String, a quoted digit represents the string that the bracketed regular expression (portion of the Search String) beginning with the *x*th \(matched.

For example, you can take a list of people in the form

```
last-name, first-name initial
```

and put it in the following format:

```
first-name initial last-name
```

with the following **vi** command:

```
:1,$s/\([^,]*\), \(.*\)/\2 \1/
```

This command addresses all the lines in the file (1,$). The Substitute command (**s**) uses a Search String and a Replacement String delimited by forward slashes. The first bracketed regular expression within the Search String, \([^,]*\), matches what the same unbracketed regular expression, [^,]*, would match. This regular expression matches a string of zero or more characters not containing a comma (the **last-name**). Following the first bracketed regular expression is a comma and a SPACE that match themselves. The second bracketed expression \(.*\) matches any string of characters (the **first-name** and **initial**).

The Replacement String consists of what the second bracketed regular expression matched (\2) followed by a SPACE and what the first bracketed regular expression matched (\1).

FULL REGULAR EXPRESSIONS

The **egrep** (a variant of **grep**) and **awk** utilities provide all the special characters that are included in ordinary regular expressions, except for \(and \), as well as several others. Patterns using the extended set of special characters are called *full regular expressions*.

Two of the additional special characters are the plus sign (+) and question mark (?). They are similar to the *, which matches *zero* or more occurrences of the previous character. The plus sign matches *one* or more occurrences of the previous character, whereas the question mark matches *zero* or *one* occurrence. You can use all three of these special characters *, +, and ? with parentheses, causing the special character to apply to the string surrounded by the parentheses. Note that these parentheses are not quoted, unlike the parentheses in bracketed regular expressions.

Regular Expression	Meaning	Examples
/ab+c/	matches a followed by one or more b's followed by a c.	y<u>abc</u>w, <u>abbc</u>57
/ab?c/	matches a followed by zero or one b followed by c	b<u>ac</u>k, <u>abc</u>def
/(ab)+c/	matches one or more occurrences of the string ab followed by c	z<u>abc</u>d, <u>ababc</u>!
/(ab)?c/	matches zero or one occurrences of the string ab followed by c	x<u>c</u>, <u>abc</u>c

In full regular expressions, the pipe (|) special character acts as an OR operator. A pipe between two regular expressions causes a match with strings that match either the first expression or the second or both. You can use the pipe with parentheses to separate from the rest of the regular expression the two expressions that are being ORed.

Regular Expression	Meaning	Examples
/ab|ac/	matches either ab or ac	<u>ab</u>, <u>ac</u>, <u>ab</u>ac
/^Exit|^Quit/	matches lines that begin with the string Exit or the string Quit	<u>Exit</u>, <u>Quit</u>, No Exit
/(D|N). Jones/	matches the string D. Jones or the string N. Jones	P.<u>D. Jones</u>, <u>N. Jones</u>

SUMMARY

A regular expression defines a set of one or more strings of characters. A regular expression is said to match any string it defines.

The following characters are special within a regular expression.

**Special
Character   Function**

.	matches any single character
[xyz]	defines a character class that matches x, y, or z
[^xyz]	defines a character class that matches any character except x, y, or z
[x–z]	defines a character class that matches any character x through z inclusive
*	matches zero or more occurrences of a match of the preceding character
^	forces a match to the beginning of a line
$	forces a match to the end of a line
\	used to quote special characters
\(xyz\)	matches what xyz matches (a bracketed regular expression)

In addition to the above special characters (excluding quoted parentheses), the following characters are special within full regular expressions.

**Special
Character   Function**

+	matches one or more occurrences of the preceding character
?	matches zero or one occurrences of the preceding character
(xyz)+	matches one or more occurrences of what xyz matches
(xyz)?	matches zero or one occurrence of what xyz matches
(xyz)*	matches zero or more occurrences of what xyz matches
xyz|abc	matches either what xyz or what abc matches
(xy|ab)c	matches either what xyc or what abc matches

The vi utility recognizes the following special characters as well as all the special characters recognized by ordinary regular expressions. Refer to Chapter 6 (page 135) for a description of regular expressions in vi.

**Special
Character   Function**

\<   forces a match to the beginning of a word
\>   forces a match to the end of a word

The following characters are special within a Replacement String in sed, vi, and ed.

Character   Function

&   represents what the regular expression (Search String) matched

\x   a quoted number, x, represents the xth bracketed regular expression in the Search String

APPENDIX
C

NETWORKING

Computers attached to a network use a common protocol, or language, to communicate at high speed. New utilities allow users to access remote computers over the network and to exchange large amounts of information quickly. This appendix describes a few of the basic networking commands, including how to log in on a remote computer, how to transfer files, and how to check the status of remote computers. Each of these commands is described in detail in Part II.

The communication facilities that link computers together are constantly improving, allowing faster and more economical connections. When the rate of transferring characters between systems was measured in the hundreds of bits per second, or even in the thousands, information sharing was limited. The development of higher speed networks, such as Ethernet, made it practical to share large quantities of data. (An Ethernet network can transfer up to ten million bits per second, though file transfer rates are typically lower, due to factors such as computer load and overall network traffic.)

At the system level, many new services have appeared and are becoming standard. On UNIX systems, daemons are usually set up to send and receive particular types of messages over the network (such as mail traffic). Several software systems have been created to allow computers to share their file systems with one another, making it appear to users as though the files are actually stored on disks attached to their local computer. Sharing remote file systems allows users to share information without knowing where the files physically reside and without learning a new set of utilities to manipulate the files. Because the files appear to be stored locally, the standard UNIX utilities (display, edit, print, move, etc.) can be used to work with them.

To take advantage of the higher speeds available on computer networks, some new utilities have been created, and existing commands have been extended. The **ruptime** and **rwho** utilities provide status information about computers and users on a local area network. The **rlogin** and **telnet** utilities allow users to connect to remote computers on their local network or at a distant site through interconnected networks. Users rely on commands such as **rcp** and **ftp** to transfer files from one computer to another, across the network. Communication utilities, such as **mailx** and **write**, have been adapted to understand remote network addresses and to set up the connections necessary to exchange information with a remote computer. An overview of some common networking utilities that are available with System V Release 4 is presented in this appendix.

Today it is common for a computer facility that contains more than one computer to include a local area network (LAN) that links the systems together. UNIX systems are typically attached to an Ethernet network. Large computer facilities usually maintain several networks, often of different types, and may also have connections to larger networks (company- or campus-wide, and beyond). The Internet is a loosely administered network, with many different types of connections, that links computers on diverse local area networks around the globe. Using the Internet, it is possible to send an electronic mail message to a colleague located thousands of miles away and receive a reply within minutes.

ETHERNET

An Ethernet network is composed of one or two types of coaxial cable (similar to the cable used by your local cable television company). Each computer is attached to the cable at a tap point and is assigned a unique address. A message, called a packet, sent by a computer includes the address of the destination computer. Each computer on the network checks the destination address in every packet that is transmitted on the network. When a computer finds its own address as the destination for a packet, it accepts that packet and processes it appropriately. If a packet's destination address is not on the local network (on the same physical cable), it must be passed on to another network by a router. A router may be a general purpose computer or a special device that is attached to multiple networks to act as a gateway among them.

To exchange information on the network, the computers communicate using a few common protocols. The protocol determines the format of a message packet. The predominant network protocol used by UNIX systems attached to Ethernet is TCP/IP, which is an abbreviation for Transmission Control Protocol/Internet Protocol. Network services that need highly reliable connections, such as rlogin and rcp, tend to use TCP/IP. Another common protocol used by UNIX systems is UDP, the Unreliable Datagram Protocol. Network services such as ruptime and rwho tend to operate satisfactorily with the simpler UDP protocol. Other network protocols developed by particular manufacturers, such as XNS (Xerox Network Software) and DECnet (DEC Network), are less widely supported.

REMOTE COMPUTER STATUS

If your UNIX system is attached to a local area network, you can use the ruptime utility to learn the status of other computers attached to the same network. This information is valuable for a system administrator who must watch over several machines. It can also be useful for individual users—for example, if you have accounts on several computers, you might choose to work on one that is lightly loaded. The ruptime utility reports the system names, the status of each system, the amount of time it has been up (or down), the number of users logged in on each system, and the load factor for each machine. (See ruptime, page 568, for more information.)

```
$ ruptime
bravo           up  29+03:42,    1 users,   load 0.37, 0.00, 1.09
hurrah        down     12:39
sobell          up   4+14:09,    2 users,   load 2.68, 2.09, 1.16
```

REMOTE USER STATUS

The rwho utility reports the login names of users who are actively using remote systems. The information this utility provides includes the user name, the name of the system and the terminal line to which the user is connected, and when the user logged in. If the last column is blank, the user is actively typing at the terminal; otherwise, the fourth column indicates how much time has elapsed since the user last typed on the keyboard. This information is especially useful when users work at individual workstations rather than on a central computer system; rwho is a who command that reports on a network-wide, rather than a computer-specific, basis.

```
$ rwho
alex        sobell:tty01      Sep 19 10:54
jenny       bravo:tty03       Sep 21 10:19    :01
roy         sobell:tty04      Sep 21 14:24    :33
```

REMOTE COMMUNICATION

Many of the standard communications utilities, such as mailx and write, can be used to communicate remotely with users. Along with the user's login name, you must specify the name of the remote computer. In the example below, the write utility on the local computer establishes a connection with its counterpart on the remote computer *bravo* and signals the user *jenny*.

```
$ write jenny@bravo
```

The *at* sign (@) separates the user name from the computer host name. Read the command line as "write jenny at *bravo*," which is a natural sequence that is easy to remember. Several standard UNIX utilities can be used for remote communication by specifying an address in "at" format. For example, you can send mail to Jenny by typing

```
$ mailx jenny@bravo
```

(Refer to page 629 for more information about the write utility.)

REMOTE LOGIN

If you have an account on a remote computer, you can use the rlogin utility to connect to the remote system and start up a login session there. When you log out, your connection to the remote computer will be broken, and you can resume using the local computer. To use rlogin, you must specify the name of the remote system you want to connect to.

```
$ rlogin bravo
Password:

Welcome to bravo!
$
```

You might choose to use a remote system in order to access a special-purpose application or device that is available only on that system or because you know that the remote system is faster or less busy than your local computer. (Refer to page 561 for more information about the rlogin utility.)

You can also use another utility, telnet, to interact with a remote computer. The telnet utility is similar to rlogin, but it can also be used to connect to a non-UNIX system. Refer to the documentation supplied with your UNIX system for more information on telnet.

FILE TRANSFER

You can use the rcp (remote copy) utility to transfer files between two computers attached to a network. The rcp utility works like cp. In the following example, given that a directory named **memos** exists in your home directory on the system named *bravo*, the file **memo.921** is copied from the working directory on the local system to your **memos** directory on *bravo*.

```
$ rcp memo.921 bravo:memos
```

(Refer to page 559 for more information about the rcp utility.)

You can also use the ftp (file transfer protocol) utility to transfer files between computers on a network. Unlike rcp, ftp is interactive—it allows you to browse through a directory on a remote system to identify files you may want to transfer. In the following example, the user *alex* connects to the remote system on the Internet called uunet.uu.net as the anonymous user and picks up an index to the archive of software source code from the USENET newsgroup named **comp.sources.unix**. Although any password is accepted for anonymous ftp, by convention you should enter your login name and system name. In this case, alex would have entered **alex@sobell** in response to the password prompt.

```
$ ftp uunet.uu.net
Connected to uunet.uu.net.
220 uunet FTP server (Version 5.99 Wed May 23 14:40:19 EDT 1990) ready.
Name (uunet.uu.net:alex): anonymous
331 Guest login ok, send ident as password.
Password:
230 Guest login ok, access restrictions apply.
ftp> ls
200 PORT command successful.
150 Opening ASCII mode data connection for file list.
lost+found
comp.std.unix
comp.sources.games
comp.sources.x
net.sources
```

```
comp.sources.unix
.
.
.
226 Transfer complete.
830 bytes received in 0.16 seconds (5.1 Kbytes/s)
ftp> cd comp.sources.unix
250 CWD command successful.
ftp> ls
200 PORT command successful.
150 Opening ASCII mode data connection for file list.
volume1
volume2
.
.
.
index
FILES
226 Transfer complete.
240 bytes received in 0.043 seconds (5.5 Kbytes/s)
ftp> get index
200 PORT command successful.
150 Opening ASCII mode data connection for index (35425 bytes).
226 Transfer complete.
local: index remote: index
36262 bytes received in 0.85 seconds (41 Kbytes/s)
ftp> quit
221 Goodbye.
$ ls -l index
-rw-r--r--  1 alex    pubs  35425 Sep 21 15:57 index
```

The ftp utility can also be used to exchange files with a non-UNIX system. While using ftp, you can type **help** at any ftp> prompt to see a list of valid commands. Refer to the documentation supplied with your UNIX system for more information on ftp.

REMOTE FILE SYSTEM

When there are many similar systems on a network, it is often desirable to share common files and utilities among them. For example, to conserve disk space a system administrator might choose to keep a copy of the system documentation on one computer's disk and to make those files available for all remote systems. In this case, the system administrator would configure the files so that users who needed to access the online documentation would not be aware that the files were actually stored on a remote system. A file system that is stored on a remote computer's disk can be mounted on the local system using either the Network File System or Remote File Sharing packages available for System V Release 4. Refer to the documentation supplied with your UNIX system for detailed information on configuring remote file systems.

SUMMARY

Support for high-speed network communication was introduced in Berkeley UNIX 4.2 and was soon added to other versions of UNIX by individual manufacturers. UNIX systems today usually communicate on Ethernet local area networks, which may be linked in turn to other networks. Networking tools are included as a standard part of UNIX System V with Release 4. Basic networking tools allow users to check on the status of remote computers and their users, to log in on remote systems, and to copy files quickly from one system to another. Standard UNIX tools have been extended to recognize network addresses, thus allowing users to exchange mail messages or establish interactive conversations. Newer applications, such as remote file systems, have simplified information sharing.

Two major advantages of computer networks are that they enable systems to communicate at high speed and that they require few connections (typically one per system, to a common cable). Two UNIX systems that are not attached to a network can still communicate over dial-up or hard-wired serial lines (it is not feasible to set up direct links from one computer to every system with which it might need to exchange data). However, dial-up lines tend to be slow and busy as more and longer connections are needed, and long-distance, hard-wired connections are very expensive. Sometimes two computers that need to exchange data can do so without establishing a direct connection by using intermediary computers to forward their messages, but this approach tends to introduce long delays (days, in many cases).

Technological advances continue to improve the performance of both computer systems and the networks that link them together. This improved performance encourages the development of new applications and services that take advantage of the better performance.

GLOSSARY

Absolute pathname.   A pathname that starts with the root directory (**/**). An absolute pathname locates a file without regard to the working directory.

Access.   In computer jargon, this word is frequently used as a verb to mean use, read from, or write to. To access a file means to read from or write to the file.

Access permission.   Permission to read from, write to, or execute a file. If you have "write access permission to a file," you can write to the file. Also, *access privilege.*

Alias.   A mechanism in the C and Korn Shells that enables you to define new commands.

Alphanumeric character.   One of the characters, either uppercase or lowercase, from A to Z and 0 to 9, inclusive.

Ambiguous file reference.   A reference to a file that does not necessarily specify any one file but can be used to specify a group of files. The shell expands an ambiguous file reference into a list of filenames. Special characters represent single characters (**?**), strings of zero or more characters (*****), and character classes (**[]**) within ambiguous file references. An ambiguous file reference is a type of *regular expression.*

Angle bracket.   There is a left angle bracket (**<**) and a right angle bracket (**>**). The shell uses **<** to redirect a command's standard input to come from a file, and **>** to redirect the standard output. Also, the shell uses the characters **<<** to signify the start of a here document, and **>>** to append output to a file.

Append.   To add something to the end of something else. To append text to a file means to add the text to the end of the file. The shell uses **>>** to append a command's output to a file.

Argument.   A number, letter, filename, or another string that gives some information to a command and is passed to the command at the time it is called. A command line argument is anything on a command line following the command name.

Arithmetic expression.   A group of numbers, operators, and parentheses that can be evaluated. When you evaluate an arithmetic expression, you end up with a number. The Bourne Shell uses the expr command to evaluate arithmetic expressions; the C Shell uses @ and the Korn Shell uses let.

Array.   An arrangement of elements (numbers or strings of characters) in one or more dimensions. The C and Korn Shells and awk can store and process arrays.

ASCII.   This acronym stands for the American National Standard Code for Information Interchange. It is a code that uses seven bits to represent both graphic (letters, numbers, and punctuation) and CONTROL characters. You can represent textual information, including program source code and English text, in ASCII code. Because it is a standard, it is frequently used when exchanging information between computers.

There are extensions of the ASCII character set that make use of eight bits. The seven-bit set is common; the eight-bit extensions are still coming into popular use.

Asynchronous event.   An event that does not occur regularly or synchronously with another event. UNIX system signals are asynchronous; they can occur at any time because they can be initiated by any number of irregular events.

Background process.   A process that is not run in the foreground. Also called a *detached process,* a background process is initiated by a command line that ends with an ampersand (**&**). You do not have to wait for a background process to run to completion before giving the shell additional commands. If you have job control, you can move background processes to the foreground, and vice versa.

Baud rate.   Transmission speed. Usually used to measure terminal or modem speed. Common baud rates range from 110 to 19,200 baud. You can roughly convert baud rate to characters per second by dividing by ten (e.g., 300 baud equals approximately 30 characters per second).

Berkeley UNIX.   One of the two major versions of the UNIX operating system. Berkeley UNIX was developed at the University of California at Berkeley by the Computer Systems Research Group. It is often referred to as *BSD* (Berkeley Software Distribution).

Bit.   The smallest piece of information a computer can handle. A bit is either a 1 or 0 (on or off).

Blank character.   Either a SPACE or a TAB character, also called *white space.* Also, in some contexts, NEWLINES are considered blank characters.

Block.   A section of a disk or tape (usually 1024 bytes long, but shorter or longer on some systems) that is written at one time.

Block device.   A disk or tape drive. A block device stores information in blocks of characters. A block device is represented by a block device (block special) file. See *Character device.*

Block number.   Disk and tape blocks (see *Block*) are numbered so that the UNIX system can keep track of the data on the device. These numbers are block numbers.

Boot.   Load the UNIX system kernel into memory and start it running. Also *bootstrap.*

Bourne Shell.   The standard UNIX System V command processor. It was developed by Steve Bourne at AT&T Bell Laboratories. See *Shell* and *Job Shell.*

Braces.   There is a left brace (**{**) and a right brace (**}**). Braces have special meanings to the shell.

Bracket.   Either a square (**[**) or angle bracket (**<**). See *Square bracket* and *Angle bracket.*

Branch.   In a tree structure, a branch connects nodes, leaves, and the root. The UNIX file system hierarchy is often conceptualized as an upside-down tree. The branches connect files and directories. In SCCS (System V's Source Code Control System), a branch occurs when a Delta is made to a file and is not included in other, subsequent Deltas to the file.

BSD.   See *Berkeley UNIX.*

Buffer.   An area of memory that stores data until it can be used. When you write information to a file on a disk, the UNIX system stores the information in a disk buffer until there is enough to write to the disk or until the disk is ready to receive the information.

Built-in command.   A command that is built into a shell. Each of the three major shells—the Bourne, C, and Korn Shells—has its own set of built-in commands. When the shell runs a built-in command, it does not fork a new process. Consequently, built-in commands run more quickly and can affect the environment of the current shell. Because built-in commands are used in the same way utilities are used, you will not typically be aware of whether a command is a shell built-in or a utility.

Byte.   Eight bits of information. A byte can store one character.

C programming language.   A modern systems language that has high-level features for efficient, modular programming as well as lower-level features that make it suitable as a systems programming language. It is machine-independent so that carefully written C programs can be easily transported to run on different machines. Most of the UNIX operating system is written in C, and UNIX provides an ideal environment for programming in C.

C Shell.   The C Shell is a UNIX command processor. It was originally developed by Bill Joy for Berkeley UNIX. It was named for the C programming language because its programming constructs are similar to those of C. See *Shell.*

Calling environment.   A list of variables and their values that is made available to a called program. See "Executing a Command" in Chapter 8 and "Variable Substitution" in Chapter 9.

Case-sensitive.   Able to distinguish between uppercase and lowercase characters. Unless you set the **ignorecase** parameter, vi performs case-sensitive searches. The grep utility performs case-sensitive searches unless you use the –i option.

Catenate.   To join sequentially or end to end. Also *concatenate.* The UNIX cat utility catenates files—it displays them one after the other.

Character class.   A group of characters in a regular expression that defines which characters can occupy a single character position. A character class definition is usually surrounded by square brackets. The character class defined by [abcr] represents a character position that can be occupied by *a, b, c,* or *r.*

Character device.   A terminal, printer, or modem. A character device stores or displays characters one at a time. A character device is represented by a character device (character special) file. On System V, a character device may be part of a streams character-handling system. See *Block device* and *Streams.*

Child process.   A process that was created by another process, the parent process. Every process is a child process except for the first process, which is started when the UNIX system begins execution. When you run a command from the shell, the shell spawns a child process to run the command. See *Process.*

Command.   What you give the shell in response to a prompt. When you give the shell a command, it executes a utility, another program, a built-in command, or a shell script. Utilities are often referred to as commands. When you are using an interactive utility such as vi or mailx, you use commands that are appropriate to that utility.

Command line.   A line of instructions and arguments that executes a command. This term usually refers to a line that you enter in response to a shell prompt.

Command substitution.   What the shell does when you surround a command with backquotes or grave accent marks. The shell replaces the command, including the backquotes, with the output of the command.

Concatenate.   See *Catenate.*

Condition code.   See *Exit status.*

Console terminal.   Also, *console.* The main system terminal, usually the one that receives system error messages.

CONTROL character.   A character that is not a graphic character such as a letter, number, or punctuation mark. Such characters are called CONTROL characters because they frequently act to control a peripheral device. RETURN and FORM-FEED are CONTROL characters that control a terminal or printer.

The word CONTROL is printed in uppercase letters in this book because it is a key that appears on most terminal keyboards. It may be labeled CNTRL or CTRL on your terminal. CONTROL characters, frequently called nonprinting characters, are represented by ASCII codes less than 32 (decimal).

Control structure.   A statement used to change the order of execution of commands in a shell script. Control structures are among the commands referred to as flow control commands. See *Flow control commands.*

Crash.   The system stops unexpectedly.

.cshrc file.   A file in your home directory that the C Shell executes each time you invoke a new C Shell. You can use this file to establish variables and aliases.

Current (process, line, character, directory, event, and so on).   The item that is immediately available, working, or being used. The current process is the process that is controlling the program you are running; the current line or character is the one the cursor is on; the current directory is the working directory.

Cursor.   A small lighted rectangle or underscore that appears on the terminal screen and indicates where the next character is going to appear.

Daemon.   A process that runs in the background, independent of a terminal, and performs a function. An example is the printer daemon, which controls the job queue for the printer.

Debug.   To correct a program by removing its bugs (that is, errors).

Default.   Something that is selected without being explicitly specified. For example, when used without an argument, ls displays a list of the files in the working directory by default.

Delta.   A set of changes made to a file that has been encoded by the Source Code Control System (SCCS).

Detached process.   See *Background process.*

Device.   A disk drive, printer, terminal, plotter, or other input/output unit that can be attached to the computer.

Device driver.   Part of the UNIX kernel that controls a device such as a terminal, disk drive, or printer.

Device file.   Also called a *special file.* A file that represents a device.

Device filename.   The pathname of a device file. All UNIX systems have two kinds of device files—block and character device files. In addition, System V has fifos (named pipes), and some versions of UNIX, including System V Release 4, have UNIX domain sockets. Most device files are located in the /dev directory.

Device number.   See *Major device number* and *Minor device number.*

Directory.   Short for *directory file.* A file that contains a list of other files.

Disk partition.   A portion of a disk. A disk partition can hold a file system or another structure, such as the swap area. Also, *disk slice.*

Editor.   A utility that is used to create and modify text files. The vi and ed editors are part of the UNIX system. Many UNIX systems also come with another popular editor, emacs. Also, *text editor.*

Element.   One thing, usually a basic part of a group of things. An element of a numeric array is one of the numbers that is stored in the array.

Environment.   See *Calling environment.*

EOF.   An acronym for end of file.

Exit status.   The status returned by a process; either successful (usually 0) or unsuccessful (usually 1).

Expression.   See *Logical expression* and *Arithmetic expression.*

File. A collection of related information, referred to by a filename. The UNIX system views peripheral devices as files, allowing a program to read from or write to a device, just as it would read from or write to a file.

File system. A data structure that usually resides on part of a disk. All UNIX systems have a root file system, and most have at least a few other file systems. Each file system is composed of some number of blocks, depending on the size of the disk partition that has been assigned to the file system. Each file system has a control block, the superblock, that contains information about the file system. The other blocks in a file system are inodes, which contain control information about individual files, and data blocks, which contain the information in the files.

Filename. The name of a file. You use a filename to refer to a file.

Filename completion. Completion of filenames and user names after you specify unique prefixes.

Filename extension. The part of a filename following a period.

Filename generation. What occurs when the shell expands ambiguous file references. See *Ambiguous file reference*.

Filter. A command that can take its input from the standard input and send its output to the standard output. A filter transforms the input stream of data and sends it to the standard output. A pipe usually connects a filter's input to the standard output of one command, and a second pipe connects the filter's output to the standard input of another command. The grep and sort utilities are commonly used as filters.

Flow control commands. Commands that alter the order of execution of commands within a shell script. Each one of the shells provides control structures, such as If and While, as well as other commands that alter the order of execution (e.g., exec).

Footer. The part of a format that goes at the bottom (or foot) of a page. See *Header*.

Foreground process. When a command is run in the foreground, the shell waits for the command to finish before giving you another prompt. You must wait for a foreground process to run to completion before you can give the shell another command. If you have job control, you can move background processes to the foreground, and vice versa. See *Background process* and *Job control*.

Fork. To create a process. When one process creates another process, it forks a process. Also, *spawn*.

Free list. The list of blocks in a file system that are available for use. Information about the free list is kept in the superblock of the file system.

Function. See *Shell function*.

Group. A collection of users. Groups are used as a basis for determining file access permissions. If you are not the owner of a file and you belong to the group the file is assigned to, you are subject to the group access permissions for the file. On System V Release 4, a user may simultaneously belong to several groups. On earlier versions of System V, each user belongs to only one group at a time, although a user may temporarily change his or her group affiliation with the newgrp command.

Group ID. A number that is defined in the /etc/passwd file when a user is assigned a group number. The /etc/group file associates Group IDs with group names.

Hard link. A directory entry that contains the filename and inode number for a file. The inode number identifies the location of control information for the file on the disk, which in turn identifies the location of the file's contents on the disk. Every file has at least one hard link, which locates the file in a directory. When you remove the last hard link to a file, you can no longer access the file. See *Link* and *Symbolic link*.

Header.   When you are formatting a document, the header goes at the top (or head) of a page. In electronic mail, the header identifies who sent the message, when it was sent, the subject of the message, and so forth.

Here document.   A shell script that takes its input from the file that contains the script.

Hexadecimal number.   A base 16 number. Hexadecimal numbers are composed of the hexadecimal digits 0-9 and A-F. Refer to the following table.

Decimal	Octal	Hex	Decimal	Octal	Hex
1	1	1	17	21	11
2	2	2	18	22	12
3	3	3	19	23	13
4	4	4	20	24	14
5	5	5	21	25	15
6	6	6	31	37	1F
7	7	7	32	40	20
8	10	8	33	41	21
9	11	9	64	100	40
10	12	A	96	140	60
11	13	B	100	144	64
12	14	C	128	200	80
13	15	D	254	376	FE
14	16	E	255	377	FF
15	17	F	256	400	100
16	20	10	257	401	101

History.   A mechanism provided by the C and Korn Shells that enables you to modify and reexecute recent commands.

Home directory.   The directory that is the working directory when you first log in. The pathname of this directory is stored in the **HOME** shell variable.

Indention.   When speaking of text, the blank space between the margin and the beginning of a line that is set in from the margin.

Inode.   A data structure that contains information about a file. An inode for a file contains the file's length, the times the file was last accessed and modified, the time the inode was last modified, owner and group IDs, access privileges, number of links, and pointers to the data blocks that contain the file itself. Each directory entry associates a filename with an inode. Although a single file may have several filenames (one for each link), it has only one inode.

Input.   Information that is fed to a program from a terminal or other file. See *Standard input.*

Installation.   A computer at a specific location. Some aspects of the UNIX system are installation-dependent.

Interactive.   A program that allows ongoing dialog with the user. When you give commands in response to shell prompts, you are using the shell interactively. Also, when you give commands to utilities such as vi and mailx, you are using the utilities interactively.

Interface.   The meeting point of two subsystems. When two programs work together in some way, their interface includes every aspect of either program that the other deals with. The *user interface* of a program includes every aspect of the program the user comes into contact with—the syntax and semantics involved in invoking the program, the input and output of the program, and its error and informational messages. The shell and each one of the utilities and built-in commands has a user interface.

Invisible file.   A file whose filename starts with a period. These files are called invisible because they must be matched explicitly when you are giving the shell an ambiguous file reference. Also, the ls utility does not normally list them. Use the –a option of ls to list all files, including invisible ones.

I/O device.   Short for *input/output device.* See *Device.*

Job control.   A facility that enables you to move commands from the foreground to the background, and vice versa. The job control provided by the C, Job, and Korn Shells also enables you to stop commands temporarily. The shell layer manager, which provides one form of job control for the Bourne Shell, does not let you stop commands.

Job Shell.   A version of the Bourne Shell that includes job control features.

Justify.   To expand a line of type to the right margin in the process of formatting text. A line is justified by increasing the space between words and sometimes between letters on the line.

Kernel.   The heart of the UNIX operating system. The kernel is the part of the operating system that allocates resources and controls processes. The design strategy has been to keep the kernel as small as possible and to put the rest of the UNIX functionality into separately compiled and executed programs.

Korn Shell.   A command processor developed by David Korn at AT&T Bell Laboratories. One version of the Korn Shell is referred to as the Korn Shell-International. See *Shell.*

Leaf.   In a tree structure, the end of a branch that cannot support other branches. When the UNIX file system hierarchy is conceptualized as a tree, files that are not directories are leaves. See *Node.*

Link.   A pointer to a file. There are two kinds of links—hard links and symbolic links. System V Release 4 has both hard links and symbolic links; older versions of System V usually have only hard links. A hard link associates a filename with a place on the disk where the contents of the file are located. A symbolic link associates a filename with the pathname of a hard link to a file. See *Hard link* and *Symbolic link.*

Log in.   To gain access to a UNIX system by responding correctly to the login: and Password: prompts.

Log out.   To end your login session by exiting from your login shell; e.g., to stop using a terminal on a UNIX system so that another user can log in. Also, *Log off.*

Logical expression.   A collection of strings separated by logical operators (>, >=, =, !=, <=, and <) that can be evaluated as true or false.

.login file.   A file the C Shell executes when you log in. You can use it to set environment variables and to run commands that you want executed at the beginning of each login session.

Login name.   The name you enter in response to the login: prompt. Other users use your login name when they send you mail or write to you. Each login name has a corresponding user ID, which is the numeric identifier for the user. Both the login name and the user ID are established in the /etc/passwd file.

Login shell.   The shell that you are using when you first log in. The login shell can fork other processes that can run other shells as well as running utilities and other programs.

.logout file.   A file the C Shell executes when you log out, assuming the C Shell is your login shell. You can put commands in the .logout file that you want run each time you log out.

Machine collating sequence.   The sequence in which the computer orders characters. The machine collating sequence affects the outcome of sorts and other procedures that put lists in alphabetical order. Many computers use ASCII codes, and so their machine collating sequences correspond to the ordering of the ASCII codes for characters.

Macro.   A single instruction that a program replaces by several (usually more complex) instructions. The nroff text formatter has a macro facility and two standard macro packages, **mm** and **ms**. The C compiler also has macros, which are defined using a **#define** instruction to the preprocessor.

Main memory.   Random access memory that is an integral part of the computer. It is contrasted with disk storage. Although disk storage is sometimes referred to as memory, it is never referred to as main memory.

Major device number.   A number assigned to a class of devices such as terminals, printers, or disk drives. Using the ls utility with the –l option to list the contents of the /dev directory displays the major and minor device numbers of many devices (as major, minor).

Merge.   To combine two ordered lists so that the resulting list is still in order. You can use the sort utility to merge files.

Metacharacter.   A character that has a special meaning to the shell or another program in a particular context. Metacharacters are used in the ambiguous file references recognized by the shell and in the regular expressions recognized by several utilities. You must quote a metacharacter if you want to use it without invoking its special meaning. Also, see *Regular character* and *Special character*.

Minor device number.   A number assigned to a specific device within a class of devices. See *Major device number*.

Mount.   To mount a file system is to make it accessible to system users. When a file system is not mounted, you cannot read from or write to files it contains.

Multitasking.   A computer system that allows a user to run more than one job at a time. The UNIX system is multitasking since it allows you to run jobs in the background while running a job in the foreground.

Multiuser.   A computer system that can be used by more than one person at a time. The UNIX system is a multiuser operating system.

Network File System.   A remote file system designed by Sun Microsystems, first included in System V Release 4 but often available on computers running earlier releases of System V from certain manufacturers.

NFS.   See *Network File System*.

Node.   In a tree structure, the end of a branch that can support other branches. When the UNIX file system hierarchy is conceptualized as a tree, directories are nodes. See *Leaf*.

Nonprintable character.   See CONTROL *character*. Also, *nonprinting character*.

Null string.   A string that could contain characters but does not. A string of zero length.

Octal number.   A base 8 number. Octal numbers are composed of the digits 0-7 inclusive. Refer to the table listed under *Hexadecimal number*.

Operating system.   A control program for a computer that allocates computer resources and schedules tasks and provides the user with a way to access the resources.

Option.   A command line argument that modifies the effects of a command. Options are usually preceded by hyphens on the command line, and they usually have single character names (e.g., –h, –n). Some commands allow you to group options following a single hyphen (e.g., –hn).

Ordinary file.   A file that is used to store a program, text, or other user data. See *Directory* and *Device file*.

Output.   Information that a program sends to the terminal or to another file. See *Standard output.*

Parent process.   A process that forks other processes. See *Process* and *Child process.*

Partition.   See *Disk partition.*

Pathname.   A list of directories, separated by slashes (/), and ending with the name of a directory or nondirectory file. A pathname is used to trace a path through the file structure to locate or identify a file.

Pathname element.   One of the filenames that form a pathname.

Pathname, last element of a.   The part of a pathname following the final / or the whole filename if there is no /. A simple filename. Also, *basename.*

Peripheral device.   See *Device.*

Physical device.   A device, such as a disk drive, that is physically—as well as logically—separate from other similar devices.

PID.   An acronym that stands for process identification and is usually followed by the word *number.* The UNIX system assigns a unique PID number to each process when it is initiated.

Pipe.   A connection between programs such that the standard output of one is connected to the standard input of the next. Also, *pipeline.*

Printable character.   One of the graphic characters: a letter, number, or punctuation mark. As contrasted with a nonprintable or CONTROL character. Also, *printing character.*

Process.   The UNIX system execution of a program.

.profile file.   A startup file that the login shell executes when you log in. Both the Bourne and Korn Shells execute the **.profile** file; the C Shell executes **.login** instead. You can use the **.profile** file to run commands, set variables, and define functions.

Program.   A sequence of executable computer instructions contained in a file. UNIX system utilities, applications, and shell scripts are all programs. Whenever you run a command that is not built into a shell, you are executing a program.

Prompt.   A cue from a program, usually displayed on the terminal, indicating that it is waiting for input. The shell displays a prompt as do some of the interactive utilities, such as mailx. By default, the Bourne and Korn Shells use a dollar sign ($) as a prompt, and the C Shell uses a percent sign (%).

Quote.   When you quote a character, you take away any special meaning that it has in the current context. You can quote a character by preceding it with a backslash. When you are interacting with the shell, you can also quote a character by surrounding it with single quotation marks. For example, the command **echo *** or **echo** ´*´ displays *. The command **echo *** displays a list of the files in the working directory. See *Ambiguous file reference, Metacharacter, Regular character, Regular expression,* and *Special character.*

Redirection.   The process of directing the standard input for a program to come from a file rather than from the terminal. Also, directing the standard output or standard error to go to a file rather than to the terminal.

Regular character.   A character that always represents itself in an ambiguous file reference or another type of regular expression. See *Special character.*

Regular expression.   A string—composed of letters, numbers, and special symbols—that defines one or more strings. See Appendix B.

Relative pathname.   A pathname that starts from the working directory. See *Absolute pathname.*

Remote File Sharing.   A remote file system designed by AT&T, introduced on System V Release 3.

Remote file system.   A file system on a remote computer that has been set up so that you can access (usually over a network) its files as though they were stored on your local computer's disks. Two examples of remote file systems that may be used on System V include NFS and RFS.

RFS.   See *Remote File Sharing.*

Restricted Shell.   A shell that provides a controlled environment for a user on System V. The environment does not allow a user to change directories with cd, change the value of the **PATH** shell variable, specify pathnames other than simple pathnames, or redirect output.

Return code.   See *Exit status.*

Root directory.   The ancestor of all directories and the start of all absolute pathnames. The name of the root directory is **/**.

Root file system.   The file system that is always available when the system is brought up in single-user mode. The name of this file system is always **/**. You cannot unmount or mount the root file system.

Root login.   Usually the login name of the Superuser. See *Superuser.*

Run.   To execute a program.

Run level.   The run level describes the state of the operating system. A run level of 2 usually indicates the system is running multiuser, and 1 (or sometimes 6) indicates single-user mode.

Scroll.   To move lines on a terminal up or down one line at a time.

Session.   As used in this book, the sequence of events between when you start using a program such as an editor and when you finish, or between when you log in and the next time you log out.

Shell.   A UNIX system command processor. There are three major shells: the Bourne Shell, the C Shell, and the Korn Shell. See *Bourne Shell, C Shell,* and *Korn Shell.*

Shell function.   A series of commands the shell stores for execution at a later time. Shell functions are like shell scripts, but they run more quickly because they are stored in the computer's main memory rather than in files. Also, a shell function is run in the environment of the shell that calls it (unlike a shell script, which is typically run in a subshell).

Shell script.   A program composed of shell commands. Also, *shell program.*

Signal.   A very brief message that the UNIX system can send to a process, apart from the process's standard input.

Simple filename.   A single filename, containing no slashes (**/**). A simple filename is the simplest form of a pathname. Also, the last element of a pathname, the *basename.*

Single-user.   A computer system that only one person can use at a time. As contrasted with *multiuser.*

Sort.   To put in a specified order, usually alphabetic or numeric.

SPACE character.   A character that appears as the absence of a visible character. Even though you cannot see it, a SPACE is a printable character. It is represented by the ASCII code 32 (decimal). A SPACE character is considered a *blank* or *white space.*

Spawn.   See *Fork.*

Special character.   A character that has a special meaning when it occurs in an ambiguous file reference or another type of regular expression, unless it is quoted. The special characters most commonly used with the shell are * and ?. Also, *metacharacter* and *wild card.*

Special file.   See *Device file.*

Spool.   To place items in a queue, each waiting its turn for some action. Often used when speaking about the lp utility and the printer, that is, lp spools files for the printer.

Square bracket.   There is a left square bracket ([) and a right square bracket (]). They are special characters that define character classes in ambiguous file references and other regular expressions.

Standard error.   A file to which a program can send output. Usually, only error messages are sent to this file. Unless you instruct the shell otherwise, it directs this output to the terminal (that is, to the device file that represents the terminal).

Standard input.   A file from which a program can receive input. Unless you instruct the shell otherwise, it directs this input so that it comes from the terminal (that is, from the device file that represents the terminal).

Standard output.   A file to which a program can send output. Unless you instruct the shell otherwise, it directs this output to the terminal (that is, to the device file that represents the terminal).

Startup file.   A file the login shell runs when you log in. The Bourne and Korn Shells run a file called **.profile**, and the C Shell runs a file called **.login**. The C Shell also runs a file called **.cshrc** whenever a new C Shell or a subshell is invoked. The Korn Shell runs an analogous file whose name is identified by the **ENV** variable.

Status line.   The bottom (usually the 24th) line of the terminal. The vi editor uses the status line to display information about what is happening during an editing session.

Sticky bit.   An access permission bit that causes an executable program to remain on the swap area of the disk. It takes less time to load a program that has its sticky bit set than one that does not. Only the Superuser can set the sticky bit. If the sticky bit is set on a directory that is publicly writable, only the owner of a file in that directory can remove the file.

Streams.   A new character-handling subsystem that was introduced in System V Release 3.

String.   A sequence of characters.

Subdirectory.   A directory that is located within another directory. Every directory except the root directory is a subdirectory.

Subshell.   A shell that is forked as a duplicate of its parent shell. When you run an executable file that contains a shell script using its filename on the command line, a subshell is forked to run the script. Also, when you surround commands with parentheses, they are run in a subshell.

Superblock.   A block that contains control information for a file system. The superblock contains housekeeping information, such as the number of inodes in the file system and free list information.

Superuser.   A privileged user who has access to anything any other system user has access to and more. The system administrator must be able to become a Superuser in order to establish new accounts, change passwords, and perform other administrative tasks. The login name of the Superuser is typically *root.*

Swap.   What occurs when the operating system moves a process from memory to a disk, or vice versa. Swapping a process to the disk allows another process to begin or continue execution.

Symbolic link.   A directory entry that points to the pathname of another file. In most cases, a symbolic link to a file can be used in the same ways a hard link can be used. Unlike a hard link, a symbolic link can span file systems and can connect to a directory.

System administrator.   The person who is responsible for the upkeep of the system. The system administrator has the ability to log in as the Superuser. See *Superuser*.

System console.   See *Console terminal*.

System V.   One of the two major versions of the UNIX system. System V is a product of AT&T.

Termcap.   An abbreviation of **term**inal **cap**ability. The **termcap** file contains a list of various types of terminals and their characteristics. System V replaced the function of this file with the Terminfo directory.

Terminfo.   An abbreviation of **term**inal **info**rmation. The **/usr/lib/terminfo** directory contains many subdirectories, each containing several files. Each of these files is named for, and contains a summary of the functional characteristics of, a particular terminal. Visually oriented programs, such as vi, make use of these files.

Tty.   A terminal. Tty is an abbreviation for teletypewriter.

Usage message.   A message presented by a command when you call the command using incorrect command line arguments.

User ID.   A number that the **/etc/passwd** file associates with a login name.

User interface.   See *Interface*.

Utility.   A program included as a standard part of the UNIX system. You typically invoke a utility either by giving a command in response to a shell prompt or by calling it from within a shell script. Utilities are often referred to as commands. They are contrasted with built-in commands, which are built into the shell.

Variable.   A name and an associated value. The shell allows you to create variables and use them in shell scripts. Also, the shell inherits several variables when it is invoked, and it maintains those and other variables while it is running. Some shell variables establish characteristics of the shell environment, whereas others have values that reflect different aspects of your ongoing interaction with the shell.

White space.   A collective name for SPACEs and/or TABs and occasionally NEWLINEs.

Wild card.   See *Metacharacter*.

Word.   A name for command line arguments, which are sequences of one or more non-blank characters separated by blanks. Also, a word is a Unit of Measure in vi. In vi, a word is similar to a word in the English language—a string of one or more characters that is bounded by a punctuation mark, a numeral, a TAB, a SPACE, or a NEWLINE.

Work Buffer.   A location where ed and vi store text while it is being edited. The information in the Work Buffer is not written to the file on the disk until you command the editor to write it.

Working directory.   The directory that you are associated with at any given time. The relative pathnames you use are *relative to* the working directory. Also, *current directory*.

INDEX

T